# The Politics of
# Development

*For Diane*

# The Politics of Development

*Forests, Mines*
*&*
*Hydro-Electric Power*
*in*
*Ontario,*
*1849-1941*

H. V. NELLES

*Archon Books*
*1974*

*First published 1974 by*
*The Macmillan Company of Canada Ltd.*
*and in the United States of America*
*as an Archon Book, an imprint of*
*The Shoe String Press, Inc.,*
*Hamden, Connecticut 06514*

This book has been published
with the help of a grant from the
Social Science Research Council of Canada,
using funds provided by the
Canada Council.

**Library of Congress Cataloging in Publication Data**

Nelles, H    V
    The politics of development

    Includes bibliographical references.
    1. Natural resources—Ontario—History.
2. Environmental policy—Ontario—History.
3. Conservation of natural resources—Ontario—
History.    I. Title.
HC117.O6N44    333.7'09713    74-4038
ISBN    0-208-01450-0

*Printed in Canada*

# Contents

# Preface

✦

New books are expected to break new ground. This one is merely a new approach to an old subject. A generation ago the study of staple production in the eighteenth and nineteenth centuries attracted some of the best minds that have ever turned to Canadian history. It inspired, as we all know, some of the great books in the field, including H.A. Innis' seminal work on the fur trade and cod fishery, A.R.M. Lower's studies of the timber trade (to which he has recently added another volume), and of course D.G. Creighton's masterpiece, *The Commercial Empire of the St. Lawrence*. These were the books that led me to wonder about the politics of new staple development.

In the intervening decades new questions drew historians away from the study of the relationship of political and economic phenomena well before the subject had been exhausted. As a result, much exploratory and descriptive work was left undone. Perhaps the most conspicuous gap in research lay in the twentieth century. Historians had studied the ways in which the problems of producing the old staples had laid down the warp and woof of Canadian politics in the nineteenth century, but no extended treatment had been accorded the political dynamics of the new forest and mineral staples and hydro-electric energy that rose to dominance in the twentieth. This book began, then, as an exercise in academic housekeeping. Here was a bit of unfinished business to tidy up. What had been the impact of new staple production upon the politics of one province?

The idea for such a book emerged from the work I did on timber administration for the Department of Lands and Forests History Project in 1965. While writing that paper I discovered for the first time the exceptional authority, expressed in the terms of the Crown Timber Act, that the state exercised over such an important constituent of the Canadian economy as the pulp and paper industry. Where had this statist tradition originated? How and why had it survived an era of laissez-faire liberalism? How had this tradition altered the industrial process, if at all, along the way? In the light of this preliminary study for the Department of Lands and Forests (which was subsequently incorporated into Rex Lambert and Paul Pross's volume, *Renewing Nature's Wealth* [Toronto, 1967]) I wondered if the experience of administering the public forests might have influenced the conception of the role of the state in the development of other natural resources or the regulation of the economy. Clearly the distribution of hydro-electricity had come under even more direct state control than the production of pulp and paper. Only the mining industry seemed to enjoy the conventional free enterprise status.

The mere variety of these relationships between government and the resource industries invited further consideration. Thus, taking this curiosity about the role of the state and combining it with a notion of the importance of the new staple industries in the economic history of Canada, I set out to ask some further questions about the politics of natural resource development in Ontario. What determined the extent of the public sector in the resource economy? How had the state used its authority to promote and regulate the industrial process? How in turn did the process of development affect Ontario political traditions? Further, how did successive governments of Ontario perceive and approach the question of continental economic integration?

And finally, how did the political system adjust to the new business responsibilities of government in the twentieth century? Some of these questions had, of course, received some attention in various biographical, economic and political studies. I sought to bring them into sharper focus in the foreground.

Where did these questions lead me? To the conclusion that the positive state survived the nineteenth century primarily because businessmen found it useful. The province received substantial revenue from the development process and enjoyed the appearance of control over it, while industrialists used the government—as had the nineteenth-century commercial classes before—to provide key services at public expense, promote and protect vested interests, and confer the status of law upon private decisions. If public functions such as the distribution of hydro-electricity were to the advantage of industry, this expansion of political control was eagerly sanctioned; whereas, if businessmen resented interference (mineral royalties and forest protection regulations, for example), then the scope of government intervention narrowed. Politicians and businessmen reacted favourably to the prospects of the continental market, but sought by law to maximize the degree of manufacturing that took place in Canada before the export of staple commodities. Interestingly enough, the province and its various interest groups pursued this development strategy fitfully throughout the first three decades of this century without the understanding or support of the federal government. Finally, it seemed to me on looking at the evidence that the structures established to regulate business in the public interest accelerated the trend towards cabinet government, actuated in large part Ontario's regional protest, and contributed to a reduction of the state —despite an expansion of its activities—to a client of the business community. Yet I do not believe this was inevitable. The failure to bring the business and technical functions of the state into the framework of democratic accountability was the failure of men with choices to make to pursue the logic of responsible government into the industrial age.

Having said that, it is important here at the outset to warn the reader what this book is not, as well as what it is. It is not intended to be a political history of Ontario, though one is badly needed. It is not meant to be an economic history, old or new, of Ontario. Nor has it been conceived as an administrative or as a business history of the three major industries discussed. Rather attention falls upon an area that lies between those poles. It is merely a preliminary inquiry into the ways in which natural resource development placed demands upon the political system of the province of Ontario.

The study of this question must necessarily begin at the provincial level on account of the division of powers set down by the British North America Act. But the issues raised by the development of natural resources obviously transcend the boundaries of one province. They have a great deal to do, for example, with defining the relationship between the province and the dominion within the federal system. I am well aware of the fact that in writing such a book on Ontario I am not writing the history of Canada; this is unapologetic provincial history. Different regions and provinces cast up different development patterns. It is my hope that this limited study might encourage other investigations into the politics of resource development in other regions. When that has taken place, and only then, we might draw firm conclusions for all of Canada and draw reliable comparisons with other jurisdictions. In further limiting my inquiry I have concentrated upon the forest products, the mining and the hydro-electric industries, as being the ones most commonly thought of as the new staple industries. For that reason I exclude the study of natural gas, oil and quarrying, which remains of purely local concern throughout. My terminal dates, marked by the first Crown Timber Act and the conclusion of the Depression, include the period during which reliable primary sources in relative abundance are available.

The relative scarcity of secondary literature on this subject has necessitated the combining of topical and narrative forms of organization. Because the economic and political history of the province remains so largely unwritten, I have found it necessary to supplement the analysis of my themes with a certain amount of background material. For that reason I have attempted to look at a period through a problem. For example, the nineteenth-century foundations of Ontario's resource policies are seen from the vantage of a concern for the survival of the positive state. The events of the 1890s are integrated into a treatment of the manufacturing condition, Ontario's little National Policy. As the province enters a phase of rapid industrial expansion just after the turn of the century, successive chapters explore business–government relations associated with the promotion of resource development, its regulation, and the nationalization of the hydro-electric industry. Continental economic integration, an important theme throughout, rises as the central question during the second decade of the century. Finally, chapters dealing with business–government relations during periods of expansion and collapse bring the story through the 1920s and 1930s to a conclusion.

During the course of my work on this book I have incurred many debts to individuals and institutions. First I must acknowledge the help extended to me almost a decade ago by Rex Lambert, Paul Pross, Walter Giles, A.J. Herridge, Herbert Morrison and F.A. MacDougall of the Department of Lands and Forests; L. Carson Brown and George Wardrope of the Department of Mines, and R.N. Beattie, the archivist of Ontario Hydro. I would also like to thank Mr. D.M. McIntyre, the former secretary of the executive council, for permission to examine the Prime Ministers' papers deposited in the Public Archives of Ontario, and the staff of that archive, especially Mr. Appleby and the late Miss Jackson, who guided me through the papers. At the Public Archives of Canada I received the courtesy and generous assistance that have become the hallmarks of that estimable institution.

Research for the thesis upon which this book is based was supported by funds provided by the Ontario government, the Department of History at the University of Toronto, and the

Queen Elizabeth II Fellowship Committee. The Canada Council made it possible for me to undertake the substantial revisions and additional research that were required to turn it into a book.

Doris Brillenger at York's Secretarial Services Division typed the manuscript, and the secretaries in the Department of History, Hilda Dworkin and Geraldine Parkes, typed the index. Margaret Van Every at the Public Archives of Ontario gave me free run of her marvellous picture collection; Lesley O'Neil at Ontario Hydro and Jack Stiff at the Ministry of Natural Resources kindly provided photographs on power and mining development. I must also thank the typesetting team at Alpha Graphics who, on more than one occasion, have corrected me when I've gone astray and whose work speaks for itself in the pages that follow. Diane Mew persuaded the publisher to take on this book in the first place, and shepherded me through the complex mysteries of publication.

My colleagues in the York University Research Group, particularly Ramsay Cook, Paul Stevens, Peter Oliver, Jack Granatstein, Tim Le Goff and Joe Ernst, heard several sections of this book and gave me the benefit of their criticism. Abe Rotstein read the chapters on Canadian-American economic relations and helped me with a number of points.

With some people, however, I have piled up more than the usual number of obligations in one way or another. Many of my ideas were first tried out in conversations with Christopher Armstrong, and we have worked closely together on some of the source material. Throughout he has shared my perverse interest in the sawlogs and the toasters, and understood. From the time we were graduate students together Michael Bliss has given me invaluable help with the many knotty problems encountered along the way. He has also read the entire manuscript and his sharp, spirited critique has spared me many errors of fact and interpretation. For those that remain, of course, I am solely responsible, and Michael warned me about them as well.

Above all, I want to set down in print my indebtedness, both intellectual and personal, to Professor D.G. Creighton under whose direction I began this study. His work and his example as a teacher and writer have been my models. From those first very uncertain days he tolerated my impertinence, encouraged me to undertake a project as ambitious as this, directed me to many useful sources and steered me away from numerous pitfalls and dead ends. He nudged me gently when it seemed as if I might get bogged down and discouraged, and he spent many hours over my laboured prose, never letting me forget that if I hoped to be a historian I first had to be a writer. His kindness and inspiration I can never repay.

Lastly I would like to pay tribute to my wife Diane. Her good humour sustained me and her editorial minority report kept the whole enterprise in its proper perspective.

HVN
Wilson's Corners, Quebec
July 1973

# 1

# A Frontier of Monarchy

During the nineteenth century the simple laws governing Upper Canada's natural resources underwent a wholesale transformation. It is, of course, entirely to be expected that a force as pervasive as the industrial revolution would re-order inherited practices to conform to its needs. What is notable about the process of legal reform in Ontario, however, is the extent to which the political control over economic activity that characterized the pre-industrial, imperial legislation survived to provide the foundations of twentieth-century natural resource law. Somewhat unexpectedly the provincial government emerged from an era of political and economic liberalism with a great deal of its authority intact. It still possessed, for example, property rights whose origins could be traced back to the ancient prerogatives of the crown.

At least in the natural resource sector of the Ontario economy, the concept of the positive, interventionist state did not have to be invented when the society first encountered the problems of large-scale industrialization around the turn of the century.

Such a conception of the state—latent in the expression, crown lands—was the natural product of a colonial heritage and a unique economic history. From the outset the unoccupied region of what was to become Ontario had been thought of in proprietary terms. These "waste lands of the crown" existed to be administered in the interests of the state, either as a source of war materiel, revenue, or as a repository for settlers. Through an accident of geography much of the natural wealth of this community, its waterpowers, minerals and forests, was to be found on these lands. How these resources were to be allocated and how public and private claims upon them would be balanced became, therefore, important political questions.

The possessive individualism of an agrarian frontier made incursions upon, but did not eliminate, the tradition of crown ownership. In the woods and forests the rights of the crown were not those of eminent domain; they were proprietary. The late nineteenth-century homestead farmer on the northern Ontario frontier neither owned nor had prior right to the pine growing on his land (beyond what he needed for his buildings), the precious minerals beneath the soil, or the waterfall in his river. These natural resources remained the property of the crown and their use was regulated by statute in accordance with prevailing notions of the interests of the state. Perhaps it was this body of law that he knew so well that prompted Professor A. R. M. Lower to comment: "The perpetuation of monarchical forms, even though the life has long since gone out of them, doubtless tends to act as a curb upon the fullest expression of democracy."[1]

I

Crown ownership of natural wealth was a joint legacy of the French and British imperial traditions. In both the French seigneurial and British freehold land systems the distinction

---

[1] "The Origins of Democracy in Canada," *Canadian Historical Association Report* (1930), p. 70.

between possession of surface rights and ownership of the minerals underground was transmitted to the North American continent. Even though the New England yeoman and the seigneur on the St. Lawrence held certain rights over the use of the surface of their lands, neither could claim in their entirety the precious minerals underground. These remained the property of their respective monarchs. In New France all precious and base metals discovered became the property of the king to be exploited by a designated royal monopoly. In the colonies to the south, English law required that only a portion of the so-called royal metals (gold, silver and copper) found on either private or unoccupied land be transferred to the state in recognition of its rights. Even after the passage of the Statute of Tenures in 1660 the crown still claimed a royalty of one-fifth of all precious metals mined in Britain and her overseas colonies.[2]

Whereas fiscal need compelled monarchs to impose a royalty on minerals, military requirements necessitated the extension of their authority into the colonial forests. A shortage of structural and masting timbers forced the governments of both France and Britain to reserve for royal naval purposes the oak and pine of their respective colonies. Colbert was the first person to encourage French shipbuilders to investigate the pineries of Canada for supplies and although no continuous trade developed during his administration a regular trade in masts, spars and planking did open up later in the eighteenth century.

---

[2] For the origins of the royalty see J. U. Nef, "Mining and Metallurgy in Medieval Civilization," in M. Postan and E. E. Rich, eds., *The Cambridge Economic History of Europe*, Vol. II (Cambridge, 1952), pp. 430-93, and his study of *Industry and Government in France and England, 1540-1640* (Ithaca, 1964). On the transfer of the concept to North America, see Norman Macdonald, "English Land Tenure on the North American Continent," University of Toronto Studies in History and Economics, *Contributions to Canadian Economies*, Vol. VII (Toronto, 1934); Marshall Dees Harris, *Origin of the Land Tenure System in the United States* (Ames, Iowa, 1953), pp. 83-120; T. A. Rickard, *A History of American Mining* (New York, 1932), pp. 1-17; and T. C. Denis, "Mining Rights in Seigniories in the Province of Quebec," *Journal of the Canadian Mining Institute*, Vol. XIV (1911), pp. 591-5.

To serve this trade the seigneur was required by the terms of his grant "to conserve all the oak timber growing on his domain and cause all oak timber suitable for the construction of the King's ships to be preserved by his feudatories and tenants."[3]

Similar regulations prevailed in the American colonies. When the royal forests of England failed to meet the timber requirements of the navy other sources of supply had to be found. The urgent necessity of reconstructing the fleet following its destruction at the hands of the French in 1688 brought this timber crisis to a head. The civil war had greatly reduced the royal forests and a blockade stood in the way of securing a reliable supply of the required materials from the Baltic. Thus British officials had to call upon the readily accessible American supplies of naval timbers despite the shipbuilders' prejudices against such stock. From a wider commercial point of view this shift in the traditional sources of naval timbers was eminently desirable. Besides helping in the case of Britain to balance an unfavourable trading relationship with the Baltic ports, it brought the mother country and the colony into the classical mercantilist alignment. The colonists would have natural products to exchange for metropolitan manufactured goods.[4]

Following the appointment by the British government of a Colonial Surveyor of Pines and Timber in 1685 a number of steps were taken to promote the growth of a naval stores industry in New England. The Massachusetts charter granted

[3] T. Southworth and A. White, "A History of Crown Timber Regulations from the date of the French Occupation to the Year 1899," reprinted from the Clerk of Forestry *Annual Report* (1899), published in the 1907 Department of Lands and Forests *Annual Report,* and reprinted again in 1957 with the 1907 pagination, pp. 148-54 [hereafter, Southworth and White]. The quotation is from the Hon. I. Williams', solicitor-general of Quebec, 1790 report on the terms of the seigneurial grants.

[4] Paul W. Bamford, *Forests and French Sea Power, 1660-1789* (Toronto, 1956); R. G. Albion, *Forests and Sea Power: The Timber Problem of the Royal Navy, 1652-1862* (Cambridge, Massachusetts, 1926); and J. N. Fauteux, *Essai sur l'industrie au Canada sous le régime français,* Vol. I (Quebec, 1927), chapters IV and V.

in 1691 reserved all large-diameter pine trees and imposed a one hundred pound penalty for cutting such trees without a licence. When the other colonies could not be pressured into enacting similar conservation legislation, the British government took matters into its own hands by passing in 1711 "An Act for the Preservation of White and other Pine Trees growing in Her Majesty's Colonies... for the masting of Her Majesty's Royal Navy". Henceforth all pine of over two feet in diameter from Maine to New Jersey could only be cut with a crown licence. A subsequent amendment in 1721 tightened these restrictions to include all pine trees regardless of diameter and extended the limits of prohibition to include the newly acquired colony of Nova Scotia. Finally the 1729 omnibus naval stores bill provided the effective machinery to administer the licensing system and supervise the cutting of pine. This latter act, which remained in effect up to the Revolution, was expanded by judicial interpretation to apply not only to pine growing upon wild, unoccupied lands, but also to that found on freehold land as well. In the settled districts the authorities condoned resistance to broad arrow laws[5] but in the more heavily forested regions of New England more rigorous enforcement provoked widespread resentment among the colonists. Though the regular petty transgressions of the lumbermen upon the crown preserves were winked at, flagrant abuses brought down the full weight of the law. While this imperial forestry policy could not be counted among the colonists' major grievances, it did create chronic irritation and at the local level provoked defiance which was as continuous as the constitutional and commercial opposition to the empire [6].

The forestry and mining laws which British colonial officials brought to the new colony of Quebec were primarily designed to promote the same objectives as the former French laws; namely, an income from the monetary metals for the Treasury,

---

[5] The Surveyors of Pines and Timber marked their trees with what was called a broad arrow: three hatchet blows which left a scar vaguely similar to a crow's foot.

[6] J. J. Malone, *Pine Trees and Politics: Naval Stores and Forest Policy in Colonial New England, 1691-1775* (London, 1964).

and a supply of structural and masting timber for the Royal Navy and merchant marine. In order to avoid the ceaseless controversy that had surrounded the broad arrow laws in New England, the new governor of Quebec was instructed in 1763 to set aside a distinct naval forest reserve within each township. The Surveyor General of Woods and Forests hoped that if these exclusive reserves were established before the arrival of settlers, then the kind of turmoil raised by the pre-emption of pine in New England might be circumvented. Taking stock of available timber supplies after the Seven Years' War, which like all the great naval campaigns had strained the supply of domestic oak and cut off the Baltic trade in masts, imperial officials regarded New Brunswick and Quebec as their most significant holdings of naval stores.[7]

The guidelines issued to the Quebec Land Office in 1789 reaffirmed the long-standing mineral and forest reservation policies, and went on to suggest that the Canadian lands of the crown were to be held and managed in much the same way as the English royal estates. Freehold grants would be made for agricultural purposes only; all lands valuable for other reasons were to remain vested in the crown. To prevent individuals from "monopolizing such spots as contain mines, minerals, fossils and conveniences for mills and other singular advantages of a common and public nature, to the prejudice of the general interest of the settlers," the regulations required the Surveyor General to reserve the aforementioned locations along with "all such as may be fit and useful for ports and harbours and works of defence, or such as contain valuable timber for shipbuilding...." Lord Dorchester's instructions of 1791 gave an even clearer indication that the authorities in London expected the state to exercise more effective control over Canadian resources than had been the case in the American colonies. Dorchester was directed to reserve, in addition to naval timber, gold and silver, lands containing coal, copper, tin, iron and lead. The base metals provisions in the new Canadian policy clearly exceeded the bounds of prevailing English practice

---

[7] Albion, *Forests and Sea Power*, pp. 346ff.; Southworth and White, pp. 154ff.

which withheld only the royal metals from the title deed. Plainly, in the altered strategic and political circumstances following the collapse of the first empire, the British colonial administrators were doing everything in their power to shore up the authority of the state, including withholding from private ownership not only all strategic and monetary resources, but also all things thought to be "singular advantages of a common and public nature."[8]

Similarly, water rights in the colony were retained in the public domain. By English common law the authority of both the state and the individual to restrict the flow of a natural stream was strictly limited and the crown was bound to protect the community of users against the monopolistic use of a stream by any of the riparian owners. According to ancient custom, water flowing across private property belonged to nobody, or rather to the "negative community"; therefore, it could not be privately appropriated. The ownership of property along a non-navigable stream generally implied ownership of the land underwater to the middle of the stream. But this property right did not convey ownership of the water above. Rather, the opportunity of access to the flow of water afforded by possession of property along the bank formed the basis of the right of *usufruct*. A riparian owner could use the flow of the stream as long as he did not prejudice the similar rights of his downstream and upstream neighbours to a normal flow. The water, simply by virtue of passing over private property, was not itself private property; it could be used only in passage.[9]

Dorchester actually did keep for the crown the riparian rights to several key Upper Canadian waterpowers in accordance with his instructions. At a time when the scattered and poor inhabitants could not themselves build and equip essential

[8] Southworth and ·White, p. 156; A. G. Doughty and D. A. McArthur, *Documents Relating to the Constitutional History of Canada*, Vol. II (Ottawa, 1914), p. 43.

[9] Samuel C. Wiel, "Running Water," *Harvard Law Review*, Vol. XXII (1908-9), p. 199; H. S. W. Coulson and A. F. Urquhart, *The Law Relating to Waters: Sea, Tidal and Inland* (London, 1880), p. 120; and H. S. Theobald, *The Law of the Land* (London, 1902), pp. 141ff.

services such as grist and sawmills, a paternalistic colonial administration stepped in to keep important waterpowers from falling into the hands of speculators and, more positively, it supplied building materials and even millstones for some of the sites. But as immigration swelled the population and the colonists were increasingly able to provide for their own needs, the government retreated from this role and discontinued its waterpower reservation policy. Thus for the rest of the nineteenth century the use of water for power continued to be governed by only the common law of riparian ownership. That is to say, the crown guaranteed free navigation in open waters and protected the rights of downstream riparian owners. As long as the right of usufruct remained a local matter, and as long as there were numerous unused waterpowers, this narrow frame of reference sufficed. However, later in the century when technological change transformed the significance of waterpowers, there would be a return to these early notions of reservation in the wider public interest.[10]

While waterpowers remained conditionally attached to the land by virtue of the common law, the precious minerals of Upper Canada were emphatically segregated from the ownership of land in the interests of the crown. Every deed to land issued in the colony carried the stipulation that both base and royal metals were not conveyed with title. However, since neither gold nor silver was discovered in significant quantities, mineral reservation continued to be a principle without actually becoming an operative policy. But the law did exist and was nonetheless real, despite the absence of cause for its application. Through habitual repetition, the principles of imperial mineral law were passed down to the post-Confederation province of Ontario substantially unaltered.[11]

By way of contrast with mining, a strong demand for colonial

[10]  William Canniff, *History of the Settlement of Upper Canada (Ontario) with special reference to the Bay of Quinté* (Toronto, 1859), pp. 206ff.; Ontario Hydro-Electric Inquiry Commission, 1922-4, *Memorandum Re: Riparian Rights on the Niagara River* (typescript, University of Toronto Library), p. 1.

[11]  Lillian Gates, "The Land Policies of Upper Canada" (Ph.D. thesis, Radcliffe College, 1955), pp. 66, 209.

timber ensured that the principles behind the imperial forestry laws would have to serve the actual needs of the trade and the administration if they were to survive. In the St. Lawrence and Great Lakes lowlands, just as in New England, settlement conflicted with naval policy. But the Upper Canadian authorities managed, before a crisis developed, to arrange a compromise that maintained the spirit of the broad arrow laws and yet permitted unimpeded settlement. Had the naval reservation laws been rigidly enforced in the verdant pineries of southern Ontario, colonization would have been brought to a standstill; or had they been arbitrarily enforced, the reaction of the Upper Canadians would probably have been similar to that of the former colonists to the south. Fortunately, Upper Canada contained such an enormous expanse of forested land that timber and settlement policies could be geographically separated as as they could not have been in the crowded New England colonies. In the southern parts of Upper Canada, officials did not pretend to enforce the naval reservation laws. Frontiersmen girdled, axed and burned the huge pines, lesser conifers and hardwoods with the full approval of the colonial officials. But up the river valleys in the vast northern forest, either in advance of settlement or in the rocky, inhospitable regions, the reservation and licensing system continued to supply the timber requirements of the Royal Navy. Because the areas in which they operated were isolated from the press of settlement, lumbermen and colonial administrators could easily modify imperial military law to meet the needs of an increasingly civilian timber trade. Yet in this process of adaptation, the central aspect of former forest law—crown ownership—was not discarded, as it was in the United States.

II

The services rendered by the Canadian forests during the Napoleonic Wars completely justified the imperial timber policy. With Baltic supplies again in jeopardy and the New England forests in American hands, navy contractors fell back upon the British North American colonies. And as the accessible

Maritime forests became depleted the focus of their timbering operations shifted to the Canadas. By 1815 British North America was producing 72 per cent of the oak planks and joints used by the Royal Navy and the Canadas supplied over 89 per cent of that amount. In the masting trade the removal of activity from the Maritimes to the Canadas was equally pronounced. Between 1806 and 1814, 68 per cent of the masts stepped into British ships came from British North America, and of those over 82 per cent were of Canadian origin. Yet in the long run the shift in the demand for civilian timber from the Baltic to Canada, also caused by wartime stringency, was the most significant development of the period. In order to raise revenues to pay for the war the Board of Trade placed import duties on all European commodities, including timber. By 1810 these tariffs had risen to prohibitive levels. Thus at first by accident, and subsequently by design, the colonial timber producers enjoyed the benefits of preferential treatment in the British market. After the war Britain imported twice as much Canadian as Baltic timber, and by 1835 the proportion had risen to three to one.[12] But despite the fact that in 1825 alone over five million cubic feet of squared timber bound for the newly sprawling British industrial cities moved through the port of Quebec, the only persons legally authorized to cut timber on the Canadian public lands were the contractors of the Royal Navy. Aside from a few regulations to establish a grading system and to guide the navigation of timber rafts on the St. Lawrence River, no attempt had been made to bring the civilian trade within a legislative framework. The naval contractors merely turned their attention to this new trade and they were joined by many others who cut crown timber without a shadow of a right.

---

[12] Albion, *Forests and Sea Power*, pp. 346, 353, 355, 419-22; Southworth and White, pp. 156-62; A. R. M. Lower, "The Trade in Square Timber," in W. T. Easterbrook and M. H. Watkins, *Approaches to Canadian Economic History* (Toronto, 1967), pp. 30-5; R. Lambert and P. Pross, *Renewing Nature's Wealth: A Centennial History of the Public Management of Lands, Forests and Wildlife in Ontario, 1763-1967* (Toronto, 1967), pp. 29, 31 [hereafter, Lambert and Pross].

As the timber trade became less military and more civilian, the forests came to be regarded as a provincial rather than an imperial resource. In 1826 the Executive Council of Upper Canada legalized this existing state of affairs by simply extending the military licensing system to include the more important civilian trade. Thereafter a commercial timber operator could obtain a licence to cut timber within a stated area on the crown lands upon the deposit of a personal bond, and upon agreeing to pay for the timber cut according to a schedule of duties. Since the trade at that time was located mainly along the Ottawa River, one government inspector strategically located at the Chaudière timber slides could perform all the required functions. He could issue the licences, collect and hold cash bonds, charge up the passing timber rafts to the accounts of the licencees, and collect final payment either there at Bytown or later at Quebec. The 1826 regulations brought no changes in the forest tenure system: the crown continued to *own* the land covered by the cutting licence. A timber licence was not a deed to land; it was an authorization to cut trees, and to pay for that right according to a specified rate per board foot. Colonial officials were thus able to adjust the terms of timber licences in such a way that they became, along with land sales, productive sources of revenue beyond the control of an unmanageable Legislative Assembly.[13]

During this period of executive regulation, from 1826 to 1849, the state itself acquired an interest in forest control subtly different from that of the timber trade and the settlers. In view of the fiscal and political circumstances of the colony, the primary concern of the administration was to maximize its revenues. It was in the interest of the state, therefore, to keep a firm hold on legal title to the forest and regulate the lumber industry for its own revenue purposes. Furthermore, the larger interest against which all public policies were measured, the

[13] Lower, "The Trade in Square Timber," pp. 35-46; *idem*, *The North American Assault on the Canadian Forest* (Toronto, 1938), pp. 38-46. See especially his *Great Britain's Woodyard: British America and the Timber Trade, 1763-1867* (Montreal, Kingston, 1973), for the most complete description of the timber trade and its structure.

rapid promotion of agricultural settlement, also inclined the state towards retaining ownership of the forest lands. Through its property rights and terms of licensing, the state could limit the life of a timber licence and require thorough cutting to clear the land for rapid settlement. Against these considerations politicians had to weigh the requirements of the colony's largest industry. Lumbermen never seriously challenged the principle of crown ownership of the forest partly because they were primarily interested in timber rather than land, but more important, because they were able to use the licence system—which deferred payment for the timber until it could be sold—as yet another means of lengthening their lines of credit. The fourth interest seeking satisfaction in public policy was that of the Quebec timber merchants. These timber buyers, in order to guarantee competition among the producers, encouraged the government to allow free access to the forests, thereby prohibiting consolidation of timber limits into a few hands. Balanced between these competing interests, the principle of crown ownership weathered the complex transition from empire to province, from executive to responsible government, and from a military to a civilian trade.[14]

Removal of the imperial preference on timber in 1846 plunged the Canadian timber trade, and indirectly the Canadian government, into a financial crisis. The resulting reduction in demand for Canadian timber, coincident with a general European depression of prices, occurred at the moment when the bias of crown timber regulations was towards maximum output from an ever-increasing number of operators. During 1847 almost 45 million feet of square timber arrived at Quebec to meet a demand for only 19 million feet. The following year the supply dropped off sharply to a little over 39 million feet, but the demand had also sunk to a mere 17 million feet. The collapse of the colony's largest industry, and the one which converted natural wealth into private and social capital, not only shook the economy, but was also in large measure

---

[14] Southworth and White, pp. 190-5; J. E. Hodgetts, *Pioneer Public Service* (Toronto, 1955), pp. 130, 141-2.

responsible for a crisis in the public finances. For when the booming grounds in the coves below Quebec groaned with unsold stock, revenues suffered and, moreover, the government encountered resistance in its attempts to borrow.[15]

A legislative committee struck to look into the causes of the depression in the lumber trade drew up the first statutory framework for the forest industry, the Crown Timber Act of 1849.[16] Prominent among the members of the committee were Scott, Egan, Bell and Johnson, the political spokesmen for the Ottawa lumber community, who naturally strove to modify the regulations to meet the needs of the trade. But the 1849 act, while it did reflect the hand of its lumbermen draftsmen, bore a strong resemblance to the former order-in-council regulations: the state permitted the industry relatively free access to timber and gave the lumbermen assurance of the security and permanence of their rights. But at the same time, the state demanded swift removal of timber from property under licence and surrender of exhausted limits so that settlement might proceed without undue delay in order that the timber limits of the crown would not stand idle but would produce a regular and substantial revenue to the public treasury.

The fact that the first statutory provisions for the province's forest industry confirmed the fundamental principle of crown ownership inherited from earlier imperial and executive regulations was of enormous significance for subsequent Ontario forest law. With only two minor adjustments, the 1849 Crown Timber Act formed the legislative foundation for the forest industry for the remainder of the nineteenth century. The actual property upon which the industry depended for its raw materials continued to be possessed by the state, and the continuation of governmental property interest in the licence areas conferred upon the state a broader access to regulation of the

---

[15] Evidence of W. W. Dawson, Select Committee on the Lumber Trade, John Scott chairman, *Journals of the Legislative Assembly of Canada*, 1849, Appendix P.P.P.P.; Lower, "The Trade in Square Timber," pp. 46ff.; D. G. Creighton, *The Empire of the St. Lawrence* (Toronto, 1956), pp. 362-3.

[16] *Canada Statutes*, 12 Vict., c. 30; Southworth and White, 195-209; Second Report of the Select Committee on the Lumber Trade, *op. cit.*

industry to satisfy competing interest groups than it would have had if the lumbermen had owned their own land.

During the 1849 committee hearings several influential lumbermen had advocated replacing the initial cash deposit—or personal bond—with a system of rent charges. Such a small annual payment, they argued, would free capital for use in the cutting operations and at the same time provide ample security against monopoly and speculation. The ground rent system was not included in the 1849 Crown Timber Act, but in 1851, as a result of continuous pressure both from the industry and from within the public service, it was incorporated into the regulations. The ground rent system, in effect, further extended the credit of the industry. For a modest annual payment of 2s. 6d. per square mile, the lumberman obtained the right to cut crown timber without having to pay for it until the timber could be sold, thereby permitting the scarce capital of the colony to be applied to the essential tasks of transporting the timber to market.[17] The rental system, while it released the capital of the industry, provided tangible evidence of the landlord-tenant relationship of the state and the industry.

In 1854 the lumber community had ample opportunity to recommend changes in the provisions of the Crown Timber Act but used the occasion to defend the act instead. That year another committee, numbering among its members Francis Hincks, John Sandfield Macdonald, John Rolph, William Hamilton Merritt, Augustin Morin, and chaired by Alexander Galt, conducted extensive hearings on reforming the method of disposing of all crown lands. Alexander Galt, in his capacity as manager of the British American Land Company, argued in a letter to the committee that pine timber should be considered part of the land and that the American system of land sales for cash become government policy. Spokesmen for the railroad interests also advocated a land sales system which, it was claimed, would prevent the lumbermen from retarding the settlement of the country with their obstructive licences. A Michigan lumberman, Jonathan R. White, also recommended

---

[17] For details, see Southworth and White, p. 209.

adoption of the American procedure of selling clear title to the land which carried full rights to both the minerals and the timber found on the land.

Canadian lumbermen and timber administrators disagreed sharply with the representatives of the railroads, land companies and American timber interests. James H. Burke, a Bytown lumberman, conceded that a sales policy might be desirable in Michigan or in areas primarily suited to agriculture, but he emphasized its inadequacies when dealing with lands that consisted of "nothing but pine and rock." Other lumbermen feared that a sales system would favour the wealthy and permit a few people to buy up all the best lands for speculative purposes. David Roblin, another lumberman, argued that the government would receive only a portion of the revenue it would otherwise have collected in ground rent and timber dues if it sold its lands outright. A. J. Russell, the crown timber agent at Bytown, echoed his concern. If Canada adopted the sales system, he warned, the government would lose the control over the land it presently exercised and "the immediate interest of the speculator would overrule the interest of the Province."[18] When faced with an attack by the railroad and settlement interests, or when threatened with competition from American firms, the strategy of the lumber community was to stress the close connection between the revenue of the state and the continued well-being of the industry. A system of land sales would have dramatically reversed the very successful campaign of the lumber industry to reduce to an absolute minimum the capital required to obtain a timber licence.

The conservatism of the industry at this point in time was a function of uncertainty during a period of market reorientation. After 1849 the market for Canadian timber shifted rapidly to the United States and simultaneously the nature of the product changed from squared timber to sawn lumber. Like any business community facing uncertainty, the lumbermen

[18] Report of the Select Committee Appointed to Enquire and Report Upon the Present System of Management of the Public Lands, A. Galt, chairman, *Journals of the Legislative Assembly of Canada*, 1854-5, Appendix M.M., pp. 26-33, 123-5, 132-6, 147-9, 160-81.

strove to minimize the number of variables.[19] They defended a forest tenure system which had been designed by them in 1849 to meet their own particular needs, and exaggerated, perhaps naturally given the tendencies of the market, the menace of American competitors in what they considered their territory.

The spread of settlement posed another challenge to the lumbering industry. For the first half of the century the farmers and lumbermen of the St. Lawrence and Ottawa River valleys had shared a symbiotic relationship. On the lowlands, where the first task was the removal of the forest cover, the lumbermen were allies of the farmers who flooded onto the cleared land in their wake. The timber crews in turn required supplies, and often the pioneer farmer's first crop was sold up-country in the lumber camps. These same camps provided the agricultural community with employment during the long winter months. But by mid-century, when both settlement and the lumbering industry had moved out of the valleys onto the rocky Laurentian plateau, for the first time the interests of the two groups clashed. The lumbermen resented the incursions of homesteaders who invariably came spreading fire. Their indignation at this invasion grew in direct proportion as the value of their timber limits and the amount of capital tied up in them increased. As one of the most prominent lumbermen complained to the Commissioner of Crown Lands: "I cannot see why, when there is so much equally good land denuded of pine, squatters should be allowed to pursue the course of destruction of pine lands which inevitably points out their location. The internal economy of the revenues of Ontario and the interests of the licensee are identical on this one point viz. the preservation of the forests." Speculative farmers, Mossom Boyd claimed, chose the best pine on a limit, stole it, then moved on. Genuine farmers were hardly more desirable. In their vain attempts to scratch a living from the rocky soil they set clearing fires that tended to get out of control and spread onto the lumbermen's limits.

[19] Lower, *Great Britain's Woodyard*, pp. 111-25.

In both cases the provincial government and the lumber industry were the losers.[20]

The lumbermen also challenged the view that the timber trade was nothing more than a clearing operation in advance of settlement and called instead for a land classification policy that would separate agricultural from non-arable land, leaving the latter for the permanent exploitation of the lumber business. The granite ridges of the Shield, the lumbermen never tired of pointing out, were totally unsuited to farming, whereas the thick forest cover would sustain a prosperous industry forever. As tenants of the state the lumbermen consistently urged the government to maintain "a fair line of separation between the lumbering and agricultural regions, as nature has laid down."[21] Although the state could not entirely deny settlers access to the Laurentian forest, to a considerable extent the civil servants and politicians agreed in principle that a land alienation system should take into account the non-agricultural character of the northern forest. And as the revenue sources open to the province were strictly limited by the Confederation settlement, the community of interest shared by the industry and the state became increasingly clear. The lumbermen's strategy of identifying themselves with the growing income from the forests paid them handsome dividends in their struggle against a land sales system that would open up their forests to both settlers and American speculators.

The rental form of forest tenure allowed the government to balance the contending forces of lumbermen and settlers while at the same time maximizing its revenues. Lumbering provided one of the principal sources of provincial revenue during the last half of the nineteenth century. Between 1852 and 1857 the forest income of Canada West never fell below £53,000 a year and averaged closer to £60,000. From 1858

---

[20] PAC, Mossom Boyd Papers, Mossom Boyd to the Commissioner of Crown Lands, undated (but from the context probably the early 1870s), Box 131.

[21] James H. Burke, testimony before the Select Committee Appointed to Enquire and Report Upon the Present System of Management of the Public Lands, p. 134.

to 1866, when the figures were quoted in dollars, the forests regularly returned about $350,000 annually.[22] After Confederation, when the province's sources of income were reduced to licences, fees, direct taxes and the crown lands, the financial importance of the forests increased tremendously. Whenever the provincial treasurer required additional revenue to meet his obligations (this usually happened just before an election), the Commissioner of Crown Lands merely auctioned off another batch of timber limits. By this time good timber was in such demand that lumbermen were prepared to bid against one another—paying what was called a bonus—for cutting rights. Timber dues (paid on the amount cut at the time of cutting) and ground rent (paid annually on the area under licence) were, of course, in addition to the initial bonus payment. Good reasons could always be found for holding a timber limit auction. The usual one was to protect the area from fire. Encroaching settlers or railroads as a rule supplied the necessary menace. Better the timber be cut over than burnt over. But one of the most obvious and persistent pressures for such sales, succinctly stated in E. H. Bronson's (a lumberman, Minister without Portfolio in the Mowat cabinet) notes for a speech defending the 1892 auction was simply: "WE WANTED THE MONEY." To help pay for railroad subsidies, roads, public institutions, hospitals, public works and the Parliament Buildings, Sandfield Macdonald's government sold off 635 square miles of timber; Edward Blake's ministry parted with 5,031 square miles in one year, and over the next 20 years Oliver Mowat disposed of 4,234 square miles.[23] Between 1867 and 1899 bonuses, dues and ground rent from the lumber industry produced in excess of $29 million, or approximately 28 per cent of the total provincial revenue. Only the federal subsidy brought in a larger sum. In large measure the flourishing state of Ontario's public finances after Confederation can be traced to this extraordinary income from forest regulation.[24]

As a result, politicians were not overly eager to pass on this paternity free of charge to homestead farmers if the lumbermen would literally pay millions for it. And while the state had sold rights to the lumbermen and was to a certain extent bound to protect those rights, they were not those of exclusive possession. No politician dared to appear to exclude the pioneer, the symbolic embodiment of all civic virtue, from the northern forest. The device of crown ownership and licensed rental gave the lumbermen access to the forest, returned a welcome revenue, and under ideal circumstances generated cut-over lands that could then be recovered from the lumbermen and passed on free to the homesteaders. The visibly temporary tenure of the lumberman, expressed in his annual licence and ground rent charges, allowed the state to open up desirable lands when pressed to do so. Because it served the political and economic interests so well, crown ownership continued to serve as the basis of Ontario's forest law on into the twentieth century.

## III

Within the formula of public ownership embodied in the Crown Timber Act, the lumbering industry and the government established a dynamic equilibrium during the latter nineteenth

---

[22] Commissioner of Crown Lands Reports, *Journals of the Legislative Assembly of Canada*, various years.

[23] Timber limit sales, 1867-1892:

| Date | | | Area | Bonus | Dues | Ground rent | Av. price per mile |
|------|---|---|------|-------|------|-------------|--------------------|
| Dec. | 23, | 1868 | 38 | 14,446.50 | .75 | 2.00 | 380.17 |
| July | 6, | 1869 | 98 | 25,564.50 | .75 | 2.00 | 260.86 |
| Feb. | 15, | 1870 | 12 | 7,680.00 | .75 | 2.00 | 640.00 |
| Nov. | 23, | 1871 | 487 | 117,672.00 | .75 | 2.00 | 241.62 |
| Oct. | 15, | 1872 | 5031 | 592,601.50 | .75 | 2.00 | 117.79 |
| June | 6, | 1877 | 375 | 75,739.00 | .75 | 2.00 | 201.97 |
| Dec. | 6, | 1881 | 1379 | 733,675.00 | .75 | 2.00 | 532.00 |
| Oct. | 22, | 1885 | 1012 | 318,645.00 | .75 | 2.00 | 314.87 |
| Dec. | 15, | 1887 | 459 | 1,312,312.50 | 1.00 | 3.00 | 2,859.00 |
| Oct. | 1, | 1890 | 376 | 346,256.25 | 1.00 | 3.00 | 919.00 |
| Oct. | 13, | 1892 | 633 | 2,315,000.00 | 1.25 | 3.00 | 3,657.18 |

SOURCE: PAC, E. H. Bronson Papers, Memoranda on Timber Sales, 1892, Vol. 704.

[24] *Report of the Commission on Finance* (Toronto, 1900), pp. 6, 24.

century. However, on account of the weakness or non-existence of the mining industry throughout most of that time, no similar continuity of fundamental principle stabilized Ontario's mining law. As the development of a mining industry assumed greater urgency with the passage of time, the state gradually liberalized the terms of access to its lands to promote exploration. However, once the long-anticipated treasure trove had been discovered, public men groped once again for a formula that would re-establish the public character of the province's mineral resources, reassert the prior social claim upon their exploitation, and at the same time not retard the development of a greatly desired industry.

Until 1845 the only regulation governing mining in Upper Canada consisted of the reservation to the crown of gold and silver contained in each land patent. That year, when the search for copper spread from northern Michigan across to the north shore of Lake Superior, the government passed a series of order-in-council regulations to license prospectors, to fix the boundaries of claims, and to establish a price for the sale of lands bearing base metals. While these regulations and a flurry of technical amendments that followed established a reasonably liberal procedure for allocating mining lands of that type, the crown continued to retain property rights to the royal metals on both agricultural and mining lands. Answering a petition from the British North American Mining Company for the inclusion of gold and silver ores in its patents issued in 1853, Attorney General Richards of Upper Canada "saw no reason for departing from the usual custom" of reserving these ores from the title deed. Should the company discover either gold or silver on its property, he replied, "I should think there would be no doubt that the Company would be permitted to work the mines on paying a small percentage in the nature of a Royalty or seigniorage to the Crown for the privilege—under such general Rules and Regulations as may be made for that purpose." Yet, despite this determination to retain ownership and control of the monetary metals, over the following decade the terms of access to base ores were regularly and systematically relaxed in response to the pleas of the mining companies. The area of each claim was reduced, the price per acre dropped to one dollar, licences and fees were either diminished or abolished, and the requirement that the claim be developed forthwith waived. Frustration with the halting, plodding progress of mining created the permissive conditions within which special pleading eroded the power of the state. Arguing that an infant, struggling industry could hardly be encouraged with taxes, the miners attacked an 1862 regulation that imposed a royalty of $2^1/_2$ per cent. In 1864 the cabinet reduced the royalty to a tax of one dollar a ton on all ores raised, and the next year removed it completely.[25]

By 1864 the policy of gold and silver reservation was under constant attack from without and, surprisingly, from within the government. A short-lived gold rush in the Chaudière region of Lower Canada led to the striking of a select committee of the Legislature to look into the proper means of encouraging a gold mining industry. From this committee's deliberations emerged the first statute governing mining in Canada East and West, the 1864 Gold Mining Act, which provided for the outright sale of gold mining lands for two dollars an acre, with unimpaired title to the gold passing to the claimant. Within two years, the crown reservation of gold and silver was withdrawn from all patents to land and, as has already been noted, royalty provisions were also removed. Compared with the California, Australian, and British Columbia gold rushes, the Chaudière rush was a bitter disappointment which undoubtedly contributed to a general disillusionment with mining prospects. It convinced legislators, as the miners had long been arguing, that mining was a costly, risky business in which a bonanza was the exception rather than the rule. This became the official attitude in 1866. For example, Alexander Campbell, the Commissioner of Crown Lands, immediately discounted the first enthusiastic reports of the Madoc gold strike:

25 Letter quoted at the June 24, 1853, board meeting of the mining company, PAC, British North American Mining Company *Minute Book*, p. 87; for a detailed narrative of these changes see Thomas W. Gibson, *The Mining Laws of Ontario and The Department of Mines* (Toronto, 1933), pp. 5-45 [hereafter Gibson, *Mining Laws*]; and the Royal Commission on the Mineral Resources of Ontario, *Report* (Toronto, 1890), pp. 263-9.

I have no faith in the gold being found in paying quantities; the Chaudière country promised much greater riches, but the only persons who have made any money there have been speculators on the delusion of others in the price of lands, and the few who have found gold in alluvial deposit. If there be any Gold in the Townships named by Mr. Flint it is *in situ* and the expense of working it will be found to reduce the affair to the laws of ordinary industrial pursuits. The lands however in the Townships named should be treated as Gold lands are in Chaudière—sold at a price of $2 per acre cash, subject to Gold Mining Act.[26]

The difficulty of mining in the Canadian Shield, in the eyes of the government, diminished the profitability of even gold mining "to the laws of ordinary industrial pursuits," leaving no possibility for the public to assert its claim upon mineral resources without seriously impairing the industry.

On the last day of the first session of the Ontario Legislature a new Gold and Silver Mining Act (31 Vict., c. 10) was introduced and read three times. Basically it re-enacted the 1864 law, extending its provisions to cover the recently discovered silver-bearing ores of the north shore of Lake Superior. In the haste, a royalty clause, calling for a contribution to the provincial treasury of between 2 and 10 per cent of gold and silver ores mined, slipped past the weary legislators. Inserted no doubt by the Crown Lands department officials and approved by the cabinet in the light of the restricted revenue sources then available to the province, the clause immediately encountered serious opposition from the tiny mining community. In reply the government frankly admitted "that it had not been able to procure sufficient information on which to base a policy and that this one was strictly experimental."[27] Chastened by criticism, the government quickly repealed the Gold and Silver

---

[26] Notation on a letter from the Hon. Bela Flint, Belleville, Nov. 6, 1866, quoted in Archibald Blue, "The Mining Laws of Ontario," Bureau of Mines, *Annual Report* (1892), p. 223; see also the *Report on the Canadian Goldfields*, Robert Bell, chairman (Quebec, 1865).

[27] Royal Commission on the Mineral Resources of Ontario, *Report*, p. 268.

Mining Act and replaced it in 1869 with the General Mining Act (32 Vict., c. 34), the terms of which were eminently acceptable to the miners. Specifically, the provisions for royalties, taxes and duties on all metallic ores were repealed, and the reservation of gold and silver in all patents voided. After 1869 any duly licensed prospector could explore any crown or private lands and by staking and surveying his locations, registering them with the Crown Lands department, and paying for them at the rate of one dollar an acre, could obtain full property rights to the minerals beneath the surface.[28] The public claim upon the resource, so important in the companion Crown Timber Act, had been completely surrendered at the request of the industry—an action sanctioned in the interest of development.

Over the next thirty years, under the beneficent freedom of the General Mining Act, the Ontario mining industry raised approximately $33 million in gold, silver, copper and nickel from the Canadian Shield without paying a penny in royalties.[29] The discovery of this long-awaited bonanza at precisely that instant when the social responsibilities of the industry had been eliminated was no mere coincidence. The owners of the Silver Islet claim—the first of the province's great mineral strikes—had held onto their property for over twelve years waiting for favourable legislation. They then explored their claim and sold out quickly for a speculator's profit. In the hands of experienced American miners Silver Islet reigned as the richest and most elegant of Ontario's mining camps in the 1870s. The mine, a mere speck of buildings floating on the surf in the lee of Thunder Cape, produced $3.5 million worth of silver

[28] Thomas W. Gibson, *Mining in Ontario* (Toronto, 1937), pp. 10-11 [hereafter, Gibson, *Mining*].

[29] Silver, $4,757,999; gold, $1,401,728; copper, $6,701,098; nickel, $20,360,326. Tables of Value of Ontario Mineral Production, 1886-1900, Dominion Bureau of Statistics, *Canadian Mineral Statistics* (Ottawa, 1957), to which I have added Gibson's estimate of the value of silver produced at Silver Islet Mine, 1870-84, of $3,500,000. Gibson, *Mining*, p. 48.

before both its pumps and its vein played out in 1884.[30] The story of Silver Islet, as told by Archibald Blue, the first director of the Ontario Bureau of Mines, illustrated the quandary in which the administrators of the crown lands found themselves. How could they draw up regulations that would allow prospectors free access and cheap locations while at the same time asserting society's claim to the resource?[31]

Discovery of a major nickel-copper deposit on the CPR right-of-way near Sudbury in 1883 sharpened the dilemma. A group of well-placed speculators quickly purchased the lands from the crown at a dollar an acre, and once again it was not until their properties could be bought out by an American that the ore body began to reveal something of its promise. The American in this case was Samuel J. Ritchie, a carriage-maker from Akron, Ohio, who had originally come to Ontario in search of lumber for wheel-spokes but stayed on to promote an iron mine and railroad in eastern Ontario with the backing of the McMullens, the MacLarens and a Cleveland syndicate. As the indomitable Ritchie began advertising the great importance of nickel and the monopoly his company enjoyed in Canada it became apparent that something of great value had passed into private hands for practically nothing. Canada, Ritchie boasted to Sir John A. Macdonald, possessed enough nickel to control the markets of the world—a fact of tremendous military importance. Scientists had only recently discovered that nickel, when alloyed with steel, produced excellent armour plate and, of course, armour-piercing shells. Sir Charles Tupper, made bold by Ritchie's extravagant rhetoric, predicted: "It really looks as if it were possible for Canada to control the character

---

30 John H. Foster, "The History of the Settlement of Silver Islet," Michigan Pioneer and Historical Society, *Reports*, Vol. XIV (1889), pp. 197-205; Janey C. Livingston, *Historic Silver Islet: The Story of a Drowned Mine, From the Rise and Fall of the Richest Silver Mine the World has ever Known, Once the Abode of Wealth and Gaiety* (pamphlet, n.d.); Mrs. G. W. Dyke, *Historic Silver Islet* (pamphlet, n.d.); PAC, T. A. Keefer Papers, "Silver Mining," (ms. 1885-6); Gibson, *Mining*, pp. 44-6, 101-2.

31 Archibald Blue, "The Story of Silver Islet," Ontario Bureau of Mines, *Annual Report* (1896), pp. 125, 158.

and efficiency of the guns and navies of the world." All of this seemed possible, to be sure, but in the meantime all Ontario could show for its famous monopoly was an ugly scar on the landscape at Sudbury. There, Ritchie's Canadian Copper Company raised the ore from the ground, heaped it onto great roasting beds, and drove its impurities off across barren hills in clouds of poisonous gas; and, what was more, they paid no royalties for these privileges. But, notwithstanding Ritchie's dreams of nickel-steel mills of unimaginable size, his financial backers did not seem to have any plans for a refinery for Sudbury or Ontario.[32]

It was precisely that differential between promises and realities that prompted the Mowat government to establish a royal commission, on May 16, 1888, to examine the province's mineral resources and to recommend the appropriate political and administrative reforms required to speed their development. After a thorough study of the province's geological formations and the economics of the existing mining operations, and after extensive public hearings, the five commissioners[33] concluded that Ontario possessed the necessary land, the know-how, and even a good deal of capital; the problem they identified was to define the legitimate role to be played by government in bringing these factors together:

[32] On the discovery and development of the Sudbury nickel field, see, *inter alia*, the Royal Ontario Nickel Commission, *Report, 1917* (Toronto, 1917); A. F. Barlow, "Nickel and Copper Deposits of the Sudbury Mining District" (Geological Survey of Canada, 1904); A. P. Coleman, *The Nickel Industry* (Ottawa, 1914); D. M. LeBourdais, *The Sudbury Basin: The Story of Nickel* (Toronto, 1953); J. F. Thompson and M. Beasley, *For The Years to Come: A Story of International Nickel* (Toronto, 1960); and O. W. Main, *The Canadian Nickel Industry* (Toronto, 1955).

[33] The personnel of the commission consisted of John Charlton, an M.P. from Norfolk; Robert Bell, assistant director of the Geological Survey; William Coe, explorer, iron miner, and friend of Samuel Ritchie; William Hamilton Merritt, an associate of the Royal School of Mines and a steel company promoter; and Archibald Blue, at that time Deputy Minister of Agriculture and secretary of the Bureau of Industries. See the Royal Commission on the Mineral Resources of Ontario and the Measures for their Development, *Report* (Toronto, 1890). Transcripts of the testimony heard by the commission may be found in PAC, Robert Bell Papers, Vol. 41.

It will always perhaps be a moot point how far the government or legislature of the province ought to go in aiding and encouraging a development of its mineral resources. The extreme view on one side would be that government ought to pursue a course of passivity, leaving the beneficent order of nature free in its operation; while the extreme view on the other side would be that the government ought to nationalise the mines and operate them for the good of the people.

Eschewing the extremes, the commissioners recommended an educational and promotional role for government: "To instruct, to inform, to ascertain and publish facts, to lighten the industry, to enlighten the men employed in it and deal with them in a generous spirit—such, in the opinion of the Commissioners, is the true national policy for governments to pursue in promoting the development of our mineral resources."

Technical ignorance was the most serious problem faced by the Canadian mining industry: "Many of the prospectors met with by the Commissioners in the northern districts were qualified to do little more than make collections of rocks and what seemed to them to be minerals." American mining companies operating in Ontario drew reluctant admiration, not only on account of their ability to raise and risk abundant capital, but also for the expertise and competence which characterized their efforts. Canadians possessed the requisite intelligence and energy, the commissioners observed, but lacked the practical experience and technical education of their American counterparts. The province could move towards overcoming this inadequacy by establishing a mining school in association with a mineral museum and a continuing geological survey.

To attract Canadian and foreign capital to the province's mineral resources, the commission recommended the creation of a Bureau of Mines which might, through collecting statistics, conducting surveys and publishing annual reports, advertise more widely the possibilities of the industry. While the province was urged to assist railway construction into the mining regions and to press for lower Canadian duties on mining equipment as well as lower American tariffs against Canadian minerals, the commissioners did not advocate any basic changes in the Ontario mining laws. The imposition of working conditions on a mining claim, they argued, would deter both monopoly and speculation. And while they recognized that the leasehold form of mining land tenure, being somewhat akin to that of the timber industry, had "strong advocates" in Ontario, they argued that past experience, the desire for clear title to the minerals, and the freehold provisions of prevailing American mining land law tended to limit the usefulness of mineral land leases in Ontario:

> ...in Ontario, where the great majority of occupiers are owners, it would be difficult to persuade people that any other system is better. ... Still less is the American or other foreign capitalist likely to invest money in a leasehold in Ontario, when in a neighbouring state he may procure a mining location under an absolute title.

If Ontario desired progress in its mining industry, the commission advised the government, both royalties and precious metal reservations should be disavowed forever:

> ...[A]s long as the mineral development in Ontario continues to depend largely upon investments of foreign capital, and especially of American capital, a liberal policy must be followed; mining lands must be not less free here than in the United States, where with the single exception of New York there is neither reservation nor royalty.[34]

Driven by powerful financial and political imperatives not felt by the commissioners, however, the Mowat government responded to the publication of their report by tightening government control over mineral resources. Taking the enthusiastic nickel promoters at their word, the government reasoned that if that industry was assured a monopolistic position in the production of strategic metals, the public ought to receive its proper portion. The Commissioner of Crown Lands, introducing a series of bills in the 1891 session of the Legislature embodying the new government policy, pointed out that nickel

[34] Royal Commission on the Mineral Resources of Ontario, *Report*, pp. xv, xvi, xviii, 208, 212, 215-8, 301, 306, 411-6.

had been transformed in the past few years from a mere ornamental metal to a vitally necessary military commodity. The implications of this technological revolution for the public revenues were enormous, he continued: "The indications are that there is in the nickel belt wealth to afford a revenue to the Province which will ward off the bugbear of direct taxation for many years to come."[35] Since 1888 the government's expenditures had exceeded its receipts; not even a wholesale increase in timber ground rent and dues in 1887 could fend off the impending deficits. For these reasons, the mining bills introduced during the 1891 session departed significantly from the recommendations of a royal commission that had been biased in favour of the industry.

In the future, the Commissioner of Crown Lands explained, "...the Government shall not too readily part with the ownership of their public lands without receiving some adequate consideration for the general uses of the Province and that when sold it shall be for the bona fide purpose of mining rather than for speculative purposes." In order to secure greater control over the remaining mineral resources, the government withdrew from location suspected nickel lands, reversed its former policy of granting minerals with title by reimposing mineral reservations on all agricultural land sales, and introduced a new form of tenure corresponding to the timber licence, a mineral lands lease. Upon payment of $1.00 per acre the first year, and substantially reduced fees per acre each succeeding year, a prospector could rent and develop mineral lands, full title to which remained with the crown. Sales, of course, still continued but on new terms. With the objective of raising revenue, the government increased the purchase price of mineral locations from $1.00 an acre to between $2.00 and $4.50 depending upon the accessibility of the property. And in its most controversial step to raise money, the government reimposed a royalty scheme, charging 3 per cent on silver, nickel,

---

[35] For the political background to the royal commission, see Margaret Evans, "Oliver Mowat and Ontario, 1872-1896" (unpublished Ph.D. thesis, University of Toronto, 1967), p. 452. The quotation is from the Hon. A. S. Hardy, *Globe*, April 9, 1891.

and copper ores, 2 per cent on iron ore, and leaving other minerals to be dealt with by order-in-council.[36]

On second reading of the mining bills Arthur Hardy summarized the problems associated with the creation of an equitable law that would on the one hand encourage development and on the other "ensure revenues for the Province for all time to come." In tightening public control of the industry he understood that he was defying the enormous influence of prevailing American practice:

> We cannot well hope to escape the influence of the laws of a country of the magnitude of the United States, for though not the earliest of miners upon this continent, they have the greatest mining production of any country in the world. I presume their mining laws have much to do with moulding our own. I am not unaware that we shall probably be reminded, by those who favour what may be called free mining, of the character of United States laws, I suppose we shall be met with the arguments used by the Liberals who sat on the other side of the House in 1868, that we ought to sell everything, leaving the benefit to the country to come in the development of the mining industry.

Anticipating this continentalist argument, Hardy appealed to conservative, anti-American instincts:

> They [the United States] have given away their public lands, their pine timber; they have practically given away the richest coal mines known to exist in the world. They have given away their gold and silver mines, yielding to individuals wealth which the fables of the past do not approximate. We may well consider whether that is a system to be followed by a people having large mining interests still in their infancy.[37]

---

[36] For details concerning these changes in the law, see Gibson, *Mining Laws*, pp. 11-7. Archibald Blue, who had been a member of the royal commission and was subsequently named first director of the Bureau of Mines recommended by it, vigorously defended the idea of a royalty in his first *Report*, "The Mining Laws of Ontario," p. 227.

[37] *Globe*, April 24, 1891.

In a little more than twenty years the Ontario government had boxed the compass as far as royalty and mineral reservation policy were concerned. Yet even in 1891, though the government stood its ground against hostile criticism from the industry, the Prime Minister confessed that his mining policy remained strictly experimental.

Opposition to the new government policy came primarily from mining land speculators, the most prominent of whom, James Conmee of Algoma, was himself a Liberal MPP. Conmee led a deputation of miners on March 14, 1891, to protest the proposed changes in the Mines Act. "We would respectfully submit," read their resolution, "that any change by which mineral lands would be disposed of in the same manner as timber lands now are would discourage the actual workers and probably lead to the mining districts of our country being locked up for many years in the hands of one large monopoly." Later Conmee and his friends fought the changes through House and committee readings, hoping to impress upon the "Cabinet of Lawyers" that their cleverly contrived regulations would kill the infant mining industry and the initiative of the independent prospector. The working conditions imposed on mining locations, he claimed, were too burdensome, the increased sale prices put lands out of reach of the small mining company, the leasehold tenure would never satisfy the financial backers and, while he agreed that the future held bright prospects, there were still "no mines making a profit." With Conservative help in committee Conmee successfully pressed the pliant government to postpone application of the royalty provisions for the first seven years of a mine's life. During the next session he led another deputation to the parliament buildings which succeeded in further restricting the royalty to net profits rather than gross income.[38]

By the end of the nineteenth century, Ontario mining policy had come full circle from the old monarchical royal metal reservation system, through a period of free mining, and back

---

[38] *Ibid.*, March 9, 14, April 16, 24, 29, 1892; PAC, Robert Bell Papers, Vol. 39, Memorandum on Mining, James Conmee, Jan. 31, 1891; PAC, Bronson Papers, Vol. 711, B. T. A. Bell to E. H. Bronson, April 16, 1891.

to strict, centralized regulation featuring separation of surface from subsurface rights, retention of the latter by the crown, and the imposition of royalties. In his subsequent modifications of the royalty clause and reduction of sale prices, Hardy claimed that the government was nonetheless maintaining "the basic policy, which it had been following since 1891, of combining the principle of inducements to mining with the principle of obtaining a financial return to the public." Over James Conmee's objection that the royalty robbed the prospector of his rights, another Commissioner of Crown Lands contended that "the community should have some interest in such a find," and defended the government's policy on the premise that the public ought "to participate in the benefits of this mineral wealth." Liberal party campaign literature for the 1898 general election proudly elaborated the government's efforts on the one hand to force speculators already in the possession of mineral lands to work them, and on the other to lighten the difficult burdens borne by bona fide prospectors, justifying the modest (and at that time temporarily suspended) royalty with the claim: "Practically, only the 'bounty of nature' is taxed."[39]

The principle that a portion of the "bounty of nature" properly belonged to the public had become one of the basic political values, opposed only by those with special vested interests. Experience with the timber industry had been especially formative in this regard in the sense that it suggested that crown ownership and control of the resource was the best means of asserting this principle. Industry received as favourable terms and relatively free access to the resources as had been found to be compatible with regulatory supervision in the interest of the public and the public revenues. By establishing control over mineral resources rendered both accessible and valuable by a technological revolution, the government of Ontario consciously strove towards a balance between private rights and public responsibilities like that already struck with the forest industry.

[39] Quoted in Evans, "Oliver Mowat and Ontario," p. 457; *Globe*, April 11, 1897; *Record of the Liberal Government: 26 Years of Progressive Legislation and Honest Administration* (Toronto, 1898), p. 76.

IV

As science revolutionized the character of the province's rapids and waterfalls, this basic belief in state control and supervision asserted itself in the government's water policies. The early experience gained at Niagara Falls, the most spectacular and familiar of the provincial waterpowers, established the all important principle of state ownership and control. It should be noted, however, that the regulation of other natural resources necessarily recommended a general policy of crown reservation that would extend beyond the particular situation at Niagara. There were other good reasons, besides the fact that Niagara Falls happened to be within a public park, that determined public rather than private ownership of the major waterpowers of Ontario.

At Niagara, hydro-electric policy developed initially within the framework of parks and recreation policy. Repeated complaints about the gaudy commercialism that blighted the beauty of the cataract prompted Oliver Mowat to pass a bill in 1880 clearing the jurisdictional ground for the federal government to acquire land for a national park at the falls. When Ottawa failed to take advantage of this unusual voluntary abdication of authority by the province, Mowat himself was forced to take action during the 1885 session. A royal commission confirmed the need for such a park and recommended that the sum of $500,000 be raised to purchase the necessary lands. The subsequent incorporation in 1887 of the Queen Victoria Niagara Falls Park empowered the appointed commissioners to issue up to $525,000 worth of debentures for the purpose of buying up the lands in the vicinity of the falls. The act further stipulated that no fee be charged for entry to the grounds, and at the same time served notice that the park would have to be self-sustaining and could not expect to be financed through legislative grants. The dilemma presented by attempting to create an exemplary park without either an admission charge or provincial assistance eventually induced the commissioners to enter the hydro-electric business. The only sources of revenue available under these circumstances were souvenir, transportation and service concessions and, just as these were found to be woefully inadequate to fund the initial debt, startling advances in electrical technology transformed the falls themselves into the most lucrative concession of all.[40]

The first person to approach the parks commission with a plan to generate electricity from the falls was Col. A. D. Shaw of Watertown, New York, in 1887. His offer arrived precisely at the moment when the commissioners realized that income from rentals and concessions would scarcely meet the interest on the debentures, let alone finance a sinking fund. These desperate circumstances explain both the eagerness with which the commissioners entertained the Shaw scheme and their insistence that two years' rental payments for such an exclusive franchise ($50,000) be paid in advance. Shaw, of course, was a speculator, not a developer. He skilfully haggled the commissioners down to a $10,000 advance and then set about peddling his property among likely prospects. After initial overtures to some local New York State industrialists failed to produce a firm offer he tried to interest an English syndicate, organized around S. Z. Ferranti's technical abilities, in the hydro-electric possibilities of Niagara Falls. However, in 1892 those negotiations also collapsed. Withdrawal of this prestigious English group shattered the commissioners' faith in Shaw but not their confidence that "it will only be a short time before the unlimited force of Niagara will be sought after."[41]

Just as Shaw's option and the commissioners' patience with him were about to run out he turned up a third and surprisingly promising group of capitalists in New York City. The technical and financial credentials of the new syndicate were solid indeed. Not only had the group actually begun a similar project on the New York side of the falls, it also numbered among its principals some of the leading names in American finance. The

---

[40] PAC, *Minute Book* of the Niagara Falls Park Commission, May 18–Nov. 11, 1885; Queen Victoria Niagara Falls Park Commissioners, *Report,* 1885, 1887 [hereafter QVNFPC, *Report*]; Ronald Way *Ontario's Niagara Parks* Toronto, 1946), pp. 37ff.

[41] QVNFPC, *Report*, 1889, pp. 78-9; 1890, pp. 101, 117; Way, *Ontario's Niagara Parks*, pp. 52-4. For a biographical sketch of Col. Shaw, see *Who Was Who in America*, Vol. I, 1897-1942 (Chicago, 1943), p. 1110.

key member of the syndicate was Francis Lynde Stetson, pop-
ularly known as J. P. Morgan's attorney general. Associated
with Stetson, of Drexel Morgan and Company, in this enterprise
were Edward D. Adams, of Winslow Lanier and Company,
William B. Rankin of Brown Brothers, and E. A. Wickes, a
colleague of W. K. Vanderbilt.[42] The impressive reputation
of these men led the commissioners to overrule their chairman,
Sir Casimir Gzowski, and to continue negotiating through Shaw
despite the delays. Suddenly in March of 1892 matters began
to move. The Canadian Niagara Power Company, a wholly
owned subsidiary of the American firm across the river, was
incorporated with Col. Shaw as its nominal president. Following
this, the commissioners of the Queen Victoria Niagara Falls
Park leased the exclusive rights to produce power on the
Canadian side to this company in return for an annual rental
of $25,000 and an undertaking that construction would be com-
pleted no later than November 1, 1898. The company further
agreed to sell at least one-half of its output in Canada at prices
no greater than the lowest American contracts, and to submit
both building plans and construction schedules to the commissioners for their technical and aesthetic approval.[43]

At the conclusion of these negotiations a jubilant Col. Shaw
scribbled his gratitude to Sir Oliver Mowat, attributing the
success to the premier's generosity and "noble Christian character." "*Without your rare honesty and great good generalship*," he
exclaimed, "*it would have failed.*" The Niagara Falls project, Shaw
promised, was destined to become "a bright jewel in the crown
of your long and splendid reign," and he prayed that the premier would "live to see it become one—a new—wonder of

---

[42] E. D. Adams, *Niagara Power* (Niagara Falls, 1927) Vol. I, pp. 69-160; Harold
C. Passer, *The Electrical Manufacturers* (Cambridge, Massachusetts, 1953);
and John Dales, *Hydroelectricity and Industrial Development: Quebec, 1898-1940*
(Cambridge, Massachusetts, 1957), pp. 17-21. For detailed biographies
of the members of the Niagara syndicate, see the *Dictionary of American
Biography* and *Who's Who in America*.

[43] PAO, Niagara Falls Park papers, Sir Casimir Gzowski to Sir Oliver Mowat,
March 31, 1892; J. W. Langmuir to Sir Oliver Mowat, Private and Confidential, March 29, 1892; QVNFPC, *Report*, 1892, pp. 158-9 for the contract.

the world."[44] Three premiers would subsequently despair of living long enough even to see it completed. For the new company, though it had progressed further than any of its predecessors and had actually paid the $50,000 so desperately coveted by the commissioners, was just as speculative as the others. The American directors reasoned that when the demand for power outstripped the capacity of their American plant, then in the first stages of construction, the Canadian franchise could be brought into production. In the light of the advantages of a future monopoly at the falls, the annual $25,000 rental demanded by the Canadians seemed a marginal expense. Nevertheless, the waterpower lease granted in 1892 met the minimum requirements of all the parties. It satisfied the Ontario demand for a fixed revenue upon which to develop a park worthy of the natural surroundings and at the same time it assured the province that it would receive a hydro-electric plant built by the most capable entrepreneurs in the world. For its money, the company acquired a monopoly at the largest waterfall in the industrialized northeastern United States, a construction schedule it plainly considered negotiable, and permission to export its Canadian power to the American market.

Meanwhile, as the top-level connections between applied science and finance capitalism attracted Americans to the possibilities of Canadian waterpower, the local Canadian financial community remained preoccupied with its essentially nineteenth-century fixations: railroads of all sorts, insurance and land companies. A Canadian group had in fact been offered the hydro-electric franchise late in the 1880s but it expressed interest solely in building a "scenic railway" along the gorge.[45] It was not until Ontario businessmen took envious notice of the industrial revolution wrought by cheap electricity across the Niagara River in the state of New York that they discovered that their Niagara waterpower had been gobbled up by Americans. At that time, leasehold form of tenure, necessitated in

---

[44] PAO, Niagara Falls Park Papers, Col. Shaw to Sir Oliver Mowat, March 30, 1892.

[45] QVNFPC, *Report*, 1891, p. 117.

the first place by the undeniably public nature of a resource included within a provincial park, proved to be of enormous value in regaining some of this lost ground.

Independent of these events at Niagara Falls, leasehold rather than outright sale had been established as policy for all of the provincial waterpowers. In connection with the 1888 Royal Commission on Mineral Resources, E. B. Borron, a police magistrate for Algoma district, had drawn up a *Report on the Lakes and Rivers, Water and Water-powers of the Province of Ontario*.[46] Borron confidently predicted a brilliant industrial future for the province based upon its hydro-electric resources; the roads of the countryside would be the beds of swift, clean electric railroads, and the small manufacturing towns would rise to supplant and supply Europe. The greater the desire to replace animal and human labour with mechanical power, Borron reasoned " . . . the greater will be the demand for, and greater the importance and value of, our Provincial waterpowers." He understood the implications of the recent technological revolution and the inadequacy of Ontario's traditional land law to cope with it:

> Instead of this power being available only at the place where the water supply and fall may happen to be situated, it can now be utilized anywhere within a radius of at least twenty or thirty miles . . .and the probability is, this distance will be so increased by further discoveries and improvements, that in another ten years, there will not be a village or even homestead in the land, that will not be within range of some one or other of Ontario's magnificent waterpowers.

Borron went on to point out the importance of electricity for farmers, manufacturers, miners, employers, employees and all classes of society and concluded:

> It is thus, a franchise in which the people at large, now and hundreds of years hence, are and will be deeply, nay, vitally interested. It is one, consequently, in which the rights of the Crown, or

---

[46] Published separately in Toronto, 1891.

in other words, of the people, are to be most jealously and carefully guarded.

Under the existing land law, Borron reminded the government, a freehold owner acquired extensive riparian rights
to whatever waterpowers might be found on his property. In
the quiet streams of the settled portions of the province no
great privileges had been inadvertently conferred; in the pre-
electric age the cost of damming a river and the attendant
local implications of the act rendered the work private and
local. But in the unsettled regions of Ontario there were raging
rivers ideally suited to massive hydro-electric exploitation, and
for that reason he argued that the law should be reformed
to take into account the latest scientific achievements for the
public protection. He asked "that in all future sales of land
the water, whether of lakes or rivers (with the exception of
that which may be required for domestic and sanitary purposes)
should be reserved to the Crown as trustee for the benefit
of the people of the Province generally. And that the
waterpowers should not be sold, but leased for a term of years,
the rent charged varying according to circumstances; the position of the fall or rapid, the difficulties to be overcome before
it can be applied or utilized, and even the purposes to which
it is to be put, being all taken into consideration."[47] Such steps,
Borron claimed, would give the state adequate control over
the industry to protect the public interest and at the same time
provide, for larger public purposes, another revenue rent from
the natural resources of the province.

The government took no legislative action on the Borron
report until late in 1897, when it became clear that in spite
of careful supervision of land sales, some properties which contained waterfalls had been alienated. The same day that the
Legislature read for a second time a bill to set aside several
permanent forest reserves, the Commissioner of Crown Lands
also defended for a second time a bill reserving to the crown
all of the province's major waterpowers.[48] In the past the gov-

[47] *Ibid.*, pp. 26-7, 312, 35-6.
[48] 61 Vict., c. 8; Gibson, *Mining Laws*, p. 17; Canada, Commission of
Conservation, *The Water-Powers of Canada*, (Ottawa, 1911), pp. 23-4; *Globe*,
Dec. 29, 1897.

ernment had attempted to prevent the monopolization of waterpowers, Commissioner Gibson claimed, through the tactical manoeuvre of selling lands along only one side of a stream. But, he confessed, some waterfalls had accidentally passed into private hands simply because the crown had not known of their existence. As a result, the commissioner pointed out, "riparian proprietors have become owners of valuable privileges which might, under wise regulation, have been available to the public." The Waterpower Reservation Act under debate would rectify this situation by declaring the principle that all major waterpowers would remain vested in the crown and that the right of usufruct would not be attached to riparian ownership. Regulations drawn up under the act and approved by the cabinet June 21, 1898, stated that the development of provincial waterpowers would be by lease rather than outright sale, that the terms of the lease would stipulate a development schedule or default, and that rental terms depending upon the character of the waterpower would be subject to negotiation between the developer and the crown.[49]

Expanding upon the rationale of the waterpower regulations in his 1898 *Annual Report,* the Commissioner of Crown Lands explained that a scientific revolution had transformed falling water into one of the great undeveloped resources of the crown domain, and a potential source of public revenue. In view of these exciting possibilities the *Report* concluded that by retaining title to waterpower in the hands of the crown and by leasing waterpower privileges instead of selling them outright, the state could demand both a revenue from the industry and prompt performance of construction agreements. Initial rentals, in order to encourage the growth of the industry, would be liberal but could be renegotiated after an interval to correspond more closely to the actual value of the concession.

Thus the politicians and administrators in late nineteenth-century Ontario set out to create legislative foundations for the hydro-electric industry similar to those already established

[49] Commissioner of Crown Lands, *Annual Report*, 1898, p. vii; Bureau of Mines, *Annual Report* (1898), Pt. III, pp. 251-6, "The Water-powers of Ontario," by Thos. W. Gibson.

for forestry and mining. It was their stated intention to promote and control the growth of the industry in order to stimulate rapid utilization, prevent monopoly and speculation, and extract from this new resource a regular income for the consolidated revenue fund. Much of what was thought to be gained by public ownership of the resource was, as we have seen, bargained away in the terms of the exclusive leases governing exploitation of the resource by private interests. Nevertheless, the property rights retained by the state could be used not only to guarantee prompt development, but they also provided a wide avenue for public rate regulation once the industry went into production. Further, public ownership of the resource itself cleared a good deal of semantic and philosophical ground for the eventual debate on the question of public ownership of the industry.

V

The principles of reservation, crown ownership and leasehold tenure which characterized Ontario resource policy stood in bold contrast to their nineteenth-century American counterparts.[50] Americans placed a premium upon the rapid transfer of the public domain, either by outright sale or preemption, into unrestricted private ownership, and the retention of property rights by the state for the welfare of the community became an increasingly un-American notion with the passage of time. The public lands were public only insofar as they were waiting to become private. At mid-century Thomas Hart Benton addressed his annual free land perorations "to Senators who know this to be a Republic, not a Monarchy, who know that the public lands belong to the People and not to the Federal Government." Half a century later, Senator Frank Mondell of Wyoming, attacking Gifford Pinchot's forest and range conservation programmes, echoed Benton: "It was monarchical

---

[50] PAC, J. J. Murphy Papers, "Epitome of the Laws Relating to the Sale and Settlement of the Public Lands of Different States and the British Colonies," ca. 1900, pp. 47-141.

in theory to give only the soil to the settler and reserve everything else to the government."[51] Mondell might indeed have
had the Ontario system in mind, for the particularism of
Ontario's resource alienation policy is the measure of, and serves
to illustrate, some of the fundamental differences that distinguished two societies so superficially alike. Perhaps an
explanation for the comparative conservatism—to Americans,
monarchism—of Ontario's timber, mineral and waterpower
policies is to be found in the interplay of ideological and material
factors, between political values on the one hand and the
environmental and economic characteristics of the Canadian
Shield on the other.

Since the contrasting patterns of resource alienation in central
Canada and the United States appear to correspond quite neatly
with the value systems that are generally thought to have
prevailed in the two societies, it would be tempting to interpret
them in strictly ideological terms. It might be argued that since
private appropriation was the norm in the United States, then
the relatively greater emphasis upon public ownership in
Ontario might be attributed to the comparative strength of
conservative values in that society. And indeed, there is a
flourishing literature on the Canadian conservative tradition
that would help in sustaining such a hypothesis. However, such
an interpretation would provide only a partial explanation of
the phenomenon. A survey of this legislation regulating the
alienation of public property ought to remind us that ideas
must bear some relation to interests or, more particularly, that
the conservatism of Ontario's natural resource laws at the end
of the nineteenth century also had a material foundation.

---

[51] Thomas Hart Benton, *Thirty Years View; or, A History of the Working of American Government for Thirty Years, From 1820 to 1850* (New York, 1871), Vol. I, pp. 103-4, quoted in Benjamin Hibbard, *A History of Public Land Policies* (Madison, 1955 ed.), p. 138; Mondell quoted in Roy M. Robbins, *Our Landed Heritage: The Public Domain, 1776-1936* (Princeton, 1942), p. 387. For an elaboration of the relationship between public philosophy and land policy, see Harris, *Origin of the Land Tenure System in the United States*, pp. 1-20; James Willard Hurst, *Law and Economic Growth: The Legal History of the Lumber Industry in Wisconsin, 1836-1915* (Cambridge, Massachusetts, 1964), pp. 9-11.

Conservative values continued to be operative because they proved, to a certain extent, to be functional.

At a time when American conservative intellectuals were freeing the individual for the progressive Darwinian struggle, Canadian thinkers, owing more to Burke than to Darwin, insisted that the state should provide some measure of moral direction for the society. For them, loyalty to the British crown signified more than just a choice of a particular set of representative institutions; it implied as well an organic view of society within which the crown and the institutions of government moulded the character of the individual, measured wealth against commonwealth, and presided over just and orderly social change.[52]

The importance of this Canadian conservative tradition can be measured not only in those things done in its name, but also in the influence it has had upon the opposing traditions. A continuing dialogue with organic conservatism significantly blunted the individualism, materialism and democratic outlook of the Canadian liberal and profoundly modified his view of the role of the state. Liberals saw no contradiction in defending the authority of the state in the collective interest. It is significant too, that the Liberal government of Ontario at this time championed provincial rather than individual rights and, in pursuit of elevated status and expanded power, it also reaffirmed the importance of the "monarchical element" of the

---

[52] D. G. Creighton, *The Road to Confederation* (Toronto, 1964), pp. 142ff.; W. L. Morton, *The Canadian Identity* (Toronto, 1960), pp. 111-14; *Parliamentary Debates on the Subject of Confederation of the British North American Provinces* (Quebec, 1865), p. 59. On the importance of the monarchy as a symbol of society see also John Farthing, *Freedom Wears a Crown* (Toronto, 1957). S. F. Wise, "Upper Canada and the Conservative Tradition," in Ontario Historical Society, *Profiles of a Province* (Toronto, 1967), pp. 20-33; Gad Horowitz, "Conservatism, Liberalism and Socialism in Canada: An Interpretation," *CJEPS*, Vol. XXXII (1966), pp. 143-71. On the influence of conservatism on the liberal tradition see also F. H. Underhill, *In Search of Canadian Liberalism* (Toronto, 1960), pp. 12-15, 68-84; R. Hofstadter, *Social Darwinism in American Thought* (Boston, 1955 ed.), p. 8; C. Berger, *The Sense of Power: Studies in the Ideas of Canadian Imperialism, 1867-1914* (Toronto, 1970), pp. 155-62, 187-8.

constitution. And it is the measure of the conservative impact upon reform thinking that these same Liberals mounted a popular and successful campaign to expand the unimpaired jurisdiction of the provincial government over property and civil rights without first establishing constraints upon the use of that power.[53] So, too, the corporatist bias of Ontario's natural resource laws might be seen as a product of that tradition.

However, there were other equally important influences besides currents of thought that sanctioned the conservatism apparent in these laws. In the first place, the Canadian Shield imposed certain limitations upon the use to which the land might be put and, therefore, the manner in which it might be alienated. Secondly, the Shield supported an economy all its own and the strongest elements of that economy, the lumbermen, chose to protect and foster their interests by defending rather than reducing the power of the state. Finally, and more tentatively, an aversion to direct taxation forced politicians to expand the authority of the state in those areas where indirect taxation in various forms might possibly produce a revenue sufficient to meet the costs of necessary services.

Precisely because the Shield laid down a definite and undeniable boundary to the limits of prime arable land, it frustrated the application in Ontario of a unitary socio-political conception of the environment similar to the agrarian homestead myth which so radically affected American resource alienation policies. Philosophers, poets and politicians, setting their republican, democratic political beliefs against a physical backdrop of seemingly endless fertile land, magnified the image of the yeoman farmer to embody the political and social values of the nation. Rooted in the elemental faith that every man had a natural right to the land, that agriculture was the only true source of wealth, and that the labour spent on the land

---

[53] J. C. Morrison, "Oliver Mowat and the Development of Provincial Rights in Ontario: A Study in Dominion-Provincial Relations, 1867-1896," in Ontario Archives, *Three History Theses* (Toronto, 1961), pp. 59ff. For an attempted quantification of the conservatism of Canadian values, see Seymour M. Lipset, *The First New Nation: The United States in A Historical and Comparative Perspective* (New York, 1963), pp. 248-73.

conferred the best title to it, the "agrarian myth" spawned a
profusion of derivative values; the foremost being that land
ownership carried status and self-respect, that the independence fostered by property afforded the basis for freedom and rational judgment, and the mystical notion that the
farmer's communion with nature and the earth ensured the
permanent happiness and purity of the republic. This cluster
of values drawn from the pastoral poets and physiocrats seemed
to be confirmed by the early interaction of men with their
environment in America, with the result that the primary intent
of American land policy by mid-century was the western extension of a "fee simple empire." The homestead system imposed
that single conception of the environment as a Farmers' Frontier
upon the public lands policy. Because the object in passing
the entire public domain by 160-acre plots to professed
cultivators for either cash or their labour in fee simple was
the perpetuation of the Republic, all other forms of land tenure
were quite naturally dismissed as alien. Thus, Senator Benton's
denunciation of tenantry: "It lays the foundation for separate
orders in society, annihilates the love of country, and weakens
the spirit of independence." Thus also Frederick Jackson
Turner's disquietude at the passing of the frontier of free land.[54]

The triumph of agrarianism in the United States not only
obliterated other concepts of land alienation, it also tended
to eliminate the demonstrable distinction between lands suitable
for agriculture and those suitable for other, industrial uses.
In Wisconsin, for example, agrarian values limited the
"imagination and will which men brought to handling the
timbered public lands," with the result that "policy derived from
the disposal of lands primarily valuable for agriculture
dominated the disposition of lands that were in fact primarily
valuable for timber."[55] The point is not simply that agrarian
land policies were applied to natural resource lands and ma-

[54] Benton, *Thirty Years View*, Vol. I, pp. 103-4; Henry Nash Smith, *Virgin
Land: The American West as Symbol and Myth* (New York, 1950), pp. 151ff.;
Leo Marx, *The Machine in the Garden: Technology and the Pastoral Ideal in
America* (Boston, 1967), pp. 73ff.

[55] Hurst, *Law and Economic Growth*, pp. 13, 127.

nipulated by timber and mining barons with scandalous consequences, but rather that the freehold tenure system became the norm for natural resource allocation. The idea that lands should be transferred outright, the state abandoning all encumbrances, converted questions of resource use and management into private decisions; whereas in the centralized Ontario system they remained public along with ownership of the resources. American liberal agrarianism dispersed decision-making power amongst innumerable freeholders, while the Ontario government retained some of that discretion over the non-agricultural resources for itself.[56]

In Canada the interaction between political values and geographic environment did not permit one conception of land use to dominate the entire framework of resource alienation. The liberal, philosophical foundations for agrarianism were weaker, and the rocky margin of the Shield clearly limited the very conditions of its existence, namely prime arable land. Like democracy itself, Canadian agrarianism was more a condition and less of a theory than in the United States. The 1868 Ontario Free Grant and Homestead Act, which marked the watershed of agrarian influence in land policy, represented at best a drawn battle with the Shield and its economy. The north of the Free Grant Act was not to be the west of the American Homestead Act; the homestead townships were only to be located in areas not primarily valuable for minerals or pine timber. Furthermore, all the pine not required for homebuilding remained the property of the crown along with "all gold, silver, copper, lead, iron and other mines or minerals." Later, of course, waterpower rights would also be stripped from the land. Ontario politicians used the rhetoric of the pre-emptive frontier, but the fine print guaranteed that no natural resource windfalls would pass unwittingly into the possession of Ontario's yeomen.[57]

---

[56] Hibbard, *A History of Public Land Policies*, pp. 243, 411-72; Robbins, *Our Landed Heritage*, pp. 243-7; John Ise, *The United States Forest Policy* (New Haven, 1920), p. 48; M. Clawson and B. Held, *The Federal Lands: Their Use and Management* (Baltimore, 1957), pp. 400-73.

[57] William McDougall, the former voice of radical Grit opinion, thought a Homestead Act would only attract "pauper immigration" rather than an independent yeomanry; H. M. Morrison, "The Background of the Free Homestead Law of 1872," *CHAR*, 1935, p. 63.

Secondly, an agrarian, freehold conception of land alienation not only conflicted with the physical reality of the Canadian Shield, but also the vested interests dependent upon it. The most important of these interests, the lumbermen, held under licence vast tracts of forested Shield land for present and future use. The leasehold system, as we have seen, ideally suited their needs. They were interested in timber not land, and they preferred to pay for the bulk of that timber as it was cut and sold. Their licence met their immediate needs and also, it should be noted, gave them a moral claim on the government for services and protection, the latter mainly in the form of protection against settlers. They regarded freehold tenure, as well as the agrarian philosophy upon which it rested, as a threat. The quality of the land which supported the lumbering economy repelled, by its very nature, a large-scale invasion of the licensed forest by settlers. Though there were scattered pockets of good land to be found there, the generally thin soil and rock of the bulk of the Shield precluded its being parcelled out to a permanent farming population. No amount of agrarian rhetoric could transform the wilderness Shield into the garden of the freehold farmer. Whenever the farmers of the southern part of the province demanded the opening up of more land in the north the lumbermen reminded them of the cold, inhospitable nature of the land and the government of the revenues that would be lost if such a course of action were followed. The Shield itself and the economic interests dependent upon it challenged a unitary, agrarian view of the environment. Indeed, together they generated a competitive myth of a solemn, empty, resource-rich northern land.[58] Instead of the homesteading philosophy changing established ways of thinking about land in Ontario, quite the reverse occurred. Interest groups and authoritarian instincts profoundly altered it.

Finally, fiscal need might be considered the third of the material forces underlying the apparent conservative bias of

[58] Gates, *Land Policies of Upper Canada*, p. 302; F. B. Murray, "Agricultural Settlement on the Canadian Shield," in *Profiles of a Province*, pp. 178-88; Cole Harris, "The Myth of the Land in Canadian Nationalism," and Carl Berger, "The True North Strong and Free," in Peter Russell, ed., *Nationalism in Canada* (Toronto, 1966).

Ontario's natural resource law. Was Ontario fiscally poor compared to neighbouring regions in the United States from which
its population tended to derive its expectations of the kinds
of services governments ought to provide? Were there enough
tax dollars per capita to support the schools, roads, public works
and social services that Ontario citizens were in the habit of
demanding? Or, the question might be framed another way;
were Ontarians generally more reluctant to tax themselves to
pay for the services they expected and, therefore, were they
more prone to think of their natural resources as the proper
source of revenue to relieve themselves of their obligations?
Certainly whenever Ontario politicians justified a timber sale,
or the principle of royalties and public ownership of waterpowers, they did so on the grounds that these indirect
measures would allow Ontario to avoid what was always referred
to as the "bugbear" of direct taxation for the immediate future
at least. When, for example, on one occasion the editor of the
*Globe* suggested that timber dues be rebated to encourage home
manufacturing into sawn lumber, the Premier of the province
quickly lectured him on the facts of fiscal life. "For God's sake,"
Arthur Hardy wrote to J. S. Willison, "don't press your suggestion of this morning that we should abandon all timber dues.
Are we to commence to levy direct taxation upon the farmers
to feed the lumbermen? . . . The whole country would rise in
arms against us, except the lumbermen."[59] This deep-seated
aversion to direct taxation, which might have been a function
of comparative underdevelopment or a resistance to suffer
taxation when other revenue sources lay at hand, might serve
to illuminate the persistence of political authority, even public
ownership, in the natural resource, export-oriented sector of
the economy. However, it would require an extended study
in comparative public finance to establish fully the tentative
hypothesis advanced here. What can be said at this point is
that Ontario politicians and civil servants thought of public

[59] *Globe*, Thurs., Nov. 4, 1897; PAC, Willison Papers, Vol. 38, A. S. Hardy
to J. S. Willison, Nov. 4, 1897, private and confidential. On the Canadian
aversion to direct taxation, see also J. H. Perry, *Taxation in Canada* (Toronto,
1951), p. 11.

control over the natural resource sector as one way of delaying or deflecting the incidence of direct taxation.

What could explain, Professor A. R. M. Lower once asked, the disparity in the relationship of the individual to the state reflected in the terms of land tenure on the Canadian and American frontiers? Did so much land and authority remain in the hands of the crown simply because of the vast expanse of land involved, or was this the consequence of a "long, consistent and pertinacious public policy," or had it come to pass merely by chance?[60] In response it might be submitted that maintenance of the old, imperial habit of authority into the industrial age stemmed primarily from the interaction of interest groups and moderately conservative ideology, within an agriculturally barren environment. The lumbermen, the Shield, and the threat of direct taxation sanctioned a set of resource laws that preserved the germ of an earlier collectivist, conservative conception of the state. The interaction of these ideological and material forces blunted the individualistic, appropriative, liberal qualities—in short the "Americanness"—of the northern Ontario frontier.

[60] *Settlement on the Forest Frontier* (Toronto, 1936), pp. 49, 77.

# 2
# The Manufacturing Condition

The resource developers of Ontario were enthusiastic con-
tinentalists during the late nineteenth century for substantially
the same reasons as the province's farmers. The United States
was their best market and the cheapest source of the manufactured goods they required to produce more efficiently. But
unlike the farmers, they went further to observe that Americans
also possessed the requisite capital, technology and experience
to initiate the proper development of the provincial resource
base. Yet the federal governments of these two countries wilfully
impeded what they considered to be a natural flow of trade
and investment between neighbours. Thus both the resource
developers and the proprietor of the resources, the provincial
government, believed continental free trade in natural products
to be their optimal development strategy.

Not surprisingly Ontario mining promoters and lumbermen
were the moving spirits of the Commercial Union movement
of the late 1880s. Samuel J. Ritchie and his friend, the ex-
patriate Canadian New York financier, Erastus Wiman virtually

dreamed up the trade liberalization movement to open up markets for their Ontario iron and copper mines. They were energetically abetted in their campaign by the lumberman-politician John Charlton and his colleagues in the forest industry whose objectives were identical. Goldwin Smith and Edward Farrer supplied a thin gilding of intellectual respectability to what was basically a businessmen's pressure group.[1] In 1888 the newly organized Ontario Lumberman's Association unanimously endorsed a resolution calling for "free commercial intercourse between the United States and Canada" by whatever means possible. Shortly afterwards the Ontario Royal Commission on Mineral Resources issued a ringing appeal for an end to what it called the "commercial belligerency" that had so retarded the growth of the Canadian mining industry. Trade barriers, in the opinion of the commissioners, had excluded Canada from the mainstream of progress: "The tariff wall serves like a wing-dam to direct the current from us. Remove the dam and the current will reach us full force." At the end of their investigation they could only conclude sadly, in words borrowed from Samuel J. Ritchie, "that what God had joined together man had rent assunder."[2] About the same time the leading Ontario Liberals were busily at work converting Laurier and the federal party to a policy of unrestricted reciprocity.[3]

Twenty years later all of this had changed. When the reciprocity issue was again joined in 1911, the mood of Ontario, more particularly its government and resource sector, had undergone a profound shift. The then premier, Sir James

---

[1] R. C. Brown, "The Commercial Unionists in Canada and the United States," *CHAR* (1963) p. 117; Ian Grant, "Erastus Wiman: A Continentalist Replies to Canadian Imperialism," *CHR*, Vol. LIII (1972), pp. 5-7; G. M. Adam, ed., *Handbook of Commercial Union* (Toronto, 1888), pp. 131-41, 190-295; John Charlton, *Speeches and Addresses, Political, Literary and Religious* (Toronto, 1905), pp. 129-50.

[2] PAO, Ontario Lumberman's Association, *Minute Book*, Feb. 8, 1888, p. 130; Royal Commission on the Mineral Resources of Ontario, *Report*, pp. xvi, xvii, 212, 215-30.

[3] Paul Stevens, "Laurier and the Liberal Party in Ontario, 1887-1911" (unpublished Ph.D. thesis, University of Toronto, 1967), pp. 10-84; C.R.W. Biggar, *Sir Oliver Mowat*, Vol. II (Toronto, 1905), pp. 577-81.

Whitney, introduced a resolution in the House condemning reciprocity for the usual reasons—that it would smash the empire and lead directly to annexation—but also because it would "jeopardize the continuance of the present satisfactory condition." Laurier's program of trade liberalization would, Whitney pointed out, " . . . reverse the policy which has brought Canada to her present enviable position, would cause widespread and revolutionary disturbance in her business, would curtail and hamper her freedom in developing her own resources in her own way. . . ." Sir George Ross told the Toronto Board of Trade that he believed that the free exchange of natural products would cripple Canadian industry.[4] Even some of those lumbermen who in the early 1890s had urged reciprocity upon the Liberal party, like E. H. Bronson of Ottawa, had publicly changed their minds.[5] By 1911 neither the provincial government nor the bulk of its resource developers considered reciprocity in natural products to be either a realistic or desirable development policy.

During the debate over commercial union it had been possible for a spokesman for the Ontario mining industry, contrasting the undeveloped mines of Ontario with the ore-hungry smelters just across the border, to remark: "If the duty were removed this trade would find its natural channel, to the great benefit of the United States furnaces and of our mines." By 1911 it was no longer advisable to talk like that in public. "Reciprocity," the member for Sault Ste. Marie bluntly told the Legislature, "would result only in an outright American robbery of our resources." It made no sense, William H. Hearst continued, to struggle to establish resource-based industries only to undermine them with reciprocal free trade in natural products. "I have a higher idea than merely getting money for our raw material. I want to see it manufactured into steel rails and pulpwood [he meant woodpulp] by Canadian workmen . . .

---

[4] *Sir James Whitney on American Reciprocity: The Parting of the Ways* (Toronto, 1911) and Sir George Ross, *Speech Before the Toronto Board of Trade* (Toronto, 1911).

[5] PAC, Bronson Papers, Vol. 704, E. H. Bronson to Sir Wilfrid Laurier and W. S. Fielding, Mar. 3, and Mar. 8, 1911.

Canadian raw materials manufactured by Canadian workmen who will receive Canadian money in return."[6] Twenty years of experience with resource development problems and a genuine industrial boom had conditioned people in Ontario to demand both the mines *and* the furnaces. In the interval something akin to a provincial version of the National Policy had evolved.

Within those two decades Ontario had acquired a new image of itself. The barren north suddenly became New Ontario and the province an Empire. The phrase "Empire Ontario"[7] described the natural resource wealth and entrepreneurial energy that had been recently discovered within the boundaries of the province. It implied extraction and manufacture, the creation of a new pattern of industrialization linked to the northern resource base. It was the same white water, granite and endless spruce forest that had defied penetration in the nineteenth century, but technological change had transformed these former disappointments into the foundation of industrial greatness in the twentieth, or at least so it seemed. The first stage of this rethinking process involved the exploration and reappraisal of the environment in the light of technological changes, followed by the propagation and assimilation of this new information. Then, while technology gave value to the Ontario landscape, impatient businessmen formed an alliance with an equally impatient provincial government to accelerate the second stage, the actual coming of industry. The emergence of this "manufacturing condition," both the frame of mind and the development strategy, forms the subject of this chapter.

---

[6]  T. D. Ledyard, "Commercial Union and the Mining Interests of Canada," in Adam, *Handbook of Commercial Union*, p. 85; Hearst quoted in Brian D. Tennyson, "The Political Career of Sir William H. Hearst" (unpublished M.A. thesis, University of Toronto, 1963), pp. 33-5.

[7]  The phrase is taken from Harold Innis, "An Introduction to the Economic History of Ontario from Outpost to Empire" (1934), reprinted in M. Q. Innis, ed., *Essays in Canadian Economic History* (Toronto, 1962 ed.), pp. 108-22. It was also current at the time; see PAO, Whitney Papers, J. J. Cassidy, editor of the *Canadian Manufacturer,* to J.P. Whitney, Jan. 16, 1899.

I

An awareness of the character of the northern regions of Ontario had been gradually accumulating since mid-century. Before then the north had been a land of mystery, a silent kingdom of fur-trading companies and Indians, a massive, indistinct blur on the maps marked "Immense Forests." As late as 1854 Orillia boasted that it was the closest "European" town to the North Pole. The questions raised by the possession of that enormous territory beyond the settled districts running all the way to the height of land somewhere north of Lake Superior did not become central issues in Ontario politics until the region itself became the battleground, quite literally, of an impassioned and protracted dominion-provincial dispute over the northern and western boundaries of the province.[8]

This conflict tended to raise contradictory images of the nature and content of the north. For the people of the farms, villages and towns of the south, northern Ontario became "New Ontario" in two senses: from one point of view its massive dimensions provided land for the permanent renewal of the pioneer cycle, bringing in its wake increased commercial prosperity for the metropolitan south. Yet from another vantage this barren, northern wilderness seemed destined to remain forever empty, to repel by its very nature the expansion of agricultural settlement. Instead it gave the promise of a new experience, the creation of an industrial economy based upon its unique natural resources. It was in this double sense that the north was new: it furnished new ground for the extension of familiar activity, and raw materials for the growth of a whole new generation of modern industries.

[8] J. E. Hodgetts, *Pioneer Public Service* (Toronto, 1955), p. 120; R. I. Wolfe, "The Summer Resorts of Ontario in the Nineteenth Century," *Ontario History*, Vol. LIV (1962), p. 66; Morris Zaslow, "The Ontario Boundary Question," in Ontario Historical Society, *Profiles of a Province* (Toronto, 1967), pp. 107-17; K. MacKirdy, "National vs. Provincial Loyalty: The Ontario Western Boundary Dispute, 1883-1884," *Ontario History*, Vol. LI (1959), pp. 191-8.

It is entirely to be expected that a predominantly agricultural community would define its new lands in its own image. If the thick forest that had covered southern Ontario hid bountiful, arable land, then surely the vast pineries of the north would yield similar riches. Thus, at the beginning of this period the conception of the north as a farming frontier seemed the stronger image and the Free Grants Act of 1869 represented the most forthright expression of this sentiment in policy, though it was a policy heavily qualified by the timber interests. Thereafter the government, in pamphlets such as the Department of Agriculture publication, *The Province of Ontario, Its Soils, Climate, Resources, Institutions and Free Grant Lands,* Alexander Kirkwood's catalogue of *The Undeveloped Lands in Northern and Western Ontario,* and *Ontario as a Home for the British Tenant Farmer Who Desires to Become His Own Landlord,* vigorously promoted the farming possibilities of the north.[9] To that end as well the Mowat government pursued a program of building colonization roads, subsidizing railroads, establishing immigration bureaux in Great Britain, and maintaining experimental pioneer farms in the remote regions to demonstrate the feasibility of northern agriculture. And, of course, just as agricultural interest in the north compared to the west seemed to flag at the turn of the century, politically inspired surveys of New Ontario discovered an unbroken expanse of superb farmland, fully three-quarters of the area of the settled parts of Ontario, the Great Clay Belt.[10] In spite of rampant speculation in these free grant lands and the almost criminal suffering endured in the thousands of failures, the conception of the north as a colonization frontier proved to be a durable constant of the Ontario psyche. In 1901 lands were set aside for Boer War and Fenian Raid veterans; in 1917 the Ontario Returned Soldiers and Sailors Land Settlement Act made homesteads available in the north for postwar rehabilitation; finally the 1932 Dominion Relief Land

[9]  Toronto, 1869, 1878 and 1888 respectively.
[10] Margaret Evans, "Oliver Mowat and Ontario" (unpublished Ph.D. thesis, University of Toronto, 1967), pp. 446-7; Sir George W. Ross, *Getting into Parliament and After* (Toronto, 1913), pp. 196-210; *Report of the Survey and Exploration of Northern Ontario, 1900* (Toronto, 1901), pp. xvi, xvii.

Settlement scheme, a dominion-provincial shared-cost program, offered thousands on relief the opportunity of a free
farm on the northern frontier. No Ontario government could
escape the pressure of such back-to-the-land movements until
1935, when Mitch Hepburn broke the tradition with characteristic directness: "We are going out of the business of colonization.
It is unsound in principle and simply throwing good money
after bad."[11]

All along, of course, there had been another view, a minority
report on the north that acquired adherents with the passage
of time. The lumbermen always did their best to challenge
the agricultural vision of the Shield country. They mounted
a persistent agitation against what they felt to be foolish and
destructive settlement programs. In 1905, for example, they
reminded the new government that over two-thirds of the
homesteaders had utterly failed and fewer than 25 per cent
had carried out the minimum improvements required for a
patent. Again and again they insisted: "Where the land is fitted
for timber growing, and for that only, timber is what should
be grown upon it, and properly managed, would be much the
most valuable use to which the land could be put." Similarly,
government officials, who knew the land well, tended to stress
the industrial rather than the agricultural potential of the north.
Thomas Gibson, of the Bureau of Mines, pointed out that what
farmland could be found in the north lay scattered between
"countless rocky ridges and great stretches of peat morass."
As for the prospect of supporting an agricultural community
in those areas, Gibson wrote, "The idea is preposterous."[12]

But from a different perspective the north was a region of
tremendous physical and cultural richness. No book on Canada

[11] R. S. Lambert and Paul Pross, *Renewing Nature's Wealth* (Toronto, 1967),
pp. 300-12; see also, PAC, Willison Papers, Vol. 40, W. H. Hearst to
J. S. Willison, Nov. 4, 1915; PAO, Drury Papers, Memorandum on the Kapuskasing Colony, Jan. 20, 1920.

[12] PAO, Ontario Lumberman's Association Papers, Memorial to the Provincial
Government, April 6, 1905; *Canada Lumberman*, Feb., 1906; Thomas
Gibson, "The Hinterland of Ontario," Bureau of Mines, *Annual Report*,
1894, pp. 101-38.

published late in the century could avoid at least one chapter heavily freighted with statistics revealing "The Nature and Extent of Its Resources." These natural endowments and their northern location kindled great enthusiasm, especially in literary quarters. Canadians were in the process of discovering, George Parkin told his London *Times* readers in 1892, that they possessed "precisely that combination of condition and resources which history has proved most favourable to human progress." The possibilities of the north led F. A. Wightman to boast that Canada was situated on "the best half of the best continent God ever made," and he confidently predicted that Moose Factory was destined to become "the new Chicago of the North." Writers such as these worshipped not only the recently discovered natural abundance of the region but also its northern location. If the land was innately promising the climate would guarantee energy and intelligence required to realize that promise. For, it was commonly thought, the sharp geographical and climatic contrasts of the northern environment bred hardy, red-cheeked, self-reliant men, through whose bodies coursed a warming intelligence and vigour, and an abiding love of Anglo-Saxon liberty.[13]

The north needed capital more than farmers; it was more of an industrial than an agricultural frontier. That was the message percolating out from government publications and the financial press during the 1890s to form part of the popular conception of the north.[14] The endless spruce forests would support scores of pulp and paper mills; rivers could be harnessed with great dams and generating stations, and of course the Shield could be made to yield up the vast hordes of precious minerals it was known to be hiding. Silver Islet and Sudbury, surely, had been the merest glimpses of what

[13] George R. Parkin, *The Great Dominion: Studies of Canada* (London, 1895), p. 90; Rev. F. A. Wightman, *Our Canadian Heritage* (Toronto, 1905), pp. 7, 107; Carl Berger, "The True North Strong and Free," in Peter Russell, ed., *Nationalism in Canada* (Toronto, 1966), p. 5.

[14] Bureau of Mines, *Annual Report*, 1892, p. 30; 1894, pp. 7-9; 1895, p. 11; *Monetary Times*, May 20, 1892; Nov. 25, 1892; Sept. 18, 1896; Feb. 26, 1897; Jan. 27, 1899; March 10, 1899.

was to come. These were the fragments of the new industrial image of the north. No better example of the integration and popularization of this vision of New Ontario at the turn of the century could be chosen than the speeches of an American industrialist-promoter, Francis Hector Clergue.

In a widely reported address to the Toronto Board of Trade on April 2, 1900, Clergue astounded the Toronto businessmen with the exciting message that Ontario possessed all the essential requirements of a self-sufficient industrial state. His fifty-minute oration, aptly entitled "An Instance of Industrial Evolution in Northern Ontario," synthesized this new spirit of optimism. He linked familiar commonplaces of abundance with the popular belief in progress through social and industrial evolution. He confidently rested his case on the ingenuity of modern applied science, the virtues of technical efficiency, the richness of Canadian natural resources, and the transcending will of the individual. After his address to the Board of Trade Francis Hector Clergue became, for a brief time, a living symbol of the fullness of the industrial potential of New Ontario.

An archetypal rugged individualist, equally at ease in the northern bush and the hushed boardrooms of New York and Philadelphia, the robust, handsome and supremely self-confident F. H. Clergue seemed then as now a figure drawn more from literature than from life. Even the sombre *Monetary Times*, after losing its customary equilibrium in praise of his Board of Trade address, felt constrained to reassure its readers: "Mr. Clergue does not look at all like a fairy prince, but he does look and talk like a level-headed man with much practical knowledge and business sense, plus an unusual degree of courage and strong faith in his country." With a promoter's effortless eloquence, Clergue had cast a magic spell of calculated understatements, drawing his listeners in and conveying to them the smug camaraderie of being on the inside. His unsinkable optimism, generosity and soothing flattery made him a hard man to deny. Many years later Sir Wilfrid Laurier (himself no easy mark) advised the premier of British Columbia asking for a letter of recommendation for Clergue to exercise "extreme caution": "Clergue is a man of remarkable power," Laurier wrote. "He has a faculty of conception of ideas and ability to put them forth which I have met in the course of my long career in very few men, even if any." The great danger in dealing with Clergue was his inability to follow his grand schemes through; as Laurier put it, he was "not strong in execution."[15]

However, in 1900 Clergue was at the height of his power, strutting, posing and publicizing his achievements like the hero of a second-rate romantic novel. In fact, the character of Clark in Allan Sullivan's *The Rapids* is a thinly disguised portrait of Clergue. At the time he was Ontario's only fully animated "captain of industry" and he played the part with the boldness and audacity of a Robber Baron to be sure, but also with some of the endearing absurdity of Leacock's Idle Rich.[16]

"It fell to my fortune," Clergue began modestly after his initial pleasantries, "to be associated with some gentlemen who were possessed of some means more than they could find profitable investments for and it was agreed between us that we should begin a prospecting tour along the basin of the St. Lawrence . . . in order to ascertain what opportunities there existed along this frontier for hydraulic development."[17] As he told it, he passed through Sault Ste. Marie, Ontario, on this "prospecting tour" in 1894—though other evidence would suggest 1892—and discovered the flooded ruins of that town's half-completed municipal power plant. The site was plainly ideal: "with Lake Superior as a mill-pond and a fall of about twenty feet," Clergue realized the tremendous hydro-electric potential of the St. Mary's rapids. The town fathers on the other hand were eager to unload their debt-ridden misfortune in municipal enterprise and quickly assigned their power rights to Clergue and his colleagues for $225,000 in cash. Clergue then completed the power plant and opened it for business.

[15] *Monetary Times*, April 6, 1900; PAC, Laurier Papers, Laurier to H. C. Brewster, March 5, 1917, 195013.

[16] Sullivan, *The Rapids* (Toronto, 1920), reprinted with an introduction by J. M. Bliss, 1972.

[17] The speech was reprinted several times as a pamphlet with the title, *An Instance of Industrial Evolution in Northern Ontario, Dominion of Canada* (Toronto, 1901). This account follows the verbatim report of the *Globe*, April 3, 1900.

"In our simplicity at that time it seemed to us that we had simply to go on, construct the dam, establish the water-wheels in place, and that all the manufacturers in the world would come to us to seek for power." But this expected migration of consumers which the owners had witnessed time and again in the northeastern United States did not take place, and as a result the power company itself had to diversify its interests to finance and build power-using factories to consume its own production:

> We began the development of that water-power, and having gotten the water-wheels into position, we then began to study the natural resources of the region, to determine to what uses that power could be profitably put. And that is a study which I advise any gentleman to make before he makes any investment in water power.

No doubt the wholesalers and smallwares manufacturers of Toronto nodded in agreement as they relit their cigars, squinting and knitting their brows as they made a mental note of Clergue's experience for the next time they risked a million or more in hydro-electric developments.

The "industrial evolution" set in motion by the power installation began with a pulp mill which consumed great quantities of readily available electricity and spruce, using the former to grind the latter into mechanical pulp for American papermakers. Pressed by heavy transportation costs, Clergue himself invented a drying machine that allowed his product entry into the competitive American market; then there followed in rapid succession a foundry to forge parts for the huge grinding machines, and a chemical pulp mill to produce a more profitable form of sulphite pulp. But it was the search for sulphur that stimulated even more dramatic evolutionary changes, leading the original power company by a circuitous route into the steel business. When the cost of importing sulphur from Sicily, the only major source of supply in the world, proved prohibitive, Clergue confidently turned to the Algoma that had already supplied him with so many raw materials for the then rare element: "I went up to the works at Sudbury and found they were racing sulphurous acid gas off into the air at a value of $2,000 a day at an expense and loss....I was not going to Sicily to find sulphur with all the sulphurous acid gas going into the air at Sudbury." Dismissing incredulous pulp experts, and brushing aside unco-operative mine owners, Clergue went ahead and bought his own nickel property at Sudbury for the sulphur, confident that he and his staff could solve the many problems involved just as they had the pulp drying:

> I have had the good sense to assemble about myself practical and scientific men from all parts of the world, who are supposed to represent the latest knowledge and experience in every class of scientific and practical undertaking which we have to engage in, and my own staff, at my call day and night—numbering over one hundred men—so that you can see that among the technical and scientific men in different departments of engineering, the resources available to us for information are broader, more ample, than are usual in places so far distant from civilization as Sault Ste. Marie, Ont.

His Toronto audience, already drawn in by the magnetic, almost hypnotic power of his voice, exploded with delight when Clergue revealed that his engineers were able to obtain a perfect sulphur liquor for the chemical pulp mill from the Sudbury ore. More amazing still, the sulphur reduction process left a rich ferro-nickel alloy which Clergue exported to Europe to the great Krupp works. However, the alloy, it turned out after the applause had died down, was *too rich* in nickel; alas, it seemed as if American iron ore would have to be imported to bring the iron-nickel constituents of the alloy into better proportion from the European armsmakers. That would never do:

> ...I had made up my mind never to ask for anything that had to be procured outside of Algoma. (Applause) I was bound that we should not be under the necessity of using American iron ore in Algoma, and so we looked around in Algoma for iron. (Applause) Nor had we far to look for red hematite. It was as I had always convinced myself that nature had not so disposed matters that all the hematite was placed on the American side. It was ready. It was at hand, and I assure you, as good as any iron in America. (Applause)

A huge iron mine was then opened in Algoma, and blast furnaces rose at the Soo. From deep in the forests and mountains of the interior, armies of men extracted nickel, iron ore, pulpwood and construction timbers which were hauled to the shore on Clergue's railway, then transferred to Clergue's ships for the journey to Clergue's smelter, pulp mills, reduction works, and the latest in the evolutionary chain, a steel rail mill. When he neared the end of his narrative, the practised spellbinder wondered aloud whether his audience might be tiring of the long cycle; from the audience rose a clamour, "No, No,...Go on." Relenting just long enough for one last grandiloquent flourish of self-congratulation, Clergue "resumed his seat amid great applause."

In the brief question period that followed the chairman asked the distinguished speaker's opinion of the proper public policy to encourage enterprises such as his own. Speaking "entirely from a commercial standpoint," Clergue replied: "It seems to me that the preservation to Canada of the raw materials which now exist there is one of the simplest principles about which children could not dispute, much less grown men"—an assertion that evoked loud cheering. Canadians ought to resist the temptation, he continued, of exporting raw materials to the United States when in fact these could be easily turned into manufactured products in Canada. And, in the long-term Canadian interest, it was of the greatest importance that Canadians not export raw materials to the United States if the manufactured forms faced stiff tariff barriers at the American border. There should be no trade in raw materials, he insisted, unless there was also a fair interchange of manufactures as well. Such a policy would simultaneously attract more Americans such as himself to Canadian opportunities and restore the confidence of Canadian businessmen in their own resources and their capacity to develop them.

Back at Sault Ste. Marie and in Toronto again in February 1901, Clergue repeated his triumph, stressing again that the Canadian stock of natural, industrial materials was, as each day passed, putting the country in a more favourable position to trade finished manufactured products with the United States. What industry required from government was assistance in the form of bonuses, so that manufacturing could get under way, a patriotic policy of using Canadian-made goods, and a resolute will to resist exporting unmanufactured raw materials to the

United States until that country relaxed its duties against Canadian goods. Most important, Canadians needed confidence in their natural wealth. Was it not ironic that Clergue, an American, should be standing before an audience of Canadians informing them of their own patrimony? At long last the message had managed to get through. "We have pestered the government so persistently," he told the Toronto Board of Trade, "with arguments in favour of Canada that they are reasonably well impressed with their own assets...." But, he claimed, the financial community, businessmen and industrialists in traditional lines still stood back, leaving others, outsiders like himself, to lead the way.[18]

Clergue's speeches made a deep impact on the Canadian press; the *Globe* and the provincial dailies reprinted the 1900 Board of Trade Speech in full. The irony of it all was not lost on the *Monetary Times*: "The enterprise and faith of this man and his Philadelphia associates are at once a rebuke and an encouragement to Canadians. A rebuke to those who, having capital were afraid to risk it, and an encouragement to such as would like to do something worthy in the way of exploration or industrial enterprise, to apply themselves to the development of the resources we possess." The *Globe*, while it showed warm enthusiasm for Clergue's message of industrial prosperity, struggled at the same time to reconcile its own free trade principles with the economic nationalism advocated by Clergue: "The lesson impressed by this development [Clergue's Soo industries] is the great value of our national resources and the folly of being in haste to alienate them. If we have the wealth in the forest, in mineral deposits, in the wasted energy of great waterfalls, or even in agricultural land, it is certain to be developed as the world's demands and the discoveries of science make such development remunerative.[19]

---

[18] *Address by F. H. Clergue at a Banquet Given in his honour by the Citizens of Sault Ste. Marie, Ontario*, February 19, 1901, pamphlet, n.d., pp. 4-5; *Address Delivered by Francis H. Clergue at a Banquet Given in his honour at Sault Ste. Marie, Michigan*, February 21, 1901, pamphlet, n.d., p. 7; *Canadian Annual Review*, 1901, pp. 97-8.

[19] Berlin, *Daily Telegraph*, April 21, 1900, March 31, 1900, March 23, 1901; *Monetary Times*, April 6, 1900; *Globe*, April 3, 1900.

As this brief quotation from the *Globe* would suggest, by the turn of the century industrialism had subordinated the idea of the north as an agricultural frontier. However, it is important to note that just as the agricultural view of the nineteenth century dominated but did not rule exclusively, so also the industrial conception gave way from time to time in the twentieth century to agrarian enthusiasm. Indeed, the discovery of the Clay Belt at this time opened another chapter in the halting history of northern settlement. But by 1900 the emphasis in newspaper articles and editorials, pamphlets, departmental reports, speeches by prominent industrialists such as F. H. Clergue, and provincial politicians such as E. J. Davis, J. R. Stratton, and the Premier himself, George Ross, fell increasingly upon the industrial future that lay ahead in the north.[20]

## II

Just as the public conception of the north changed with the passage of time, so also did ideas of how best to develop it. For better or for worse, after having once publicly dreamed the dream of the northern empire of mines, smelters and steel mills, pulpmills, paper factories and huge hydro-electric dams, all linked together and to the south with busy railroads, neither the government nor the opposition could afford the Olympian patience of the *Globe*. Inevitably, as resource wealth became the object of public optimism, the subject of promoting the industrialization of those natural resources moved closer to the centre of gravity of Ontario politics. In sharp contrast with their opinions a decade earlier, by 1900 resource developers such as Clergue, S. J. Ritchie himself, the Ontario lumbermen,

[20] See, for example, the Department of Crown Lands pamphlets, *Our Northern District* (Toronto, 1894); *Northern Districts of Ontario* (Toronto, 1899), and *A Statement concerning the extent, resources, climate and industrial development of the Province Ontario* (Toronto, 1901). See also the speeches by E. J. Davis, Commissioner of Crown Lands, 1899-1904, *Land Settlement in New Ontario* (Toronto, 1901); J. R. Stratton, *Monetary Times*, March 10, 17, 1899; *Canadian Engineer*, Vol. VII, Dec., 1899, p. 213.

and the Liberal government no longer spoke of free trade in the natural products of the farm, forest and mine as the most constructive development policy. Instead home manufacturing had become the new dogma. Industrialists strove to use the power of the state to encourage and protect, through its control over natural resources, manufacturing in Ontario. For eager, impatient men, the operation of impersonal market factors seemed either too painfully slow, or too ineffective. Americans, in defiance of all economic principles, appeared content to import Canadian raw materials indefinitely.

The lumbermen of the province were the first to experience a change of heart on the question of an appropriate development strategy. In that sector the shift from a free trade to a restrictive temperament also corresponded with the entry of a large number of new producers into the market, the migration of the centre of gravity of the trade away from the Ottawa valley towards the northwestern districts of the province, and the sudden rise in exports of unprocessed logs in the 1890s. There were, of course, relationships between these factors. The relocation of the trade in a region with greater access to the Upper Lakes explained the new export pattern and the appearance of new operators on the scene. Ultimately a deterioration in trade relations between Canada and the United States in 1897 as a result of the Dingley tariff brought retaliatory feeling within the trade to a head.

Until the late nineties control of the export of logs and lumber was considered to be a responsibility of the federal government. In fact, during the 1880s the Macdonald government had imposed a number of export duties, ranging from between one and three dollars per thousand feet board measure, both as a response to American tariff increases and as an encouragement to home manufacturing. In 1890, however, the lumbermen convinced the government to remove its export duties as a *quid pro quo* for more attractive American duties on Canadian sawn lumber imports. Having won this opening, John Charlton, the self-appointed spokesman-diplomat for the trade, lobbied tirelessly in Washington for reciprocal concessions. His efforts and the Canadian initiatives immediately paid off. As a first step the McKinley tariff cut American duties on Canadian lumber in half and subsequently the Wilson-Gorman tariff of 1894 removed them altogether. With the aid of his friends in the American Senate, Charlton claimed credit for inaugurating what he hoped would be an era of uninterrupted free trade in forest products.[21]

Against this narrative of tariff liberalization it is important to keep two factors in sharp focus in the foreground. The first is John Charlton's unusual success in temporarily overcoming the normal retaliatory reflex of his industry in trade matters; the second is the relative failure of freer trade, in contrast at least with the expectations held out for it, to bring prosperity to the Canadian timber trade. All exports of timber—finished lumber and logs combined—in the comparatively free trade years between 1891 and 1896, averaged only 15 per cent higher than the totals for the previous tariff-ridden five years, a fact that can be attributed primarily to a serious recession in the United States beginning in 1891 and a consequent softening of all Canadian exports to that country.

During this interval important changes had been taking place within the Ontario lumbering industry. In the first instance the Ottawa valley lumbermen were beginning to run out of prime timber. By their own admission they were working over second-grade timber limits and producing a cheap, coarse lumber, primarily for the American market. By the mid-decade some of the large operators had begun to run down their lumbering operations and to transfer their accumulated capital to other businesses, mainly insurance, railroads, municipal utilities and pulp mills.[22] The growth area of the industry lay

---

[21] PAC, Bronson Papers, Vol. 704, "Departmental [Crown Lands] Memo. re: Export Duty on Logs," pp. 1-3; University of Toronto Archives, John Charlton Diaries, Vol. 5, 1890 summary, Vol. 7, Feb. 25-28, 1894, Vol. 8, summary; A. R. M. Lower, *The North American Assault on the Canadian Forest* (Toronto, 1938), pp. 154-9; R. C. Brown, *Canada's National Policy, 1883-1900* (Princeton, 1964), pp. 188-211, 241; Southworth and White, "A History of Crown Timber Regulations," pp. 249-51.

[22] PAC, Bronson Papers, Vol. 707, E. H. Bronson to Aubrey White, Assistant Commissioner of Crown Lands, Feb. 17, 1897; Vol. 127, Levi Crannell to Aubrey White, Aug. 16, 1897; Vol. 723, Levi Crannell to O. H. Ingram,

on the Lake Huron shoreline and in the far western Lake-of-the-Woods region. This decline of the Ottawa valley industry and migration northwestward can best be seen in the relocation of provincial revenue from the forests. In 1884 the western and Ottawa districts were on a par, each contributing approximately 42 per cent of the total Woods and Forests revenue. But by 1889 the Ottawa share had slipped to 31 per cent and the western portion had risen to 50 per cent. By 1894 the gap had widened; Ottawa district produced only 25 per cent of the revenues, whereas the western district paid 64 per cent of the total gathered. The comparative eclipse of the old, Ottawa valley lumbering barons, a redirection of their interests into other areas, and the rise of a newer, less secure group of small lumber operators in the western regions of the province account in part for the new mood of the trade.[23]

The combined effects of a shift westward in logging activity and increasingly freer trade conditions in the early nineties produced a significant alteration in the character of the export trade. It now became possible to cut timber in the Georgian Bay watershed, or along the north shore of Lake Superior on a large scale, raft it into great booms of sawlogs, and tow those booms across Lake Huron to established sawmill centres such as Saginaw, Bay City, and Alpena, Michigan. There the Ontario timber would be cut, dried, sorted and shipped. Such a trade had been in existence for some time, but the mutual reduction in tariffs at the beginning of the decade suddenly increased its importance. Export figures from an extended, unpoliced shoreline are dubious at best, but the Department of Crown Lands estimated that in 1892 about 33 per cent of Ontario's exports of forest products took the form of logs rather than lumber. The sudden appearance of this trade attracted attention in the Ontario Legislature in 1890 and again three years later in the federal House. However, neither the trade nor the

---

Aug. 22, 1898. See also Peter Gillies, "The Ottawa Lumber Barons and the End of the Great Pine in Eastern Ontario" (unpublished MS., 1972, forthcoming in the *Journal of Canadian Studies*), pp. 5-12.

[23] Crown Lands, *Annual Reports*: 1885, p. 10; 1890, p. 13; 1895, p. 17.

provincial government could find cause for complaint at that time. It was felt that the greater advantages of free trade outweighed whatever particular disadvantages might spring from the export of unprocessed raw materials and, moreover, the new trade did create jobs and stimulate a demand for agricultural products that had not hitherto existed.[24]

This reorientation of the trade also opened up opportunities for new entrants. For a generation the industry had been ruled by the old, crusty family firms on the Ottawa, whose fortunes and reputations had been made during the days of the square timber trade. The westward migration brought new men into the industry. Of course, in the eyes of the Ottawa men these new operators lacked the necessary cachet. They had to scrounge for timber limits, financial backing and markets. They were an erratic, strident bunch who depended entirely upon the American export market. Consequently, they lacked the stability—financial and social—afforded by British business connections of long standing. Although they were more numerous, they operated on a much smaller scale with less capital tied up in limits and mills. In short, they worked closer to the margin, but what they lacked in size and importance, the Ottawa men thought, they more than made up for in noise.[25] These characteristics that distinguished the Georgian Bay from the Ottawa valley lumbermen, the established and declining from the struggling and ascendant, would in large measure determine the quite different responses of the two groups to the crisis that was about to break upon them.

The Dingley tariff of 1897 effectively restored the trade conditions that had prevailed during the 1880s. It reimposed the former two dollars per thousand duty against incoming Canadian lumber, but continued to allow Canadian sawlogs to enter the country free. Moreover, and this was a new twist, the protective duties were reinstated in such a way as to thwart in advance any Canadian retaliation. If Canada chose as a

---

[24] PAC, Bronson Papers, Vol. 704, "Departmental Memo," pp. 3-7.

[25] *Ibid.*, Vol. 129, Levi Crannell to O. H. Ingram, Aug. 11, 1897; Levi Crannell to John Bertram, July 4, 1898.

countermeasure to re-establish export duties on sawlogs, the sum of those levies would automatically be added onto the American tariff against sawn lumber. The Dingley tariff put Canada back in the position of being able to supply the American demand for raw materials, but not for semi-processed goods. Naturally, it caught most of the Ontario lumbermen in the sawmilling business with large stocks of common lumber on hand that would not bear the weight of the new duties. Many of them faced the bleak prospect of either selling at distressed prices in the small domestic market—there was no overseas trade in such grades—or going bankrupt waiting for better conditions.[26] Of course the operators cutting sawlogs for export were unaffected by the tariff; if anything, they probably benefitted moderately for a time.

The Ottawa valley men reacted in time-honoured form. During the hearings on the tariff bill in the early summer seven of the biggest lumber firms raised about $17,000 to maintain a lobbyist in Washington.[27] Then John Charlton swung back into action. As a sawlog exporter himself, he was not deeply hurt by the terms of the tariff. However, the prospect of a revival of protectionism offended the sensibilities of an international businessman such as himself—his mills were in Tonawanda, New York—and rubbed against his Manchester liberal, free trade grain. In January, April and again in July of 1897 Charlton haunted the Senate lobby in Washington, an entirely unofficial vigil that caused his own government some considerable embarrassment. But his interviews with all the important senators and, on three occasions, chats with his old friend the President, were to no avail. A continuation of free trade in forest products was hopeless and even Charlton's second line of attack, restoration of the McKinley schedules, proved

[26] *Ibid.*, Vol. 723, Levi Crannell to O. H. Ingram, Aug. 22, 1898; Vol. 127, Levi Crannell to Aubrey White, Aug. 16, 1897.

[27] *Ibid.*, Vol. 722, Levi Crannell to McLachlin Bros., Gilmour & Hughson and W. C. Edwards, July 6, 1897. The money was apparently refunded when the lobbyist—who was also working for Michigan interests—failed to have the tariff reduced; see *ibid.*, Vol. 722, Levi Crannell to Gilmour & Co. Aug. 2, 1897.

to be a lost cause.[28] When it became apparent that these direct measures would not work the organized lumbermen petitioned the federal government of Canada to restore the old export duties on sawlogs. The Laurier government adopted a sympathetic posture, but shrank from acting decisively even though pressed by some of the most important businessmen in the country. W. S. Fielding had a bill passed authorizing export duties on sawlogs, pulpwood and ores, but in fear of the extra-territorial implications of the Dingley tariff and in the hope of opening up talks with the Americans concerning trade liberalization on a much wider range of goods, the government did not proclaim the legislation.[29] In the meantime, as the inevitable bore down upon them, the Ottawa men curtailed their woods operations, closed up their mills and settled themselves in to wait out the storm as they had so many times before. They still had a certain amount of British business and some trade in the better grades of lumber to fall back upon. Their strategy, to the extent that a coherent strategy existed, was to adopt a retaliatory posture while bargaining for better terms.[30]

The Georgian Bay lumbermen could not afford the gentlemanly resignation of the Ottawa men. They had no such cushion against the crisis and their credit would not carry an extended wait for better times. They also encountered the injustice of the American tariff in a particularly agonizing way. While they perched on the brink of bankruptcy the sawlog exporters cutting on neighbouring limits carried on as if nothing had happened. Unlike the Ottawa men they could not rationalize this contradiction so easily. Their circumstances demanded a more militant response.

Throughout the Dingley hearings the western Ontario lumbermen were consistently more intransigent and belligerent

---

28 University of Toronto Archives, John Charlton Diaries, Vol. 9, Jan. 16-20; April 29 to May 3; July 9-11, 1897; R. C. Brown, *Canada's National Policy*, pp. 271-2.

29 *Ibid.*, Feb. 23-24, June 11, 17-8, July 20, 28, 1897; Canada, House of Commons, *Debates*, 1897, Vol. II, pp. 3872-3.

30 PAC, Bronson Papers, Vol. 707, E. H. Bronson to Aubrey White, Feb. 17, 1897.

than their Ottawa valley colleagues. Led by John Bertram, the Toronto industrialist who numbered the Collins Inlet Lumber Company among his many interests, and E. W. Rathbun, who, aside from being chairman of the Ontario Royal Commission on Forest Protection, also owned a multi-product wood manufacturing plant at Deseronto and timber limits near Gravenhurst, the western lumbermen petitioned the Laurier government to retaliate regardless of the consequences. A simple division of labour was worked out. Bertram organized the lumbermen and worked on his friends in the Liberal cabinets at Ottawa and Toronto, while Rathbun handled publicity, writing numerous pamphlets and letters to influential newspaper editors.

When the lumbermen set out to justify their claim to protection in general terms they naturally returned to that great wellspring of Canadian protectionist thought, the National Policy. From time to time during the 1890s the *Canadian Manufacturer*, the leading protectionist organ in the country, had urged that the principles of the National Policy should be extended to encourage the manufacture of raw materials within the country. In this case an export duty on outgoing unprocessed resources would promote processing industries in much the same way as the tariff on incoming goods stimulated secondary manufacturing in the country. Moreover, the connection between the emerging manufacturing condition school of thought and the National Policy tradition was both intellectual and personal. Bertram's brother and business associate was one of those responsible for bringing the Liberal party around from its former platform of unrestricted reciprocity to a moderate protectionist position. John's efforts on behalf of the Ontario sawmilling industry at this time coincided with his brother's tutoring of Laurier on the tariff. The Bertram brothers and Rathbun, a National Policy Conservative, provided the key linkages between protectionist thinking at the federal and the provincial level. In their minds the manufacturing condition was the provincial counterpart to the National Policy.[31]

---

[31] R. C. Brown, *Canada's National Policy*, pp. 264-70; J. M. Bliss, "A Living Profit: Studies in the Social History of Canadian Business, 1883-1911" (unpublished Ph.D. thesis, University of Toronto, 1972), p. 386.

Rathbun's first pamphlet, *Shall We Place an Export Duty on Sawlogs and Pulpwood?*, suggested something of the mood of the western lumbermen. "It would be far better," he argued, "that the American mills should stand closed, their workmen remain idle and the traffic of their railways be lessened, than that corresponding interests in Canada should so suffer because of their unfair discrimination." Their strategy consisted of trying to shut off all trade in sawlogs to force the American government to reconsider its tariff on sawn lumber. For his part John Charlton thought this "wild craze" on behalf of retaliation the sheerest folly. He believed, and many of his friends on the Ottawa were inclined to agree, that since a tariff of one dollar per thousand was probably the best Canada could expect from a protectionist Congress, that the Canadian lumbermen should do their best to fight for this compromise. The Georgian Bay men thought that treason. Bertram reminded the Prime Minister that Charlton was, after all, a sawlog exporter and that his views were not those of the trade in general. Bertram insisted that the United States should not be permitted "to fix up the lumber duties to entirely suit themselves without Canada taking some action and the key of the position is largely in our hands."[32] Following the passage of the Dingley tariff in July of 1897 the Georgian Bay lumbermen grew more determined and their plight aroused considerable public sympathy. Even John Charlton was surprised at the extent of strong feeling. On a trip to Toronto late in July he found the president of the Bank of Toronto, which was deeply involved in financing lumber operations, "very much excited over the export duty question and most unreasonable. He would put the export duty on tomorrow if he had the power."[33] However, the Laurier government, which had provided itself with the power to impose retaliatory export duties to satisfy the trade, was not inclined to use that power for the time being while it kept the option of wider trade talks open.

[32] E. W. Rathbun, *Shall We Place an Export Duty on Sawlogs and Pulpwood?* (Deseronto, 1897), p. 7; PAC, Laurier Papers, John Bertram to Laurier, Jan. 15, 1897, 11046.

[33] University of Toronto Archives, John Charlton Diaries, Vol. 9, July 30, 1897.

At that point the lumbermen turned to their landlord, the province, to supply a suitable remedy for the ills they suffered. Since the Dingley tariff referred only to federal export duties and said nothing of provincial regulations, the lumbermen seized upon the device of mobilizing provincial legislation to countervail against the American tariff. Provincial action had a further advantage; if necessary the province could close off its borders with appropriate legislation and completely halt all sawlog exports. On August 19 the lumbermen of the province convened in Toronto to debate a course of action. In the discussions the Ottawa lumbermen and John Charlton found themselves increasingly isolated from the majority opinion in favour of retaliation expressed by their more numerous and vociferous Georgian Bay colleagues. Levi Crannell, speaking for the Bronsons and Weston Lumber Company, held the view that " . . . matters should be left as they now are, hoping that in the meantime the government may possibly make some favourable arrangement with the United States which may include the lowering of possible abolition of the duty; and trade may adjust itself so as to make any action unnecessary."[34] But what Charlton called the "lumber jingos" carried the day. The revived Ontario Lumbermen's Association that emerged from this August meeting in effect represented only the Georgian Bay lumbermen.[35]

Bertram, Rathbun and John Waldie, who had been elected president of the association, planned a second convention of lumbermen for October to court the provincial government. The leading members of the Hardy government found the warmth of this sudden embrace and its circumstances positively embarrassing. In the hope of forestalling any overwhelming pressure being brought to bear upon them, Hardy and his ministers adopted the tactic of trying to keep the lumbermen divided among themselves. When John Gibson, the Commissioner of Crown Lands, heard that there was a

[34] PAC, Bronson Papers, Vol. 127, Levi Crannell to Aubrey White, Aug. 16, 1897.

[35] University of Toronto Archives, John Charlton Diaries, Vol. 9, August 19, 1897, and year-end summary, Vol. 10.

possibility that the Ottawa valley men would not attend the
second meeting, he frankly begged them to come. "We think
it very important that all the lumber interests of the Province
be fully represented," Gibson wrote Levi Crannell:

> Public feeling and sentiment is becoming wonderfully strong
> and excited over this question and it is still a matter of serious
> consideration on our part what course we shall be obliged to
> take....One thing is certain,—we cannot have too much in-
> formation and we are extremely anxious to have all that is to
> be said, or can be said, on both sides, and I would regard it
> as extremely unfortunate if there should be any understanding
> on the part of the Ottawa lumbermen not to attend this meeting
> or not to be very *fully* represented at it. It would be very
> advantageous to have possession of information showing how
> far the lumber interests of the Province as a whole, taking the
> extent of the limits as the base of representation, are in accord
> with the resolution passed on the 17th August meeting. That
> is information which can be obtained and presented to the
> Government, but so far has not been presented in anything like
> a definite tangible shape.

Gibson went on to ask Crannell to meet with W. C. Edwards,
another prominent Ottawa valley lumberman opposed to
retaliation, to help organize an Ottawa contingent. But, he
cautioned, "Let me however ask you to avoid very carefully
intimating or letting it be understood that any such request
has emanated from the Government. It should be your own
spontaneous action." If the substantial lumbermen of the
province stayed away, Gibson feared that the meeting would
be close to unanimous in demanding government action: "In
view of the very strong public sentiment, even if it is uninformed
sentiment, on the question, there is no saying what we might
be obliged to do. For every reason, therefore, it is most desirable
that both sides of the question should be fully represented."[36]
Some time later Arthur Hardy confided to Willison of the *Globe*

---

[36] PAC, Bronson Papers, Vol. 734, John Gibson to Levi Crannell, Oct. 1, 1897,
private and confidential.

that he considered Bertram's campaign extremely dangerous and he too hoped that the lumbermen might be kept divided.[37] On October 16 the Ontario Lumbermen's Association reconvened in Toronto and, as the government expected, the convention unanimously approved a federal export duty. A second resolution demanding a provincial ban on the export of unmanufactured sawlogs passed by 42 votes to 4 with only the sullen Ottawa delegation dissenting.[38] The provincial government now faced the situation it dreaded most—an unequivocal call for action from the trade and a rising tide of public opinion in its favour. To make matters worse, this all converged in an election year.

In the fall session the premier himself introduced a bill requiring that pine timber cut on crown lands be sawn into lumber in Canada. This amendment to the Crown Timber Act, called the manufacturing condition, was to take effect upon issuance of the annual licences on April 30, 1898. Hardy preferred to introduce a separate bill rather than act by order-in-council, which he had the power to do, because that course allowed him greater room to manoeuvre, he explained to Willison. "Furthermore," Hardy continued confidentially, "we think it much better that the House—the whole House—should take the responsibility of dealing with a matter which may possibly provoke international complications. It is a hundred times more serious a matter than the Canadian lumbermen who are interested think."[39] The Government resented being forced into a policy that did not have the confidence of its Ottawa valley supporters. Privately, caution, timidity and resistance were the watchwords.

But publicly it was another story—it had to be! In the Legislature the premier made a bold face of it, explaining that

[37] PAC, Willison Papers, Vol. 38, A. S. Hardy to Willison, Nov. 4, 1897, private and confidential.

[38] *Canada Lumberman*, Nov. 1897, for verbatim report; PAC, Mossom Boyd Papers, Vol. 132, Aubrey White to Mossom Boyd, Oct. 9, 1897; Crown Lands, *Annual Report*, 1899, p. xi.

[39] PAC, Willison Papers, Vol. 38, A. S. Hardy to Willison, Oct. 14, 1897, confidential.

the manufacturing clause had been introduced "to protect Canadian industry and workmen against American aggression." Just in case, he covered his flank by attacking the leader of the opposition for the anti-American tone of remarks in which he had referred to the American sawlog exporters as "thieves and plunderers." Surprisingly, the bill met little substantive opposition in the House, yet another sign of the prevailing mood. The only difference between the government and the opposition on the question, George F. Marter claimed, was that the government wished to put off implementing its legislation for a year whereas the opposition wanted it adopted immediately.[40] In private, members of the government expected defeat in the coming spring elections if they so much as appeared to waffle. Long-standing associations with the Ottawa men, whom the government considered to be the most substantial and sensible in the trade, irritation at being pushed so hard, and the inertia of uncertainty under the circumstances determined the course of action followed. A bold and popular position had been taken in the months immediately preceding an election and the consequences of that policy would not become apparent until some time in the future. The waffling could take place quietly after the election. However, the result of the March contest was so close that even that proved impossible. The government, clinging to its slender majority, did not dare back down or appear to retreat for fear of influencing the outcome of the by-elections.[41] Thus, with the utmost reluctance on the part of the government responsible for it, the manufacturing condition became law on April 30, 1898. All pine timber taken from crown lands during the coming season and thereafter would have to be made into sawn lumber in Ontario.

The injured parties reacted immediately. For their part the American exporters holding Canadian limits challenged the

40 PAO, Newspaper Hansard, Dec. 2, 20, 1897, Jan. 12, 1898.

41 PAC, Willison Papers, Vol. 38, Hardy to Willison, Oct. 14, 1897, Confidential; University of Toronto Archives, John Charlton Diaries, Vol. 10, Aug. 19, Dec. 27, 1897, May 5, 1898.

manufacturing clause in the courts, protested to their own Secretary of State, and joined some of their Canadian colleagues in petitioning the federal government to disallow the provincial legislation. Now the Laurier government found itself in a tight spot. It was under considerable pressure both from the United States government and the Ottawa valley men within the Liberal party to take the embarrassing step of disallowing the retaliatory legislation of the government of Ontario. The fact that a Joint High Commission had just been created to wipe from the slate all outstanding differences between the two countries, including the trade hostilities that had produced the retaliation in the first place, made Laurier's position even more uncomfortable.

Counsel for the American lumbermen argued that the government of Ontario had violated its own contract by imposing extraordinary performance conditions upon licences long after they had been granted. So burdensome were these new conditions, the lawyers for the sawlog exporters argued, that the substantial investments of their clients had been "virtually confiscated," an action which impugned the good faith of the Ontario government and undermined the validity of all its contracts. As an afterthought, these American lawyers also stumbled upon the question of the constitutionality of the manufacturing condition: since it clearly trenched upon the federal trade and commerce power it must be, therefore, *ultra vires*. In relaying these complaints to the British ambassador and through him ultimately to the Canadian government, Secretary of State William R. Day proposed that the federal government temporarily stay the hand of the province while the whole question of trade in forest products was referred to the Joint Commission for a decision.[42] To sawlog exporters, John Charlton (who was a member of the Joint Commission), and some of the Ottawa valley men, this seemed to be an eminently sensible thing to do. Even Sir Richard Scott, Laurier's Secretary of State and

---

[42] PAC, Sir Richard Scott Papers, Vol. 4, Sir Julian Pauncefote to Lord Aberdeen, June 17, 1898, enclosing D. M. Dickenson and R. Lansing to William R. Day, Secretary of State, June 11 and 13, 1898, and Day to Pauncefote, June 15, 1898.

an old Ottawa valley lumberman himself, thought the ploy of using the Ontario legislation to pry concessions from the Americans a good one. "There should be reciprocity in logs and lumber," he advised the Prime Minister. "We have put lumber on the free list and if the United States adopted an equally liberal policy we might induce Ontario to remove the present restrictions on timber licenses."[43]

But a new mood had overtaken the province that made free logs for free lumber no longer a tenable position. This spirit had been inspired in part by the public relations efforts of the western lumbermen, but it was itself also in keeping with a much broader feeling of national self-confidence on all economic matters that welled up with the first wave of prosperity after 1896.[44] When at last the Liberal party had an opportunity to discuss liberalizing trade in natural products with the United States the tide had begun to run strongly against reciprocity. Many people in Ontario at least had come to regard the export of logs, for example, as the export of jobs. Why not adopt policies in the national interest to foster the manufacture of natural resources into finished products? Even according to the testimony of its critics, the manufacturing condition—the frame of mind discussed above—had begun to take hold.

During the summer of 1898 the western lumbermen stepped up their protectionist campaign, primarily to steel the will of a wavering provincial government now facing pressure from above, and to restate for the benefit of the federal government their determination that free logs for free lumber was no longer good enough. E. W. Rathbun dashed off a second pamphlet for the cause in which he argued that the Joint Commission, about to convene at Quebec, had no business tampering with the provincial manufacturing condition. Whatever vested rights the "absentee limit-holders" may have acquired, he insisted, they were clearly subordinate to the national interest in this

---

[43] University of Toronto Archives, John Charlton Diaries, Vol. 10, May 5, 1898; PAC, Willison Papers, Vol. 15, Charlton to Willison, July 30, 1898, Private and Confidential, PAC, Scott Papers, Vol. 4, Scott to Laurier, July 23, 1898, copy.

[44] R. C. Brown, *Canada's National Policy*, pp. 350-401.

case. Instead of using the Ontario legislation as a bargaining tool, Rathbun suggested that Ottawa take a positive view of the matter: "The government have it in their power, by their treatment of this question, either to foster and encourage a class of Canadian industries which are specially deserving of such encouragement, or to destroy the measure of prosperity now existing in the lumbering districts and effectually depress and discourage native enterprises by giving a premium to the pursuit of such enterprises abroad." After some pandering to anti-Americanism and a great deal of specious nonsense about the manufacturing condition being a conservation measure, Rathbun rested his case for its retention on the grounds of moderate, economic nationalism:

> A sound and sensible policy of protection, whether by tariff or otherwise, seeks not to encourage the introduction of industries which are pursued here at a relative disadvantage, but to develop what may be termed natural, as distinguished from exotic manufactures....To carry forward and develop the manufacture of forest products in the highest degree, sending forth the finished article into the markets of the world in the place of raw material, is the only way in which we can realize the full value of our forest resources.

In addition to the native industries that would be stimulated by such a policy of sensible protection, Rathbun calculated that Canada would also acquire those sawmills in the United States already dependent upon Ontario resources: "Debarred from the opportunity of cutting logs for export, it is an absolute certainty that the American lumberman, in default of other sources of supply, will transfer his sawmill enterprises to Canadian soil."[45] Thus in the process of expanding a private interest into the public interest, retribution became a positive development strategy.

In the gathering mood of popular economic nationalism that characterized the Joint High Commission phase of Canadian-

[45] PAO, Ontario Lumberman's Association, *Minute Book*, Aug. 2, 1898, pp. 158-64; E. W. Rathbun, *The Conference and the Lumber Question from a Canadian Standpoint* (Deseronto, 1898), pp. 2-7.

American economic relations, and amid diplomatic circumstances of the utmost delicacy, the manufacturing condition question moved towards resolution. After considerable prodding from Ottawa the Ontario government finally moved to defend its actions against American complaints late in July. Arthur Hardy's memorandum repudiated the contention that the government had violated a contract with the lumbermen. A timber licence was not a contract in which the terms and conditions prevailing at the time of first issuance remained in force in perpetuity. Instead, Hardy pointed out, timber licences were renewed annually subject to such regulations as might from time to time be imposed under the Crown Timber Act. In the past these regulations had been changed many times without anyone suggesting that a contract had been broken because, in law, no such breach had occurred. As for the manufacturing condition being beyond the competence of the provincial legislature, the Ontario brief maintained that the commerce clause remained inoperative in matters pertaining essentially to the management of the public lands in which the province had undoubted plenary powers. Shortly afterwards Mr. Justice Osler, of the Ontario Court of Appeal, upheld this view. The legislation only incidentally affected trade and commerce, he decided, as any legislation bearing upon property and civil rights within the province might. Accordingly, the judicial committee of Laurier's cabinet, notwithstanding its views on the wisdom of the policy, recommended that the government allow the legislation to stand.[46]

That disposed of the formal question of disallowance, but what of the much more subtle proposal that Ontario withdraw its legislation as a *quid pro quo* for whatever trade agreement might emerge from the Joint Commission? As has been seen, the western lumbermen had placed themselves in opposition to such a plan. So had influential papers such as the *Globe*. Sir William Van Horne also weighed in to prevent "any

---

[46] PAC, Scott Papers, Vol. 4, Hardy to Scott, July 25, 1898; Memorandum of the Attorney General (A. S. Hardy); Supplementary Memorandum, Aug. 22, 1898; J. M. Gibson to David Mills, Dec. 20, 1900, in *Provincial Legislation 1896-1920*, Vol. II (Ottawa, 1922), p. 22.

backdown." And at length so also did a most reluctant Ontario government. Responding to just such a proposition from Sir Richard Scott, Hardy admitted that before and during the election the question had been debated. But, he indicated to Scott, things had now reached the point that no compromise of that sort was tenable. "It is, too," he continued, "quite obvious that whatever the American tariff may be in the future, an unlimited right of lumbermen, American or Canadian, to cut and carry away logs from the lands of the Crown to be sawn in the United States, would not satisfy public opinion." In support of this position Hardy took the high ground that conservation of the forest was a higher goal than maximizing trade, apparently unmindful of the contradiction involved in hoping the legislation would compel the Michigan men to move their mills to Ontario.[47] Plainly, having gone so far it was politically impossible to turn back. Incidentally, too, the policy was not only popular, it also appeared to be having the desired effect. Thus the federal government had to decline a request to place the question of the manufacturing condition on the agenda of the Joint Commission and in their discussions at Quebec and Washington the commissioners, unable to deal with one of their major differences, failed to arrive at any agreeable understanding on a reduction in forest products tariffs.[48] On the impasse over trade in lumber, it has been said, the hopes for reciprocity in natural products—by this time mutually lukewarm—foundered.[49]

When the first returns of the manufacturing condition began to come in the caution that had characterized its implementation quickly melted away. According to John Bertram's presidential address to the Ontario Lumbermen's Association in 1900, the Ontario legislation appeared to have reversed the trend of declining prices and demand that had typified the middle nineties: "1899 will be remembered," he announced, "as one

[47] *Globe*, Nov. 4, 1897; July 29, Aug. 29, Sept. 15, 1898; PAC, Scott Papers, Vol. 4, Hardy to Scott, Aug. 1, 1898, Private.
[48] *Ibid.*, Vol. 4, Governor General to Secretary of State for the Colonies, copy, n.d.; L. H. Davies to Scott, Jan. 16, 1899, Private and Confidential.
[49] R. C. Brown, *Canada's National Policy*, p. 371.

of the most eventful in the history of the trade. Opening with low prices and a moderate demand it closed with higher prices for common lumber than had ever been obtained either in Canada or the United States." Both Bertram and the Department of Crown Lands pointed proudly to the accomplishments of the manufacturing condition; all along the Lake Huron and Georgian Bay shorelines new sawmills were either under construction, or already in production. The new mills had a combined capacity, the *Canada Lumberman* estimated, of over 265 million board feet annually and provided employment to about 1,000 men at an average rate of pay of $1.50 a day. And, contrary to the dark prophecies of the Michigan lumbermen, Ontario timber limits brought much higher prices after the imposition of the export ban than ever before.[50]

The provincial government, of course, preened itself while taking full and unqualified credit for its wise, statesmanlike and far-sighted policy. By the 1902 election the Liberals were boasting arrogantly of the results of *their* manufacturing policy, tracing its paternity beyond Alexander Miscampbell's 1893 resolution, where the opposition claimed it lay, to a more respectable regulation introduced by Arthur Hardy that had lived briefly and quietly died in 1890. Evidently the manufacturing condition, whose application had been inspired by the western lumbermen, satisfied the needs of the industry and, moreover, the idea of it "took....with the bulk of the people."[51] It struck a responsive chord with the press and the public and thus, within a year of its inception, an opportunistic provincial government began to look into other areas where its application might produce similar results.

[50] PAO, Ontario Lumberman's Association, *Minute Book*, Feb. 21, 1900, p. 181; *Canada Lumberman*, March, 1902; Ontario Department of Lands and Forests, Woods and Forest Report Book No. 3, Memorandum on the Benefits of Sawing Logs in the Province, pp. 407-8; Crown Lands Department, *Annual Report*, 1900, p. v; *Mail and Empire*, Sept. 8, 1899.

[51] E. J. Davis, *Speech in the Budget Debate* (Toronto, 1902), pp. 9-10, 19-20; compare with [Liberal Party of Ontario], *Ontario General Election* (Toronto, 1894), pamphlet number 10, "Export of Sawlogs to the United States," pp. 1-4, and *Ontario General Elections* (Toronto, 1898), "The Export of Sawlogs," p. 1.

III

Pulpwood was the obvious next step. In the first instance the physical analogy with sawlogs was strong. If spruce pulpwood, like pine sawlogs, could be towed across the lake to American mills, then surely a similar embargo would also produce a reverse migration of American pulp mills to Ontario.[52] Secondly, a nascent pulp and paper lobby was in existence demanding protection in one form or another. And finally, a social revolution that had greatly increased the size and importance of daily newspapers had combined with technological change to alter completely the character of a once slumbering industry. These technological changes had rendered northern Ontario an ideal location for a pulp and paper industry, at least in theory. How might that promise be realized?

During the third quarter of the nineteenth century a series of rapid advances in paper-making technology, all financed and executed abroad, changed the potential of the Canadian Laurentian forest. Until that time pine had been regarded as the most valuable species, but the news that spruce, a wood which grew in even greater profusion than pine, had become the most desirable raw material for the fabrication of paper, laid the foundations of a new forest industry. Equally rapid and dramatic changes in electrical technology in the last quarter of the century heightened these expectations by turning the ragged, white rivers rushing through the northern spruce forests into a cheap, convenient source of power close to the supply of raw materials.

The standard process of making paper in the early nineteenth century combined vegetable fibres with rag stock, and although the process had been mechanized successfully early on in the industrial revolution, the difficulty and expense of obtaining its raw materials made paper a relatively scarce commodity. The discovery that wood could be made to produce the required fibres changed all that. By the mid-nineteenth century a machine had been perfected that would simply grind bolts of wood into a mechanical paste which would then be added to

[52] *Shall We Place an Export Duty on Sawlogs and Pulpwood?*, p. 6.

the traditional rag mixture, thereby reducing the cost of manufacture. Subsequent research by American, German and Austrian scientists uncovered several methods of chemically separating the fibres in wood, rather than grinding them into a paste, so that wood might completely replace the rag content of paper. Following these inventions the late nineteenth-century papermaker could manufacture a wider and more inexpensive range of products by varying the proportions of groundwood, chemical pulp and rag stock, from fibreless tissue at the one extreme, through newsprint, to the many grades of fine paper at the other.[53]

The industrial era of Canadian papermaking did not get under way until after 1866 when the A. & J. Buntin Paper Mill at Valleyfield, Quebec, installed the first Canadian groundwood pulp machine. Or perhaps its advent should be dated from 1888 when J. R. Barber, in his Georgetown, Ontario, mill became the first papermaker on the North American continent to use hydro-electric power and thus began the close identification of the industry with its energy source. To Francis H. Clergue must go the credit for instituting, in Ontario at least, the modern pattern of the industry; namely, a pulp mill built close to and in association with a hydro-electric project, drawing its raw material, sprucewood, from a huge hinterland of crown lands forest. Up until his time paper mills had been located in the older, more settled parts of the province, closer to the consumers and sources of rag fibre than to the spruce forests.[54]

Being the first, naturally the agreement entered into between Clergue and the Crown Lands Department for the supply of

[53] The best survey of papermaking technology from a Canadian viewpoint is to be found in George Carruthers, *Paper in the Making* (Toronto, 1947). Carruthers was the president of Interlake Tissue Mills, and the book was ghost-written for him. Part one treats the first one hundred years of paper manufacture by machine, and part two deals specifically with the early history of Canadian paper companies.

[54] For an analysis of the economics of location of the pulp and paper industry, see J. A. Guthrie, *The Newsprint Paper Industry: An Economic Analysis* (Cambridge, Mass., 1941), or Nathan Reich, *The Pulp and Paper Industry in Canada* (Toronto, ca. 1926).

spruce for his mill became the prototype for the others that followed. According to their 1892 agreement the Department allowed Clergue's company to cut spruce, poplar, tamarack and jack pine at a rate of twenty cents dues per cord, and other species (except, of course, pine) for ten cents a cord, on any fifty square miles of territory "running back upon either side of one or more rivers flowing into Lake Superior and West of Sault Ste. Marie." As a condition of the licence, Clergue had to post a cash bond, agree to spend at least $200,000 on construction before December 1895, and bring a mill employing three hundred men for ten months of the year into production by that date. In return for these performance guarantees written into the terms of the pulpwood concession, the company could be assured a source of spruce pulpwood for twenty-one years, the life of the agreement. In the pulp and paper industry, as had been the case with lumbering, crown ownership of the forest lands formed the basis of tenure. The industry received a lease from the government to cut pulpwood on publicly owned lands only after having agreed to specific terms and conditions.[55]

After Clergue's groundwood pulp mill began production in 1895—on schedule and over twice its planned size—the number of agreements between company promoters and the government rapidly multiplied. Nevertheless, the progress of the industry from the promotional stage to actual production disappointed both government officials and the public. The villain of the piece for the Canadian pulp men, as with the western lumbermen, was the American tariff which admitted raw materials at considerably lower rates than manufactured products. Thus, for the time being the pulp and paper mills remained on the American side of the Great Lakes and the Ontario forests were towed over to them.[56]

[55] Department of Lands and Forests, Wood and Forests Report Book No. 2, p. 196, and draft agreement between the province and F. H. Clergue, October, 1892, pp. 224-8.

[56] Generally the agreements were negotiated with local mining or timber developers then sold to American or British interests; see *ibid*., April 24, 1895, p. 235; undated, 1898, pp. 298-303; Sept. 12, 1899, pp. 341-3; Sept. 8, 1899, pp. 343-5; Crown Lands, *Annual Report*, 1900, p. vi; *Monetary Times*, Mar. 24, 1893.

When in 1878 the introduction of groundwood pulp compelled the American papermakers to combine to maintain stable prices, the organization that emerged naturally turned its attention to the tariff. By 1883 the papermakers' association had succeeded in having both pulp and paper added to the dutiable list. The McKinley tariff of 1891 maintained a 15 per cent *ad valorem* rate against imports of Canadian pulp and paper, although pulpwood, like most other raw materials, was permitted free entry. However, by the mid-nineties the newspaper owners had organized themselves into a consumers' association and lobby as well. Under the leadership of John Norris the newspapermen campaigned on behalf of lower duties on newsprint although, ironically, most of the membership editorially supported the notion of industrial protection. The competitive aims of these two groups were met in one clause of the Dingley tariff which permitted free entry of pulpwood, thereby keeping the price of paper down, while at the same time it levied a schedule of specific duties against imported pulp and paper, thus satisfying the papermakers' desires for increased protection. As with the lumber−sawlog sections of the tariff, this clause also contained a retaliatory proviso designed to prevent Canada from imposing export duties on pulpwood.[57]

The dog-in-the-manger terms of the Dingley tariff angered Canadian papermakers as much as it did the western Ontario lumbermen. Sir William Van Horne, who was himself a director of the Laurentide Pulp and Paper Company, raged at the impertinence. "The United States *must* have Canadian pulpwood or they must buy Canadian pulp and paper," he explained to Israel Tarte. "So long as we permit them to have our pulpwood and let them put any duty they like on our pulp and paper we will have stumps to show for it." He went on to argue that an export duty on pulpwood would lead directly to the construction of a large number of pulp mills and hydro-electric plants in the Laurentian region and concluded: "...if I had my way about it, I would put on an export duty and

---

[57] Guthrie, *The Newsprint Paper Industry*, p. 40; L. E. Ellis, *The Print Paper Pendulum: Group Pressures and the Price of Newsprint* (New Brunswick, New Jersey, 1960 ed.), pp. 16ff.

keep it on without regard to any reciprocal offers. . . . I believe that Canada can easily command the paper making industry of the whole world within a very few years and that alone would be sufficient to make it a wealthy country."[58] But Van Horne made no greater impression on the federal government than had the lumbermen.

When W. S. Fielding asked the House in 1896 for the authority to apply export duties on Canadian sawlogs, he also asked for and received power to impose export restrictions on Canadian pulpwood bound for the United States. However, the extra-territorial terms of the Dingley tariff, and then the deliberations of the Joint High Commission, interceded to hamper implementation of the authorized duties. Thus, with the federal government diplomatically immobilized, public attention shifted to the provincial level where, in the case of sawlogs at least, some possibility of action in self-defence remained. The leading Canadian pulp manufacturers, E. B. Eddy of Hull, John McFarlane of the Canada Paper Company, J. F. Patton of Dominion Fibre, J. Davy of the Riordon Company, F. H. Clergue of the Sault Ste. Marie Paper Company, W. G. Jones of the Acadia Pulp and Paper Mills, and J. R. Barber of Georgetown unanimously agreed at a meeting in September 1898 "that an export duty be immediately placed on all pulp wood exported from Canada (no matter what size or shape), which would be equivalent to the present import duty on Canadian pulp entering the United States, unless the United States admit all Canadian pulp, both chemical and mechanical, free of all import duty." They obviously had the sympathy of the federal government, but they did not receive any satisfaction from meetings with the Prime Minister. Meanwhile, in the press, the pulpwood issue was being swept along with the wave of support for the sawlog manufacturing condition. The normally staid *Monetary Times* probably best summed up that popular mood:

[58] PAC, Canadian Pacific Railway Papers, Van Horne Letterbooks, Vol. 53, Van Horne to Israel Tarte, May 15, 1897, personal; see also Van Horne to W. S. Fielding, June 22, 1897; Vol. 55, Van Horne to Miss Flora Shaw, Nov. 1, 1898.

If the American people are not pleased to purchase our wood-pulp as a finished product, they should not be allowed to take it in the form of spruce logs. Taxes prohibiting international commerce are generally objectionable, but under circumstances such as the present, it is difficult to see what other course could be followed by a government desirous of preserving the property of its citizens and maintaining its own dignity.

Into this power vacuum the provincial government eventually moved. In the Ontario Legislature during the 1899 session, J.R. Stratton, in an emotional and widely praised speech on the industrial potential of New Ontario, demanded a spruce manufacturing condition as well: "We should decide to sell them [the U.S.] our paper," the *Monetary Times* reported him saying, "but not one stick of spruce." He scorned the "selfish and huxtering attitude of the Americans toward us." Ontario could, he firmly believed, go out into the markets of the world and beat the Americans with paper and other products just as it had done with cheese![59]

Buoyed up by the tremendous success of the pine manufacturing condition, a similar self-confident, almost strident tone began to creep into official documents such as the Department of Crown Lands *Annual Report*. The 1899 issue, which proudly calculated the number of new sawmills rising along the Lake Huron and Georgian Bay shoreline, also drew attention to the exciting new pulp mills at Sault Ste. Marie and Sturgeon Falls which cost over two and a half million dollars to build and between them paid out $300,000 in wages to over nine hundred men. The implication of this juxtaposition was plain: the pulp industry would be equally well served by a manufacturing condition on spruce wood. All across the province, the leader of the opposition discovered a rising feeling that native industry would have to be protected "if New Ontario is ever to amount to anything more than a rocky solitude, even if that policy prevents present holders of mining and pulp land from realizing upon their properties immediately." Even the free-trade

---

[59] *Monetary Times*, April 2, 1897; Sept. 16, 1898; March 10, 1899; PAC, Laurier Papers, Sir William Van Horne to Laurier, Nov. 28, 1898, 28423-4.

*Globe* was prepared to set aside its principles temporarily in support of the Ontario government's policy of restricting the export of pulpwood from crown lands.[60]

By a quiet order-in-council passed in 1900 the Ontario government, without fanfare or flourish, extended the manufacturing condition of the Crown Timber Act to include spruce pulpwood. Thereafter, all spruce cordwood taken from crown lands, though not of course from fee simple, private lands, had to be manufactured into mechanical or chemical pulp in Canada. Since the industry did not yet exist in the province on a large scale, the manufacturing condition effectively established new ground rules for location. The pulpmen were quite satisfied with the Ontario action and only wished that it might be imitated by the province of Quebec, the scene of the most intensive pulpwood export operations. Until that border was also sealed off, and until the industry turned its attentions in a serious way to the Ontario forest, the manufacturing condition could not begin to do its work. Nevertheless, the almost voluntary adoption of the pulpwood manufacturing condition by the provincial government did reflect the increasingly militant mood of Ontario opinion on the subject of a proper resource development strategy.

IV

Application of the manufacturing condition to nickel ore revealed the complex emotional appeal of that policy, its practical limitations, and more particularly the dark and intricate network of self-interest that underlay it. Ontario had embarked upon its program of encouraging the final manufacture of its raw materials within the boundaries of the province not out of any systematically worked-out theory, and not under the pressure of any overwhelming popular mandate (though

[60] Crown Lands, *Annual Report*, 1899, p. xii; PAO, Whitney Papers, J. S. Macdonald to Whitney, enclosing clipping from the Toronto *News*, Dec. 17, 1899; *Globe*, April 30, 1900.

certainly the climate of opinion was such that the policy could be enthusiastically supported), but rather because special interest groups who stood to gain from such a policy had managed to impress their opinions upon government. Acting on the advice of the sawmilling industry, the government had launched its manufacturing policy tentatively, almost negatively, in 1897. Then on the basis of its apparent success the principle was extended, once again at the request of pulpmen. When, however, the government moved, by this time more positively and confidently, to force the location in Ontario of the strategically important nickel refining industry, it failed miserably. Widespread publicity of nickel's hardening properties, particularly the United States Navy trials with nickel-steel armour-plating, briefly brought competition into the Sudbury mining field. However, Ritchie's personal influence with senior U.S. Navy officers won for his Canadian Copper Company the critical contract to supply the Navy with the nickel required for its experiments. A second Navy contract to Colonel Thompson's Orford Copper Company in New Jersey, to solve the refining problems of the Sudbury ore, established that company as the leading buyer of Sudbury nickel-copper matte and supplier of refined nickel for the Carnegie and Bethlehem armour-makers. Orford's possession of a secret refining process meant that power and initiative passed to it; the Canadian Copper Company, though it held massive ore deposits, did not have an effective refining process of its own. To consolidate its dominance in the mining end of the business at least, Canadian Copper entered a long-term agreement with the Orford refiners through which it became the latter's sole supplier. Its technical success gave the Orford Company a monopolistic position within the American nickel market, and this power, working backward through the exclusive supply contract, ensured the overwhelming supremacy of Canadian Copper at Sudbury. For this reason, in spite of the 1890 excitement when over ten companies were launched to mine nickel ores, only two significant competitors to Canadian Copper actually entered production: The H. H. Vivian Company, shipping its ore to its own refinery in England, and a Canadian syndicate headed by Louis S. Forget, the Dominion Mineral Company, which sold its output to Joseph Wharton's small electrolytic refinery in New Jersey. But in a European market controlled by the French Rothschild's Le Nickel, with mines in New Caledonia, and in a North American market ruled by the tight Orford−Canadian Copper combination, the excess capacity of the mining operations fell primarily upon these two small competitors. Thus, despite the tremendous strategic importance of nickel and the fact that providence had laid down the world's finest ore body in Ontario, one company monopolized the mining of the metal, and the all-important refining and armour-plate fabrication industries remained firmly planted in the United States.[61]

By the mid-nineties actual development based upon nickel mocked the glowing promises of its early Ontario promoters. At least part of the reason for this disappointment, as well as the slow growth of the pulp and sawmilling industries, could be isolated in American tariff policy. In 1883, at a time when the primary use of nickel was still decorative, the American refiners and nickel-mining companies, both relatively small operations, obtained protection from the giant Le Nickel monopoly in the form of a 15-cent per pound import upon refined nickel, upon the nickel ore, and upon the partly smeltered product, matte. By 1890 the Canadian Copper Company and the Navy succeeded in placing both ore and matte on the free list. While this gave Sudbury a monopoly in the American ore market, with equal certainty it guaranteed that the refining industry would remain behind the tariff wall in the United States where, comfortably insulated against Le Nickel, it could both meet the needs of the American steelmakers and dump its surpluses into the European market without fear of retaliation. However much Ritchie might weave an Ontario nickel-steel industry in the air, his own representations before the Ways and Means Committee belied the hope.[62]

[61] O. W. Main, *The Canadian Nickel Industry* (Toronto, 1955), pp. 19-32; J. F. Thompson and N. Beasley, *For the Years to Come: A Story of International Nickel of Canada* (Toronto, 1960), pp. 39-59.

[62] Main, *The Canadian Nickel Industry*, pp. 51-3; A. P. Coleman, "The Sudbury Nickel Region," Bureau of Mines, *Annual Report*, 1905, Part III, pp. 136-43.

Undoubtedly the main reason for the absence of a Canadian nickel-refining industry could be found in the combination of financial conservatism on the part of the Canadian Copper Company and the difficulty of obtaining a successful alternative to the secret Orford process. Although Ritchie publicly boasted of the day when his railway would link Sudbury nickel with Hastings County iron—which he was also developing—in a huge nickel-steel complex somewhere on Lake Ontario, his vision was that of a promoter who lived by continuous spectacular successes rather than of a manager who moved ahead by stages. While Canadians might thrill to his words, Ritchie's Ohio backers quickly tired of his rhetoric. Doubting the quality of Hastings iron for steel, and embarrassed by Ritchie's repeated promises of a Canadian refining industry, the Ohio group withdrew its financial backing and froze him out of the nickel business but left him in charge of an unfinished railway and an idle iron mine.[63]

Sam Ritchie immediately engaged his former Ohio colleagues in a lengthy legal battle to regain control of Canadian Copper. When his action failed, he then combined forces with a group of Hamilton industrialists, consisting of John Patterson, A. T. Wood and John Gibson. Together they organized three companies: the Nickel Copper Company, to mine and smelt Sudbury ore; the Hoepfner Refining Company, with rights to Carl Hoepfner's new electrolytic refining process; and the Nickel Steel Company of Canada, to manufacture nickel steel alloys. Inasmuch as the Hamilton men had been operating a successful smelting company since 1895, already owned coal, iron and manganese properties, and possessed both the financial resources and the practical desire to build Canada's first nickel-steel complex, they could apply considerably more pressure for that all-important export duty on nickel matte to protect home industry than Ritchie could alone—not the least of the reasons being that to a man they were substantial supporters of the new Laurier Liberal government.[64]

---

[63] Main, *The Canadian Nickel Industry*, pp. 29-32, 52.
[64] William Kilbourn, *The Elements Combined* (Toronto, 1961), chapters 3, 4; Main, *The Canadian Nickel Industry*, p. 40.

Publicly Ritchie embarked upon a pamphlet campaign for a nickel export duty, while privately he and his principals begged Laurier to help them. Contrary to what the Canadian Copper Company said, Ritchie claimed that nickel refining could be carried on in Canada, and he discounted the possibility of Americans turning away from Ontario to New Caledonian ore supplies. A mere 10-cent a pound export duty on nickel, he pleaded in numerous letters to Laurier, would bring iron mining to life in Canada and create a viable nickel-steel industry. John Patterson, the president of the Nickel Steel Company, and J.M. Gibson, the lawyer for the company and at this time Ontario's Commissioner of Crown Lands, also applied political pressure to Laurier, but to no avail. Parliament granted permission for such duties in 1897, but the government refrained from imposing them. "I must tell you in all sincerity," Laurier replied to Gibson, "that the Government is not prepared, at this moment, to impose such a duty. The matter must be very carefully looked into before such a conclusion is arrived at."[65]

The reasons for resisting such strong influences must have been overwhelmingly convincing, as indeed they were. Canadian Copper, the Orford Company, and Orford's own newly established mining company, the Canadian Mining and Metallurgical Company, answered the export agitation with pamphlets and pressure of their own. New Caledonian ore could be used by American refiners, Robert M. Thompson, of the Orford Company, reminded Laurier, and any Canadian export tax would only hasten the shift to that source. In its pamphlets the Canadian Copper Company reiterated the sobering point that Canada had no monopoly on nickel ore, then demonstrated the necessity, in a keenly competitive international market situation, of refining in the most economical location, New

[65] S. J. Ritchie, *The Question of Export Duties on Nickel and Copper Mattes: The Anonymous Circular Answered* (Ottawa, 1898), pp. 2, 8; PAC, Laurier Papers, Ritchie to Laurier, Dec. 22, 1897, 20177-89; Jan. 29, 1898, 20171-6; Feb. 18, 1898, telegram, 20745-8; June 18, 1898, 24343; John Patterson to Laurier, July 19, 1898, and enclosed petition, 25116-48; July 23, 1898, 25246-347; June 28, 1899, 24612-13; Gibson to Laurier, Personal June 27, 1898.

Jersey. Nickel-steel was neither in great demand in Canada, nor could it be economically manufactured there when the coke, iron and coal required had to be imported from the United States. Answering Ritchie's pamphlet directly, Thompson pointed out to Laurier that his company was paying out as much in wages to Canadians as it was dividends to its American owners and attributed Ritchie's campaign to one of private malice: "He has an axe to grind, a feeling of revenge to gratify against his associates in the Candian Copper Company, who ejected him from the management of the Company."[66] The Americans held much stronger cards than their opponents; against the problematical nickel-steel industry, Laurier had to weigh the possibility that the existing mining companies would shut down rather than pay the export duty.

Rejected by the federal government, Ritchie, Patterson and company then turned to the provincial government with which, through their solicitor, J. M. Gibson, the recently appointed Attorney General, they had strong personal ties. Although the government's subsequent dramatic action was prompted by the direct influence of Gibson, it seems equally clear that it could not have moved as sharply and quickly had its will not been stiffened by the apparent success of the sawlog manufacturing condition, which, ironically, Gibson had opposed. In a memorandum to the Commissioner of Crown Lands dated November 23, 1899, Archibald Blue, the director of the Bureau of Mines, stated the case for expanding the manufacturing condition to include nickel ores. In addition to the strategic importance of the metal, which even the Admiralty now recognized, there were sound financial reasons for compelling refining in Ontario. Between 1892 and 1898 Blue calculated that over ten million dollars, or more than two-thirds the value of the ores mined at Sudbury, had been distributed in wages and expenses at the refineries in the United States, and his figures did not include processing to armour plate. On the basis of Blue's

---

[66] *Ibid.*, Stevenson Burke to Laurier, Feb. 22, 1898, 20847-52; R. M. Thompson to Laurier, May 5, Nov. 2, 1899, 23070-5, 27734-5. See also the Canadian Copper Company Pamphlets, *The Nickel Question* and *The Practical Side of the Export Duty Question* (Ottawa, 1898).

memorandum the cabinet adopted a three-pronged policy to encourage refining in Ontario. The government would re-open discussion with the British Admiralty to see if it might be interested in establishing a refinery of its own; secondly, the federal government would be pressured to impose export duties on raw and semi-processed ores; and finally the cabinet agreed that all future grants of mining lands would carry the provision that "copper and nickel ores upon or in such lands shall be treated and refined in the Province so as to produce fine nickel and copper of marketable quality. . . ."[67] Nothing came of the first two proposals, and since most of the nickel lands were already in private hands the third resolution was of no importance.

However, at the next session of the Legislature the new Ross government did move decisively to force the American mining companies to refine their ores in Canada and to assist the Hamilton group. By an amendment to the Mines Act the government imposed conditions that virtually precluded the economic export of nickel ore and matte. Rather than a total ban or an export duty, which it had no authority to impose, the government settled upon a licence fee graded to punish exports. In the case of nickel matte the licence fee would amount to $60 per ton. If, however, the ore was eventually refined in Canada (and this was the clause designed to penalize the Canadian Copper—Orford combination and protect the Nickel Steel interests), the entire licence fee would be refunded.[68]

The amendment drew a sharp and immediate response from the American mining companies. Through Wallace Nesbitt, a staunch Conservative and one of the few Canadian shareholders in the company, Canadian Copper bore down upon the

---

[67] Memorandum for the Commissioner of Crown Lands, Nov. 23, 1899; Order-in-Council on Copper and Nickel Mining in Ontario, Nov. 24, 1899, both in *Papers, Orders-in-Council and Correspondence on the Mining and Treatment of Nickel and Copper Ore in the Province of Ontario* (Toronto, 1899); see also for earlier attempts in 1891 to interest the Admiralty in Ontario nickel.

[68] *Statutes of Ontario*, 63 Vict., c. 13; Thos. Gibson, *The Mining Laws of Ontario* (Toronto, 1933), p. 20; Royal Ontario Nickel Commission, *Report* (Toronto, 1917), p. 13.

Conservative opposition in the hope of defeating the offensive clauses of the bill. The Attorney General had forced the government, Nesbitt wrote James P. Whitney, the new leader of the opposition, "to adopt a policy that is absolutely suicidal towards the Province and...you can make great capital by opposing it...." The best evidence that the Canadian Copper Company had been operating "on a business basis," Nesbitt continued, was that it alone had survived where more than six others had failed. The mine workers of Sudbury, fearing for their jobs, called a public meeting to protest the amendment and a number of mining promoters urged the leader of the opposition to "stand up for the mining industry" during this great time of trial. But Whitney refused to be caught in the crossfire between Hamilton and Sudbury. He agreed entirely with the idea of refining Ontario nickel and copper in Ontario, but attacked the government for not acting sooner, before "the best nickel lands in the Province . . .[had been] gobbled up—he could not say improperly—to be purchased by foreigners." Whitney bore no brief for the Canadian Copper Company, which he called "this great financial octopus," and he condemned the Attorney General for his contemptuous, partisan behaviour. Perhaps public ownership, Whitney hinted, might be the best solution to the refining question; at least the idea warranted exploration. But on the whole, his party approved of the application of the manufacturing condition to nickel-copper ores. The Conservatives restricted their criticism to previous neglect and the government's late conversion by its friends.[69]

The main arguments against the legislation originated with R. G. Leckie, manager of the Canadian Mining and Metallurgical Company, and B. T. A. Bell, editor of the *Canadian Mining Review*. In the columns of his journal Bell criticized the amendment as being wrong in principle and a practical discouragement to mining; it was, he argued, both vindictive and unconstitutional. If the government wanted to raise

[69] PAO, Whitney Papers, Wallace Nesbitt to Whitney, Jan. 18, Mar. 5, April 11, 1900; J. A. Orr to Whitney, April 12, 1900; J. F. Black to Whitney, April 2, 1900; George T. Marks to Whitney, April 21, 1900; S. J. Ritchie to Whitney, April 25, 28, 1900; *Globe*, Feb. 20, 1900.

revenue based upon the mineral resources of the province it should tax net profits and leave the business decisions to the mining men themselves rather than government officers. Francis H. Clergue, speaking to a hostile Ontario Mining Protective Association meeting in defence of the licence system, argued that "refining was not commercially practical in Canada until some one attempted it," and he was fully prepared to do just that. Otherwsie, if the protection was not provided, he would build a duplicate refinery across the St. Mary's River to supply the American market. His confidence on the refining problem and his proudly professed Canadian patriotism drew heavy fire from the assembled miners. In reply B. T. A. Bell claimed the licence system served no useful purpose; it merely prejudiced the investment of capital in an industry that stood in desperate need of it. Other critics contented themselves with *ad hominem* attacks on Clergue, "the glib-tongued Yankee."

In his summation of the sense of the meeting, R. G. Leckie saved his sharpest words for Clergue and his impenetrable metallurgical ignorance. The only two men supporting the government policy, Ritchie and Clergue, Leckie reminded the miners who needed no telling, were "foreigners and aliens":

> They have come here to make money and it matters not to them if Ontario and Canada bring discredit and ridicule upon themselves. Mr. Clergue goes further and threatens to erect his furnaces, which are still "castles in air" on the Michigan side, if this iniquitous Mining Bill is not made law. This is a bluff which may have some effect in his own locality, where sycophants are looking for favours, and railway contractors for profitable jobs, but it cannot influence the independent mining men of Ontario. Rather than submit to threats and intimidations coming from such a quarter, in speaking my own mind, I feel that I am voicing the loyal and true sentiment of every Canadian in this room, that I should prefer to see Mr. Clergue carry out his threat, pack his carpet bag and firebricks and re-migrate to the other side of the noble river.[70]

---

[70] *Canadian Mining Review*, Jan. 1900, p. 7; Feb. 1900, p. 33; April 1900, pp. 61-7, 92-7; May 1900, pp. 101-11; Ontario Mining Protective Association, *The Ontario Mines Act* (Ottawa, 1900) for a verbatim report of this meeting.

But the ferocity of these patriots proved to be of no avail. The next day the Legislature approved the bill and it awaited only the proclamation of the cabinet to become law. Undaunted, the miners steeled themselves for a disallowance fight.

On the positive side the government's refining policy found its strongest support in the daily press, the *Toronto World,* the *Mail and Empire,* and the *Globe.* The *Globe* saw a logical development from sawlogs to pulpwood to nickel: "What such a policy means to labourers, to the farming community and to the traders of the country can hardly be overestimated." Encouragement came as well from the financial and technical trade papers, while the *Canadian Mining Review* continued its spirited but on the whole moderate objection to the bill. The *Canadian Manufacturer* thought the monopoly nature of the industry forced government action and called the amendment "the most significant political development which has appeared in late years." The *Monetary Times* feared a reaction of capital but approved the intention of the government's action. "The policy of the new Ontario ministry on the nickel question," commented the *Canadian Engineer,* "is in fine contrast to that of the Dominion Government which—in spite of the protests of individuals of its own party—has played into the hands of the foreign corporation which has held a monopoly on our nickel industry in such a questionable manner." It, too, saw the connection between sawlogs, pulpwood and nickel, noting that the government embarked on its nickel policy immediately on hearing the favourable decision of the Ontario Court of Appeal on the sawlog manufacturing condition.[71]

For the year following the passage of the Mines Act amendment in April 1900, the scene of battle shifted from Toronto to Ottawa. In September, W. R. P. Parker, a Toronto barrister engaged nominally by twenty-eight citizens of Nipissing but actually by the Canadian Copper Company, filed an appeal for disallowance, principally on the grounds that the

[71] *Globe,* Jan. 15, Feb. 15, 21, Mar. 31, April 30; Berlin *Daily Telegraph,* Feb. 16, April 10, 1900; *Canadian Manufacturer* quoted in the *Globe,* Dec. 25, 1899; *Monetary Times,* May 11, 1900; *Canadian Engineer,* Dec. 1899, p. 213.

design of the amendment was the regulation of trade and commerce which was plainly beyond the authority of the Legislature. Replying to this petition, the Ontario Attorney General denied the trade regulation intent of the act. Its sole object, he argued, was to raise revenue using the licensing power and crown lands authority undeniably in the possession of the provinces, and he warned the Minister of Justice not to interpret the federal commerce power to "hamper, impair or interfere with the right of the province to raise revenue under the powers given by the [B.N.A.] Act in that behalf." Then in March 1901, J. M. Clark of Toronto, acting for Ludwig Mond, submitted a second petition which repeated at length the Parker argument and built a forceful case that the Ontario Act amounted to "virtual confiscation without compensation."[72]

It is difficult to understand such strong objections coming from this source inasmuch as the Mines Act amendment, which echoed the earlier concern for the state of the imperial fleet, specifically exempted British companies. On the face of it, this British reaction suggests either collusion with the Canadian Copper and Orford interests, or that the attempt of a small principality to regulate its own industrial future offended all capital. The resistance of Ludwig Mond weighed heavily in the balance. So did that of Stevenson Burke, the new president of the Canadian Copper Company, who once again repeated the threat to close up the Canadian mining operations of his company. How could the opinions of those who had raised the clamour for the licence system carry any authority with the federal government, Burke asked Richard Cartwright, when none of them was a successful businessman like himself? "They have theory, theory, theory,—nothing else. Let them produce something marketable before you destroy by your orders this industry you have now." Publicly the Copper Company worked through the Canadian Mining Institute, under Bell's direction,

---

[72] *Provincial Legislation*, Vol. II, W. R. P. Parker to Governor-General in Council, Sept. 13, 1900, pp. 9-12; Report of the Attorney General of Ontario, Dec. 20, 1900, pp. 20-2; J. M. Clark Memorandum, Mar. 1901, pp. 27-34; see also PAC, Laurier Papers, Parker to Laurier, Mar. 19, 1901, 54486; R. V. Sinclair to Laurier, April 22, 1901, 56072-6.

which at its annual meeting in 1900 condemned the legislation as "fatal to the nickel and copper industry," and sent a deputation to Ottawa a year later in support of the disallowance plea.[73] Countering these arguments the Ontario government and the Nickel Steel Company urged Ottawa to allow the Mines Act amendment to stand just as it had done the sawlog manufacturing condition. Otherwise, A. T. Wood, the president of the company lamented, "our buildings in Hamilton...will be a scrap heap." However, John Bertram, the one man primarily responsible for the sawlog case, argued precisely the opposite. While he claimed ignorance of the legal niceties, Bertram did know from his constant contact "with Capitalists and their representatives . . . that the present condition of affairs is very detrimental to further investment." For that reason alone, he confided to Laurier, there were many friends of the Ontario government who had taken "the responsibility of urging them against their will to take action in the sawlog matter, who are just as strongly opposed to the continuation of the Mines Act in the Statute Book." But by this time the federal government had made up its mind to challenge, if not disallow, the Ross legislation. "I am of your opinion that the legislation is very objectionable," Laurier replied to Bertram, "and it seems to me to be clearly beyond the powers of the Legislature of the Province. But I do not like exercising the power of disallowance, and I think it should be reserved for very extreme cases."[74]

Noting the objections of Parker and Clark, the Minister of Justice forewarned Premier Ross on April 11, 1901, that he intended recommending disallowance. Startled by this unexpected news at the eleventh hour, Ross angrily repeated the formal position of his government that the licence was not intended to interfere with trade but rather to regulate the provincial crown lands for revenue purposes, and he suggested

---

[73] On Mond's influence, see *ibid.*, E. S. Clouston, General Manager of the Bank of Montreal to Laurier, May 6, 1901; *ibid.*, Burke to Cartwright, Jan 20, Feb. 8, 1900, 225455-60; *Canadian Annual Review*, 1901, p. 45.

[74] PAC, Laurier Papers, A. T. Wood to Laurier, April 29, 1901, 55790-2; Bertram to Laurier, April 11, 1901, 55278-9, May 15, 1901, confidential, 56232-3; Laurier to Bertram, May 16, 1901, 56233.

an alternative to disallowance: " . . .let the Mines Act stand as was done with the Act respecting the manufacture of pine logs, and let the parties who claim to have a grievance contest its validity in the Courts." When he addressed himself to the political implications of disallowance, however, Ross conceded the whole federal case with the contradictory question: Was the Laurier government prepared to use its powers on behalf of home industry?

> You will be asked to impose an export duty where we impose a license fee. Both political parties have accepted the policy of developing our mineral resources along the lines of the Mines Act. Are you prepared to take the responsibility which may follow such a course? We will certainly have to resist it and oppose it and antagonize it by every means in our power, and with the decision of the Court of Appeal, already cited [the sawlog case], we think our position sufficiently strong constitutionally to make a good defence.

In a letter to Laurier, Ross spelled out more frankly the political consequences of his contemplated action: "This disallowance would lead to a rupture between the two governments that might lead to disastrous results. We could not, you can easily see, acquiesce in disallowance now any more than we did when the 'Rivers & Streams' Bill was disallowed by Sir John. . . ." The history of that case, Ross suggested, "tells all that need be known" of the political effect of such a dispute.[75]

In a similar letter to Laurier in which he, too, repeated the threat of open warefare, J. M. Gibson, the Attorney General, insinuated "that before your general elections took place the Canadian Copper Company had an understanding with your Government that this Act would be disallowed." Laurier did not relish exercising the power of disallowance, but in his carefully measured replies to the Ontario arguments he made it clear that he considered the Mines Act amendment one of those

---

[75] PAO, Ross Papers, Special Series, David Mills to Ross, April 11, 1901; Ross to Mills, April 27, 1901; PAC, Laurier Papers, Ross to Laurier, April 27, 1901, private, 55769-70; *Provincial Legislation*, Vol. II, 34-6.

"very extreme cases" in which the power should and must be used. Laurier admitted to Ross that he was "very much prejudiced" against the legislation because it seemed to him to be "absolutely prohibitory," and he advised the Ontario government to reconsider its position. "It seems to me, on reflection," he told Gibson, "that your legislation is one which cannot be successfully defended on general principles." As for Gibson's reference to the Canadian Copper Company's arrangement with the government, that was "sheer nonsense."[76]

The formal reply by David Mills, the Minister of Justice, to Ross's letter of April 27 removed the last prop from the Ontario case. The sawlog argument could not apply to the mines legislation, he pointed out, because the minerals were not being taken from crown lands, as was the case with sawlogs, but were taken from private property. The sawlog manufacturing condition did not, and could not be made to, apply to private lands. The licence plainly attempted to regulate trade and as such clearly transcended the provincial competence. Since both parties were eager to avoid a collision, Ross, Gibson, and the Minister were able at a conference on May 8, 1901, to arrive at a workable compromise. The federal government would not disallow the Mines Act amendment as long as the provincial government withheld proclamation of the offensive portions pending an immediate reference to the Supreme Court.[77]

For some considerable time, his bluster notwithstanding, Premier Ross had been aware of both the legal and political vulnerability of the Ontario case. Ever so gradually, Ross began the painful business of backing away from an untenable position. With a view to calming the tone of debate surrounding a long series of discussions between the Ontario cabinet and the American nickel companies, Ross asked his friend John Willison in May of 1900 "...not to allow Mr. Ritchie to attack the Canadian

---

[76] PAC, Laurier Papers, Gibson to Laurier, April 27, 1901, private and confidential, 55760-1; Laurier to Ross, April 29, 1901, 55763; Laurier to Gibson, April 29, 1901, 55762.

[77] *Provincial Legislation*, Vol. II, Mills to Ross, May 7, 1901, pp. 37-9; Mills' Memorandum, May 10, 1901, pp. 47-8; PAC, Laurier Papers, Laurier to E. S. Clouston, May 7, 1901, private, 55951.

Copper Co. through the columns of the *Globe* for the next two
or three months or perhaps for a longer period. He has already been heard by the people of Canada pretty fully through
the press with regard to nickel matters; it would be an advantage
to us, we think, if he were not heard from again just now."[78]
In those talks with the Ontario government Stevenson Burke
no doubt sympathized with the provincial desire for a nickel-
refining industry, but also indicated that the Orford Company
had just acquired several nickel properties in New Caledonia.
Canadian Copper had spent a great deal of money testing refining methods, Burke probably reminded the cabinet, but in the
end all had been rejected as uneconomical in the Canadian
setting, the Mond and the Hoepfner processes included. Mond
himself was on the record on this point. In all likelihood, the
Copper Company represented itself as being in the same position as the government; it wanted to do its own refining, but
without a method of its own it had to submit to the will of
the more powerful Orford Company which absolutely refused
to budge from its American location behind the tariff wall.
Therefore, if the government took strong repressive measures
against Canadian Copper, it would merely succeed in plunging
fifteen hundred men into misery, hand a monopoly of the North
American nickel market to New Caledonia, and force a flight
of both American and British capital from Ontario and Canada.

Probably for the first time during these discussions, the new
Premier realized the extent to which his Attorney General, John
Gibson, as an instrument of the Hamilton group, had minimized
the real strength of the Canadian Copper position. Curiously,
only after the amendment had passed the Legislature did Ross
clearly see the possible consequences of his policy. By that
time, while the dialectic of dominion-provincial relations
demanded a defiant reaction to the threat of dominion disallowance, the provincial government saw the advantages to
be gained by consigning the whole problem to that dreary
netherland of dispute jurisdiction. Premier Ross was just as

---

[78] PAC, Willison Papers, Vol. 70, Ross to Willison, May 14, 1900, confidential;
PAC, Laurier Papers, Stevenson Burke to E. J. Davis, Jan. 26, 1900, copy,
225461-5.

eager to reach a compromise with the federal government on the disallowance question as Laurier himself was to avoid a direct confrontation over mining legislation. When finally a court reference had been decided upon, Ross expressed tremendous relief that the collision had been averted, but he had no apparent interest in actually testing the substance of the legislation, although both Laurier and Mills, hoping to vindicate their original judgment, urged him to do so.[79] From Ross's point of view, success consisted of avoiding the trial and certain ignominy of disallowance. He had no intention of prejudicing that victory by pressing ahead with the court reference.

Thus the provincial government's attempted application of the manufacturing condition to nickel and copper ores ended as a non-event: the federal government did not disallow it, nor was it referred to the courts. Instead, the Ontario government simply withheld proclamation by the Lieutenant-Governor; it remained on the statute books, reduced to a pious intention, until ultimately repealed in 1907. By 1901 the Ontario government had resumed its former position of accepting the official excuses of the Orford—Canadian Copper axis with only mute protests and helpless hand-wringing. The manufacturing provisions of the Mines Act proved ineffectual for two reasons: on the one hand because the government had responded too hastily without sufficient tactical consideration to the solicitation of its Hamilton friends, and on the other hand because those parties injured most by its action were financially and politically powerful enough to play off the federal and provincial governments.

V

Industrial promotion was the first major use made of the authority of the state over its natural resources in the modern era. Between 1897 and 1900 the government of Ontario attempted to alter the legal framework of resource exploitation

---

[79] *Ibid.*, Ross to Laurier, May 14, 1901, Private, 56180-1; Laurier to Ross, May 15, 1901.

in such a way as to compel users of natural resources to locate their manufacturing establishments within the province. One of the most notable features of this mobilization of the state on behalf of economic goals was the largely passive role played by politicians. Special interest groups made demands upon the government, which responded if sufficiently coerced or led forward by its friends. The development strategy that emerged, therefore, was a sum of group interests, not a clearly thought out program deduced from fundamental political beliefs. It would not be too much of an exaggeration to suggest that as far as the manufacturing condition was concerned the provincial government merely acted as the political extension of certain—not all—business groups. There were, of course, some niceties to be observed. A public sanction had to exist, or be made to exist, before political action became possible. Likewise, no government could safely fly in the face of clearly articulated public opinion. However, public opinion could be courted and manipulated by those seeking redress. Nor could political intervention be seen to be nothing more than political favouritism. However, the compromising role of John Gibson in the nickel affair suggests how extraordinarily tolerant Ontario opinion might be even in that regard.[80]

Once the government tried to use its power to influence economic behaviour in this way, what limited its effectiveness? Not surprisingly, orthodox market conditions require first consideration. Protective policies such as the three manufacturing clauses could do nothing to lower factor costs. People tended to associate the expansion of sawmilling with the advent of the manufacturing condition, and those responsible for the policy naturally fostered that belief. But rising prices and stronger demand were clearly independent phenomena and they must be credited with a large percentage of the responsibility for the rapid growth of sawmilling in the western part of the province after 1897.[81] With the passage of time through shifts

[80] There were some notable exceptions; see the Toronto *World*, Feb. 22, 1900; *Monetary Times*, Dec. 1, 1899; PAO, Whitney Papers, A. H. U. Colquhoun to Whitney, Feb. 2, 1900.

[81] For lumber price indices, see M. C. Urquhart and K. A. H. Buckley, *Historical Statistics of Canada* (Toronto, 1965), p. 292, col. 26; J. A. Guthrie, *The Newsprint Paper Industry*, pp. 40ff.

in the location of resources and demand, that part of the province began to acquire a comparative advantage that made the manufacturing condition work so well for the sawmilling industry. Neither nickel-refining nor paper-making had arrived at that point by 1900. Given the particular refining technique employed by the Orford Company, its argument that Canadian production would have been more costly was technically correct. When that technique changed from a process requiring heat, in which the eastern United States with its abundant coal had an advantage, to an electrolytic process, in which Ontario with abundant hydro-electricity held a comparative advantage, then Ontario would acquire a nickel-refining industry. Coercive legislation would not be effective until this technological shift had taken place. And the monopolistic character of the marketplace tended to postpone that development. In 1900 the United States papermakers still had access to pulpwood supplies within reasonable distance from their mills. Until scarcity of raw materials drove prices up and alternative sources of supply were closed off, the Ontario prohibition on pulpwood exports would not dislodge any American mills. Thus market factors remained necessary conditions of industrial location but were not, it must be noted, sufficient in themselves.

The second limitation arose, ironically, from the very success of the business lobbyists. After having been turned down by Ottawa they succeeded in convincing the Ontario government to intercede on their behalf, as has been seen. That represented an initial victory, but it also created another problem. Henceforth, if a development strategy were to be expressed as a national policy, all of the provinces would have to act in concert. In the case of pulpwood exports, for example, Quebec declined to join Ontario, which left a gaping hole in the barrier being raised between Canadian raw materials and American industrial consumers. Quebec, being somewhat nearer to the wood-using industries of the American northeast, had already developed an extensive export business in sawlogs and more particularly, pulpwood, as a result of extensive commercial operations and an aggressive northern settlement program. Ontario could make sweeping policy statements without confronting established powers, which accounts for the ease of application of the manufacturing condition to pulpwood compared with sawlogs and nickel. But in Quebec vested interests and the church, the inspiration behind the settlement program, confounded attempts to regulate sawlog and pulpwood exports for another decade.[82] Formulation of an effective national policy thus depended upon the co-ordination of provincial policies, and without such a co-operative national policy the provincial policies were ineffective.

The inertia of capital was the third impediment hindering the work of the manufacturing condition. Capital-intensive, technologically complex industries resisted pressures toward mobility. It was an easy enough thing to move a sawmill, but a nickel refinery or a pulpmill was another matter. Even though paper-making technology had stabilized by the turn of the century, it remained complex and still best understood by the Americans who had perfected it. Canadians could see readily enough the applicability of that technology, but they had not yet mastered the technique themselves to any great extent, nor had a sufficiently large body of native capital come forward to underwrite the effort. On the other hand nickel-refining technology had not yet stabilized by 1900. Financing research was as risky and expensive a proposition as tackling an American corporate giant. Thus, it might be argued, the more complex the technology and the greater the capital intensity embodied in the desired industry, the more difficulties would be encountered attempting to foster its location in the resource hinterland.

In that connection, if Canadian businessmen seriously hoped to move sophisticated, capital-intensive industries or launch some of their own in competition, they surely had to form a united front to do it. Cracks in the façade could be taken advantage of; internal divisions made a determined policy in the face of determined resistance almost impossible. Such a degree of unanimity on a development strategy did not exist within the Canadian business community. Only minor internal opposition arose as a result of the sawlog and pulpwood export

[82] *Speech of the Hon. S. N. Parent, Prime Minister, On the Question of Pulpwood and the Policy of His Department*, delivered in the Legislative Assembly, April 25, 1903 (Quebec, 1903), pp. 8-10, 18-22.

clauses, but the nickel restrictions raised a storm of protest, not all of which came from interested quarters. Nor, given the fact that Canada was a major capital-importing country, could these protests be lightly dismissed. When the general manager of the country's largest chartered bank weighed in against economic nationalist development policies, as E. S. Clouston did in the nickel case in 1901, the government of Canada had to consider that advice seriously. Even the resource developers themselves were far from unanimous. As has been seen, John Bertram, the foremost advocate of the forest products manufacturing condition, strongly urged the federal government to disallow its nickel counterpart. The fact that so many companies and all levels of government depended upon foreign borrowing, made the coercion or even coaxing of capital an enterprise fraught with peril. A dependence upon outside capital led inevitably to an immobilizing anxiety whenever "a flight of capital" was threatened.

The relative legal access of the state to an industry also appeared to set limits on the manufacturing policy. Direct access was more effective than indirect. The sawlog and pulpwood manufacturing clauses were made conditions of tenancy. The government merely wrote these conditions into the crown timber licences and the courts upheld this as a legitimate use of the provincial proprietary right. However, because the nickel deposits had been converted into fee simple, private property, that manufacturing condition had to work through a more circuitous route. With private property, the arbitrary powers of the state were strictly limited. The only device at hand, a prohibitive licence fee to discourage exports, appeared to most observers—including some responsible for imposing the licence—to be *ultra vires* of the provincial government. Its jurisdictional right to license was of a much lower power than its proprietary right in the woods and forests.

Finally, the effectiveness of the manufacturing condition depended upon the power and skill of its opposition. Orford Copper, soon to become International Nickel, demonstrated the influence and ingenuity of concentrated economic power. Its opinions, resting as they did upon monopoly and expertise, simply possessed greater credibility. If its directors made up their minds to refine Canadian ore in New Jersey, they were not easily moved by criticism. They knew how to defend themselves and they could afford a good defence. A well-advertised purchase of a New Caledonian ore body, no matter how inferior, gave them a second source of supply with which to silence Canadian critics. Everything could be moved to New Caledonia, a threat that proved remarkably envigorating to the Canadian mining fraternity and public opinion around Sudbury. Orford had strength and knew how to use it. Through an apparent arrangement with Mond, the American company was able to bring the forces of the old world into the fray to restore order in the new, even though Mond's company was expressly exempted from the Ontario regulations. Moreover, Orford knew how to work the dominion-provincial machinery. By an exceptionally skilful playing of the dominion-provincial game the company mobilized the senior level of government against the junior. In the face of many extremely serious threats from the province of Ontario, Laurier stood his ground. It would require a great deal of cunning and self-confidence on the part of any level of Canadian government to erect a durable policy to contain the power of a corporation as determined and well-endowed as Orford. The coils of federalism that had given rise to the provincial manufacturing condition in the first place could also be engaged to nullify it.

# 3
# Promoting
# New Ontario

New Ontario more than lived up to its abundant promise during the first decades of the twentieth century. As had been predicted, hydro-electric plants and pulp mills appeared along the northern rivers; iron mines, smelters and steel mills were opened; and the miners of the province, in a wild, exhilarating succession of rushes, uncovered a series of fabulous gold and silver bonanzas. Nor could the bare figures of capital invested, new plant capacity, miles of railroad added annually and population increase, do justice to the story. So remarkable were these developments in New Ontario that they could not be scaled by such mundane categories; they could only be measured in myths.

Legends of discovery and development have been among the most enduring legacies of this era. Most of the mines have long since been boarded up, the mills have turned into decrepit polluters, but the myths they spawned in their youth are still with us. The transformation of the northern economy has generally been described by its chroniclers in individualistic terms. The self-made, self-sufficient man, driven forward by a sense of destiny, an inspiring self-confidence and an irrational faith in the land, was the stock symbol in the literature of the northern as well as the western frontier. Railroad barons served as the prototypes, and then business tyrants like F. H. Anson, George Mead, E. W. Backus, and that captain of all industries, F. H. Clergue, were cast in their mould. But in mining the mystique of the individual, in this instance the solitary prospector, has been especially pronounced. Countless virile legends and touching homilies of faith have been inspired by the exploits of Fred Larose, James McKinley and Ernest Darragh, M.J. O'Brien, David Dunlap, the Timmins brothers, W.G. Tretheway, Benny Hollinger and Sandy McIntyre, W.H. Wright and Ed Hargreaves, the Tough brothers and Harry Oakes. All men of humble origin, they lived and, in several cases, died in princely style. Their careers have become testimonials to the infinite capacity of individual initiative in a rich land of opportunity.[1]

But in reality the development of New Ontario was a joint public and private venture, a provincial equivalent to the opening of the west. The exaggerated individualism of the northern narratives has almost totally obscured the role played by the far from silent partner in the enterprise, the government of Ontario. Long before these spectacular industrial developments transpired, the government had established ambitious promotional programs to stimulate and assist enterprise. The manufacturing condition was only one, albeit one of the most aggressive, of many such policies. This exceptionally supportive

---

[1] See for example: G. R. Stevens, *Canadian National Railways*, Vol. II (Toronto, 1962); D. W. Ambridge, *Frank Harris Anson (1859-1923): Pioneer in the North* (Toronto, 1952); Augustus Bridle, *Sons of Canada* (Toronto, 1916); Peter C. Newman, *Flame of Power* (Toronto, 1959); E. L. Chicanot (ed.), *Rhymes of the Miner* (Gardenvale, ca. 1930); George Lon, *The Mine Finders* (Toronto, 1966); B. F. Townsley, *Mine-Finders: The History and Romance of Canadian Mineral Discoveries* (Toronto,1935); Anson A. Gard, *North Bay: The Gateway to Silverland* (Toronto, 1909), *The Real Cobalt* (Toronto, 1908), and *Silverland and Its Stories* (Toronto, 1909); D.M. LeBourdais, *Metals and Men: The Story of Canadian Mining* (Toronto, 1957); S.A. Pain, *Three Miles of Gold: The Story of Kirkland Lake* (Toronto, 1960); O.T.G. Williamson, *The Northland Ontario* (Toronto, 1946).

environment within which entrepreneurs launched their initiatives deserves some study, if only to restore the balance of the heroic myths. For early in the century the state had gone to considerable trouble and expense to create a proper matrix of policies within which enterprise could be rewarded. Promotion, embracing the improvement of access to resources, the extension of financial assistance whenever necessary, and the provision of information and technical education, was the public contribution to resource development.[2]

I

How could businessmen be encouraged to take up the numerous opportunities that faced them? Few people disputed the right of the state to concern itself with that question. How then might the province foster the industrial development of its natural resources? In the first instance by improving the accessibility of those resources.

Access had a legal and physical dimension. Improving the accessibility of natural resources involved both better laws and better transportation facilities. To that end the government of Ontario adjusted its statutes and regulations to remove the legal obstacles in the way of those with capital seeking land. But more positively, the provincial government strove to bring land, labour and capital into productive combination in the north by improving transportation to the region. In the case of the Temiskaming and Northern Ontario Railway this required the construction and operation of a railroad as a public work.

---

[2] This classification owes a great deal to a number of administrative studies, especially: Marver H. Bernstein, *Regulating Business By Independent Commission* (Princeton, 1955); Merle Fainsod *et al.*, *Government and the American Economy* (New York, 1959 ed.); Robert E. Lane, *The Regulation of Businessmen: Social Conditions of Government Economic Control* (Hamden, 1966); Gerald D. Nash, *State Government and Economic Development: A History of Administrative Policies in California, 1849-1933* (Berkeley, 1964); and Paul Pross, "The Development of a Forest Policy: A Study of the Ontario Department of Lands and Forests" (unpublished Ph.D. thesis, University of Toronto, 1967).

It was no easy task, one observer reminded the members of the Canadian Mining Institute, to devise a mining law that would satisfy "poor prospectors and rich capitalists, men with little and those with large experience; those who want to find something to develop and those who desire merely to get something to sell; the miner who wants to work the land for the valuable mineral he expects it to produce and the speculator who desires only to hold it while neighbouring development increases its value. . . ."[3] Amid this maze of competing interests, what then was the best policy for a government to pursue in allocating its mineral lands? The contortions performed by various governments to answer that question illustrate some of the problems and paradoxes involved in trying to enhance the legal accessibility of the provincial natural resources.

At first, in order to offer "liberal encouragement" to miners of every sort, the government established a different policy to meet the needs of each group. By 1905, for example, there were three recognized methods of obtaining mining properties: by purchase, lease and exploration permit. Once a prospector bought a licence for a nominal fee he could stake mining locations ranging from 40 to 320 acres on any crown lands or 22$\frac{1}{2}$ to 40 acres within areas of potential mineralization called mining divisions. After signing an affidavit certifying that he had discovered "valuable mineral in place" and had done exploration work on the property for at least two years, a miner might obtain a freehold patent to his lands by purchasing them from the crown at prices ranging between $1.00 and $3.50 per acre. However, the prospector could follow another procedure to a freehold patent. As early as 1891 the Mowat government had recognized that outright sale favoured the mining companies and well-supported exploration crews at the expense of the legendary "poor prospector." In order to broaden opportunities to include this less-favoured class of miners the government established a leasehold system; after the required two years of working the location had been met,

[3] Samuel Price, "The Mining Law of Ontario," *Journal of the Canadian Mining Institute*, Vol. XIV, 1911, p. 574.

the crown would issue a ten-year lease to the property at a rental of at least $1.00 an acre for the first year, receding to as little as 15 cents during the final year. If at that time occupation had been continuous, the rent paid up, and working conditions fulfilled, then the impecunious prospector might obtain clear title to his mine. For as territorially possessive an industry as mining, this leasing system proved remarkably popular—perhaps because in addition to its democratic intent, it incidentally reduced the financial risk for mining companies. From 1892 until 1906, when the program was abolished, revenues from leases usually equalled, and sometimes surpassed, returns from mining lands sales. In any event, by selling lands cheaply, by reducing the working conditions and discovery requirements (if not by law then by lax administration), by renouncing royalties for all time finally in 1900, and by alleviating the burden upon small prospectors through the rental arrangements, the Ontario government sought to attract Canadian and foreign miners to its unexplored territories.[4]

From time to time the government also issued exclusive exploration permits to entice large mining companies into exploring specific areas in northern Ontario. During 1896 an English syndicate received one such permit covering 46,000 acres of potentially gold-bearing land in the Lake of the Woods region. In return the company agreed to spend at least $120,000 over a three-year period exploring the properties involved; should it discover mineral-bearing formations then it would have to stake locations in accordance with the regulations. The Minister of Crown Lands at the time, John M. Gibson, defended moving "outside the beaten track of mining laws" on the grounds that extraordinary measures were required to attract experienced developers.[5] However, the failure of the syndicate

---

[4] For a detailed survey, see Thomas Gibson, *The Mining Laws of Ontario* (Toronto, 1933), pp. 13-24; 63 Vict., c. 13 abolished all royalty provisions contained in earlier mining lands patents. Henceforth the government recognized that its revenues from the industry would of necessity consist of returns from sales, land taxes, and other direct taxes on mining operations. This was in keeping with standard American practice.

[5] *Globe*, April 6, 1897; Bureau of Mines, *Annual Report*, 1896, pp. 8-9; Thomas Gibson, *Mining Laws*, pp. 24-9.

to perform the terms of its agreement immediately discredited this avenue of access. The event simply serves to illustrate the extent to which Ontario governments were prepared to bend regulations in order to accommodate timid capital.

However, once the North American mining community, attracted by these liberal terms and the success of Cobalt, turned its attention to Ontario, the miners themselves demanded uniformity in the law rather than the variety that had formerly been necessary to meet their various needs. In 1905 the new Conservative government sought the advice of the rapidly expanding mining industry on reform of the Mining Act. Following informal regional meetings in the main mining camps, 113 delegates convened in Toronto in mid-December. Their first and most insistent resolution asked for "one uniform mining law for the whole Province" and the assurance that it would not be manipulated by order-in-council. Shortly thereafter, the government introduced a consolidated Mines Act, which among other things eliminated the leasehold system, decentralized administration, and established one sale policy for the entire province, as the miners had requested.

An informal, pluralistic approach to resource alienation seemed to be the most likely method of attracting capital during the preliminary stages of industrial development. For mining the government established a variety of mineral land disposal programs to satisfy a number of different circumstances. In fact, the government was so eager that it was prepared to entertain almost any exploration proposal. However, once an industry became established, all that changed. An expanding, confident mining industry after Cobalt demanded and quickly received systematization, equality of treatment, stability and uniformity in the law and the administration of the law—still, it must be added, on terms liberally favouring the industry.

The practice of allocating pulp concessions to potential developers underwent a similar cycle. There, however, political rather than business considerations led to a rationalization of procedures. During the 1890s the government had entered into a number of pulpwood agreements with various syndicates without attracting much notice. The Spanish River pulp concession, leased in 1900 to a group of Ontario lumbermen with American backing, provoked the first serious debate on public policy towards the industry. "The time had come," Whitney said, "when the public domain should not be given out blindfold in secret contracts when the people, in whose behalf the Government was acting, were unaware of what was being given away." Such contracts, several of which had been negotiated during the late nineties, were especially suspect when, as in the Spanish River case, "the Government held the capitalists who were seeking concessions in the hollow of their hands and could compel them to yield to improper demands." Rather than continue the private deals with a small group of Liberal developers, Whitney moved an amendment demanding public competition for pulp concessions, full disclosure of the terms and conditions, and a full-scale inventory of pulpwood resources in order that the House and the people might know the true value of timber limits and could then grant them intelligently.[6]

The *Globe*, in defending the government, chided Whitney, the leader of the opposition, on the narrow legalism of his argument. It was the essence of statesmanship, surely, to encourage struggling industries by treating them generously. The *Globe* explained that "it is not an easy matter to induce capitalists to go into such enterprises if they have to risk everything and get no concessions, such as they are always offered to secure the investment of capital in new and untried fields." Later, "when the industry gets more firmly established," there would be ample opportunity to establish more stringent conditions such as open bidding. But in the meantime the government quite properly should give the pulp and paper industry every possible encouragement. W. F. Maclean's ever-vigilant Toronto *World* called the Ross government's behind-closed-doors methods "Hayforking the People." The industry had long since advanced beyond the stage that it required the kind of coddling that the Premier could only give in private, the *World* observed. "Instead of taking the people into their confidence the Government hoodwinks them and conceals the true extent of its secret deals by hayfork clauses. The concessions which the grafters are now obtaining from the Government

[6] PAO, Whitney Papers, draft amendment, March, 1900.

Poster announcing an auction
of timber limits, 1872
*Public Archives of Ontario*

Rafting sawlogs on Georgian Bay near Parry Sound, 1895
*Public Archives of Ontario*

James Playfair's mill, Midland, 1896
*Public Archives of Ontario*

Francis Hector Clergue
*Public Archives of Ontario*

Right: Members of the Ontario legislature and guests
pose in front of F. H. Clergue's residence, a restored blockhouse
from the fur-trade era, during a tour of Algoma in June 1899
*Public Archives of Canada*

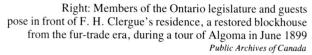

The Ontario legislature inspects F. H. Clergue's
pulp mill at Sault Ste. Marie in June 1899
*Public Archives of Canada*

Right: The Soo industries as they appeared in 1906
showing the powerhouse and iron works
*Public Archives of Canada*

The Joint High Commission at Quebec, 1898. Sir Wilfrid Laurier is standing
right centre. John Charlton is seated second from the right.
*Public Archives of Canada*

Interior of an early smelter at Sudbury
*Ministry of Natural Resources, Mines Information Branch*

Mining in the Cobalt district: McKinley-Darragh Mine
*Public Archives of Ontario*

Nickel mining at Sudbury, 1887
*Public Archives of Ontario*

Two views of the town of Cobalt, the top taken in 1905, the bottom one in 1906
*Public Archives of Ontario*

Cobalt Lake Silver Mine. *Public Archives of Ontario*

*Public Archives of Canada*

Diamond drilling at the Hollinger Mine in the 1920s.

Tipping ore cars underground in the Dome Mine in the twenties.
*Ministry of Natural Resources, Mines Information Branch*

Interior view of INCO's
Port Colborne refinery in the twenties
*Ministry of Natural Resources,*
*Mines Information Branch*

INCO Smelter, Copper Cliff, *circa* 1917
*Public Archives of Canada*

will net them millions without their embarking in the industry at all. . . . Any trustee who would deal with his client's property as the Ontario Government has dealt with the people's timber limits would be amenable to criminal prosecution." According to the *World's* sinister view of the matter the government, in the name of free access, merely distributed the pulpwood of the province among its friends, who in turn set about peddling *their property* to legitimate developers, skimming something off the top, of course, for themselves and their party.[7]

The annual debates thereafter merely restated the arguments advanced for and against the Spanish River concession in 1900. Temporarily, the government could play both ends against the middle, claiming that the infant industry needed special treatment and at the same time that its success with the Soo Industries clearly vindicated such a policy. Newton W. Rowell, who had made something of a reputation for himself as a negotiator of pulp concessions, emerged as the most able and best informed apologist for the government's approach. His research into American timber laws, he claimed, revealed the Ontario legislation to be "wise and progressive and states-manlike," the opposition policy "discredited in its administration, disastrous in its practical results, and inimical to the best interests of the people." In reply, the leader of the opposition accused the government of being in league with the corporations and at each session demanded an inventory of existing timber reserves, legislative control over pulpwood contracts and concession by public auction.[8]

---

[7] *Globe*, Mar. 30, April 10, 11, 1900; Toronto *World*, April 6, 9, 10, 11, 12, 13, 1900.

[8] PAC, Rowell Papers, Box 35, Memos and Notes regarding Pulpwood and Lumbering. Politicians might emphasize the public ownership aspect of pulpwood concessions, but pulp and paper companies in their prospectuses always stressed the "perpetual" nature of their agreement with the government. See *ibid.*, Mossom Boyd Papers, Vol. 130, Peabody Houghteling & Co., Circular No. 843, Feb. 1914, advertising the Abitibi Forest Mortgage, 6% Serial Bonds. *Canadian Annual Review*, 1901, pp. 69-70, and for a poetic statement of the Conservative charges against the government, see the election pamphlet, *Build Up Ontario: The Campaign Songs of the Ross Minstrels* (Toronto, 1902), especially, "The Political Robin-Son," the "Song of the Builders," and "True Liberalism (New Variety)."

For all its colourful language, the *World* had been correct in suspecting the speculative nature of the majority of these first concessions. Notwithstanding the solemn covenants to build pulp mills and employ so many men, the holders of these timber rights had no such intentions. But for a number of reasons, the two most prominent being the recession of 1903 and the persistence of the American tariff against Canadian pulp, paper and newsprint, buyers could not be located as quickly or as easily as they had expected. The three companies that did get under way collapsed almost immediately and the five speculative limit holders failed to interest any developers in their properties. An embarrassed government could do nothing more than grant their petitions for an extension of their agreements. By 1905, then, the Liberals were defenceless against Conservative attacks on their pulp policy: three mills were in ruins and the five promised seemed unlikely ever to materialize. Those who had claimed the success before 1902 as their own could not now shift responsibility for the failures.

Not unexpectedly, when the Conservatives took office in 1905 they abruptly cancelled the lapsed Nipigon, Keewatin, Montreal River, Dryden, and Blanche River concessions. Then, after seeking the advice of Judson F. Clark, a professional forester in the government service, Premier Whitney and Frank Cochrane, the minister of the new Department of Lands, Forests and Mines, reopened the concessions under a new, "businesslike" auction system. Industrialists were invited to submit sealed bids on the confiscated concessions stating how much they would be willing to pay in addition to the normal crown dues (which incidentally had been doubled to 40 cents a cord) in order to obtain the advertised timber rights. Announcement of the change, which ended the "hole-in-the-corner" methods of the former administration, drew praise from spokesmen for the industry. "At such times when trade is depressed," the *Pulp and Paper Magazine* editorialized, "we know what use such favoured people have made of their 'pull', and only on this ground alone will the Premier be publicly justified in keeping concessionaires and franchise holders to the fair fulfillment of a fair bargain." Aside from the increase in dues and the auction system, the new government made no fundamental changes in the terms and conditions; it merely formalized an access procedure. In itself, such a measure could do nothing to stimulate the industry during difficult times; indeed, only two of the re-offered concessions attracted suitable bids. The government could boast of housecleaning Liberal "behind-the-door" methods in 1908 but could not claim any new expansion. For a time, the departmental reports even ceased mentioning the pulp industry.[9]

Public investment in railroads helped more than anything else to open up northern resources to southern capital and entrepreneurship. On railroads, the province spent prodigiously. George Ross often boasted that under Liberal governments railroad mileage in New Ontario had risen from a mere 12 miles in 1881 to almost 1,750 in 1904. The impulse was so strong and the Liberal commitments so binding that even under reduced assistance from the subsequent Conservative governments new construction proceeded with unabated enthusiasm at a rate of 300 miles per year. Rare indeed was a line built without a provincial subsidy, bond guarantee, or land grant; some obtained all three! Between 1867 and 1914 the province aided the construction of 2,783 miles of track to the extent of $7,969,406 and pledged at least that much of its credit again in support of various railroad bond issues. Over and above their cash subsidies, Mackenzie and Mann received a $5 million bond guarantee from the province and more than three million acres of crown land in support of their Canadian Northern. An equally persuasive F. H. Clergue convinced the Ross government to increase the usual 5,000

[9] Woods and Forests Report Book, No. 3, July 10, 1906, pp. 120, 126, 191-3. For cancellation, see *ibid.*, Feb. 7, 1906, pp. 194-6; for terms and conditions of re-offered limits, see *ibid.*, Feb. 19, 1906, and an advertising circular in PAC, Mossom Boyd Papers, Vol. 133. Judson Clark's "Memorandum on Methods of Selling Pulpwood Stumpage" can be found in PAO, Whitney Papers, February 3, 1906, Special Series. See also, *Pulp and Paper Magazine*, Vol. IV, February, 1906, pp. 28, 45-6; *Greater Ontario, Results of the Practical Administration of Crown Lands, Forests and Mines by the Whitney Government, A Record and a Contrast* (Toronto, 1908), p. 14. For regranting of the concessions to J. R. Booth and Robt. McLaughlin, see Woods and Forests Report Book, No. 3, pp. 233-5.

acre per mile grant to 7,400 acres for his Algoma Central line and to throw in the timber and mineral rights which usually remained vested in the crown.[10] Clearly the provincial government could assume no responsibility for the transcontinentals, but it could claim the initiative for three north-south lines (the Northern, the Algoma Central and the Temiskaming and Northern) which, as it turned out, were much more important factors in the industrialization of the north.

These "development roads," and especially the Temiskaming and Northern Ontario, exposed the north both physically and psychologically to the energies of the Toronto business community. By the end of the nineteenth century Toronto had firmly established itself as the pre-eminent regional metropolis of southern Ontario, organizing and financing the trade and commerce of a prosperous, agricultural hinterland. Rail penetration of the Canadian Shield necessarily expanded that hinterland and changed its character. At first the railroads were driven northward simply to tap new agricultural areas to the north and west, but the incredibly rich silver and gold deposits unearthed by railroad construction redirected attention to the much greater opportunities presented by the natural resources of the Shield. Railroads thus brought the Shield under the dominance of Toronto, which developed in response the techniques, facilities and in a sense the energies to finance resource industries, especially mining, with a vigour that Montreal, for some reason, seemed to lack. Toronto's initial advantages of transportation and experience on the Canadian Shield imparted a powerful thrust to its rise from regional to national metropolitan stature. Indeed, as Professor Careless has observed in this connection, the "successive opulent suburbs of Toronto spell out a veritable progression of northern mining

---

[10] Liberal party, *The Ross Government Has Kept Ontario in the Lead*, p. 10; *Public Accounts*, 1915, pp. a65-7, "Aid to Railways—Confederation to Oct. 31, 1914;" G. R. Stevens, *Canadian National Railways*, Vol. II, pp. 30-81; D.M. McCalla, "The Department of Lands and Forests and Railway Building" (unpublished ms.), pp. 22-5, 36; PAO, Whitney Papers, J. P. Whitney to E. C. Whitney, March 19, 1909.

booms."[11] Much of the credit for initiating this mutually profitable relationship must rest with Ontario governments of this time, which in addition to extending the normal generous subsidies to private railroad companies, intervened even more positively to build and operate as a state enterprise the strategically important Temiskaming and Northern Ontario Railway.

Without a transcontinental of its own, the Toronto business community seized upon a railroad to Hudson Bay as a cheap and ready, if not entirely rational, substitute. En route to tidewater, so it was argued, the railroad would necessarily expand the city's agricultural hinterland, and by offering a third outlet to Europe, the northern seaport would reduce Toronto's dependence upon Montreal and New York. One promoter actually proposed that a Hudson Bay railroad in conjunction with a northwest passage shipping company would make Toronto the headquarters for the Klondike. In due course Hudson Bay became a self-justifying symbol of Ontario manifest destiny and metropolitan commercial ambition. Although several such schemes were projected with the usual civic éclat, each failed miserably in accomplishment; the James Bay Railroad managed to reach only as far as Parry Sound, and the Toronto and Hudson Bay, among others, remained gloriously stillborn. Eventually both Toronto businessmen and northern resource promoters turned to the provincial government for help.

Taking an "average business man's point of view with no axe to grind," John Bertram told the Toronto Board of Trade in 1901 that it was both necessary and sensible that the state should build the northern railways. "The chief thing to be considered was transportation," he said, "and the government would be lacking in its duty, to give away such a rich inheritance [in land grants] to any railroad corporation." On January 15,

[11] D. P. Kerr, "Metropolitan Dominance in Canada," in J. Warkentin, ed., *Canada: A Geographical Interpretation* (Toronto, 1968), pp. 541-2; H. A. Innis, *Problems of Staple Production in Canada* (Toronto, 1933), p. 64; J. M. S. Careless, "Limited Identities in Canada," *CHR*, Vol. L (1969), p. 6; Jacob Spelt, *Urban Development in South-Central Ontario* (Toronto, 1972 ed.), pp. 101-149.

1902, just on the eve of a provincial general election, the Ross government introduced a bill to build a railway from North Bay into the Temiskaming district which, it hoped, would give access to the vast arable lands of the Clay Belt discovered only two years earlier, extend the operations of the lumbering industry and expose, in the Minister of Public Works' prophetic words, "deposits of ores and minerals which are likely upon development to add greatly to the wealth of the province." Announcement of the planned intersection of the Ontario government line with the National Transcontinental gave Toronto, at long last, its national connections. "I believe it [the T. & N. O.] will prove of inestimable value," J. F. Ellis remarked in his presidential address to the Toronto Board of Trade, "in developing and settling the fertile wheat lands of New Ontario and the West—lands that are now practically valueless because of the want of railway facilities. Ontario and particularly Toronto, will be the great gainers."[12] But on their way to Hudson Bay and the West, Toronto businessmen suddenly discovered the Canadian Shield. The T. & N. O. and Cobalt taught Toronto to see its new northern hinterland in its own terms.

Late in 1903, construction crews blasting a level through the rough Laurentian ridges uncovered veins of natural silver so rich that sheets of pure metal could be peeled from the surrounding rocks. The rush began at first slowly in 1904, but with the first shipments of silver ore and the first flurry of Cobalt paper in 1905 the stampede began in earnest. By 1906 there were more than two thousand prospecting teams at work scouring the rugged Cobalt landscape.[13] The government railroad, running right through the centre of the camp, made Cobalt one of the world's most accessible mining fields and

---

[12] *Monetary Times*, Feb. 26, 1897; Jan. 27, 1899; April 15, 1901; Mar. 18, 1904; *Globe*, Jan. 16, 1902; C. C. Farr, *The Lake Temiscamingue District, Province of Ontario, Canada* (Toronto, 1894); Pain, *The Way North*, p. 89. For details of the financing and construction of the Temiskaming and Northern Ontario Railway, see PAC, Latchford Papers, Vol. 6, file 25 and Vol. 7, 26.

[13] *Monetary Times*, July 20, 1906; for details of the discovery and development of the Cobalt camp, see the work of Gard, Townsley, LeBourdais, Pain and Lon cited above, footnote 1.

Toronto its metropolitan capital. By the T. & N. O. it was but a short, comfortable excursion from the stock exchange to pithead. In the daycoaches hardened veterans of Virginia City, Australia, Rossland and the Klondike shared lies with excited clerks, labourers and stock promoters from the city; in the parlour cars wealthy owners and promoters talked quietly of the market as farms, small towns, and then the endless forests and small lakes passed in review. In 1906, forty-four stockbrokers made a one-week round trip in three luxurious private cars between New York and Cobalt; similar expeditions from Toronto formed a regular part of the railroad's business. These were the trains, Stephen Leacock tells us, of which the citizens of Mariposa were so proud: "On a winter evening about eight o'clock you will see the long row of Pullmans and diners of the night express going north to the mining country, the windows flashing with brilliant light, and within them a vista of cut glass and snow-white table linen, smiling negroes and millionaires with napkins at their chins whirling past in a driving snowstorm." A pleasant train ride united Toronto physically and psychologically with the booming mining frontier. After the shipment of more than $8 million of silver ore by 1906 the Toronto Board of Trade needed no convincing of what a few years earlier it would not have thought possible: "It is upon the prospector and the miner, rather than the home seeker, that New Ontario must depend [to] increase in population and wealth."[14]

On account of the ease with which the surface ores could be mined, Cobalt was often called "a poor man's camp." But this phrase could also be said to reflect the promotional nature of government resource development policies which consciously sought to encourage the combination of the factors of production. The state offered cheap and readily available land, permitted free incorporation and unimpaired capital-seeking and supplied inexpensive transportation to and from the heart

---

[14] *Monetary Times*, Aug. 10, 1906; *Sunshine Sketches of a Little Town* (Toronto, 1965 ed.), p. 4; see also "The Speculations of Jefferson Thorpe," for the impact of mining fever in a small town; and F. C. Loring to the Toronto Board of Trade, *Annual Report*, 1906, p. 45.

of the camp. Low rates favoured the movement of heavy timber, pulpwood and ore; the government willingly absorbed a $20,246,451.99 capital account charge for the T. & N. O. railway between 1902 and 1914 knowing that the development stimulated by the railway would indirectly make up these losses.[15] Through liberal regulations convenient and agreeable to industry and through an aggressive transportation policy, successive Ontario governments sought to render their resources as attractive and accessible as possible to both capital and labour.

II

In the further interest of encouraging development, the province maintained what today would be called an industrial research program and provided at public expense a variety of industrial services. To stimulate the more complete manufacture of raw materials, which would in turn provide greater employment opportunities, the state offered bonuses and bounties as incentives. In especially difficult circumstances, government could be called upon for bail. When one overprotected, "hot-house" corporation fell into foreign receivership, the silent provincial partner in the enterprise arranged an emergency transfusion of public capital to prevent a total collapse and to protect its own considerable investment. Here again, both political parties agreed upon the basic ends of such a policy; they differed only slightly upon the amount of public assistance and the means by which it was provided.

Government research consisted for the most part of detailed reports on the engineering and economics of resource exploitation and the scientific exploration of the vast northern territories. When the province established a Bureau of Mines in 1891, following the recommendation of the Royal Commission on the Mineral Resources of Ontario, its primary responsibility was to supervise the "collection and publication of information

[15] *Public Accounts*, 1915, "T. & N. O. Expenditure to Oct. 31, 1914," p. a58; Innis, *Problems of Staple Production*, pp. 61-3.

which will be of service to those actually engaged in the business of mining as prospectors, miners or mine owners, as well as to promoters and capitalists looking for opportunities. . . ." The Department of Crown Lands (after 1905 the Department of Lands, Forests and Mines) maintained similar, if less prominent, services for the pulp and paper industry. Perhaps confidence that the pulp industry would be compelled by dwindling American forest reserves to migrate northward tended to minimize the need for government aid. Perhaps, too, the obvious problems associated with the expansion of the lumbering industry emphasized the necessity of determined regulation rather than of promotional assistance. However, the mining situation differed substantially. The trees were there for everyone to see; the minerals first had to be found. Bureaucrats, politicians and voters found unlimited potential an unsatisfactory substitute for measurable accomplishment. In the realization of mineral wealth, the *Monetary Times* complained in 1892, "Canadians never are, but [seem] always *to be* blest."[16]

Consequently, first notice of any promising mineral formation was usually to be found between the bulging covers of a Bureau of Mines or Crown Lands annual report. At first the Bureau published the findings of professors and students hired for the summer months, but after 1903 a provincial geologist with a small staff directed the research. Every annual report came well freighted with the notes of wideranging general explorations[17] and considerably more detailed studies of particular rock formations[18] or mining regions.[19] The Bureau

16  Mines, *Annual Report*, 1902, p. 3; *Monetary Times*, Nov. 25, 1892.

17  Mines, *Annual Reports*, "A Tour of Inspection of Northwestern Ontario," and "The New Ontario," 1895; "The Nipissing-Algoma Boundary," 1899; "Niven's Base Line," 1900; "Lake Nipissing to the Height of Land," 1902; "Up and Down the Mississaga," 1903; "The Abitibi Region" and "The Economic Resources of the Moose River Basin," 1904; "Exploration in Mattagami," 1906; "The Geology of the Thunder Bay–Algoma Boundary," 1908, and "The Patricia District," 1912.

18  *Ibid.*, "The Laurentian and Huronian Systems North of Lake Huron," 1891; "The Goldfields of Ontario," 1893; "Copper and Iron Ranges of Ontario," 1900; "Iron Ranges of the Lower Huronian," 1901; "Cobalt-Nickel Arsenides and Silver," 1904, among many others.

19  *Ibid.* Each issue reported in great detail on the actual mining operations

also published weighty technical papers on the engineering or metallurgical peculiarities of various mines and ore bodies.[20] Crown lands reports invariably bore similar thoroughly documented studies by its surveyors and field staff on the forest cover, geology, wildlife and waterpowers of the northern townships. Each year scientific investigations of government agencies added to the accumulating store of information concerning the nature and extent of the provincial resources; in effect, the province of Ontario did its own preliminary prospecting. On one occasion, a highly publicized expedition of scientists to survey the Hudson Bay Slope in 1900, an imaginative method of collecting information was enough to accomplish the objective of attracting public attention to the northern resources. However useful such expeditions might be politically, the mining community deplored what it called "distant voyages of adventure." Rather, it preferred the plodding, less dramatic, but far more useful studies conducted annually by the Bureau of Mines. Comparing the Bureau's reports with those of the federal Geological Survey, the *Canadian Mining Review* found the latter altogether too scientific and too preoccupied with purely theoretical considerations that seemed totally irrelevant to the day-to-day problems of actual miners. On the other hand, the provincial Bureau kept its prime objective, the advancement of the mining industry, more firmly in view when selecting its areas of study. Indeed, the *Review* often encouraged the Bureau to expand the scope of its research activities to include metallurgical experiments, and during one long slump urged

---

being carried on in each region of the province, and from time to time the Bureau published exhaustive studies on particular industries or mining regions: "Nickel Steel for Armour," and four reports on the iron industry, 1892; "Nickel and its Uses," 1894; "The Metallurgical Industries at Sault Ste. Marie," 1901; "The Sudbury Nickel Field," 1905; "The Iron and Steel Industry of Ontario," 1908. In 1906 the Bureau issued over 10,000 copies of Professor W. G. Miller's report on the Cobalt ore body first published in 1904.

[20] *Ibid.*, "Treating Iron Ores," 1892; "The Sudbury Nickel Deposits," 1903; "Temiskaming District Mines," 1906; "The Iron Ranges of Lake Nipissing," 1908; "Magnetic Concentration of Low Grade Hematite," 1910.

the government to open up mines of its own for promotional and research purposes.[21]

Once prospectors had been attracted to the available land, the state provided specialized services to assist them in the accurate evaluation of their properties. When most mining companies could not afford complex machinery and continued assessing their claims by pick and shovel surface trenches, the Bureau of Mines purchased two diamond drills, the first in 1894 and the second in 1901, for use by government geologists and rental to private developers. Then, in the hope of inducing more thorough exploration by diamond drill, the Bureau relieved prospectors of some of the financial hardship entailed by absorbing 45 per cent of the modest rental. To assist in the speedy and accurate chemical analysis of mineral samples submitted by both private and government explorers, the province established its first assay office at Belleville in 1898. Soon afterward, when the northern camps came into their own, the government opened regional branches of this office to serve the immediate needs of the mining community. There government technicians evaluated the mineral content of drill cores and rock samples, judged the final determination of disputed mineralization values, and passed out a variety of technical and geological information to enquiring prospectors.[22]

All levels of government, in their eagerness to hasten the location of certain strategic or especially desirable industries offered direct cash incentives such as bounties, bonuses and subsidies, as well as a variety of other inducements. A great deal has already been written concerning the tariff and bounty policies of the federal government. At the other pole of government, municipalities competed with each other in extending the most generous terms to interested industrialists. For instance, the promise of a small but important municipal bounty was enough to move Adam Beck's cigar box factory from Preston to London; Hamilton won a virtual competition for

[21] *Canadian Mining Review*, Jan. 1, 1908.
[22] Mines, *Annual Report*, 1894, pp. 167-76; 1895, pp. 221-34; 1899, pp. 284-9; 1901, pp. 148-9, 167-76.

the favours of a blast furnace company by offering a free 75-acre waterfront site, tax exemptions, and a cash bonus of $100,000.[23] Similarly, the development impulse justified the provincial government's bounty programs aimed at securing the location within the province of iron, nickel and silver refineries.

"The relation of the various attempts to make iron in this country," James H. Bartlett unhappily concluded in 1885, "presents a sad record of loss and disappointment, of blasted hopes and shattered fortunes":

> If under the dispensation of Providence, the successful and profitable manufacture of iron in Canada was an impossibility or even a dangerous or difficult venture, we would be compelled philosophically to accept the position, just as we all of us, with repining, submit to the veto of nature against the cultivation on our lands of sago, tea or oranges.

But, as Bartlett, the Royal Commission on the Mineral Resources of Ontario, and the Bureau of Mines repeatedly emphasized: "Nature . . . has *not* placed any such veto on the manufacture of iron in our Dominion." Canada, and especially Ontario, was liberally endowed with the preconditions of successful enterprise; namely, abundant ore, fuel, skill, capital and transportation. Six years later the Ontario Royal Commission recommended that "every proper means should be taken" to secure the location of this "first-class" industry in the province. "It is unquestionably in a country's interest not only to smelt its own ores," the commissioners pointed out, "but to refine and manufacture the metals, providing always that the various operations can be carried on economically and without taxing other interests indefinitely for their maintenance." William Hamilton Merritt, himself one of the commissioners, was profoundly disappointed by the reluctance of the commission to make specific proposals for government assistance. "We

---

[23] W. J. A. Donald, *The Canadian Iron and Steel Industry* (Boston, 1915), pp. 114, 171; William Kilbourn, *The Elements Combined* (Toronto, 1960), p. 48; W. R. Plewman, *Adam Beck and the Ontario Hydro* (Toronto, 1947), pp. 212.

cannot point to any nation in the world that amounts to anything," he declared in 1892, "which does not manufacture its own iron and steel":

> One who has never visited a "black country" cannot conceive the stupendous scale of each member of the family of industries that goes to make up the creation of iron and steel. First the underground world teeming with miners to produce the iron and coal, or the busy neighbourhoods where the forests supply charcoal, the great traffic of these products to the railroads to some central point for smelting, the men day and night round the blast furnaces, the swarm of workmen at puddling and rolling the product, if iron, or converting the pig into steel and then rolling it. In all these the consumption of nearly every product is so prodigious that a thousand other trades are permanently benefited, from the farmer, who produces food for the workmen, to the cloth maker who turns out his Sunday clothes.

Ontario, too, might enjoy this prosperous activity, Merritt concluded, if the provincial government joined with the federal government in providing liberal cash incentives in the form of bounties or bonuses to entice capitalists into taking the necessary risks.[24] That same year, the redoubtable James Conmee, MPP for Algoma, appealed for provincial aid towards the construction of an iron smelter through loans, bond guarantees or "a good direct bonus."

Within the small circle of the new Bureau of Mines there was a major difference of opinion on the subject of government assistance. Archibald Blue, the director of the Bureau and formerly a member of the Royal Commission, blamed the failures of the industry not upon the want of capital, but rather upon the "lack of men with confidence and enterprise to invest

---

[24] James Herbert Bartlett, *The Manufacture, Consumption and Production of Iron, Steel and Coal in the Dominion of Canada* (Montreal, 1885), pp. 109-11; Royal Commission on the Mineral Resources of Ontario, *Report* (Toronto, 1891), pp. xx-xxii, 223-6; William Hamilton Merritt, *Notes on the Possibilities of Iron and Steel Production in Ontario* (Toronto, 1892), pp. 12-15; see also G. G. Mackenzie, "The Iron and Steel Industry of Ontario," Mines, *Annual Report*, 1908, pp. 190-342.

their money in the business of iron mining as they do in other manufactures, in trade, or farm lands, or bank stocks, or corner lots." Conditions had taught Canadian capitalists to invest in those lines, but in due course, Blue suggested, the tremendous possibilities of the mineral resources would also attract their attention: "Self-reliance is of infinitely greater value to a business man than the best devised scheme of Government bounty alone can be; and there are many who believe that the bounty on pig iron provided for by the Canadian Government, in connection with the measure of protection afforded by the tariff, is ample in its liberality." Canadian governments, he warned, ought to guard against overprotectiveness stemming from an eagerness for development; the close dependence of businessmen upon governments brought to his mind the caricature of the Australian: "Whenever he stands he leans against a post." Ironically the most vigorous opponent of this sort of direct government intervention in economic affairs was not a free enterprise businessman, but a civil servant. "There are ways doubtless in which Government help can and should be given," Archibald Blue wrote summing up this case, "the most natural and useful of which would appear to be the collecting and publishing of information on all the natural resources of the country, and on the best economic methods whereby raw material may be utilized and converted into the finished article, to the mutual advantage of producer and consumer."[25]

Yet in the same *Annual Report* Dr. A. P. Coleman, a distinguished professor of geology at the University of Toronto, insisted that the state must provide more tangible assistance than Blue was prepared to grant if its future growth, wealth and prominence "in the front rank with the rest of the World" depended upon the development of its natural resources. "In a purely agricultural country like Ontario," Coleman contended, "encouragement is particularly needed, since our people have not yet developed the skill and experience required for success in this direction; and the foreigners who might be

[25] Mines, *Annual Report*, 1892, pp. 29-30.

expected to undertake the work are already interested in the success of rival establishments in the United States, England and other countries."[26]

Although the professional counsel divided over the ethics and economics of bonuses, the Mowat government faced no real choice once it had been set upon by friends among the interests. It quickly and willingly succumbed to pressure from those connected with dormant iron properties and the Hamilton Liberals who were promoting a furnace company in 1894. In short order the opinion of the Bureau of Mines became the opinion of the industry. "This is an age of iron and steel," the first chairman of the mining section of the Toronto Board of Trade declared in 1899, "and in the race for national supremacy, it is that country most richly endowed with these blessings of nature that will stand preeminent." Two years later the *Report* of the Bureau echoed that same Darwinian sentiment: "So important are iron and steel in modern civilization that they may be said to constitute the material basis upon which the structure of society rests."[27]

In 1894 the Mowat government created a $125,000 Iron Mining Fund to be distributed at a rate of $1.00 (a deputation of miners had earlier asked for $2.00) per ton of pig iron manufactured from ores mined in Ontario on the condition that in any one year draughts upon the Fund might not exceed $25,000. While the aid was aimed directly at the mining and miners of Ontario ores, from the outset both the government and the smelting industry regarded the protection afforded as a complement to existing federal programs. With the blessing of the provincial government the smelters demanded that the miners assign their bounty rights to them; in any event, fierce competition naturally reduced the market price of ore by the amount of the bounty. The Bureau of Mines itself, in explaining the intent of the new program, emphasized the benefits that

[26] *Ibid.*, pp. 95-122.
[27] Toronto Board of Trade, *Annual Report*, 1899, p. 33; Mines, *Annual Report*, 1901, p. vii. See also John Birkinbine, "Commercial Progress as Influenced by the Development of the Pig Iron Industry," *Journal of the Federated Mining Institutes*, 1898, pp. 87-95.

would accrue to the smelting companies: "The aid thus provided, together with the bonus of $2 per ton granted by the Dominion Government and the customs duty of $4 per ton, is the equivalent to an advantage of $7.00 per short ton. . . ."Surely this protection and inducement would bring a native iron industry into existence.

Coincident with the provincial bonus, but certainly not solely on account of it, smelters were located at Owen Sound, Midland, Port Arthur and Deseronto, new iron mines were opened in the Nipissing, Algoma and Lake of the Woods region, and two major iron and steel mills went into production at Sault Ste. Marie and Hamilton. Ontario, which had neither mined nor smelted any iron ore in 1895, claimed an iron ore production of 62,387 tons and pig iron output of 82,950 tons by 1900 valued respectively at $111,805 and $936,066. Between 1900 and 1905 ore production slightly more than doubled to 193,464 tons ($227,909), while pig iron production more than quadrupled to 256,704 tons ($3,909,527).[28]

Plainly very little of this expansion could be credited to the provincial bonus of $150,000 paid out between 1896 and 1905. It was a mere mote compared with the mountainous $17,396,434 in subsidies transferred to the iron and steel industry by the federal government between 1884 and 1912, not to mention the incalculable tariff protection also provided. Indeed, according to W. J. A. Donald the primary responsibility for growth in the iron and steel industry could not be claimed by federal policies either. But perhaps the Iron Mining Fund did make a small contribution to the revival of iron mining in the province after 1896. For example, between 1896 and 1904, during which the Fund assisted the smelting of Ontario iron ores, the consumption of native ore averaged 30 per cent of all ores smelted within the province; during the following nine years before the First World War the percentage of Ontario ore used fell off to only 19 per cent. But here also the refractory qualities of Ontario ore and a general shift to American sources

---

[28] *Globe*, April 27, 1894; Mines, *Annual Report*, 1894, p. 32; Donald, *Canadian Iron and Steel Industry*, pp. 327-8; Ontario, Iron Ore Committee, *Report* (Toronto, 1923), p. 14; E. S. Moore, *American Influence on Canadian Mining* (Toronto, 1941), p. 122.

of supply must be taken into account in any explanation of this decline. Nevertheless, it is interesting to note that after iron ore mining ceased again in 1921 a renewed series of provincial subsidies played a part in the subsequent revival.[29]

In due course the provincial government expanded its bonus strategy in the hope of attracting to Ontario those American smelting and refining companies that consumed the majority of its copper, nickel and silver ores. It seemed only just that Canadian rather than American labour should be provided with the opportunities of manufacturing domestic natural resources and the Canadian economy the benefit from the increased value thus imparted to its exports. In 1900, for example, the Liberal government promised to use the receipts from its proposed tax on the export of nickel-copper matte to establish a fund for the encouragement of Ontario copper-nickel refineries. Unfortunately, that fund disappeared along with the ill-fated manufacturing stipulation into the jurisdictional limbo already outlined. The Conservative opposition, after first claiming the policy as its own, then turned during subsequent sessions to attack the repressive aspects of the manufacturing condition mentality. Whitney and his colleagues argued that the government should offer positive inducements in the form of bounties instead of restrictive pre-conditions. Such a "give away" approach united both those currently involved in mining and those proposing to enter the refining business, whereas the manufacturing condition had provoked the Sudbury miners (whose fears had been greatly exaggerated by the Canadian Copper Company) to oppose government policy.[30]

---

[29] Mines, *Annual Reports*, 1903, p. 25; 1904, p. 19; 1905, p. 14-5. The Hamilton Iron and Steel Company derived the most substantial benefit from the provincial bounty, receiving a total of $47,088 between 1902 and 1904 when the payments were itemized, or a total of 72% of the available grant. The nearest competitor was the Drummond Canadian Iron Furnace Company of Midland which managed only 26% or $17,234 during those years.

[30] The Conservatives in opposition and in office were strongly influenced by mining opinion, especially from Sudbury, through Frank Cochrane; PAO, Whitney Papers, Cochrane to Whitney, Mar. 15, 1901; J. F. Black to Whitney, Dec. 15, 1904; J. M. Clark to Whitney, May 5, 1905.

After sounding out the mining community on the subject, the new Whitney government passed the Metal Refining Bounty Act in 1907 which was designed to assist the location of copper, nickel, silver and cobalt refineries in Ontario. At that time all of the nickel-copper matte produced at Sudbury was being exported to the United States for refining, and, according to the Temiskaming and Northern Ontario Railway, about 71 per cent of the ore shipped from Cobalt was destined for American smelters. The act provided a bounty of six cents per pound upon the refinement within the province of metallic nickel, nickel oxide, metallic copper, and cobalt oxide to be limited in any one year to $60,000 for copper or nickel and $30,000 for cobalt which formed an important constituent in the Temiskaming silver ores. Subsequently, five silver refineries were established at Copper Cliff, Orillia, Thorold, Deloro and Welland; but no nickel-copper refineries could be moved by the comparatively small incentive provided. During the ten years the act was in effect the province paid out $170,140, principally to the Thorold, Deloro and Welland companies. In silver as in iron, the Ontario bounty cannot be said to have directly caused the location of a silver-refining industry. Rather it provided those already interested in the business with slightly more attractive prospects, greater security on which to incur capital debts, and decreased risks. In the case of silver the province assumed a portion of the cost of producing cobalt oxide, a useful but unprofitable by-product.[31]

When, with some justification, the Ross government proudly adopted Francis Clergue's mushrooming Soo Industries as the natural children of its resource development policies, it also inadvertently assumed some great unforeseen liabilities of paternity. Those same arguments advanced to justify a program of generous incentives in the first place, and the conspicuous credit Liberal politicians claimed for the initial success of the enterprises, carried within them the justification for even further massive aid to secure mere survival in the event of a general collapse. The province was, as George Ross said, a

---

[31] Gibson, *Mining Laws*, pp. 25-6, 79-80; Gibson, *Mining in Ontario*, p. 95; Mines, *Annual Report*, 1911, pp. 25-6.

partner in the success story of the Consolidated Lake Superior complex of companies; it had practically given away the iron ore and pulpwood that fed the huge integrated mills and then had lavished cash subsidies, mineral-rich land grants, and bond guarantees upon the railroads being laid to tap the resources and colonize the hinterland. The Consolidated Lake Superior Company and its transportation arm, the Ontario Lake Superior Company, financed by Philadelphia industrialists and jointly capitalized at $65 million, ruled the vast empire that had risen in less than a decade at Sault Ste. Marie. The Consolidated Lake Superior Company capped one organizational pyramid consisting of the Nickel Steel Company, the original Lake Superior Power Company, a pulp and paper company, the Canadian Electro-Chemical Company, and the company supplying water and light to the town. The Ontario Lake Superior Company controlled the Algoma Central Railway, the Algoma Commercial Company—a traction, forest products, real estate, and mining property holding company for the group—and a fleet of sixteen ships. In December 1901 the directors amalgamated the two divisions into one grand Consolidated Lake Superior Corporation, doubling the capitalization in the process in accordance with the optimistic merger spirit of the day. Finally, in 1902 the last element, the Algoma Steel Company with a capital of $20 million, was fitted into the magnificent design. At the head of this vast, sprawling organization stood Francis Hector Clergue, its architect, manager and tireless promoter.

Like a fictional colossus Clergue strode across the eager but undeveloped province leaving a trail of prophetic dreams, memorable Board of Trade banquets, and civic receptions in his wake. Inspections of his works by politicians and businessmen invariably featured plenty of good, strong drink, elaborate meals, cigars, and a fireworks display afterwards. On his promotional abilities alone, it is little wonder that the *Canadian Engineer* and the whole province looked upon Clergue as "one of the great captains of industry, who are seizing upon the forces of nature and making them minister to the comfort and convenience of man. The story of Mr. Clergue's developments at the Sault reads like a romance." Understandably, the Ross government eagerly basked in Clergue's reflected glory.

But it could not magnify its role in the affair without at the same time incurring accompanying moral and financial obligations as well. The expectation of electoral approval necessarily implied the assumption of partnership responsibility. And in harness with Francis Clergue, the risks were very high indeed.[32]

Disaster struck in December 1902 when serious difficulties in the new steel mill, coinciding with a "disturbed stock market," forced the company to lay off five hundred men and the directors to suspend the usual dividend. The company's preferred shares immediately plunged from $80 to $37 and its common stock, which had sold as high as $40 earlier in the year, plummetted to below $10. Ironically, there were numerous contracts available, even while German steelmakers dumped their surpluses into Canada, but contractors were compelled to reject Algoma rails because they were substandard. Throughout the spring and summer of 1903 the company scrambled desperately to convert the furnaces and find better grades of ore before a $5,050,000 loan from Messrs. Speyer and Company, the New York commercial bankers, fell due in September. In April Cornelius Shields, formerly general manager of Dominion Iron and Steel replaced Clergue at the head of the Lake Superior Corporation, but even his managerial expertise could not accomplish the miracle. An emergency plan to launch a $5 million bond issue failed, so it was said, on account of Morgan and United States Steel hostility in the New York money markets. The loan matured; Speyer and Company foreclosed, and on September 18, thirty-five hundred Sault Ste. Marie workmen were thrown out of work with several months of back pay still owing.

At first most people, like the *Canadian Engineer*, refused to believe what was happening: "Too much capital has been expended to permit of any temporary embarrassment putting

---

[32] *Canadian Engineer* (January, 1903), p. 15. For the story of the Soo Industries, see: *Financial Post*, August 10, 1907; Donald, *Canadian Iron and Steel*, pp. 212-8; Eldon, "American Influence in Canadian Iron and Steel" (unpublished Ph.D. thesis, Harvard University, 1952); J. Ferris, *Algoma's Industrial and Trade Union Development* (Sault Ste. Marie, 1951), and Margaret Van Every, "Francis Hector Clergue and the Rise of Sault Ste. Marie as an Industrial Centre," *Ontario History*, Vol. LVI (1964), pp. 191-202.

a stop to the developments. . . ." Then as the situation steadily deteriorated the formerly silent doubters had the field to themselves. "Such enterprises cannot be run on wind," the *Canadian Mining Review* moralized; the *Globe,* while remembering Clergue's "intelligence, courage and versatility as a promoter," laid the blame for failure on his inability to delegate executive responsibility. Similarly, the *Monetary Times*, reporting "A Banker's Opinion of the Soo," credited the collapse to Clergue's attempt at "striking 12 o'clock all at once."[33]

Bankruptcy fell like a hammer blow upon George Ross's government with its narrow majority. None of the provincial politicians who had traded so heavily upon the reputation of the Soo Industries could share the smug satisfaction of the cautious bankers who had resisted involvement. This was especially true after September 28, when the angry workmen under the influence of militant lumberjacks, who had just arrived in town from the bushcamps, mobbed the company office and rioted for the rest of the day. The local police and militia lacked the will to intervene decisively; in any event they were vastly outnumbered by the enraged and drunken workmen. Eventually four hundred militiamen dispatched from Toronto restored order. Then, as a group of Canadian and American businessmen negotiated for financial control, the provincial government loaned the company $250,000 to pay the salaries owing the workers.[34] This provincial intervention relieved some of the immediate, explosive difficulties, but it would require a much greater financial commitment from the public treasury to reassemble the pieces of the Consolidated Lake Superior Corporation in any permanent way.

Rumours that the Morgan and United States Steel interests were at work behind the scenes preventing a reorganization of their Canadian competitor further complicated orderly

---

[33] *Canadian Engineer*, January, 1903, pp. 15, 19; *Canadian Mining Review*, November 1903; *Globe*, April 3, 1903; *Monetary Times*, Oct. 9, 1903, Dec. 18, 1903.

[34] Van Every, "Francis Hector Clergue," p. 201; for a fictional account of the crisis, see Allan Sullivan, *The Rapids* (Toronto, 1920), pp. 296ff., and for a brief study of both the novel and Clergue, see the introduction by J. M. Bliss to the 1972 edition.

refinancing. However, the apparent antagonism of American interests did help to smooth the way for inevitable government action. E. H. Bronson, for example, urged his old friend the Premier to take "heroic measures in defence of the interests of Ontario," and he, for one, was prepared to accept public ownership of the Soo Industries if necessary. At length George Ross decided upon a decidedly unheroic but definitely prudent course of action: the province would guarantee a $2 million bank loan to the Toronto, Montreal and New York syndicate now in charge of the companies.

On April 8, 1904, George Ross rose on second reading to defend the loan, ostensibly to the Algoma Central Railway.[35] On general principles, the Premier explained, the government should do everything in its power to ensure the survival of such a giant corporation as Consolidated Lake Superior. Although many such organizations had been successfully established in the United States in recent time, this one was the first to locate in Canada and in a sense the reputation of the country, by implication, depended upon it. Moreover, each of the industries in the complex drew upon, helped to publicize, and therefore developed "the latent resources of the country." Premier Ross reviewed the progressive expansion of the works, a story that had been told so often before, in better times, by Clergue himself. Ross accepted the bankruptcy calmly and with almost pious resignation. Ignoring management's fatal neglect of all matters relating to marketing, the Premier explained the collapse exclusively in terms of a downturn in the stock market. A promising firm had been struck down in the strange and unfathomable ways of an almighty market and not even all the wealth of America could save it.

"The question which confronts the House chiefly," the Premier explained as he got to the point, "is whether it would be in the public interest, whether it would be expedient to

[35] PAC, Bronson Papers, Vol. 695, Bronson to G. W. Ross, Oct. 2, 1903, Private. For details of the provincial loan and the complex reorganization, see *ibid.*, Dunn Papers, Vol. 386, *Agreements and Documents Relating to the Reorganization of the Consolidated Lake Superior Company* (Toronto, 1906), pp. 107-98.

assist the Company in reorganization by coming to its relief by guaranteeing the bonds of the Company to the extent of two millions, or to any extent, at once. . . ." The alternatives, an absolute collapse of the companies and abandonment of the incomplete railway, argued convincingly for the affirmative. Furthermore, the honour of the province and its economic future depended upon saving the corporation:

> Leaving out of the question for the moment that American capitalists had been getting little for their investment and that it would be desirable to encourage such investments in Canada for the future, I think the House must feel that it is of great importance to the people of Ontario, and, perhaps, to the people of Canada, that the industries should be revived and put on a strong financial footing, and carried on on the lines originally projected, as it would encourage the investment of American capital for the development of Ontario resources.

Finally, within a strictly business context, the financial security offered amply justified the undertaking. In return for its two-year, $2 million guarantee, the government received a first mortage on the property and two seats for its appointees on the board of directors. At length, over the sarcasm of the opposition, which had not approved of the original 1901 railroad land grant and subsidy, the Legislature approved the government's action. Subsequently, the steel company reorganized its finances and production and, aided by new rail tariffs, anti-dumping laws, and practically government-guaranteed contracts, it managed fitfully for the next decade.[36] Gradually, as the opportunities arose, the new directors dismembered Clergue's magnificent creation, selling off the con-

---

[36] PAO, Ross Papers, Special Series, stenographic typescript of speech on the Bill to Aid the Algoma Central Railway and Associated Companies, April 8, 1904; *Monetary Times*, June 3, 1904. George Drummond and Raoul Dandurand were the contact men between the company and the federal cabinet. Ottawa contributed to the reorganization through a guarantee of rail orders for the Intercolonial. See, for example, PAC, Laurier Papers, Laurier to Drummond, Jan. 18, 1904, Private and Confidential, 81388, and an extensive correspondence follows; *ibid.*, Dunn Papers, Vol. 257, Dunn to W.K. Whigham, Jan. 17, 1910.

stituent elements to a number of companies primarily interested in the separate business of what had once been an integrated whole.

During the debate, A. J. Matheson, the Conservative financial critic, asked the Premier what the government would do should the company not meet its obligations? "That will constitute a default," came the formal reply, "and we can take over. We can foreclose and then it might be a case of Government owner-ship." "I think my hon[ourable] friend is prophetic," J. P. Whitney interjected, "I think it will be a case of Government ownership." However, the Liberal Premier thought otherwise: "I am not fond of owning a great deal of property," he told Whitney, "particularly if I think it can be managed as profitably by a private corporation. I think you can overload a Government in that way." But in spite of the fact that the two parties did disagree fundamentally on the question of public ownership at this time, a Conservative government curiously enough had to face that contingency in 1906, and it behaved very much like its Liberal predecessor, Whitney's prophecy notwithstand-ing. That year, when the company repaid only one half of its debt, Col. A. J. Matheson, now the provincial treasurer, went down to New York to extend the provincial guarantee for the remaining million for one more year. To be sure the transaction, coupled as it was with a request for further assist-ance for another of the company's railroads, provoked a mild crisis of conscience among some members of the new govern-ment. But even Tories could find no real alternative to continu-ing public support.[37]

III

As a complement to its policies of free access and generous assistance the government of Ontario also maintained an

[37] *Canadian Annual Review*, 1906, p. 340; PAO, Whitney Papers, E. B. Rykman to Whitney, Mar. 24, 1905; J. S. Hendrie to Whitney, May 31, 1905, Personal; Whitney to Hendrie, June 3, 1905, Personal. Whitney later encouraged James Dunn and his associates to take over the government's position in the enterprise, PAC, Dunn Papers, Vol. 254, Dunn to Robert Fleming, Sept. 18, 1908.

education program to familiarize a conservative business community with the rich but unfamiliar prospects of resource
development and to upgrade the skills of the labour force.
In the settlement process the Ontario population had become
thoroughly acquainted with lumbering, agriculture and trading;
but it had yet to learn the new industrial arts and opportunities.
These would not spring naturally from the normal course of
daily experience. A traditional pattern of life tended to reinforce
the psychological barriers against unconventional enterprise:
"A purely farming people, earning their bread and laying by
a modest competence by steady industry," the director of the
Bureau of Mines wrote in 1903, "have neither the skill to discover the mineral wealth of the rocks around them, nor the
boldness to venture their hard-won earnings in the business
of extracting it from the ground." Professor Coleman explained
the restrained progress of the mining industry during the 1890s
in similar terms of social conditioning. The Ontario
environment had bred, he conceded, "a fine, sober-minded,
moderately prosperous race of countrymen, progressing quietly
but steadily, afraid of hazardous ventures in business, knowing
nothing of mines and minerals and the fortunes won and lost
in them." Recognizing this situation, the provincial government
purposefully set about to change it, to convert an agricultural
into an industrial people.

Formal educational programs were begun at both the voca-
tional and professional levels. In 1890 the Crown Lands Department established culler's courses in the major lumbering towns
to teach the basic skills of estimating, timber ranging, and vol-
umetric scaling. From this group of licensed cullers the
Department recruited its part-time field staff, numbering 1,264
men in 1907, and lumbering companies a cadre of skilled woods
rangers. With the professionalization of the Department of
Lands and Forests in the twentieth century these annual cullers'
courses were expanded into broader public conservation programs and eventually into the Forest Rangers' School.[38]

---

[38] Department of Lands and Forests, *Annual Report*, 1907, appendices 6,
51; *Statutes of Ontario*, 52 Vict., c. 7; Lambert and Pross, *Renewing Nature's
Wealth*, chapters 10, 24.

The *Report* of the Royal Commission on Mining, published in 1891, expressed astonishment at the incompetence and ignorance of Ontario's prospectors, miners and mine managers, and the commissioners specifically requested the government to undertake the responsibility, in the interest of stimulating mining, of "enlightening" the men employed in the industry. That same year the Geological Section of the Canadian Institute approved a resolution from the Port Arthur and Rat Portage Boards of Trade calling for the creation of mining schools: "We have mined by rule of thumb long enough," these businessmen confessed, "and need economical methods, guided by experience and modern discovery, in order to make the most of our mineral wealth." Almost immediately the newly created Bureau of Mines responded directly to the needs of the miners and prospectors already in the field by setting up its first Summer Mining Schools in 1894 at Sudbury and Rat Portage to teach these men the basic principles of geology and the practice of scientific prospecting. During the summer of 1895, 131 men received instruction from William Hamilton Merritt in four northern mining camps. For many of these men, W. L. Goodwin (who succeeded Merritt) reported in 1902, the Summer Mining School constituted their first and only formal education; for the other, the program "made up for the lack of instruction in mineralogy and geology in our public schools and high schools." By 1906 the classes were reaching more than 500 miners in five centres and a year later, swelled by the flood of amateur prospectors into Cobalt, the numbers rose to 950.[39]

In the universities, at the other end of the education spectrum, the provincial government also established schools of mining and forestry. On the recommendation of the Royal Commission on Mining, the Mowat government supported the foundation

---

[39] Royal Commission on the Mineral Resources of Ontario, *Report*, pp. xvi, xxiii, 415-20, 513-21; *Monetary Times*, April 10, 1891; Mines, *Annual Report*, 1894, pp. 216-22; 1895, pp. 212-20; 1902, pp. 61-9; 1906, pp. 39-46; 1907, pp. 49-54. Gilbert LaBine, one of the famous Canadian prospectors, learned his geology at these Department of Mines Summer Schools; Newman, *Flame of Power*, pp. 153, 157.

of the Kingston School of Mines in 1893 with a $5,000 annual grant. This school, which later became affiliated with Queen's University, offered "a complete scientific education of both a theoretical and practical character to young men studying for metallurgists or mining engineers." Although the University of Toronto had offered geology courses for some time, the provincial university lagged considerably behind Queen's and McGill in providing for mining in its engineering program. In 1895 the School of Practical Science acquired a collection of mining equipment, but the imperatives of inter-university rivalry did not force the creation of a chair of mining and metallurgy until 1908.[40]

Scientifically trained, professional mining engineers were necessarily required to penetrate the complex mysteries of the earth's crust. Scientific forestry, however, emerged not from a concern for "mere development" of the forest resources, as in mining, but rather from a second-order intellectual urge towards the "best" or "most efficient" use of those resources. "The difference between the logger and the forester," one of Ontario's pioneer foresters explained, "is that the former is a harvester of nature's crop, and exploiter of natural resources, cashing the accumulated wood capital, a mere converter into useful shape of a crop to the production of which he has contributed nothing and to the reproduction of which he does not give any thought, while the forester is a producer of wood crops, just as the farmer is a producer of food crops.... The main difference, then, between the forester and the lumberman is their *attitude toward* the future."[41]

[40]  Mines, *Annual Report*, 1893, pp. 178-80; 1895, pp. 212-20; *Canadian Mining Journal*, Jan. 1, 1908, Oct. 15, 1908; J. B. Porter, "The Education of Mining and Metallurgical Engineers," and Mr. Douglas' commentary, *Journal of the Canadian Mining Institute*, Vol. IX (1906), pp. 143-52; J. C. Gwillim, "The Status of the Mining Profession," *ibid.*, Vol. X (1907), pp. 321-39.

[41]  B. E. Fernow, *Lectures on Forestry* (Kingston, 1903), p. 52; "The Relation of Mining to Forestry," *Journal of the Canadian Mining Institute*, Vol. XII (1909), p. 375; "The Education of Foresters," *Canadian Forestry Journal*, Vol. III (1907), pp. 143-53; S. P. Hays, *Conservation and the Gospel of Efficiency* (Cambridge, 1959), pp. 27-48.

Recognition of the forestry profession in Ontario around the turn of the century stemmed in part from widespread anxiety about the wanton destruction of the forests by fire and logging, and in part from the scientific re-evaluation of the character of the forest as a renewable resource. Gradually the idea radiated outward from a small group of international scientists, to forestry movements and eventually into popular currency, that under professional supervision the forest need not be cut over or burned over only once, then to be abandoned to an eternity of sub-marginal farming, second-growth scrub, or pitiful erosion by the elements. Professional foresters could save the forest from fire and ruthless exploitation while still permitting extensive cutting; they would stabilize a hitherto extractive, migratory industry; and thirdly, they would ensure the permanence of the public forest and the revenues from it. For their part, the lumbermen regarded the foresters primarily as insurance against forest fires. The foresters supported their crusade against the notion of the moving agricultural frontier and were thus valuable allies in the old struggle with the farmers over occupancy of the northern forest. Science legitimized the lumbermen's claim that their industry could be permanent and their argument that their tenure should be more secure. Nor did the professional foresters threaten the forest products industries as directly as many urban nature preservationists believed. "A forester is not a mere botanist let loose to air his facts at the expense of others," the head of the Yale Forest School told a Canadian audience in 1906, "neither is he a fire ranger, a lumberman, a sportsman, an arboriculturalist, a dendrologist, a silviculturalist, or any other ist....His business is to grow crops of trees, AND MAKE THEM PAY."[42] From a lumberman's point of view, those were not exactly fighting words.

[42] A. H. D. Ross, "Canadian Forestry Education," *Canadian Forestry Journal*, Vol. II (1906), pp. 71-2; Peter Gillies, "The Ottawa Lumber Barons and the End of the Great Pine in Eastern Ontario: An Aspect of the Conservation Movement, 1880-1914" (unpublished ms. Forthcoming in the *Journal of Canadian Studies*). For a contrasting view of the lumbermen's attitudes towards conservation, see Paul Pross, "The Development of Professions in the Public Service: The Foresters in Ontario," *Canadian Public Administration*, Vol. X (1967), pp. 377-8.

W. L. Goodwin, of the new Kingston School of Mines, was the most instrumental figure in carrying the American forestry movement into Canada. His essays and reports continually emphasized the need for a professional forestry school. In 1901 he had the terms of reference of his own School of Mines expanded to encompass forestry education, and it was at Goodwin's invitation and at his institution that Bernhard Fernow, the most distinguished of the American foresters, delivered his famous *Lectures on Forestry* in 1903. Such vigorous activity at Queen's provoked an immediate response at the University of Toronto, which announced a one-year diploma course in forestry in 1904. Outside of the universities there was also a great deal of pressure urging a forestry school and accumulating evidence that the new profession was being readily accepted. From its inception in 1900 the Canadian Forestry Association called for a school and the public application of forestry principles. Leading lumbermen, trade periodicals and prominent businessmen, most notably Clifford Sifton and B. E. Walker, general manager of the Bank of Commerce, actively supported the idea. In 1903 the provincial agricultural college named a professional forester to its faculty, and a year later the Crown Lands Department appointed the first fully qualified forester to its staff. As for the school of forestry, B. E. Walker's presence and influence on the Royal Commission appointed by Premier Whitney in 1905 to resolve the tangled affairs of the University of Toronto practically ensured a favourable outcome. The commission's *Report*, brought down in 1906, strongly urged the government to provide the university with sufficient funds to establish a forestry school and one year later just such a faculty was created within the reorganized University of Toronto, with Bernhard Fernow as its dean.[43]

[43] J. W. B. Sisam, *Forestry Education at Toronto* (Toronto, 1961), pp. 9, 13-4; A.D. Rogers, *Bernhard Eduard Fernow* (Princeton, 1951), pp. 381-519; W. L. Goodwin, "A School of Forestry for Ontario," Queen's Quarterly, Vol. X (1902), pp. 77-80; "Principles of the Canadian Forestry Association," *Canadian Forestry Journal*, Vol. I (1905), p. 4; *Pulp and Paper Magazine*, Dec., 1903; *Canadian Annual Review*, 1904, p. 538; PAC, Bronson Papers, Vol. 695 and 764, E.H. Bronson to Thomas Southworth, Director of Forestry, Dec. 24, 1903; PAO, Whitney papers, Judson F. Clark, Provincial Forester, to Whitney, April 27, 1906.

At the Great Crystal Palace Exhibition of 1851, the Province of Canada, on the instigation of Lord Elgin, presented a display of its natural resources in the hope of stimulating interest in Canadian opportunities. After Confederation, both the federal government and the province of Ontario continued the tradition. Ontario attempted to draw the attention of the world to its undeveloped resources at the Cincinnati Centennial Exposition in 1888, the World's Columbian Exposition in 1893, and at several Buffalo fairs after the turn of the century. Naturally the expenditure of effort on the education of foreigners in the opportunities of Ontario resources suggested similar programs for the edification and encouragement of Ontario's own citizens. During the hearings of the Royal Commission on the Mineral Resources of Ontario in 1889, Walker emphasized the need for a provincial museum as a repository of an educational collection of provincial natural life and resources. A decade later, before the Canadian Institute, he reaffirmed the necessity: "It should not be forgotten that a museum is about the most profitable investment a government can make...I can only repeat that we are rich enough to bear the cost with ease, but we are not intelligent enough to see our own interest in spending the money." In 1905 a somewhat impatient Dr. W. A. Parks pointed out that the Bureau of Mines' travelling collection required a permanent home which could quite easily be in a provincial museum at Toronto, "the heart of the educational system." "It is high time," he concluded, "that the example of all progressive states were followed and a thoroughly complete provincial museum established." Shortly thereafter, the government did found a museum in which the mineral resources of the province were prominently displayed, and in 1908 it began what was to become a permanent exhibit at the Canadian National Exhibition, publicizing to a much wider public the natural resources and their industrial applications.[44]

---

[44] Audrey Short, "Canada Exhibited, 1851-1867," *CHR*, Vol. XLVIII (1967), pp. 353-64; Archibald Blue, *Mineral Exhibit of the Province of Ontario* (Cincinnati, 1888); A. P. Coleman, "Ontario's Minerals at the World's Fair,"

Upon occasion, the provincial government adopted the opposite strategy; instead of collecting samples of resources and carrying them to public exhibitions at home and abroad, it sponsored excursions by various influential groups into northern Ontario itself. Both the government and the north received a great deal of favourable publicity following a tour of New Ontario by the Canadian Press Association. In 1907 a group of visiting British financial journalists enjoyed a splendid railroad excursion into the mining camps as guests of the Ontario government; and government agencies—including of course the T. & N. O. railway—regularly accommodated groups organized by the Canadian Mining Institute and the Toronto Board of Trade. In a constant search for ways of bringing both the resources and the successful methods of developing them before the general public, and particularly the investing public, the provincial government demonstrated considerable skill at news management, or what is today referred to as "public relations."[45]

Through the medium of its exhaustive departmental annual reports, which were themselves conceived as massive advertisements for Ontario resources and were always eagerly received and thoroughly summarized by the press, the provincial government hoped to accomplish the considerably more delicate task of educating capital. Canadians, who were, for the most part, habitually unconcerned with mining and pulp, had to be attuned to these profitable opportunities; experienced foreign capitalists in search of new sources of raw materials had to be shown Ontario's abundant resources. Although Ontario largely

---

Mines, *Annual Report*, 1892, pp. 185-94; "Ontario at the Pan-American Exposition, Buffalo, 1901," *ibid.*, 1902, pp. 83-90; Royal Commission on the Mineral Resources of Ontario, *Report*, pp. 411-3, and Walker's testimony, pp. 420-3; *Monetary Times*, April 6, 1900; Dr. W. A. Parks, "The Need of a Provincial Museum in Ontario," *Journal of the Canadian Mining*, Vol. VIII (1905), pp. 68-75; and *Canadian Mining Journal*, Sept. 15, 1908.

[45] Canadian Press Association, *New Ontario* (Welland, 1903); *Canadian Mining Journal*, Oct. 1, 1907; PAC, Willison Papers, Vol. 16, F. Cochrane to J. S. Willison, Sept. 16, 1907; *Quarterly Bulletin of the Canadian Mining Institute*, January, 1909; Toronto Board of Trade, *Report*, 1911, pp. 10-12.

succeeded in attracting quantities of mobile international capital during these prewar years, overcoming the inertia that ruled the domestic capital market proved a somewhat more frustrating experience and only a qualified success. Officials in the Crown Lands, and later Lands, Forests and Mines Departments, alternately prodded, implored, and tried to shame Canadians into investing in their own natural resource industries. The mere provision of information was simply not enough. For example, during the mid 1890s "Canadian moneyed men, with their $187,000,000 deposited in banks," drew down the wrath of Archibald Blue in the Bureau of Mines. Canadians, and especially Canadian bankers, congratulated themselves on these record per capita sums "lying in banks" invested in low-yield but eminently secure businesses: To the director of the Bureau of Mines it seemed unforgivable "that where nature has been so bountiful the citizen folds his arms and the enterprising foreigner is invited to step in to win and carry away the treasure." The conclusion to be drawn was obvious; the need for prompt action was essential: "Unemployed money in the bank or the safe, and ores of gold, nickel, copper or iron in the earth, are in that form alike useless to the service of man. The money must go into circulation, and the ores must be won and their metals made ready for the purpose of commerce and the arts."[46]

The financial press, often taking as its point of departure information found in government reports, also commented upon the financial conservatism of Canadians. The *Monetary Times* proffered the usual excuses and explanations for Canadian reticence, but placed its faith in education:

> Our universities have taken up the subject and provided means for imparting knowledge in mineralogy. The theoretical training will greatly aid in the practical working out of success in mining, so that it will not be so much a wild venture as formerly, but a practical business carried on upon legitimate principles, such as have made it attractive elsewhere, because of the profits yielded.

[46] Mines, *Annual Report*, 1894, pp. 8, 9; 1895, pp. 7-9.

Nevertheless, it could not help but wonder at what it considered the resolute irrationality of Canadian investors: "In grain and real estate people will invest their money whether they gain or lose, and they will continue to do so in a most persistent manner; while even one loss in mining operations seems to discourage them for a lifetime, so they will not touch the thing again." In the Kootenays, where Americans were reaping fortunes from the mines, Canadians monopolized the town lots, because Canadians "understand more about a town lot than they do about a mine." R. M. Horne-Payne, a visiting British financier, reported to the Toronto Board of Trade that Canadians had not even dominated those activities in which they allegedly excelled in the Kootenay camps. Canadian firms were represented there by "young men of little experience," whereas American companies dispatched "the best and most active men they can command."[47]

The initial insensitivity of Canadians to Cobalt silver occasioned a great deal of bewildered comment in mining and financial circles. No one seemed to be taking mining seriously, the *Canadian Mining Review* complained in July 1905. The daily press consistently ignored the "extraordinarily rich and promising finds" which were being made almost every week. Happily for the *Review*, "in spite of this apathy...prospectors, largely from the United States are flocking to the locality, while, too, capital is beginning to make investigations." When the first wave of popular excitement finally broke a year later, the *Monetary Times* paused in its narrative of remarkable occurrences to consider the moral of the "homily" being played out at Cobalt. We must "play our own hand on our own land with all the ability of, and even with greater confidence than those who, seeing great opportunities for their own enrichment, come to us from outside," the *Monetary Times* exhorted its readers. Much of the Canadian conservatism displayed at Cobalt could be traced to those environmental conditions which produced a

---

[47] *Monetary Times*, May 20, 1892; Nov. 6, 1896; *Canadian Annual Review*, 1902, p. 282; University of Toronto Archives, Walker Papers, Byron Walker to S. F. Walker, June 9, July 4, 1900.

"strong-brained and strong-bodied" specimen possessing "natural capacity ahead of the average native of any other country." Regrettably, that same climate also bred a limited vision and a preoccupation with "the dust of routine." Cobalt clearly demonstrated that the time had come for vision, for "a grasp of large affairs." Canada First, the *Times* recommended, was a text "we need to rub into each other often and vigorously." However, it bore no brief against those American companies who had made such a success at Cobalt; rather the *Times* used their presence to jolt Canadians from their lethargy: "It ought not to be necessary for us to learn the value of our own possessions from the friendly, far-seeing, quick acquiring, alien."

Ironically, many of the most profitable properties had originally been held by Canadian prospectors or turned down by Canadian businessmen before the arrival of enterprising Americans:

> The president of the Nipissing Mines Company is understood to have paid $250,000 for the properties which were chiefly of prospective value. The sellers thought they had outwitted a Yankee. Now, probably, they are assuring themselves that they were foolish to part with so great a property at so small a price. It is not the business of this paper to encourage speculation. But it is proper to point out that almost every chance which has been taken in Canada by Yankees to their own enrichment has first gone begging to Canadians. Many who refused to touch Nipissing stock at $5 a share...are no doubt envying those who went and saw and invested.

Caution and discretion, the *Times* remarked a few weeks later, were excellent business qualities, but they should be subordinated to a natural enterprising instinct, a willingness to take promising risks. Canadian businessmen ought to know their resources better than they did and ought to use them for their own country's advantage. "The best sections both of agricultural and mineral-bearing lands in Canada," the *Monetary Times* repeatedly warned, "are falling into the hands of our enterprising neighbours, while we ourselves are waiting Micawber-like to see how things will turn out. By the time we know the

Americans will know, and Canadians will be listening open-mouthed to the tales of wondrous wealth in foreign lands."[48]

Despite this crisis of conscience, Canadians continued to welcome the investment of foreign capital. No one of any significance ever concluded from the foregoing that alien capital should be excluded. Indeed, most commentators were quick to concede the benefits that accrued, particularly from American investment. In 1891 the Royal Commission on the Mineral Resources of Ontario proudly reported that Americans owned one-half of the mines in the province. This was encouraging news because the commission found that as a rule Americans ran their mines with intelligence and efficiency. Dr. W. G. Miller, the provincial geologist, thought that it was probably just as well that Cobalt was being worked "so largely by Americans" because they were experienced and possessed much better judgment on the worth of properties. On the other hand he considered that the inexperienced Canadians in the business were too eager "to make a mine"—a dangerous frame of mind. Similarly a booster of the Algoma district, recording the alarming fact that Americans skimmed the cream off resource opportunities, was able nevertheless to conclude his story happily: "Our American friends are doing invaluable service to this country in reclaiming our lands from the original state imposed upon them by nature; for it is they who are developing the resources of the country, showing up its true mineral character, placing a proper value upon our lands by their operations; and by these means are advertising the country in the markets of the world." Sometime later B. E. Walker summed up what he thought to be the attitude of Canadians towards foreign investment. "Taken as a whole," he wrote, "we have always been glad to see American manufacturing concerns establish branches in Canada. They have been in the main successful, and some of them very successful, while British Companies,

---

[48] *Canadian Mining Review*, July, 1905, p. 153; *Monetary Times*, "Cobalt and a Homily," Aug. 10, 1906, see also Sept. 21, Oct. 5, 1906 and May 25, 1907; F. W. Field, *The Resources and Trade Prospects of Northern Ontario* (Toronto, 1912).

because of lack of understanding have not as a rule done very well." All too often, the *Monetary Times* complained, British financiers plunged into disasters that experience or even intelligence might have easily avoided "and once stung they become blind."[49]

Generally speaking, a spirit of irrepressible optimism characterized Ontario thinking on the foreign investment question. In the first place the introduction of capital from outside usually brought long-dormant opportunities to life. It was always assumed that Canadian capital would eventually rise to the occasion and in the process inherit all of the skill and experience that had accompanied earlier migrations of foreign capital. For this reason both the government agencies and the press were able to use incoming American capital as a good-humoured prod to encourage the traditionally reticent Canadian investor. This optimism precluded any thought of restricting American investment for purposes of self-defence.

That optimism would appear to have been reasonably well justified; if Americans dominated the first wave of mining and pulp investment, Canadians learned very quickly, joined and even surpassed the Americans in the second wave. For example, three American companies established the reputation of Cobalt: Nipissing Mines, owned in New York by E. P. Earle and the directors of International Nickel; Buffalo Mines, controlled by a group of Buffalo capitalists led by C. L. Denison; and McKinley-Darragh-Savage, a Rochester company owned by Kodak directors.[50] They were the first on the field, the largest, and paid the highest dividends. But following these successes a number of well-placed Canadians, impressed by the possi-

---

49  Royal Commission on the Mineral Resources of Ontario, *Report*, pp. xviii, 208; W. G. Miller, "Mines of Northwestern Ontario," Mines, *Annual Report*, 1903, p. 74; W. Roland, *Algoma West, Its Mines, Scenery and Industrial Resources* (Toronto, 1887), pp. 36-8; F. R. du Caillaud, *Le Nouvel-Ontario (Canada)*(Paris, 1906), p. 17; University of Toronto Archives, Walker Papers, Walker to W. A. Beddoe, Feb. 21, 1922.

50  Details of ownership collected from *Monetary Times*, especially July 20, 1906; *Cobalt Daily Nugget*, Mining Industry Edition, September, 1910; L. Carson Brown, *Cobalt: The Town with a Silver Lining* (Toronto, 1967); and Gibson, *Mining in Ontario*, pp. 51-69.

bilities, launched several very profitable companies and founded Ontario's first mining dynasties. From his vantage on the board of the T. & N. O. Railway, M. J. O'Brien came into possession of a claim so rich that he was able to set up a private company and consolidate the fortune within his own family circle. On the advice of their friend Dr. W. G. Miller, who was returning from his first examination of the Cobalt region, the Timmins brothers and David Dunlap bought out Fred La-Rose's claim. After a lengthy defence of their rightful title to the property (in which political influence would appear to have played an important role, though this was vigorously denied by both the Timmins group and the Whitney government) this Ottawa valley syndicate absorbed the properties on their periphery then sold out at a tremendous profit to New York interests and moved on to even greater glory in Porcupine gold. Among the producing companies, leaving aside the welter of speculatives, Toronto money controlled Tretheway, Te-miskaming, Beaver Consolidated and Cobalt Lake; Montreal men predominated in the Crown Reserve Mine and shared ownership of Coniagas mining and refining companies with Col. Leonard of St. Catharines. Thus, Canadians appear to have recovered much of the initial advantage that had gone to American firms. Taking as a guide to control the admittedly crude indicator, national distribution of share ownership, by 1921 Canadians held 71 per cent, Americans 19.2 per cent, and Britons 8.2 per cent of Ontario silver-cobalt mining and smelting company securities.[51]

If nothing else, these figures suggest how rapidly Canadians lost their traditional reserve in these matters. As the Bureau of Mines noted hopefully in 1895, "mining begets mining." Cobalt established an independent financial base for further Canadian-owned mining ventures. Drawing upon the experience and the profits gained at Cobalt, Canadian miners and Toronto financiers dominated the development of

[51] S. and A. Young, *O'Brien* (Toronto, 1968), pp. 37-57; Townsley, *Mine Finders*, pp. 53-5; Gibson, *Mining in Ontario*, pp. 54-5; *The Larose Payment* (Toronto, 1908); Moore, *The American Influence on Canadian Mining*, p. 85.

Porcupine and later Kirkland Lake gold. In 1921, of the $143,705,374 worth of extant gold mining stocks and bonds, Canadians owned 70.2 per cent, Americans 27 per cent, and Britons only 2.6 per cent. Almost total American and British control of the nickel mining industry, 48 per cent and 43 per cent respectively, reduced the ratio of investment in all Ontario mining concerns from a Canadian point of view to 52 per cent Canadian, 31.2 per cent American, and 14.5 per cent British. In the capital-intensive pulp and paper business the Canadian recovery proceeded at a somewhat slower pace. Of the nine Ontario mills either in production or under construction at the outbreak of war, eight were American-owned. The Canadian company compensated slightly by being for a short time the largest in the world, and during the 1920s its ambitious management built Abitibi into one of the "Big Three" newsprint consolidations. Canadian capital did not respond as quickly to pulp and paper as it did to mining during the initial phases of growth, but it did participate enthusiastically in the major expansion of the industry which followed the First World War.[52]

In this development process government agencies acted as intellectual entrepreneurs, carrying information, ideas and opportunities to labour and capital. The continuous stream of information and statistics from the Bureau of Mines and, to a lesser degree, the Woods and Forests branch of the Crown Lands Department, had as its prime objective the education of domestic and foreign capital. Then, to render the eventual application of capital to resources as effective as possible, the government adjusted the formal education system to improve the professional and technical skills of the labour force. Finally, the publicity of government agencies and its echo in the press strove to heighten popular awareness of resource development for the long range purposes of broadening the horizon of acceptable occupations and loosening the conservative savings

[52] Mines, *Annual Report*, 1895, p. 7; Innis, *Settlement and the Mining Frontier*, p. 403; Moore, *The American Influence on Canadian Mining*, p. 85; H. Marshall *et al.*, *Canadian-American Industry* (Toronto, 1936), pp. 40ff.

and investment patterns as well as for the immediate purpose of explaining and justifying public spending. Education, in this broad sense, thus became the most dynamic and probably most permanently influential of the state's promotional functions.[53]

---

[53] Mines, *Annual Report*, 1892, p. 185; 1903, p. 7; *Monetary Times*, April 6, 1900.

# 4

# Claiming the "People's Share"

Promotion was by no means the only function of government. Other groups and other values required satisfaction besides those of business. Once development had been stimulated, the question of how the state would use its proprietary and statutory authority to regulate that process in the public interest inevitably arose. But what was the public interest? Who defined it? How and to what extent would it be asserted? Those, of course, were vexing political questions.

The problem of framing and administering any laws for such a vast area, especially under conditions of rapidly changing technology and industrial organization, proved a difficult enough challenge. So, too, did the development of a system of taxation which would realize the public claim upon the exploitation of crown resources. The resources themselves and the labour employed in their extraction needed statutory protection against wasteful and dangerous practices. Nor could any of these concerns be pursued in isolation. Each of the regulatory functions, for example, impinged upon the promotional responsibilities of the state. An administrative bureaucracy necessarily complicated free accessibility, assistance had to be balanced against revenue requirements, and the exploitive urge towards mere development was often at odds with rational conservation methods. The early phases of growth emphasized the government's role as a promoter, but later, once large-scale operations had commenced, the regulation of industry became the more dynamic function. Yet the contrasting promotional and regulatory activities of the state were never as discrete, exclusive or sequential as this analysis makes them appear. Regulations perforce existed at the outset and promotion was a continuous responsibility.

In time politicians imposed a myriad of regulations upon resource developers. Some of these were prompted by the developers themselves; others they bitterly fought. Some required the mere collection of statistics, others (which will not be dealt with here) controlled operating procedures, still others regulated hours and conditions of work and protected the health and safety of workers. Eventually, almost every aspect of the industrial process came under public purview. But in the early stages of resource development the public interest was usually conceived of in terms of a satisfactory revenue from the profits of exploitation and the observance of suitable conservation practices. The dominant issue in the regulation of mining was the question of obtaining an adequate public return from the development of what was thought to be a public property. In forestry regulation debate centred upon the question of conserving a diminishing resource.

I

Ontario governments exercised the public interest in mining primarily, though by no means exclusively, by taxing it. "On this side of the line at least," O. D. Skelton, guest speaker at an American accountants' convention in Toronto, explained in 1908, "there is general agreement that...the mineral wealth of the nation be made in some form or another to pay toll to the treasury."[1] Yet despite the passion of this conviction, whose medieval and imperial origins have already been examined, for most of the nineteenth century the very poverty of the mining industry limited the state to merely theoretical tollkeeping. For if the minerals remained below ground, how could they be taxed? Twice the province imposed royalties when the outlook seemed promising and twice repealed them following disappointment. But not too long after this second disavowal of royalties, the remarkable silver discoveries at Cobalt reopened the vexing question of how a toll might be collected and how much that toll should be.

Similarly, the attendant staking rush raised serious questions about the bureaucratic procedures of mines administration in the province. A variety of land titles accumulated in response to the particular requirements of "poor" prospectors, and a solitary recording office in Toronto probably accommodated the casual explorations of the late nineteenth century quite adequately. But suddenly the province had been overwhelmed by an influx of miners making for a relatively small, fabulously rich, body of ore. The government's genial, general-store manner hardly suited this new set of circumstances. Thus the first problem to be faced was administrative. How could the process of transferring land from public to private hands be carried out in an equitable, orderly and efficient manner? Then consideration could be given to maximizing public revenues in the extraordinary situation at Cobalt. The richness of that ore body seemed to require rules all its own. Finally, the matter of devising a permanent mineral taxation policy had to be dealt with. Now that the pattern of exploration and development had been established, what would be the most satisfactory method and the optimum rate of taxing the mining industry in the future?

On the basis of the provincial geologist's report confirming the richness of the silver ore uncovered during the construction of the Temiskaming and Northern Ontario Railway, the Ross government in 1903 withdrew from occupation or staking all

---

[1] "The Taxation of Mineral Resources in Canada," a paper read before the International Tax Conference, Toronto, Oct. 8, 1908, reprinted in the *Canadian Mining Journal*, Nov. 1, 1908, p. 551.

of the lands not already claimed for ten miles on either side of the route. Over the winter of 1903-4 the government considered its future policy. The deputy minister of Crown Lands recommended special consideration for what was clearly an unprecedented situation. "If the search should be rewarded by finding other deposits," he suggested to the cabinet, "they might be offered for sale to the highest bidder... or, if as rich as those already discovered, might be worked by the Government. A few such finds as those already made... might be made to yield money enough to materially assist in building the railway." However, the government ignored his advice and, in April 1904, adopted the somewhat more conventional course of declaring the Temiskaming District a Mining Division, thereby reopening the withdrawn lands for prospecting. Essentially, the new regulations reduced the size of a claim to forty acres, limited the number of claims to four per person in any calendar year, demanded somewhat more stringent working conditions, and established a regional mining recorder's office to deal with claims on the spot. Thus after April 6, 1904, anyone possessing a valid miner's licence could claim up to 160 acres of silver-bearing lands for $3.00 an acre.[2]

During the election campaign J. P. Whitney had promised a thorough review of mining policy. On assuming office in February 1905 his government faced immediate difficulties at Cobalt. Briefly, after the district had been reopened by the April order-in-council, speculators and insiders had taken advantage of a priceless opportunity and had literally blanketed the region with their claims. When the first flood of prospectors poured into the field during the spring of 1905, they discovered that everything worth taking had already been claimed. Pending an overall examination of policy, the Whitney government revived a hitherto ignored section of the Mines Act first introduced in 1897 which forbade anyone staking a claim unless

---

[2] W.G. Miller, "Cobalt-Nickel Arsenides and Silver," Mines, *Annual Report*, 1904, pp. 96-103; *Greater Ontario* (Toronto, 1908), p. 31; *Monetary Times*, April 15, 1904; T. W. Gibson, *The Mining Laws of Ontario* (Toronto, 1933), pp. 22-3; PAO, Whitney Papers, June 26, 1906, Gibson's memorandum on Cobalt policy.

he had actually discovered a vein, lode, or other deposit of mineral. By another order-in-council, on July 14, 1905, the government appointed a corps of competent mining engineers to inspect every claim. Rigorous examination quickly dissolved the Cobalt monopoly. Unless the licensee could prove his discovery to the satisfaction of an inspector, the mining recorder refused to grant a patent and threw open the property once again to legitimate prospectors. Suddenly the camp came to life:

> On a claim being thrown open on an inspector's report other prospectors immediately put their picks and shovels to work upon it. Half a dozen parties might be seen working on a claim at the same time, and as they realized that to secure the land they were obliged to make a discovery that would pass inspection, every cranny or crack in the rock was searched with care for cobalt bloom or traces of silver. It is doubtful whether any area of equal size anywhere on the continent has been prospected more minutely or intensely than the Cobalt silver field.[3]

Naturally the dispossessed complained bitterly of the "muddle and uncertainty as to titles," "Order-in-Council Government," and "Government Claim Jumping," but after the inspectors demonstrated their integrity and impartiality, the miners heartily endorsed the policy. Without it, W. G. Trethewey claimed, the entire countryside would have been "blanketed and gobbled up by speculators and boomsters . . .there would not have been a vacant piece of land within ten miles of Cobalt." He was delighted, as well he might have been, that the government had been "equal to the occasion."[4]

Still, the question of a permanent mining policy remained open. In convention late in December, the miners themselves

---

[3] *Greater Ontario*, p. 32; *Canadian Annual Review*, 1905, p. 266; Gibson, *Mining Laws*, p. 24; *Monetary Times*, July 20, 1906.

[4] *Canadian Mining Review*, Sept. and Oct., 1905; *Canadian Mining Journal*, June 1, 1908; J. M. Clark, "The Revision of the Mines Act of Ontario," *Journal of the Canadian Mining Institute*, Vol. IX (1906), p. 113; Samuel Price, "The Mining Laws of Ontario," *ibid.*, Vol. XIV (1911), p. 576; *Monetary Times*, May 25, 1907.

petitioned the government for one uniform law throughout the province, cheaper mining lands, an impartial mining commissioner to settle disputes, and the permanent renunciation of royalties and special mines taxes. At the other extreme the *Globe* demanded as a matter of principle that public revenues should be proportionate to the amount of ore extracted and that title to mining lands, "like that of timber lands, should remain vested in the Crown for the advantage of the people. . . . There is only one sure way to safe-guard the public interest in minerals and that is to lease mining franchises, not sell them. . . . In no other way can speculation on the unearned increment be eliminated, and this kind of speculation is absolutely incompatible with public rights."[5]

But in its new Mining Bill presented to the legislature in the spring of 1906, the government chose to meet the miners' requests for administrative reform (discussed in chapter three) while leaving undecided its method of extracting greater revenues from the industry. The Mines Act, which received the approval of the opposition, standardized the mining law by extending the Mining Division principle across the entire province; it abandoned royalties and regulated the working conditions within the mine and those required for a patent. It included provisions for a mining commissioner, as the miners had requested, made inspection and discovery permanent features of claim staking, and doubled the licence fee to $10, against the miners' wishes.[6]

Although the Whitney administration specifically repudiated royalties, there was no doubt in anyone's mind that it fully intended taxing the industry in some other manner. The apparent act of self-denial meant merely that the government concurred in the widespread belief that in order to raise the volume of capital required to explore and develop a claim, the industry depended upon clear title to its lands. Henceforth

[5] *Monetary Times*, Dec. 15, 1905; Gibson, *Mining Laws*, pp. 24-6; *Canadian Mining Review*, Aug., 1905; *Globe*, quoted in the *Canadian Annual Review*, 1906, p. 336.

[6] *Statutes of Ontario*, 6 Edw. VII, c. 11; Gibson, *Mining Laws*, pp. 27-31; Mines, *Annual Report*, 1907, pp. 36-47.

the government would base its charge upon the industry not upon domain or property right, but rather upon what O. D. Skelton called, "the good old Jack Sheppard basis of faculty, or ability to pay." Furthermore, there was pressure from every quarter—excepting of course the miners—to appropriate a much larger public share of the millions being raised at Cobalt than the mere $10 licence fee and $3.00 an acre sale price. Again, according to Skelton,

> The popular demand for action was all the more insistent because it was through the building of a Government railroad that the silver field had been discovered, and largely by the aid of Government officials that it was developed. The further fact that the indirect benefits received were less than usual owing to the low cost of working, the Cobalt deposits being extremely low, and the ore being nearly all shipped out of the country for treatment made the case overwhelming.[7]

After a furious summer of prospecting around Cobalt in 1905, the Conservatives reconsidered their action, and they too withdrew from location that fall all of the unclaimed portions of the Cobalt townships, the beds of Cobalt and Kerr lakes, and the nearby Gillies Timber limit, a rich stand of virgin pine which in itself represented substantial crown revenues. Whitney ordered the pause for three reasons: to give the lumber company time to get its timber off before eager prospectors burned it down; to allow his harried cabinet time for thoughtful consideration of the situation; and finally, to serve notice to the mining community that henceforth all claims would be subjected to taxes yet to be decided upon. Within a matter of weeks of this warning of taxes to come, the government reopened *all but* the lake beds and the timber limit for prospecting as usual.

Just before Frank Cochrane introduced his new Mining Bill in the spring of 1906, the Premier announced the extraordinary measures his government would take to maximize income from Cobalt and Kerr lakes, the Gillies Limit, and mining rights to

[7] Skelton, "The Taxation of Mineral Resources in Canada," p. 552.

the four miles of T. & N. O. right-of-way which cut straight across the heart of the camp. For the mining properties on the right-of-way Whitney invited tenders from groups willing to pay a $500 yearly rental for building locations, a $50,000 annual bonus for a lease to the concession itself, and a royalty of 10 per cent on ore valued at $400 per ton or less, 20 per cent on values over $400, and 50 per cent on ore valued at over $1,000 per ton. These were minimum conditions, the Premier joked half-seriously: "If any higher offers are made we shall, of course, be prepared to consider the highest." At the same time he announced that clear title to the lake beds would be auctioned to the highest bidder; but it was his ambiguous reference to the Gillies Timber Limit which stirred up the greatest excitement: "The Government, after considering the circumstances and conditions up there," he told the Legislature on April 3, "have decided that after the timber is removed on Oct[ober] 1st they will not dispose of this valuable area, it being our property. We will keep it, and we will use it, for the benefit of the people of the Province of Ontario."[8]

The purposefully vague but forceful statement received immediate, universal and, for the Premier, bewildering acclaim. His intention had been to say the government had not yet decided what to do with the property, whether to parcel it up and sell it to individual miners as the mining community requested or to auction it off to large companies. But everyone interpreted him quite literally, he quickly discovered, in trading upon the currently fashionable public ownership rhetoric. "From one end of the Province to the other the action is cordially endorsed by the press of both sides of politics," the Ottawa *Citizen* reported on April 6. "It is a radical departure which appeals to the spirit of enterprise in the people who believe that the public should benefit directly from the great natural resources of the Province, and not merely turn them over at a nominal figure to enrich private corporations." Understandably, the largely disappointed prospectors appealed to Whitney to allot portions of the 6,400-acre limit to the licensed

[8] *Monetary Times*, July 20, 1906; *Saturday Night*, April 7, 1906; *Canadian Annual Review*, 1906, pp. 334-5.

miners, veterans of 1905 and 1906; Andrew Broder, the Premier's close friend and federal member for his constituency, suggested parcelling it in 10- and 20-acre lots, then auctioning them, "giving some time for capitalists to get into it. . . ."[9]

However, enthusiastic public ownership advocates read considerably more into the Premier's statement than he ever intended. "It is all the talk down town to-day the Gov't. will work Cobalt ores for the people," wrote one supporter looking for a job on the expected Mining Commission. "The newspapers invented that portion of my remarks about the Gillies limit property being developed by a Commission," Whitney replied. But the warm and influential praise he received from close political friends and senior civil servants clearly impressed him. "You have given thousands of us who never expected to have it in any other way, an interest in a silver mine," wrote the assistant Receiver General. Thomas Southworth, the director of the Bureau of Colonization, added his congratulations: "I have never been able to see why the whole people of this Province should not share in the wealth that lies under ground as they have long shared in the timber wealth above ground." And finally Robert Borden, in the course of discussing organization for the coming elections, complimented Whitney on his bold but shrewd political stroke:

> The policy which you have laid down with regard to the mineral wealth of the Province is a splendid departure from the traditions of the past. I commend it in every way and thoroughly congratulate you upon it. There appears to me no good reason why great resources of this character should be handed over for the upbuilding of huge private fortunes instead of being reserved for the benefit of the whole community—for the establishment and maintenance of great educational institutions or otherwise for the benefit of the people at large.[10]

[9] *Canadian Annual Review*, 1906, p. 334; PAO, Whitney Papers, Broder to Whitney, April 4, 1906.

[10] *Ibid.*, R. Grass to Whitney, April 4, 1906 and reply April 5, private; see also Dr. T. F. Francis to Whitney, same dates and private reply; Francis Clergue to Whitney, April 9, 1906; George Ritchie to Whitney, April 4, 1906; D. Creighton to Whitney, April 4, 1906; Southworth to Whitney, April 19, 1906, private; Robert Borden to Whitney, April 19, 1906, private.

The overwhelming response, Whitney confessed to a correspondent, opened up a new line of thought. While substantial doubts still lingered in his mind, clearly the idea of a government-operated mine appealed to him. "There seems to be one unanimous expression of approbation of our course with regard to the Gillies Limit," Whitney wrote his brother shortly after the announcement. "It will not be turned over to us until next October, so that we will have plenty of time to decide on the best methods of running it. I have no doubt it will meet with general satisfaction, and while there is no certainty with reference to it, still Cochrane believes that there are great riches in it." But in writing to Borden later in the month, Whitney denied adopting "what is called Government ownership." His government was going to use something which it already owned in the public interest and, he emphasized, "we have no idea as yet just how we will do it." It was too soon to make any firm decision on the merits of a government-run mine, he claimed. But through it all the Premier remained optimistic: "There is so much exaggeration in the air with reference to such questions that one hesitates to express an opinion, but there is no doubt that we would realize a number of millions of dollars tomorrow for the Gillies limit."[11] Then on July 26, a government surveying party led by the provincial geologist reported the discovery of a rich vein of silver during its examination of the timber limit. That decided the issue. When the lumber company finally relinquished its rights on October 1, 1906, the Ontario government entered the mining business.

From the outset the Whitney government extracted more political capital than silver from its mine. Daily newspapers praised the public-spirited action; even the crusty financial press generously approved. For a short time the province preened itself on possessing the only publicly owned and operated mine on the continent. As O. D. Skelton explained the phenomenon to his American audience, "...public ownership has a romantic glamor when it is a silver mine which we the people, control, lacking when the more prosaic gas works or street-car line is

---

[11] *Ibid.*, Whitney to D. Creighton, April 5, 1906, private; Whitney to E. C. Whitney, April 6, 1906, private; Whitney to Borden, April 20, 1906, private.

concerned." Conservative election propaganda in 1908 hailed
the mine as "a triumph for honest government" and boasted
that "an item of $100,000 appears in the estimated revenue
of the Province for the current year from that source." And
Sam Hume Blake, in one of his pompous commentaries on
the work of the Legislature, gave thanks that "the lands, the
pulpwood regions, the mines and minerals, now go without
graft to the persons entitled, and the Province receives as large
a share as is compatible with due regard for the rights of the
explorers, the purchasers, and the miners."[12]

Unfortunately, the intensely political character of the experiment rendered its ultimate failure all the more tragic
and permanently harmful to the idea of public ownership. To
encourage thorough prospecting of its area, the Bureau of
Mines offered a bonus of $150 per inch of any silver vein dis-
covered on the property. But that incentive turned up only
one very small outcropping. When a shaft sunk into it proved
disappointing, the government decided to quit while it was
ahead. In the spring of 1909 the Bureau of Mines sold the
accumulated ore from its operations for $128,578, an excess
of $34,893 over expenses, divided up the northern portion
of the limit into eighty-one parcels, and auctioned them off
during the late summer and early fall for a total of $711,458
and a future 10 per cent royalty on gross proceeds.[13] Inevitably,
the failure of the experiment confirmed the suspicions lurking
in several quarters about the wisdom of public ownership.
"Nothing beyond a rather indecorous auction sale has come
of the Ontario Government's attempt to operate the Provincial
Mine on the Gillies Limit," scoffed the *Canadian Mining Journal*.
And the retreat disappointed many advocates of the principle.
Whitney, in replying to the Toronto *Daily Star*'s censure of his
reversal, revealed the tentative, almost flirtatious spirit which
had governed the experiment throughout. He had never

[12] *Financial Post*, Aug. 10, 1907, Nov. 28, 1908; *Monetary Times*, Aug. 31,
   1907; *Canadian Mining Journal*, Mar., 1907, pp. 7-11; Skelton, "The Taxation of Mineral Resources in Canada," p. 552; *Greater Ontario*, p. 30; PAO,
   Whitney Papers, S. H. Blake to Whitney, May 25, 1908.
[13] Mines, *Annual Report*, 1910, pp. 40-1.

intended committing the government to any permanent, specific course of action, he replied, returning to his position of before April 4, 1906. "I think I said, that we would hold the property and work it and administer it for the benefit of the Province," he reminded the editor. Regarding the portion of the limit which remained in government hands, the Premier admitted that his government had "no settled policy, whatever, ...we will endeavour to be guided by developments or results just in the same way as a businessman would conduct any enterprise." But for John Lewis of the *Daily Star* and the many devoted public ownership supporters, Whitney's statement represented a considerable come down from the boastful enthusiasm manifest before the 1908 provincial general election. "Some of us," Lewis replied, "are very enthusiastic about public ownership, and regard it as the most hopeful movement now before the public. We rejoice when we see it making headway, and we are sorry to see it receive any check."[14]

The long-term effects of the "indecorous auction" were perhaps more significant, if more difficult to assess. Here the clue is to be found in the deputy-minister of Mines' comment long after the affair: "So ended with a small profit the first and only attempt at governmental mining in Ontario, leaving to Soviet Russia the monopoly of this form of official activity."[15] Despite appearances, the Whitney government had never taken its government ownership policy very seriously. Only after it had announced an auction for the only truly valuable properties left, those under the railroad and the lakes, right in the middle of the camp, did the government comprehend the extent of the public belief in the principle, and then the only area left was the Gillies Limit off on the southern margin. But the government soon discovered, along with a host of mining speculators, that its property was more than close enough to the Cobalt camp to raise baseless expectations.

The government's lack of genuine conviction condemned the principle of public ownership for a long time to come. Shortly

[14] *Canadian Mining Journal*, Oct. 1, 1909; PAO, Whitney Papers, Whitney to Lewis, Aug. 10, 1909, private, and Lewis to Whitney, Aug. 15, 1909.

[15] T. W. Gibson, *Mining in Ontario* (Toronto, 1937), p. 64.

the very concept, so universally acclaimed in 1906, would become associated with a discredited ideology, as Thomas Gibson's candid remark would indicate. How much different would the history of Ontario mining have been if the government had believed in the policy? Between 1906 and 1915 the Crown Reserve Mine on the Kerr Lake property paid $771,883 in royalties alone to the provincial treasury; over the same period the six producing mines on the railroad right-of-way leases contributed a total of $666,915 in royalties. Between 1904 and 1914 Cobalt mines produced $113,751,261 in silver and just under 50 per cent of that amount, $55,228,964 in dividends. And a conservative estimate of the undisclosed profits of the two private companies, O'Brien and Drummond, would raise the latter figure by another $10 million.[16] Cobalt was a phenomenally rich field and if the state had mined the central Cobalt Lake, Kerr Lake, and railroad properties it had retained instead of the marginal Gillies Limit, it would have reaped a much larger proportion of the harvest. By its casual, almost off-handed manner of deciding upon a policy of government ownership, the Whitney administration inadvertently destroyed the utility of the policy for mining.

## II

The government's other money-raising expedients caused it even more grief than the unfortunate mining adventure, but returned proportionately higher rewards as well. When, for example, the Timmins interests challenged the validity of the patents of their rival, M. J. O'Brien, in the courts, the Whitney government saw its chance to cash in as well. M. J. O'Brien had learned of the Cobalt discoveries almost immediately through his political friends in 1903; he quickly purchased Neil King's four claims for $4,000 and promptly sued the owners of the adjacent LaRose claim for a piece of conflicting property. The Ross government settled the issue by dividing the disputed portion between the parties. With the change in government

[16] Mines, *Annual Report*, 1915, p. 55.

in 1905 the Timmins brothers, Duncan McMartin, and David Dunlap, owners of the LaRose property, counterattacked. This battle of "The Big Cobalters," the "O'Brien crowd," and the "LaRose people" over a multi-million-dollar silver mine caught the Whitney government in the cross-fire. Apparently David Dunlap marshalled enough evidence to convince his brother-in-law Frank Cochrane, the Minister of Lands, Forests and Mines, that "there seemed a fighting chance" of overturning at least one of the O'Brien patents on the grounds that King's claims had been blanket claims and that he had never actually discovered mineral in place as the Mines Act required. Since, as a later Conservative apologia delicately explained, "the spectacle of the province attacking its own patents in the Courts was one to be avoided in the interest of the provincial credit if possible," Cochrane and Whitney sought an out-of-court compromise acceptable to all three parties, the O'Briens, LaRoses and, of course, the province.

A nervous M. J. O'Brien offered concessions to the crown to keep the affair out of the courts and after he had increased terms to a 25 per cent royalty, the crown accepted. Then, in view of the considerable trouble and legal expense incurred by the LaRose group, whose challenge had forced O'Brien to concede a royalty, the appreciative crown awarded them $135,000. This generosity raised a number of eyebrows—the *Globe* called it "a disgraceful surrender"—and the Conservatives felt moved to provide an elaborate justification before the 1908 election. The Whitney government would not have been involved in the affair at all, the argument went, had it not been for the "blundering or crooked work of their predecessors." But no one escaped unspattered from this dirty business. The government lost a little grace but gained a total of $700,966 in royalties; the Big Cobalters on the other hand, all became millionaires.[17]

The regulations covering Cobalt townsite, the lake and the railway right-of-way announced on April 3, 1906, returned even

---

[17] Mines, *Annual Report*, 1907, pp. 26-7; *The LaRose Payment* (Toronto, 1908); S. and A. Young, *O'Brien* (Toronto, 1967), "How to Become a Millionaire," pp. 37-57.

more impressive sums to the provincial treasury. Mines sunk on the right-of-way and townsite lands leased by the railroad paid $666,915 in royalities between 1906 and 1914. A Montreal syndicate eventually won clear title to the bed of Kerr Lake for $178,500 cash and a 10 per cent royalty which brought in $771,833 over the same period. Finally, in December 1906, Whitney revealed his most astonishing sale: a group of Toronto capitalists led by Henry Mill Pellatt and Britton Osler had agreed to pay an incredible $1,085,000 for outright title, no royalties attached, to the bed of Cobalt Lake. Compared with mining incomes under the Ross administration these figures were positively spectacular, and during the 1908 and 1911 election campaigns the Conservatives traded heavily upon the "Wonderful Progress of the Mining Industry" and, of course, the "Results of the Practical Administration of the Assets of the Province by the Whitney Government."[18]

Although the government's shrewd capitalization on the Cobalt opportunity was manifestly popular there were some disappointed parties who disputed both the manner and right of government intervention. The most serious challenge came in 1907 when a group of Toronto capitalists calling themselves the Florence Mining Company sought an injunction restraining the operations of Pellatt's Cobalt Lake Mining Company. They also appealed for disallowance of the provincial legislation which validated the withdrawal of the lakebed in 1906 and then its sale in 1907. Counsel for the Florence Mining Company, J. M. Clark, argued that a W. J. Green had actually discovered valuable ore when drilling through the ice of the lake in March of 1906; that he had properly recorded his claim and was, therefore, legally entitled to it; and that the government had by its actions confiscated rights, subsequently assigned by Green to the Florence Mining Company, without due compensation. Clark's attack hinged upon the argument that when the government had reinstated Coleman Township for staking on

---

[18] Mines, *Annual Report*, 1915, p. 55; *Monetary Times*, Dec. 29, 1906; *Canadian Annual Review*, 1906, pp. 334-5; *Greater Ontario, passim*, and *Good Work for Ontario: Splendid Record of the Whitney Government: Seven Years of the Square Deal* (Toronto, 1911).

October 30, 1905, it necessarily reopened the bed of Cobalt Lake contained within its limits (see above, page 160). The government considered the charges "trivial and baseless," since its August 14, 1905, order-in-council had specifically reserved the lakebed from all claims thereafter. Nonetheless, it was compelled to defend itself before the federal government and in appeal courts all the way to the Judicial Committee of the Privy Council before finally establishing its case. Not only did the government's one million dollar profit on the sale of the property depend upon the successful resolution of this dispute, but so also did an important constitutional principle. Furthermore, irony alone justifies examination of the Cobalt Lake case; for as the Ontario government defended itself and Pellatt's mine against attack from the Florence Mining Company, it had to contend simultaneously with an identical constitutional challenge to its hydro policy led by Pellatt's Electrical Development Company![19]

The provincial geologist had originally recommended withdrawal of the lake in November of 1903 primarily to protect a supply of fresh water for the future town and an expected reduction works.[20] On January 4, 1904, and June 8, 1905, W. C. Chambers and Milo Bessey respectively claimed the lakebed, but in each case the mining recorder refused their claim because the lake and the land beneath it had been withdrawn. Frank Cochrane reopened the lake on July 13, 1905, with the provision that a valuable discovery had to be proven. Bessey immediately restaked his claim, but it failed to pass inspection on August 17 on two grounds: the inspectors denied that a discovery had been made, and stated that the claim had been improperly staked on the road allowance around the lake. In the meantime,

[19] PAO, Whitney Papers, T. W. Gibson's memorandum to Whitney, June 26, 1906; Whitney to Rev. Charles W. Gordon, June 12, 1906, enclosure; *The Cobalt Lake Case* (Toronto, 1908), see below, chapter 7.

[20] However, the concern for drinking water and sanitation evaporated quite rapidly in the heat of fortune hunting. A decade later one of the town doctors, A. E. Munro, wrote a pamphlet, *An Era of Progression: The Draining of Cobalt Lake and and Its Effect on the Town* (Cobalt, 1913), in which he provided a rhapsodic justification for removing all of the water from the lake, as the mining company proposed.

the August 14 order-in-council withdrawing Kerr Lake and the Gillies Limit also removed Cobalt Lake once again. Thus, for one month in 1905 it would have been possible to claim the property. Already two claims had been refused, and the third staked during the legally open period failed to pass inspection. The government stated that W. J. Green set up his diamond drill on the ice in January 1906 in full knowledge of what had gone before. Cochrane, the mining recorder, and the local townspeople all informed Green and his colleagues that the lake had been withdrawn, but intent upon a piece of sharp practice, they refused to listen. When they tried to record their claim in March, George T. Smith, the mining recorder for the district, naturally denied it, whereupon Green and company launched an acrimonious attack on the government by letter, then through the press, and ultimately in the courts. Knowing of Green's spurious claim, the government confirmed and ratified the August 14 order-in-council by a special statute, 6 Edw. VII, c. 12, at the next session. When the property was subsequently sold to the Cobalt Lake Mining Company, the government passed yet another act in 1907 conferring positive and undisputed title. Aside from being retroactive, this legislation precluded the possibility of appeal to prevent nuisance suits. If anyone had cause to complain it was the luckless Bessey, not the devious W. J. Green.

Opinion divided along the usual lines. Feeling itself to be genuinely deprived, the Florence Mining Company found its champion in the Liberal opposition, which in turn brought influence to bear upon the federal government to nullify Whitney's seemingly arbitrary behaviour. The company and its friends denounced the 1906 legislation, charging that the withdrawal of the lakebed was "a direct interference with vested rights without compensation." H. W. Maw, secretary of the company, angered the Premier with his repeated assertion that "if a South American Republic treated a European investor as we have been treated his Government would undoubtedly send a gun-boat to prevent the confiscation of his rights." A similar sharply worded letter of protest from the author Ralph Connor (the Rev. C. W. Gordon), whose brother had been a colleague of W. J. Green, evinced an equally forceful rebuke from the impatient Premier on "the intolerable language . . . from a gentleman in your position and of your calling."[21] A Dr. Milligan invoked the frightening wrath of a Presbyterian God from the pulpit of St. Andrew's in Toronto against what he termed "these amateur anarchists in Queen's Park":

> They are making Ontario an unsafe place for capital to invest in. I don't know but what I'll write to the Glasgow *Herald* and the Edinburgh *Scotsman* telling my friends not to put a dollar in this province. I wouldn't invest a dollar here myself. Oh, that men would remember to do justly and then we would have no trouble with the greed of monopolists who are largely to blame for this craze of the people for their rights.[22]

Goldwin Smith, growing more befuddled with each passing day, warned the Premier: "This is not an ordinary nor in fact a political question. It is a question of moral and social principle, touching, as one great authority after another declares, the foundations of civil society." Whitney patiently drafted a long memo in reply, setting down the complete history of the affair for the aging Regius Professor in which he concluded: "The legislation . . . was passed for the purpose of putting an end to attempts to attack the title to Cobalt Lake by persons having pretended claims good as it is believed neither in morals [n]or law."[23] Mining fever had smitten all levels of society from clerks to professors of classics; the extent of this madness partly explains the avid public interest in the case.[24]

---

[21] PAO, Whitney Papers, C. A. Masten to Whitney, May 15, 1906; Masten to Frank Cochrane, May 17, 1906; H. W. Maw to Whitney, June 28, 1906, Feb. 12, 1907; Whitney to Rev. C. W. Gordon, June 28 and July 12, 1906.

[22] PAC, Laurier Papers, quoted in J.M. Clark to Laurier, Jan. 30, 1908, private, 135739-44.

[23] PAO, Whitney Papers, Goldwin Smith to Whitney and memo in reply, July 18, 1908; Goldwin Smith, *Reminiscences* (London, 1910), pp. 458-9; University of Toronto Archives, Walker Papers, B.E. Walker to Goldwin Smith, Feb. 17, Mar. 1, 1909; PAC, Willison Papers, Vol. 76, Goldwin Smith to Willison, May 4, 1910.

[24] PAO, Whitney Papers, Professor A. R. Bain to Whitney, July 13, 1906.

The federal Liberals were easily convinced of the iniquity of the Cobalt legislation, but could not be so readily moved to disallow it. J. M. Clark contended with some force that this policy of what he called confiscation destroyed the credit of the province, prejudiced the reputation of the dominion, and represented a repudiation of provincial obligations. J. J. Foy, the Ontario Attorney General, denied that an injustice had been perpetrated and reminded the federal government that this was an affair having to do with the administration of the crown lands, a field of provincial paramountcy. Laurier declined to intervene, but in doing so he made his own views unmistakably clear. "It was confiscation, nothing else," he admitted to Clark, but in the light of recent constitutional interpretation the Legislature of a province possessed even that unchecked power:

> If the legislation passed by the Whitney Government, or anything approaching it, had been passed by Ross, when he was in office, or by us in Ottawa, the whole Conservative press, the *Mail,* the *News,* the *Telegram,* the whole Conservative party, Foster, Borden and the rest, would have made the country ring with their indignation. We did not think that it was good interpretation of our particular Constitution to disallow this iniquitous legislation and I doubt that any amendment in this direction would be effective. Our people have been too apathetic in the Province of Ontario against this nefarious act, but therein is a remedy.[25]

Aylesworth's formal memorandum on April 29, 1908, advising against disallowance left no doubt where he stood on the matter either. With noticeable reluctance the Minister of Justice deferred to the doctrine that "it is not the office or right of the Dominion Government to sit in judgment considering the justice or honesty of any Act of a provincial legislature which deals solely with the property or civil rights within the province."

---

[25] PAC, Laurier Papers, Laurier to J. M. Gibson, Jan. 5, 1909, 134636; Laurier to Clark, Feb. 3, 1908, private, 135743; Clark to Laurier, April 15, 1908, private, 139084-7; Laurier to Clark, April 17, 1908, 139088; Laurier to Clark, Nov. 20, 1908, 147916-7; Clark to Laurier, Nov. 19, 1908, private, 147913.

Then, after citing the four principles which justified disallowance, Aylesworth concluded: "The Legislation in question,
even though confiscation of property without compensation
and so an abuse of legislative power, does not fall within any
of the aforesaid enumerations."[26]

The courts upheld both the constitutionality and the justice
of the legislation and thoroughly vindicated the action of the
Whitney government. Nevertheless, the verdict provided an
ominous revelation of the fullness of provincial power. Unlike
the Minister of Justice, Mr. Justice Riddell dismissed the
Florence Mining Company's claims for damages as unfounded.
The government could not confiscate rights the company had
never possessed. Yet, following the argument of counsel for
the plaintiffs, the judge added an extraordinary footnote: "In
short, the Legislature within its jurisdiction, can be anything
which is not naturally impossible and is restrained by no rule,
human or divine. If it be that the plaintiffs acquired any
rights—*which I am far from finding*—the Legislature has the power
to take them away. The prohibition 'Thou shalt not Steal,' has
no legal force upon the sovereign body, and there would be
no necessity for compensation to be given."[27] Notwithstanding
Riddell's substantive judgment, Aylesworth continued to brood
upon his powerlessness in the face of what he called a "flagrant
violation of private rights and natural justice." Before 1896,
he told the House on March 1, 1909, "this legislation would
have been disallowed." But if the courts in their wisdom subordinated the eighth commandment to the discretion of the
provincial Legislature, mere human injunctions paled to
insignificance as well. "I am willing to go thus far in the enuncia-
tion of the views I am stating to this House," Aylesworth said,
"that a provincial legislature . . . might if it saw fit to do so,
repeal Magna Carta itself." Taking note of the "remarkable

[26] For the arguments and decisions on this disallowance case, see Canada,
Minister of Justice, *Correspondence, Reports of the Minister of Justice, and Orders
In Council upon the Subject of Provincial Legislation*, Vol. II (Ottawa, 1922),
pp. 80-5.

[27] Emphasis added; *Canadian Annual Review*, 1908, p. 286; *ibid.*, 1909, p.
382.

and violent outbreak of the Minister of Justice," Whitney reminded Aylesworth the next day in the Legislature that his duty was solely to determine the constitutionality of legislation and not "to give *ex parte* judgment after hearing one side of the case":

> He may vilify the Provincial Government and the people of Ontario, but I am glad to know that the people don't pay much attention to what Mr. Aylesworth may say or do in his capacity of statesman—except as a curiosity. (Government laughter and renewed applause.)[28]

On April 5, 1909, Chief Justice Sir Charles Moss handed down the decision of the Ontario Court of Appeal which upheld the lower court's decision and found, moreover, that the claimants did not hold a miner's licence, that they had made no discovery upon the crown lands, and that in any event, the 1907 legislation precluded further consideration of their supposed claims.[29] Now, fully confident and vindicated, the triumphant Whitney government eagerly retaliated upon the federal government and the Florence Mining Company. The Premier ordered a thousand copies of the Appeal Court judgement printed and freely distributed, then arranged to have the decision read into Hansard in its entirety. Both Whitney's correspondence and actions reveal his genuine excitement at the favourable verdict. It showed "in conclusive language that there was no good faith or honesty of purpose behind the claims," he told his brother. "Further, it defends and approves the Statute passed by us. This, I think, will settle the pirates for a while." The government seemed almost eager, B. E. Walker cautioned J. M. Clark, to see the matter taken to the Judicial Committee of the Privy Council,

---

[28] Canada, House of Commons, *Debates*, Mar. 1, 1909, 1750-8; The *Globe* reported Aylesworth's speech under the inflammatory headline, "May Repeal Magna Carta," Mar. 2, 1909; see also, *ibid.*, Mar. 3, 1909, "Sir James Stirred by Mr. Aylesworth's Comments."

[29] *The Florence Mining Company* v. *The Cobalt Lake Mining Company: Ontario Court of Appeal* (Toronto, 1909); *Globe*, April 6 and 8, 1909.

and despite Walker's advice, the company did so with humiliating results.[30]

The ability of vested interests to mobilize one level of government against another necessarily discredited the federal power of disallowance. In the Rivers and Streams, Manufacturing Condition, Cobalt Lake, and as we shall shortly see, the Hydro disallowance cases, the federal government's threatened use of the power confronted sound, just and, what is more important, popular provincial legislation. In the double context of crown lands administration and the imperatives of Ontario politics, nothing could have been more ill-advised than to be put into the position of even contemplating disallowance of the Cobalt Lake and Hydro bills. Yet the federal government was seen to have submitted to the special pleading of the allegedly victimized parties. The Cobalt Lake and Hydro cases did not develop into another Rivers and Streams knock-down, dragged-out fight between the province and the dominion, as George Ross had warned Laurier over the Manufacturing Condition appeal. But the Laurier government just as effectively compromised itself in both cases. Its partisan animus confirmed the suspicion of the Ontario government and electorate that no federal government could be expected to possess the high-minded impartiality required in the exercise of the disallowance power. Regrettably, it is a matter of the record that the federal government was not on the side of the angels in any of these cases.

## III

Meanwhile, as the Whitney government was launching and defending those special programs designed to take advantage of an immediate situation, it was also formulating a permanent

[30] PAO, Whitney Papers, A. C. Boyce to Whitney, April 7, 1909; reply, April 8, 1909, private; Whitney to E. C. Whitney, April 7, 1909; PAC, Willison Papers, Vol. 16, Cochrane to Willison, April 8, 1909; University of Toronto Archives, Walker Papers, Walker to Clark, Feb. 17, 1909.

system of taxation to replace the totally ineffectual royalties system disavowed in 1906. Until then the state had based its right to an income from the mining industry upon proprietary rights in mining lands which it withheld from the title. But as we have already seen, both the principle and the income remained largely theoretical. Frank Cochrane's Supplementary Revenue Bill introduced in 1907, which imposed a 3 per cent tax on mining profits over $10,000, a two-cent acreage tax on mineral lands, and a modest tax upon the production of natural gas, represented a major departure from former policy.[31] The 3 per cent profits tax did not rest upon any reserved property right; like any other specialized business tax it was founded simply upon the ability to pay. And unlike the *ad valorem* systems characteristic of the United States, the Ontario scheme taxed output, not capital. Canadians, traditionally less concerned with equity, O. D. Skelton explained, preferred output rather than capital taxation:

> The negative reason for this is found in the fact that our constitution leaves more scope for legislative discretion than the American State consitutions. As our cabinet system of government makes it possible to fix responsibility more definitely, we feel free to grant power more freely, assured that all will be well, so long as, in Palmerston's phrase, there is someone to hang. This results sometimes in short cuts to justice, as, for example, in the Ontario Government's handling of various Cobalt disputes, which would send a shudder through the American trained in awe of rigid constitutions and courts committed to outworn economic shibboleths.[32]

Since the equity constraint need not be considered, the level of the Ontario tax on mining represented a balance of political power. The answer to the question how much *should* be charged, reduced itself to the answer to how much *could* be charged.

---

[31] *Statutes of Ontario*, 7 Edw. VII, c. 9; Mines, *Annual Report*, 1908, pp. 32-3; Gibson, *Mining Laws*, pp. 30, 49-51; J. H. Perry, *Taxation in Canada* (Toronto, 1953), pp. 236-9.

[32] Skelton, "The Taxation of Mineral Resources in Canada," p. 554; W. A. Roberts, *State Taxation of Metallic Deposits* (Cambridge, Massachusetts, 1944) is the best survey of this subject.

That answer measured the influence and resistance of the industry on the one hand, and the power and determination of public opinion on the other.

The *Canadian Mining Review* led the counterattack against what it called the "ignorant and loud clamour" which arose once the public realized the richness of Cobalt. Any special levy upon the industry would most certainly discourage capital, ruin the small investor, and burden even further the heroic "poor prospector." Instead the state should give the pioneering explorer every encouragement: "Prospecting is hard work, and it would be unattractive work were it not for the indomitable will, energy and love of adventure of the race. But we need the services of thousands of hardy, tireless, sharp eyed and sharp witted men...." The *Review*'s prospector scarcely resembled the men encountered by the royal commissioners in 1890, or the Summer Mining School instructors thereafter. Spokesmen for the mining industry urged the government to "Cherish the Prospector," and recommended "a careful study of the provisions of the mining laws of Mexico"—by any standards the most scandalously lenient on any continent.[33] J. M. Clark, who had reasons of his own for disliking Ontario mining laws, told the Canadian Mining Institute in 1906 that the industry would not object to carrying its fair share of the burden of taxation; but the next year before the same institute, he revealed that a little tax was, nevertheless, a little too much:

> The great need of Northern Ontario is capital which cannot be secured unless faith is kept with investors. The immense injury which will result to the business, manufacturing and agricultural interests if the tremendous inflow of capital into this country is seriously checked, is so obvious as to require no argument to emphasize it.

Nor could he resist the fairy-tale imagery which the industry clung to in justification of its role. "In short," Clark concluded, "it is a foolish thing to kill the goose which lays the golden

---

[33] *Canadian Mining Review*, Aug. and Sept. 1905; Oct. 1906; Mar. 1907; Marvin D. Berstein, *The Mexican Mining Industry* (Albany, 1969), pp. 17-94, 277-84.

egg."[34] Both the Canadian Mining Institute and its Ontario branch vigorously condemned the proposed 3 per cent profits tax which it said would lead directly to a general depression and the virtual ruination of persons with small means. Representatives from the Standard Stock and Mining Exchange protested against what they considered "partial confiscation," and a deputation of Cobalt miners claimed that the industry already paid enough in the form of licences and fees.[35] According to the main theme of the miners' logic, any tax would discourage both prospecting and investment with tragic results for the farmers and businessmen of southern Ontario, a lamentable train of consequences usually symbolized by the tiresome Beanstalk metaphor.

The gloomy outlook forecast by the miners did not move the government to reconsider its tax. "We think public opinion demands it," Whitney replied to its critics. Frank Cochrane even lectured the deputation of mining men from his own constituency upon their responsibilities in protecting the investment of capital:

Let me tell you straight, as a man, that I believe the present conditions of speculative boom which you deplore are caused by the mining men and brokers themselves. They have gone on filling the papers with reckless statements not calculated to help your district. And not one mining man rose to contradict or counteract this attempt to manufacture a stock boom out of what should be an honest enterprise. Let me tell you men of my own district that this was far more injurious to the getting of capital to develop the mineral resources of this Province than any tax we can put on your profits.[36]

34 J. M. Clark, "The Revision of the Mines Act of Ontario," *Journal of the Canadian Mining Institute*, Vol.IX (1906), pp. 113-4; *ibid.*, "Royalties on Minerals in Ontario," Vol. X (1907), pp. 340-1.

35 *Canadian Annual Review*, 1907, pp. 507-9.

36 PAO, Whitney Papers, Whitney to Dr. T. S. Sproule, Mar. 1, 1907, private; Whitney to E. C. Whitney, Mar. 5, 1907, private; *Canadian Annual Review*, 1907, pp. 508-9; Royal Ontario Nickel Commission, *Report* (Toronto, 1917), pp. 509 ff.

Defending his tax in the Legislature, Cochrane argued that the mining industry depended just as heavily upon the state for protection and redress and relied upon the services of stable government as the other moderately taxed enterprises. Historically, mining development depended more than most other businesses upon government-owned or at least publicly aided railroads. As the industry established itself, which it was most certainly doing after Cobalt, it ought to bear its reasonable share of the burden of civil government. Indeed, the government regarded the 3 per cent profit tax as particularly lenient; local taxes could be deducted, as could legitimate expenses, and marginal mines were completely exempt. This very liberality reflected a concern to encourage future investment and recognized that in many remote areas mining companies had to provide some of the public services usually expected of the state themselves. The separate levy of two cents an acre on all mining lands in the unorganized districts was frankly designed to discourage long-term speculative holdings while providing at the same time an income to support schools and law enforcement. Some of the funds thus raised, Cochrane told J. S. Willison, might also be used to provide the funds for the nickel and silver smelting bonuses which he introduced during the same session.[37] Once passed, the acreage tax and the profits tax became permanent features of the Mines Act. And, despite its protestations to the contrary, the mining industry discovered that it could live quite comfortably with the modest toll.

Growing from strength to strength as it moved from Cobalt silver to Porcupine and Kirkland Lake gold, the mining industry quickly blossomed into a bright and important component of the Ontario economy. From 1902 to the end of 1906, Ontario mines yielded a total output valued at $77,977,533; during the next five years (1907-11) production soared 111.5 per cent to $164,929,057, and between 1912 and 1916 it increased yet another 62.1 per cent to $267,419,383. The average annual output within each of these five-year periods best illustrates

[37] PAC, Willison Papers, Vol. 16, Cochrane to Willison, Feb. 20, 1907.

the steadily rising fortunes of the industry:

| | |
|---|---|
| 1902-1906 | $15,595,510 |
| 1907-1911 | $32,585,811 |
| 1912-1916 | $53,583,876 |

Then again, perhaps the $111,476,521 in dividends declared between 1905 and 1916 conveys a more vivid impression of the "fortunes" being made in nickel, silver and gold mining:

| | 1905-1916 |
|---|---|
| Silver | $65,181,743 |
| Gold | $ 9,786,625 |
| Nickel | $36,508,153 |

Profits equalled almost 25 per cent of total production, and in some sectors, silver mining for example, they soared to more than 50 per cent. After Cobalt it was no longer necessary to speak hopefully of Ontario's mineral potential, for in the space of a few short years the province witnessed the rise of a brash, boisterous and rich mining industry.[38]

Of course the Whitney government modestly assumed credit for the "wonderful progress of the mining industry" and crowed mightily about the vastly enlarged "people's share" it had garnered from this new found wealth. Indeed the royalties and the mining taxes, which the government had established in response to the "loud and ignorant clamour" for greater public revenues from this source, delivered handsome returns to the public treasury, particularly when compared with the pre-1907 revenue record. Annual income from all phases of mining activity averaged only $82,511 between 1902 and 1906, but during the following five-year interval it climbed to average almost a million dollars a year!

Whitney's new taxes figured largely in the increase; during the decade following 1906 mining royalties of $2,798,096 and profit taxes of $1,341,159 accounted for 58.1 per cent of total

---

[38] For Ontario mining statistics, see Mines, *Annual Reports*, various years; Royal Ontario Nickel Commission, *Report*, p. 526.

revenues—the remainder coming, as before, from the sale of mineral lands and prospectors' licences. Along with the rapidly increasing revenues, the ratio of provincial revenue from mining to the total value of mineral output also rose from a miniscule 0.52 per cent during the Ross years to a level of 3.02 per cent for 1907-1911.[39] That percentage illustrates most graphically the extent to which the Whitney government tried to satisfy the public demands for greater revenues from mining enterprises.

However, figures for the last years of the Whitney administration and the beginning of W. H. Hearst's term indicate just as dramatically the tendency towards patronage by aging governments. Between 1911 and 1916, when the value of mineral production was increasing by 62.1 per cent, public revenues were falling by 50.5 per cent to an average of only $487,775 a year. With this decline the public share of production slipped back to only 0.91 per cent, close to the much-maligned former Liberal level. Over time a strong, confident mining industry accommodated itself to the new regulations, and the regulatory body—in this case a pliant government—interpreted the regulations in the interests of its clients. Gradually the royalties were negotiated downwards to between 3 and 5 per cent. The International Nickel Company argued successfully that its profits should be distributed over the smelting and refining processes, which did not fall under the profits tax, rather than be attributed entirely to mining.[40] Nor did W. H. Hearst demonstrate the same enthusiasm for royalties from the rich Porcupine and Kirkland Lake discoveries as his predecessors had at Cobalt. Accommodation[41] and lack of determination permitted the "people's share," once so proudly championed, to fall back to earlier unacceptable levels.

---

[39] Mines, *Annual Report*, 1917, pp. 61-4; Royal Ontario Nickel Commission, *Report*, p. 525.

[40] *Ibid.*, Appendix, pp. 198-203; text, pp. 520-3.

[41] For a study of this process of regulatory accommodation to vested interests, see Marver H. Bernstein, *Regulating Business by Independent Commission* (Princeton, 1955), especially pp. 269-79.

# 5
# Conserving
# the
# Forest

✤

The problem with the forests was not that the public drew
too little revenue from their exploitation, but rather too much.
Various governments, it began to appear, had sold timber to
pay their bills. The depredations of loggers, settlers and fire
had at length raised serious concern about the permanence
of the public forest and, accordingly, the employment and
revenues dependent upon it. Could the forest resources of the
crown be saved? The conservation movement that arose in
response to the crisis believed so, if the state administered its
property properly. The regulations required to save the forests
were more detailed and specific than those imposed upon the
mining industry; they would require a much larger government
bureaucracy to administer, and would necessitate much more
assertive activity in the business sector on the part of the state.
Moreover, the pressure for these reforms emanated not from
some diffuse assertion of popular opinion, but instead from
a genuine movement of progressive businessmen, professionals
and intellectuals. All too often those closest to the resource,

the loggers and millhands, conceived their own welfare in narrow company terms, especially before the organization of labour. Instead, the business and professional middle classes, the opinion-making groups in distant urban centres, were the ones who initiated the demand for the "business-like management"—a revealing phrase—of the crown timber.

I

Under the influence of changing scientific ideas and social conditions, the extractive attitude towards the forest which had prevailed during the "Golden Age of Forest Exploitation"[1] underwent a thorough reformation after the turn of the century. Previously a frontier community, finding itself surrounded by an oppressive expanse of forest stretching for unimaginable distances in almost every direction, set out to remove it as the first task of orderly agricultural settlement. Lumbermen conveniently led the assault, slashing their way through the finest timber stands, while pioneer farmers swarmed in behind, burning everything that remained. That such para-military destruction might be part of a golden rather than a dark age was to be explained by the fervour of the civilizing instinct within a context of apparent abundance. No matter how wanton the attack of the lumberman or the settler, it seemed as if the area of cleared land wrenched from a state of nature would remain, for some time to come, a mere notch on the southern margin of an immense wilderness. The simple vastness of the forest ensured that man might not wholly prevail against it for centuries.

Despite this vision of the eternal forest, the nineteenth-century community did not look upon it as a living organism, perpetually growing, dying and regenerating itself. Rather the forest was conceived of as a static concept, as a unique historical event. People believed that once it had been cut over or burned

---

[1] The phrase is a chapter heading in R. Lambert and P. Pross, *Renewing Nature's Wealth* (Toronto, 1967), pp. 124-49.

the forest could never renew itself to its original quality except through human reforestation. Instead, it would naturally deteriorate in stages of inferior weed, second growth. In summary, the nineteenth-century image of the forest was that of an enormous non-renewable resource, not unlike a giant mineral deposit, which was permanent simply by virtue of its size and could be exploited only once and then passed on to the farmers.

Officially at least, this extractive mentality governed Ontario forest policy long after the symbiotic relationship between the lumbermen and the settlers had ceased to be an operative reality. Even as late as 1901 a deputy minister of Crown Lands confessed that the settlement of an "industrious thrifty people who intend to farm" was still the first principle of forest administration, to which was subordinated—and note the emphasis—the "conservation of the revenue derived from lands and timber." However, within a few years the notion of the forest as a permanent, renewable resource became the new orthodoxy. A tightly knit, ably directed, and well-financed conservation movement, drawing up and feeding the shock and righteous anger provoked by the disparity between wasteful habits and imminent scarcity, was almost totally responsible for this sudden reversal of the old priorities.[2]

Conservation was pre-eminently a scientific movement. Professional foresters and civil servants initiated it, stimulated it intellectually, and directed its reforming energies. Men such as Elihu Stewart of the Department of the Interior, Thomas Southworth and Judson Clark of the Ontario Forestry Branch, J. C. Gwillim and G. Y. Chown of Queen's, Bernhard Fernow, C. D. Howe, and James White at Toronto and E. J. Zavitz at the Ontario Agricultural College vitalized the Canadian Forestry Association, central agency of the movement. These were the men who launched the conservation crusade to max-imize the social efficiency of the public lands and forests by bring-

---

[2] Department of Lands and Forests, Woods and Forests Report Book No. 3, Memorandum on Settlers and Timber 1901, pp. 453-5; David M. Potter, *People of Plenty: Economic Abundance and the American Character* (Chicago, 1954).

ing them under public and professional management. Their objectives were much the same as those of Gifford Pinchot and Theodore Roosevelt, the guiding spirits of the American conservation movement. "We base our whole policy on a principle stated by the President," Pinchot told the Canadian Forestry Convention in 1906, "that we must put every bit of land to its best use, no matter what that may be—put it to the use that will make it contribute most to the general welfare."[3]

The concept of efficiency as it applied to the forests rested upon the natural and the social sciences, upon biology and the application of scientific techniques to the problems of management. Trained scientists employing the latest managerial and organizational methods could best determine the most efficient allocation of natural resources; they could put an end to the waste inflicted by fire, disease, lumbermen and improvident governments and in so doing improve upon nature's own work. "Nature's method of waiting an age for the trees to disappear after they had passed their prime was wasteful alike in time and material," Judson Clark explained. "The forester with his axe saved the material and the time."[4] Conservation, the foresters continually repeated, did not mean simply preservation. Foresters were not primarily interested in forest protection or reforestation; they were no mere nature lovers interested in trees for their own sake. Like the preservationists, the conservationists wanted permanent forest re-

[3]  For details concerning the American forest conservation movement, see Hays, *Conservation and the Gospel of Efficiency* (Cambridge, Massachusetts, 1959), pp. 1-4, 27-48, 122-98; J. L. Bates, "Fulfilling American Democracy: The Conservation Movement, 1907-1921," *Mississippi Valley Historical Review*, Vol. XLIV (1957), pp. 29-57; Roy M. Robbins, *Our Landed Heritage: The Public Domain, 1776-1936* (Princeton, 1942), pp. 301ff; the Pinchot quotation is from the *Report of the Canadian Forestry Convention, Ottawa, January 10, 11, 12, 1906* (Ottawa, 1906), p. 25, hereafter RCFC.

[4]  For "scientific management," see Samuel Haber, *Efficiency and Uplift: Scientific Management in the Progressive Era, 1890-1920* (Chicago, 1964); Bernhard Fernow, "The Education of Foresters," *Canadian Forestry Journal*, Dec., 1907, pp. 143-53; Judson Clark, "Forest Revenues and Forest Conservation," *ibid.*, March, 1907, p. 19, and "A Canadian Forest Policy," *ibid.*, Feb. 1906, p. 46.

serves, but unlike the preservationists, foresters and conservationists argued for the permanent *use* of the forests thus set aside. The central principle of forestry, Judson Clark wrote in 1906, was the perpetuation and improvement of the forest by "judicious lumbering." "Forests grow to be used," Bernhard Fernow assured the Canadian Forestry Assocation: "Beware of the sentimentalists who would try to make you believe differently." Gifford Pinchot added with his usual directness: "Forestry with us is a business proposition. We do not love the trees any the less because we do not talk about our love for them." But, he went on, "use is the end of forest preservation, and the highest use." Scientific management then, was the central message of the conservation movement. [5]

There were, however, two prerequisites to the application of conservation principles: recognition of forestry as a profession, and ownership of the natural resources by the state. If foresters expected to exercise such broad powers of distributive discretion they required standardized scientific training and special sanctions from the community at large. A professional stature, conferred by university training, separate degrees and professional associations, was the most effective method of gaining the trust and respect of the community. Consequently, the leaders of the conservation movement assiduously cultivated their professional image; they asked to be looked up to as a dedicated body of practical scientists using the skill and knowledge of advanced education in the management of the public forests for the public good. [6]

Secondly, only the state possessed the necessary resources and jurisdiction to implement a sound forestry program. The task exceeded both the capacity and often the will of private owners who were, more often than not, concerned primarily

---

[5] Canadian Forestry Association, *Annual Report*, 1908, p. 102; 1909, p. 77; *RCFC*, p. 26; Hays, *Conservation and the Gospel of Efficiency*, pp. 122-46; Roderick Nash, *Wilderness and the American Mind* (New Haven, 1967), pp. 96-181.

[6] Paul Pross, "The Development of Professions in the Public Service: The Foresters in Ontario," *Canadian Public Administration*, Vol. X (1967), pp. 176-9.

with immediate returns. Moreover, the effects of combined individual neglect or short-sightedness redounded upon the entire community in the form of floods, droughts, exhausted soil and scarcity. Therefore, it was the duty of the state to protect the public interest against the rapacious instincts and ignorance of its citizens. The state alone commanded the heights from which a scientific survey was possible; it alone possessed the wealth and power required to protect the forest from fire and disease, to study and take stock of its growth characteristics, and to allocate and supervise its selective exploitation. It followed that foresters would be dedicated professionals in the public service, but above all they would be professionals, men of independent spirit possessing an inner ethic and an esprit de corps, and not the docile, politically dominated individuals usually associated with the term civil servant. Conservation of the forest resources could only be accomplished, Professor Fernow argued, when "the administration of the remaining timber lands is entrusted to a technically educated staff of a bureau, or perhaps better of a forest commission after the precedent of the Civil Service, Railroad, [and] Hydro-electric Commissions."[7]

But foresters could neither obtain such extensive power nor be deferred to in its exercise without a mandate from the community at large. The professionals wished to remove discretionary power over resource use from the hands of individual owners, even from the hands of the uninformed politicians in the legislatures. But at the same time these technocrats promised to preserve their notion of democracy in this concentration of authority by maintaining a vigorous program of "public education" to let the people know what needed to be done.

Had the conservation movement been recruited solely from the thin ranks of the professional foresters and civil servants who gave it life, it would not have been so successful in changing the popular image of the forest, nor would it have been as

[7] Elihu Stewart, "Canada as a Field for Intelligent Forestry," *Canadian Forestry Journal*, Jan., 1905, pp. 10-14; Fernow, "What We Want," Canadian Forestry Association, *Annual Report*, 1909, p. 82.

politically influential. However, the conservation message did strike a responsive chord among urban businessmen, intellectuals, and some of the lumbermen out on the forest frontier. Of the 267 persons who answered Sir Wilfrid Laurier's call to the 1906 Canadian Forestry Convention for example, 58 per cent came from Canada's major cities, 12 per cent from large industrial towns, and 24 per cent from the small towns and villages of the timber regions in British Columbia, Manitoba, Ontario, Quebec and New Brunswick. The geographical distribution of the 2,510 members of the Canadian Forestry Association in 1910 showed the same heavy representation from the cities and lumbering towns and an almost total absence of representation from the farming classes which made up more than one-half of the total population. The association drew 47 per cent of its membership from cities, 19 per cent from large industrial towns, and 29 per cent from small towns or villages—5 per cent lived out of the country. If the lumbermen are considered businessmen then it could be said that two main groups dominated membership of the movement—businessmen and what might be called for want of a better word, the urban intelligentsia of clergymen, journalists, professors, civil servants and, of course, politicians.[8]

At first glance it seems surprising that a movement whose energies were directed towards the distant northern forest should draw its membership from the urban businessmen and middle classes. For instance, all 398 branch managers of Molson's Bank, the Merchants' Bank, and the Banks of Commerce, Montreal, British North America, and New Brunswick were members of the Canadian Forestry Association; the Toronto, Montreal, and Hamilton Boards of Trade, the Canadian Manufacturers' Association, and the major railways usually sent delegates to the annual meetings. B. E. Walker, George Gooderham, Hugh Graham, William Birks, George Drummond, J. W. Flavelle, R. B. Angus, and a host of lesser commercial and industrial luminaries associated themselves

[8] Membership lists may be found in *ibid.*, 1910, pp. 121-38, 1912, pp. 113-21 and *RCFC*, list of participants, pp. 189-94.

from time to time with the objectives of the movement. Businessmen understood and responded instinctively to an appeal for efficiency. Businessmen knew at first hand the virtue and utility of modern science, and they liked the flattering ring of phrases like "scientific management" and "business-like methods." Moreover, the movement called for a major reformation in the character and spirit of politics by the application of board-room methods. Conservation meant the businesslike, professional management of the public trust, which implied, in the minds of businessmen, honesty, efficiency, prudence and permanence, compared to the profligacy of strictly political management.[9]

Businessmen recognized the economic importance of the forest and were quite prepared to believe that drought, floods and pestilence would accompany the financial disaster that they knew would follow upon its destruction. Canadians had behaved "like the unprofitable servant mentioned in Scripture," a representative of the Toronto Board of Trade said after considering such a gloomy prospect: "We had wasted our talent instead of caring for it and using it to best advantage." Then he continued, gliding easily from biblical to financial metaphors, to prescribe a remedy:

> It seems to me that we are like a great commercial or banking institution receiving reports from the gentlemen in charge of its business. These gentlemen have too unobtrusively told us of the great values of our property and the work that has been done in connection with it. And because of the devotion they have shown and of the importance of the interests they have in charge we must be prepared to give them greater latitude in the future than we have given them in the past.

Clifford Sifton, on another occasion, drew a similar conclusion. "We are still largely dominated in Canada by the idea that any ordinarily capable amateur can do the work which ought to be done by a trained scientific man," the *Monetary Times*

---

[9] Haber, *Efficiency and Uplift*, p. ix; Hays, *Conservation and the Gospel of Efficiency*, pp. 142ff.

quoted him as saying, "and until we eradicate this fallacy thoroughly, and in its place implant the view that men who are technically trained are the only men competent to deal with technical problems, we shall not begin to attain to general success in making the best use of the materials which are at our disposal."[10]

Bankers in particular knew the inevitable humiliating consequences of "living off one's capital," and the most articulate of them, B. E. Walker, sensed also the broader, ecological implications of an unbalanced forest account:

> . . . there is no doubt that if we disturb the beautiful balance that nature has given us in our natural resources, the entire order of things in Canada may fall to pieces. It is not simply that our water powers will decline in value, but our coal areas will not be so valuable. Nothing will be so valuable. Nature has given us a curious opportunity for the strong northern man to exercise his brains upon, and if we disturb the equilibrium we are criminals in the greatest sense in which men can be criminals for we are criminals towards our descendants and to future generations.[11]

For men who traded daily upon the steady, accumulative virtues of a thrifty population, men who directed insurance companies and banks, the word conservation itself carried that special, reverent connotation, saving. Industrialists saw the finest image of themselves mirrored in the movement; they naturally responded to the conception of social efficiency, that business might confidently continue forever under professional, scientific management.

At the spiritual level as well, conservation merged with another notion of saving, salvation. In literature, art and poetry the forest was a place of beauty and wonderment; in the church and cathedral the forest was a divine gift placed in the stewardship of mortals. Man's treatment of this precious heritage necessarily revealed something of his intellectual sensibility or

---

[10] *RCFC*, pp. 94-6; *Monetary Times*, Dec. 7, 1917.
[11] *RCFC*, pp. 171-5.

his state of grace. Thus the spiritual quality of the conservation movement helped to bridge the widening gap between the worlds of business and the intellect, and it helps to explain the support extended to the movement by clergymen, professors and intellectuals. Men such as these were just as susceptible to the gospel of social efficiency as were the businessmen, but the point is that conservation also raised "higher questions" which were the concern of men of spirit in a materialistic age. Walker, who as a banker, geologist, art collector, literary critic and educationalist lived in both worlds, thought that this aesthetic aspect of the movement warranted emphasis, particularly when he found himself in the company of Philistines. After Gifford Pinchot's austere utilitarian confession quoted above, Walker was moved to reply: "The man who thinks that the aesthetic side of forestry has nothing to do with the practical upbuilding of the nation is simply a species of fool. That is all there is in it." Again at a special conservation meeting held at Convocation Hall in 1910, Walker subscribed to Clifford Sifton's good practical reasons for conserving the forests, but he added: "The trouble was in getting every man, woman and child to realize that it was not only an administrative and economic question, but also a great question of national morals and national character."[12]

Ethics and aesthetics drew men like the presidents of the Royal Society and Toronto, Queen's, and McGill universities into a movement of lumbermen and men in trade; these were subjects which concerned mutually the Protestant clergy of Ontario and the hierarchy in Quebec. From a forester's point of view these well-intentioned instincts verged dangerously upon the sterile sentimentalism of mere preservation of the forest for its own sake. Yet there was room within the movement for some ambivalence on certain points. The motives of the recruits need not correspond exactly to the rationale of the founders. And as long as no crises arose to divide the two groups, preservationists, beautifiers, moralists and urban reformers might continue to feel reasonably comfortable in the company

[12] *Ibid.*, p. 173; *Canadian Forestry Journal*, June, 1910, p. 54.

of hard-headed businessmen, lumbermen and professionals.

The conspicuous absence of farmers from the movement can be readily explained. Invariably the farmer was the villain of the conservation piece. Even Sir Wilfrid Laurier, in opening his Forestry Convention in 1906, assailed the farmers' "merciless" destruction of the forest. In many respects conservation represented a frontal assault upon both the practice and myth of agrarianism. It had been the farmers who had denuded the watershed and thus loosed the devastating spring floods; they had stripped Norfolk, Simcoe and Prince Edward counties bare, mined the soil, then abandoned their exhausted, eroded farms to the elements. Now a vast expanse of sand dunes, shells of buildings, rusting equipment and arid, wind-swept wastes marked their passage. Up in the north country the settlers had wrought even greater destruction with their clearing fires. Because the homestead farmer either burned timber accidentally, or stole it purposefully, he was looked upon by both foresters and lumbermen as an especially pernicious enemy of the forest.

Conservation challenged the farmers' traditional agrarian ideology at precisely the same time as urbanization and industrialization challenged their traditional place in society. Rural depopulation, the relative deprivation of rural life, and the changing social composition of the population all combined at this time to threaten the farmer and undermine his self-respect. Farmers, then, could hardly be expected to respond immediately to the conservation movement's message of censure. However, in due course, the foresters did get their message to the farmers through the farmers' own progressive organizations, the agricultural colleges, and Experimental Unions. Much later the conservation movement and the Farmer's Progressive movements would converge. Through E. J. Zavitz's work with the farmers' clubs, the most progressive members of the Ontario farming community came in time to recognize the value of water-table maintenance, farm woodlots and reforestation. Ironically, this later friendship of the farmer and the forester, personified in the friendship of E. C. Drury and E. J. Zavitz, produced more impressive results than the early conservation movement. But that is getting ahead somewhat. It is only necessary at this point to note that the anti-agrarian tone of the most outspoken conservationists tended to discourage farm membership in the movement at the outset.[13]

Since the foresters went to great pains to project the message that conservation meant the permanent *use* of the forest, it is not surprising that lumbermen quickly jostled their way to the front of the movement. At the annual meetings of the Canadian Forestry Association, lumbermen usually comprised the second largest contingent—civil servants were always the most numerous—and between 1907 and 1914 lumbermen served as presidents of the association for six of the eight terms. The lumbermen were irrepressibly visible, always a high-spirited gang of wealthy, robust men whose rough-hewn humour manifested itself however sombre and genteel the surroundings. The amiable, indomitable Senator W. C. Edwards, a Liberal lumberman from the Ottawa Valley, was their unofficial leader and names like Booth, Miller, Snowball, White, Hendry, Rathbun, Bigwood, Charlton, Price, Power, Barber, Ellis and Riordan were prominent in the ranks. To be sure all of these men professed a deep concern for sound conservation principles; each felt that he was a fast friend of the forest and, to be fair, some were in fact genuine, well-informed proponents of forestry. Nevertheless, it is also perfectly clear that both the lumbermen and the pulpmen tried to use the conservation movement either in self-defence, or in pursuit of tactical objectives. For example, the lumbermen usually interpreted forestry to mean preservation from fire, which they quickly identified with the elimination of settlement in the forest regions. For Canadian papermakers, good forestry always seemed to turn on the question of halting the export of pulp logs to American paper mills. The men of the forest products industries sought to direct the enthusiasm and influence of the wider membership of the Canadian Forestry

[13] *RCFC*, pp. 8-9; foresters repeatedly pointed out that many formerly heavily forested sections of southern Ontario bore even less forest cover after the settlement process than some seriously deforested areas of Europe. See, for example, the *Canadian Forestry Journal*, May-June, July-August, 1911, October, 1913, and June-July, 1914. For the farmers' movement and conservation, see E. C. Drury, *Farmer Premier* (Toronto, 1966), pp. 99-100.

Association into support for their immediate demands upon reluctant governments. More often than not they were jovially contemptuous of the "theoretical men" [they considered themselves to be practical men] and learned professors whose papers they seldom understood, who kept advocating "scientific forestry"—whatever that meant.

"The lumberman . . . is not the enemy," Senator Edwards reminded the Canadian Forestry Convention, "but the legitimate lumberman is the very best friend of the forests." Before an appreciative audience of colleagues at an annual meeting of the Canadian Forestry Association, the genial senator expanded upon the virtues of men who cut down trees; then and for some time to come, he said, the "practical, sound lumberman" would continue to be "the salvation of the forests. (Hear, hear and applause.)" Any forester could heartily second J. B. Miller's assertion that self-interest alone compelled the lumberman to take a serious interest in the permanence of the forest, "as upon it depends the duration of his industry," but at the same time Miller's conclusion that the lumberman was "more sinned against than sinning" must have raised knowing smiles among the "theoretical men" present. Senator Edwards was even bolder: "I believe there is more timber dying of old age in Canada to-day than there is being cut by lumbermen," he told an applauding audience in Toronto. From time to time the lumbermen would admit that there might be the odd delinquent in their midst, but each confession usually came accompanied by a rider that lifted the burden of guilt from the industry as a whole. The most wasteful loggers, Miller claimed, were those with small operations forced by government regulations to clear their limits within a specified time. These men, with very little equipment and no investment at all to speak of in standing timber, threatened the crown lands and neighbouring limits with trespass and fire. They were a class, Edwards said, "whom I am personally in the habit of calling thieves."[14] Thus denying all responsibility for the perilous

[14] *RCFC*, pp. 103, 106, 108-9, 111; Canadian Forestry Association, *Annual Report*, 1909, pp. 125, 129; for a somewhat different view of the

condition of the forests, the lumbermen accused settlers and governments as the two outstanding agents of destruction.

Lumbermen were of the general opinion that if they could have the forests to themselves and public assistance in preventing forest fires, the forestry question would to a considerable extent solve itself. "If fires are kept out of the forests," an aging J. R. Booth told his excursion guests at the Madawaska limit, "there will be more pine in this country 100 years from now than there was fifty years ago, and we shall have lots of timber for the generation to come." And lumbermen invariably associated fire with frontier farming. "The greatest engine of destruction that the forests of Canada have suffered from," Senator Edwards claimed, was "illegitimate settlement." It was not enough to maintain fire-ranging systems to put out fires, he added, "the man who most frequently starts the fires, the pretended settler, must be eliminated." Both the Ontario and Canadian Lumberman's Associations petitioned the federal and provincial governments for a systematic classification of lands that would set precise boundaries around those areas suitable for agriculture and those better suited to other purposes. The Hon. George H. Perley told the Canadian Lumberman's Association in 1913 what it hardly needed reminding, but it was no doubt reassuring to hear it from a politician and former lumberman:

> The public does not as yet know that a large part of every country, and of Canada in particular, is fitted only to grow trees and that devoted to that purpose it will produce wealth for the whole nation; while to attempt to farm such areas or to leave them to take care of themselves has resulted and always will result in barrenness, waste, depopulation and poverty. [15]

---

lumbermen's participation in the conservation movement based mainly upon the Bronson Papers, see Peter Gillies, "The Ottawa Lumber Barons and the End of the Great Pine in Eastern Ontario: An Aspect of the Conservation Movement, 1880-1914," forthcoming in the *Journal of Canadian Studies*.

[15] *RCFC*, pp. 188; *Canadian Forestry Journal*, August, 1906, p. 109; Feb., 1913, p. 17.

In the lumbermen's view the foresters and the conservation movement, in calling for forest inventories and elaborate land classification schemes, merely restated in a new jargon what they had been asking for years, a "fair line of demarcation" between agricultural and forest districts.

Although the lumbermen believed that settlers created the immediate problem, they also claimed that governments ought to bear the greater share of responsibility. Governments had failed to provide adequate fire protection systems or to classify their lands properly; they had imposed inconsiderate terms and conditions upon the lumbermen and were, after all, responsible for the presence of the settlers on unsuitable lands in the first place. Politicians not lumbermen had passed the Homestead laws and written the extravagant immigration propaganda. "Thousands of abandoned clearings," dotting the north that had been once occupied by Englishmen "who came here in the hope of becoming landed gentry," remained as a grim testimonial, according to J. B. Miller, to the futility and tragedy of free grants. Moreover, he continued, if logging operations did result in waste, it was the government's own fault. The sale of small timber berths for very high bonuses to be cut over and then returned to the crown within a specified number of years practically forced the owners to slash their way through the properties as quickly as possible to protect their investment from thieving neighbours and the inevitable fires that accompanied lumbering operations. Permanent forest tenure combined with large-scale industrial exploitation would compel lumbermen to protect their limits in their own self-interest, Senator Edwards alleged: "What I hold is that the best condition of all is to have a lumberman who has a permanent and large investment to sustain and maintain and one who desires to conserve the timber for the supply of his establishment." The big timber operators reasoned that if the politicians would adjust the law to meet their long-term economic interests, conservation would naturally follow. When that degree of progress had been accomplished, then, Senator Edwards suggested,

> ...if they will just shoot about half of their Provincial members, and another class of members that I will not name here—

(Laughter)—there will be every opportunity for perpetuating those forests. But unfortunately we have that enemy, and it is the greatest enemy of the lumber trade. DELEGATE: How about shooting the Senators? (Laughter.) SENATOR EDWARDS: If he is not a worthy preserver of the forests, shoot him, for heaven's sake. (Laughter.)[16]

It was to be expected that the professional foresters would protest the bold expropriation of "sound forestry principles" by their opportunistic lumbermen colleagues, while the latter deeply resented being reminded of their impertinence and their misdeeds by the former. When Professor Fernow suggested in a paper to the Canadian Forestry Association that scientific forestry was somewhat more involved than merely cutting mature trees and hinted that the lumberman might be one important element in the way of its practice, the redoubtable senator rose and "fired back" at him: " . . . coming for a moment to our friend, Dr. Fernow, I must say I didn't understand him this morning. That is, if I understand him correctly, I don't know what he means. (Laughter.)" Theoretical men might know something of theories, Edwards continued, but the "practical lumberman" was the only person who "understood the question so far as practical operation is concerned." He knew from experience that pine would regenerate quickly and he was equally confident that the forest would last forever if the mature trees were cut when they came of age so that the younger trees could grow in their place. Far from being an obstacle, the senator said, the lumberman "is an element above all elements, who will join in the heartiest way to co-operate for the preservation of the forests—the very reverse of what the Doctor said. He simply does not know the boys as he ought to know them. (Laughter.)" But on this occasion the professor had the last word. With almost arrogant precision Fernow exploded the senator's optimistic notions concerning forest

[16] PAO, Ontario Lumberman's Association Papers, Memorial to the Provincial Government, April 6, 1905; *Canadian Forestry Journal*, June, 1905, p. 126; *RCFC*, pp. 103, 110; Canadian Forestry Association, *Annual Report*, 1909, p. 128.

regeneration, then attacked the distinction, repeatedly drawn, between "practical" and "theoretical" men: "The Senator has not realized that every man is a theorist as well as a practical man. (A voice—"Good.") He is a practical man in some things and a theorist in others. Now, I agree that the Senator is a practical lumberman; but he is a theorist of the worst kind in Forestry." [17] It is not surprising that the trained foresters quickly established their own Canadian Society of Forest Engineers where their papers received a somewhat more sympathetic, less patronizing hearing. But, at the same time, they did not leave the Canadian Forestry Association; rather they stayed in to provide professional guidance and maintain their links with the broader public.

Notwithstanding their protestations to the contrary, there remains something vaguely unconvincing about the lumbermen's advocacy of conservation. Blaming the evident destruction upon settlers and the government was a good ploy, but the lumbermen must be judged by their work, not their words. Conditions approaching the lumbermen's ideal on the upper Ottawa failed to save the forest, even that part of it under the trusteeship of some of these latter-day conservationists. The great pine forests were gone. It is true that representatives of the biggest companies tended to be promoters of professional forest management in the best progressive tradition, but by the same token the most ardent conservationists in the industry were also old men, industrial statesmen like Edwards and Bronson to be sure, but men on the brink of retirement from the trade who had perhaps forgotten the methods of their youth. Geographically, lumbermen of the conservationist persuasion tended to come not from the booming western part of the province, but instead from the declining east. These circumstances suggest that for some of them at least conservation was not a program meant to be projected forward as a guide to action in the future, but rather it served as a rationalizing ideology to justify and sanctify what had gone on in the past. In the ideal conservationist's world the lumberman was

[17] Canadian Forestry Association, *Annual Report*, 1909, pp. 124, 129, 150-2.

not a pariah. Active participation in the movement dignified a business then under popular censure. At the end of his career the lumberman, if he chose, could transform himself from a logger into a forester. He could stand among the stumps and pretend.[18]

## II

Although the Canadian conservation movement coincided with an impassioned American conservation crusade and even drew upon its ideas, experiences and leadership, it was not a mere pallid northern reflection of the ongoing Progressive struggle to the south. Admittedly, the American crusade was much better theatre; and clearly, this continental drama did influence the Canadian movement. The very presence of Bernard Fernow at the University of Toronto, public interest in President Roosevelt's assertive exploits, and the occasional lightning visits of Gifford Pinchot to Canadian forestry conventions indicate the internationality of conservation ideas and personnel. The President always invited Canadian representatives to his conservation conferences, and invariably the excited Canadian delegates returned to the provinces full of information, enthusiasm and gossip to shock Canadians into a recognition of the seriousness of the problem. The United States furnished Canadian conservationists with innumerable examples of resource exhaustion to lay before their compatriots as stern warnings of what lay ahead. The soil erosion problems of eastern Canada paled to insignificance, apparently, compared to the "deserts" that had formerly been Wisconsin, Michigan and New York. Canadians seemed quite prepared to believe that the United States would be treeless within twenty years.

---

[18] E. H. Bronson's fervent espousal of conservation rhetoric did not prevent him from fouling the Ottawa River with his mill wastes even though he knew this to be wrong; see PAO, Bronson Papers, Vol. 128, F. P. Bronson to E. B. Eddy Company, April 18, April 19, 1898; on the deterioration of the forest, see Jacob Spelt, *Urban Development in South-Central Ontario* (Toronto, 1972 ed.), p. 104.

But for all that they shared in common, the Canadian conservation movement differed significantly from its American contemporary. Even though conservation in Canada acquired a similar moral overtone and attained the status of popular gospel, the movement never developed the crusading spirit of its American counterpart because Canada did not share the American crisis over ownership which did so much to inflame emotions within the United States. Indeed, Canadian observers took a cool, superior, almost patronizing interest in the agonizing struggle Americans had to undergo merely to establish government-owned forest reserves. Canadians never missed an opportunity to congratulate themselves that their much more sensible governments had never permitted private citizens or corporations to appropriate vast kingdoms of the public domain. Even the legendary Gifford Pinchot complimented this apparent Canadian foresight in keeping title to the forests vested in the state.[19]

The Canadian movement concerned itself with the more prosaic problems of what to do with the forests which the state already controlled. Thus the conservation campaign was principally educational. It poured out alarmist informational pamphlets and bad poetry, staged elaborate conventions and excursions, and lobbied incessantly in Ottawa and the provincial capitals. The Canadian Forestry Association published the *Canadian Forestry Journal* which became a standard source of editorial inspiration for the daily and financial press. Taking stock of the progress of the conservation movement up to 1913, the *Canadian Forestry Journal* noted the numerous professional foresters in the public service and the new forestry schools at the universities, but it concluded that a great deal of "foundation work" remained to be accomplished. Although the conservation movement found much to criticize in government policy, it did not blame politicians for everything. On the contrary, the *Journal* observed that it had always found politicians "open to argument and ready to advance as fast

---

[19] *RCFC*, p. 25; *Financial Post*, Sept. 19, 1908; Lambert and Pross, *Renewing Nature's Wealth*, pp. 208ff.

as the people. So we come back to the point," the editorial concluded, "that the chief work of the Association is education."[20]

The Canadian Forestry Assocation, therefore, restricted its activities to the mundane business of disseminating information. Foresters in the public service fed ideas and proposals to their influential journalist friends; others in the universities gave governments the benefit of their opinions in learned articles, magazine polemics and private correspondence. Civil servants pressed their schemes upon reluctant political superiors, and the most prominent supporters of the movement proselytized their friends in high places. Agents in the new Canadian Clubs, Canadian Manufacturers' Assocation, and local Boards of Trade bent the will and prestige of their organizations towards the cause.[21]

The score of annual reports and technical monographs from the Canadian Commission of Conservation stand as an imposing monument to the power of the conservation lobby. Because the federal government was not encumbered by the immediate, practical considerations of having to administer vast areas of highly productive forest, it succumbed painlessly to the conservation gospel. Following Theodore Roosevelt's example, Laurier convened his own Canadian Forestry Convention in 1906 to publicize the plight of the forests. Then in 1909, after further communication with Roosevelt and the leading Canadian conservationists, Laurier established a Canadian Commission of Conservation chaired by Clifford Sifton—appropriately enough a businessman—to study and give advice upon the entire range of Canadian resource problems. He merely intended to carry on the work of the private con-

[20] Canadian Forestry Association, *The Forests and the People* (Toronto, 1906), *passim*; *Canadian Forestry Journal*, issues of Jan., 1905, Oct., 1913, Nov., 1913.

[21] PAC, Willison Papers, Vol. 16, Judson Clark to Willison, June 7, 1906; PAO, Whitney Papers, Bernhard Fernow to Whitney, Nov., 15, 1907; N. F. Davidson to Whitney, Oct., 18, 1905; PAC, Laurier Papers, Senator Edwards to Laurier, Sept. 7, 1901, 58753; Edwards to Laurier, Jan., 13, 1906, 105968-9, for examples.

servation movement under the prestigious office of a public commission. There was no intention, Laurier explained to an aloof Whitney, of trenching upon areas of provincial jurisdiction: "The Commission itself is not intended or expected to have any administrative capacity. Its work will consist rather of investigation, so as to acquire knowledge on which to base recommendations or findings which may be considered and studies by the various authorities under whose administrative charge the natural resources of the country are. . . ." While the federal government possessed direct power in these matters only in the prairies and the Territories, Laurier served notice that he would use the publicity function that he did possess to influence the responsible provincial jurisdictions.[22]

The conservation movement aimed at something more than a shelf full of books, however impressive that might be. Power to halt a deteriorating situation lay with the provinces which actually owned the endangered forests. From provincial politicians conservationists demanded more than sympathy and study; they expected action. Ontario's politicians, like all men of reason, immediately recognized a just cause and associated themselves rhetorically with it. Suddenly the most unexpected people became "good friends of forestry." But conservation sentiment operated at three different levels more or less in tension with each other. On the technocratic plane the professional foresters conducted research and advocated reform programs; many of the urban supporters of the movment were far more interested in the aesthetic plane on which the forests were to be protected, for basically moral reasons, from all forms of predators, human and divine. Administrators, politicians and lumbermen found themselves on a third plane, the practical level of the movement. They shared responsibility for implementing change; they were the ones most likely to ask how much the conservation programs would cost and who would pay for them. We have already noticed how the lumber-

---

[22] PAC, Laurier Papers, President Roosevelt to Laurier, Dec. 24, 1908, and reply, 149351-2; Laurier to Whitney, July 20, 1909, 158411; PAO, Whitney Papers, R. H. Campbell, Dominion Superintendent of Forestry, to Whitney and reply, Oct. 27, 1905.

men attempted to use conservation as a justification for their own business drives. Politicians, hardly less callous, had to weigh the desirable against the possible, count the costs, then dress up the resulting policy in an appropriate conservationist disguise.

The technocrats' programs of scientific management always seemed to involve massive field staffs of highly trained, well-paid foresters and fire rangers. This was an almost ludicrous idea at a time when a score of laymen, political appointees at Toronto and in the half-dozen regional Crown Timber Agencies, administered the sprawling forest operations in the province, and the lumbermen looked after their own fire protection. Taking the view from the cabinet, scientific forest management appeared to be an expensive, visionary proposition which would weigh heavily upon the lumbermen and the crown revenues. Thus the politicians eagerly made grand declaratory gestures of no cost or consequence, but demonstrated great reluctance in creating adequate fire prevention methods, taking forest inventories, drafting timber laws with sensible cutting regulations attached, and then recruiting the qualified field staffs to enforce them. At the root of the American crusade for public ownership lay the assumption that ownership necessarily implied rational management, but the Canadian conservationists learned from experience that was not so. "Ownership," Bernhard Fernow wrote in 1912, "is a snare and a delusion." For the state, and here he referred directly to Ontario, continued to rent out its property to lumbermen "under conditions which make ownership of doubtful value."[23] At the "practical" political level, as amongst "practical" lumbermen, there were always good reasons for compromises. Reasons of economy would compromise sound management in Ontario for another two generations.

The ideas of the conservation movement began to be translated into legislation at the turn of the century. Following a particularly bad forest fire season, Premier Arthur Hardy

[23] PAO, Hearst Papers, "Forest Resources and Problems of Canada," offprint from, *Proceedings*, Society of American Foresters, Vol. VII (1912), p. 141.

appointed the Royal Commission on Forest Protection on the advice of Thomas Southworth, to determine what might be done "without at the present time incurring much expenditure" to restore the forest in burnt and cut-over areas and to preserve it in those districts unsuited to settlement. In 1899 the commission, made up of progressive lumbermen and civil servants, recommended the creation of permanent forest reserves and government control of all fire ranging. The same year the Legislature passed the required Forest Reserves Act under which crown lands "deemed advisable for the purpose of future timber supplies" could be set apart from settlement and "kept in a state of nature as nearly as possible." Since these lands were already under the jurisdiction of the government, it was an easy and inexpensive matter to map out and declare large areas to be forest reserves. So, between 1899 and 1905 Liberal governments declared a total of 10,437,520 acres of forest in eastern and northern Ontario reserved for the purpose of supplying a permanent source of both forest products and revenue. On the matter of fire protection, those same governments moved considerably slower. The government did assume responsibility for the forest reserve lands, but the fire control amendments passed in 1900 governing licensed land merely rendered compulsory what had been law since 1878; namely, that the lumbermen appointed fire rangers for their limits and the government paid 50 per cent of the costs. These new policies, especially the grand forest reserves gesture—a Minister of Crown Lands in Ontario could with the stroke of a pen create more forest reserves than all of Pinchot's army—gave the appropriate conservationist impression, but what really mattered was what would be done with those reserves besides keeping out settlers.[24]

[24] Department of Lands and Forests, Woods and Forests Report Book No. 2, Memorandum on Regeneration, June 6, 1897, pp. 499-502; *ibid.*, Memorandum on Forest Reserves, Mar. 21, 1899; Royal Commission on Forest Protection in Ontario, *Report* (Toronto, 1899), p. 20; *Statutes of Ontario*, 61 Vict., c. 10; Lambert and Pross, *Renewing Nature's Wealth*, pp. 184-5, 201.

Timber in these reservations would be auctioned and cut like any other crop when it matured, the Minister of Crown Lands explained on a number of occasions, thus ensuring lumbermen a permanent supply of raw materials, the crown a permanent revenue, and the province a perennial forest. However, Thomas Southworth, from his little Bureau of Forestry and Colonization, pointed out in a long memorandum to the Minister in 1901, that such a policy contained inherent contradictions since the existing Crown Timber Regulations were at odds with all principles of permanency. But his superiors ignored his recommendations. The 1902 regulations governing the disposal of timber in crown forest reserves did not provide for an adequate staff to administer the property nor did they impose any cutting restrictions that did not already apply to licensed lands. Lumbermen were notably enthusiastic about the program; now they had their exclusive timber reserves, access to them on their own terms and the government paid for fire protection.[25] Nevertheless, this did not prevent the government from keeping up appearances by making extravagant claims for its forest reserve policy. Moreover, in 1904 it appointed a professional forester, Judson F. Clark, to a powerless, advisory position with Southworth in the Bureau of Forestry. Otherwise, it was business as usual. On the pretext that the T. & N. O. railroad, then under construction, would endanger rich pineries in the Temagami district, the government held its usual pre-election timber limit auction in 1903.

[25] Department of Lands and Forests, Woods and Forests Report Book No. 2, Memorandum re: Temagami Forest Reserve, Jan. 7, 1901, pp. 441-8; Report Book No. 3, Regulations Respecting Forest Reserves, 1902, pp. 22-4. For the lumbermen's support of the forest reservation program, see PAO, Bronson Papers, Vol. 698, E. H. Bronson to Hon. E. J. Davis, July 27, 1901, personal; Vol. 695, E. H. Bronson to Hon. G. W. Ross, Dec. 14, 1903, private; Vol. 695, E. H. Bronson to Hon. E. J. Davis, Dec. 24, 1903, and Jan. 2, 1904, both private. Bronson wanted some of his limits included in the Temagami Reserve: "The inclusion of this territory in the reserve would give us additional fire protection, and protection that would also be of value to the government to the extent of the Crown dues of the timber within the licensed area."

It was the same old convenient arrangement: the lumbermen needed the timber, the government needed the money, and the party could use the inevitable rewards that passed its way following such events. The Liberal government talked a good conservation policy, but its actions belied its words.[26]

The overwhelming Conservative victory in the 1905 general election raised the hopes of both the timber administrators and the conservationists. "The present government with its large majority," Judson Clark wrote in 1906, "is certainly in a position to adopt any policy that can be shown to be for the public advantage," and Clark urged his friend J. S. Willison to press the demand for reform "which can hardly be undertaken unless asked for, because of the sure and certain opposition with which it would be met in certain influential quarters." In opposition the Conservative party had been considered reasonably "sound" on the forestry question. Even under the leadership of W.R. Meredith back in the 1880s the party had protested the inclusion of timber revenues in the current revenues of the government on the ground that timber represented capital. Every year during the budget debate the Legislature endured a lengthy disquisition on this subject, until in 1900 the Royal Commission on Finance temporarily scotched the argument. Nevertheless, the Conservatives remained suspicious of the tremendous revenues pouring into the public treasury from lumbering operations—a sum which totalled $40,000,000 between 1867 and 1905—and questioned whether large timber sales, like the one conducted in 1903, were entirely consistent with the government's avowed program of conservation. By 1905 even the *Globe* had begun to criticize the Ross government for its lack of a "provident timber policy."[27] Thus, in spite of the Liberal's

---

[26] *Canadian Annual Review*, 1901, p. 454; Hon. E. J. Davis, *Budget Address, 1902* (Toronto, 1902), p. 18; Hon. E. J. Davis, *Ontario's Forest Wealth: A Hundred Years of Revenue* (Toronto, 1904), p. 6; *The Ross Government and Progressive Ontario* (Toronto, 1905), p. 10; *The Ross Government Has Kept Ontario in the Lead* (Toronto, 1905), pp. 4-5.

[27] PAC, Willison Papers, Vol. 16, Clark to Willison, June 7, 1906; Royal Commission on the Financial Position of the Province of Ontario, *Report* (Toronto, 1900), pp. 6-7, 15, 26; PAO, Ross Papers, Memorandum on Timber, Proceeds of Sale.

dramatic forest reserve policy, the Conservatives came to power as the conservationist party. Their traditional insistence that timber represented capital now fitted perfectly with the new notion of the forest as a renewable resource. Moreover, they assumed office with an impressive mandate for change at a time when earnest civil servants and the conservation movement stood waiting in the wings with new programs.

From the outset the new government struck the necessary conservationist pose, but its overall accomplishments fell considerably short of expectations. On the recommendation of the University Commission it did establish a Forestry School within the University of Toronto and also expanded the reforestation research already under way at the Ontario Agricultural College. To meet the growing menace of fire, the Whitney government further amended the Fire Act in 1906 compelling railroads to maintain fire rangers along their rights-of-way and, at public expense, expanded somewhat the patrols within the forest reserves. To offset this latter cost, the government shifted the full cost of fire protection on licensed areas to the lumbermen in 1910.[28]

However, the government's most widely heralded reforms, those involving the method of selling rights to crown timber, related only incidentally to forest conservation. On the advice of senior civil servants within the new Department of Lands and Forests, the Whitney government replaced a system of sale and administration that had been evolved to meet the requirements of the Ottawa square timber trade in the mid-nineteenth century with a new procedure more suited to the sawlog and pulpwood industries that now extended from the upper Ottawa, across the north shore of Lake Huron, through the Lakehead to the Lake of the Woods district in the most westerly corner of the enormous province. The needs of these widely scattered operations could not be met with casual timber sales, usually before elections, nor could the government keep track of cutting from an office in Ottawa and another at Quebec.

[28] Lambert and Pross, *Renewing Nature's Wealth*, pp. 186, 207; J. W. B. Sisam, *Forestry Education at Toronto* (Toronto, 1961), pp. 13-14; *Canadian Forestry Journal*, May, 1910, p. 44.

Moreover, the Conservatives hoped to be able to maximize their revenues from licensed lands without having to increase the total area under licence. Some of these changes were long overdue, and political change merely hastened them. Aubrey White, long-time deputy minister of Crown Lands—now the Department of Lands, Forests and Mines—designed a system that met most Conservative objections to former Liberal policies. In 1907 he imposed several impressive but inconsequential cutting regulations to protect younger trees, and in 1909 raised the dues on square timber to prohibitive levels to bring an end to that wasteful and hazardous type of operation.[29]

But White's most important changes were not with the regulations; rather they dealt with the method of selling rights to timber. In the past lumbermen had bid on areas at open auctions at the Parliament Buildings, stating how much cash they were willing to pay over and above the annual dues and ground rents charges for rights to that area. White shifted the bonus calculation from area to volume actually cut and changed the payment from one lump sum at the auction to an annual payment, along with the dues and ground rent, proportionate to the lumberman's actual production. Since the bonus depended upon volume, the government would have to know precisely how much timber was being cut on each limit each year. To gather this information, White expanded the number of part-time cullers attached to the regional Crown Timber Agencies. Henceforth, lumbermen would submit a sworn declaration of their cut; this would then be verified by the cullers, most of whom were simply lumberjacks in the employ of the very men whose timber they were checking. On this total, the local Crown Timber Agent calculated the amount of dues and bonus owing.

But the system introduced by Aubrey White, unaccompanied by any reform of the civil service, placed a great deal of discretionary power in the hands of that tightly knit clique of lumbermen and placemen who had always ruled field opera-

---

[29] Lambert and Pross, *Renewing Nature's Wealth*, p. 207; T. Southworth, "Ontario's Progress Towards a Rational Forestry System," *Canadian Forestry Journal*, Dec. 1907, pp. 157-63.

tions. Ultimately, the accuracy of the returns upon which the public revenues would be based rested upon the lumberman's sworn declaration. Lumbermen were not above a little harmless deception, especially when bonus charges rising with timber prices amounted to four or five times the nominal dues; the cullers lived in mortal fear of dismissal from their full-time jobs, and the notoriously corrupt Crown Timber Agents, accepted the lumbermen's affidavits at face value. All of the field staff owed their jobs to the influence of their lumbermen clients—not a very healthy regulatory situation. The Conservatives reformed administrative procedures without, however, reforming the administration.[30]

In addition to the free advice heaped upon him by the press, Whitney actually solicited the advice of his senior civil servants on forestry matters upon assuming office. As has just been noted, his government quickly implemented Aubrey White's administrative proposals, but other equally important suggestions received no satisfaction whatever. Thomas Southworth, who shared the major responsibility for the existence of the forest reserves, reminded the new Premier that the government had yet to establish special regulations for lumbering operations within the forest reserves to distinguish them in any way from any other licensed crown lands. He suggested that his tiny publicity bureau be expanded into an adequately staffed Department of Colonization, Forestry and Parks with full authority to manage the forest reserves separate from the other crown lands on a permanent, sustained yield basis.[31]

---

[30] Lambert and Pross, *Renewing Nature's Wealth*, pp. 260-2, for details of the administrative changes. For the lamentable story of corruption in the Department of Lands and Forests field staff, see PAO, J. P. Bertrand, "Timber Wolves" (unpublished ms., circa 1961); Royal Commission on Timber, 1920, *Hearings*, 12 Vols., and *Reports* (Toronto, 1921 and 1922). For manuscript evidence, see *inter alia*, PAO, Whitney Papers, G. H. Macdonnell to Whitney, Feb. 17, 1900; J. S. McDonald to Whitney, Jan. 1, Mar. 29, 1900; E. C. Steele to Whitney, April 2, 1900, private and confidential; J. J. Foy to Whitney, Nov. 26, 1902; Charles Hartley to Whitney, Feb. 12 and 23, 1904; W. A. Osler to Whitney, August, 1905, telegram; James Conmee to Hon. J. M. Gibson, Oct. 23, 1908.

[31] PAO, Whitney Papers, T. Southworth to J. J. Foy, Mar. 31, 1905, marked private by the author and important by the Premier.

Although Judson F. Clark was Southworth's subordinate, he was nevertheless an aggressive, crusading personality following the professional example set by Gifford Pinchot. He put his case before the Premier somewhat more forthrightly and much more often. "I have found," he wrote to the Premier in February 1906, "that the forestry movement after developing so far along sound lines, has come to a parting of the ways where a decisive move must be made if progress is not to be indefinitely stalled. The move necessary is two-fold, educational and administrative—theoretical and practical." By creating a School of Forestry, he observed, the government was meeting its educational responsibilities. He regarded his memorandum as "a plea for the administrative change necessary to make the educational work of real value to the Province." From his point of view sound management demanded a staff of professional scientific administrators with the power to draft strict laws and regulations and a competent, honest field organization to enforce them. He knew full well that left to themselves the lumbermen would not behave according to proper conservation procedures. *"It is impracticable to introduce forestry measures,"* he emphasized for the Premier's benefit, *"without conflicting with privileges which have long been regarded as rights."* He suggested closer supervision of lumbering operations to ensure that the minimal cutting regulations in force were being followed, and proposed further that the lumbermen be compelled by law to dispose of the debris from their operations rather than leaving it on the forest floor to dry out and eventually catch fire. But the government, if it paid any attention to him at all, was more interested in his memorandum on the subject, "How Forest Revenues can be Increased." Meeting constant opposition from the laymen in the Woods and Forests Branch of the Department of Lands, Forests and Mines, as well as indifference from the leading political figures in the government, Clark decided to make his opinions more widely known in two highly critical papers, one of them delivered to the 1906 Canadian Forestry Convention. This indiscretion led ultimately to a parting of the ways.[32]

[32] PAO, Whitney Papers, Memorandum re: Pulpwood Stumpage Selling, Feb. 3, 1906; Memorandum re: Forestry Education, Feb. 16, 1906; Mem-

Whitney's suspicion of "professionals" and "movements" was entirely understandable under the circumstances. At this time he was, as we shall shortly see, deeply entangled in the coils of the public power movement and preoccupied with reining in the independent professionals associated with that crusade in his government. No doubt he shuddered in horror at the very thought of removing responsibility for huge sections of the public forest from the small, highly profitable and eminently placid Department of Lands, Forests and Mines, and placing it in the hands of a group of uncontrollable, arrogant young professionals, like Judson F. Clark, in a Department of Forestry. Between Adam Beck and Judson Clark, who could say how long his government could stay solvent? Whitney did, however, follow up Southworth's proposal of a Bureau of Forestry and Colonization, but he refused to give it jurisdiction over the forest reserves. In fact, since the prime responsibility of the Bureau would be the reforestation of desolate, abandoned farmlands in southern Ontario, Whitney moved the Bureau right out of the Department of Lands, Forests and Mines, away from those pedestrian bureaucrats in charge of selling timber, into the Department of Agriculture where philosophizing would kindle no animosities. An obviously disappointed Thomas Southworth slipped quietly into a job in private industry shortly after, and the mercurial Judson Clark fled to a position with a British Columbia lumber company. Behind the proud conservation rhetoric, all the government really had to show for its boasting about businesslike management was the resignation of its two most capable, if a little outspoken, advocates of the principle. [33]

Lumbermen could hardly be expected to practise the proper forestry methods without close government supervision. The forest reserves as it turned out were little more than private

---

orandum re: Section 140 (i) of the University Bill, April 27, 1906; "How Forest Revenues Can Be Increased," marked cabinet only, April 30, 1906; *Canadian Forestry Journal*, "Woodland Taxation," 1905, pp. 160-72; *RCFC*, pp. 164-70.

[33] Lambert and Pross, *Renewing Nature's Wealth*, pp. 186-93; *Greater Ontario*, pp. 10, 33; *Northern Ontario: Its Progress and Development Under the Whitney Government* (Toronto, 1913).

preserves for the lumber industry which could be raided and plundered by anyone with political influence—especially after 1914. Nor could the government be expected to fulfill its conservation pledges without making provision for the strict enforcement of protective legislation—which it did not. Yet neither the government nor the public at large would sanction the expenditure of large sums on forest management; the forest was something from which revenue was derived, not something upon which money was to be spent. While concerned about the problem, everyone wanted to believe that it could be legislated out of existence by passing a few mild, completely unenforceable cutting regulations which Thomas Southworth, for one, feared were "such as to be unnecessary, and from a forestry standpoint ineffective."[34]

This was the age of industrial innocence and good feeling, a time when a man's honour—even a lumberman's—still counted for something. This is probably best symbolized by that flimsy affidavit upon which the revenues of the crown depended. Perhaps the enlightened self-interest so prominently on display at the annual Forestry Conventions would carry the day. Overwhelming popular support, a clear legislative mandate, and effective political leadership are the prerequisites of government regulation in a liberal, democratic society.[35] The conservation movement could not stir Ontario society that deeply; it raised feeling but did not rouse passion and had more impact upon rhetoric than policy. It has been argued that regulatory bureaucracies arise not from an accumulating series of administrative pressures, but rather as a response to an exogenous "concatenation of circumstances," usually a sudden, often catastrophic exposure of some social evil.[36] It took a terrifying sequence of forest fires (42 people died at Rainy Lake in 1910, 73 at Porcupine the next year, and 224 persons perished

---

[34] Southworth, "Ontario's Progress Towards a Rational Forestry System," *Canadian Forestry Journal*, Dec., 1907, p. 163.

[35] Bernstein, *Regulating Business by Independent Commission* (Princeton, 1955), p. 284.

[36] Oliver MacDonagh, "The Nineteenth Century Revolution in Government: A Reappraisal," *Historical Journal*, Vol. I (1958), p. 58.

at Matheson in 1916) to lay the foundations for a rational public fire protection system.[37] Tragedy could elicit the response that the conservation movement could not prompt by itself.

Certainly the wanton destruction by fire and waste did not pass without commentators. Bernhard Fernow sniped continually at the administrators of the crown domain over at Queen's Park from his nearby ivory tower at the University of Toronto. "Economic reforms, like social reforms," he pointed out in one of his regular attacks on the Department of Lands, Forests and Mines, "find their greatest obstacles in the conservatism, or less euphemistically, in the inertia which the daily usage, the routine, imparts...." He even used his contribution to *Canada and Its Provinces* as a platform for some uncomplimentary remarks concerning timber management in Ontario: "As yet the forests are viewed solely as a source of current revenue, not as capital, and the rights of the people and of posterity are sacrificed." And he could say this after almost a decade of rule by a party that claimed to regard timber as capital. Whenever self-important Ontario cabinet ministers delivered themselves on the subject of "The Progress of Forestry in Ontario," the *Canadian Forestry Journal* could be relied upon to provide a sobering tonic.[38] And so it went.

The conservation message did not penetrate deeply enough into the conscience of the province. It would not make any significant progress into legislation for another generation. Ironically, the very advantage the Canadian conservation movement possessed over its American counterpart, a settled forest ownership situation, tended to impair its effectiveness. The ownership question is what gave the American movement its momentum. Public ownership of forest lands was a relatively simple issue which ordinary, non-professional people could understand, with which they could readily identify. It was the formula that reduced all the technical language to a simple,

---

[37] Lambert and Pross, *Renewing Nature's Wealth*, pp. 212ff.

[38] Bernhard Fernow, "Forest Resources and Problems of Canada," p. 133; A. Shortt and O. Doughty, *Canada and Its Provinces*, Vol. XVIII (Toronto, 1914), p. 599; *Canadian Forestry Journal*, Dec. 1913, pp. 181-3; Dec. 1914, p. 122.

clear-cut choice. The professionals who had aroused that indignation, that sense of intolerability, stood ready to channel it into constructive programs. The absence of the ownership issue emasculated the Canadian conservation movement—the Canadian forests were already publicly owned—and reduced it to a prodding and not particularly effective conscience. As an educational movement it could continue to accumulate evidence, but without a crusading issue it could not bring about that all-important "concatenation of circumstances." Under these conditions the will and interests of the client industry governed the degree to which conservation ideals would influence government policy. Thus it was the lumberman's rather than the professional forester's view of conservation that triumphed, and would for a long time to come.

# 6
# Hydro
# As Myth

❖

When T. C. Keefer, professional engineer and transportation philosopher, delivered the last presidential address of the nineteenth century to the Royal Society of Canada, it might have been expected that he would reflect back upon the industrial progress he had spent the better part of a full life promoting.[1] Instead, he chose to look forward to yet another industrial revolution which, he predicted, lay just ahead in the dawning century. Surveying the advances in the science of electrical generation and transmission that had taken place during the eighties and nineties, Keefer foresaw that hydro-electricity

---

[1] T. C. Keefer, "Canadian Water Power and Its Electrical Product in Relation to the Undeveloped Resources of the Dominion," May 23, 1899, Royal Society of Canada, *Proceedings and Transactions*, 2nd Series, Vol. V., 1899, pp. 3-40. This speech was reprinted in consecutive issues of the *Canadian Engineer,* August 1899, pp. 91-4, and September, pp. 124-7. For a brief survey of his ideas and career, see my introduction to T. C. Keefer, *The Philosphy of Railroads* (Toronto, 1972).

would soon provide a cheaper, more versatile energy source for existing industry. But even more significantly, he anticipated that the by-products and applications of electrical technology would bring to Canada entirely new manufacturing processes. In a steam-driven age central Canada had naturally lagged behind Great Britain and the United States because it lacked coal; however, the electrical twentieth century forecast an imminent redress of that imbalance. The development of Canada's superabundant waterpowers using existing technology would draw industries to Canada, such as aluminum, paper, carbide, abrasives, chemical, and electro-metallurgical factories, that had not even been in existence a decade earlier.

Over and above the employment benefits provided by this new industrialism, Keefer declared its most important characteristic would be the use of raw materials which Canada also possessed but which, until the advent of hydro-electric power, could not be economically utilized. Taking the paper industry as an example, Keefer explained: "Heretofore we have cut our spruce into deals and exported it to Europe, and more recently into pulp wood and exported that to the United States; but manufactured by our water power into paper, the raw material would yield this country ten times the value it is now exported for." In the future Canada's own "white coal" of falling water would deliver the dominion from its "hewer of wood" servitude to American industry and its bondage to American coal; it would speed smokeless, silent trains over vast distances; mine and electrolytically refine the complex ores of the Shield, raise new cities in the forest, brighten the streets of existing cities, and lighten the drudgery of menial tasks. The application of modern electrical science to Canada's unique combination of natural resources practically guaranteed the coming, Keefer proclaimed, of a second industrial revolution. Hydro bore the promise of greatness in this, the engineer's counterpart to Laurier's "Canada's Century" speech.

I

In a coal-starved province, businessmen, manufacturers, investors, newspapermen and politicians eagerly seized upon hydro as a symbol of the anxiously awaited new industrialism. Water-power, the Toronto *News* confidently predicted, would "make Ontario the Pennsylvania of Canada and build up a flourishing industrial community where good wages and profitable investments would be the general order." Furthermore, hydro had distinct advantages over coal, for it was available in infinite supply and left no sooty, offensive residues. Years later Hector Charlesworth, the Toronto journalist and editor, remembered the exhilaration of learning that "a source of energy as vast as the entire soft coal deposits of Pennsylvania had by some miraculous process been transferred to Canadian soil and by another miracle made not only clean but inexhaustible as the widow's curse." An excited engineer foresaw a giant grid of hydro-electric generating stations stretching from Labrador to the Lakehead: "Indeed, by the end of the twentieth century the Ottawa Valley may be the power heart of the world and the centre of a delightful district unsullied by coal smoke and beautified by reservoirs of unrivalled natural beauty."[2]

It was this curious transcending quality of hydro as a symbol that charged its utility with mass, emotional fascination. Because it existed in harmony with the rational and the romantic world, hydro-electric power could resolve the paradox of ugliness that had blighted nineteenth-century industrialism; it could create factories *and* natural beauty. Since hydro was at once a triumph of rational scientific progress and a mysterious elemental force, the myth of hydro appealed to both practical and poetic instincts.

At the practical level, the great "Coal Famine" of 1902 transferred the engineer's frustration at Canada's dependence upon foreign sources of energy to the businessman, workingman and homeowner in terms they could understand. During the summer a series of bloody strikes in the Pennsylvania coalfields halted all coal shipments to Ontario. Looking ahead to a chilly October, the Berlin *Daily Telegraph* noted the empty coal bins about town and expressed the anxiety of every householder

---

[2] *News*, May 12, 1905; Hector Charlesworth, *The Canadian Scene* (Toronto, 1927), p. 208; engineer quoted in John Dales, *Hydroelectricity and Industrial Development: Quebec, 1898-1940* (Cambridge, Massachusetts, 1957), p. 257.

on the threshold of a Canadian winter. In its columns Smyth Brothers Cheap Cash Store advertised temporary domestic substitutes for scarce coal, "Fine Wool Blankets and Iderdown Comforts." But for factory owners and workmen the situation was considerably more serious, for inordinate power costs occasioned by rapidly rising coal prices closed down the mills, throwing hundreds out of work. In the spring of 1902 a ton of coal could be bought in Toronto for $5, but by July the price had risen to $6.50, and by September to $9.50. A boatload of Welsh coal arriving in October was emptied at $10 a ton. The coal famine dramatized in cruelly simple terms the Ontario dependence upon American energy. Hydro promised deliverance from this expensive and degrading subordination. Even before the coal strikes the *Globe* had chuckled: "There will be a very comfortable feeling in the knowledge that the gentlemen who sit in their parlor in New York and fix the price of bituminous coal for all of eastern North America will take less toll of the people of Toronto."[3]

The very magnitude and mystery of the tunnels, turbines and, of course, the Niagara Falls themselves were enough to captivate the public imagination. Never before, the promoters of the developments reminded their audiences, had works of such gigantic proportions and scientific complexity been attempted anywhere in the world. In their efforts to explain the undertakings, publicists and newspaper reporters drew upon familiar agricultural images, such as "tamed" and "harnessed," and freely mixed in the military metaphors of "conquest" and "triumph" to convey the co-ordination and power required to accomplish such mythological "labours." The reputation of this Wonder of the World, the frightening rush of its dark waters and the fearsome roar of its cascade, were known to almost every citizen of Ontario. Drawing upon this personal knowledge, the promoters of the hydro-electric works were thus able to hold their after-dinner audiences spellbound

³ Berlin *Daily Telegraph*, Oct. 8, 1902; *Monetary Times*, Sept. 19, Oct. 3, 10, 17, 1902; *Globe*, April 13, 1900; E. B. Biggar, *Hydro-Electric Development in Ontario* (Toronto, 1924), p. 27; Merrill Denison, *The People's Power* (Toronto, 1906), p. 27; see also PAO, Whitney Papers, municipal resolutions in support of the 1906 Power Bill, each of which mentions the dependence upon Pennsylvania coal.

with stories of battle against seemingly irresistible forces. Frederic Nicholls' tale of the adventure of his Electrical Development Company's engineers groping their way behind the curtain of water, over slime-covered rocks, through thundering whirlwinds of spray to the very centre of the Horseshoe Falls, was unquestionably the best of this genre.[4] The romantic aura of Niagara itself imparted a special appeal to the hydro myth.

The epic of Niagara had implications that transcended the private ambition of a group of companies; it represented another episode in the continuing struggle "for the possession of power—not the mere animal power of political rule, but the actual subjection of the forces of nature." Victory in this engagement with the elements assured Ontario a place in the mainstream of civilization and success in the Darwinian "struggle for eminence": "The wealth of an imperial dominion and the progress and prosperity of a powerful people," the *Globe* proclaimed, "solicit the attention of all who are joined to mankind in the subjugation and enjoyment of nature."[5]

On the one hand the engineer was locked in mortal combat *against* the forces of nature, yet at the same time he consciously strove to be in harmony *with* nature's mysteries. Capitalists, engineers and workmen, operating with military precision, battled valiantly against the "furious waters" that threatened and often succeeded in sweeping their feeble schemes to destruction over the brink. Their aim was the subjugation of the raw and wild, the domestication of elemental forces to man's ordered plan. The *Globe*'s description of the Electrical Development Company's powerhouse, a "stately building of classical design" constructed "to house the monster generators," unintentionally conveyed that intent.[6]

---

[4] Speech to the Toronto Empire Club, Jan. 19, 1905, "Niagara's Power: Past, Present, Prospective," in *Empire Club Speeches* (Toronto, 1905), pp. 159 ff.

[5] *Globe*, Aug. 5, 1905, a special Saturday issue on Power, Light and Heat; see also the *Monetary Times*, Sept. 30, Oct. 7, 14, 28, 1904.

[6] *Globe*, Aug. 5, 1905; on conceptions of nature, see Leo Marx, *The Machine in the Garden* (New York, 1967); Hans Huth, *Nature and the Americans* (Berkeley, 1957); A. A. Ekirch, Jr., *Man and Nature in America* (New York, 1963), and Roderick Nash, *Wilderness and the American Mind* (New Haven, 1967).

While this struggle for mastery formed the dominant theme of the Niagara imagery, a conscious effort to co-operate with nature's awesome master plan sustained a continuous counterpoint. An Ontario Power Company engineer stressed the essential unity of his work and nature's landscape as he outlined for his fellow engineers "a long but unobtrusive building, its farther end obscured by the spray from the great cataract. It [the powerhouse in the gorge] is of modest though massive design and its colours almost blend with those of the overhanging cliff." The Vice-President of the same company, Major-General Francis Vinton Greene, a charming former military historian and distinguished police commissioner of New York city, claimed compatibility not only with the physical setting, but more especially with God's own managerial intent:

> It is a spectacle second only to the Falls themselves as a mighty manifestation of the works of God upon earth, to walk through one of the great power houses at Niagara, and in profound silence, with only a half a dozen operators in sight, watch the wires and transformers and recording instruments through which is invisibly and noiselessly passing a titanic force on which depend the light, the transportation, and many of the industries of hundreds of thousands of people scores of miles away.

Like a "genie out of the bottle," Frederic Nicholls explained for the benefit of the Toronto Empire Club in 1905, the electricity from his powerhouse at Niagara would fly invisibly and mystically through slender copper wires to factories and homes in Toronto where it would "expand into a force that is terrifying when uncontrolled." In the same vein, one reporter covering the construction phase of a powerhouse paused momentarily in his technical narrative to note the "strange subterranean silence" that attended the underground work: "Strange men from far countries with quaint beliefs helped to dig and build. The rats were safe among them, for the bloodshed might bring evil on the place. No man dared whistle in this cavern, because the spirits of air are at enmity with the spirits of earth and water."[7]

---

[7] Paul N. Nunn, *The Development of the Ontario Power Company* (Niagara Falls, 1905), p. 5; General Francis Vinton Greene, "Niagara Power and the Future

Although the mysticism of hydro-electric development represented but a minor theme in the larger opus of conquest and scientific triumph over the forces of nature, its presence serves to represent the basic ambivalence of North Americans towards nature. Within the imagery of hydro the symbols of reverence for nature and war against it constantly clashed. This clash of rational and romantic elements is probably best illustrated by an artist's impression of the Shawinigan Falls power development which featured a Christ-like figure draped in flowing classic robes, its head uplifted and ringed with a halo of lightning bolts, rising as if just unchained from the spray of the base of the falls. On the river bank could be seen the triumphant outcome of this emancipation, a perfect rectangular grid of a town, which a headline revealed to be "A Dream Realized; From Primeval Forest to Busy Mart in Seven Years." The *Globe* captured the two worlds in which the hydro symbolism moved, with its felicitous description of the industry's brief history as a story of "magic merged in business."[8]

Although the complex sensual appeal of its symbolism and the importance of hydro-electricity as a vehicle for rapid industrialization help to account for the warmth of public interest in the question of hydro-electric development, it does not explain why the Ontario government would in time nationalize the industry. Why did Ontario, at such an early date, chart a course of public ownership for this key industry, or to use the words of the Hydro-Electric Power Commission's official historian: "What impelled one Canadian province among all the states of North America...to embark on such a novel experiment?"[9] All that could be said of the impact of Niagara as a symbol in Ontario could also be said of New York State, for example. All regions of North America shared the monopolistic tendencies of the industry; it was generally conceded that both the economics and mechanics of electrical dis-

---

of Ontario," Jan. 10, 1907, in *Empire Club Speeches* (Toronto, 1907), p. 163; Frederic Nicholls, "Niagara's Power," *op. cit.*, p. 151; *Globe*, Aug. 5, 1905.

[8] *Globe*, Aug. 5, 1905; see also the *Monetary Times'* series on the Electrical Development Company during Sept. and Oct. 1904.

[9] Denison, *The People's Power*, p. 2.

tribution made the business, in the American utilities magnate Samuel Insull's happy phrase, a "natural monopoly." But even for a man with his enormous appetite, who claimed "all the electrical energy for a given area must be produced by one concern," Insull restricted the "given area" to mean one metropolitan region. Also, in many regions the public regulation that had come early to the business, often encouraged by the developers themselves, had been quickly extended to the logical conclusion of public, municipal ownership.[10] A select committee of the Ontario Legislature found in 1903, for example, that 126 municipalities within the province operated their own water, gas or electric light plants; a similar study in 1906 for the American mid-west disclosed over 1,250 municipally owned electric light installations.[11] Thus the monopolistic nature of the industry and a tendency towards public ownership at the local level, though significant contributing factors to Ontario's unique state intervention, were continental, even international, phenomena and not in themselves decisive.

In view of the monopolistic character of the industry and its overriding public importance, it might be expected that the province would be called upon to establish a regulatory framework for the distribution of electrical energy in the public interest. But in extending public regulation to provincial owner-ship of the means of distribution, Ontario deviated sharply from the North American norm. The building of provincially owned transmission lines, followed in due course by the na-tionalization of the privately owned powerhouses, depended upon no borrowed precedents, either British or American, but

[10]   Samuel Insull, *Central Station Electric Service* (Chicago, 1915), p. 75; Forest McDonald, *Insull* (Chicago, 1962), p. 114; C. H. Mitchell, *Canadian Hydraulic Power in Canadian Industry*, Water Resources Paper No. 17 (Ottawa, 1916), pp. 36 ff; Walter H. Voskuil, *The Economics of Water Power Development* (Chicago, 1928); Ben W. Lewis, "Public Policy and the Growth of the Power Industry," *Journal of Economic History*, Supplement, Vol. VII (1947), pp. 47-55.

[11]   McDonald, *Insull*, p. 119; Ontario Select Committee on Municipal Trading, *Municipal Trading and Municipal Ownership or Operation of Public Utilities* (Toronto, 1903); see also Blake McKelvey, *The Urbanization of America, 1860-1915* (New Brunswick, 1963), pp. 107-13, and C. N. Glaab and A. T. Brown, *A History of Urban America* (New York, 1967), pp. 183ff.

was rather a product of the unique social and political environment of early twentieth-century Ontario.

The frustrations of retarded development and metropolitan social tensions operating within a statist political tradition—best reflected in public ownership of the waterpower itself—were the key causal factors. These anxieties, charged with the emotional symbolism of Niagara and anti-monopolist feeling, given direction by a charismatic leader, led directly to public ownership of first the distribution facilities and then the generating stations. Adam Beck's mastery of these economic, social, psychological and political forces determined the unique and controversial outcome of public regulation of the hydro-electric industry in Ontario.

## II

As T. C. Keefer's address to the Royal Society of Canada would suggest, the broader implications of hydro-electric development had begun to receive publicity outside of the Niagara district by the late nineties. Of course, interest within the district had been intense for a number of years. The spectacular growth sparked by hydro-electric development on the American side of the Falls exasperated the residents of the Niagara peninsula who had long since grown suspicious of the endless excuses advanced by the Canadian Niagara Power Company for the total lack of progress on its monopoly concession within the park. By the time the first generators turned in the Niagara Power Company plant across the river in 1895, an aluminum company, a carborundum company, and a half a dozen other electro-chemical companies had opened up close by, making the formerly non-existent Niagara Falls market, rather than Buffalo, the company's prime sales area. By the end of 1896 over 13,500 h.p. was being consumed within the city of Niagara Falls, New York, and half of that by new companies using electro-chemical processes which had not even existed only a decade earlier.[12]

[12] Harold Passer, *The Electrical Manufacturers, 1875-1900* (Cambridge,

Presented with this industrial renaissance just across the river, the citizens of the Niagara district became, in the cautious language of the Queen Victoria Niagara Falls Park commissioners, "clamorous for power development." An organization known as the Canadian Niagara Power League, a thinly disguised popular front for a competitive electric company hoping to break the Canadian Niagara Power Company monopoly, quickly sprang up to feed the popular indignation. One of the league's pamphlets, issued in 1897, listed twenty-eight new companies that had recently been set up in Niagara Falls, New York. On the facing page there was a list intended to represent similar newcomers to Niagara Falls, Ontario. The page was blank.[13]

The Canadian Niagara Power Company had filed its plans with the park's commission in 1894 according to the agreement. These plans were duly approved by the commission and the government. But that was where development began and ended. In 1896, after having done nothing at all towards development, the company applied to the commission for an eighteen-month extension, which the latter granted on the grounds that a market for power did not yet exist in the vicinity of Niagara Falls and would not for years to come. The commissioners also took note of the fact that long-distance transmission techniques had not yet been perfected nor generating equipment decided upon. They therefore urged the government to confirm the extension in spite of the "local opposition" that had arisen in the Niagara district. But by this time the local campaign against the phantom Canadian Niagara Power Company and its monopoly had begun to attract widespread sympathy in the press and in the Legislature.[14]

Massachusetts, 1953), pp. 287-93; E. G. Adams, *Niagara Power, 1846-1931,* Vol. I (Niagara Falls, 1927), pp. 202-35; Harold Sharlin, "The First Niagara Falls Power Project," *Business History Review,* Vol. XXXV (1961), pp. 59-73.

[13] *The Situation of Niagara Power in Canada* (Niagara Falls, 1897), pp. 6-7; Queen Victoria Niagara Falls Park Commission, *Report,* 1898, p. 5 [hereafter, QVNFPC, *Report*].

[14] QVNFPC, *Report,* 1894, p. 24; 1895, p. 298; 1896, pp. 24-8; 1897, p.

Premier Hardy, forced by the strength of public opinion to take action, overruled the park's commissioners' decision and ordered the company to stand by its 1892 promises. To clarify his own position and give a hint of what might result, he also asked the Supreme Court of Ontario to rule whether the total absence of construction prescribed by the agreement at the 1897 deadline constituted a breach of contract which would thereby void the company's rights. The court found that the terms of the original 1892 agreement made it impossible to cancel the company's privileges until November 1, 1899, when the power plant would have to exist as promised or the water rights could be revoked. Nevertheless, before the final showdown could take place the government and the company worked out a satisfactory compromise. In July of 1899 the company relinquished its monopoly on the Canadian side of the Falls. In return the government extended the company's time limit, allowed it to proceed with its works, and reduced the rental rates to compensate for the competition being allowed. The compromise satisfied all of the parties. The company could develop its franchise practically at its leisure, the eager rivals that had sprung up would be given opportunities to apply for their own power concessions, the government had averted another confrontation, and the Niagara district could be pacified with the assurance of major hydro-electric development at the Falls in the very near future.[15]

The furor raised by the Canadian Niagara Power Company defiance served to further publicize the significance of hydro-electric development in the province. After the monopoly at the Falls had been broken the *Monetary Times* confidently predicted that within two years the city of Toronto would be receiv-

---

5; Niagara Falls, Board of Trade, *Niagara Power: Report Containing Information Concerning the Development of Electrical Power at Niagara Falls* (Niagara Falls, 1897); *Monetary Times*, July 8, 1898; Nov. 24, 1899.

[15] QVNFPC, *Report*, 1897, p. 10; 1899, pp. 4, 11; PAO, Whitney Papers, J. Harrison Pew to Whitney, Feb. 9, Mar. 8, 11, 1899, private; *Globe*, Mar. 8, 1899; Hector Charlesworth, *Candid Chronicles* (Toronto, 1925), pp. 176-7.

ing its power from far-off Niagara. And that was one of the least extravagant predictions. Within this atmosphere of excitement and conflicting claims the Toronto Board of Trade set up a special committee on April 25, 1900, chaired by W.E.H. Massey to get the facts about the new power source that was generating so much interest. In their report, the cautious businessmen who made up the committee warned their colleagues against the many exaggerations in circulation. They concluded that electricity would remain "a secondary force, a handmaid or servant of steam or some other primary power." Its use would be confined to small plants whose limited power requirements rendered a large steam plant uneconomical. Ultimately, however, in its own unenthusiastic manner, the Massey committee confirmed the importance of the new energy source:

> While electric power is not the all-important inducement in procuring new industries that is generally supposed, your Committee believe that cheap electric power would be a great boon to our city, especially to smaller manufacturers, and that reasonable measures should be taken to procure a power connection with one of the companies operating at Niagara Falls.[16]

Hydro generated the greatest excitement amongst the smaller manufacturers who used mechanical power rather than heat in their industrial processes. Within the Boards of Trade of the industrial towns of Toronto's hinterland, where this class of manufacturer predominated, this enthusiasm was heightened by the anxiety that "Hogtown" would be able, through its advantages of size and influence, to capture the entire output of Niagara to serve its own metropolitan ambitions.

---

[16] Toronto Board of Trade, *Annual Report*, 1900, Report of the Special Committee on Electric Power, April 25, 1900, pp. 7-8. Besides Massey, the committee included Elias Rogers, a prominent fuel merchant; William Stone, who owned a small manufacturing firm; and A. E. Kemp, a metal wares manufacturer and trust company director.

The power question took on greater urgency with the letting of new concessions and an actual start on the construction of the powerhouses. A syndicate of Buffalo industrialists which had been waiting in the wings since 1887 received the second hydro-electric franchise from the Ontario government for their Ontario Power Company in April of 1900. John Joseph Albright, a graduate of Rensselaer Polytechnical Institute and a successful coal supplier of the steel industry, was the moving spirit behind the Ontario Power Company. The board of directors consisted of men much like him, from wealthy second or third generation commercial families. The Toronto law firm of Blake, Lash and Cassels had negotiated the agreement with the Ontario government, but after 1905 General Francis Vinton Greene assumed major responsibility for the company's public and political relations. Ownership of the Ontario Power Company differed markedly from that of the Canadian Niagara Company. The leading directors of the former were the most prominent industrialists and financiers of the Buffalo region rather than, in the latter case, of the national metropolis, New York.[17]

As the new Ontario Power Company and the older Canadian Niagara Power Company broke ground for their separate projects in 1902, the commissioners of the park opened a series of public hearings to determine whether another waterpower lease, in addition to the two already in existence, might be let. The two hydraulic engineers retained by the commission to study how much water could be diverted without a serious reduction in the beauty of the cascade reported that there remained both water and a site for one more company. Accepting their advice and dismissing the defensive objections of the two companies that had just begun construction, the commissioners—supported by the government—granted a third concession in 1903 to three Toronto financiers: William Mackenzie,

[17] QVNFPC, *Report*, 1899, p. 25; 1901, pp. 19-24; *Poor's Manual of the Railroads of the United States*, Vol. XLI, 1908; Ontario Hydro Archives, Ontario Power Company, Minutes of Meetings of Directors, Vol. III, *passim*; PAC, Laurier Papers, Lord Grey to Laurier, May 10, 1906, 203628-38; *Dictionary of American Biography*, Vol. VII, p. 565.

Frederic Nicholls, and Henry Mill Pellatt, the first Canadians to obtain rights at Niagara Falls.[18] Amid much éclat their Electrical Development Company began tunnelling during 1904.

Ironically the Canadian obsession with railroads, which had led to the refusal by Canadian interests of the waterpower franchise in 1891, eventually had led Canadian entrepreneurs by a distant and circuitous route back to Niagara Falls a decade later. At the end of the Spanish American War, Dr. F. S. Pearson, a street railroad promoter from New York who had met the leading members of the Canadian financial community in connection with the flotation of bonds for the maritime iron and coal industry, succeeded in turning Canadian investors towards Caribbean and South American business opportunities. According to the *Monetary Times*, Sir William Van Horne had been the first Canadian "to take advantage in a large way of the change that took place in Cuba," and the success of his Cuban railways led to an immediate proliferation in Latin America of street railways financed in Canada.[19] Toronto capital invaded Brazil, Argentina and Mexico; Montreal dominated Jamaica and Cuba. Because these tramways were the first industries to use electricity, the traction companies also had to provide their own thermal or hydro-electric power stations, with the happy result that the railway franchises generally contained clauses granting monopolies of steam heat and electric power service, a characteristic reflected in their titles: Sao Paulo Tram-

---

[18] QVNFPC, *Report*, 1902, for full text of hearings, pp. 51-105; Pellatt–Nicholls–Mackenzie agreement, Jan. 29, 1903, in *ibid*., 1903, pp. 30-40. Former contracts had specifically forbidden the transfer of rights from one party to another, or one company to another, but this syndicate received permission to convey their rights to a corporation. Accordingly, when the Electrical Development Company received its letters patent, Mar. 21, 1903, the aforementioned sold their rights to the company for $6,100,000. The first $6,000,000 was paid in stock and the $100,000 in cash, all of this for an original outlay for the franchise of only $30,000. See Ontario Hydro Archives [hereafter, OHA], Electrical Development Company of Ontario Ltd., Minute Book, No. 1, pp. 1-9.

[19] *Monetary Times*, Oct. 19, 1900. Van Horne attributed his initiatives to a chance meeting with the Cuban Ambassador to the United States; see PAC, Sr. Gonzala de Quesada y Arostegui Papers, Memoire, "The Iron Horse in East Cuba," 1929; Van Horne to Arostegui, Oct. 15, 1901; April 21, 1909; July 16, 1910; Jan. 17, 1911; Jan. 12, 1912.

way, Light and Power; Mexican Light, Heat and Power; and Trinidad Electric and Railway Company.[20]

These tropical investments, B. E. Walker told an English correspondent, possessed the distinct advantage "of being based upon charters given by countries very anxious indeed to have development take place and not having socialist views or envy of those who may make money out of such charters."[21] Whatever the risks of "political revolutions, etc.," which Walker conceded were very real, the profits were appropriately phenomenal. In 1905 the *Monetary Times* reported that the interest alone from these securities amounted to more than a million dollars annually.[22] Canadian finance discovered not only the electrical industry in the tropics; it also developed confidence and self-respect. As a result of these investments, the *Monetary Times* boasted, "Canadian finance is becoming a power in the world which has to be reckoned with."[23] The confidence and technical skill required to launch an enterprise as large as the Electrical Development Company flowed directly from this flowering of Canadian capitalism. All of the key promoters of the company had participated in the Latin American traction boom; furthermore, their ambitions at Niagara were prompted by the necessity of supplying power to their existing street railway and electric light franchises in Toronto.

---

[20] All of these companies were promoted by the mysterious Dr. F. S. Pearson, a key figure in the history of Canadian entrepreneurship and high finance, about whom very little is known. For a brief description of the financing of these utilities and the marketing of their securities, see Lord Beaverbrook, *Courage: The Story of Sir James Dunn* (Fredericton, 1961), p. 61; PAC, Dunn Papers, Vol. 252, Dunn to Martin Schiff, Feb. 28, 1907; Vol. 249, Dunn to Robert Fleming, Sept. 14, 1906 among many.

[21] University of Toronto, Walker Papers, Byron Walker to Henry J. Gardiner, Feb. 27, 1908; see also, PAC, Porteous Papers, Vol. 20, C. E. L. Porteous to James Ross, Mar. 17, 1898.

[22] *Monetary Times*, July 7, 1905. For rapid increases in the value of South American traction stocks, see Toronto Board of Trade, *Annual Report*, 1902, 1903, 1904, 1905, "Highest-Lowest Stock Quotations." See also the *Monetary Times*, Nov. 4, 1904; Feb. 10, 1905; Nov. 10, 1905; March 16, 1906. Sao Paulo shares quoted at $50 in 1902 tripled in value in three years.

[23] *Monetary Times*, July 7, 1905.

From the outset the financial press beamed with pride that Canadian capital had sufficiently matured to be able to undertake such a "Colossal Industrial Enterprise." Commenting on a tour of a group of engineering students through the Electrical Development Company excavations, the *Monetary Times* noted: "It is not many years since great industrial works like these, if attempted at all, would have been supplied with American and British money, and probably conducted entirely by foreign engineers. Canadian energy and Canadian capital are here giving a lesson to the world." What is more, the promoters were not only Canadians, they were worthy of the highest compliment the financial press could bestow; they were "practical men...for each of them has had experience in railway building or electrical works."[24] It had been a long but profitable excursion through tropical tramway and hydro-electric investments, but at long last Canadian capitalism arrived at Niagara in 1903.

William Mackenzie, a railroad man, Frederic Nicholls, an electrical engineer, and Henry Mill Pellatt, a general financier-entrepreneur, personified the three worlds which had converged to make the Electrical Development Company possible. Hydro-electric development demanded technical competence and a heavy capital investment, and for the first time, through the men of this generation, Canada could provide both.

In 1892 Mackenzie left his western railroad contracting partnership with Donald Mann, James Ross and Herbert Holt to modernize and take over the management of Toronto's street railroad. In combination with his Toronto and Montreal friends, Mackenzie moved on to do the same in Winnipeg, Montreal, Saint John, Birmingham, and of course, in the Caribbean. With the profits from these street railway investments, Mackenzie would later return to trunk railroading with his former partner, Donald Mann, but this time as an owner.[25]

Frederic Nicholls, who had only arrived from England in 1874, had managed to raise enough money amongst the

---

[24] *Ibid.*, Sept. 30; Oct. 7, 14, 28; Nov. 4, 1904.

[25] G. R. Stevens, *Canadian National Railways* (Toronto, 1962), Vol. II, p. 36; H. J. Morgan's *Canadian Men and Women of the Time* (Toronto, 1912), pp. 701-2.

Toronto merchants and manufacturers to establish the steam-powered Toronto Incandescent Light Company which went into business in 1891. When it merged with a failing arc light company under the title of the Toronto Electric Light Company, Nicholls' group held a monopoly over the supply of steam-generated electric power and the municipal street lighting franchise. From this success Nicholls led a larger group of Torontonians into an electrical equipment manufacturing business which went on to greater heights under the name the Canadian General Electric Company. As a secretary of the Canadian Manufacturers' Association in the 1880s, editor of the *Canadian Manufacturer*, and president in 1896 of the National Electric Light Association of America, Nicholls was a highly regarded spokesman for both manufacturing and the hydro-electric industry. To the *Canadian Engineer* he represented its ideal; with a full-page portrait it entered Nicholls in the "gallery of men who have 'done things'...to develop the resources and shape the destinies of the greatest colony of the British Empire."[26] Nicholls' electric company and Mackenzie's street railway naturally complemented each other, and although the two companies remained separate, in short order the director-ships merged.

In contrast with Mackenzie and Nicholls who had worked their way up, Henry Mill Pellatt, the son of a stockbroker, had been "born to be a director, to sit on boards, to preside at meetings...." The investment of other people's money for mutual profit came effortlessly to him. He got his start in north-west lands, then bought into Toronto utilities, promoted Nova Scotia coal and steel, jumped eagerly into South American utilities, and moved in Alberta coal and Cobalt silver when those fields opened up. A commanding and pompous figure of baronial habits, Pellatt became involved in Niagara power for two reasons: his investments had gained him the presidency of the Toronto Electric Light Company, and in that capacity he was interested in securing a cheap supply of electricity to

[26] E. N. Ashworth, *Toronto Hydro Recollections* (Toronto, 1955), chapter one; and Morgan, *Canadian Men and Women of the Time*, p. 861; *Canadian Engineer*, Vol. XII, July, 1905, p. 195.

meet the expanding needs of a growing city. Secondly, as a broker with experience in Latin American hydro-electric securities, Pellatt recognized the enormous profits to be reaped from the successful flotation of an enterprise the size of the Electrical Development Company. To all three men, whose businesses had become indistinguishably merged in the public mind, Niagara power was both a business and a speculative proposition.[27]

It would appear that the principals planned to organize the Electrical Development Company according to the pattern set by the South American and Caribbean utilities flotations. In the first place construction would be financed from the sale of bonds; the stock was to be distributed *pro rata* as a bonus. As a rule, a large and representative syndicate would be organized to take the bonds of the company (at a discount and on a 10 per cent margin) with the bonus stock thrown in to sweeten the deal. A second and usually much larger block of bonds and bonus stock would be placed with a group of English investment houses on the same terms for distribution among their clients. During the next stage of promotion the stock of the company would be manipulated by insiders trading to induce wider public interest and confidence. Then, ever so gradually, the syndicate would begin to unload its bonds and stock—at a considerable premium—onto the market thus created. Profits from these transfers, plus interest on the securities held, allowed the members of the syndicate to retain substantial holdings without having to pay any more than the initial margin. Of course, on a successful venture, the insiders' profits would be enormous. It was thought that in the immature Canadian capital market of the time this was the only way to float an

---

[27] Augustus Bridle, *Sons of Canada* (Toronto, 1916), p. 246; Morgan, *Canadian Men and Women of the Time*, p. 894; Frederick Griffin, *Major-General Sir Henry Mill Pellatt, V. C. O., D. C. L., V. D.: A Gentleman of Toronto* (Toronto, 1939). For details of organization, the varieties and proportions of credit instruments used, see C. A. S. Hall, "Electrical Utilities in Ontario under Private Ownership, 1890-1914," (unpublished Ph.D. thesis, University of Toronto, 1968, pp. 52-94), 155-89.

enterprise of any magnitude. The plan had worked many times before, and it would certainly be tried many times again.[28]

The prosperity of the late nineties had built up a respectable pool of capital, especially in the hands of the insurance companies, which sought profitable outlets. Securities like those of the Electrical Development Company would ultimately be taken up by these institutions partly as a result of interlocking directorates but partly on their own merits. The stock and bonds of the company would also find a small but eager market among the Toronto business classes already familiar with the successes of Mackenzie, Nicholls and Pellatt.[29] In London the underwriting was to be handled by the firm of Chaplin, Milne, Grenfell and Co., who had previously placed a number of Canadian and South American utilities issues.

Membership in the Electrical Development Company syndicate was drawn from an identifiable social group, centred in Toronto, whose interests were related through a number of varied companies. At the top, besides the principals, the

[28] For a description of the formal instruments and institutions of the market, see E. P. Neufeld, *The Financial System of Canada: Its Growth and Development* (Toronto, 1972), pp. 468-90. My conception of the process of corporate finance is based upon a reading of the Porteous and Dunn Papers. C. E. L. Porteous was financial secretary to James Ross and William Mackenzie between 1884 and 1900. By 1906 James Dunn had graduated to London where he, in association with Dr. F. S. Pearson and Robert Fleming, carried on the business of floating utilities and traction companies. Professor Hall, who takes a somewhat more sympathetic view of the "innovative" financial manoeuvrings of the Electric Development Company promoters, nevertheless provides information confirming that capital stock, which accounted for 37.4% of the company's liabilities, brought no cash whatever into the company treasury before 1908. Hall, "Electrical Utilities in Ontario under Private Ownership, 1890-1944," tables, pp. 82, 136-8.

[29] The exotic South American stocks aside, the solid, respectable Toronto Electric Light $100 shares never paid less than 7% after 1891 and in 1903 traded as high as 160, see *Poor's Manual*, 1909, No. 42, p. 1806; see also, Ian Drummond, "Canadian Life Insurance Companies and the Capital Market, 1890-1914," *CJEPS*, Vol. XXVII (1962), pp. 204-24, and Hall, "Electrical Utilities in Ontario under Private Ownership, 1890-1914," pp. 155-174.

syndicate was led by the Hon. George Albertus Cox, senator, insurance company president, and capitalist. From there the list of Electrical Development Company shareholders ran down through the middle ranks of Toronto manufacturers to the small retailers who had bought into the original electric light company in the 1880s. Included were the Lieutenant-Governor, Sir Mortimer Clark, the Postmaster General, Sir William Mulock, B. E. Walker, the general manager of the Bank of Commerce, and directors of Sun Life, Canada Life, Manufacturer's Life, National Trust, and the Toronto Electric Light Companies. Members of the Montreal financial community who were both personal friends of the Toronto promoters and associates with them in the Toronto Railway Company, men like James Ross, Herbert Holt, Sir William Van Horne, Senator Forget, Sir F. W. Borden, and C. E. L. Porteous, · were also given a position in the flotation. A web of interlocking directorships, then, linked the Electrical Development Company directly with the Bank of Commerce, which arranged its banking, the National Trust, which took up some of its bonds, the Toronto Electric Light and Toronto Railway companies, Toronto General Trusts, Canadian General Electric, the Canadian Northern and the life insurance companies already mentioned. More often than not the individuals holding bonds and stock of the Electrical Development Company had also invested in Havana Traction, Sao Paulo Tramway, Mexican Heat, Light and Power, Rio de Janeiro Tramway, Dominion Lands and the maritime coal and steel companies. Their offices could be found buried behind the new Greek façades ranged along King Street, and their homes in the ultra-respectable sections of the city, along St. George, around the crescent at Queen's Park, the north end of Sherbourne, and the middle stretches of Jarvis streets.[30]

---

[30] OHA, Electrical Development Company, Minute Book No. I, List of Shareholders at Oct. 2, 1905 special general meeting, pp. 107-10; bondholders, pp. 27-8.

   A comparison of the social origins of American and Canadian businessmen involved in hydro-electric development at Niagara Falls superficially suggests the greater opportunity for upward social mobility in Canada's relatively backward yet expanding economy at the time. A survey of 24 prominent businessmen associated with the Electrical Development

High finance preoccupied these aggressive men in mid-career. They knew how to buy franchises, manipulate stock, and borrow from a multitude of sources on the slightest assets, but unfortunately for the Electrical Development Company, they discovered too late the ultimate foundation of public support upon which the success of their enterprise depended. They ignored Samuel Insull's warning to his colleagues in the electrical distributing business: "Unless you can so conduct your business as to get the good will of the community in which you are working, you might as well shut up shop and move away."[31] The brusque habits picked up in negotiating contracts with Latin American dictatorships and pliant colonial administrators hardly suited the management of such an important public service industry in Ontario. Moreover, the record of bad service and arrogance established by both the Toronto Street Railway and the Toronto Electric Light companies had built up a substantial stock of public ill will which the Electrical Development Company inherited through its identical directorate. Thus, despite its popularity in financial and professional circles, the Electrical Development Company grew up in an environment of public hostility.

At the company's cornerstone-laying ceremony in 1906, Walker felt compelled to remind Canadians of the debt they owed the millionaires, the pilots of industrial progress:

---

Company reveals 12 former farm boys, 8 sons of businessmen, 7 immigrants, and 2 ministers' sons; only two of the total were born in Toronto. Aside from the immigrants, 15 had moved to Toronto during the 1880s from Ontario's sleepy farm towns. Eight came from what might be considered "well-off" families, 6 possessed some form of higher education according to the standards of the day, and almost all had a grammar school background. Nine had risen through various corporations, railroads or banks; 3 had made their initial capital in railroad finance. All were of British extraction, all were Protestant, the breakdown as closely as could be determined: 7 Anglicans, 7 Presbyterians, and 9 Methodists.

Although the sample is admittedly small, one might draw the tentative conclusions from it that the educational attainment of the group was significantly lower than that of the American group and that the proportion of farmers' sons and immigrants was noticeably higher. Upward social mobility through business would seem to have been more likely in late nineteenth-century Canada than in contemporary United States. See above, chapter one, note 44.

[31] McDonald, *Insull*, p. 114.

I know of no way in which we can reach the complex industrial condition we hope to reach unless the people are grateful for having the great captains of industry who possess expert ability and experience for the carrying out of great works. It often irritates me when I hear people talking lightly of great works of industry, people who never put their minds to it to understand what it means to carry such works to completion.

Works such as those at Niagara, he warned, "...are not the kind of works which it is given to commissions and politicians to carry on." Frederic Nicholls used the same occasion to recount the tremendous financial risks and personal perils that the project had entailed. "And do you suppose," he asked, "that the men who provided this money could be induced to take the risk for a mere paltry bank interest on the par value of their bonds?...No capital can ever be found to develop a country unless it be given some commensurate return based upon the risk it has to run." A spirited attack on the company's critics by W. R. Brock, Toronto's leading drygoods wholesaler and a major shareholder in the enterprise, indicated just how deeply their unpopularity troubled the directors on what should have been a joyous celebration. Brock denounced first "the thousands of men with little money" whose carping criticism diminished in the public mind the true measure of his company's success; then he turned with special fury upon the "little politicians" who toured the country "trying to make political capital of the cry against them."[32]

There had been times when these men might have abided criticism without dampening the spirit of such an event; it was, after all, the cornerstone-laying of a monument to Canadian financial and engineering achievement. Yet even the thick-skinned directors of the Electrical Development Company had sensed the new chill in the climate of enterprise and considered the change sufficiently grave to warrant comment. They were not particularly disturbed that their keen pursuit of an honest profit had generated hostility in many quarters; that was to be expected from an incurably mean and thankless public. Rather, they were alarmed that the radical changes in the public

---

[32] *Globe*, May 10, 1906, report of proceedings.

mood had been just as rapidly directed into political channels, and at that moment threatened the very survival of their enterprise. Standing literally on the brink of Niagara, angered and confused by bewildering currents of dangerous new ideas, these proud, defiant captains of industry prepared to engage a mass movement that was about to descend upon them, fortified by a provincial election victory demanding public ownership of the hydro-electric industry.

III

The public power movement began modestly at a meeting of the Waterloo Board of Trade on February 11, 1902. In a reply to a toast to the Manufacturing Interests, E. W. B. Snider, a miller, farm implement manufacturer, lumberman, and former provincial politician, reasoned: "If Waterloo could offer cheap power to manufacturers it would greatly assist its further progress." Toronto, on its own merits, could attract a power line from the plants at Niagara, but the scattered towns of southwestern Ontario were certain to be left behind unless, as Snider suggested, the Boards of Trade banded together to create an attractive, co-operative market for Niagara power. To an inquiring Daniel B. Detweiler, a shoe wholesaler and past president of the Berlin Board of Trade, Snider explained: "I thought it a good time for the several Towns like Waterloo, Berlin, Preston, Hespeler, Galt and Guelph as a 'Hive' of industries joining hands and with a united effort, in conjunction with Toronto, might in that way secure some special privileges that might not be secured later on."[33] After starting the idea,

---

[33] W. Snider, "E. W. B. Snider, 1842-1921: An Appreciation," *Waterloo Historical Society Annual Report*, Vol. XLIV, 1957, pp. 9-11; Plewman, *Adam Beck*, pp. 32-6; Biggar, *Hydro Electric Development*, p. 42. See also Beck's campaign pamphlet *The Genesis of the Power Movement* (Toronto, 1907) which stresses the importance of the early Toronto investigations, a defect the Kitchener Light Commission purposefully set out to correct in its eulogy of the local initiatives: *The Origin of the Ontario Hydro-Electric Power Movement* (Kitchener, 1919). Berlin *Daily Telegraph*, Feb. 12, 1902, for a report of the Waterloo Board of Trade's "Most Successful Banquet In Its History." PAC, Detweiler Papers, Vol. I, Snider to Detweiler, Feb. 14, 1902.

Snider forsook the Canadian winter for an "extended trip south," leaving Detweiler to pursue the issue before the Berlin manufacturers' annual meeting in May.

In the light of previous experiences with Detweiler's zealous schemes, the Berlin Board of Trade responded coolly to his proposition, but eventually authorized him to confer with Snider and prepare an appropriate resolution. On Snider's return from Florida a meeting of the regional manufacturers was arranged for the beginning of June to hear the popular temperance orator and alderman F. S. Spence speak on Toronto's difficulties in obtaining a municipal power line to Niagara and to listen to Mr. C. H. Mitchell, a former resident of Waterloo and an engineer with the Ontario Power Company, discuss the possibility of transmitting power to the inland towns. As he set down his thoughts before this meeting, Snider remained undecided on the critical question of the means of distribution. Should the power companies build a line to the towns, or should the power users form a company to "secure a water privilege and supply their own power," or thirdly, should the "Government develop and sell the power at a trifle over cost"? He seemed inclined towards the second possibility but recognized that the third would involve less expense; at any rate, he concluded, Premier Ross would have to be consulted before any of the possibilities could be examined.[34]

At the gathering of manufacturers in the Berlin council chambers, June 9, 1902, Detweiler, Spence and Mitchell set out the facts, and Snider set out the three possibilities. If the municipalities of Ontario ever hoped to reap the extraordinary harvest of "white coal," the "great heritage of Niagara," they would have to "bestir" themselves quickly before the Americans monopolized the Falls. Either the two existing companies would have to build a transmission line to the municipalities; or a manufacturers' power company would have to be formed with municipal utilities and private factories subscribing stock in proportion to their consumption; or thirdly, the government

---

[34] Berlin, *Daily Telegraph*, May 9, 1902; W. V. Uttley, *A History of Kitchener Ontario* (Waterloo, 1937), pp. 337ff.; PAC, Detweiler Papers, Vol. II, clipping, Feb. 27, 1903.

would have to step in and distribute power equitably to the dispersed towns of the province. The assembled civic and business leaders of southwestern Ontario, on the basis of Snider's urgent appeal, chose a central committee of twenty-one led by Snider and representing the major manufacturing communities to explore further the various possibilities and bring down a report. A subsequent meeting of the central committee, now strengthened by representation from London, dispatched Detweiler to obtain information from the municipalities and the Niagara power companies, and a sub-committee of three, headed by Snider, was to determine the attitude of the provincial government on the power question.[35]

In their meeting with Premier Ross during the fall of 1902, Snider and his colleagues restated the case against coal—the "famine" was then at its height—suggesting that should the provincial government release the manufacturers from this bondage by distributing hydro-electricity, the initial expenditures would be amply returned in rapid industrial expansion. In the event that the government would not act the least that it could do, the sub-committee concluded, would be to preserve a waterpower privilege at Niagara for a manufacturers' co-operative power company. But Ross could not justify such a large expenditure of public money for the benefit of a few manufacturers. Nor could he understand the petitioners' fear of monopoly. "In addition to the two companies already preparing to do business," he replied, "there is ample room there for three or four others, so that private capitalists are still free to project such Works as would meet the prayer of your Petition. I mention this in order to open the way for local enterprise in the meantime."[36]

Thus when the central committee reconvened on October 20, 1902, in the presence of a large number of interested man-

[35] Kitchener Public Library, Snider Papers, Minutes of Meeting Re: Niagara Falls Power, Berlin, 9 June, 1902; Berlin *Daily Telegraph*, June 9, 10, 26, 30, July 2, 1902; PAC, Detweiler Papers, Vol. II, Minutes, June 7, 9, 30, 1902.

[36] Kitchener Public Library, Snider Papers, Snider to Ross, Sept. 19, 1902; Ross to Snider, Personal, Oct. 1, 1902.

ufacturers from Galt, Snider was compelled to report "that it was unlikely that the Ontario Government would undertake the development and transmission of Electric Power"; if the municipalities and manufacturers wanted cheap power, they would either have to generate and distribute it themselves, or induce the power companies to do it for them.[37] Undaunted by this temporary check, the committee authorized Snider and Detweiler to continue gathering data on the power requirements of the region. The ever-energetic and enthusiastic "Dan" Detweiler enlisted commercial travellers to circularize industries on their power needs and peddled around to the interested municipalities on his famous bicycle, keeping up spirits and the lines of communication. Above all, the towns would have to maintain a united front; Snider personally urged the factory owners not "to commit yourself to any company offering you power, for joint action is necessary to secure the most advantageous rates and conditions, and to properly conserve and safeguard the interests of the various municipalities." While their initial efforts of 1902 had proven unsuccessful, Snider and Detweiler had succeeded in welding the scattered and divided municipalities and manufacturers of southwestern Ontario into a strong, centralized organization which could deal as a unit with the problem of obtaining cheap hydro-electric power from Niagara Falls.

Throughout December and on into January of 1903, the public hearings conducted by the Queen Victoria Niagara Falls Park Commissioners on the advisability of issuing new franchises intensified public interest in the power question. In Toronto especially, W. F. Maclean at the *World*, and Joseph Atkinson at the *Star*, along with the mayor and city council, all joined in a vocal campaign to defeat the efforts of the Toronto syndicate in the hope that a municipal scheme might be approved instead. Then in February, the Toronto section of the Canadian Man-

---

[37] PAC, Detweiler Papers, Vol. II, Minutes of Galt Meeting, Oct. 20, 1902; G. M. McLagan to Detweiler, Oct. 27, 1902; London Users of Power (Beck's factory was not named), in Detweiler Papers, Vol. I; see also Snider and Detweiler to . . . . . . . (blank of form letter), Jan. 13, 1903, in both Detweiler and Snider Papers.

ufacturers' Association swung its support behind Toronto and the other municipalities in their endeavours on behalf of cheap power.[38]

Thus, from the moment he proudly announced the chartering of the first all-Canadian power company, the Electrical Development Company, Premier Ross faced a relentless clamour from the organized municipalities and manufacturers against his power policy. Speaking in Newmarket shortly after granting the franchise, Ross back-tracked, raising for the first time in public the possibility of a municipal co-operative. But at the same time he stoutly defended the former policy on sound business principles: "We are willing to allow the municipalities, Toronto and the rest to develop energy there and they will not be curtailed." Surveys carried out by the Parks Commission indicated that there were several more major sites on the Canadian side of the Niagara River which, Ross suggested, could be occupied by either municipal co-operatives or private companies. However important hydro might be, the Premier bluntly stated: "Ontario must not get into debt because of it. Niagara power can only reach a small portion of the population of the Province. All and any municipalities desiring to go into the business of developing electric power may do so, but the Government will not involve the Province in debt unless for the substantial benefit of all."[39] Ross simply found it impossible to identify the public interest and the manufacturers' interests as closely as had the municipalities.

With consummate timing, the Snider–Detweiler subcommittee called a meeting for February 17 to outline its plan for a municipally owned distribution system. Since the municipalities had demonstrated a "disposition to get together," *Saturday Night* commented, the Legislature at the coming session would "have to take sides definitely with the corporations or with the people." The power question, it noted condescendingly, was far too important to be left in the hands of either the

---

[38]  Toronto *Daily Star*, Jan. 27, 1902, quoted in G. L. Spalding, "The Toronto *Daily Star* as a Liberal Advocate, 1899-1911," (unpublished M. A. thesis, University of Toronto, 1954), p. 297; Plewman, *Adam Beck*, p. 41.

[39]  Plewman, *Adam Beck*, p. 39.

monopolists or confounded by the "airy schemes" of a "rabble of small municipalities." But under Snider's smooth management the municipalities proved, even to *Saturday Night*'s satisfaction, that they were something more than a "rabble."[40]

On Tuesday, February 17, 1903, sixty-seven delegates, including the mayors of all the main towns and cities of the region, answered the call to meet in the Berlin YMCA. In the morning Snider presented a detailed plan which recommended that the municipalities should build a transmission system only, purchasing their power from one of the existing generating plants at Niagara for about $8 per horsepower per year, and selling it at the municipal boundaries for approximately $15. In that way the municipalities could avoid the heavy capital costs involved in building a generating station but at the same time would be assured of hydro-electric power at very close to actual cost. Discussion during the afternoon revealed three distinct currents of opinion. The Toronto deputation wanted immediate, preferably government action; Beck of London, Halloran of Brantford, Hamilton of Guelph, and Hepburn of Stratford professed simply spectators' interest but were inclined towards provincial ownership of the transmission line; and Cant of Galt supported by Noxon of Ingersoll opposed collective ownership. The last-mentioned argued that since the science of transmission was in its infancy the government should not undertake any risks but should instead regulate the private utilities through a rates commission. Mayor Cant added an ideological clincher to his contention that public ownership was both unwieldy and uneconomical: if the government were to go into business, he argued, "that would be class legislation." But these two men were outstanding exceptions to the broad consensus that public ownership of the transmission lines provided the most practical solution to the problem.[41]

---

[40] *Saturday Night*, Jan. 31, 1903; PAC, Detweiler Papers, Vol. II, Snider and Detweiler to . . . ., Feb. 11, 1903.

[41] *Ibid.*, Vol. II, Minutes of February 17, 1903 Meeting; Berlin *Daily Telegraph*, Feb. 19, 1903; Berlin *News-Record*, Feb. 18, 1903; Kitchener Public Library, Snider Papers, draft resolutions.

The overwhelming presence of an aggressive contingent of Toronto businessmen sharply differentiated this meeting from the others that had preceded it. Both Mayor Urquhart's motion to appeal again to the provincial government and Alderman Spence's resolution to go ahead with the municipal plan were nervously defeated, according to the Berlin *News Record*, by an "under current of feeling that the Toronto representatives were attempting to railroad through some scheme favouring that city. . . ." As much as the cautious provincial burghers might favour collective action, they were not going to be rushed, especially by Toronto. The meeting did agree, however, to establish a committee of mayors to resolve the difficulties and present a specific proposal to the Legislature that session. Once again democracy had delegated its responsibility to a committee, but in this case the delegation of authority marked a distinct advance for the public power movement. Initiative had now passed from the informal group of civic politicians and manufacturers that Snider and Detweiler had rallied in 1902 into the practised hands of mayors representing the bulk of the province's population. As Detweiler noted at the foot of the minutes, "this practically concluded the work of the preliminary organization. . . ."[42]

All of the provincial dailies gave the Berlin Convention, as it was called, extensive and favourable coverage. Even Toronto *Saturday Night* lost its sense of equilibrium in praising the "earnestness and conviction" that marked the debate:

> The very name, "Berlin Convention," has a curious significance. Historically it suggests a gathering not of tribunes of the people, but of representatives of royalty and age-long privilege, come together to discuss not public needs but the interests of dynasties and the conflicting claims of armed and aristocratic Governments. "Berlin Convention" to the people of Ontario at least, are the words which henceforward will possess a new and better

---

[42] *News-Record*, Feb. 18, 1903; Detweiler had been the dynamo behind the organization of the manufacturers, Snider its guiding genius. When the movement advanced to the delicate political phase Detweiler found little scope for his talents and he went on to other good causes.

significance. They will now connote a declaration of popular
right as opposed to monopoly privilege. . . .They will inspire
with new hope and purpose all advocates of industrial and political progress who believe that the many are not designed to
be forever bled and bullied by the few. . . .

The Toronto *World* happily joined in applauding this populist
revolt against the corporations: "Capitalists get together and
create monopolies. The municipal representatives at Berlin
yesterday gave practical effect to the belief that the people
should get together and create monopolies. . . .Corporate
oppression has been possible largely because of the diffusion
of the strength of the oppressed. The Berlin Convention is
a sign of an awakening."[43] At the Berlin talks, held the very
month that the Electrical Development Company was chartered,
the public power forces officially surmounted their mutual
metropolitan suspicions and coalesced into a powerful pressure
group whose opinion, unlike that of an informal group of manufacturers, Premier Ross could ignore only at his peril.

On February 27, 1903, the Premier and three of his ministers
received the twelve-member deputation. As spokesman for the
group, Snider begged the province either to distribute hydro-
electricity itself or permit the municipalities to do it themselves.
Southwestern Ontario and Toronto, he claimed, had become
suddenly alarmed "on learning that the powers [of Niagara]
might possibly go into the hands of a few corporations." A
monopoly of that magnificent waterpower, Snider stressed,
would not, and ought not to be tolerated and would meet strenuous objection in the towns of Southwestern Ontario which
"would dwindle down in a short time and lose their prestige"
without cheap hydro-electricity. Fully supported by his deputation, which included Mayor Cant of Galt, Snider pressed the
government to take immediate action. Ross, in replying to this
appeal, repeated his refusal: "Ontario is a large Province with
many great industries, and we must not pledge the future of
the West without being prepared to take similar responsibility

[43] *Saturday Night*, Feb. 21, 1903; Toronto *World*, Feb. 18, 1903.

for the east and for the centre." He had no objection to Toronto and the other municipalities launching a co-operative venture under a public commission, provided of course this met with the approval of the ratepayers, and he pledged legislation to that effect immediately. Whether this commission generated its own power or bought it from the existing companies was for it to decide; once it was established, Ross gave the impression that he would be pleased to see it go its own way fully separate from the authority of the provincial government: "You supply the money, and you control the commission; they will serve you satisfactorily and if not you can change them; you will be responsible for the success of the scheme. . . ." Despite the fact Ross had pledged only minimal co-operation, the delegates came away pleased; they had obtained permission to go ahead on their own, and had created the impression that the impatient and indignant government had fallen out of step with popular opinion and was reacting to a pressure that it could not resist. As the leader of the opposition observed to an old supporter, "there is no doubt that Mr. Ross has been slow to move and will now go only as far as he is compelled to go."[44]

While the public power circles exalted over the triumph, the Premier, in close consultation with his old colleague Snider, drafted and introduced "An Act to Provide for the Construction of Municipal Power Works and the Transmission, Distribution and Supply of Electrical and Other Power and Energy." It authorized the creation of the Ontario Power Commission, consisting of an electrical engineer and several businessmen whose job it would be to conduct detailed feasibility studies. The commission would then report directly to the co-operating municipalities which, after a vote of the ratepayers, could then establish a second, permanent Board of Commissioners to undertake the actual construction and management of the transmission lines. A general meeting of the interested municipalities and manufacturers in the Toronto City Hall, August 12, 1903,

---

[44] Toronto *News*, Feb. 28, 1903; PAC, Detweiler Papers, Vol. II, clipping, Feb. 27, 1903; PAO, Whitney Papers, Whitney to Dr. Kaiser, Mar. 3, 1903.

selected commissioners under the act. E. W. B. Snider, the retiring guiding genius of the campaign, was naturally selected as chairman of the commission, to be assisted by P. W. Ellis, a Toronto wholesale jeweller, W. F. Cockshutt, a farm implement manufacturer from Brantford, and Adam Beck, factory owner, mayor of London, and Conservative MPP. With the first meeting of this commission, December 8, 1903, at which the firm of Ross and Holgate was retained for the engineering work and the $15,000 expenses of the commission were parcelled out to the seven municipalities that had agreed to bear them, the public power movement underwent a further metamorphosis, changing from a political pressure group into a legally constituted public power authority.[45]

In its pressure-group phase the power movement had lacked a conspicuous leader. *Saturday Night*, on the eve of the Berlin Convention, in an issue that featured a cartoon showing a Lilliputian George Ross grubbing in the pockets of a bulbous, cigar-chomping capitalist clutching a fistful of franchises, noted that "what is needed is some public man who will make himself an expert on this question and give to the public the advantage of his knowledge ordinarily possessed by, and used on behalf of, those who desire to monopolize what the public has not yet learned to value." This urgent need was felt within the power movement as well, and Detweiler went as far, during the fall of 1902, as attempting to recruit the much-lionized Francis Hector Clergue, "the wizard" of Sault Ste. Marie. "I could not possibly give attention to opportunities at Niagara Falls even if my activities were needed there," Clergue replied to Detweiler, adding, "which I do not think to be the case."[46] During the Ontario Power Commission phase of the power movement such a man did emerge, and from within its own ranks.

---

[45] PAC, Detweiler Papers, Vol. II, Snider and Detweiler circular letter, May 14, 1903; Kitchener Public Library, Snider Papers, Hon. G. W. Ross to Snider, Mar. 4; April 24; May 4, 12, 1903; *ibid.*, Minutes of the Ontario Power Commission meetings.

[46] *Saturday Night*, Feb. 7, 1903; PAC, Detweiler Papers, Vol. I, F. H. Clergue to Detweiler, Oct. 29, 1902.

Adam Beck made his first appearance at the Berlin Convention in February of 1903, and he had come, at least so he said, primarily to observe. But for Beck that was a most unnatural role. He had been a forceful and aggressive competitor in everything he had undertaken up until that point: tennis, lacrosse, horsemanship and politics. In 1898 he had tried without success to move from a minor local office into the provincial arena; now his persistence and growing popularity overcame that initial set-back with the result that by 1902 Beck occupied both the mayorality of London and a Conservative seat in the Legislature. As a manufacturer (cigar boxes), and especially as a mayor of an aspiring manufacturing city, he sincerely felt the need for cheap, Niagara power; and within him these impulses were joined to a canny instinct for the political possibilities of the public power movement. Beck was too complex a personality to ascribe his vigorous activity in the movement to mere personal ambition, yet vanity and love of authority were his two foremost weaknesses. However tangled his motives, Adam Beck quickly mastered the ins and outs of the power question after the Berlin Convention and just as rapidly rose to leadership of the Ontario Power Commission. In his person the movement acquired what it had long needed—assertive leadership unrestrained by modesty or self-consciousness. To the mannerisms of a populist orator Beck adapted the rhetoric of the Niagara industrial myth, and he emerged as the most dynamic of the spokesmen for public ownership. Off the platforms and in the close quarters of the commission his star was also rising. Since a good part of Snider's influence derived from his close relationship with Premier Ross, his power naturally suffered an eclipse during the last agonies of Liberal government. Beck, on the other hand, claiming the ear of the prospective government, gradually replaced him. Thus during the political uncertainties and Power Commission investigations of 1904, Adam Beck vaulted into the leadership of the public power movement.[47]

---

[47] Biographical material can be found in a variety of secondary sources, though no one has yet felt the need to write a full-scale biography of

IV

Hydro made its deepest impression upon the businessmen and small manufacturers in the provincial towns. The thought of boundless, cheap hydro-electricity inspired these men of property and industry with evangelical zeal. To the moderately well-to-do, socially prominent bourgeoisie who invariably manned the town councils and local boards of trade, hydro came as divine recompense for persevering through the agonizing trial of years of slow growth. These tireless "boosters," who embodied the highest values of commercial society, instinctively came forward to champion the new power source in fulfilment of their role as the natural leaders of men and opinion. They were the impulsive memorialists and petitioners; their views had always been canvassed and conspicuously given on all matters of local, even national importance. Hydro seemed to them a marvellous engine of progress and they welcomed it with the same generosity and eagerness as they had the railroads to which they had willingly mortaged their future. Yet the manufacturers' enthusiasm for cheap hydro (the emphasis always fell on its abundance and thus inexpensive quality) far exceeded their narrow concerns as the major power users and real estate speculators. A deep and abiding local pride had long since blurred the distinction between their own interests and those of the communities around them. They freely contributed their considerable energies to "boosterism" and the unswerving promotion of industrial expansion. Because they conceived the public interest as indistinguishable from their own private interests, the manufacturers and businessmen of Ontario ardently embraced hydro-electric power as the materialization of their fondest hopes for their beloved towns.

From the outset the crusade for public power was a businessmen's movement; they initiated it, formed its devoted,

---

Beck: see Plewman, *Adam Beck*; Biggar, *Hydro-Electric Development*; Denison, *The People's Power*; chapter in Augustus Bridle, *Sons of Canada*; and the eulogy by Percy Graham, *Sir Adam Beck* (London, 1925). See also Hector Charlesworth, *The Canadian Scene* and *Candid Chronicles* (Toronto, 1925) for the observations of a contemporary.

hard-core membership and, most importantly, they provided it with brilliant leadership. By the phrase "the people's power," the businessmen meant cheap electricity for the manufacturer, and it was assumed that the entire community would benefit as a result. The socially and politically influential manufacturers turned readily to public ownership primarily because the private electric companies at Niagara refused to guarantee them an immediate, inexpensive supply of a commodity on which they believed their future prosperity depended. In this, as in countless other cases in both Canada and United States, when the market economy failed to satisfy the immediate necessities of the business community, it appealed without the slightest qualm to the state for public provision of the service.[48]

In a very real sense public ownership was a function of economic backwardness, of suddenly liberated expectations of industrial growth after a period of stagnation. Compared to the states just south of the Lakes, Ontario had languished; if cheap hydro would stimulate the long awaited industrial expansion, the local manufacturing elites of Ontario's small towns demanded that its benefits should be distributed equally and instantly.[49] But two of the Niagara companies planned to dis-

[48] On the role of the state in American economic growth see Goodrich, *Government Promotion of American Canals and Railroads, 1800-1890* (New York, 1959); Oscar and Mary Handlin, *Commonwealth: A Study of the Role of Government in the American Economy: Massachusetts, 1774-1861* (New York, 1947); Louis Hartz, *Economic Policy and Democratic Thought: Pennsylvania, 1776-1860* (Cambridge, Massachusetts, 1948); see also contributions by Hartz and O. Handlin to the Symposium on Laissez-Faire, *Tasks in Economic History*, Vol. III, 1943. For Canada see H. A. Innis, *Problems of Staple Production in Canada* (Toronto, 1933), pp. 1-16, 30-81; *Essays in Economic History* (Toronto, 1956), pp. 78-96; and H. G. J. Aitken, "Defensive Expansionism: The State and Economic Growth in Canada," reprinted in W. T. Easterbrook and M. Watkins, eds. *Approaches to Canadian Economic History* (Toronto, 1967), pp. 183-221.

[49] For comparisons of the performance of the Canadian and American economies in the 1890s, see Simon Kuznets, *Modern Economic Growth: Rate, Structure and Spread* (New Haven, Connecticut, 1966), pp. 352-3 and John Dales, *The Protective Tariff in Canada's Development* (Toronto, 1966), pp. 111, 125-9. Dales calculates that Canada's population, GNP, value added in secondary and primary manufacturing, all fell as a percentage of similar

tribute the bulk of their power in New York State, selling in effect their surpluses to industrial parks in the vicinity of the Falls. And when the third company finally entered the field, its intended objective was Toronto, the largest concentration of population and industry in the province, where the lighting and street railway companies already assured a profitable market. The high costs and low profits of servicing the widely scattered demand of the provincial towns diminished their competitive position, rendering them a secondary consideration by any commercial calculation.

The struggle for hydro renewed the old metropolitan tensions of the Ontario economy. As Toronto's grip on Niagara, represented by either the city council's abortive plan for a municipal transmission line or by the flotation of a private company by the city's financiers, seemed to tighten, the sensitive municipalities of its hinterland grew proprotionately more resentful and desperate. One way or another, Toronto seemed to be on the verge of adding the benefits of cheap electric power to its other metropolitan advantages at precisely the same instant that the American coal strike dramatized the provincial manufacturers' vulnerability to fluctuations in the price of their steam power. Frustrated envy drove the peripheral towns together to counterbalance the well-publicized designs of the metropolitan centre upon Niagara power. The subsequent failure of Toronto's efforts to acquire a municipal power line, and the chartering of the Electrical Development Company instead to meet the city's needs, established the essential common ground between the manufacturers of the hinterland and their counterparts in the city. Toronto's municipal leaders viewed this entrenchment of the electrical and street railway monopolists to be antipathetic to that city's best interests just as

---

United States levels. Only in agricultural productivity did Canada improve at a faster rate than did the United States. From 1891 to 1901 the population increased at the slowest rate recorded in the nineteenth century; emigration almost exceeded immigration. See, W. E. Kalback and W. W. McVey, *The Demographic Basis of Canadian Society* (Toronto, 1971), p. 35. These and other disappointments led the inhabitants of Mariposa about this time to the conclusion that the census was largely the outcome of "malicious jealousy."

surely as the regional towns regarded the focusing of Niagara's power in Toronto as detrimental to their industrial welfare. The mere existence of the Electrical Development Company, owned as it was by men of known reputation, united the business classes of the hinterland and the centre.[50]

Ontario's public power movement drew extensively from the intellectual and emotional residuals of assertive, "civic gospel" feeling and the sensationalist popular alarm at the suddenly giant corporations.[51] Municipal leaders argued with the fervour of religious converts that if a public service was a natural monopoly and yet run for private profit, the user of the service paid more than if it were operated at cost in the public interest. Private utilities implied poor service at high cost, an axiom that Toronto consumers knew from first-hand experience: transit service was inadequate, streetcar tracks were used as freight railways, the electric company raised poles and strung wires where it pleased, gas and light rates were exorbitant, and all the services were monumentally indifferent to public criticism and city council.[52] Beginning as early as 1895 the city took steps to establish its own lighting plant only to be ultimately checkmated by James Conmee's 1899 amendment to the Municipal Act, which forbade competition between public and private utilities. Before the city could provide a municipally operated street lighting or electrical service it would first have to purchase the already existing private utilities and their franchises.[53] And in large cities where economies of scale made

[50]  This line of thought is prompted by J. M. S. Careless' two articles "Frontierism and Metropolitanism in Canadian History," *CHR*, Vol. XXXV (1954), pp. 1-21, and "Metropolitanism and Nationalism," in *Nationalism In Canada* (Toronto, 1966), pp. 271-83. For background to Toronto's growth see D. C. Masters, *The Rise of Toronto, 1850-1890* (Toronto, 1947).

[51]  Asa Briggs, *Victorian Cities* (New York, 1963 ed.), pp. 187-243. Blake McKelvey, in his survey of American urbanization, *The Urbanization of America, 1860-1915* uses the somewhat more grandiloquent phrase "civic renaissance" to describe this phenomenon, pp. 99-114, and 75-98.

[52]  Biggar called this era "Toronto's Struggle for Responsible Government," *Hydro-Electric Development*, p. 88; Paul Rutherford, "Tomorrow's Metropolis: The Urban Reform Movement in Canada, 1880-1920," Canadian Historical Association, *Historical Papers* (1971), pp. 207-8.

[53]  *Statutes of Ontario*, 62 Vict., c. 26, s. 35, ss. 4.

utilities a profitable investment, and where their owners were invariably more powerful, municipal ownership met more determined opposition. With the Toronto Electric Light Company paying 8 per cent, its owners were understandably reluctant to sell. But in smaller centres the owners of marginally profitable operations welcomed the opportunity to unload their properties at more than a fair price to eager, crusading councils, and in these towns the "civic gospel" was fervently proclaimed. When, for example, Berlin's municipal waterworks recorded a $4,000 surplus on its first year's operation, the *Daily Telegraph* encouraged the town fathers " . . . to reach out for the other franchises. The lighting question comes up next and the Council should be able to act wisely in fuller knowledge of the waterworks lesson." By 1903 the town ran its own street lighting and gas distribution systems as well, a phenomenon which the Legislature's Select Committee on Municipal Trading reported that year to be the rule rather than the exception. The press played a key role in the propagation of the gospel, in long, thick columns of type both respectable and sensationalist newspapers carefully documented the inevitable reductions in cost and improvements in service brought by public ownership in other British, American, and Canadian cities.[54]

Prominent among the other topics receiving detailed scrutiny in the press was the advent of "an age noted for gigantic trusts and combines." The presence of huge corporations shattered the familiar confidence in the natural laws of the marketplace; even the most conventional of newspapers recognized the necessity of "combatting" these mammoths that now controlled the marketplace itself.[55] While a great deal of the anti-corporate tone of the press was imported bodily from the United States, the behaviour of suddenly mature Canadian capitalism pro-

[54] Ontario, Legislative Assembly, *Select Committee on Municipal Trading and Municipal Ownership of Public Utilities* (Toronto, 1903), tables at the end; Spalding, "The Toronto Star," p. 295; Charlesworth, *The Canadian Scene*, pp. 215 ff; Berlin *Daily Telegraph*, the most notable being: Jan. 18; Nov. 13, 1900, May 18, 1901; April 2, July 9, 1902; *Canadian Engineer*, Feb., 1904.

[55] Berlin *Daily Telegraph*, Mar. 22, 1900.

vided editors with ample opportunities to berate the home-grown Canadian trusts as well. As early as 1900 debaters from the Toronto Liberal Club and the Cartwright Club deplored the "making of a host of millionaires" by the great corporations and called for public ownership of the railways as a remedy. The Toronto *Daily Star* traced the growth of the corporation back to the nineteenth century's short-sighted eagerness for mere development which resulted in the giving away of franchises for nothing and the provision of bonuses to companies which accepted them:

> [T]he twentieth century will be kept busy wrestling with million-aires and billionaires to get back and restore to the people that which the nineteenth century gave away and thanked the plutocrats for accepting. . . . The nineteenth century shirked its duty, humbugged and defrauded the common people, played into the hands of the rich, and left the twentieth century with a host of perplexities.[56]

Hydro-electric companies were doubly vulnerable: on the one hand they were strategic, yet privately owned natural monopolies; and secondly, the tremendous capital required to build them rendered these enterprises the exclusive property of the Morgans, Vanderbilts, Rothschilds, Albrights, Mac-kenzies, Nicholls and Pellatts. Niagara Falls was no longer a public asset; henceforth it would be wrung until dry for the profit of the aforementioned gentlemen, or at least so it seemed in an emotionally charged Ontario before the triumphant crusade.

Another important quality of Ontario's economy permitted the manufacturers, once propelled by anti-monopoly and civic gospel indignation, to forge ahead with an untroubled con-science. Unlike their American counterparts who had to keep glancing nervously over their shoulders at the stirring masses, the Canadian businessmen reformers could take dead aim on their objective without the disquieting suspicion that their rhetoric might be turned against them. Industrialism had raised

---

[56] *Globe*, Feb. 10, 1900; quoted in Spalding, "The Toronto Star," p. 296.

the corporate menace to the right of the Canadian business Progressives, but it had yet to beget, in the same measure as in the United States, massive industrial unions and frightening social revolutionaries on the left. Feeling themselves caught between the corporations and the workers' movements, the American middle-class Progressives had to choose their words very carefully. They could not endorse public ownership as unequivocally as the Ontario reformers when they found themselves in the company of a vital socialism advocating nationalization of the tools of production. Where labour and leftists were vocal and militant, public ownership of utilities made the least headway, because advocacy of the principle from these quarters tended to frighten a defensive middle class into an alliance with the financial community in defence of all private enterprise.[57]

In Canada, labour was relatively weaker, and in the east more conservative. At a time when the American Socialist party was growing to its eventual 6 per cent presidential vote and when there were socialist mayors and state assemblymen in profusion, a socialist mayoralty candidate in Toronto received only a few hundred votes. Labour and radicalism, while they were sources of concern for Canadian businessmen, were not the objects of terror they were to many middle-class Americans. Had labour been more militant or the socialists more active, as they were in California, Chicago and New York, the outcome for public ownership in Ontario might have been very different.[58]

The interests of the manufacturers and the people were not entirely identical: P. W. Ellis might declare himself to be a friend of the workingman when he advocated public power as a member of the Ontario Power Commission in 1904, but as president of the Canadian Manufacturers' Association the same year, he was hardly a true friend of labour.[59]

---

[57] Richard Hofstadter, *The Age of Reform* (New York, 1955), pp. 135-66, 240-1; D. A. Shannon, *The Socialist Party of America* (Chicago, 1967 ed.), pp. 1-80.

[58] George Mowry, *The California Progressives* (Chicago, 1963 ed.) pp. 288-95; R. Fogelson, *The Fragmented Metropolis: Los Angeles, 1850-1930* (Cambridge, 1967), pp. 224-46; McKelvey, *The Urbanization of America*, p. 113.

[59] S. D. Clark, *The Canadian Manufacturers' Association*, University of Toronto Studies in History and Economics, Vol. VII (Toronto, 1939), p. 42; Seba

The conditions that made public ownership necessary and those that made it possible were identical. Economic backwardness drove the manufacturers to use the state, in Harold Innis' phrase, to throw a bridge "from a retarded development to an advanced stage of industrialism."[60] And those same circumstances permitted the businessmen to use the state and identify themselves with the masses without anxiety and without fear of contradiction.

---

Eldridge *et al.*, *Development of Collective Enterprise* (Lawrence, Kansas, 1943), pp. 227-42, 419-46, 541-60.

[60] Innis, *Problems of Staple Production in Canada*, p. 30.

# 7

# Power
# Politics

The Conservatives had acquired an inclination towards public
ownership during their long years in opposition but had not
developed that tendency into a detailed program. In 1902, for
example, the party had introduced a resolution calling for the
cessation of hydro-electric exports to the United States and
public ownership of the Niagara generating stations. This
surprise policy, summarized by Beattie Nesbitt as "the
Government at the switch and not the corporations," had been
introduced into the debate on the speech from the throne in
the hope of raising a groundswell of popular support just before
an election when the Liberals could not act quickly enough
to steal the idea. However, the hydro myth had only just begun
to stir up expectations and anxieties among the businessmen
and manufacturers of the province. Thus, hydro-electric policy
was not the important issue in the election that year that party
strategists thought it would be. Three years later the acquisition
of cheap power had become a matter of some urgency, but
the deliberations of Snider's Ontario Power Commission had

temporarily removed the issue from politics. Nevertheless, the Conservatives were known to be sound on the power question and assumed office in 1905 with the full confidence of the public power movement.[1]

On taking office, Premier Whitney repeated in the House what he had said many times before on the hustings: "The waterpowers of Niagara should be as free as air."[2] That implied, he explained, that "these powers should be as free as air not only to the monopolist and the friend of Government, as it used to be, but every citizen under proper conditions should be free to utilize the powers that the Almighty had given to the Province." Henceforth his government would not simply multiply the companies exploiting Niagara as the Liberals had done, but would rather take action to ensure the equitable distribution and inexpensive consumption of the product of those magnificent and publicly owned waterpowers. While Whitney roasted the Liberals and the "monopolists" to the general satisfaction of the power enthusiasts, significant ambiguities regarding the all-important method of carrying out that inten-

[1] PAO, Whitney Papers, Whitney to Dr. T. E. Kaiser, Aug. 16, 1901; Miscampbell-Carscallen motion, Feb. 5, 1902; *Globe*, Feb. 6, 12, 1902; *Canadian Annual Review*, 1902, p. 46.

[2] *Globe*, April 20, 1905; for first use of this phrase, see *ibid*., Dec. 12, 1900. The phrase is of course meaningless as it stands and is open to several contradictory interpretations. Professor Humphries suggests that the Liberals, so long in power, developed an inclination towards the view of the power producers, while the Conservatives, in opposition, understood the problem from the consumer's point of view. He argues further that the Liberals, with their predominantly rural political foundations did not sense the importance of the hydro question in contrast with the Tories, who under Whitney's leadership were gaining control of the growing urban vote and were thus able to articulate what was largely an urban issue. The Liberals also were tied personally to the corporate viewpoint through Gibson's interests and through the Premier himself, who was president of Mackenzie's Manufacturers' Life Insurance Company which extended loans to the Electrical Development Company. C. W. Humphries, "The Political Career of Sir James P. Whitney" (unpublished Ph.D. thesis, University of Toronto, 1966), p. 505, and "The Sources of Ontario 'Progressive Conservatism,' 1900-1914," *CHAR* (1967), p. 124.

tion remained. In fact these ambiguities would persist for another three years.

I

In May 1905, as a first step towards the development of a policy of its own, the Whitney government cancelled a contract, negotiated during the last hours of the Liberal administration, which would have granted the Electrical Development Company rights to all the remaining waterpowers at Niagara Falls. On that occasion Adam Beck, stressing the enormous importance of hydro-electricity as an instrument of development, delivered a devastating critique of the former government's policy. George Ross had wilfully abandoned the consumers of Ontario to stock-watering monopolists. Beck charged: "It is the duty of the Government to see that development is not hindered by permitting a handful of people to enrich themselves out of these treasures at the expense of the general public." In order to carry out that responsibility, Beck asked that a provincial commission with "the most extensive powers" be established to "build up a policy which will commend itself to the people of the Province."[3] Accordingly, the government created the Hydro-Electric Commission of Inquiry on July 5, 1905, with Beck as its chairman, empowering it to make a thorough inventory of the provincial waterpowers, to gather information on the capital costs of hydro-electric production and the probable rates of service, and to bring down recommendations to the government on the best method of distributing hydro-electricity.

As a member of the Ontario Power Commission, Beck had discovered the difficulties on the one hand of getting information from the private power companies, and on the other of

[3] *Globe*, May 10, 1905; Adam Beck, *The Public Interest in the Niagara Falls Power Supply* (Toronto, 1905). George Ross completed his identification with the power companies in this debate by stressing the great uncertainty that faced the industry and the need for strengthening the one Canadian company in the field.

keeping the mercurial municipalities in harness together. He also became convinced that since the province would have to act as banker and co-ordinator of the municipal co-operative at any rate, it might as well take an active role in the running of whatever system might be decided upon. Thus during 1905 there were two public bodies looking into the power question with two men, Beck and Ellis, a former president of the Canadian Manufacturers' Association, on both: the Ontario Power Commission of the municipalities operating under the 1903 Ross Power Bill, and the provincial government's Hydro-Electric Commission of Inquiry carrying out its investigations under the Public Inquiries Act.

As both commissions were drafting their final reports during the early spring of 1906, Adam Beck initiated a publicity campaign to prepare the public mind to receive their recommendations. Speaking in Toronto on February 7, he claimed Niagara power could be delivered to the city for as low as $17 per horsepower per year. At large public meetings in London, Galt, Guelph, Berlin, Woodstock and Stratford, he exposed the methods of the private power interests, documenting his case by referring to the exorbitant prices Montrealers had to pay for their power on account of watered stock of the Montreal Heat, Light and Power Company. But Ontario had cried halt; the people's interests would henceforth be protected. Then Beck would extol the virtues of cheap power; it would bring new industries, clean, rapid transportation, and the massive development of northern resources. And for the first time the revolutionary potential of electricity in the home received attention; if electricity were cheap enough, it could be used not only for domestic lighting, but also for farm machinery, and household appliances. Beck also noted the connection between lower rates and higher demand, pointing out that because of the economies of the industry, the greater and more diversified the demand, the cheaper the power could be. He would then conclude his address at these meetings with the argument that a publicly owned transmission line could deliver electrical power to the municipalities most efficiently; but, he emphasized, the people would have to demand it "as Governments were not willing to move out of their ordinary course without strong public pressure."[4]

The already well-organized municipalities responded im-mediately to Beck's thinly disguised call to direct action by form-ing the Municipal Power Union of Western Ontario on March 23, 1906, to co-ordinate the agitation for "cheap power." When the Beck Commission brought down its recommendation of a publicly owned distributing network a month later, fifteen hundred demonstrators representing the Boards of Trade of Ontario, the Canadian Manufacturers' Association, the city of Toronto, and twenty-nine municipal corporations with a com-bined population of over a million people, descended on Queen's Park under the auspices of the Power Union to support Beck's stand.[5] By appealing to mass opinion outside the confines of the party, Beck strengthened his position in the cabinet where, unexpectedly, he encountered serious opposition.

After the first flush of victory had faded, the new Premier seemed to draw back from his earlier certainty about public ownership. In his answer to the mass demonstrations on April 11, for instance, Whitney repeated the pledge that his gov-ernment would protect the people's interests by either develop-ing its own power or by securing distribution at a fair price by other means; but he added the sobering warning that the expropriation of the existing generating plants would involve the people of Ontario in an expenditure of between $15 and $25 million. Some observers attributed the subtle shift to the presence in the cabinet of two ministers who had close connec-tions with private power companies; Frank Cochrane owned a major interest in the Wahnapitae Power Company that supplied the town and mines of Sudbury, and John Hendrie was known to be associated with the private utilities in Hamilton. It seems more likely that Whitney's new conservatism on the power question was prompted by a better understanding of the difficulties facing the Electrical Development Company and the financial chaos that its collapse would most certainly create.

[4] *Canadian Annual Review*, 1906, p. 117; PAO, Whitney Papers, J. P. Lyon to Whitney, Mar. 29, 1906, enclosure.

[5] *Canadian Annual Review*, 1906, p. 178; W. R. Plewman, *Adam Beck and the Ontario Hydro* (Toronto, 1947), pp. 48-49; PAO, Whitney Papers, Whitney to E. C. Whitney, private, April 11, 1906.

Whitney had promised both Pellatt and Nicholls that the private companies would be consulted before any policy was decided upon. But the spectacle of Beck, a minister of the crown, attacking them in public and advocating public ownership at the same time raised doubts in their minds that Whitney had kept his word. The more Whitney kept them at arm's length, pleading that the "great press of public business" prevented him receiving a deputation from the company, the more insistent their protests grew. Denied an audience, Pellatt laid his views before Whitney by letter. The people had heard only one side of the power question; Beck's facts, especially the $17 figure quoted for Toronto, remained unsubstantiated even by the commission's report; and the prices quoted for the other towns were merely opinions. Before the government even contemplated legislation it must hear the company's case and take special note of the influence of its actions upon the future investment of capital which up until that time had been "accorded reasonable protection and security."[6]

From the beginning the private companies had ignored the Snider Commission and absolutely refused to co-operate with the potentially more dangerous Beck Commission. The Electrical Development Company took the stand that since it was simply carrying on its lawful business it need not submit to "an inquisitorial investigation." Frederic Nicholls, claiming the sanctity of a commercial contract, refused to release the details of the contracts his company had negotiated either to the commission or privately to Premier Whitney. The board of directors of the Toronto Electric Light Company categorically rejected the notion that the Electrical Development Company should make public its contract on the grounds that "the giving of information to the public...is an unheard of thing in commercial circles; and any attempt to extort such information would not be tolerated in Great Britain or the United States." No business could be carried out, no money invested, the directors claimed, without this secrecy. Eminent counsel advised Nicholls that his company was under no compulsion "to make

<hr />

[6] PAO, Whitney Papers, H. M. Pellatt to Whitney, Jan. 9, 1906; Whitney to Scott Griffin, Feb. 16, 1906.

public or communicate to other parties, confidential business dealings." Sam Hume Blake, Nicholls' personal lawyer, added: "...while I think it always well to take the public into one's confidence and turn on the searchlight, yet there are occasions when the particular circumstances demand privacy and where even angels fear to tread." Aemilius Jarvis, a prestigious Toronto banker and stockholder, told the Premier: "We find our clients are becoming nervous at the attitude...the Commission is taking towards this Company, and if anything were to now occur that would ultimately upset the transaction we might be heavy losers...." And he warned Whitney of the "far reaching consequences that premature enquiries into the affairs of this Company (which is not yet a going concern)" might have upon the financial position of the province.[7]

Whitney appealed to the business community for reason and good sense. "The Government," he declared, "is anxious to avoid doing anything which will have an injurious effect upon the Company," but in order to arrive at a sound opinion it needed information which only the companies possessed. When the necessary statistics were still not forthcoming, Whitney signed an order-in-council compelling the Electrical Development Company to reveal to the commission the prices at which it had contracted to sell power. Only after that company reluctantly admitted its intention to sell electricity in Toronto at between $25 and $35 per horsepower did Sam Hume Blake (who was also the corporation counsel for the Ontario Power Company) reveal confidentially that his company was selling power in Niagara Falls, New York at $12.50 per horsepower, and $12.75 in its industrial park at Niagara Falls, Ontario. Mass demonstrations by the Power Union and release of the Hydro-Electric Commission's report brought a panic-stricken plea from Nicholls that the government not be "stampeded" by "pop-

---

[7] *Ibid.*, Solicitor of the Electrical Development Company to Whitney, undated, but from internal evidence, Feb., 1906; F. Nicholls to Beck, Feb. 21, 1906; Nicholls to Whitney, Feb. 24, 1906, Mar. 7, 1906 with enclosures, Mar. 13, 1906; Memorandum of the Board of Directors of the Toronto Electric Light Company, Feb. 25, 1906; S. H. Blake to Nicholls, Mar. 13, 1906; A. Jarvis to Whitney, Feb. 21, 1906.

ular clamour" into repressive legislation and a voluntary offer by the Electrical Development Company to build the transmission line as a private venture with the price of electricity being regulated by the cabinet. Whitney's immediate reassurance that the Beck position had not become government policy and would not until the private interests had been previously heard provided little comfort, particularly after his staunch support of Beck over the disclosure controversy. In the increasing public clamour the power companies had begun to doubt whether Whitney was in fact his own man.[8]

The great groundswell of popular enthusiasm that greeted the publication of the two power commission reports in March of 1906 obviously made a deep impression upon the Premier. The Snider Commission, reporting first, recommended that a municipal co-operative build and operate the transmission system linking the major towns with Niagara. The commissioners decided that for the time being they could not afford to build a generating station of their own at Niagara. Instead, they proposed buying and distributing it at cost through their own system. Their *Report* also called on the government to repeal the Conmee clauses of the Municipal Act which prevented competition between publicly and privately owned electrical utilities. Finally, the commission recommended the appointment of a permanent power commission to be run as "a purely business institution and absolutely divorced from politics" to regulate the entire hydro-electric industry.

Within a matter of weeks Adam Beck's commission brought down its first report. As might be expected, the Beck Commission placed greater emphasis upon provincial participation in

---

[8] Ontario Hydro Archives [hereafter OHA], Minutes of the Board of Directors Meeting, Mar. 1, 1906, Toronto Electric Light Company Minute Book, p. 103; Contract between Toronto and Niagara Power Company and the Toronto Electric Light Company, pp. 40-61. Prices ranged from 4,000 h.p. per annum at $25 to 6,000 h.p. per annum at $35; PAO, Whitney Papers, Whitney to A. Jarvis, private, Feb. 22, 1906; Nicholls to Whitney, Mar. 24, Mar. 29, 1906, private and confidential; Blake, Lash and Cassels to Whitney, Mar. 30, 1906; Whitney to Willison, private, May 17, 1906; Nicholls to Whitney, Mar. 29, April 1, April 3, 1906, private and confidential; Whitney to Nicholls, April 7, 1906, private.

the distribution of power. Instead of a municipal co-operative Beck proposed a provincial hydro-electric commission to regulate the affairs of the private companies and to distribute its own power to the municipal utilities.[9] In addition to the impressive public demonstrations organized by Beck's Power Union, hundreds of petitions flooded in upon the Premier in May supporting the conclusions of the investigating commissions. Private companies, these documents claimed in the same monotonous phrases, could not be entrusted with such an important public service as the distribution of electricity. Only a public agency, operating beyond all thought of profit, could supply power truly at cost.[10]

This massive outpouring of support for public ownership in the spring of 1906 coincided with a distinct sinking in popular esteem of the entire financial community, and especially those closely connected with the power companies, as a result of the investigations of the Royal Commission on Insurance. "Mackenzie & Mann and Sir Henry Pellatt," Whitney informed his brother, "have been doing queer things with reference to loans with insurance money." What they were doing was straightforward enough. In their capacity as directors of the country's largest insurance companies the aforementioned and Senator George Cox of Canada Life simply diverted large sums of the pooled premiums in their care into their own companies. The Electrical Development Company, among many others, depended to a large extent upon such connections for both short and long-term financing. However, notwithstanding the merit of some of these transactions from the point of view

---

[9] *Report of the Ontario Power Commission to the Mayors and Municipal Councils of Toronto, London, Brantford, Stratford, Woodstock, Ingersoll, and Guelph* (Toronto, Mar. 28, 1906), pp. 11-15; the Beck Commission issued five reports, the first in April, 1906, dealing with the power sources and requirements of the Niagara district, with others following in rapid succession treating the Trent Watershed, Lake Huron and Georgian Bay, the Ottawa–St. Lawrence region, and Algoma–Thunder Bay–Rainy River; *Reports of the Hydro-Electric Power Commission of Ontario* (Toronto, 1906-1907).

[10] PAO, Whitney Papers, flat file of municipal petitions dated February to May, 1906.

of the policy-holders, such an intimate relationship between borrower and lender was obviously open to abuse. Yet despite the bad odour which surrounded the owners of the Electrical Development Company, the Premier of Ontario felt obliged to come to their assistance. The company was in serious financial trouble. No matter how wrongheaded its management or frenzied its financing, Whitney was in the last resort responsible for the survival of a corporation of this magnitude. Hydro-electric companies were the most capital-intensive enterprises that had ever been organized in the province. No Premier could stand aside and watch the collapse of one with equanimity, whatever his private feelings may have been. Therefore, in order to prevent a general loss of investor confidence in Ontario's public and private securities, Whitney hoped to be able to strike a satisfactory compromise between the extremes of public and private ownership.[11]

For that reason Whitney could not wholeheartedly support Beck's *Report* and the draft legislation based upon it. His evident procrastination brought a gentle prodding from his mentor, Chief Justice W. R. Meredith. "I sincerely hope that you will not be, shall I say, stampeded into withdrawing or emasculating your Power Bill," Meredith wrote early in May. "It is a safe and conservative measure. Nothing can be done without the action of the Commission on which the Government will be represented if it has not a majority of its members." Reluctantly, caught between a commitment to public ownership and a growing awareness of its possible consequences in the impressionable financial world, the Premier pressed on with the legislation.[12]

---

[11] *Ibid.*, E. Coatsworth, Mayor of Toronto, to Whitney, April 12, 1906; W. S. Connolly to Whitney, May 2, 1906; Whitney to E. C. Whitney, Mar. 24, 1906, private; Royal Commission on Life Insurance, *Report* (Ottawa, 1907), and *Minutes of Evidence*, 4 Vols. (Ottawa, 1907), particularly the evidence of Hon. G. A. Cox, pp. 937-1068. See also, Ian Drummond, "Canadian Life Insurance Companies and the Capital Market," *CJEPS*, Vol. XXVIII (1962), pp. 210ff.; C. A. S. Hall, "Electrical Utilities in Ontario Under Private Ownership, 1890-1914" (unpublished Ph.D. thesis, University of Toronto, 1968), pp. 159-65, 186-9, 206-10.

[12] W. R. Meredith to Whitney, May 9, 1906, quoted in Humphries, "The Political Career of Sir J. P. Whitney," pp. 377-378, from papers in his

In picking his way through the surrounding dangers Whitney demonstrated a degree of skill that many people did not think he possessed. His reputation had improved remarkably, both in the province and within his own party, from the low point in 1902 when John Ross Robertson was said to have remarked bitterly: "You can throw a brick through the window of any country law office and hit a J. P. Whitney."[13]

Choosing the members for the all-important permanent Hydro-Electric Commission was, as Chief Justice Meredith implied, the most critical decision. Obviously, Whitney would have to give the chairmanship to Beck. But Beck needed someone of sufficient power and stature to control his enthusiasms. John S. Hendrie, a minister-without-portfolio from Hamilton, seemed to Whitney to be such a man. Inclined towards the private power point of view, Beck's equal as a horseman, and a determined committee infighter, Hendrie would balance Beck's radical populism. But at first Hendrie balked. "I think it would be better to leave me off this commission," he wrote to the Premier in May 1906, "not that I do not desire to serve the Government or the Province, but it might have the effect of starting friction in your Cabinet that I always had and always will have every desire to avoid. I am perfectly satisfied with my present position and work and would not in any way wish, to use a vulgar phrase, to butt in on another man's work." However, that is precisely why Whitney needed him, and after a private interview on the subject, Hendrie eventually agreed

---

possession. Whitney did not have much patience for the Electrical Development Company management and he was not entirely fair in dealing with them. When he was reminded of his word that he would consult the power company before introducing legislation based upon the Hydro-Electric Power Commission Report, he gave Henry Pellatt only a brief weekend's notice and a merely formal hearing on Monday morning; see PAO, Whitney Papers, Pellatt to Whitney, May 5; Whitney to Pellatt, May 5, private; Pellatt to Whitney, May 7; Whitney to Pellatt, May 7, private, S. H. Blake to Whitney, May 7, all 1906.

[13] Quoted in Hector Charlesworth, *Candid Chronicles* (Toronto, 1925), p. 175; for other assessments of the new Premier, see PAC, Lord Grey Papers, Grey to the King, May 3, 1905; Grey to Joseph Chamberlain, May 5, 1905, private.

to serve. Cecil B. Smith, a former general manager of the Temiskaming and Northern Ontario Railway, and a professional engineer, was selected as the third member.[14]

The permanent Hydro-Electric Power Commission would have to carry out the regulation of private utilities and, by means to be decided upon, undertake the distribution of electric power to the municipalities. As a sign the government meant business, and to guarantee co-operation from the companies, the commission was armed with powers of expropriation. In selecting its membership, Whitney set out to curb the boundless energy of the public power movement just as surely as that movement hoped to control the private power companies. The government intended to direct the pace of developments in the future, as Whitney made plain to Hendrie: "The Government will be so close to the work which may have to be done that the Commission must practically [be] a Committee of the Cabinet with certain statutory power."[15]

Angered by Whitney's apparent indifference to their interests and the betrayal of his pledge, the management of the Electrical Development Company opened a two-front campaign in the British capital markets and in the Canadian press against the government's hydro-electric policy. Late in May, 1906, H. E. Gordon, a British bondholder in the E.D.C. and friend of the Governor General, arrived in Canada to support Henry Pellatt's contention that government intervention in the power field would lead directly to a flight of English capital. The press dismissed the argument with jocular disdain. "If English capitalists are going to rise like a covey of scared partridges and quit the country whenever citizens stand up suddenly and object to being skinned," observed *Saturday Night*, "why, let them scare."[16] But Premier Whitney, whose government had just turned to the London money markets to finance capital projects and who would in all probability have to go there again to borrow capital for the very works that were in such unanimous

---

[14] PAO, Whitney Papers, Whitney to Hendrie, May 12, 1906; Hendrie to Whitney, May 14, 1906, both private.

[15] *Ibid.*, Whitney to Hendrie, May 15, 1906, private.

[16] *Saturday Night*, May 12, 1906.

demand, took the threat more seriously. The power legislation, he told the *Mail and Empire*, in no way endangered any capital invested in the province. Then he took great pains to explain the worrisome expropriation clauses of the power act for H. E. Gordon:

> The Government does not look forward to being compelled to exercise the power of expropriation given them by the Act—and without which such legislation would be entirely useless—but in the event of its being compelled to take such action, you may safely rely upon it that the interests of all holders of Bonds or other charges upon the property expropriated will be safe in the hands of the Government and that the security, which they now hold on the property, will not be impaired by the expropriation proceedings.

Whitney sent along a copy of his letter to Earl Grey, Gordon's friend, emphasizing the importance of the Commission to both the consumers and producers of power in Ontario. Lord Grey confirmed that Gordon, during his stay at Rideau Hall, had been "apprehensive" about the legislation in question, but the Governor General reassured him that the Ontario cabinet was one of "businessmen who fully appreciated and understood ...the importance to Ontario and the Dominion of the London market."[17]

London was still Canada's major source of long-term capital. In 1906 British investments in Canada totalled more than £3 million, mostly in railways and government issues, but a growing proportion was in industrial enterprises such as the Electrical Development Company.[18] Because London was such an important source of public and private borrowing, Whitney took extra precautions to counteract the alarmist propaganda

---

[17] PAO, Whitney Papers, Lord Grey to Whitney, May 29, 1906, private; Whitney to Lord Grey, May 28, private; Lord Grey to Whitney, May 29, private, 1906; Whitney to Gordon, May 23, 1906, private; *Canadian Annual Review*, 1906, p. 181; *Mail and Empire*, May 15, 1906.

[18] *Canadian Annual Review*, 1906, p. 196; F. W. Field, *Capital Investments in Canada* (Montreal, 1911), pp. 193ff., for details of company flotations between 1905 and 1911.

being circulated in London by the private power interests. To ensure that the gentlemen responsible for making investment decisions in London were in full possession of the facts, Whitney met with the representatives of the financial houses doing business in Canada during his vacation in England during the summer of 1906 and personally tried to clarify the power situation in Ontario.

What the Premier heard in London of the misrepresentations perpetuated by the power companies, and their press campaign back in Ontario, frankly disgusted him. "I have no hesitation in saying to you," Whitney wrote to Nicholls, "that certain of the gentlemen interested in the production of Power at Niagara have not only endeavoured to make capital against the Government unfairly but have also possibly injured the cause, or object they, apparently, desire to serve." From his secretary in Toronto Whitney learned that the Electrical Development Company, working through an advertising agency, was buying space in the letters to the editor and editorial columns of the daily press. A terse note in the board minutes of the company for September 27 reports: "The Third Report of the Hydro-Electric Commission was laid upon the Table and a discussion ensued upon the attitudes of the Newspapers towards the Company."[19] It was at about this time that John Ross Robertson of the *Telegram* confirmed the largely successful efforts of the company to purchase favourable opinion in the Toronto dailies. Apparently the *Canadian Engineer* also came under the influence of the Power Company for a brief time in 1906.[20]

The American-owned Ontario Power Company, counselled by Sam Hume Blake, chose to co-operate with rather than fight the Hydro-Electric Commission. Following an interview in May with Premier Whitney, General Greene had come away con-

---

[19] PAO, Whitney Papers, Whitney to Nicholls, June 2, 1906, private; same to same, July 9, private; Horace Wallis to Whitney, July 23, 1906, private; OHA, Electrical Development Company Minute Book No. 1, p. 149.

[20] PAO, Whitney Papers, Whitney to J. R. Robinson, Oct. 6, 1906, private; see also, Charlesworth, *Candid Chronicles*, p. 175; only in July and August of 1906 did the *Canadian Engineer* break with its traditional policy of municipal ownership of utilities and in 1907 it returned to that position.

vinced that the legislation proposed would do no harm to his company, and thereafter the management seems to have decided to make the best of the situation rather than aggravate it. Thus, during October, Blake and Greene laid three propositions before the Premier: the Ontario Power Company would sell power to the Hydro-Electric Commission at Niagara for under $12 per horsepower per year; or it would itself build a transmission system, retailing power at rates to be determined by the commission; or, thirdly, the company would act as a contractor and build the system for the government agency. The second proposal, not unlike the earlier suggestion by the Electrical Development Company, appealed to Whitney. "It seems to me," the Premier wrote to Beck, "that the propositions of this Company are remarkably reasonable and that without doing any injustice to the other Companies we should be glad to deal with them." In asking Beck to report on the desirability of coming to terms with the company, Whitney stressed: "They agree to ask no profit whatever out of the transmission. This offer, it seems to me, is a very reasonable one from our point of view." If the private companies would build the lines and operate them at cost while the commission controlled the rates, why should the government undertake the expense and at the same time risk the wrath of the English capitalists?[21]

However reasonable the suggestion appeared to Whitney, to Adam Beck and his near-fanatical allies, then in the throes of a great electoral struggle at the municipal level against "the interests," any suggestion of compromise amounted to heresy. The mere attendance of the Lieutenant-Governor at the Electrical Development cornerstone-laying in May generated a storm of protest; these same watchful forces on behalf of public ownership also interpreted the leasing in July of a waterpower on the Trent River to a private power company as further evidence that the people's interests were being neglected by the Whitney government. It appeared, the sec-

[21] PAO, Whitney Papers, General Greene to Whitney, May 29, 1906; Blake to Whitney, Oct. 19, 1906; Whitney to Beck, Oct. 20, 1906, confidential; Blake to Whitney, Nov. 29, Dec. 21, 1906; Whitney to Blake, Nov. 30, 1906, private.

retary of the Western Ontario Municipal Niagara Power Union pointed out to Whitney, that the government was withdrawing its confidence from Adam Beck and his proposed system. Whitney's support for the Ontario Power Company's privately owned scheme intensified that suspicion.[22]

Characteristically, Beck fought and won his point at the ballot box rather than in the cabinet. Before the Hydro-Electric Commission could proceed with its own transmission network as provided in the Power Act, the municipal voters would have to approve a by-law empowering their local councils to enter a contract with the commission to deliver electricity at the town limits at a specific price. In July the interested municipalities gathered at Galt to draw up a standard by-law to submit to their respective electorates at the regular elections on January 1, 1907. Throughout the fall and winter Adam Beck and Cecil Smith toured the province addressing meetings organized by the Power Union in support of the hydro by-law. The future of hydro and Beck's bargaining position within the Cabinet depended directly upon the outcome of these municipal elections.[23]

The press of the province lent Beck and his power by-laws almost unanimous support; in Toronto, for example, only the *Globe* and the *News* expressed any reservations. Then, on the eve of the polling, the most respected defender of the private interests, the *Monetary Times*, defected to the other side. After a careful examination of the conflicting evidence, and a reappraisal of the methods and motives of the private companies, the *Monetary Times*, in the interests of capital, set out the facts as it saw them, taking as its maxim the proposition: "The wise man of business is he who has an unfailing judgement as to what is inevitable." Since hydro had unshakable popular

---

[22] *Ibid.*, J. W. Lyon to Whitney, Sept. 13, 1906; Whitney to Lyon, Sept. 19, 1906, private; W. H. Greenwood to Whitney, Sept. 22, 1906, private; *Canadian Annual Review*, 1906, p. 182.

[23] *Canadian Annual Review*, 1906, pp. 181-5; C. B. Smith, "The Hydro-Electric Power Question," Dec. 27, 1906, *Empire Club Speeches, 1906-1907* (Toronto, 1907), pp. 131-44.

and political foundations, and since the by-laws were certain
to pass, further resistance was folly:

> The captain of industry is often an indifferent politician; which
> possibly, is one of the reasons why he is a captain of industry.
> When his business brings him into the region of public con-
> troversy, he is apt to make blunders which a ward worker, earning
> nine dollars a week, would avoid. It begins to look as though
> some of the power companies of Ontario have missed their way
> because of their inability to foresee the tendencies of public opin-
> ion operating through Government channels.

A publicly owned system had merit; it would provide healthy
competition without endangering capital already invested. The
superiority of the public power argument had been apparent
for some time; under the circumstances the *Monetary Times*
counselled the financial community to recognize the inevitable
and yield.[24]

The outcome was never really in doubt. In Toronto, the
key city, ratepayers voiced overwhelming approval for the
power by-law in the municipal elections. "The very fact that
the power companies seemed to be working so strenuously
against the by-law," the *Monetary Times* observed mordantly,
"must have cast thousands of votes on its side." All over the
province, in Ottawa, Hamilton, Galt, London, Guelph,
Ingersoll, Stratford, Paris, Preston, Weston, St. Thomas and
Waterloo, voters enthusiastically endorsed the principle of
public ownership. Beck had won the first round.

## II

After his great victory at the polls Adam Beck was eager to
press ahead with construction; but Whitney and the more conservative members of cabinet procrastinated in the hope that a
compromise might be arranged that would spare the financially troubled Electrical Development Company. Impatient with

[24] *Monetary Times*, Dec. 29, 1906.

the repeated delays, Beck stormed off to London. Whitney, whose temper was every bit as short, demanded that he return: "The Companies are now ready, if not anxious to treat with the Government by means of the Commission, and I hope you will come down prepared to discuss further progress in the matter." But even after the engineers of the commission had laid a detailed comparison of bids tendered by the Electrical Development and Ontario Power companies before the cabinet, recommending acceptance of the latter's offer of 25,000 horse-power delivered at Niagara for $10.40 per annum (the best the Electrical Development Company could do was $12.00), the government contined to stall. The difficulties of the Electrical Development Company became public knowledge after its February annual meeting. Privately its manager begged Whitney to do something for the only Canadian company, and more ominously still, Joseph Flavelle and Thomas White of the National Trust Company, trustees for the bondholders, supplied the Premier with the inside story of the troubles into which the company had been plunged.[25]

Without consulting the cabinet, Whitney asked Blake if the Ontario Power Company, although it had submitted a lower tender, would be willing to share the contract. His government felt committed to doing "anything reasonable" for the Canadian company, especially since it was in such perilous straits: " ...on abstract business principles, this might be considered as not fair to the Ontario Power Company, but perhaps such an arrangement could be arrived at." However, the company argued that it had co-operated fully with the government when the Electrical Development Company had been and was continuing to do the opposite, and it expected nothing less than fair treatment in return. "I cannot but think," Blake replied,

[25] PAO, Whitney Papers, Whitney to Beck, Mar. 9, 1907, private; Whitney to Beck, April 26, 1907, private; Beck to Whitney, April 27, 1907, personal; Whitney to Beck, April 27, 1907, private; see also the memorandum prepared by P. W. Southam comparing the Electrical Development and Ontario Power tenders, dated incorrectly Feb. 15, 1906; OHA, Electrical Development Company Directors' Minute Book No. 1, Minutes of the Annual Meeting, Feb. 25, 1907, p. 182.

"that the Electrical Development Company very much exaggerates all matters with which they deal. Of course the representatives propose to make themselves millionaires no matter at what cost it might be to others, and they naturally are disappointed when they fail in accomplishing this object. They have refused to listen to reason and appear to be manufacturing all kinds of reasons and statements to compel a result which they should never have asked." Without a realistic alternative, Whitney reluctantly agreed to the signing of a contract between the Hydro-Electric Commission and the Ontario Power Company on April 30, 1907. Nevertheless, he continued the negotiations even after the contract had been signed, only to fail once again on account of the Electrical Development Company's stubbornness.[26]

Premier Whitney's prolonged mediation, all against Beck's will and much of it without his knowledge, attest to his concern for the welfare of the Canadian company, or perhaps more accurately, for Ontario's credit rating in London. For there again, in spite of his visit the summer before, the renewed propaganda efforts of the company added to the fears of a financial community already apprehensive at the onset of a mild recession. These are "anxious if not critical times in the City," Arthur M. Grenfell, whose firm had placed about $3 million in EDC bonds, grumbled to his father-in-law, Earl Grey. The new troubles were "partly due to the want of confidence which has been gradually growing up as a result of State Socialism and the interference by Municipal and Government bodies in trade and against Capital." Whitney's own Lieutenant-Governor, in passing on the message, noted philosophically: "It may be absurd and narrow but nevertheless the managers of these big concerns are narrow."[27]

From his London financial agent, F. W. Taylor of the Bank of Montreal, Whitney learned the full extent of the mis-

---

26 PAO, Whitney Papers, Whitney to Blake, April 29, 1907; Blake to Whitney, April 30, 1907, private; F. V. Green to Blake, May 1, 1907, telegram; Beck to Whitney, Aug. 14, 1907; Whitney to E. C. Whitney, Oct. 9, 1907, private; *Canadian Annual Review*, 1907, pp. 518-520.
27 *Ibid.*, Sir Mortimer Clark to Whitney, April 2, 1907.

representations that had succeeded to a large extent in discrediting both the government and the company. During the summer of 1907 he made a second pilgrimage to London, but according to Taylor, his earnest explanations, even his protestations that he had not come for a loan, proved unconvincing. A stiff note from Arthur Grenfell confirmed the futility of the Premier's mission. "When we see the credit of the Province being used in favour of a foreign institution," Grenfell complained, "to provide lines for distribution of power in preference to the Canadian Company, we can only say the impression which will be produced in the mind of the investor will be in the highest degree detrimental to the interest of all concerned."[28] Despite Whitney's daring and protracted attempts to reach an accommodation with the company during the year, the reputation and credit of his province in the London markets had deteriorated dangerously. Upon his return he could only stand helplessly by as the company and the public power legions advanced relentlessly towards a head-on collision.

Toronto was an essential element in Beck's plan; without its concentrated commercial, industrial and domestic demand his system could not provide inexpensive power to the scattered western towns. Yet Toronto, the key city, did not possess a municipal electric system. There the private Toronto Electric Light Company (in reality the Electrical Development Company by another name) repeatedly thwarted city council's successive efforts, dating back to 1895, to take over the utility. In 1907, after the voters had indicated a desire to participate in the public power scheme, the long-drawn out negotiations came to a head.

Anticipating an expropriation attempt by the city, the company appealed to the Legislature to increase its capitalization in the spring of 1907. Whitney granted a $1 million increase, over the strenuous objections of the city council, but at the same time he permitted Beck to re-enact as a separate Power Bill those sections of the 1906 legislation that rendered

---

[28] *Ibid.*, Whitney to Taylor, July 5, 1907, private; Taylor to Whitney, Aug. 1, 1907; Arthur Grenfell to Whitney, Aug. 10, 1907.

inapplicable the Conmee clauses of the Municipal Act which, it will be remembered, forbad municipal competition with private utilities. The company received permission to increase the value of its property, and the city obtained the right to establish its own municipal distributing system without first having to expropriate the Toronto Electric Light Company.[29] After a tempestuous series of talks stretching over the summer and fall during which it became increasingly clear that the company would never surrender its property at anything near what the city considered a reasonable price, council refused to buy or expropriate the private utility but decided instead to establish a competitive system of its own. Therefore, on January 1, 1908, the ratepayers were asked to approve a $2,750,000 bond issue to build a municipal network which would distribute the Hydro-Electric Commission power that the electorate had committed the city to taking the previous year.

Both the company and the commission threw themselves into what each considered a life and death struggle. The Toronto Electric Light Company feared competition from a municipal system which could obtain its power from the Hydro-Electric Commission much cheaper than it could from the Electrical Development Company. By the same token, the commission itself could not exist without the strategic Toronto market. Meanwhile, unnoticed by everyone except Whitney and the distressed bondholders, the Electrical Development Company tottered on the brink of collapse.

Advocates of the by-law cleverly addressed themselves to the religious convictions and thriftiness of the ordinary man. Righteous allusions permeated Beck's own pamphlet, *The*

---

[29] The 1907 Act, 7 Edw. VII, c. 19, removed the Conmee clauses of the Municipal Act from operation against the Hydro contracts with the municipalities and repeated the safety clause of the 1906 Power Act which prevented legal action against the commission contracts: "Without the consent of the Attorney-General, no action shall be brought against the Commission or against any member thereof for anything done or omitted in the exercise of his office" (s. 24). For the long and bitter discussions between the T.E.L. Co. and the city, see the *Canadian Annual Review*, 1907, pp. 519-525.

*Genesis of the Power Movement*, and a proven religious format provided the structure for the Power Union's booklet, *Catechism on the Power Question*. Through municipal and public ownership, these pamphlets argued, the citizen would receive the compound benefits of more numerous, more prosperous industries, cleaner shops, safer streets, brighter homes, and lighter loads, and he would receive these advantages at a lower personal cost and a much greater social saving than through private ownership. However, the municipal power campaign depended as much on an appeal to the heart as it did to reason. The religious rhetoric fused to the hydro myth transformed the public power movement into a crusade against evil forces and villainous men who were constantly scheming to deprive the working man of his inalienable right to hydro-electricity at cost. The editorials of the Toronto *World* especially presented the campaign alternatives with compelling, fundamentalist simplicity:

> The greatest light that God gave to man is the pure white light generated by God's greatest masterpiece—Niagara Falls. Do not let the middlemen—the Gibson's, the Pellatt's, the Jaffray's, the Nichollses—get between the people and this great blessing and make it dear and limit its use, so that they may be rich.
>
> Let us keep it forever for all the people, and let us put it in the house of every citizen however humble, at cost price. We want no electric barons here as we now have coal barons of Pennsylvania, tolling us and tithing us at $7.00 a ton for coal, that public ownership of the mines and railways would give us for $2.50 a ton, or less.

Through the careful manipulation of an emotionally charged rhetoric Beck and his allies replaced a confusing, complex maze of ambivalent technical arguments with a simple world of heroes and scoundrels ("the Electric Ring...The Most Dangerous Ring in Canada"). In Beck's exciting fictional world it was so much easier to choose sides.[30]

---

[30] Both pamphlets were published in Toronto during 1907; for a detailed description of the campaign, see the *Canadian Annual Review*, 1907, pp. 522-525; Plewman, *Adam Beck*, p. 51; E. B. Biggar, *Hydro-electric Development in Ontario* (Toronto, 1924), p. 89ff.; *World*, Nov. 21, Dec. 14, 1907.

Opponents of independent municipal action, particularly the *Globe* and the *News* (both of whose owners had financial interests at stake), quietly asked for fair play for the investors, balanced potential savings against senseless duplication, discounted the immediate boon to the working man, and rebuked the by-law's supporters for their immoderate language—Willison of the *News* called it their "adjectival insanity." In their sometimes fervent plea for reason and justice, the *Globe* and the *News* were, more often than not, shouted down by the *Star*, the *Telegram*, the *Mail & Empire*, and especially the *World*. When the *Globe*, a constant supporter of the principle of public ownership, demanded on October 17 that the city first come to terms with the company, the *World* bellowed across its front page the next day: "The Mask is off; the Charlatan stands revealed!" When the *Globe* asked for justice for the eight hundred stockholders of the Electric Light Company back came the bold type, front page reply: "...*they* [the company and the *Globe*] *are one in the same crowd....Both have broken faith, both are extortionate, both give dear and poor service. Both are public enemies.*" As the voting day drew closer the *World* demanded to know: "Who Shall Rule, the 800 or the 80,000?"[31]

Over at the *News*, John Willison conducted, as might be expected, a reasoned but not entirely unemotional defence of private enterprise. While the *News* believed in public ownership, it would not tolerate competition between the state and private companies. As far as Willison was concerned, that amounted to confiscation of vested rights, and he urged Whitney and Beck to expropriate both the Toronto Electric Light and the Electrical Development Companies. "We are a borrowing country," he warned, "and if we plunder British investors it will be at our cost...when regulation is invited or expropriation under fair terms of arbitration may be arranged, duplication at the public cost is wasteful, unjust and immoral." State competition not only violated the unwritten rule governing international investment, it most certainly violated the spirit of the

---

[31] *Globe*, Oct. 17, 21; *World*, Oct. 18 (front page); *Globe*, Nov. 8; *World*, Nov. 9, Nov. 15, Dec. 20; *Globe*, Dec. 13, 17, 30; *World*, Dec. 17, 20, all 1907.

original franchise contract in which the government bound itself not to generate its own power. If the city and the government went ahead, "the revenues of the private company may be impaired, its securities depreciated, its ruin accomplished...." That was "neither British, honourable, nor decent."

> The transaction would be condemned in a South American Republic.... Moreover, capital would shun such communities, and they would sink to the level of outlaw states. Is a Conservative Government, the hereditary guardian of the rights of property, to persist in a course of action which is admitted to be unjust even by British Socialists?

The *World* simply cut through the fine distinctions and high moral tone of the *News* and the *Globe* with the blunt reminder: "They seek to muddle the public, befog the voter, frighten him with bogey men and bogey widows and orphans, ruinous outlay and the like, and to curry it with 'We are the true friends of public ownership.' "[32]

Premier Whitney had by this time lost whatever sympathies he formerly had for the management of the private company. He was angered by both its misrepresentations of government policy and its blatant purchase of editorial opinion. The leaders of the *News*, Whitney wrote his brother in Ottawa, were not those of Willison, the editor, but rather Flavelle, the owner: "It would be all right for us to repudiate our contract with the Ontario Power Company and then spend ten or twelve million dollars in expropriating the other people's property, in order that the pocket of Mr. Flavelle may not be injured." E. B. Osler tried vainly "to use some influence on the excitable people in the Crowd," but the management blundered foolishly onward. When a Boston broker wrote to complain that the

---

[32] Toronto *News*, Nov. 28, 29, Dec. 10, 12, 24; Toronto *World*, Nov. 13, 16, Dec. 9, 20, 1907. The *Monetary Times* supported the by-law, and the newly established *Financial Post* opposed it. The Toronto branch of the Canadian Manufacturers' Association announced its support December 20. On Saturday, December 28, four thousand people pressed into Massey Hall to hear Adam Beck argue emotionally for passage of the by-law.

power legislation was "more socialistic than any action taken against the corporations in this country," Whitney finally lost his temper. "I am only acquainted by hearsay with the methods of stock jobbers," he replied, "but the language used in your letter renders superfluous any explanation as to the motives which underlie the arrangement evidently made between your associates here and yourselves with a view to affecting the vote on a By-law of the City of Toronto."[33]

From W. H. Greenwood at the *World* Whitney learned that the *Mail*, *Globe*, *News* and *Star* were getting advertising rates for letters, articles and editorials favourable to the interests of the private utilities and that the *World* itself had been offered $350,000 to change its policy. Moreover, offended businessmen were withdrawing advertising from the *World*, which was at the best of times only a marginally profitable operation. Greenwood's request was straightforward enough: "I think it is reasonable to suggest that the government should see its friends through." A hundred thousand lines of government advertising at twenty-five cents a line seemed a reasonable compensation for losses suffered because of its views. Perhaps the government might also deposit $100,000 for one year in the *World*'s account at the Sovereign Bank. "It is a rough road for principle," moaned the hard-pressed editor, "and we want your encouragement." Although Whitney could not accommodate the *World*, he did raise the question at a cabinet meeting and visited Greenwood privately to explain his refusal.[34]

The long and heated campaign against his government by the very capitalists he was trying so hard to help eventually wore the Premier down. On December 21 he publicly chastised the company and its friends for flooding the press with "silly falsehoods," and especially for using their influence in the British markets to intimidate the government:

---

[33] PAO, Whitney Papers, Whitney to E. C. Whitney, Dec. 4, Dec. 5, 1907, private; Baker, Ayling & Co. to Whitney, Dec. 26, 1907; reply, Dec. 27, 1907.

[34] *Ibid.*, W. H. Greenwood to Whitney, Dec. 3, 1907, enclosures; Greenwood to Whitney, Dec. 5, 1907; reply, Dec. 27, 1907.

I hope and believe that the people of Toronto will not be led away by the array of anonymous false and discordant objections to the power scheme.... I pass over for the present the attitude of those who insist that the conduct of the Government in this matter is that of foot-pads and that it is neither British nor honest nor decent, and who, rejoicing in the possession of the rich vocabulary their language indicates would drive us if possible into spending from ten to fifteen million dollars of the people's money in a way which their own language shows would be unjustifiable.

The government was not going to confiscate anyone's rights or threaten anyone's investments; it was simply "an onlooker in this matter." Once the voters had made their will known, the government would act "simply [as] the go between or conduit pipe," buying power at Niagara and selling it at the municipal boundaries. The Premier took considerable satisfaction from the resounding vote of confidence the government's program received in the municipal elections. In Toronto 76 per cent approved the contentious by-law, and comparable majorities in other towns authorized municipal contracts with the Hydro-Electric Power Commission. It seemed like a promising harbinger for his own imminent provincial general election.[35]

Yet, though it seems incredible, even after the municipal elections in January Whitney did not think himself committed to a government-owned power transmission line as proposed by Beck! As a matter of fact, behind the façade of antagonism the bondholders and the Premier mounted a massive effort to save the Electrical Development Company. Their joint plan, had it worked out, would *not* have involved government ownership of the all-important transmission lines.

The financial problems of the Electrical Development Company stemmed primarily from the fact that the initial sale of bonds had not brought enough cash into the treasury to

---

[35] *Globe*, Dec. 21, 1907; *Canadian Annual Review*, 1907, pp. 523-524. The reference to "footpads" was an attack on Willison who had argued in the campaign: "The footpad who attacks and robs an unarmed citizen on the streets may get a cheap watch, but the transaction is generally not approved of by moralists." *News*, Nov. 29, 1907.

complete the works. This state of affairs arose in part from the techniques employed in the placing of these securities and the hostile atmosphere within which the company had been promoted which made it impossible to sell all of the bonds issued. Thus, the company had to scramble about trying to finance the remaining construction with expensive, short-term notes, using its unsold bonds as collateral. Late in 1906 the Bank of Commerce was prevailed upon for $400,000 and in April of 1907 Senator Cox's Canada Life Assurance Company agreed to loan the company another $100,000 at 7 per cent. In June the company obtained a further $900,000 from the Bank of Scotland to meet expenses and to pay off the note called by the Bank of Commerce. Although this large loan from the Bank of Scotland was renewed in December (Dominion Securities of Toronto accepting half of it at 7 per cent) there remained the difficulty of meeting $203,750 in bond interest falling due in March, 1908. Under normal circumstances this relatively small sum might have been raised with ease, however the by-law contest in Toronto had created a great deal of uneasiness in the financial community. Notwithstanding the adverse political circumstances, its policy of renewing short-term notes could not be pursued for long, even among friends. No company without income-generating assets could expect to borrow indefinitely to meet bond interest and to build what the bonds should have paid for in the first place. Thus, as 1907 drew to a close and as the municipal elections reaffirmed the influence of the public power movement, the Electrical Development Company appeared headed for a certain crack up.[36]

Early in December 1907 the bondholders informally took over effective management of the company and approached Whitney with two propositions: either the Electrical Development Company might rent its existing system at cost plus a fair return on the investment, or the government and

---

[36] OHA, Electrical Development Company, Directors Minute Book No. 1, minutes of meetings, April 15, 1907, p. 195; June 17, 1907, p. 198; Nov. 7, 1907, p. 204; see also Hall, "Electrical Utilities in Ontario Under Private Ownership," pp. 80-3.

the company could go into a partnership to supply power to the municipalities at cost plus maintenance and interest. Either way the government would obtain a hydro system without cost to itself, and would at the same time avoid unnecessary duplication of facilities and discredit in the capital markets. Although both proposals overlooked the fact that a contract had already been signed with the Ontario Power Company, Whitney was inclined to agree with the deputation of bondholders that an immediate and amicable settlement was more desirable than giving the American firm its due—at any rate, something could always be worked out later.[37]

At about this same time J. S. Willison (who, according to Whitney, felt "pretty badly over the situation") and E. B. Osler were working with great determination to moderate the public differences between the actual management of the company and the government. After consultations with the bondholders and the management Osler asked Whitney to broach the subject of either a revision of the Ontario Power contract or a merger of the Electrical Development and Ontario Power companies: "The Toronto Companies, I think, are hard pressed just now in connection with some of their loans falling due in Scotland, and I think they would be willing to come to a reasonable agreement if they could in any way see that there would be an end to the present condition which is hampering them." Cochrane, Hendrie, and Hanna supported Osler, but Whitney, ever cautious, counselled delay. "I think the Electric Power matter will come out all right in the end," he wrote his brother on December 13, "although that may mean that action will have to be postponed. It seems to me that with the chances in favour of new inventions every day . . . a little delay may turn out best for the interests of all parties concerned."[38]

While Whitney took some considerable pleasure from the electoral blow dealt Pellatt, Nicholls, Flavelle, White and the

---

[37] PAO, Whitney Papers, E. R. Peacock, manager of Dominion Securities, to E. A. DuVernet, Dec. 4, 1907, enclosure; same to same, Dec. 11, 1907.

[38] *Ibid.*, Whitney to E. C. Whitney, Dec. 4, 13, 26, 1907, all private; E. B. Osler to Whitney, Dec. 12, 1907, confidential.

others, he still did not see any pressing need to go ahead with construction of the Hydro-Electric Power Commission transmission line just yet. "There is no question that the public feeling is unanimous," Whitney explained to his brother on January 7, "and this of course, while it renders it easier to do what ought to be done, does not excuse us from acting very slowly and taking every possible step to prevent anything unfair or extreme." Instead, on January 11 he opened secret negotiations with the Ontario Power Company through Sam Hume Blake to determine whether "any step can be taken in the direction of a reasonable and desirable adjustment. . . ." Blake agreed to "absolutely private" discussions with E. B. Osler and W. D. Mathews but warned that Whitney would be held responsible if his participation were "regaled in the newspapers." At any rate, after two weeks of negotiations, during which Blake rejected every proposal advanced by the spokesmen for the bondholders of the Electrical Development Company, the talks collapsed. If the company had properly employed the money that it had raised according to the terms laid down in its prospectus, Blake indignantly explained to Whitney, there would be no need for either government assistance or help from the competition. Plainly, a great deal of the capital had not been applied to the works. "If these matters get noised abroad," Blake suggested coyly, "it strikes me that it will make people in England very slow to entrust Canadians with their money." The only hope for the Electrical Development Company, in Blake's view, was for it to pass "into the hands of persons of such wealth as can afford to make large advances to pay the floating debt, to extend the undertaking, and who will be willing to pass the payment of a dividend for some years."[39]

The second effort to save the private company late in January 1908 involved the Premier directly. Following preparatory talks with Earl Grey, B. E. Walker, and J. S. Willison, Major Guy St. Aubyn (Arthur Grenfell's brother-in-law) paid a call upon

[39] *Ibid.*, Whitney to E. C. Whitney, Jan. 3, 7, 1908, private; Whitney to Blake, Jan. 11, 1908, private; Blake to Whitney, Jan. 13, Jan. 18, Jan. 23, 1908, reporting the discussions with W. D. Mathews.

the Premier to inform him that the Association of American Bondholders and Shareholders was about to remove Ontario securities from the favoured list as a result of the government's attitude towards the Electrical Development Company. In St. Aubyn's opinion, the government had no choice but to expropriate the private company "in the public interest." The Premier, as he explained to his brother, refused: "I told him just what we told Osler and Mathews, that we will do all in our power to help any reasonable scheme by which this matter may be reasonably settled. . . . From what he says I think the Electrical Development Company has been given a chance until the month of March when it will probably go under if nothing is done." But in his bold explanation of the mysterious interviews with the British financier before the House in March, Whitney denied both the idea of expropriation and the thought of a compromise: "We had practically accepted the tender of the Ontario Power Company, the lowest tender offered, for the sale of power at a lower rate than the offer of the competing company, and therefore, we could not in honour retire from our position."[40]

It had become clear that either the government or some private individual would have to take over the Electrical Development Company or else it would expire with calamitous consequences for everyone concerned. When the government refused to move, William Mackenzie came forward to save the company. On February 14 he reorganized his Toronto railway empire and assumed direct control over the Electrical Development Company. Previously the company had been nominally independent, notwithstanding a directorate that linked it to Mackenzie's utilities complex. This reorganization merely brought the Electrical Development Company formally into the family. The process went as follows: Mackenzie created the Toronto Power Company as a holding company to control the Electrical Development Company, the Toronto and Niagara

---

[40] University of Toronto Archives, Walker Papers, Walker to Lord Grey, Jan. 28, 1908; Lord Grey to Walker, Jan. 27, 1908, confidential; PAO, Whitney Papers, Guy St. Aubyn to Whitney, Jan. 30, 1908, Feb. 6, 1908; Whitney to E. C. Whitney, Jan. 29, 1908, private; notes for speech in Legislature, Mar. 10, 1908; *Canadian Annual Review*, 1908, p. 301.

Power Company, and eventually, the Toronto Electric Light Company. The Toronto Power Company was itself controlled by the Toronto and York Radial Railway Company, which was in turn a subsidiary of the Toronto Railway Company. The object of all this manoeuvring was to permit the Toronto Railway Company to guarantee a sufficient number of Electrical Development Company bonds to complete its works. This consolidation, Walker hastily informed Major St. Aubyn, meant that the company would meet its bond interest on March 1, indeed his bank intended to loan the money for that very purpose.[41]

Nevertheless, between the announcement on February 14 and the actual takeover on the 26th, Whitney was under a great deal of pressure to acquire the company himself. Osler and Mathews "made a tremendous effort to come to an arrangement with us," the Premier told his brother, and their offer was "not altogether unreasonable either." In the meantime, as the government pondered the situation, the shareholders met and placed the company in Mackenzie's hands. "This saves the bondholders, and, in my opinion," wrote the Premier, "will make matters comparatively easy for us. Mackenzie will be so situated that it will be altogether in his interest to endeavour to meet our views." Clearly, Whitney's views were still not Beck's views. He fully expected that Mackenzie might "furnish us with power cheaper than anybody has expected" in the hope of obtaining generous government assistance in building his railways in northern Ontario.[42] Even after his speech in the House on March 10 Whitney thought

---

[41]   The Premier readily granted the letters patent to facilitate these changes in the hope of avoiding what he called a "smash up"; see PAO, Whitney Papers, Whitney to E. C. Whitney, Feb. 7, 1908, private; University of Toronto Archives, Walker Papers, Walker to St. Aubyn, Feb. 10, 1908; OHA, Electrical Development Company Directors Minute Book No. 1, Feb. 24, 1908, p. 207; Hall, "Electrical Utilities in Ontario Under Private Ownership," pp. 83-95.

[42]   PAO, Whitney Papers, Whitney to E. C. Whitney, Feb. 27, Feb. 28, 1908, both private; OHA, Electrical Development Company, Directors Minute Book No. 1, Mar. 10, 1908; Toronto Power Company, Directors Meetings, April 26, 1908, p. 2.

Mackenzie would arrange a merger with the Ontario Power Company, then volunteer to build the transmission system with the government merely controlling the rates. "If he offers this, with satisfactory conditions," the Premier confided to his brother, "it seems to me it would be desirable but, of course, there will be a great outcry against it and we will be accused of giving in to him [Mackenzie]. The *World* and the *Telegram* will no doubt take that line, as nothing will satisfy them but government ownership and management."[43] This possibility did not materialize immediately; Mackenzie concentrated instead on the pressing problems of settling the company's finances, drawing his empire into a tight, thoroughly integrated utilities complex, and improving personal relations with the government without extending or asking for firm commitments.

Nevertheless, with an election bearing down upon the government, it had to take some bold, substantive steps. In the absence of the expected better offer, the Hydro-Electric Commission completed its contract with the Ontario Power Company on March 21, 1908. Immediately thereafter the municipalities each signed their final contracts with the commission, but since this final contract differed slightly from the by-laws approved by the local ratepayers, a special bill had to be rushed through the House in May making the mayors' signatures "sufficient, legal, valid and binding."[44]

In the ensuing general election Beck was able to mobilize massive and enthusiastic popular support for the government's exertions against the interests and on behalf of cheap power. Yet, amazingly enough, Whitney was still not committed, nor was the commission, to public ownership of the critical transmission lines. The government had not yet let the contracts for the lines, nor would it until after the election. This key ambiguity soothed the private interests for the moment and at the same time allowed the public ownership supporters to think that the contracts would be let as a matter of course. To most observers

---

[43] PAO, Whitney Papers, Whitney to E. C. Whitney, Mar. 18, 1908, private; see below, note 47 for details of the attempted accommodation.

[44] *Ibid.*, Blake to Whitney, Mar. 21, 1908; Hydro-Electric Power Commission, *Annual Report*, 1909, p. 23, 128ff.

it seemed as if the government had no choice but public ownership. In fact, there remained a narrow, but substantial, range
of possible alternatives. Publicly it appeared as if a united government had striven with singular purpose toward public ownership; but privately, without Adam Beck's knowledge, the
senior members of that government had been continuously
exploring a whole series of compromises in the mutual interest
of the province and the industry. For the time being at least,
William Mackenzie thought that he had an understanding with
the Premier; so also did the voters of Ontario who returned
the reforming Conservative administration on June 8 with an
astonishing 66-seat majority.[45]


## III

An announcement on August 13, 1908, that the McGuigan
Construction Company had signed a contract with the Hydro-
Electric Commission to build a transmission line from Niagara
Falls to Dundas with branches running to Toronto in the east
and the municipalities in the southwest finally ended the long
period of uncertainty. It also brought an angry protest from
the Toronto Power Company. But this time Adam Beck and
James Whitney stood as one man in their determination to
resist the renewed attacks of the private company. After signing
the transmission line contract there could be no further indeci-
sion. "We must go forward no matter what happens," Whitney
explained to his Attorney General, J. J. Foy, in October, "and
it is possible that circumstances may occur in addition to those
which have occurred already which may justify some further
legislation next Session. No matter how we look at it, it all
comes back to this, that we must go on and not look back.
There may be danger in the former, but there would be practical
ruin and humiliation in the latter."[46]

William Mackenzie received the news with shocked dismay.
Immediately he reminded Whitney of their meeting in London

---

[45] *Canadian Annual Review*, 1908, pp. 332-350.
[46] PAO, Whitney Papers, Whitney to J. J. Foy, Oct. 8, 1908, private.

the summer before. Had the Premier not given him assurances then that he would not go ahead with a government line? "I assumed responsibility in connection with the Company's affairs," he wrote, "mainly through my belief that you and I could satisfactorily adjust matters." Since taking over he had done nothing without first informing the government; he had co-operated fully only to be betrayed. Whitney flatly denied Mackenzie's recollection. Far from coming to any agreement at their meeting, Whitney had merely suggested that the Electrical Development Company would have to approach the Ontario Power Company, with which the government was under contract, "with a view to acting together in case you wished to proceed further. To this you agreed...."[47] Apparently

[47] *Ibid.*, Mackenzie to Whitney, Aug. 7, 1908, personal; Whitney to Mackenzie, Aug. 10, 1908, private; Mackenzie to Whitney, Aug. 10, 1908, private. There is an undated memorandum on the power question (but probably February or March, 1908) from William Mackenzie in the Whitney Papers. This memo is likely the basis of Mackenzie's belief that an understanding had been reached between himself and the Premier. In the memo Mackenzie argued that a government transmission line would result in more expensive power than if the private companies and government co-operated in a mutually advantageous agreement. Duplication of facilities would prove very costly to both parties, he suggested; for example, the municipal utilities on the government line would have to pay for their power, the line losses, insurance, operating costs, and repairs of the system, plus 4 per cent interest, and sinking fund contributions. Instead of competition between two systems, one public one private, Mackenzie proposed that the Electrical Development and the Ontario Power companies merge to form a common distribution company which would build its transmission lines "as the Government may require." Then, Mackenzie noted, "let contracts be entered into between the Power Companies and the municipalities. ..." If the government wished it could set up a commission to control rates, and if it did so, that would remove the necessity for a competitive publicly owned municipal system in Toronto. Finally, the government could help lower the capital costs of the transmission system by guaranteeing the bonds of the company. That way it would have effective control without risk or expense, the company would have low interest rates, and the municipalities cheap power all without unnecessary duplication and the bitterness of competition. But this document also bears the evidence that no agreement had in fact been reached between the Premier and Mackenzie. For in the sentence, "let contracts be entered into between the Power Companies and the municipalities ..." Whitney had stroked out "Power Companies" and inserted "Gov't."

Mackenzie had listened only to what he wanted to hear; if he had interpreted the Premier's conciliatory manner as an admission of defeat, he had been sadly mistaken. "Your recollection is at fault," the Premier replied, "when you suggest that a proposition came from me to allow the matter to stand until a more reasonable time." Mackenzie scurried to make contact with the Ontario Power Company, but that opportunity had fled with the spring.

The British bondholders raised the predictable cry of "confiscation," but that tiresome story lost a good deal of its impact on the third telling. "If the investing public on this side could be satisfied once and for all," an exasperated Arthur Grenfell wrote Whitney in November, "that there was no question of the Ontario Government experimenting with public ownership in competition with private enterprise, and to the injury of vested interests, money could be more readily found here for high class industrials and the difficulty of financing the many concerns which are ready for expansion would be considerably lessened." But Whitney had already made two pilgrimages to London and had carefully explained, then repeated, his policy both in letters and in private talks. With this third attack he unleased his considerable temper. The transmission system, he reminded Grenfell, had been public knowledge for years and at no time had he given any assurances that it would be changed in any way. Surely Mackenzie's action had satisfied the English security holders; in any event, his government, he frankly admitted, had grown tired of the persistent whimpering of the ill-informed, unbelieving British investors: "We will protect all vested rights, and the rights of investors as far as we can, but not against the folly and stupidity of these owners and investors, and we will not be deterred by any talk of state competition—which has no relation to the situation—from carrying out an agreement to act as the agents and intermediaries for the municipalities in this matter."[48]

On November 20 the Premier granted an interview to Mr. W. R. Lawson of the *Financial Times* of London. During this

---

[48] *Ibid.*, A. M. Grenfell to Whitney, Nov. 17, 1908; reply, Dec. 4, 1908, private.

interview Whitney took violent exception to the reporter's impudent tone and especially his impertinence in asking where the government thought it could possibly borrow the money to build the line. Mr. Lawson was shown the door, and the Premier, infuriated by both the insult and perhaps the fact that he could not answer the question, dashed off a memorandum account of the incident for his own personal reference:

> I declined to discuss the matter with him when he finally said with a very superior air "That the Government did not know what it was doing." I told him that in this country language such as he used was considered to be impertinence. He evidently felt that he had gone too far, but I closed the interview.

This interview, noted the *Monetary Times*, "would have formed an excellent prologue for a farce."[49] It also dramatically ended Whitney's patient humouring of the London capitalists.

Two days before this suspended interview, Whitney and Beck had proudly reviewed the government's power policy for two hundred and fifty municipal representatives gathered at the sod-turning for the transmission line. Driven into the Horticulture Building of the Toronto Exhibition grounds by torrential rains, Beck confidently projected a vision of Ontario Hydro stretching from Belleville in the east to Windsor in the west. Over its municipally owned but government-financed lines would run the cheap power that would maintain Ontario's "supremacy as a manufacturing centre" and break its dependence upon "a foreign nation for our coal supply." Premier Whitney used the occasion to describe the many obstacles that had blocked the way. A municipal co-operative like Ontario Hydro was a unique institution, and he thanked the municipalities for standing by the government as it sought, without precedent, the best method of going ahead. "We have not gone thus far to be stopped in the good work," he concluded, "we will not be discouraged and will not be deterred by any such thing as technicalities or difficulties of an ordinary

[49] *Ibid.*, memoradum, Nov. 20, 1908; *Monetary Times*, April 10, 1909.

nature."[50] Like its predecessor before it, the Toronto Power Company had chosen to fight when resistance was folly.

This time the battle was fought out in the courts. Actions were launched against Toronto and London to prevent those cities taking power from Ontario Hydro, but inasmuch as the commission was a co-defendant, the permission of the Attorney General was required before the suits could proceed. The Premier, acting in that capacity, refused to grant a fiat. Then the mayor of Galt refused to sign a contract with the commission on the grounds that its terms did not correspond with those of the by-law empowering him to act, and Mr. Justice Anglin refused an appeal to make him sign. "I do not agree," wrote Judge Anglin in his judgment, "in the view that the mayor...is a mere automaton, bound to place his signature to any document or instrument, however vicious or illegal, merely because he has been directed to do so by the Municipal Council."[51]

During the 1909 session the government met this challenge with legislation that simply declared that the contracts were both valid and beyond the jurisdiction of the courts. Thus the Toronto Power Company had its only means of redress cut off. In bowing to the will of the Legislature Mr. Justice W. R. Riddell explained the position of the court:

> This Legislation is within the limits fixed by the British North America Act and so is perfectly valid. I have not to tell the Legislature what to do; I am a creature of the Legislature— though not a subservient creature. If the Legislature says, it is your duty not to try such and such an action, it is my duty not to try it. I am here to carry out the laws.

Chief Justice Falconbridge also confirmed the constitutionality of the government's harsh legislation in dismissing a related action:

> We have heard a great deal recently about the jurisdiction of the Province, a good deal of complaint about the exercise of

---

[50] *Canadian Annual Review*, 1908, p. 305; Plewman, *Adam Beck*, p. 53.
[51] *Canadian Annual Review*, 1908, p. 307.

its powers; but there is no doubt that the highest authority has declared that within its own jurisdiction it is supreme; in fact, while it seems rather severe I suppose there is not any doubt it has been conceded in recent cases that if the Legislature had chosen to confiscate—the word that is used—the farm of the plaintiff without any compensation they would have a perfect right to do it in law, if not in morals.[52]

At this late stage the government could brook no opposition from the private company even if it meant removing its right of access to the courts.

The next threat to the government power policy may only have existed in Beck's fertile imagination. The chairman of the Hydro-Electric Commission refused to accept the lowest tender for an equipment contract from the Canadian General Electric Company, whose directorate interlocked with that of the Toronto Power Company. Sam Hume Blake shared Beck's opinion that if the General Electric people were granted the contract to supply transformers and equipment for the power lines, especially the trunk section from Niagara to Dundas, it would sabotage the entire system: "The very anxiety shown by the antagonistic Company to obtain this key to the situation should be a warning that danger may be anticipated, and that what is really sought is such a position as will largely give control to General Electric."

Whitney dismissed that conspiratorial view and ordered Beck to arrange a sharing of the contract between Westinghouse and General Electric. But Beck absolutely refused to have anything to do with his old enemy, Frederic Nicholls, the general manager of the latter company, and promptly sulked off to London. Whitney demanded his presence at a cabinet meeting to discuss the matter and insisted that General Electric, by virtue of winning the bidding, should be given two-thirds of the territory, and Westinghouse the remainder. "I fully appreciate your earnestness in the matter," Whitney explained to his petulant minister, "and only wish to impress upon you the absolute necessity of the matter being closed up now at once

---

[52] Hydro-Electric Power Commission, *Annual Report*, 1909, pp. 305ff.; *Canadian Annual Review*, 1909, pp. 373-379.

without further dragging. . . . I cannot find words to express more strongly what I mean when I say that this proposition ought to be accepted by the Commission, and the Westinghouse people told that it must be accepted by them." In other words, Whitney recommended giving the Niagara to Dundas, Dundas to Toronto contracts to General Electric. But Beck stubbornly held out; he would not permit the crucial trunk of the Y-shaped system to fall into the hands of the old private power crowd. After several more "retreats" Whitney finally gave in. The cabinet agreed to letting the two arms of the Y to General Electric, and the Niagara–Dundas trunk to Westinghouse. Nicholls once again complained bitterly that Whitney had betrayed him, but the Premier had no choice but to stand behind his Hydro chairman no matter how frightening Beck's nightmares.[53]

Federal disallowance of the 1909 legislation was a much more tangible and menacing possibility. In support of its appeal for disallowance, the Toronto Power Company lawyers gathered the hostile "Views of English and Canadian Writers and Correspondents" into a pamphlet entitled *The Credit of Canada: How it is Affected by the Ontario Power Legislation*. They used these opinions to support their main contention that Ontario had acted unconstitutionally, primarily because its precipitous action had threatened the financial standing of the entire dominion. Professor A. V. Dicey opened with the view that although the province was within its jurisdiction the "injustice and impolicy" of its action was "almost patent." Inevitably, there was space reserved for "Goldwin Smith's Opinion," a senile fulmination against another transgression of a British freeman's rights which, he had to confess, was fully to be expected in a colony: "It is perhaps not wonderful, considering the mixture of elements here, and the general circumstances of a colony, that there should be a change in the political spirit. . . . It is a land

---

[53] PAO, Whitney Papers, S. H. Blake to A. F. Lobb, Feb. 13, 1909; Whitney to Beck, Jan. 28, 1909, private; same to same, Feb. 1, 1909, private; Nicholls to Whitney, Feb. 15, 1909; Whitney to Nicholls, Feb. 15, 1909, private; A. F. Lobb to Nicholls, Feb. 15, 1909.

of graven images, and they are mad upon their idols." From that high point the intellectual tone of the pamphlet rapidly descended to the tiresome pleading of the Duchess of Marlborough's estate manager and the prosaic drone of the minions of corporate finance.

Of all the London financial papers, the *Financier and Bullionist*, the *Statist*, the *Economist*, the *Investor's Review*, it was W. R. Lawson in the *Financial Times*, as might be expected, who supplied the most scathing condemnation of Ontario's power legislation. Playing upon the Minister of Justice's reluctant admission in the Cobalt Lake case that a provincial government had the authority to repeal Magna Carta if it so wished, Mr. Lawson fantasized that:

> Sir James Whitney would have been a Prime Minister and Attorney General after King John's own heart. As the Pooh-Bah of Runnymede he would have been in his element, and an interview between him and the bold, bad barons of Magna Carta would have been worth listening to. Few men are born at the proper time and live in the century they really belong to. There is, at least one Ontario politician of today who is seven hundred years behind his age.

The *Investor's Review* explained it all quite simply: "The [Canadian] Legislatures, nine in number, are filled with country lawyers, storekeepers and farmers, usually honest enough personally, but always ready to follow their leaders when their leaders are doing wrong, on the principle that party loyalty is then more admirable than when the leaders are doing what is right."[54] These critics constantly restated with varying degrees of vigour, two main themes: that the Ontario legislation had created competition between the state and industry, contrary

---

[54] *The Credit of Canada: How it is Affected by the Ontario Power Legislation* (Ottawa, 1909), *passim*. The *Monetary Times* was conspicuous by its absence. Throughout it contended that the government might have acted a little impetuously but thought the idea of Henry M. Pellatt defending Canada's credit abroad absurd. See, in particular, the delightful jousting parody in the April 11, 1909 issue.

to vested rights; and that the 1909 legislation in particular removed the traditional, constitutional guarantees of legal redress. In both cases, the credit of Canada had been impaired; Lawson calculated the loss at about £ 600,000. "They can hardly feel flattered as a nation," he wrote, "when a 3 per cent. Dominion guarantee is not valued in London higher than 82½. Even the Ontario Ministers see something wrong with that."

Before launching his counterattack, Whitney first took the pulse of the London market through Frederick Williams Taylor, manager of the Bank of Montreal in the City. Discontent was limited to those holding Ontario electrical securities, Taylor reported: "I am quite satisfied that in no respect has your credit been impaired." His confidence renewed, the Premier answered the pamphlet in a series of public speeches. The legislation had been necessary, he explained, to expedite the will of the people which had been expressed so unequivocally in two by-law campaigns and a general election. Action had been taken at the request of the municipal councils themselves who wished to get on with the project without further expense or delays. Nor was there anything extraordinary about the clauses removing the contracts from the judgment of the courts without the permission of the Attorney General; these terms were part of a great deal of legislation both in Ontario and Great Britain, and here he quoted the English Education Act with telling effect. Then he denounced in turn the English financial press for depending solely upon interested parties for its information, and the power company—though he did not name it—for using its influence so scurrilously: "All the watered-stock experts and stock gamblers in Canada are on the side of our opponents in this matter and the latter are paying full rates for every line, for every word, published in their interest by the newspapers in this country. . . ."[55]

---

[55] PAO, Whitney Papers, Frederick Williams Taylor to Whitney, Dec. 29, 1908, private and confidential. When it came time to sell bonds to finance the transmission line the government chose to place them in the Canadian market just in case. It was good business if bad faith. *Monetary Times*, April 30, 1910; Plewman, *Adam Beck*, p. 94; *Canadian Annual Review*, 1909, p. 380.

Whitney wanted desperately to reply to the London papers just as bluntly, but Frederick Williams Taylor, in restraining him, explained that many judicious gentlemen of finance, though they felt that Ontario had gone a little too far, would welcome a calm statement of policy, but would react strongly to an explosion of temper. The Premier took the advice, drafted a moderate, but forceful letter to the *Economist* and *Standard of Empire*, and passed on a similar recommendation to his Provincial Secretary, W. J. Hanna, who was preparing for a trip to England that summer:

> We feel that we are not bound to answer to charges of every Tom, Dick or Harry who chooses to attack us. You will, therefore, be pretty careful of the newspaper men. There will be no harm in your saying something like this—the Ontario Government declines to make any answer to the ridiculous charges of confiscation, etc., which have appeared in the newspapers. While this may not seem satisfactory it is the only course we will take, because, the full explanation will be too long a story and would only cause further attacks.

From London both Hanna and Taylor reported that the offensive behaviour of Pellatt, Nicholls, Mackenzie and H. H. MacRae (who had been in London all spring using his influence with the press) had genuinely alienated the London capitalists and that they were now inclined to sympathize with the government.[56]

On October 7, 1909, Sir Wilfrid Laurier, William Pugsley, and E. L. Newcombe for the Minister of Justice, heard the petition for disallowance of the 1909 Ontario power legislation. F. H. Chrysler, counsel for the petitioners, contended first of all that since the Niagara was an international waterway, it lay outside the jurisdiction of the Ontario government. Furthermore, he argued that the Ontario Hydro-Electric Commission, which threatened the investment of a multitude

---

[56] PAO, Whitney Papers, Taylor to Whitney, May 12, 1909, confidential; Whitney to W. J. Hanna, June 17, 1909; Hanna to Whitney, July 26, 1909, and Whitney to Taylor, Aug. 9, 1909, private and confidential.

of private investors, had been thrust upon the municipalities which would have to pay for thirty years whatever the commission chose to charge them without any right of appeal in the courts. The action of the province amounted to virtual confiscation of private property, and while he was aware that such action was not a violation of the letter of the British North America Act, it did contradict its "spirit and purport":

> It may be unconstitutional without being prohibited in the British North America Act. The B.N.A. Act is not a complete category of the constitutional rights either of the Dominion or of the Province, or of the citizens either. If it is possible for the Province to legislate to the extreme limit of its power, so long as it does not break an express stipulation of the British North America Act, is it to be said that the power of disallowance does not exist?

Newcombe raised this matter again in questioning later; did counsel mean that the Ontario legislation was unjust rather than *ultra vires*? Chrysler replied: "Yes, exactly, unconstitutional in a political sense." The Prime Minister then asked him: "Would that be one of the grounds upon which you would appeal to the court, that you thought you had a right to be tried?" Somewhat discouraged by the turn of questioning, Chrysler responded: "I am afraid that is not a ground upon which the court would relieve us. I use the word 'constitutional' in a sense other than legal." The power company asked the federal government to exercise its power of disallowance in defence of human rights and natural justice; but unfortunately, the Judicial Committee of the Privy Council had swept away that authority in 1896, along with the right to legislate on behalf of "peace, order and good government."[57]

The Ontario reply, drafted by J. J. Foy, Adam Beck, and Whitney, which was heard on December 7, dismissed the international waterway contention with a mild jest: "The rights

---

[57] *Ibid.*, argument before the Privy Council on the Petitions for vetoing of the Power Legislation of Ontario, pp. 28, 37, 55, 57, 68-69.

of the Dominion over the River are only so far as it is navigable, and the River's non-navigability at the points referred to, is apparent and notorious."[58] Had the 1909 act been imposed upon the municipalities against their will, then Ontario conceded that there might have been a case for disallowance. But far from opposing the government's action, the municipalities had demanded it to avoid the delay of a third vote on a principle already overwhelmingly approved. "Careful consideration of the facts must result in the conclusion that the Legislation in question was desirable and necessary in order to prevent great injury to the Power Scheme." J. J. Foy cited thirty-four instances in Great Britain where access to the courts was restricted without apparent damage to that country's credit, and he concluded by quoting Osler, Mackenzie and Walker—surely judicious choices—on the buoyant financial condition of Canada. In short, the Ontario laws were popular and constitutional, the alleged damage to Canada's credit rating manufactured for the occasion, and the plaintiff's legal argument specious.

So confident was the Ontario government of the outcome that the construction work went ahead without interruption, Whitney's presumption was fully warranted. Although Sir Wilfrid let it be known that he disapproved of the legislation, he had also admitted Ontario's right to pass it. Just after the formal hearing, in November 1909, Laurier expressed his candid opinion on disallowance to Hugh Blain, a prominent Toronto businessman and Liberal who had an interest in the Electrical Development Company appeal:

> You say that as a Liberal you have always . . . thought we should be guided by principle rather than policy. In this I altogether agree with you. Allow me to remind you of this. Is it not a

---

[58] *Ibid.*, Ontario brief before the Privy Council on the Petitions for vetoing of the Power Legislation of Ontario, pp. 1-6; the light touch was added by Whitney himself. On this point of disallowance, see Eugene Forsey, "Disallowance of Provincial Acts, Reservation of Provincial Bills, and Refusal of Assent by Lieutenant-Governors since 1867," *CJEPS*, Vol. IV (1938), pp. 47-59.

fact that for more than forty years, under the guidance of Mowat and Blake, the Liberal party has stood by the principle of no disallowance of provincial legislation? Our party has had many a fight under Sir Oliver Mowat and Mr. Blake for the maintenance of this principle and after many years of conflict it finally prevailed and was practically endorsed by the whole community.

The local legislature has certain powers vested in it. These powers may be abused, but we have always held that the remedy was not in the exercise of the power of disallowance by the stronger government at Ottawa, but by the people of the Province themselves. The legislation of which you complain has been passed unanimously by the Legislature of the province without a word of dissent from anybody. Were we to disallow this legislation, it would be re-enacted again by the Whitney government, disallowed again, re-enacted once more, and when would that end?

Principles and prudence recommended a policy of non-interference. Certainly Laurier's views would have been public knowledge in the Toronto business community well before the final announcement on March 29, 1910. The Minister of Justice's declaration that the petition had been dismissed merely confirmed the obvious. In the case of an abuse of power by a provincial legislature, even to the extent of confiscation of property without compensation, Aylesworth pointed out echoing Laurier's letter, an appeal against such action lay not to the federal government but rather, and he quoted Lord Herschell, "to those by whom the Legislature is elected."[59]

Aylesworth's report removed the last of a long series of obstacles against a publicly owned hydro-electric distribution system for the province of Ontario. The Hydro chairman and the

---

[59] PAC, Laurier Papers, Laurier to Hugh Blain, Nov. 23, 1909, 162331-162332; PAO, Whitney Papers, A. B. Aylesworth, Minister of Justice to Governor-General in Council, Mar. 29, 1910, Report on Disallowance, pp. 7-8, 10-12. For details of this disallowance fight, see Christopher Armstrong, "The Politics of Federalism: Ontario's Relations with the Federal Government, 1896-1941" (unpublished Ph.D. thesis, University of Toronto, 1972), Chapter Four.

Premier were naturally elated. "When, if ever," the Premier declared on hearing the news, "the secret history of the fight of the corporate electric interests to destroy the Hydro-Electric Power Project is made public the people will indeed be amazed."

> The unfair and dishonest methods adopted against this legislation prove clearly that when men's pocketbooks govern their actions they are not as a rule particular as to the nature of the means they are willing to adopt. From the beginning the electric interests in Toronto and elsewhere were the bitter opponents of this legislation. All the stock gamblers were against it. An emissary was sent over to England and the so-called financial journals there blossomed out with editorials made up very largely of misrepresentation and frigid, calculated falsehood. Every imaginable influence over there, social, political, private and public, was retained where possible and all who realize the strength of such combined influence in London, will at once appreciate what this meant.[60]

In Ontario, Adam Beck was the man of the hour. He personified the hydro system and certainly did not underact his part. Beck personally transformed the "switching on" of the publicly owned network that autumn into an ecstatic celebration of Niagara mythology and a symbolic re-enactment of the righteous crusade. These ceremonies further served, it might be added, as a chilling demonstration of Beck's rapidly growing extra-parliamentary power.

For the first "switching on" ceremony on October 11, 1910, the Berlin *News Record* bore a yellow headline—THE POWER BUND —ringed with electric sparks. Beneath this banner a transmission line connected a sketch of Niagara Falls on the left with a brilliantly lit, smokeless factory on the right. Underneath that, bold type broadcast A GREAT DAY FOR ONTARIO; the inside pages blazed, NIAGARA FALLS—BERLIN RISES; and everywhere columns shouted unstinted praise for Adam Beck, "the human dynamo," "the doer of things." The more conserv-

---

[60] Quoted in Plewman, *Adam Beck*, pp. 97-98.

ative *Daily Telegraph* the next morning simply carried a full front-page portrait of Adam Beck and inside devoted itself fully to reporting the previous day's carnival happenings. Banners were strung between light standards already draped with bunting; thousands lined the streets to catch a glimpse of Beck and Whitney passing in open motor cars. Late in the afternoon the crowds jammed the dim Berlin arena for the real show. Hilda Rumpel, swathed in red, white and blue, carried the button, which would summon the electric genie from Niagara, atop a plush red cushion. Playing his part magnificently, Premier Whitney took the hand of Beck, his Minister of Power, and guided it toward the button. The crowd hushed as the Premier solemnly announced: "Gentlemen, with this hand, tried and true, this hand which has made this project complete, I now turn on the power." Suddenly the arena blazed with light, the current from Niagara surged through the mass with one great cheer. Little Hulda Rumpel's crown of tiny light bulbs glowed proudly, and the crowd roared itself hoarse.

The mayor of Berlin thanked Beck effusively in German, and Beck responded by praising Berlin's own hydro pioneers, his own technical staff, the united municipalities, and the Whitney government. "You say our work is done. I say that it has only begun. We must deliver power to such an extent that the poorest working man will have an electric light in his home. No more oil and gas, and soon, I hope, no more coal." That evening at a banquet at the Market Hall, five hundred dignitaries sat down to an "excellent dinner cooked by electricity generated at Niagara." Dan Detweiler proposed a toast to the commission, and upon rising to reply Beck received a standing ovation. When the tumult died he re-lived the old struggle against the "Electric Ring," the glorious triumph that had been won by dint of hard work and pre-ordained municipal virtue, and he stressed again that neither the work nor the fight was finished. As he resumed his seat the band in attendance struck up "See The Conquering Hero Comes" and played it through four times before the cheering let up. When his time came Whitney briefly recapitulated the tremendous campaign that had been mounted to crush the government's power policy: "We have been attacked, vilified and even slandered." Men of influence, he claimed, "from the humblest man in the land up to the Prime Minister of Great Britain were approached in the endeavour to destroy our power legislation. . . ." And at what was the ending of one struggle and merely the beginning of another, the Premier mustered a moving word of praise for Beck: "We, Adam Beck's colleagues, can never forget his steady confidence in the result and the bravery and pluck with which he stood up against all attacks."[61] It was Beck's day, and the Premier stayed contentedly on the sidelines. It was also Beck's day when the morality play was staged again and again in the nine other participating hydro municipalities.

IV

The Hydro-Electric Power Commission that finally went into business in 1910 was a monument to the energy of Adam Beck and the influence of his movement. Beck the strategist identified the immediate goals and Beck the charismatic leader galvanized a group of small businessmen and municipal politicians into a crusading movement. The capacity of the leadership and the ownership question to convert a dissatisfaction into a movement with clear-cut political objectives distinguished this progressive crusade from its contemporary, the conservation movement. The question of ownership opened up temporary class divisions in Ontario. Hydro-electric power was too important to be left in the hands of those who had been able to seize it. The confrontation over the ownership issue in successive electoral contests infused the movement with righteousness and built up mass support for it. Beck framed the conflict in these terms, mobilized the forces, and in election after election carried the day. Because he had to work from a minority position within his party, Beck relied upon his bi-partisan, extra-parliamentary authority to induce the required majorities. Whenever the procrastination of the Premier or the obstruction of his col-

---

[61] Berlin *News Record*, Oct. 11, 1910; Berlin *Daily Telegraph*, Oct. 12, 1910; Plewman, *Adam Beck*, pp. 66-67.

leagues exceeded the limits of patience, Beck would retreat to his power base in western Ontario and wait behind the ramparts of the Municipal Power Union until he had won his point.

The public power movement that Beck led was a progressive businessmen's crusade which, in the course of its struggles, acquired mass support. In very simplified terms the power question pitted the haute against the petite bourgeoisie of Ontario. The capital-intensive character of the hydro-electric industry necessarily allied the agents of finance capitalism—the investors, brokers, banks, insurance companies—on one side against the consumers of power—merchants, manufacturers and ratepayers—on the other. The ensuing contest of interests was conducted in such a way that the most powerful individuals in the society could not form the most powerful group; namely, a majority in an election. In the Ontario of the time the forces that separated these business groups were stronger than the ideology that united them. The clearly visible intentions of the haute bourgeoisie in the power business were perceived to be antagonistic to the welfare of the community as a whole—as that interest was conceived and articulated by the small businessmen of the public power movement. Moreover, the petite bourgeoisie could demand public ownership of electrical distribution as a means of promoting rapid industrialization without feeling any strong ideological anxieties. Under the circumstances, their psychic and practical need for cheap and immediate delivery of electricity effectively overrode their traditional laissez-faire, liberal capitalist sentiments. Since there was no one to their left advocating the same goal in the name of socialist principles, the manufacturers, merchants and ratepayers could press their class interest with extraordinary vigour. Imputations of socialistic behaviour were readily dismissed by both the movement and the government. "It is indeed a ghastly joke," Whitney once told a British journalist, "to charge the Ontario Government with being socialist, etc., when it is the bulwark in Canada by means of which such influences will be shattered."[62]

[62] PAO, Whitney Papers, Whitney to A. J. Dawson, July 7, 1909.

Public ownership as eventually practised by the Whitney administration, from the unobstructed point of view of the urban businessman, was the most effective method, as Harold Innis once observed, of "tempering the more recent advances of the industrial revolution to a thinly populated, relatively non-industrial area." In that respect it was a function of economic backwardness. Public power was also a classic, radical democratic cause. As well as being a practical method of obtaining an immediately desirable economic objective, it was also a defensive measure against one of the more obvious abuses of capitalism.[63]

Throughout this intra-class struggle the Premier was forced into the role of conciliator in order to protect the provincial credit. The haute bourgeoisie, having been rebuffed at the polls, turned their considerable personal influence upon him with telling effect. Notwithstanding his open support of Beck, Whitney conceived his main function between 1905 and 1908 to be the arrangement of a mutually satisfactory settlement between the opposing groups. Though from time to time he took private delight from the discomfort of some of the more pompous and foolish members of the embattled elite, he also feared the consequences of their total defeat. As far as he was concerned there were many positions short of outright public ownership upon which both parties might be made to agree. However, the intransigence of the desperate financial community and the persistence of the zealous power crusaders precluded such a compromise. When an accommodation proved impossible—though it was a near enough thing at times—for better or for worse the unpopular and foolhardy financiers had to be abandoned to their fate.

However reluctantly, the Whitney government pushed the state into a new and important role. The beginnings of the provincial power utility, though noisy, were nevertheless modest enough. The commission bought its power from one of the

---

[63] H. A. Innis, *Problems of Staple Production in Canada* (Toronto, 1933), pp. 76-81; Alexander Gershenkron, *Economic Backwardness in Historical Perspective* (Cambridge, Massachusetts, 1962), pp. 5-30, Samuel H. Beer, *British Politics in the Collectivist Age* (New York, 1965), pp. 34-43.

private companies at Niagara and merely distributed it over its own lines to a handful of municipal utilities. But in the superior legal and political position of the Ontario Hydro-Electric Power Commission, in the relentless ambition of its chairman, and the monopoly characteristics of the industry, one could discern the shape of things to come.

# 8
# Joining the
# New Empire

The rise of the new staple industries during the early decades of the twentieth century permanently reshaped the contours of the Canadian economy. The insatiable appetite of America's cities for paper and its industries for non-ferrous metals ultimately reared enormous mills and mines in the northern forests of central Canada, and huge power projects that gave them life in its rivers. A new axis of continental integration, symbolized by the ownership, technique and market orientation of the new staple industries, cut across the east-west lines of national consolidation laid down by the wheat economy. This almost exclusively North American movement of capital and industrial raw materials, by multiplying and accentuating lines of continental force, drew Canada irresistibly into an ascendant American empire. By a curious and perhaps cruel dialectic, the National Policy created its opposite.

— Traditionally the government of Ontario welcomed the example and initiative of American capitalists, especially in the resource sector, where Canadians habitually demonstrated such reluctance themselves. With the exception of the hydro-electric industry, Ontario never resisted American ownership. At no point—again with the exception of hydro—did the people of Ontario demand or their government articulate any policy designed to reduce the level of foreign ownership or investment. However, on numerous occasions the provincial government did impose conditions upon both foreign and domestic enterprise with the aim of altering the pattern of resource exploitation to bring it into harmony with a national or provincial (spokesmen always seemed to equate the two) industrial strategy.

In these instances the Ontario developmental objectives could be expressed in two words, more jobs. But within that end economists have discerned three separate goals: a desire to increase the general level of economic activity by expanding one sector; an attempt at stimulating the growth of industries using staple outputs as inputs; and the promotion of secondary industry serving the requirements of the staple-producing sector. Of these three, the Ontario strategy consistently emphasized the second, or "forward linkage," goal. Assuming that for a long time to come the market would be the United States, then the object of government policy was to export these materials in as close to their finished state as possible. The location within the province of finishing industries would create wider employment opportunities involving more sophisticated skills and increase the returns from international trade proportionately by raising the overall value of exports.[1]

Thus beneath the process of continental economic integration lay fundamental differences in national interest. The United States wanted cheap, secure, raw materials; Canada hoped to export more expensive, semi-processed goods. As early as the 1890s it had become apparent that Canadian objectives would

---

[1] M. Watkins, "A Staple Theory of Economic Growth," in *Approaches to Canadian Economic History* (Toronto, 1967), pp. 49-73. On continental economic integration, see *inter alia*, H. G. J. Aitken, *American Capital and Canadian Resources* (Cambridge, Massachusetts, 1961), Chs. II, III, and "The Changing Structure of the Canadian Economy," in Aitken *et al.*, *The American Economic Impact on Canada* (Durham, 1959), pp. 9-35.

not be met within the ordinary workings of the market system, or more particularly, within the boundaries laid down by American commercial policy. Satisfaction could only come with struggle. This became evident during the first decade of the century. But only during the Great War, as the pace of industrialization picked up, national consciousness heightened, and the shift of capital markets from Great Britain to the United States accelerated, did the problem of asserting national goals within the continental economy become critical.

The initial attempt at an industrial strategy, the turn of the century manufacturing condition, had to be considered a qualified failure. Eventually, it was true, hydro-electric generating stations did appear on the Canadian side of the Niagara River, but only on the condition that 50 per cent of their output could be exported to the nearby American market. The nickel interests successfully confounded the manufacturing clauses of the Mines Act by pitting the federal government against the province. Then, shortly afterward, the leading manufacturer of nickel-steel armour plating and its banker, United States Steel and the House of Morgan, merged the Canadian mining company (Canadian Copper) and two American refineries (Wharton and Orford) into one huge, integrated corporation, the International Nickel Company. Thus the Morgans and United States Steel held a virtual monopoly of the mining, refining and marketing of nickel within North America through INCO and, by virtue of the richness of the Sudbury orebody, they were also able to challenge the Rothschilds' Le Nickel for world control.[2] The province now faced an infinitely stronger opponent. Only on sawlogs and pulpwood could the Ontario government make the manufacturing condition stick. There it proved quite successful in forcing the Michigan, Wisconsin and Minnesota sawmilling industry into Ontario, but it could not dislodge the paper mills as easily.

Although the idea of the manufacturing condition lived on after 1900, the actual policy itself lay in pieces. Paradoxically, the federal government continued to be one of the greatest

---

[2]  O. W. Main, *The Canadian Nickel Industry* (Toronto, 1955), p. 45.

obstacles in the way of implementing a viable provincial development strategy. As a friend of capital and the private power interests, the Laurier government let itself be manoeuvred into a position of tactical opposition to the public power movement. At the same time the reorganized International Nickel Company continued to rely upon the sympathy of the government at Ottawa to parry threatening legislation originating in the province. And finally, during the reciprocity negotiations of 1910-11, the federal government once again showed its ignorance or disapproval of provincial initiatives in the resource sector. The province—now in league with Quebec—had to insist upon maintaining its prohibition upon pulpwood exports in the long-term industrial interests of the country against the better judgment of the federal government. Often during these early years the struggle against continental integration on American terms resolved itself into a struggle between the province of Ontario and the federal government. The drawn battles of the first decade of the century discussed in this chapter were a fitting prelude to the crises that would blow up over resource policies during the Great War.


I


According to the terms of their waterpower leases, the companies at Niagara were permitted to export electricity to the United States as long as they agreed to make at least one-half of their output available to Canadian consumers, *when that power was required*, at a price no higher than the lowest charged in the United States. This meant in effect that the power companies possessed export privileges limited only by conscience. Both the Canadian Niagara Falls and the Ontario power companies were American-owned and had located in Ontario primarily to serve the lucrative American market across the river. Therefore, both exported almost their entire production to the United States where they maintained hundreds of miles of transmission lines, but neither owned nor intended to build similar systems in Canada. The late-blooming, Canadian-owned Electrical Development Company, as we have seen, planned

to distribute the bulk of its power within Ontario, but it expected
to be able to export a significant percentage too.

At length, however, a most curious international alliance of
Canadian economic nationalists, big businessmen, American
electric and coal interests, and the progressive beautifiers of
the American Civic League joined forces to regulate the growing
export of Ontario hydro-electric power to the United States.
The strongest and most persistent complaints arose from the
American electric companies who used steam as a source of
power and their suppliers of coal who understandably objected
to the incoming flood of "cheap" Canadian electricity. In private
they demanded strict limitations on hydro-electric imports and
an international agreement freezing generating capacity at
existing levels on both sides of the Falls. The power companies
on the American side willingly endorsed these proposals which
would have the immediate effect of stabilizing prices, and the
long-range effect of confirming their control at Niagara.
Publicly, however, the interests cloaked their objective with the
more obviously public spirited rhetoric of those Progressive
organizations dedicated to beautification and preservation.

Although the crusading Colonial Dames of America, the
American Scenic and Historical Society, and especially Horace
McFarland's American Civic Association, gave the impression
that they intended a complete purge of moneychangers from
the temple of beauty (the power barons, they claimed, would
in time reduce Niagara to a trickle!), in actual fact all they sought
was a promise from government that no more franchises would
be issued and no more water diverted for power generation.
That is to say, they wished the status quo to be made permanent.
Here surely was a cause to which the greediest power baron,
for the moment at least, could subscribe.[3] Under the combined

[3] Samuel P. Hays makes this point that very often the business community
found the esthetic sentiments and drives towards social efficiency prevalent
amongst Progressive organizations to be useful complements to their own
special pleading; *Conservation and the Gospel of Efficiency* (Cambridge, Mass.,
1959), pp. 4, 31-32, 65, 143-145, 263-265. See also Robert Wiebe, *Businessmen and Reform* (Cambridge, Mass., 1962), pp. 16-100; PAO, Ferguson
Papers, Horace Wallis to Ferguson, Sept. 28, 1925; W. H. Price to Ferguson,
Sept. 24; and Scovell's memorandum attached.

influence, then, of the preservationists *and* the power interests, President Theodore Roosevelt directed the American section of the International Waterways Commission to examine the depletion problem at Niagara, and in his message to Congress early in 1906 announced that he would take immediate steps to preserve "unharmed" the "scenic beauty" of the cataract.[4]

At about this same time, Elihu Root, the American Secretary of State, opened discussions with the British Ambassador to Washington, Sir Mortimer Durand, aimed at settling all of the outstanding Canadian-American differences. Root proposed that the two governments conclude a comprehensive treaty governing the use and diversion of boundary waters. While these talks progressed Roosevelt introduced an interim measure based upon the recommendations of the American section of the commission. Significantly, this first substantive step towards the preservation of the scenic beauty of Niagara took the form of government-imposed quotas upon the importation of Canadian hydro-electric power. Not unexpectedly, the licences issued by the Secretary of War under the Burton Act of 1906 authorized the two American companies on the Canadian side of the Niagara River to export 60,000 horsepower each and limited the Canadian-owned Electrical Development Company to only 37,500 horsepower—a discriminatory action that restricted even further the range of profitable opportunities open to the hard-pressed company.[5] Still, Roosevelt emphasized

---

[4] PAC, Laurier Papers, J. Horace McFarland to Laurier, Jan. 26, 1906, 106503-106505. See also, Canada, Commission of Conservation, *Water-Powers of Canada* (Ottawa, 1911), pp. 56-9.

[5] For details of the Burton Act, see *Water-Powers of Canada*, pp. 60-5; Captain Charles W. Kutz, *Reports Upon the Existing Water-Power Situation at Niagara Falls, So Far as Concerns the Canadian Power Companies and Their Associated Transmission Companies* (Washington, 1906), p. 15. Capt. Kutz's logic bears brief notice. He argued that since the Electrical Development Company planned a distribution system in Ontario and the two American companies did not, then the American companies should be permitted to export greater amounts of power to the United States. For the reports of the Canadian and American sections of the International Waterways Commission see, Canada, House of Commons, *Sessional Papers*, 1906, 19a, Reports of the International Waterways Commission, Vol. XLI, No. 8.

that the Burton Act represented a temporary arrangement pending a full-scale treaty defining the total volume of water that might be diverted on either side of the international boundary.

This American initiative caught both the federal and the Ontario governments in extremely delicate circumstances. Canadians had just begun to realize that Americans had been first in the field at Niagara, that they had seized tremendous opportunities when Canadians had not been interested, and that American companies thoroughly dominated the generation of hydro-electric power. Now it seemed as if those same enterprising Americans were attempting to stabilize politically and make permenent the advantage they already held, precisely at the moment when both Canadian entrepreneurs and governments were beginning to take an interest in this increasingly important source of industrial energy. Moreover, the province of Ontario had successfully claimed jurisdiction at Niagara, leaving Ottawa very much on the outside looking in.

Premier Whitney held serious misgivings about limiting his own powers to grant further franchises by treaty. What if it were found to be necessary to counteract the American presence on the Canadian side of the river by granting new franchises to Canadians? At the same time he could not wholeheartedly identify himself with the grievances of the Electrical Development Company or defend the export of Ontario power in view of the political situation examined in the preceding chapter. Unfortunately, the opportunity of establishing an international agreement on the utilization of boundary waters, which incidentally stabilized development at Niagara Falls, arrived just a little prematurely for Canadians.

However, the British officials at Washington—before 1907 Durand and after James Bryce—and the "restless and interfering" Earl Grey at Ottawa, were desperately eager to wipe the Canadian-American slate clean.[6] Clearly, the boundary waters

---

[6] Peter Neary, "Grey, Bryce and the Settlement of Canadian-American Differences, 1905-1911," *CHR*, Vol. XLIX (1968), pp. 357-80. See also, C. J. Chacko, *The International Joint Commission Between the United States of America and the Dominion of Canada* (New York, 1932), pp. 71-85.

question was one of the most important of the unsettled matters standing in the way of complete Anglo-American accord. Still, there was suspicion in some British quarters. From the Foreign Office Alfred Mosely warned Laurier against tying his hand regarding the future utilization of Canadian waterpower. If Canada bound herself by a strict treaty, Mosely pointed out, "she might find herself in considerable difficulty in the endeavour to check aggression (in the shape of extortionate rates for their energy) by the monopoly already granted." With Earl Grey, Mosely was even more forthright: " . . .this 'cute band of Yankees,' having secured the rights for enormous water power, now desire to make it a monopoly by agitating for the 'preservation of the beauties of Niagara' and so preventing any further concessions. . . ."[7]

Even so, Grey was anxious to press ahead. "Mr. Root spoke to me twice on the subject of Niagara," he wrote his Prime Minister in April 1906. "He and the President have that subject very near their heart." The Burton legislation coming in the midst of the treaty overtures compounded Laurier's embarrassment. Without yet having decided its own policy on the subject of export let alone the thorny dominion-provincial question of waterpower diversions, his government was forced into the position of having to support the Electrical Development Company's vigorous protest against Washington's overt discrimination. Even James Whitney added his perfunctory request for redress, though quietly. In forwarding the Minister of Justice's official memorandum on the Electrical Development case through the Governor General to Durand in Washington, Laurier explained the extreme delicacy of his position:

> The political consideration is this. If this unfair discrimination is maintained, there will be pressure brought to bear upon us to prevent completely the exportation of electrical energy from Canada into the U.S., and a new cause of friction will arise. I would respectfully ask Your Excellency to forward Mr.

---

[7] PAC, Laurier Papers, Alfred Mosely to Laurier enclosing the opinion of the Foreign Secretary, Feb. 19, 1906, 107300-107304, and Mosely to Grey, same date, 107301-107304.

Aylesworth's Memo. to Sir Mortimer Durand, with a note to press upon Mr. Root and Mr. Taft, the expediency of not bringing this new cause of irritation between us.[8]

As both Grey and Laurier well knew, the sentiment against all exports and the pressure for federal intervention was not problematical; it already existed.

A variety of interests were pressing in upon Laurier demanding that he act. The reasons advanced were as opposite as the interests proposing them. First there were the extremists demanding a complete severance of hydro-electric exports to New York State and use of that power in Ontario. Fortunately for Laurier, most of these men were Conservatives, with the maverick Tory W. F. Maclean as their spokesman. Although this argument did not weigh heavily upon his counsels, Laurier did recognize that the sympathy of the Ontario masses tended increasingly in that direction. At the other extreme the American power companies sought federal legislation confirming the principle of their export rights just in case the very unpredictable Ontario situation took a turn for the worse.[9] B. E. Walker advocated a federal power commission to regulate this and other problems related to the new form of energy; plainly he and his colleagues at National Trust and the Electrical Development Company felt more secure, and with just cause, in Laurier's hands than in those of Adam Beck. Other Liberal supporters urged Laurier to reassert federal primacy over such important matters and, as an incidental bonus, allay "the socialistic progress in Ontario."[10]

---

[8] PAC, Grey Papers, Box 1, Grey to Laurier, April 14, 1906; Box 7, Laurier to Grey enclosing Aylesworth's memorandum, Nov. 10, 1906; PAO, Whitney Papers, Whitney to Aylesworth, Nov. 2, 1906; H. H. MacRae for the Electrical Development Company to Whitney, Nov. 1, 1906.

[9] PAO, Whitney Papers, S. H. Blake to Whitney, May 11, 1906.

[10] University of Toronto Archives, Walker Papers, Walker to Aylesworth, Jan. 11, 1907; PAC, Laurier Papers, E. W. Thomson to Laurier, undated, 100212-100213. On national regulation of power development, see C. Armstrong and H. V. Nelles, "Private Property in Peril: Ontario Businessmen and the Federal System, 1898-1911," *Business History Review*, Vol. XLVII (1973), pp. 158-76.

Passage of the Burton Act forced some kind of formal Canadian reply. The Prime Minister's most sensible and fully informed adviser on this question was George Gibbons, the chief Canadian representative on the International Waterways Commission. Gibbons was in the front lines negotiating the first stages of a comprehensive treaty with the Americans; he knew at first hand the methods and goals of the American power companies. The 50 per cent domestic requirement written into the Ontario waterpower leases, Gibbons told Laurier, practically amounted to nothing as long as the American companies refused to construct adequate distributing networks in Ontario. Furthermore, his American counterparts were insisting that Canadians recognize the American right to at least one-half of the power generated on the Canadian side of the river as a precondition of any comprehensive boundary waters treaty. "The trouble is," he wrote Laurier, the Americans "do not want what is fair and do not care at all for the public interest." And he impressed upon the Prime Minister the need for a firm declaration of principle on the export question, stressing the practical and tactical utility of such a course:

> The whole remedy . . . is in your hands. You have a perfect right to say to the three Companies operating on the Canadian side, "Unless you get busy and within a reasonable time, build transmission lines, and take care of the Ontario market, within a practical distance of the Falls, we will withdraw your Permit to export." They should never be allowed to export anything excepting the surplus after the Ontario demand is supplied.
>
> Nothing could be more aggravating than that after we have made an arrangement exceedingly advantageous to this country with the Americans [regarding the division of water at Niagara], that our people should obtain no benefit.

However, the real genius of the aggressive policy Gibbons pressed on the Prime Minister was that it would steal a march on the public power movement and protect the interests of the power magnates. Laurier could seize the opportunity to assert himself in the utilities regulation field and at the same time dash Adam Beck's schemes of "doubtful practicability" by compelling the power barons to perform their proper public duties: "They would be simply doing what they should have done long ago, in carrying out the spirit of their agreement with the Ontario Government."[11]

As the Burton Act moved through Congress in May 1906, the Canadian Minister of Justice, Charles Fitzpatrick, introduced corresponding legislation to give the government control over the exportation of gas, electric power and other gaseous fluids. However, Fitzpatrick's energy export bill was an exceptionally cautious document: it purposefully avoided a declaration of principle; it set no limit on exports; nor did it presume to affect export rights already conferred. Ontario's ambivalent reaction exposed an underlying confusion and embarrassment. Whitney protested on the one hand that the federal government should clarify the jurisdictional ambiguities with the provincial government before pressing ahead with unilateral action. Yet at the same time he welcomed the federal initiative, emphasizing that Ontario felt a much stronger bill was required. The real difficulty lay with those rights already granted which were specifically excluded from Fitzpatrick's draft. "It may be," Whitney's Deputy Attorney General observed, "that some occasion will arise where joint action between the Dominion and the Province may be necessary to secure a proper supply of electric energy in the Province, and the section referred to would interfere with any such action as it excepts from the Bill such Companies as already have power to export."[12]

---

[11] For a general view of Gibbons' role in the Waterways affair, see Peter Neary, "Grey, Bryce and the Settlement of Canadian American Differences, 1905-1911," pp. 365ff; PAC, Laurier Papers, Gibbons to Laurier, Nov. 29, 1906, 116166-116171. No doubt much of Gibbons' antagonism towards Beck was that of a patrician Liberal from an old, established London family towards a rising Conservative from the same city, an immigrant's son, a cigar-box maker with aristocratic pretensions, who pandered unconscionably to the mass taste.

[12] Canada, House of Commons, *Debates*, 1906-1907, May 10, 1906, pp. 3077-3101; May 29, 1906, pp. 4035-4077. PAO, Whitney Papers, Fitzpatrick to Whitney, May 11, 1906; Memorandum of J. R. Cartwright, May 14, and May 17; Whitney to Fitzpatrick, May 17, 1906; and Fitzpatrick to Whitney, May 18, 1906, agreeing that the Bill should be laid over until the next session. This correspondence was later printed and appears also in PAO, the Hearst Papers, Box A-D, 1918.

Not wanting to court a contest of jurisdiction at that particular moment, Laurier withdrew the bill but served notice that he intended to present another at the next session. In the meantime Allan Aylesworth, the new Minister of Justice, set about drawing up a new Fluid and Electricity Export Act to meet the Ontario objections; but plainly George Gibbons was the guiding spirit behind the new draft. Aylesworth's bill extended federal regulation to the existing companies and proclaimed the general principle that "the quantity of power or fluid to be exported shall be limited to the surplus." Moreover, one clause permitting export only after the Canadian market had been served seemed to provide an entrée into the wider field of domestic utilities regulation. According to the new bill, if any company failed to meet Canadian needs satisfactorily, its export licence would be revoked. Gibbons insisted that plain language was demanded by the circumstances and urged a reluctant Laurier to press on ahead: "The Bill is strong but it is better so. The sooner they [the power companies] find out you are in earnest, the sooner they will accept the situation."[13]

The remarkable progress of the public power movement during 1906 added a special sense of urgency to demands for federal action. Private property was in peril and federal regulation appeared to be the only way to prevent a collision between the Electrical Development Company and the provincial government. "I have talked the matter over with the leading bankers in Toronto," Gibbons reported early in 1907, "and every one is favourable to the action of the Government, but in introducing it are all anxious that you should emphasize in the strongest way your intention to protect legitimate capital investment." The public ownership campaign of the Becks and MacLeans had terrified the capitalists of the country. But firm leadership from Laurier, "a Conservative respector of property rights," would command respect in every quarter and restore order. Gibbons, in the name of the "Toronto bankers," encouraged the Prime Minister to step in quickly to protect capital, spare the business community from the folly of a few, and at the

---

[13] *Statutes of Canada*, 6-7 Edw. VII, c. 16, reprinted in *Water-Powers of Canada*, pp. 341-2; PAC, Laurier Papers, Gibbons to Laurier, strictly private, Dec. 10, 1906, 116504-116505.

same time, "prevent corporate greed overlapping into extortion":

> ...there is no subject as to which the public mind is more agitated all over the continent than the relationship between public corporations and the people. I thought then and I think now that you could do the party great service by a clear and emphatic declaration of policy. The demagogue is making headway and gaining popular favour because of the mistaken attitude assumed by many of those Corporations who seem to think they can wholly ignore public interests. Through their stupidity a feeling is being created of hostility to capital, which is very liable to do great injury to the country.

Unquestionably the power companies were behaving badly and the financial community knew it. Yet if Laurier played a Canadian Roosevelt by declaring strict ground rules of corporate conduct, the deteriorating situation could still be saved. Gibbons saw clearly that: "Roosevelt's great strength with the people is the fact that he has convinced them that he is on their side as against the Rockefellers and others who utterly ignored their rights and whose motto up to date has been 'the public be damned.'" If Laurier pledged himself to guaranteeing the security required for massive foreign investment and at the same time "announced that the dishonesty which would lead to repudiation of obligations, or the anarchism which would destroy vested interests, should never have any footing on our soil," Canada might avert the impending double disaster of public ownership and a consequent flight of capital. Clearly Gibbons and the financial community hoped to out-flank the rapidly advancing public power forces with the federal export legislation; for them Laurier was the guardian of the capitalist system. "The sooner the Corporations wake up to the realization of their obligations to the public the better for themselves," Gibbons concluded, "otherwise the pendulum will swing the other way and smash things."[14]

---

[14] PAC, Laurier Papers, Gibbons to Laurier, Jan. 7, 1907, 117937-117945; Gibbons to Laurier, Jan. 22, 1907, confidential, 118550-118552. It is interesting to note that the American government officially protested this

When the new bill came before Parliament in January 1907, the Conservative members from Ontario immediately sensed this strategy. In committee stage W. F. Cockshutt, H. Lennox, E. A. Lancaster, Edmund Bristol, John Barr and W. F. Maclean argued strenuously that the Aylesworth bill, in the name of regulating exports, in actual fact merely licensed the good behaviour of the power companies. "I would be in favour of a Bill that would really regulate the exportation of electric power," Lancaster claimed: "But . . .this Bill does not do anything of that kind. This Bill creates a disposition, makes it *prima facie* for export, and provides for the export of our power to the United States instead of trying to use it for the development of Canadian industry." At the practical level, they attacked the very notion of surplus and argued generally from a doctrinaire economic nationalist point of view heavily tinged with anti-Americanism. A surplus today, Lancaster pointed out, would not always be a surplus. After expensive cables and conduits had been laid and long-term contracts signed, Maclean and Lennox claimed, an attempt to reclaim the exportable surplus would be met with argument from vested interest and charges of confiscation.

But the basic differences between the Ontario Conservatives and the federal government policy lay at the level of principle. The Aylesworth bill permitted export; for essentially nationalist reasons, the Conservatives denied that premise. "The Province of Ontario is admirably adapted to be the workshop not only for its own people," Maclean asserted, "but for the West as well. One of the prime necessities of a workshop is cheap power. Can we hope for cheap power if we allow this export to the United States? And if we are exporting to the United States a raw product which we need at home, can this be called a national policy? . . ." W. F. Cockshutt, a plain-spoken manufacturer from Brantford, wholeheartedly agreed with his colleague W. F. Maclean, the mercurial member of York South: "What we want is that a certain amount of power should be bottled up on our side, and then capitalists will start up works

---

apparent Canadian attempt at limiting power exports; see *ibid.*, Grey Papers, M. Howard (British Embassy at Washington) to Grey, Jan. 9, 1907.

which will consume that power. See what happened at the Soo. . . . That is what should happen at Niagara." An undeniable anti-American animus underlay their argument, which during E. A. Lancaster's contributions to the debate, became something of a battle-cry. Perhaps it had something to do with his being from the border riding of Lincoln: "Well," he asked, "whom are we legislating for?"

> Are we sitting here for the sake of having another banquet with somebody from the United States so that he may call us good fellows, for allowing them to use our power? Let us be serious about this matter. Some of us are getting sick and tired of passing legislation here simply in order to win the commendation of the United States and prevent its great men from calling us greedy. We have a right to be greedy nationally with that which is our own. We must protect ourselves, for it is certain that the United States will not protect us, but will do their best to place us at their mercy.[15]

From Toronto Whitney continued to demand intergovernmental consultation to avoid "some of the possible complications," but in private he admitted bewilderment. "This is the most difficult subject with which we have had to deal," he wrote Borden, the leader of the opposition, "and the more one tries to consider it the more difficult the question appears." The Ontario government, then, did not object to the passage of the bill, and Borden, who maintained close contact with Whitney throughout, limited his protest to a technicality. He proposed an independent commission, like the Railway Commission, instead of the cabinet to grant export licences: "The Minister of Customs when he comes to administer this Bill will likely have to deal with warm personal and political friends and with uncompromising opponents."[16]

Defence of the bill fell to the new Minister of Justice from eastern Ontario, Allan Aylesworth. He explained the new

[15] Canada, House of Commons, *Debates*, 1906-1907, Jan. 29, 1907, pp. 2229-2280; Mar. 19, 1907, pp. 4946-4964.

[16] PAO, Whitney Papers, Aylesworth to Whitney, Jan. 30, 1907; Whitney to Aylesworth, Feb. 28, 1907; Borden to Whitney, Jan. 30, 1907; Whitney

clauses that had been added; noted that the Ontario objections had been met; and argued that the bill, despite Conservative claims to the contrary, did establish an important principle of national energy policy. Had there been a shortage of electricity, he would have agreed with demands for an absolute prohibition of exports; but such was not the case:

> The three companies have the rights . . . to generate 415,000 horse-power . . . and we have a market at the present time for at most one-tenth of that amount. What is to be done with the other nine-tenths? These companies are but men who have banded together and put their money into that enterprise; must they allow that property, for it is literally that, to go to waste? If they supply the 40,000 horse-power of Canadian demand, and have 360,000 to spare, must they waste it, or may they sell it in a foreign country? If it were any other product no one would hesitate to answer that this country is in no sense injured if its needs are in full supplied, and it could be the worst kind of dog in the manger policy to say that the surplus which otherwise would go to absolute waste as it has done through all the ages, might not be sold in a foreign country.

Yet this defence tended only to vindicate Conservative charges that the bill was designed to facilitate exports rather than regulate them. And W. F. Cockshutt immediately challenged the Minister of Justice's calculations. Adam Beck, he pointed out, already had firm orders for 100,000 horse-power.

Aylesworth merely confirmed the opposition view that a surplus was very difficult to determine and that the Liberal government lacked the will to intervene decisively in the national interest. Then, tiring at last of the incessant barrage of criticism from the friends of public ownership—a principle with which he had no sympathy—Aylesworth blurted out that capital investment required just as much protection as the interests of Canadian power consumers. No government of which he was a member, he said, would be "stampeded by silly newspaper

---

to Borden, Feb. 26, 1907; Canada, House of Commons, *Debates*, 1906-1907, pp. 4947ff.

outcries against the encroachments of aggressive companies."[17]
His candour and unmistakable disdain for a movement that
was carrying all before it in his home province disclosed where
the real concern of the federal government lay and whose
interests its bill sought to protect.

Although the critics failed to alter the substance of the bill
by its amendments, through its close identification with the
Ontario public power crusade it was able to establish the impression that it was the Conservative government in Toronto rather
than the Liberal government at Ottawa which was the true
defender of the national interest. While the federal authorities
licensed exports, provincial politicians were struggling to obtain
cheap power for home industry. The federal government
promised the power companies entry into the rich American
market if they were good, just at the moment when Ontario
voters had all but convinced themselves that good service from
private utilities was a contradiction in terms. Despite its Fluid
and Electricity Export Act, the federal government could not
define a credible national energy policy worthy of the name and,
as we have already seen, the rapid movement of events in
Ontario froze the federal government out of the utilities regulation field and the federal stance in the Hydro disallowance case
completed its identification with the private power interests.

Because of the overriding concern for hydro-electric power
from Niagara, the conclusion of the International Boundary
Waters Treaty in January 1909 represented no great triumph
of diplomacy from an Ontario point of view. Although George
Gibbons' hard bargaining had established the principle of
a permanent International Joint Commission, his second
victory—a 36,000 to 20,000 cubic feet per second diversion
ratio at Niagara Falls favouring Canada—was not what it
seemed. Existing American rights to channel 10,000 cubic feet
per second through the Chicago sanitary system reduced the
overall differential to only 6,000 cubic feet per second at Niagara,
and that volume was more than compensated for by the long-

---

[17] Canada, House of Commons, *Debates*, 1906-1907, pp. 2237-2241, 2256-
2257.

term export contracts by which Americans could claim up to one-half of the power generated on the Canadian side. As early as 1906 the American section of the International Waterways Commission recognized that the Canadian export commitments more than negated whatever geographical claim Canadians might have to a larger volume of water at Niagara, and that surely explains why the American negotiators conceded the point so readily.[18]

When the proposed terms of the treaty became known early in 1908, Ontario officials reacted sharply to its clauses limiting hydro-electric diversions at Niagara Falls. Whitney lodged an immediate protest in Ottawa pointing out the importance of Niagara hydro-electric power for Ontario's future industrial growth. Adam Beck demanded access to Niagara for his Hydro-Electric Power Commission, "untrammeled with treaty restrictions," and he, too, warned the federal government not to shackle "an asset which should enable us to attain a degree of industrial development unsurpassed in any other portion of the world." Laurier quickly arranged a meeting between the discontented Ontario politicians, the federal cabinet, and James Bryce on February 21, 1908. Then, one year later, when final approval was being considered, George Gibbons met with the Ontario cabinet to explain the pressing need for such a treaty and that he had done the very best he could. At length the Ontario government reluctantly conceded his argument, and Whitney even complimented Gibbons on his negotiating skill. Nevertheless, Adam Beck "grouched away" at the terms, and Gibbons, despite their great differences, could see his point:

> The question at Niagara is a very troublesome one. Power never should have been permitted to be developed there until we had a market for it. Inside of 20 years we will have a market likely for the whole 440,000 h.p. one half of that they [the companies] have a right to export. That will be irritating enough; but certainly the other half should be retained for the use of our people, and when this treaty is through, it seems to me that these corporations ought to be told *formally* that in making their con-

---

[18] The treaty is reprinted in *Water-Powers of Canada*, pp. 331-9. Section 5 relates to Niagara. For the details of negotiations, see Neary, "Grey, Bryce and the Settlement of Canadian-American Differences, 1905-1911," pp. 363ff.; Chacko, *The International Joint Commission*, pp. 71-85.

tracts they must bear in mind their obligations to this country, and that it will be no excuse for their failure to do so that they have, in the meantime, made contracts in the United States. I think it would be very dangerous to let them export power without putting formally on record the position which we must assume towards them when it becomes necessary to assume it.[19]

Neither the Fluid and Electricity Export Act nor the Boundary Waters Treaty settled the troublesome electricity export question; both merely delayed the inevitable confrontation between Canadian needs and the companies' export privileges. That collision would occur, not as George Gibbons thought, twenty years hence, but within a decade. Nevertheless, both the debate and the treaty served to consolidate Canadian opinion on the principles involved. In journals as widely separated as the *Monetary Times* and the *University Magazine*, Canadians drew the same moral from their experience. "Unless the Government adopts some means to ensure that this power, with its immeasurable advantages to the community, does not escape us," the former editorialized, "it will be an absurdity to talk of Canada's water power at the Falls. Geographically it may be but commercially and practically it will belong to the American manufacturer." "A Canadian" warned the readers of the *University Magazine* in 1910 against repeating the Niagara mistake with the St. Lawrence water powers that American speculators were fairly bursting with schemes to develop. Then in the very next issue, Arthur V. White, the Commission of Conservation's authority on these matters, added the weight of his informed opinion to the growing nationalistic consensus. "Let the people of Ontario and Canada inform themselves upon what is taking place by way of effort[s] to control or take away their best and largest waterpowers," he admonished his readers, "and realise what all such deprivation may mean in the future."[20]

---

[19] PAC, Laurier Papers, Whitney to Laurier, Feb. 15, 1908, enclosing Beck to Whitney, Feb. 14, 1908, and some clippings from the Toronto *World* to indicate popular feeling on the question, and an exchange of telegrams, Feb. 18, Feb. 20, 1908, 136379-136385, 136486-136488; *ibid.*, Gibbons Papers, Box 8, Letterbook, Gibbons to Laurier, Feb. 6, 1909.

[20] *Monetary Times*, Jan. 19, 1907; "The Long Sault Dam," April, 1910, *University Magazine*, pp. 255-264; Arthur V. White, "The Exportation of Electricity," October, 1910, *ibid.*, pp. 460-7.

Finally, W. K. McNaught, an Ontario Hydro commissioner, lamented the sins of the fathers in a pamphlet entitled, *Ontario's True National Policy in Regard to Black and White Coal*. So far as the true interests of the people of Ontario were concerned, he declared, " . . .not a single horse-power of hydro-electric power should ever have been allowed to be exported from this province to any foreign country." He claimed further that if the demand for electricity continued to grow as rapidly as it had following the creation of the Hydro-Electric Power Commission, Ontario would soon need all of the power it was capable of producing: "The time is coming, and perhaps it is not so far distant as some people imagine, when we shall need all of this hydro-electric power for our own use. Will we then be able to secure its return without economical or actual warfare?"[21] Within the province of Ontario at least, the public was largely convinced that a "true national policy" governing the use and exportation of hydro-electric energy could be devised, and was just as firmly convinced that the provincial government alone was capable of asserting it.

## II

Although the federal government had possessed the authority since 1897 to regulate the export of nickel matte in the national interest, good and sufficient reasons could always be found why that power should not be exercised. In effect, federal authorities accepted International Nickel's argument that it had spent thousands of dollars testing every refining process known to man and each, for one reason or another, had proven uneconomical in Canada. Even if it had been successful in that quest, the company often reminded inquiring Canadians, manufacturing costs were much higher in Canada and the refined nickel thus produced would have to overcome a stiff American tariff that the semi-refined matte did not have to bear. Under those circumstances it would be much cheaper for Americans

[21] Reprinted in *Canadian Forestry Journal*, Nov.-Dec., 1911, pp. 150-1.

to import New Caledonian ore than refined nickel from Canada. In spite of the fact that Canada contained tremendous nickel ore reserves, its international competitive position as a refiner was not as strong as its position as a primary producer. When the company discovered an acceptable process and had solved the tariff problem, then a refinery would be built in Canada. But in the meantime, Canadians enjoyed substantial wage and subsidiary benefits from the busy mines, smelters and railways of the Sudbury district and by implication should be satisfied with that.

On more than one occasion International Nickel warned that any political pressure directed towards forcing it to locate a refinery in Canada would lead directly to the closing down of its existing works at Sudbury and a wholesale shift to its allegedly vast New Caledonian holdings. Although Ontario's strong imperial sentiment insulated the Mond Nickel Company in Wales from the intermittent agitation for "home refining," for reasons known only to themselves the officers of that company upheld everything that International Nickel had to say on this question.[22] This threat of dislocation, substantiated by INCO's only real competitor in the field, effectively stayed the hand of the federal government. But the somewhat more presumptuous Ontario government under George Ross actually called the company's bluff, with the Mines Act of 1900, only to have its ace trumped in Ottawa. Eventually it, too, came to realize the weakness of its position and grudgingly learned to live with the situation. After the dismal failure of its bounty strategy in 1907, the Whitney government all but abandoned hope that a nickel refinery would ever locate within the province. When the British Admiralty inquired as to the provincial government's power to control the export of nickel matte in times of national emergency, Frank Cochrane, admitting total defeat, replied that provincial authorities had never possessed such powers.[23] At length, both the federal and

---

[22] Professor Main suspects collusion between Mond and Canadian Copper; see *The Canadian Nickel Industry* (Toronto, 1955), pp. 56-7, 149.

[23] Royal Ontario Nickel Commission, *Report* (Toronto, 1917), pp. 15-7 (hereafter, RONC, *Report*).

provincial governments capitulated completely to the will of International Nickel.

Though it provided little consolation, by 1905 Canada permanently overtook New Caledonia as the world's most important source of nickel and by 1910 produced three times as much as its rival. Still, the bustle in the mines and smelters could not satisfy the industrializing impulse of Ontario; nor could the poisonous pall that weighed down upon Sudbury hide the fact that the really important jobs were being exported, with the semi-finished matte, to the United States. The popular opinion of the nickel affair was perhaps best summed up in the Toronto *Telegram*'s tart observation: "A few boarding houses around two or three holes in the ground, plus Sudbury, represent all that Ontario has to show for a monopoly of 90 per cent of the world's nickel supply."[24]

International Nickel intimidated Canadian politicians and ruthlessly crushed potential Canadian competitors. J. P. Morgan and Company, it was alleged at the time, played an important role in bankrupting Francis Clergue's combined nickel and steel operations; then, after the Hamilton Nickel-Copper Company failed in its bid for political protection, Morgan successfully prevented the leading American smelting companies from purchasing the company's property. Every Canadian effort at challenging this tight monopoly was checkmated by International Nickel's political influence at Ottawa or control of the New York capital markets, or discouraged by the intractable qualities of the Sudbury ore, the capital-intensive nature of the refining industry, and the American tariff.[25]

The only weakness of the Mond-INCO axis was that it did not own all of the Sudbury nickel deposits. But as long as no other purchasers of nickel ore came forward, these properties in themselves posed no particular threat. Besides, in other

---

[24] Quoted in the *Canadian Mining Journal* (hereafter, *CMJ*), Sept. 1, 1916, p. 406.

[25] Main, *The Canadian Nickel Industry*, pp. 68-9. The suggestion of collusion between INCO and the federal government is not to be discounted if the obvious conclusions are to be drawn from correspondence between R. M. Thompson, president of the company, and Laurier. On October 18,

people's hands they served the more useful purpose of demonstrating that in actual fact a monopoly did not exist. Nevertheless, as a purely speculative undertaking, M. J. O'Brien and J. R. Booth, under the name of The Dominion Nickel-Copper Company, went ahead and consolidated the abandoned workings of the Nickel-Copper and Lake Superior Corporations with several undeveloped private properties. While these men did not command either the will or the wealth to enter competition with the Morgans, Monds, and Rothschilds, they could afford to wait until time and the tide turned up a genuinely interested purchaser. At least the continued existence of their important holdings outside of the control of the Mond-INCO axis gave wing to the hope that a third company might someday be formed, perhaps with its refinery in Ontario.

The international armaments race, which both increased the demand for nickel and dramatized its strategic importance, rekindled entrepreneurial interest in nickel refining. At the same time higher prices and increasing exports of the semi-refined nickel matte heightened Canadian irritation with the foreign International Nickel Company. Periodic rumours that a new company was in the process of formation, jointly financed by Anglo-Canadian capitalists and backed by the British government, stirred public interest in what had come to be known as the nickel question, and brought back old memories of previous struggles. Over the years it had become brutally apparent that International Nickel could not be shaken without political assistance in the form of massive bounties, export restrictions, or both. Therefore, anyone interested in breaking into the industry had first to establish the absolutely essential political alliances, and to do this it was necessary to incite, then appeal to, popular indignation at Canada's foreign bondage. From International Nickel's point of view, the most serious of these inspired outbreaks of public concern over the nickel question occurred in 1910, when the House of Commons Select Standing

---

1906, Thompson sent Laurier a cheque for an undisclosed amount which included a "profit" of $5,000 on stock which Thompson claimed to have purchased for the Prime Minister. For Laurier's effusive reply, see PAC, Laurier Papers, Laurier to Thompson, October 20, 1906, 114779, 114780.

Committee on Mines and Minerals heard expert testimony that the operation of a nickel refinery within Canada would be both possible and profitable.

Arthur Wilson, a Toronto engineer claiming to represent some British manufacturers that had been "looking at nickel properties all over the world," told the committee that an international market-sharing and price-fixing aggreement existed between Mond, Le Nickel and International Nickel. Without such an agreement, he said, the New Caledonian ore would not have been able to compete so effectively with Sudbury ores. He also charged that the price policy of the combination had the double effect of restraining European governments from entering the refining business, while at the same time driving prospective competitors to the wall. According to his calculations, International Nickel received a profit of 18 cents a pound on nickel it produced for less than 15 cents a pound. Yet in spite of the tremendous profitability of the business and the availability of nickel desposits, this combination had succeeded, through ruthless control of both the nickel and capital markets, in choking off all serious competition. When he was asked by committee chairman James Conmee (who no doubt had an interest hidden in the affair somewhere), what the probable result of a federal export duty on nickel matte would be, Wilson replied: "It would have the effect of causing all the nickel matte to be refined in Canada instead of as at present in the United States and Great Britain. It would be the equivalent of a revenue of a million dollars in this country." In conclusion, all he asked by way of government assistance in establishing a viable Canadian nickel refining company was an export duty on nickel matte and a bounty on the production of nickel-steel. Almost as an afterthought he added an extra-ordinary request that "a company composed of all Canadian or English Capital [be] protected from undue competition on the part of foreign corporations."[26]

John Patterson, the disgruntled promoter of the ill-fated Hamilton Nickel-Copper Company testified personally to the

[26] Canada, House of Commons, 1909-1910, *Journals*, Vol. XLV, App. No. 5, Proceedings of the Select Standing Committee of the House of Commons on Mines and Minerals, Arthur Wilson, pp. 12-21.

power of International Nickel. All he could say in 1910 at the conclusion of his long and painful narrative of the trials his company underwent at the hands of the Morgans was: "The combination was a little too hard for us." He complained most bitterly of the $120 a ton American tariff that had to be borne by Canadian nickel refiners and he begged Ottawa either to impose an export tax that would lead to the elimination of that crushing toll, or to prohibit the export of nickel matte entirely. Finally, in his somewhat less obviously partisan evidence, Thomas Gibson, the Ontario Deputy Minister of Mines, ventured the opinion that in the near future nickel-refining technology would rely more heavily upon electricity than heat and when that occurred, the economic balance would shift quite rapidly in favour of refining in Ontario.[27]

Speaking for International Nickel, A. P. Turner, E. F. Wood, G. M. Colvocoresses and Wallace Nesbitt vigorously denied every one of Wilson's contentions. They denounced his allegation that an international conspiracy to fix prices existed by pretending that Mond, Le Nickel and INCO were in desperate competition and that even as late as 1903 "it was a question of which one would survive." Perhaps profits on a pound of nickel reached $7^{1}/_{2}$ cents during good market conditions, these officials admitted, but these returns were quickly eaten up by expensive metallurgical research. Wilson's claims of enormous profits were obviously fabrications; if they were true, why was it that the company passed dividends on its common stock until 1909?

International Nickel maintained its refinery in New Jersey, its spokesmen explained, for the simple reason that the fuels and chemicals used in its Orford process could be obtained most cheaply there. Once again Canadians were bluntly warned that the Sudbury works would be closed at the first hint of political pressure and that the company could switch over to New Caledonian ores which were, after all, much cheaper and easier to use. Indeed, Canadians were reminded that the only reason that the Sudbury properties had undergone such extensive development during the past decade was the

[27] *Ibid.*, John Patterson, pp. 44-56; T. W. Gibson, pp. 59-69.

sentimental inclination on the part of the owners " . . . to spend their money and build up an industry on British soil near home than in a French penal colony on the other side of the world, all things being equal."[28] Again in 1910, as he had in 1900, Ludwig Mond weighed in on behalf of the International Nickel Company. In a letter to James Conmee he confirmed the richness and competitiveness of New Caledonian ores, suggesting that any export duty would cripple Canadian mining and at the same time "favour the products of convict labour in the penal colony of New Caledonia."[29]

Confused by such a direct conflict of testimony, the Committee merely reported its investigations to the House without making any recommendations. However, even though the laymen legislators were unable to render a judgment, their hearings did revive public debate on the nickel question. The *Globe*, for example, alarmed by the onrushing events in Europe, urged the government to take over the nickel deposits in the interest of imperial defence.[30] Other papers renewed the long-standing agitation for "home refining." But the most damaging indictment of company policy was delivered by the director of the federal Bureau of Mines before the prestigious Commission of Conservation. Dr. Eugene Haanel not only questioned the necessity of refining in New Jersey, but he informed the commissioners that the Sudbury smelting operations were the most wasteful of by-products he had ever seen:

> Whenever we speak of our mineral wealth we grow eloquent in describing our vast nickel resources, and we may well be proud of possessing the deposits of the Sudbury region. But really, of what particular and special benefit are these deposits to our country? We mine the ore, smelt it into matte and send it as such out of the country. If we want nickel or nickel steel we have to import it.

[28] *Ibid.*, see especially the testimony of A. P. Turner who was questioned by Wallace Nesbitt. Turner was the general manager of the Canadian Copper Company, pp. 26-36.

[29] Main, *The Canadian Nickel Industry*, pp. 80, 153.

[30] Quoted in *CMJ*, Feb. 1, 1910, p. 68.

Experiments conducted by the Mines Branch indicated that an electrolytic method was best suited to the Sudbury ores, which of course implied that refining could be carried on most economically in Canada.[31]

The *Canadian Mining Journal* responded to his reasoned argument with a stern lecture on the indiscretion of civil servants. "Dr. Haanel has neither the right nor the technical knowledge," it assured its readers, "to offer criticisms on one of the most modern and most effective metallurgical plants." For its part, the company replied to this challenge with a vicious personal attack on the director of the Mines Branch. "For the last ten years," J. J. Harpell commented in an article entitled "Political and Mischievous Interference with Industry," "the mining men of Canada have tolerated Dr. Haanel with an indulgence that is eloquent in its prayer for a strong reforming hand or the sickle of Father Time."[32]

Instead of changing its policies to meet scientific and mounting public criticism, International Nickel merely hired a public relations expert to weave the grand deception that henceforth the company would bring the public into its confidence.[33] However the hounds might bay, the company seemed assured of a safe refuge in Ottawa. In a graphic illustration of International Nickel's confidence on that account, Robert Thompson, the company president, hardly disturbed his African holiday to deal with the Canadian uproar. Reclining in the mid-morning sun in the finest Robber Baron tradition, Thompson dictated a letter to his close personal friend Sir Wilfrid Laurier in distant, frozen Ottawa, as "ten brawny oarsmen" pulled his barge up

---

[31] "Possible Economies in Production of Minerals of Canada," Commission of Conservation, *Annual Report*, 1910, pp. 67-8.

[32] *CMJ*, Jan. 15, 1910, p. 66; Feb. 1, 1910, pp. 68-70. Parenthetically it is worth noting that Dr. Haanel was absolutely right and the company itself vindicated him by its actions. The Hybinette electrolytic process was eventually acquired by INCO through the purchase of another company and it was upon this strategic technology that the later success of the company rested. Those with the technology before the war could not get capital or political assistance; those with capital and political support used both to get along without the technology.

[33] Main, *The Canadian Nickel Industry*, pp. 80-1.

the Nile. For two pages he picked holes in Wilson's facts and quibbled with his vocabulary—generally giving the impression that both Wilson and Haanel were ill-informed troublemakers hardly worth bothering about.

"But I am cruelly wasting your time," he broke off, "and had much better undertake to describe to you the beautiful scene that I am looking at." And indeed the scene might well have been created by Mathew Josephson, Gustavus Myers, or Frederick Lewis Allen. As the oarsmen chanted softly, Thompson described the great sweeping curve in the river ahead, the broad green fields on either side, and in the distance what appeared to be a small town, "its minarets and domes shining in the sun." Then as his barge passed through the town, Thompson could not resist a long postscript on the European habits of the Copts, the colour of the houses, pigeon raising, and the crowded market. But soon he was out of town, back into the wheatlands with the blue hills of the Libyan desert off in the distance:

> The sky is blue without a fleck of cloud, although along the horizon there is a smoky appearance due to the fact that early this morning there was a fog, which has not yet entirely disappeared. We are sitting on the upper deck of the dahabeah, dressed in summer clothes, but if the sun gets a little more powerful we shall begin to cry for our awnings.

Soon Sir Wilfrid, and Canada, and nickel matte, and all the carping critics would reassume their proper places, and like the quaint village, vanish into the quivering haze.[34]

As long as the president of International Nickel felt confident enough to devote the bulk of his correspondence with the Prime Minister of Canada to travel writing rather than reasoned argument, or even veiled threats, quite plainly his company was in no danger from that source. Nor could there ever be a national mineral policy if Canadian governments, both federal and provincial, continued to accept company testimony ahead

---

[34] PAC, Laurier Papers, Robert M. Thompson to Laurier, "On Board Dahabeah Maat, On-the-Nile," Feb. 10, 1910, 166821-166827.

of that from their own fully competent officials. And finally, as long as the home refining issue provoked irritation rather than outrage among Canadians, the nickel question would remain unanswered—a question rather than a policy. The company's great skill at parrying every political thrust generated frustration, anger and resentment, but after a time those very emotions contributed to a mood of despair. Political action depended upon that despair becoming desperation, and that transformation required a crisis, some irrational or hysterical response, that would justify action at whatever cost. Without that sense of intolerability the nickel question would continue to be a puzzle that did not seem to have any clear-cut solution.

Meanwhile, an American tariff frankly designed to promote the industrialization of the United States and the servitude of its trading partners neatly complemented International Nickel's New Jersey refining policy. While the company held Canadian governments in line with the New Caledonian trump and crushed competitors in the New York money markets, the American tariff of $120 on a ton of refined nickel materially reduced the possibility of competition growing up within Canada or the empire independent of American capital.

## III

While the tariff was just one additional discouragement for hopeful Canadian nickel refiners, it was an operative reality for existing Canadian papermakers. In that sector, too, the tariff had the effect of promoting the importation into the United States of raw rather than finished goods, pulpwood rather than paper. American papermakers, just like International Nickel, owned expensive mills in the United States which they were reluctant to abandon despite much cheaper Canadian raw materials, labour and energy. The tariff represented and perpetuated that inertia. However, Canadians were much more confident of their monopoly over pulpwood than they were about nickel ore. Consequently, the Canadian bargaining position with American industrialists was stronger and Canadian policy much more resolute.

After the initial success of the sawlog manufacturing condition the province of Ontario also forbade the export of raw pulpwood with the intention of compelling American papermakers, in search of new sources of pulpwood supply, to move their installations northward to Ontario's waterpowers and forests. But Ontario could not act in a vacuum. Since Quebec possessed much larger spruce forests closer to the existing mills and markets of northeastern United States, it was the first and busiest centre of Candian pulp and paper activity. In view of that geographical situation, Ontario's provincial manufacturing policy had no hope of success until it could become a national policy, and since Ontario had seized the legislative initiative in this area, a national policy would require interprovincial policy co-ordination rather than unilateral federal action.

When the Ross government introduced its pulpwood manufacturing condition in 1900, it did so on the understanding that the province of Quebec would shortly institute a similar policy. Ross explained privately to Willison that Premier Marchand had promised the Ontario government that Quebec would demand the manufacture within Canada of pulpwood cut from the crown lands: "He says however he cannot announce this change till the House rises in order to avoid a collision with some of his friends. This would justify you in letting him alone in the *Globe*."[35]

Marchand's sudden death could possibly explain the subsequent failure of his plan. But probably just as significant was the fact that Quebec was not Ontario. Instead of imposing a manufacturing condition, the government of Quebec merely raised the stumpage modestly on pulpwood destined for export and in doing so promised not to modify its export legislation for a full ten years at the request of the lumbermen. The circumstances that had produced the Ontario policy were not present within the province of Quebec, and unlike Ontario the advocates of the manufacturing condition within Quebec

---

[35] PAC, Willison Papers, Box 70, Ross to Willison, private, undated, but probably early 1900.

faced strenuous opposition. Pulpwood was one of the most important by-products of the church's Laurentian colonization program. It was the colonist's first cash crop, often his only one, and no government could easily tamper with the shaky Laurentian economy by closing the pulpwood market just because it was to be found within the United States. Moreover, conditions favoured the fabrication of a resource development strategy by the Ontario business community in advance of large-scale American exploitation of the provincial resources. But by 1900 Quebec had already experienced this American demand and many of its lumbermen had responded by branching out into the pulpwood export business. These "friends" of the government proved to be much more influential than the handful of Canadian paper manufacturers. Ontario businessmen could anticipate changing conditions without having to deny the livelihood of their lumbermen colleagues, but within Quebec any restriction of pulpwood exports, even for long-range industrial goals, conflicted directly with several powerful vested interests.[36]

Over the next decade the half-dozen Canadian paper companies organized a crusade to prohibit the export of unmanufactured pulpwood. In their repeated petitions to Ottawa and Quebec, Carl Riordan, J. R. Booth, E. B. Eddy and Sir William Van Horne appealed principally to nationalist sentiment to justify their request for some protective legislation along the lines of the Ontario manufacturing condition. The papermakers' primary concern, Van Horne explained, was to "save Canada's spruce forests from Americans." For in the absence of export prohibitions, American industry would strip Ontario and Quebec just as it had already denuded New England and the Lake states. "Enterprising capitalists of the United States are pressing upon us," warned Clifford Sifton, "and reaching out to make use of our resources for their own

[36] For the influence of the pulpwood exporters, see PAC, Bronson Papers, Vol. 711, *Speech of the Hon. S. N. Parent, Prime Minister, on the Question of Pulpwood and the Policy of His Department, April 25, 1903* (Quebec, 1903), pp. 4-15. See also, A. R. M. Lower, *Settlement and the Forest Frontier in Eastern Canada* (Toronto, 1936), pp. 93, 124-5.

purposes. They will not come for a purely philanthropic purpose but for their own financial advantage."[37]

Obviously this kind of nationalism had economic as well as intellectual or emotional origins, though often the three factors were inseparable. "Why should we contribute to the building up of this industry in a foreign country?" J. F. Ellis asked delegates to the Canadian Forestry Convention: "Would it not be far better for us to conserve and build up our own industries by manufacturing the raw material into commercial shape?" E. B. Biggar frankly slanted the editorial content of his *Pulp and Paper Magazine*, much of which appeared in pamphlet form, "to...demolish the frivolous pretensions of those...who are ruining the Canadian spruce forests for the benefit of American manufacturers...." His magazine and the petitions of the papermakers repeatedly pointed out that a Canadian pulp and paper industry would not only create new employment opportunities, it would also increase the value of Canadian exports. Sir William Van Horne calculated that a cord of pulpwood returned $6 when it was exported in its raw state, $19 as newsprint, and $24 in the form of chemical pulp. If Canadian governments were not afraid to use their "whip hand," Carl Riordan complained, then Canada and not the United States would retain the full benefit of the industry. Nor should Canadians fear American retaliation, Van Horne pointed out. The tariff situation could not be any worse than it actually was; moreover, "Canada is becoming too big a customer to be lightly treated." American sales in Canada, he noted shrewdly, were greater than in Mexico, the West Indies, Central, and South America combined.[38]

Predictably, the appeal for protection won the wholehearted support of the Canadian Manufacturers' Association, and the

---

[37] *CAR*, 1902, p. 286; 1903, pp. 473-4. Van Horne is quoted in William Banks and J. S. Crate, *Pulpwood and Its Problems* (Toronto, 1907), pp. 13-7; Sifton quoted in *Canadian Forestry Journal*, June, 1910, p. 52 (hereafter, *CFJ*).

[38] *Report of the Canadian Forestry Convention* (Ottawa, 1906), pp. 128-9; Canadian Forestry Association, *Annual Report*, 1909, pp. 132-6; PAC, Laurier Papers, E. B. Biggar to Laurier, Dec. 21, 1907; Jan. 3, 1911, 134069, 179163-179165; *Pulpwood and Its Problems*, pp. 13-7, 38-41.

tale of rapacious Americans having their will with the Canadian forests rallied the indignation of the Canadian Forestry Association to the cause. Nevertheless, some people, especially within the latter organization, disagreed. Senator W. C. Edwards, a pulpwood exporter himself, and a self-confessed "uncompromising free trader," argued at tiresome length that the pulp and paper industry "would grow naturally if left alone." Was he more culpable than the others whose principles also served their interests? Edwards believed in the home manufacture of Canadian raw materials, but he held serious reservations about what he called "Chinese legislation" aimed at forcing that result: "If the Canadian people, with the most numerous and best waterpowers in the world, the greatest quantity of available spruce for the making of pulp, and labour as good as that which can be found anywhere else, cannot get along in that particular industry without such help, they had better go and die, if they are not fit to live."[39]

However, the mean and retaliatory characteristics of the American tariff robbed the senator's argument of its convincing simplicity. In metropolitan Canada even the free trade press considered pulpwood export restrictions warranted by the circumstances. In 1907 the *Globe* commissioned an extended study of the pulpwood question from which its editors concluded: "The Americans will take as a gift, beg, borrow or steal all the raw material they can get from any other country, and use it to beat that country out in the world's market, secure themselves in the protection of a tariff wall strewn along the top with broken glass, barbed wire and sharp nails." On another occasion the *Monetary Times* suggested that a pulpwood export prohibition would be "a natural event in the course of Canadian development" that should not interfere with any steps that might be taken towards wider trade liberalization with the United States. "It is almost generally recognized throughout the Dominion," the journal concluded, "that one of our chief assets is natural resources. To allow our neighbour to strip

---

[39] *CFJ*, April 1910, p. 13; University of Toronto Archives, Walker Papers, Walker to Edwards, Mar. 15, 1911; *Pulpwood and Its Problems*, p. 39.

these and take them home purely for their benefit is obviously unfair to the growth of the Dominion."[40]

Nevertheless, Laurier would not act. Perhaps he did not want to jeopardize his chances of eventual American tariff concessions, but probably he did not want to intrude upon what had become a field of provincial jurisdiction, particularly to assume responsibility for unpopular legislation. At Quebec City, Premiers Parent and Gouin, in keeping with their earlier promises of a moratorium of a decade on changes in forestry legislation, held firm against the competing demands for change coming from the church, lumbermen, and papermakers. But all the while the papermakers, and the growing number of those interested in building mills within the province, were becoming more influential.

At the same time a major crack appeared to be opening in the American tariff wall. Ironically, the best friends of the Canadian papermakers were American newspapermen. The rapid growth of mass circulation newspapers bulging with display advertising had pushed American newsprint consumption steadily upward until by 1909 demand exactly equalled domestic production capacity. Driven by the rising prices that accompanied this convergence of consumption and production, the American Newspaper Publishers' Association, led by John Norris of the New York *Times*, launched a dual assault upon combinations within the paper industry and the high tariff on newsprint which, it claimed, taken together accounted for the inflated newsprint prices. Whatever their editorial position on the tariff as a general proposition, American newspaper publishers mounted a spirited campaign for free trade in newsprint which, they believed, would lower prices. On the other hand, the American Pulp and Paper Association protested against what it called the "unfair discrimination" proposed by the publishers, arguing that a removal of the tariff would inevitably lead to a migration of paper mills to Canada where production and raw material costs were lower.[41]

---

[40] *Pulpwood and Its Problems*, p. 25; *Monetary Times*, April 23, 1910.

[41] This struggle has already been studied in detail by L. Ethan Ellis, *Print Paper Pendulum: Group Pressures and the Price of Newsprint* (New Brunswick, New Jersey, 1948), pp. 3-38; see also J. A. Guthrie, *The Newsprint Paper Industry* (Cambridge, Massachusetts, 1941), pp. 3-46.

In their testimony before the Mann Committee investigating
the newsprint controversy in 1908, the publishers effectively
challenged protectionism with their view of continentalism. The
publisher of the Syracuse *Post Standard*, in a respresentative
statement, conceded that free trade would "transplant the newsprint industry to Canada," but he also recognized that it would
be the existing American paper companies which would finance
and direct that northward expansion:

> I have thought that our American mill owners would probably
> re-establish their plants in Canada, but I do not think the
> Canadians would ever initiate a movement large enough to
> supply the newsprint demands of this country. I think Canada
> may do it, but through American enterprise and American
> capital. And I think that is the impression that quite widely
> prevails in Canada.

Still, the continentalism of the American Newspaper Publishers'
Association, which was directed primarily against the American
tariff, could also be used against the Canadian restrictions on
pulpwood exports. At length—one year and six volumes—the
Mann Committee recommended substantial tariff reductions
to satisfy the publishers, but on terms which would also
"perpetuate the American newsprint industry." In a report
which President Taft described as "a diplomatic proposition
to Canada," the committee suggested a reduction in the duties
prevailing against Canadian newsprint, from $6 to $2 a ton, on
the condition that Canada, "as a matter of neighbourly
courtesy," also eliminate provincial pulpwood export restrictions thereby permitting American papermakers and "the great
reading population" of the United States unlimited access to its
spruce forests.[42]

Canadians were not as impressed by the modest victory won
for them by John Norris and company as they were by the
evidence uncovered, and emphasized by the papermakers
themselves, that the American paper industry was becoming
increasingly dependent upon Canadian raw materials. More-

[42] U.S. House of Representatives, 60th Congress, Doc. No. 1502, *Pulp and
Paper Investigation Hearings* (Washington, 1909), 6 vols.; testimony of
W. E. Gardner, pp. 579-81; *Final Report*, pp. 3313-19.

over, the vicious attack of the American Pulp and Paper Association against the "medieval" Ontario manufacturing condition, and the insignificant Quebec pulpwood export tax, served as a clear indication that these restrictions were finally bringing results. The heavy-handed Payne-Aldrich tariff of 1909 supplied convincing proof. This new tariff, the papermaker's idea of continentalism, retained the duties against Canadian paper and threatened double rates unless the provinces removed their pulpwood export limitations. But in the light of the Mann Committee revelations, its desperate retaliatory provisions looked like a "stuffed club" that merely confirmed Canadian opinion that the American paper industry would soon be compelled to migrate to its natural source of raw materials. By maintaining the duties and imposing retaliatory rates as well, the Payne-Aldrich tariff posed a greater threat, in the form of higher newsprint prices, to the American publishers than it did to the Canadian provinces. Thus, a tariff which had been designed to bring the provinces to their knees only strengthened their determination to resist; they had nothing to lose and perhaps a newsprint industry to be gained by calling the bold American bluff. Ontario, which had never wavered since 1900, continued to stand firm, and on September 6, 1909, Sir Lomer Gouin announced that he too would prohibit the export of pulpwood cut from crown lands. At long last Ontario and Quebec presented a united front on the pulpwood question.[43]

After the battle had been joined but a short time, the *Paper Trade Journal* admitted failure: "The maximum tariff failed to frighten the Canadians into letting us have free pulpwood, so the whole tariff revision scheme fell flat...."[44] And not only were the united provinces able to establish their point in this international poker game, their determination was quickly rewarded by a flood of new pulp and paper company promotions during 1910. Yet just as the interprovincial alliance seemed to be making considerable headway against the

---

[43] *Pulp and Paper Investigation Hearings*, pp. 1884-5, 2014-7, 2143; *Monetary Times*, Aug. 13, 1910 for Gouin's announcement.
[44] Quoted in Ellis, *Print Paper Pendulum*, p. 188.

American papermakers, it had to ward off a potential threat from the Canadian federal government.

Under extreme pressure from the low tariff wing of his party as well as from the high tariff eastern newspapers in search of cheap paper, President Taft initiated a series of talks aimed at averting a major trade war with Canada over the terms of a recently concluded trade agreement with France and the proposed Quebec pulpwood embargo. To satisfy the insistent newspaper publishers, Taft took the forceful step of offering Canada free entry for its newsprint in return for the free export of pulpwood. He was willing to make a sacrifice of the paper industry in order to settle, for once and for all, the troublesome newsprint question.[45]

James Bryce fully understood Taft's great anxiety to reach a swift agreement. "If anything could be done in the way of a concession of woodpulp," he appealed to Lord Grey during the first weeks of the talks, "tha[t] would be the best way of easing off the position and letting the U.S. down with just enough to save their face." But Grey correctly doubted that Laurier would "weaken his hand by playing his ace of trumps, unless he is satisfied that by doing so he can secure several tricks."

> The Government here, as you know, have resisted the pressure put upon them to prohibit the export of pulp. *They are opposed to any such prohibition* [my italics]. The power of prohibiting the export of pulp is of course a whip in the cupboard, which it is undesirable to give away....There is every desire to help the United States, but Canada realizes the strength of her position and does not feel inclined to give anything away.[46]

---

[45] L. Ethan Ellis has also written extensively on this role of newsprint in reciprocity, *Reciprocity, 1911* (New Haven, 1939), pp. 38-44. Aside from repeating the main details, this study adds the Grey-Bryce and Laurier-Foster correspondence to the picture filled out by Prof. Ellis. The Canadian treaty, extending most favoured nation terms to France, automatically invoked sanctions written into the American tariff structure that would have punished Canada for discriminating in favour of France and against the United States.

[46] PAC, Grey Papers, Box 10, James Bryce to Grey, Mar. 6, 1910; *ibid.*,

Provincial intransigence on the pulpwood embargo clearly weakened Laurier's bargaining position. If the provinces had already imposed prohibitions, then the federal government had nothing to hold back to entice wider tariff concessions from the United States. Thus, in the interests of a broad reciprocity treaty, Laurier used his influence to delay the implementation of Gouin's new policy until the fall of 1910.

Understandably, Ontario and Quebec did not consider the free paper for free pulpwood offer to be as generous as the federal government and the Americans. As the reciprocity talks advanced along other fronts, the two provinces insisted upon the absolute necessity of a pulpwood embargo and reminded the federal authorities of the unquestionable provincial jurisdiction over such matters. Thus, in his official letter to Philander C. Knox setting forth the terms of their final agreement, W. S. Fielding plainly regretted that it had not been possible to settle the pulp and paper issue satisfactorily:

> It is necessary that we should point out that this is a matter in which we are not in a position to make any agreement. The restrictions at present existing in Canada are of a Provincial character. They have been adopted by several of the Provinces with regard to what are believed to be Provincial interests. We have neither the right nor the desire to interfere with the Provincial authorities in the free exercise of their constitutional powers in the administration of their public lands. The provisions you are proposing to make respecting the conditions upon which these classes of pulp and paper may be imported into the United States free of duty must necessarily be for the present inoperative.[47]

Fielding's apologetic tone and Laurier's compromising attitude indicated quite clearly the kind of assistance that the provinces could expect from the federal government in their

---

Laurier Papers, John G. Foster (U.S. Counsel General, Ottawa) to Laurier, April 15, 1910; Laurier to Foster, April 29, 1910; 170002-170003; Ellis, *Print Paper Pendulum*, p. 187; *Reciprocity*, pp. 40-1.

[47] PAC, Foster Papers, Vol. 37, "Confidential Prints on Canadian American Relations," Fielding to Knox, Jan. 21, 1911.

struggle to relocate the North American newsprint industry. From the federal point of view, the provincial regulations were a source of embarrassment. But in Toronto and Quebec City the politicians and promoters sensed that if the American newspaper publishers could force the concession of half a loaf—free paper for free pulpwood—then the whole loaf would follow shortly. In 1911 alone, eighty-one new companies, capitalized at over $83 million, had been formed to exploit Canadian pulpwood resources. And the newspaper publishers, disappointed with their reciprocity failure, now lobbied unmercifully for unqualified free entry of newsprint.

The provincial strategy of waiting for the ultimate resolution of the conflict between the American publishers and papermakers was fundamentally sound. Even after the defeat of reciprocity in the Canadian general election of 1911, the Taft administration unilaterally lowered the tariff against Canadian newsprint at the same time as it reinstated former duties against other Canadian commodities. James Bryce explained that the reduction followed from a "constant, unfailing desire on the part of Congress and the Government generally, to favour and win the support of the newspaper interests of the country by giving them cheap paper. Such a line of action becomes all the more tempting at the present moment in view of the forthcoming election." With the publishers well in charge of the writing of the tariff, it was just a matter of time before the long-term Canadian strategy achieved its goal—the free entry of pulp and paper into the American market.

After the Democratic victory in 1912, the provinces did not have to wait much longer. As one of the defeated papermakers grumbled, his industry was now "a poor relation at the tariff table, its place being very far below the salt." The Underwood tariff, not unexpectedly, was a complete triumph for the publishers. Senator Reed Smoot remarked on its passage: "My friend [John] Norris is safe in leaving the Senate gallery, in abandoning the corridors of the Capitol, and going back to New York to-night and reporting the successful termination of the fight he has been waging for so many years. . . ." Henry Cabot Lodge, reflecting the disappointment of the New England papermakers, was somewhat less jubilant; he correctly perceived the Underwood tariff, which established unqualified and unprecedented free trade in mechanical pulp and newsprint, merely enabled Canada "to force the erection of paper mills by American capital on Canadian ground."[48]

This remarkable concession of free trade could be considered as much a triumph for the provinces of Ontario and Quebec as it was for the American Newspaper Publishers' Association. They had stuck to their manufacturing strategy even against federal pressure and their persistence ultimately paid off. October 3, 1913, the date President Wilson signed the Underwood tariff, may be taken as the founding of the Canadian pulp and paper industry.


IV


Prewar Ontario consciously resisted the American conception of continental economic integration, that trading strategy that encouraged the duty-free importation of Canadian energy and raw materials but prohibited the export of finished products and manufactured goods to the United States market. Continentalism had several faces. On the assumption that Canadian trade with the United States would continue to expand, and that industrial raw materials would be in particular demand, the province of Ontario demanded full benefit from the manufacturing opportunities created by the exploitation of its natural resources. Taking this view of the changing character of Canadian-American economic relations, Ontario considered massive exports of raw materials and hydro-electric power detrimental to its own long-term growth. Instead the province tried by a variety of measures to persuade investors to build the processing plants, refineries and finishing industries within its boundaries.

Guidelines aimed at bringing this result about were established during the prewar years, but for a variety of reasons

[48] Quoted in Ellis, *Print Paper Pendulum*, pp. 86-9; see also Guthrie, *The Newsprint Industry*, pp. 45-6, 57.

could not be fully applied. The principle of exporting only surplus hydro-electricity had been agreed to, but the difficulty of defining a surplus in a dynamic situation had yet to be faced. Neither the provincial nor the federal government could get enough leverage on the multinational nickel refining industry, and after repeated efforts both appeared to give up trying. With newsprint the province did experience some success with its development strategy. Economic conditions certainly favoured the location of this industry, but the critical change in the American tariff that laid the basis of the Canadian industry came when it did and in the way it did mainly because of Ontario's determination—in association with Quebec—to control forest exploitation according to its conception of equitable continentalism.

# 9

# War
# and the Canadian
# Quandary

The strain of World War I eventually brought the latent conflicts within the continental resource economy to a climax. Munitions consumed vast quantities of metal and electricity and the reports of their explosion at the front blackened millions of miles of newsprint in the North American cities. In response to wartime demand Ontario nickel and newsprint production doubled and the Ontario Hydro-Electric Power Commission load tripled. By 1919 the value of Canadian pulp and paper exports had reached almost $100 million, enough to supply 30 per cent of the U.S. market. The war also helped New York displace London as the financial centre of the world and, notwithstanding the intensity of imperial sentiment in Canada, this shift was reflected in the changing pattern of Canadian borrowing. In 1913 Canada had raised 74.2 per cent of its foreign capital requirements in London and only 13.5 per cent in New York. Within two years those proportions were almost exactly reversed.[1]

[1] R. S. Rife, "Canada and the United States," *Monetary Times*, Jan. 3, 1919: see also August 31, 1917, November 16, 1917; and W. W. Swanson,

Yet even as the war speeded up the integration of the Canadian and American economies, on another level it re-affirmed their separateness. The intense nationalism it excited reinforced Candian convictions that there were still important national interests worth pursuing. War sharpened the distinction between allies and neutrals, and for much of the duration Americans were counted among the latter. War imposed new industrial priorities that unquestionably transcended the imperatives of ordinary inter-American commerce.


I


International Nickel reacted to the uncertainties of war by closing down its Sudbury mining and smelting operations because, as the ever-apologetic *Canadian Mining Journal* explained, "this is usually a dull season with the Nickel Co., but the war in Europe with the resultant tie-up of shipping has brought about unusual dullness." Three months later its mines reopened, but at half staff. By contrast the British-owned Mond Nickel Company, after only a momentary hesitation, doubled its capacity.[2] Ultra-patriotic Canadian newspapers, already exasperated by International Nickel's past behaviour, were more than eager to draw invidious conclusions from its conspicuous idleness. Obviously, the company must have sold most of its production to Germany where it had been stock-piled ready for war. Thus Canadian nickel, refined by Americans, and forged into shells by Germans, was now being fired back at the Canadian soldiers and sailors defending the Empire. It was but a short step to believing that International Nickel was itself enemy-controlled.

These exaggerated but believable suspicions fed a sense of public outrage that finally compelled Canadian governments to face the nickel question squarely. The sensational Toronto

---

"London and New York as Financial Centres," *ibid.*, October 11, 1919. See also, *Financial Post*, November 4, 1916; March 3, 1917.

[2] *Canadian Mining Journal*, August 15, 1914, p. 536 [hereafter, *CMJ*]; University of Toronto Archives, Walker Papers, Byron Walker to C. V. Corless, August 10, 1914; Walker to the Rt. Hon. Sir Alfred Mond, Bart., August 12, 1914.

*World*, with the unanimous support of the metropolitan press, led a crusade for an immediate embargo on nickel exports to the United States to ensure that no more Canadian nickel would reach the enemy. Now the imperatives of national security, not just common sense, demanded government control over nickel mining. This being the case, the press insisted upon the construction of a Canadian nickel refinery, perhaps even government-owned, with sufficient capacity to supply the requirements of the entire British Empire.[3]

To these appeals Premier W. H. Hearst replied with an apparent lack of interest. "Ontario has no control over the two companies in question."[4] For its part the federal government declared its complete confidence in the integrity of International Nickel. In a special memorandum on the subject issued on December 21, 1914, the Borden government pointed out matter-of-factly that the company was American-, not German-owned, and revealed that federal agents, with the full support and co-operation of the imperial authorities, already maintained a strict and perfectly adequate surveillance over its sales. The memorandum went on to suggest that an export ban would only further hinder the war effort by reducing the supply of refined nickel available to British industry, and concluded with a warning that such an embargo would most certainly strain Canadian-American relations at a particularly critical juncture. In a letter addressed to "the Canadian public," the president of International Nickel flatly denied the existence of any European influences within his company and reassured Canadians that he would continue to co-operate fully with their government. But just for good measure, Ambrose Monell concluded his declaration of sympathy with an impolitic allusion to the old New Caledonian canard.[5]

---

[3] See the running debate between the Toronto *World*, the *Daily Star*, *Mail and Empire*, *Evening Telegram*, and *Globe* on the one side and the *CMJ* on the other, Oct. 15, 1914, pp. 661-2; Dec. 1, p. 757; Dec. 15, pp. 789-90. See also Main, *The Canadian Nickel Industry* (Toronto, 1955), pp. 82-3.

[4] *World*, Dec. 25, 1914, quoted in the Ontario Liberal party pamphlet, *Nickel* (Toronto, 1919).

[5] *Financial Post*, Jan. 1, 1915; *CMJ*, Jan. 1, 1915, p. 15; PAC, Borden Papers, Loring Christie, Control of the Export of Nickel, Feb. 27, 1916, pp. 58279-

This united front in defence of the status quo confirmed the long-standing impression that the company held both the federal and the provincial governments in its palm. Neither the bland response of government nor the company's threatening disclaimer could dispel the mounting popular anxiety. Hysterical newspaper headlines continued through the winter and by the spring of 1915 Boards of Trade had begun to pass laboured resolutions demanding an embargo on nickel matte.[6] As an indication of the unprecedented force of public opinion, even the obedient *Canadian Mining Journal* abandoned INCO when a respected, "practical mining man" argued in its columns that refining could be economically carried on in Ontario. The deterioration of the company's public relations had become so serious, the *Financial Post* claimed, that its conduct endangered the entire capitalist system. Nor was the *Post* above contributing its own stories of "notoriously immoral" behaviour and political corruption to the mounting evidence of INCO's villainy.[7]

Although B. E. Walker considered the whole affair a newspaper fabrication—"I do not really believe that it will amount to anything serious"—he wisely advised the Mond Nickel Company, of which he was a director, not to enter the refining controversy this time.[8] Outside of the Conservative cabinets at Ottawa and Toronto, the International Nickel Company could not claim any respectable public defenders. Consequently, when N. W. Rowell attacked the government's know-nothing policy that spring in the Legislature, Hearst retreated behind the promise of a royal commission to look into the matter.[9] At Ottawa, the Borden government was no longer quite as confident either. About the same time it established the first

---

80; see also correspondence tabled Feb. 11, 1915, pp. 58281ff. for details of Canadian, American and British surveillance.

[6] PAC, Borden Papers, reels C-4337-8, clippings; *CMJ*, Jan. 1, 1915, pp. 3-4; Jan. 15, pp. 34-5.

[7] *Financial Post*, July 15, 1916, where it is reported that two Liberal cabinet ministers received free stock during the INCO consolidation in 1902.

[8] University of Toronto Archives, Walker Papers, Walker to Bernard Mohr, Feb. 23, 1915; Walker to C. V. Corless, Aug. 11, [1915]. This severing of the former Mond-INCO axis was especially important.

[9] For the debate, see the *Globe*, Feb. 23, 1915.

of two Munitions Resources Commissions to study the whole question of base metal refining in Canada. This first angry tide of public opinion at least forced both the federal and provincial governments to take the nickel question more seriously than either had since 1900.

Behind this curtain of popular indignation a newly formed third nickel company struggled desperately to turn events to its own advantage. Back in 1913 that shadowy New York entrepreneur who had led Canadian capital into steel, street railways, and South American utilities, Dr. F. S. Pearson, announced in association with E. R. Wood and James Dunn the formation of the British American Nickel Corporation.[10] After a series of shrewd, discrete, and remarkably thorough studies, the Pearson syndicate purchased the Booth-O'Brien consolidated properties at Sudbury and North American patents for the Hybinette electrolytic refining process.[11]

To the Mond people in England the new company resembled just another Canadian company promotion. But Walker, who knew the principals personally, convinced his colleagues that the British American Nickel Corporation meant business: it knew the value and extent of its ore body; it owned a superb refining process and had hired the best technical management available; and what is more, it possessed brilliant financial

[10] Very little is known about Dr. Frederick Stark Pearson even though he was probably one of the two or three most important figures during the formative stages of Canadian finance capitalism. Born in Lowell, Massachusetts, in 1861, he received his university engineering degrees at Tufts. There he taught mathematics, and at MIT, chemistry. After a short career as a Brazilian mining engineer he managed a small electric company in Massachusetts for two years and then became chief engineer for a major New York city street railway. From that post he expanded into promoting the Dominion Coal Company in Nova Scotia and the Metropolitan Street Railway in New York. After the turn of the century Pearson concentrated on mobilizing Canadian capital for South American and Caribbean utilities promotions until 1913, when he turned his attention to nickel. *Who Was Who in America* (Chicago, 1942), Vol. I, p. 949.

[11] PAC, Borden Papers, W. T. White to Borden, Feb. 2, 1915, pp. 58691-2. White, who ought to have known, thought that the British American Nickel interests were the ones behind the anti-export agitation. On the organization of the company, see Main, *The Canadian Nickel Industry*, pp. 70-2.

leadership. "I have known Dr. Pearson for years," Walker confided to Bernard Mohr of Mond Nickel:

> He gets his capital for his various enterprises from the public in the manner of company promotions, but he is not an ordinary promoter. I do not remember anything he has taken hold of which has not been a success except the Mexico and North Western Railway and Timber Company, which being in Chihuahua is interfered with by the revolution at the moment. He is not working in any way in the interest of the Booth-O'Brien people but is undoubtedly purchasing from them, and although he may be mistaken in the estimate of the value of the property, that he believes in its value there can be no doubt. I mention this because there is no use in deceiving ourselves by thinking too little of our opponents.

Walker's sober intelligence, coming as it did during a mild recession and a period of price instability, caused a slight panic among the English directors. Mond himself urged Walker to come to some kind of working agreement with the syndicate or, failing that, to arrange a merger. Walker promptly began the delicate approaches to Pearson, advising him "on general principles" to consult fully with Mond before spending large sums on the construction of a refinery, but the syndicate obviously sensed its opportunity and pressed ahead alone.[12]

War removed the danger as far as the Mond Nickel Company was concerned, but then, for the first time, the upstart British American Nickel Corporation seriously threatened the giant International Nickel monopoly. Ferocious Canadian patriotism had already placed the American company under a cloud and its directors feared that the Pearson syndicate, which with its ore, patents and personnel had everything but solid financial backing, might capitalize upon their misfortune by using that wrath to induce embarrassed governments to supply the

---

[12] University of Toronto Archives, Walker Papers, Walker to C. V. Corless, Confidential, Jan. 2, 1913; Walker to Bernard Mohr, Confidential, Jan. 3, 1913; Mohr to Walker, Confidential, Jan. 17, 1913; Walker to Mohr, Jan. 30, 1913; Alfred Mond to Walker, Feb. 1, 1913; Walker to Mond, March 14, 1913; Walker to F. S. Pearson, March 3, 1913.

required capital. Lurking behind the refining convulsion, International Nickel foresaw the grave possibility of genuine, government-supported competition rising to replace the token and largely prearranged rivalry with Mond.

Just as International Nickel expected, E. R. Wood launched a major campaign late in 1914 to enlist the support of the federal government behind a thoroughly Canadian enterprise. In return for a mere 3 million bond guarantee, Wood and Pearson promised the Prime Minister a nickel refinery with sufficient capacity to serve the entire Empire. He laid a whole series of propositions before Borden and the Minister of Finance, Thomas White, ranging from complex dominion-provincial tax incentives to a good old reliable bounty. "I am satisfied... that the most certain way of bringing about the much desired refining of Nickel in Canada," Wood concluded his presentation, "is for the Government to give us the guarantee, and, if they do so, we will be refining Nickel successfully and economically in this country in eighteen months' time."[13] While the members of cabinet pondered the British American proposition, International Nickel hastily volunteered a host of good reasons why the government should not acquiesce. But the government stalled, waiting for the recommendations of its own Munitions Resources Commissions. Meanwhile, leaving E. R. Wood to tend the fires in Ottawa and Toronto, Pearson hurried back to England to obtain the necessary imperial guarantee, as misfortune would have it, aboard the ill-fated *Lusitania*. With the death of Pearson the company lost its promotional genius at a critical moment in its struggle for life.[14]

By the end of the year public opinion could be denied no longer. Anticipating the conclusions of his own Munitions Resources Commissions and the Royal Ontario Nickel Commission, Robert Borden asked International Nickel tactfully but publicly to give a Canadian refinery its "careful consideration and active attention." With regal condescension Ambrose

---

[13] PAC, Borden Papers, Borden to G. H. Perley, Nov. 21, 1914; Perley to Borden, Dec. 15, 1914; E. R. Wood to Borden, Jan. 30, 1915, pp. 58540, 58552, 58595-7. *Ibid.*, White Papers, Box 9, E. R. Wood to White, Feb. 2, 1915.

[14] *Ibid.*, White Papers, Box 9, J. M. Clark to White, Feb. 6, 8, 10, 1915.

Monell replied: "We will grant your request, and erect in the Dominion of Canada, at such point as seems in our judgment to be the most economical for operation, a plant for the refining of nickel...."[15] Yet Monell's grand but indeterminate promise failed to satisfy public opinion or the first Munitions Resources Commission. Reporting on February 24, 1916, it pressed the federal government to "...insist upon the International Nickel Company proceeding," pointing out that, in its opinion, "climatic conditions present no adequate cause for failure to proceed with the installation of such a refinery immediately." Two months later the second Report went even further and suggested urgent cash assistance as well as a bond guarantee to help the British American Nickel Corporation get under way immediately.[16]

Borden could accept the first recommendation; but in view of the troubled railway situation, he could hardly agree to the second. "I am not at all confident that the resolution of the Commission is feasible," he wrote to Thomas White, "possibly you might sound E. R. Wood as to the present proposals of the British American Nickle [sic] Corporation." The Minister of Finance agreed that neither loans nor bond guarantees could be justified at that particular moment. In another context he elaborated upon the reasons for his reluctance:

> There is a strong prejudice in the public mind against discrimination in favour of wealthy corporations as against private prospectors, and while from a business standpoint much can be said in favour of granting the application of this Company, I think the present an inopportune time to take it under consideration.[17]

[15] *Ibid.*, Borden Papers, Borden to Monell, Dec. 29, 1915; Monell to Borden, Jan. 7, 1916, pp. 58288-90; *CMJ*, Feb. 15, 1916, p. 96.

[16] PAC, White Papers, Box 9, Report of the Canadian Munitions Resources Commission, Feb. 23 and 24, 1916, and the second Report, April 17, 1916.

[17] *Ibid.*, Borden to White, June 6, 1916, Confidential; White to Borden, June 8, 1916; White to Borden, Aug. 18, 1916. All along White had opposed offering help to the Pearson-Wood syndicate. It was, he said, preposterous for the government to cover the risk of a commercial venture. PAC, Borden

Officially, the federal government relied completely upon the integrity of International Nickel and nervously awaited the fulfillment of its promise to build a refinery.[18]

In two provincial by-elections that summer the Liberal opposition in Ontario assumed the leadership of the continuing crusade against International Nickel. Party spokesmen circulated impressive-looking lists of the company's German-American stockholders as evidence of Krupp control. One of the Liberal candidates, Hartley Dewart, campaigned exclusively on the nickel issue and more particularly upon the intimacy of Conservative politicians and the delinquent company. Dewart drew considerable political capital from W. J. Hanna's 885 preferred shares of INCO and Frank Cochrane's business associations with A. P. Turner of the Canadian Copper Company.[19] Specifically, the Liberals charged that the corrupt "Cochrane-Hearst-Ferguson nickel plated policy" protected the company from paying its rightful tax burden, ensuring the permanent location of its refineries in the United States.[20]

While the two parties were exchanging smears, counter-charges, and denials in the August heat of 1916, news reached the province that sometime in July a German submarine, the *Deutschland*, had slipped into a port on the east coast of the United States and put out to sea with a cargo of refined nickel presumably Canadian in origin. In the wake of the *Deutschland* sensation the British Admiralty censured Henry R. Merton & Co., International Nickel's European export agents, and

---

Papers, White to Borden, Feb. 3, 1915, Confidential; White to Borden, June 1, 1915, Confidential, pp. 58689-90, 58863-4.

[18] *Ibid.*, Borden to Monell, Feb. 26, 1916, June 6, 1916, and July 17, 1916, for prodding, pp. 58292, 58294, 58298.

[19] Cochrane at least seemed to know where his duty lay. He rejected the British North American Nickel Company propositions outright, ostensibly on the grounds of their "untried" refining process. His Department of Railways and Canals was responsible for the supervision of International Nickel sales. PAC, Borden Papers, Borden to Perley, June 2, 1915; Cochrane to Borden, April 29, 1918, pp. 58861, 58835.

[20] For a compendium of Liberal charges, see the 1919 election campaign pamphlet, *Nickel*, and *CMJ*, Sept. 1, 1916, pp. 410-11.

announced the seizure of twelve shipments of nickel in prize court. And as the circle of suspicion widened to include other metal brokers connected with International Nickel, the *Deutschland* returned in November and made off with another load of Canadian nickel. The *Deutschland* incident and the revelations that followed thoroughly destroyed the credibility of the federal government's policing system. No one, not even the acting British High Commissioner, believed Arthur Meighen when he assured Parliament that the cargo in question contained no Canadian nickel, that the federal government maintained absolute control over International Nickel sales, and that the British Admiralty had complete confidence in the effectiveness of that surveillance.[21]

As a result of these sensational events, International Nickel found itself in serious trouble. That popular resentment which it had been able to restrain for so long now threatened the company's formerly unassailable monopoly. Moreover, a Canadian company stood by with adequate ore and better technology to profit from its fall. But what was more alarming still, public ownership of nickel mining and refining was being advocated not just by wild-men like W. F. Maclean and the irresponsible *World*, but by respectable, church-going corporation lawyers like Newton Rowell and solid newspapers like the *Globe*. Nor could public ownership be dismissed as a hollow threat. The very real presence of the Hydro-Electric Power Commission gave pause for thought. From an International

---

[21] For details of the *Deutschland* episode see *Nickel*; *CMJ*, Aug. 1, 1916, p. 384; Sept. 1, 1916, p. 407; Nov. 1, 1916, pp. 504-5; PAC, Foster Papers, Box 100, clippings from *Globe* and *World*. Some unguarded remarks by Lord Robert Cecil concerning this incident were taken in Canada as implied criticism of the Canadian government's handling of the nickel question and touched off an acrimonious exchange of communications between Borden, Meighen, Perley and the Colonial Secretary's office that lasted almost a year. In the end the British authorities apologized and withdrew their substantive proposals for improving the control of nickel refining. The net result was a tightening of security in the United States and closer co-operation between Canadian officials and the office of the British consul general in New York. See for details, PAC, Borden Papers, reel C-4336, pp. 58315-58418A.

Nickel point of view, it was no longer a question of continuing to hold out against hostile public opinion; events had moved so quickly that it was doubtful that even an extraordinary effort to satisfy that opinion would be enough to save the corporate skin. Could the company build its refinery soon enough and would that outflank the inevitable political attack in the Legislature? It was no coincidence that with first word of the *Deutschland* outrage International Nickel announced that it would build a new refinery at Port Colborne, emphasizing that construction would begin immediately. At the same time the militant Liberals captured both seats in the provincial by-elections. That fall the company raced to catch up with public opinion as the Liberal party mounted its own campaign to incite wider support for its legislative program of public ownership. Meanwhile, above this turmoil, the prestigious Royal Ontario Nickel Commission sat in judgment, about to deliver its definitive opinion after exhaustive study into every aspect of the question.[22]

When the Liberals presented their first public ownership resolution to the Legislature in February 1917, the government maintained that the Royal Commission would shortly present some expert recommendations on that very matter. Later it turned aside a second such resolution by pointing out that the commissioners, in their wisdom, had pronounced unequivocally against that course. In its voluminous *Report* handed down in April, the Royal Commission confirmed that Ontario truly possessed the world's most extensive and highest quality nickel deposits and need not, therefore, fear competition from any source. Documenting the widespread benefits of the refining industry for the chemical and metallurgical trades, the *Report* concluded that any refining process could be successfully worked in Ontario and that the Hybinette electrolytic method best suited Ontario conditions. Finally the commissioners praised the management of the nickel companies for their

---

[22] See Dewart's speeches, *Nickel*, pp. 7-33; *Globe*, Nov. 20, 1916; *CMJ*, Dec. 15, 1916, pp. 588-90 ("Mr. Dewart on German Control of Metals"). For N. W. Rowell's views—"Governments at Ottawa and at Queen's Park...are dominated by the International Nickel Corporation"—see the *World*, Nov. 18, 1916.

efficient mining operations and particularly for their commitment to research. Of course publication of this detailed *Report* could not be credited directly with International Nickel's decision to locate its refinery in Ontario. That had been announced almost a year earlier. Nevertheless, the selection of qualified experts to conduct the investigation, then the thoroughness and scope of their studies, must have made it clearly apparent to the company from the outset that their ultimate *Report* would reveal its case for what it was, a tissue of lies. The very appointment of a Royal Commission composed of recognized authorities prefigured the demise of the old, reliable New Caledonia ruse.[23]

Ironically, by the date of its publication, the potentially dangerous Royal Commission *Report* had become International Nickel's best defence. With the company outdoing itself to accommodate public opinion, the *Report* turned out to be a surprisingly conservative document thoroughly satisfied with the status quo. International Nickel was rushing one refinery into production as the commission deliberated, and the British American Nickel Corporation gave assurance that it planned to go ahead immediately with its refinery, probably in the vicinity of Sudbury if sufficient hydro-electric power was available. As it turned out, this basic conservatism of the commission destroyed any prospect of there ever being any genuine competition for International Nickel in Ontario from a private, public, or mixed corporation. In its most inexplicable finding,

---

[23]  The Royal Ontario Nickel Commission, chaired by George Thomas Holloway, vice-president of the British Institute of Mining and Metallurgy and a renowned scientist, which also included W. G. Miller, the provincial geologist, T. W. Gibson, the Deputy Minister of Mines, began its hearings in September 1915. See its *Report*, "Summary and Conclusions," pp. xxiii-xlii. Since the problem that it had been set up to study—namely, the absence of a refining industry in Ontario—had disappeared by the time the commission reported, it made no specific recommendations. However, partially as an outcome of its researches, the Hearst government raised the sliding scale of mines taxes to garner more of the nickel profits, and succeeded in demanding $1,300,000 in back taxes from International Nickel. See the section of the *Report* dealing with mines taxation, pp. 506-28, conclusions, p. xxv, and Appendix N, pp. 158-203 [hereafter, RONC, *Report*].

the commission declared that genuine competition already existed. If no monopoly could be found, then it followed that there was no real justification for government aid being extended to a new company trying to enter the business. Secondly, the commissioners roundly condemned nationalization because a government takeover would cost something in the order of the total paid-up capital of all the chartered banks in Canada. The expense hardly warranted the risk. Nickel, the commissioners pointed out, "is not a necessity of life nor an article of universal consumption or use, and the nickel business is in no way comparable to those connected with the operation of public utilities, where government ownership may be beneficial or expedient."[24]

In short, the sober men of the Royal Ontario Nickel Commission regarded public ownership as nothing short of an "adventure." Their views unquestionably counteracted all of the Liberal propaganda in favour of public ownership and, just incidentally, also doomed the British American Nickel Corporation. Without heavy government support it had no better hope than its predecessors of getting itself established in a hostile financial environment controlled by its competition. Eventually the British government offered a small measure of help, but both the federal and the provincial governments steadfastly refused to do so.[25] After a short time the small company exhausted its resources and collapsed into interminable quarrelling over the liquidation. In due course International Nickel acquired its assets, including its electrolytic refining technique, which, as it turned out, provided the basis for the next generation of INCO's ascendancy. A merger with Mond in the twenties made the monopoly complete. But it need not have happened that way. Both British American and public

[24] Professor Main concluded that the commission's belief could not possibly have been based on the readily available facts, "but upon the insistence of the producing companies that they were competing." RONC, *Report*, pp. xxvii-xxxi; Main, *The Canadian Nickel Industry*, pp. 86-7, 90-107.

[25] PAC, Borden Papers, E. R. Wood to Borden, April 24, 1918, pp. 58824-30.

ownership offered viable alternatives in 1917, but the Royal Ontario Nickel Commission, on slim evidence and a great deal of unscientific prejudice, obstructed those two avenues. International Nickel, by recovering quickly enough to be able to comply and demonstrate its agreement with the *Report*, was able to turn the very instrument of public opinion, a Royal Commission, against the popular will.[26] By this strange, confusing and ambivalent process, Ontario became the home of the North American nickel refining industry.

Leaving aside the question of the political influence exerted by INCO—which can never be settled definitively—what could explain the reluctance of the federal government to assert itself? Certainly the official reason given was convincing enough. Since the United States owned such a large percentage of the world's refining capacity, it made no sense to deny allied war industry access to it *even if* very small amounts of nickel fell into enemy hands—although both Borden and Meighen vigorously denied that this had ever taken place. A second, equally compelling logic also counselled inaction. As Borden candidly explained to the acting British High Commissioner on one occasion, an embargo on nickel exports "...would create strained relations with the United States and might provoke retaliation."[27] A Canadian prime minister looking at the complete web of continental entanglements recognized as perhaps the British could not, and the furious Canadian nationalists did not care to, that Canadian-American issues could no longer be treated in isolation. The relationship, even this early, had become too complex and intimate for that. Not surprisingly, when the possibility of a domestic power shortage ceased being a theoretical question, this same inertia of continental interdependence hindered the articulation of a national energy policy as well.

---

[26] Main, *The Canadian Nickel Industry*, pp. 97-8, for the importance to INCO of the British North American Nickel Company patents.

[27] Borden to the acting British High Commissioner, July 13, 1916, quoted in Henry Borden, ed., *Robert Laird Borden: His Memoirs* (Toronto, 1938), Vol. II, pp. 629-30.

II

Affluence, industrial expansion, and energetic salesmanship each contributed to the rapid growth of the Hydro-Electric Power Commission after 1910. Through a series of public demonstrations and popular, mobile "electric circuses," Beck the showman introduced Ontario householders to this new form of energy. Beck the salesman kept domestic rates low enough that electricity quickly became a necessity rather than a curiosity, thus profitably diversifying the load characteristics of his system. Beck the ruthless competitor sold his power at any price. He slandered privately owned utilities and thrust himself shamelessly into municipal politics, flattering, blustering and if necessary bribing ever-increasing numbers of ratepayers into supporting his hydro by-laws. Using all of these tactics, Beck the businessman-politician gradually enlarged his public enterprise at the expense of the private competition—mainly provided by Mackenzie's consolidated Toronto Power Company.

Beck's method resembled that of any North American power baron of the time. Indeed, an interesting comparison could be drawn between Adam Beck in Ontario and the notorious Samuel Insull in the American mid-west. They shared the same business strategy—low domestic rates to diversify the load factor and increase the efficiency of the whole system. Interesting similarities could also be found in their domineering personalities, baronial habits, and control over legislatures. The key difference between them—and this set them poles apart—was that Beck carried out his operations in the name of the public; elections were his tools and public money his means. Insull, though equally committed to the public service conception of his enterprises, was just as convinced of the inherent superiority of private enterprise. One wonders how much these champions of two forms of utilities organization knew about and learned from one another.[28]

---

[28] Compare W. R. Plewman, *Adam Beck and the Ontario Hydro* (Toronto, 1947) and Forest McDonald, *Insull* (Chicago, 1962). For further insight into the public versus private power fight in the United States during the 1920s

By the end of 1914 Beck and an eager, innovating, young engineering staff had together transformed Hydro from a small distribution company, delivering 2,500 horsepower to ten municipalities in 1910, into a major network of 95 municipalities with a load of 77,000 horsepower. After only five years of operation, that wildly optimistic sum of 100,000 hp contracted for in 1908 was no longer adequate. War opened new opportunities for expansion and Beck seized every occasion. During the first year the commission increased its load by 35 per cent and the tremendous spurt in demand expected from the hundreds of munitions factories then under construction still lay ahead. By the end of 1916 the commission was distributing 167,000 horsepower to 191 municipalities; but the next year, when the munitions factories came onto the line, the load jumped to 333,000 horsepower. Within three years the commission had tripled its service; it was well on its way to becoming one of the world's largest hydro-electric empires.[29]

Since the commission was at once the competitor and regulator of every hydro-electric installation in the province, Beck could, for all practical purposes, tyrannize the Niagara companies into selling him the power he needed at the price he was willing to pay. However, further *purchases* from private companies satisfied neither the needs nor the ambitions of the chairman of the commission. Through his near complete control over the Hearst government, Beck also managed to expand the commission's responsibilities to include the *production* of its own power at Niagara. Then, in his characteristically imperious manner, he ordered construction of the world's largest hydro-electric generating station. This wartime aggression, always carried forward on waves of municipal by-law victories, led the commission away from the modest "conduit pipe" role envisioned by Whitney towards the exclusive monopoly coveted by Adam Beck and the public power movement. During the war Hydro ceased being a mere distributing company carrying

---

and 1930s, see Ernest Gruening, *The Public Pays: A Study of Power Propaganda* (New York, 1964 edition).

[29] Plewman, *Adam Beck*, p. 475.

power as inexpensively as possible from the producers at Niagara to the municipal consumers. Under Adam Beck's dictatorial direction it rapidly developed into a fully integrated generation, transmission, and distribution organization striving towards monopoly throughout its domain.

Beck established the principle of generating his own power in a seemingly innocent way. In 1914 he received permission to buy a tiny generating station on the Severn River and then expanded that authority by building two other stations in the same district. Having established the principle, the commission acquired the power stations along the Trent Canal in 1916. During the last hours of the session that year Beck rushed a much bolder measure through the House. Notwithstanding the clauses contained in the original Niagara waterpower leases, this legislation gave the Hydro-Electric Power Commission authority to generate its own power at Niagara Falls. The next year the commission purchased the Ontario Power Company, its principal supplier, for $22,669,000. Two key considerations guided Beck in this takeover. Firstly, the commission required much more power to meet its immediate commitments, and buying up an existing company seemed the fastest and cheapest way of getting it. Secondly, the International Boundary Waters Treaty had limited the amount of water available at Niagara for power generating purposes. A further agreement between the Ontario government and the power companies in 1914 had distributed that volume among the users, the Canadian Niagara Power Company receiving permission to divert 8,225 cubic feet per second, the Electrical Development Company, 9,985, and the Ontario Power Company 11,180.[30] If he planned to build his own modern generating station Beck would have to buy out one of the companies just to get water to run it—hence his persistent objection to the Treaty in the first place. The Ontario Power Company held rights to the largest volume of water and its diversion to the proposed plant at Queenston,

---

[30] Ontario Hydro-Electric Power Commission, *Annual Report*, 1917; 1918, pp. 59-71[hereinafter, OHPC, *Annual Report*]; for the waterpower division, see PAO, Hearst Papers, Water Power Available at Niagara Falls, June 18, 1914. See also, Christopher Armstrong, "The Politics of Federalism: Ontario's Relations with the Federal Government, 1896-1941," (unpublished Ph.D. thesis, University of Toronto, 1973), pp. 199-205.

where the full difference of level between Lakes Erie and Ontario could be utilized, would yield the commission substantially more power than it would from the Ontario Power Company's turbines at the very foot of the Falls. Moreover, at the time of the takeover in April 1917, the company was not using its full allotment; therefore, as a temporary measure, the existing facilities could be quickly enlarged to meet the present emergency.

Yet not even the full output of the Ontario Power Company could accommodate the surging demand stimulated by war. Blackouts, which had started first in 1916, increased both in frequency and severity over the next three years. Thus, even with a power company of his own, Beck still was forced to rely upon private producers to supply the difference between what the commission could produce itself and what it had agreed to supply. But the private companies were also experiencing new demands upon their production, and were not eager to deliver power to Beck for a pittance when it could be sold at much higher rates in the industrial market or across the river in the United States. To strengthen his already extensive coercive powers, Beck rammed two more pieces of legislation through the House in 1917. The first granted the commission broader authority at Niagara Falls, and the second, the Water Powers Regulation Act, appointed a three-man Royal Commission to determine the amount of water being taken from the Niagara River. If the private companies were found to be using more than their allotted volume—Beck suspected they were stealing water—the Royal Commission could order sale of the excess power to Hydro at a recommended price. With just ordinary threats Beck had managed to pry 50,000 horsepower from the Canadian Niagara Power Company, but the case-hardened Mackenzie company refused to be intimidated so easily. Therefore, leaving a biased Royal Commission hand-picked by Beck to torment the stubborn Electrical Development Company, Beck opened yet another front in his campaign to obtain more power for his system while at the same time strangling the remaining private companies into total submission.[31]

31  OHPC, *Annual Report*, 1918, pp. 52-6; for details of Beck's assault first upon Canadian Niagara Power and then upon the Electrical Development Company, see Armstrong, "The Politics of Federalism," pp. 212-23.

Ontario's rapidly increasing power requirements could only be met, Beck reasoned, by shutting off hydro-electric exports to the United States. With the full support of his captive pressure group, the Ontario Municipal Electric Association, Beck called upon the federal government to halt the sale of Canadian hydro to the United States for the duration of the power crisis. The private companies on the Canadian side of the Falls, he charged late in 1917, were selling large blocs of power at enormous profits in the United States as a time when Ontario's war industries desperately needed more electricity. Beck insisted that the federal government should order these companies to bear their patriotic responsibilities. It could easily remedy this intolerable state of affairs by revoking their export licences under the terms of the 1907 Fluid and Electricity Export Act in order that this power might be released to the Ontario Hydro-Electric Power Commission for distribution. There was in this, as in all Beck's arguments, a compelling simplicity. A national emergency existed. Canada needed the power being sold at a profit to foreigners. The duty of the federal government was clear. Beck, of course, capitalized gleefully on an opportunity to wrap himself in the flag, shift responsibility for the blackouts to the federal government, and in the process, heap more popular abuse upon the embattled private companies. Beck's aggressive search for power provoked yet another dominion-provincial crisis over the energy question, and brought federal authorities face to face with those continental power relationships disclosed during the nickel refining affair. Within only a decade the eventuality prophesied by the critics of the 1907 Act had indeed come to pass.[32] Could power bargained away during a time of surplus be easily recovered during a period of scarcity? On what possible grounds could reasonable men at Ottawa resist the force of Beck's logic?

On the surface at least, Beck was simply attempting to enlist the federal government in a drive to release more power to Ontario's industries. The question of the propriety of power exports had been raised by the government of Ontario with

[32] See above, Chapter 8.

federal authorities in 1914 and again in 1916 during the protracted wrangling with the Canadian Niagara Power Company.[33] But the bombast of the 1917 campaign signalled a major escalation of dominion-provincial conflict over hydro. Nor was the issue as clear cut as on first glance it appears. Questions of principle must always be seen in their context. During the war both the Electrical Development Company and the Canadian Niagara Power Company continued to deliver power to New York distributors just as they had always done. But so did Beck's own Ontario Power Company; indeed, it was the worst offender![34] When Hydro purchased the company in 1917, included among its assets was a contract binding the owners to export 60,000 hp to an American transmission company until 2010. After lengthy negotiations, Beck arranged a reduction of the volume of power to 50,000 hp and a terminal date of 1950, but he could not escape from the contract. Certainly Beck needed the 81,000 hp being sold in New York by his two competitors, and to get it he needed federal help. Perhaps he also wanted to shift the odium of breaking his own export contract onto Ottawa. As part of Beck's long-term strategy, cancellation of exports would also remove one of the few independent supports left to the private companies and would in time throw them into complete dependence upon the commission. In any event, the transparency—if not the hypocrisy—of his motives seriously compromised the patriotic purity of Beck's appeal.

The export crisis flared up in the late spring of 1917 when a munitions supplier in New York State reported that it was unable to complete its orders for the British government on account of the withdrawal of Canadian power. Sir Joseph

---

[33] PAO, Hearst Papers, copies of extensive Beck, Hearst, E. L. Patenaude (Minister of Inland Revenue) correspondence, spring-summer of 1916.

[34] According to Sir Henry Drayton's later findings, Toronto Power exported 13,500 hp during peak periods, Canadian Niagara 30,000, and the Ontario Power Company 37,500. During off-peak hours these totals rose to a combined volume of 108,000 hp; Sir Henry Drayton, *Report on the Export of Electricity From Canada and Report of the Power Controller* (Ottawa, 1919), p. 14.

Flavelle at the Imperial Munitions Board quickly intervened. He called Beck and representatives of the private power companies to a meeting in his office on June 27 to explore possible solutions to this particular shortage. Inevitably those talks broadened out into a discussion of the entire export question. Beck argued that exports from the private companies to the United States should be shut off but that his Ontario Power Company should continue to meet its contractual obligations. Not surprisingly, the private companies complained bitterly that Beck's plan was little more than a raid upon their contracts in the name of patriotism and Flavelle sympathized with them—as he always had. He proposed that the various parties set aside their differences for the interim, pool their available supplies and match supply with demand. This, of course, was completely unacceptable to Beck. Ontario Hydro, he argued, was virtually the government of Ontario. It was solely responsible for ensuring that power be distributed in the public interest. It followed that it could not be dictated to by either the federal government or the private companies. Flavelle could not break the deadlock and the federal government ignored the matter for the remainder of the summer.[35]

The problem, of course, did not disappear. By September the export crisis had assumed international importance. Uncertainty over their power supplies led American industrialists on the Niagara frontier to complain to the State Department, and the United States government in turn let it be known that it would not tolerate further export reductions. The federal government found itself then in the uncomfortable position of being pressured by the government of Ontario on the one hand to cut off all exports, and the government of the United States on the other hand to maintain existing deliveries.[36] Caught in this difficult bind, the Borden government escaped through the usual route of appointing a one-man Royal Commission to resolve the dilemma. Sir Henry

---

[35] Armstrong, "The Politics of Federalism," pp. 223-6.
[36] PAC, Borden Papers, Sir Cecil Spring Rice to Governor General, Sept. 18, 1917, Secret, p. 124667.

Drayton of the Board of Railway Commissioners was assigned the thankless task of recommending a settlement of this episode of the continuing Beck-Mackenzie feud.

Drayton wasted no time. Within a month he managed to establish the facts of the case and draw up a report.[37] He concluded after examining the potential generating capacity of all the companies at Niagara, studying their contracts and surveying the projected demand, that a power crisis of major proportions was in the offing. He condemned both the private companies and Ontario Hydro for conduct in the past that had poisoned the atmosphere and made co-operation more difficult. Although he conceded that a critical shortage was in the making, Drayton nevertheless did not recommend cancellation of outstanding power export licences. He cautioned the federal government against acting as a "cat's paw" for Ontario Hydro in its dispute with the private companies.[38] Instead, he recommended the maintenance of existing export levels for the time being until an international conference could be convened to explore the possibility of releasing some of this power for Canadian use. Finally, Drayton's one-man Royal Commission proposed the appointment of a Power Controller under the War Measures Act to co-ordinate the matching of supply and demand during the anticipated shortage.

A federal cabinet committee chaired by Frank Cochrane, Beck's former colleague in the Whitney cabinet who did not hide his impatience with the public power movement and its leader, received the Royal Commission *Report* late in October 1917 and immediately called a meeting of federal, provincial, Hydro and company officials to discuss it. By all accounts it was a stormy affair. Beck, piqued by Drayton's criticism, rejected his recommendations and repeated his demand that the federal government stand up to the United States by cracking down upon the power exports of the private companies. The latter in their turn denied Beck's charges of wartime profiteering,

[37] *Ibid.*, Cochrane to Borden, Sept. 8, 1917, pp. 124660-1; Sir Henry Drayton, *Report on Export of Electricity from Canada*, p. 20-3.

[38] Armstrong, "The Politics of Federalism," p. 229.

pointed to the hypocrisy of his position, and accused him of hampering the war effort with his intransigence. The meeting broke up in anger without any agreement on the all-important matter of sharing power having been reached. Over the next few days the federal-provincial conflict over power exports took on a definite political complexion when the Hydro chairman hinted that unless his demands were quickly met he would run Beck-Hydro candidates against Unionists in the coming federal election. Again the federal government chose to post-pone a collision by naming Sir Henry Drayton to the post of Power Controller with instructions that he should examine the troubled relations between Hydro and the private companies. The *Financial Post* observed: "It cannot be denied that it is pretty good politics to take just this course in view of the coming elections and the fact that the Power Knight is a pretty big factor in the political situation in Ontario."[39]

The context of the confrontation tended, on the whole, to obscure the central issue. Beck's mixed motives, and of course the war itself, confused matters and exaggerated feelings. W. R. Plewman, who was close to the situation at the time, recalled much later that federal officials went so far as to try to silence Beck, or at least make him more co-operative, by letting it be known that he had a pro-German relative living in the United States.[40] Emotional extravagance such as this, coinciding with the culmination of the long struggle between public and private power forces, and of course Beck's domineering manner, all combined to blur the issue at stake. These circumstances had brought the export question to a head in the first place, but they were precisely the kind of complications that also prevented any approach to the problem based upon principles.

As expected, the power shortage became acute during 1918. To make matters worse, construction delays plagued the installation of new turbines at the Ontario Power Company plant, cancelling out at least 50,000 horsepower that Beck had

---

[39] *Monetary Times*, Sept. 14, 1917; *Financial Post*, Nov. 10, 1917; Sir Henry Drayton, *Report of the Power Controller*, May, 1919.

[40] Plewman, *Adam Beck*, pp. 202-6.

Workmen pose during construction of crib-work for the
Electrical Development Company of Ontario. *Ontario Hydro*

Henry Pellatt lays one of three cornerstones for the Electrical
Development Company generating station at Niagara Falls, May 8, 1906.
Frederic Nicholls is on the right, carrying an umbrella. F. S. Pearson
can be seen in the centre of the picture behind the cornerstone.
*Ontario Hydro*

Old and new technologies on the American side of the Niagara gorge in 1907: factories using

Aerial view of the Electrical Development Company generating station in 1922    *Ontario Hydro*

waterpower on the left and the Niagara Falls Power Company generating station on the centre right

''A stately building of classical design will house the monster generators. . . .''
The *Globe*, August 5, 1905, on the Electrical Development Company powerhouse
*Ontario Hydro*

Entrance to the Ontario Power Company
generating station at Niagara Falls

Art Nouveau control pedestals
at the Ontario Power Company
generating station, 1914
*Ontario Hydro*

"A Nervous Marksman:
Premier Whitney Dithers Over the Power Question."
Samuel Hunter, Toronto *World*, March 25, 1908
*Public Archives of Canada*

"In the 'High Finance' Sugar Bush."
Samuel Hunter, Toronto *World*, April 7, 1907
*Public Archives of Canada*

Adam Beck.

Hon. A. J. Matheson, the Provincial Treasurer,
Mrs. Beck and Adam Beck in the triumphal
"switching on" parade, Berlin, October 11, 1910
*Ontario Hydro*

Berlin, October 11, 1910. Power to the People    *Ontario Hydro*

The turning-on ceremonies at Berlin, October 11, 1910

*Public Archives of Ontario*

Queenston hydro-electric generating station under construction, *circa* 1920. *Public Archives of Canada*

Santa sells Adam Beck's hydro in London, 1911 —even Santa's truck is electric. *Ontario Hydro*

counted upon to meet his contracts with new war industries. Frustrated by repeated breakdowns and angered by delays, Beck once again turned upon federal authorities. He refused to co-operate with the federal Power Controller and insisted instead that Drayton use his authority to secure more power from the private companies for his commission. All the while American officials were applying pressure in Ottawa to restore Canadian hydro-electric service to certain key war industries. Caught between these millstones, the federal government eventually authorized the Power Controller to re-route power from the private companies to Ontario Hydro, as Beck demanded, in order that these American commitments could in fact be met.[41]

Still Beck was not satisfied. Later in the year he attacked Sir Joseph Flavelle at the Imperial Munitions Board for letting contracts for munitions in Ontario without first consulting Hydro to ensure that power would be available. Flavelle was incensed. "The Board, noting the power difficulties in Ontario, does not let contracts if the company gives Ontario Hydro as its source of power," Flavelle complained to N. W. Rowell, now in the cabinet. "True to his type he charges his troubles to the incapacity and inconsiderateness of others, and probably hoped that as before if sufficient storm were raised, he would some way secure temporary assistance which would carry him over the trying period until his new power was developed."[42]

About the same time Beck denounced the Power Controller for continuing to authorize certain hydro-electric exports during the critical shortage. But this time Sir Henry fought back—in public. Speaking from a prepared text to an emergency meeting of the Toronto branch of the Canadian Manufacturers' Association on October 18, 1918, Sir Henry Drayton reminded the Hydro chairman—who was in attendance—that he had

[41] A. M. Beale, "Power—Canada's Opportunity," *Monetary Times*, Sept. 20, 1918; Armstrong, "The Politics of Federalism" pp. 231-2.

[42] PAC, Foster Papers, Box 36, John Murphy to Arthur Meighen, Oct. 21, 1918; N. W. Rowell to George Foster, Oct. 25, 1918, confidential, enclosing Flavelle's bitter commentary on Beck's conduct.

spent every effort, with some success, to reduce power exports, that the commission had the highest priority when such power could be released, and he put it firmly on the record that Hydro was itself the leading exporter. Moreover, unlike the other contracts, Hydro's were long-term contracts for firm power which could not be interfered with:

> There was no doubt in the world but that the exportation, apart from these contracts which the province had entered into, could be reduced, but I also found that the power which was being produced and exported to the United States was being utilized in essential war work, and that it could not be recalled without grave injury and without the possibility of grave consequences. In part however, it has been reduced.

Instead of cutting the lines to the United States, Sir Henry suggested several practical remedies, the most important of which was a massive reduction of domestic consumption. In effect, Adam Beck had sold his power too well. The thousands of irons and electric heaters on the Hydro lines contributed significantly to the power shortage. "One of the most expensive ways of producing heat is by electricity," Sir Henry explained, "and a tremendous amount is required to supply heaters that are used to keep people from getting cold."[43]

The federal government could not act, and what is more, refused to act to help Adam Beck out of the crisis he had helped to create by his own ambition. Fortunately, by this time the worst had passed, and the war was almost over. The commission was able to struggle through with its own devices. Soon the extra 50,000 horsepower became available, and the giant Queenston project, to serve the province's long-run requirements, was well under way.

Beck's appeal to patriotism failed primarily because his own contractual obligations compromised his credibility. Secondly, the federal authorities, through their close connections with

---

[43] PAC, Foster Papers, Box 36, Transcript of Meeting of Toronto Branch, Canadian Manufacturers' Association, with Power Controller, Oct. 18, 1918; *Monetary Times*, Oct. 25, 1918.

the Toronto financial community, recognized the export agitation as yet another episode in Beck's unremitting campaign against William Mackenzie and the private power interests. But what were the "grave consequences" cited so ominously by Sir Henry Drayton that convinced him that it was "absolutely impossible to cut off from the American market...?" Whatever the domestic reasons for denying Beck's request, there were also sufficient continental complications which reduced an export prohibition to an absolute impossibility.

As Sir Henry Drayton carefully explained in his Toronto speech, "I believed that it was in the best interests of the country that manufacturers in the United States manufacturing war materials, ought not to be interfered with; that we should continue to send them a modicum of power and to receive from them in turn our proportionate share of coal, raw materials, etc." Although Sir Henry did not elaborate upon his discussions with American authorities, the *Financial Post* did address itself to the problem under the apt heading, "The Fuel and Power Balance." Canada had been treated as one of the states of the Union during the coal rationing; if Sir Adam disconnected the power, the Americans would simply cut off Ontario's coal. "No," the *Financial Post* advised, "we cannot afford to throw down the gauntlet to the United States on the coal and power issue....Canada is too much dependent upon her Southern neighbour to start a family row." In 1917 and again in January and February of 1918 the American Fuel Controller had actually threatened to curtail deliveries of coal to Canada in the event that power exports to the United States were cut off or substantially diminished. As W. F. Maclean and his colleagues had warned during the 1907 debate, when the time came to recover the formerly surplus power the suggestion was met with cries of confiscation from the vested interests and the Americans considered such action "a cause of offence."[44] With power, as with nickel, the extent of Canadian-American economic interdependence prevented the isolation of the difference. A

---

[44] *Financial Post*, Oct. 20, 1917; Armstrong, "The Politics of Federalism," pp. 227, 235-7.

weakness in one area could always be brought up to offset a grievance in another sector. In that way federal hands were effectively tied.

Although the 1917-18 re-examination of hydro-electric exports did not produce the practical result of more power for Ontario, it was an instructive experience. Reflecting on the problem for the Commission of Conservation, Sir Clifford Sifton suggested that the lessons of Niagara should be applied to future hydro-electric development on the St. Lawrence. Americans were preparing to build plants on the Canadian side and if successful, he warned, they would export the bulk of their power back across the river to the United States. Instead, Sir Clifford recommended that the waterpowers of the St. Lawrence River should be divided equally between Canada and the United States and no hydro-electric exports should be permitted. Sir Adam Beck expanded this prohibition to include that power developed by private Canadian promoters, like Sir Clifford Sifton and his sons, as well as Americans. He resented the postwar power development schemes not only because they were financed by Americans or because they involved massive exports, but also because they would reintroduce the baneful influence of the private interests which he had all but eradicated. Certainly the export plans of these projected companies opposed Canada's long-range best interests, but more important, the very existence of these companies conflicted with Sir Adam's grand design for the expansion of Ontario Hydro.[45]

In one of his last and most paranoid pamphlets, Sir Adam Beck denounced the Carillon Falls development on the Ottawa River as a plot against Ontario Hydro jointly conceived by the federal government and private interests bent upon exporting power. His premier, Howard Ferguson, though he supported Beck on the export question, saw matters in a slightly different light, typically more congenial to private development. "If our enterprising neighbours want Canadian electrical power, which is a great natural resource," he replied to the critical editor of *La Presse*, "let them come to the source of supply and use

[45] Sir Clifford Sifton, quoted in *Monetary Times*, Dec. 14, 1917.

it in Canada. Let them bring along their capital, employ Canadian labour and raw materials, and thereby contribute to the prosperity and development of this country. That is the proper solution of the situation. We will not sell our birthright for a mess of pottage."[46]

Bitter memories of the wartime experience at Niagara Falls prejudiced the Ontario government against all subsequent export proposals. It convinced the politicians at Toronto, if not at Ottawa, of the need for strict regulation of the exportation of hydro-electric power. Ontario Hydro discerned—with some justification though it was always oversensitive on this point—in the postwar St. Lawrence and Ottawa River development schemes the restoration of private enterprise within a jurisdiction from which it had largely been banished under provincial control. Again the federal government was seen to be the chief prop of the private interests, just as it had been during the wartime and prewar conflicts. Indeed, substantive differences with Ottawa over the energy export question and the related issue of the method (public versus private) of hydro-electric development explain, and in large measure justify, Ontario's unswerving determination thereafter to control power development on its international and interprovincial boundaries.

## III

One might have thought that passage of the Underwood tariff in 1913 would have permanently settled the pulpwood export question. That was not, in fact, the case. In 1919, for example,

---

[46] Sir Adam Beck, *A Statement by Sir Adam Beck Protesting Against the Exportation of Electric Power with Special Reference to the Proposed Lease of the "Carillon" Site* (Toronto, 1925), p. 5; PAO, Ferguson papers, Box 11, Ferguson to the editor, *La Presse*, May 19, 1925; H. H. Stevens to Ferguson, May 7, 1925; Ferguson to Fred Gaby, May 14, 1925; Ferguson to R. W. Shannon, May 16, 1925, personal; Charles Magrath to Ferguson, Jan. 8, 1926, confidential. For the political intricacies of the Carillon affair see, Blair Neatby, *William Lyon Mackenzie King*, Vol. II (Toronto, 1963), pp. 224-8, and for the federal-provincial conflict over St. Lawrence and Ottawa River waterpower, see Armstrong, "The Politics of Federalism," chapters 6, 7.

Canada exported 1,597,042 cords of spruce pulpwood to the
United States valued at $15,386,600, or enough pulpwood to
manufacture one-half of the newsprint consumed in the United
States that year. If this had been converted into paper in Canadian mills and sold at $75 a ton, the market price at that time,
the *Monetary Times* estimated that it would have returned
$79,852,050.[47] Such tremendous quantities of pulpwood could
not possibly have been taken from private lands which were
not included under the manufacturing condition, nor is it
reasonable to assume that all of this wood originated in Quebec.
A large percentage of it did come from Ontario in plain defiance
of the law.

As the American pulpwood stocks dwindled and the price
per cord increased, the temptation to break the law naturally
rose with the price. During the war, when many of the mills
on the south shore of the Great Lakes were running desperately
short of wood, Canadians could obtain about twice as much
for a raft of pulpwood delivered to an American mill as to
a Canadian one. Just at this moment when the manufacturing
condition needed vigorous enforcement, the Department of
Lands, Forests and Mines was more thoroughly dominated by
lumbermen and promoters than at any time in its history; the
Minister, Howard Ferguson, seemed content to take his instructions from lumbermen and industrialists. His Deputy Minister,
Albert Grigg, could not see what was going on around him,
and the corrupt field staff of placemen was too weak or too
frightened to do anything about it.[48]

Between 1911 and 1920 no one cut anything in the northwest-

---

[47] *Monetary Times*, June 27, 1919.
[48] For more detail see R. Lambert and P. Pross, *Renewing Nature's Wealth*
(Toronto, 1967), pp. 262 ff. In making these accusations I am relying
upon the *Hearings* and *Reports* of the Ontario Royal Commission to
Investigate and Report upon the Accuracy or Otherwise of all Returns
made Pursuant to the Crown Timber Act, section 14, by any holder of
a Timber Licence, less formally known as the Timber Commission, and
a remarkable manuscript, left unpublished because of the laws of libel,
by J. P. Bertrand, himself a lumberman and eyewitness to these events,
entitled, "Timber Wolves." A copy has been deposited in the Ontario
Archives.

ern part of the province without first doing business with Col.
J. A. Little or some member of what came to be known as
"the old Tory Timber Ring." The colonel's associates were Gen.
Don Hogarth, provincial organizer of the Conservative party,
banker, mining promoter, and timber speculator; W. H. Russell,
a young Detroit lawyer turned pulpwood exporter; and J. J.
Carrick, a former mayor of Port Arthur, Conservative MP, MPP,
real estate promoter, and mining speculator. Timber and pulp
limits could be had through the Timber Ring provided that
liberal contributions to the Conservative party were first
promised to Hogarth and Little. And since they were the political bosses of the district, all government appointments, including those in the Department of Lands, Forests and Mines whose
regulations they were flouting, passed through their offices.
It was this small coterie of speculators that seized the
opportunities presented by the differential in pulpwood prices
between the Canadian and American sides of Lake Superior.
According to one conservative estimate, pulpwood export companies organized by Russell and Little shipped $75,000 worth
of pulpwood annually between 1914 and 1920. They obtained
the wood by purchasing Returned Soldiers' lands and then
stripping them of their pulpwood, or simply by stealing it from
crown lands. A Royal Commission studying the Department
of Lands, Forests and Mines in 1920 found that Russell had
"...trespassed for many years upon government lands without
a shadow of a right and...removed therefrom such pulpwood
of great value."[49]

Ironically, the simplest method of obtaining pulpwood for
export was also technically legitimate. At that time a mining
claim conveyed rights to the timber—excepting pine—growing
on it. Since the government expected that this timber would
be used in the development of the mine, it was not expressly
included under the provisions of the manufacturing condition.
The Timber Ring eagerly seized upon that loophole. Little,
Russell, Hogarth and their associates busily registered mining

---

[49] Bertrand, "Timber Wolves," pp. 66-115; Mr. Justice F. R. Latchford and
Mr. Justice W. R. Riddell, Royal Ontario Timber Commission, *First Interim
Report* (Toronto, 1920), pp. 18-9; *Final Report* (Toronto, 1922), pp. 5-6.

claims or arranged for their wives, relatives and friends to regis-
ter claims for them. Soon afterward and sometimes before,
gangs of men would appear on the properties and promptly
strip them bald. The pulpwood cut was then gathered into
booms in the many bays along the north shore of Lake Superior
and towed across to the American side. That way the pulpwood
export companies claimed and cut hundreds of thousands of
dollars worth of pulpwood purchased at the nominal rates
charged under the Mines Act, about three dollars an acre.[50]

Even more reprehensible, this wholesale plunder of the public
domain went on with the full knowledge of the Department
of Lands, Forests and Mines. Operations as extensive as Russell's
could not have been carried out without the collusion of the
field staff, the crown timber agent, and the mining recorder
at the Lakehead. But their silence can be explained by the
nature of their appointment. Nevertheless, evidence produced
for the Timber Commission indicated that the responsible
minister, Howard Ferguson, was in full possession of the facts,
yet he delayed closing the loophole until 1918. Several people
claimed to have warned him of the fraud, but the commission
staff could not find those letters in the department files. C. C.
Hele, Ferguson's private secretary, cleared up the mystery.
Those letters were personal, he told the Latchford-Riddell
Timber Commission; they were removed from the department
with Ferguson's private correspondence, were currently entrusted to Hele in Ferguson's absence, and therefore could not
be shown to the Royal Commission.[51]

Further evidence revealed that Ferguson's private secretary
had more to do with the actual running of the department
than the nominal deputy minister, Albert Grigg. Ferguson's
evasions and the fact that Hele was on the payroll of a pulp
and paper company totally discredited their administration
of the crown lands. Russell's well-protected pulp mining
enterprises such as those uncovered by the Royal Commission
could not even rank with some of the other flagrant abuses

[50] PAO, Timber Commission, *Hearings*, pp. 178-181.
[51] *Final Report*, pp. 39-42.

perpetrated by the lumbermen with the complicity of the Department of Lands, Forests and Mines. The courts did recover some of the crown dues evaded by Russell, but the total destruction wrought by his companies could never be determined. The pulpwood exporters had not merely broken a law with the assistance of corrupt officials; they had successfully nullified its effectiveness. As the figures printed by the *Monetary Times* clearly indicated, American paper mills continued to depend upon Canada for about 50 per cent of their pulpwood throughout the war. But the manufacturing condition existed precisely to curb that dependency. Since 1900 Ontario had prohibited the export of pulpwood cut from crown lands to paper mills in Michigan, Wisconsin and Minnesota in order to force them to move across to the north shore of Lake Superior, their natural source of supply. The Timber Ring's evasion of the law and the political complicity that permitted it merely postponed even further that industrial migration. Belatedly, the Hearst government severed title to timber from mining claims (without prosecuting the offenders), and E. C. Drury rejuvenated the administration of crown lands to put a stop to this kind of pillage.[52]

However, a more legitimate pressure to relax the manufacturing condition could not be overcome as easily. Colonization and Soldiers' Resettlement programs had placed a great number of ill-equipped, poverty-stricken families on homesteads in northern Ontario. Many could not cope with the hardships of frontier farming and simply abandoned their lands, but those who could not escape, those who were too poor or too dispirited to leave, stayed to scratch a miserable living. In the summer they fought back the bush and tried to make the best of the niggardly soil, but during the long winter they had no income at all. Just like the settlers of La Laurentie, they asked permission to cut pulpwood from the vast crown lands that surrounded them. Sale of this wood to the pulpwood export companies would at least provide for their bare subsistence. The poverty

---

[52] Lambert and Pross, *Renewing Nature's Wealth*, pp. 264-5; T. W. Gibson, *The Mining Laws of Ontario* (Toronto, 1933), pp. 97-9.

of these last frontiersmen was so heart-breaking that not even
the most determined administrator could dismiss their appeals
without feeling some sympathy for their plight. Amendments
to the Crown Timber Act in 1913 first permitted lifting of
the manufacturing condition from small areas at the discretion
of the minister. For humanitarian reasons the Hearst government occasionally permitted pulpwood exports, and
although there had been many abuses of this privilege, the
Drury government continued the practice. There were other
grounds besides poverty for the exercise of that discretionary
power. In 1920, to take just one case among many, the South
Porcupine Board of Trade petitioned the government to
remove the manufacturing requirement temporarily. There was
no market for pulpwood and therefore no winter employment
for the settlers because there were no pulpmills in the vicinity.
The Premier's secretary recommended compliance:

> The enforcement of the Manufacturing Condition in such cases
> means that the Province obtains a much less price [*sic*] for its
> pulpwood. Owing to the extensive mining which is going on
> in some localities and in close proximity to townships containing
> more or less pulpwood it is desirable that the timber should
> be disposed of with the least possible delay, and to ensure an
> adequate price for the timber so situated it is desirable that power
> should be had under legislation to permit export of the wood,
> by which means the price of the wood would be greatly
> enhanced.[53]

He strained logic and grammar to justify an opportunity which
the law had been designed specifically to withhold. But sometimes principles, however firmly held, are terribly hard to live
with. And sometimes the burden of principle falls most heavily
upon the poor, who are always the least capable of bearing
it. The provincial government learned, just as Quebec had
earlier, that once it had encouraged settlement in the northern
forest it could not deny those settlers their chance for survival.

[53] PAO, Drury Papers, South Porcupine Board of Trade Petition, Jan. 21,
1920; see also reports by Albert Grigg, Jan. 8, and Feb. 20, 1920, and
memorandum by F. Niven, quoted, May 28, 1920.

The war heightened Canadian consciousness of resource export problems and exposed the ambiguity of continentalism. It supplied the crisis required to settle the nickel question once and for all, but that very solution revealed Canada's vulnerability to retaliation should it ever be necessary to support principles with action. Canadians also learned to their grief that hydro-electric power, sold to the United States during a period of temporary surplus, could not be recalled even during an emergency. The Canadian-American economic relationship had become too intimate, the continental connections too complex even at this early date, for the federal government to take a strong nationalist stand on any isolated issue. It would appear that Ottawa's consciousness of the strength of the American bargaining position acted as a self-censoring device to neutralize beforehand the issue-oriented nationalist pressures coming from Ontario. Finally, the premium on Canadian pulpwood, created by rising newsprint consumption and decreasing pulpwood supplies in the United States, posed a cruel test first to the honesty and then to the conscience of government officials.

These experiences demonstrated the need for national resource policies or manufacturing conditions, but at the same time they also illustrated the difficulty of maintaining such policies in any absolute manner. As economic ties with the United States became more complex, it became more difficult to isolate, much less defend, any national or provincial economic interest. Whatever one thought about the situation, clearly there was little or nothing that could be done about it. And for that reason there is an insubstantial quality to the discussion of continental economic matters between the two levels of government during this period. But on balance the integration of the continental economies went ahead satisfactorily, without widespread discontent. There were, however, isolated cries of anguish —such as those about hydro and nickel. If on occasion principles had to be modified for domestic or diplomatic reasons, the totality of the relationship ensured overwhelming compensating advantages. Being a northern province in the American empire conferred new prosperity, but it also entailed its share of compromised ideals and aspirations.

# 10
# Responsible Government Revisited

Preceding chapters have examined the origins and some of the dimensions of political authority in the natural resource economy. Taking state ownership of resources in the nineteenth century as a point of departure, we observed the gradual modification of that principle during the first decades of this century into three methods and degrees of state intervention. The provincial government controlled the development of natural resources either by direct management, property right, or statute. Waterpower regulation grew to include the distribution of hydro-electricity and ultimately public ownership of the industry. The principle of crown ownership of the forest survived intact and was used by the landlord state to bind its industrial tenants to contractual manufacturing commitments. The risks of mining and the will of its promoters gradually forced paternal governments to relinquish all exceptional powers over that industry until the conventional boundaries between private enterprise and public authority in a liberal state had been reached.

This examination of the powers of government and the use made of them to promote and regulate resource development raises the further question: what impact did this expansion of government control have upon the political process? How did these new institutions and responsibilities of government react upon the political system that gave rise to them? These questions can be narrowed to the specific problem of ministerial accountability within a parliamentary democracy. If cabinet ministers were responsible for the well-being of enormous industries, and if, as in the case of Hydro, the government itself operated a giant corporation, how did obligations arising therefrom affect the relationship between the executive and legislative branches of government? Did responsibility *for* an industry necessarily imply responsibility *to* it, and if so, would that conflict with a minister's parliamentary responsibilities? Were the imperatives of business conduct compatible with the principles of responsible government, or more simply, could businesslike government be democratic government?[1]

Perhaps no better illustration of the interdependence of government and industry could be given than Howard Ferguson's explanation of the role of government, as he conceived it, written for the benefit of the Spruce Falls Pulp and Paper Company shareholders. In 1926 the company met some resistance selling its preferred shares in the United States, primarily because of American unfamiliarity with the terms of Canadian pulpwood contracts. Like all similar pulpwood agreements with the Ontario government, the Spruce Falls contract carried a long list of detailed stipulations governing the amount of money the company must spend on building its mill, when the company should begin production and how many jobs it must provide. In the event of non-performance, a final

[1] This chapter draws heavily upon the following works on government enterprise and the problem of ministerial accountability: A. H. Hanson, *Parliament and Public Ownership* (London, 1961); J. E. Hodgetts, "The Public Corporation in Canada," in Wolfgang Friedmann, ed., *The Public Corporation* (Toronto, 1954); G. Marshall and G. C. Moodie, *Some Problems of the Constitution* (London, 1961 edition), and Lloyd D. Musolf, *Public Ownership and Responsibility: The Canadian Experience* (Cambridge, Mass., 1959).

clause provided for cancellation of the agreement. Apparently, the American investors could not understand why the government leased its pulpwood instead of selling it, and why it used this superior legal position to make specific demands upon a private company. To dispel these fears, Strachan Johnson, the Canadian counsel for the company, asked his old friend the Premier to consider removal of the offending clauses, particularly the forfeiture provisions.

In reply Howard Ferguson pointed out that the crown always reserved extensive enabling powers to protect itself, and these powers would never be used in a hostile way against a legitimate business enterprise: "What the Crown expects is reasonable compliance with the covenants and obligations, and it is always ready and willing to give consideration to difficulties that may arise to prevent the strict observation of the letter of a contract. Personally, I think your clients are shying at a shadow." Since the company had already begun construction it could safely consider the clauses "surplusage."

After relieving Johnson's anxiety on that account, the Premier continued in a rare philosophical digression to describe his government's interest in and responsibility for the success of the Spruce Falls Pulp and Paper Company:

> The Crown expects to receive a large income from the timber cut by such companies as yours, and is of course deeply interested in their maintenance. One of the very purposes of the recent timber sale was to enable your Company and others of a similar character to enlarge their capacity and put themselves on a sound financial basis, so that they may be perpetual industries. There must be co-operation between the contracting parties. In a sense we are just as deeply interested in the success of your Company as its shareholders. In fact, *we are in a way the largest shareholders*, because we contribute the power and the timber at a very reasonable price, that will undoubtedly enable your organization to flourish. We want it to succeed so that you need not be nervous about anything occurring that will embarrass or retard your development.[2]

---

[2] PAO, Ferguson Papers, Strachan Johnson to Ferguson, April 17, 1926, emphasis added.

If the Ontario government was the largest shareholder in the pulp and paper industry it was the only shareholder in the hydro-electric industry. How could government reconcile its business role as a shareholder with the constitutional process? This question was especially acute, since such involvement naturally tends to create a disposition on the part of any government, whether Conservative, Liberal, or even United Farmer, towards seeing industrial problems through the eyes of management. Would government, now that it had become so closely tied to industry—particularly the resource industries—be ruled by its business associates or by its constitutional responsibilities to the Legislature and the community?

The magisterial independence of the Minister of Lands, Forests and Mines and the chairman of the Hydro-Electric Power Commission raised the problem of political accountability in a characteristically theatrical manner at the end of the First World War. Evidence presented before the Timber Commission showed that Howard Ferguson had repeatedly defied the regulations of the department in the course of negotiating agreements with its clients. Adam Beck's disdain for the Legislature was notorious; he simply requisitioned enormous sums of public money without ever accounting for it, or for that matter thinking it necessary to account for it to the representatives of the people. Both Beck and Ferguson, by their own admission, presumed themselves to be authentic agents of the people's will, and therefore above accountability. But was it proper for a minister to break the law in the name of businesslike administration? Should the Legislature rest content as the passive instrument of the Hydro chairman? Or were both men servants of the Legislature, wholly answerable to it for their estimates and actions?

I

After a two-year investigation of the Department of Lands, Forests and Mines, W. R. Riddell and F. R. Latchford emphatically condemned the "very objectionable, as well as illegal, practice" followed by the late Minister of granting timber limits to lumber companies by private agreement. The commissioners, reporting in 1922, discovered that in the two months prior to the 1919 general election, Howard Ferguson had parted with 962 square miles of timber without advertisement or public competition as required by the Crown Timber Act. Nor was this an isolated incident; earlier in the year he had disposed of 103 square miles in a similar manner, 171 in 1918, and 322 during 1917. But those iniquities paled beside two other totally illegal transactions with the Shevlin-Clarke Lumber Company, whose president, J. A. Mathieu, also happened to be a Conservative member of the Legislature. Without recourse to the instruments provided by statute, Ferguson sold a timber limit in the Quetico forest reserve to that company in 1917 for dues of only $6.26 per thousand board feet, or about $10 less than the prevailing rate. Two years later Mathieu acquired rights to two more limits for $9.50 per thousand board feet. A subsequent evaluation of these limits established $20 as a more appropriate price. In a flagrant abuse of his discretionary power and in plain contradiction of the statute governing timber sales, Howard Ferguson transferred three valuable blocks of timber to a political associate for less than half of the $2 million they should have returned by law to the public treasury.

Of course both the Minister and the company protested that there was a good reason for this apparent generosity—the company was supposed to test new forestry techniques—but a Royal Commission and the courts found the justifications advanced to be thoroughly counterfeit. Because the company had agreed to perform some expensive burning "experiments" with the slash left behind in their lumbering operations, the government as compensation lowered the regular dues by private negotiation. But the company never carried out the operations; furthermore, even if it had, the information was hardly worth the millions the government seemed willing to pay for it. The same data could have been obtained from the federal Department of Indian Affairs or the United States Forest Service, or the Minister could have found it in his own files, for Shevlin-Clarke had undertaken a similar study for the Department in 1911. The courts levied a $1,500,000 fine on the company for its deception, and the Timber Commission severely censured the responsible Minister:

We are of the opinion that no officer, Minister or otherwise, should have the power to grant rights over large areas of the public domain at will without regard to Regulation; that power was never contemplated by the statutes; it does not at present exist, and should not be given to any individual. Such an arbitrary power subject to no control is obviously open to abuse.[3]

Ferguson's private deals with the lumber companies were simply political corruption of the time-honoured sort. But his equally unauthorized negotiations with two pulp and paper companies could not be classified and dismissed as easily.

When George H. Mead, president of Spanish River Pulp and Paper, investigated the possibility of expanding his company's Espanola mill in 1918, his investment banker, Alex Smith of Peabody, Houghteling and Co. of Chicago, agreed to finance the project but only if the government could guarantee the company much larger pulp limits. Following a series of talks with Ferguson, George Mead formally applied for exclusive rights to an area of approximately 5,000 square miles on September 19, 1919. The company was "anxious to have matters brought to a head," Mead explained, "because of pending financial matters"; namely, a $3,500,000 loan from Peabody, Houghteling. On September 25 Howard Ferguson approved the request: "There can be no doubt that industries such as yours can be more economically and efficiently conducted on the basis of large units, and it is to the best interests of the Province as a whole that a reasonable number of large mills should be maintained, rather than a large number of small mills which means an increase of overhead and operating expenses and short life of the industry." Although the law clearly stated that pulp limits must be sold by public tender, Ferguson concluded: "it is in the public interest that you should be assured an additional supply of wood. . . ." On his own initiative he waived the normal provisions of the law and reserved the designated territory for the exclusive use of Spanish River Pulp

---

[3] PAO, Ontario Royal Commission to Investigate and Report upon the Accuracy or Otherwise of all Returns made Pursuant to the Crown Timber Act, section 14, by any holder of a Timber Licence [hereafter, Timber Commission], *Hearings*, pp. 259 ff.; *Final Report*, pp. 35-6.

and Paper, leaving the question of price and the "other details in connection with the transaction" for some indefinite discussions in the future.[4]

At about the same time Frank Anson of Abitibi Pulp and Paper received similar advice from his Chicago bankers. They agreed to underwrite an expansion of Abitibi's manufacturing capacity, Anson told the Timber Commission, but at the same time explained that "it would be impossible and inadvisable to go on with this construction without . . .further reserves of wood and water." After a number of informal meetings with his friend the Minister of Lands, Forests and Mines, Anson received the required "personal promise" of additional pulp limits and waterpower concessions. "My ambition has been to see the largest paper industry in the world established in the Province," Ferguson confessed to Anson in a letter approving the reservation of 1,500 square miles of pulpwood for Abitibi, "and my attitude towards the pulp and paper industry has been directed towards assisting in bringing this about."[5] Thus without advertisement, public tenders, or even an agreement on a price, the Minister of Lands, Forests and Mines set aside almost 7,000 square miles of crown forest to assist two paper companies finance their growth. But was this as much an illegitimate use of ministerial discretion as the lumber company deals?

Solely upon the security of Howard Ferguson's letter, Peabody, Houghteling loaned the Spanish River Pulp and Paper Company $3,500,000. Abitibi raised a like amount with similar collateral. "We had nothing but Mr. Ferguson's assurance or the Government's assurance," Anson told the astonished Royal Commission, "that we were going to get this wood and power." However, by the time George H. Mead reported the successful completion of his company's financial arrangements, the Ontario election of 1919 radically altered the relationship

---

[4] Timber Commission, *Special Report on the Spanish River Pulp and Paper Mills*, pp. 63-5.

[5] Timber Commission, *Hearings*, pp. 10, 422-80. Frank Anson explained that there was so little actual correspondence on file between himself and the minister because the two of them were such good friends they could rely upon verbal agreements.

between businessmen and the government. "You will readily understand," Ferguson apologized to Mead, "that since the election the matter has passed out of my hands, but the proposition is such a sound business one that I am quite sure that whoever my successor may be will take the same interest, and pride, as I have taken, in encouraging the growth of such an excellent and beneficial enterprise as yours."[6] But the United Farmers were more concerned with the illegality of Ferguson's action than its business merits; they were more impressed with his grossly irresponsible and unparliamentary behaviour than with the advantageous consequences it might bring. Since Ferguson had never shared any of his confidence with the Legislature to which he was nominally responsible, Premier E. C. Drury called him before the Latchford and Riddell Royal Commission to render a complete, if somewhat belated, account of his stewardship of the public trust.

How could a minister possibly justify, the commissioners wanted to know, taking such exceptional liberties with the timber and pulpwood of the province? In reply, Ferguson claimed that he had treated every case "as a business proposition";

> I worked out that policy along the lines which I think are sound business methods and in the best interests of this province; I have not any hesitation, I am not afraid of these criticisms, because I stand behind these arrangements absolutely anywhere, that these are sound business arrangements made with competent business men with the sole object of developing the forestry interests of the province for the benefit of the people.

But, the two commissioners protested, Ferguson's private judgment flatly contradicted the statutes and regulations. "We have heard about the King being above grammar," Mr. Justice Riddell interjected, "but we have not heard of a departmental officer or officer of the Crown being above the law before."

---

[6] *Ibid.*, pp. 7608ff, 10435, 11614-57; the correspondence between Ferguson and Mead was reprinted in the Timber Commission, *Special Report on the Spanish River Pulp and Paper Mills*, pp. 63-5.

Whatever the appearances, Ferguson replied calmly, the guiding principle of his administration of the crown lands had been the development of the vast northern regions of the province. "Law or no how?" Mr. Justice Riddell inquired. Ferguson readily admitted: "I was superior to the regulation[s] where I thought it was in the interests of the province"; if the law forbad businesslike negotiations with respectable industrialists, then plainly the law was in error: " . . .as developments go on and the timber and forestry business expands, conditions alter and the situation had to be dealt with, and if to meet that the regulations should have been altered why I suppose it was an error that they were not altered, but no regulation should hold up the development of the country; that is the point."

It was all very well to say that timber limits should be thoroughly advertised then sold by public tender—that was the most democratic and honest method of disposing of public lands to private citizens—but that was not the best method for business agreements when there were millions at stake. Advertisement and tender, Ferguson explained to the commission, were sacred "from an arm-chair oracle's point of view," but such preliminary arrangements did not always produce the desired results. He might have illustrated his point (though he chose not to) by reminding the commissioners that when the department opened up pulp limits to supply the Provincial Paper mill at the Lakehead, the company was outbid by speculators. Democratic methods had not produced a desirable result in that instance. Summing up Ferguson's testimony, the commission counsel suggested that as a minister Ferguson had done what he pleased with the public lands. The confidence and candour of Ferguson's reply offer the best insight into the supremely self-assured kind of mentality that overrode statutes and regulations at will:

> No, not as I pleased. That remark is entirely unwarranted. My judgment was dictated in the interests of the province and the public of this province, I am quite prepared, notwithstanding what may occur here, to leave my record with the public and the people of the northern country as to whether my administration was good or bad.[7]

Howard Ferguson pretended, in all honesty, that he knew better than law or the Legislature how to promote the development of the northern districts. He claimed to understand when others could not the requirements of modern industry, and he knew that its affairs, particularly when vast sums of capital were involved, could not be undertaken in the glare of publicity. In his considered view, it was the duty of government to provide businessmen with every reasonable assistance in creating large-scale, efficient industrial enterprises, giving direct employment to thousands and indirect employment to thousands more. That, he argued, was a minister's first responsibility; everything else was secondary.

Ferguson's boldness and arrogance scandalized the United Farmers' government. The law had been drafted to protect the public interest, Premier Drury argued, and it must, therefore, be scrupulously adhered to. Any deviation from its terms necessarily involved action hostile to the best interests of the people. When one energetic Lakehead lumberman proposed a private timber agreement to "cut out the speculators," Drury replied in horror: "I believe that the practice of selling by private arrangement is so dangerous, both to the mill owner and to the Government, and so liable to lead to corrupt practices, that it should not for one moment be considered."[8] Nevertheless the new government did discover in due course that democratic procedures were sometimes an embarrassing encumbrance during negotiations with potential investors.

In 1914 E. W. Backus, a Minnesota lumber baron, bought the Lake of the Woods pulp limit, but he was unable to begin

---

[7] Timber Commission, *Hearings*, pp. 6147-362; for details of the Provincial Paper scandal, see R. Lambert and P. Pross, *Renewing Nature's Wealth* (Toronto, 1967), pp. 270-1. For a study of the impact of this investigation on Howard Ferguson's career, see Peter Oliver, "Howard Ferguson, the Timber Scandal and the Leadership of the Ontario Conservative Party," *Ontario History*, Vol. LXII (1970), pp. 163-78.

[8] PAO, Drury Papers, E. E. Johnson to E. C. Drury, Mar. 29, 1923; Drury to Johnson, April 9, 1923; on related questions see also, F. J. Niven to Drury, July 2, 1920; J. J. Carrick to Drury, Aug. 6, 1920; T. M. Kirkwood to Drury, Nov. 22, 1919; Beniah Bowman to Drury, Feb. 22, 1923.

development because of the wartime financial stringency and the difficulties he encountered with the International Joint Commission over developing waterpower. Just before the change of government in 1919 Howard Ferguson had served notice that the Ontario government would not accept any more excuses or delays; similarly when the United Farmers assumed power, they too ordered Backus to proceed or forfeit his pulp limits. But Edward Wellington Backus was an exceptionally skilful operator. [9] In spite of the fact that his generous support of the Conservative party was well known, he was nevertheless able to charm the United Farmers into an extremely favourable reorganization of his contract. Supported by a five-hundred man delegation from the Fort Frances district, Backus laid a new proposition before the provincial government in August 1920. If the government would grant him rights to the White Dog Rapids power site on the English River and to the 3,046 square-mile English River pulp limit, he would then possess enough pulpwood and hydro-electricity to embark upon a much larger project than he had previously considered possible.

Over the objections of the local United Farmers' constituency organization, E. C. Drury and W. E. Raney, the Attorney General, agreed to do business with Backus.[10] He was, after all a

[9] Christopher Armstrong, "The Politics of Federalism: Ontario's Relations with the Federal Government, 1896-1941" (unpublished Ph.D. thesis, University of Toronto, 1972), pp. 28-30, 263-70; *The Mandonian* (Fort Frances, 1954), pp., 3-10; *Who Was Who in America, 1897-1942* (Chicago, 1945), p. 41. Much later J. A. Mathieu fondly recalled his old rival: "Backus was able to use politicians irrespective of their party labels; he believed that every politician had his price and he was reported to be generous at election time . . . We didn't get along too well, although I liked him . . . He was a big borrower and a big talker too. He bragged a lot, used to come in here and brag to beat the band. But he was the best man in a witness stand in court that I ever saw, and I saw him there quite a few times." Interview with J. A. Mathieu, July 29, 1965.

[10] PAO, Drury Papers, W. J. Richards to Drury, Aug. 24, 1920, ". . . there will be a scandal and the papers will be full of it . . . . The two principal medicine men of the old Hearst Gov't., Dr. Gunn of Kenora and Mayor George Tool, Pres. of the Conservative Association are reported to be with the bunch. Old partyism is not dead yet. It takes an old politician to engineer a deal."

prominent American lumberman and papermaker, a financier of proven ability, and a brilliant promoter. He was also, as his former business competitors remembered, an extraordinary negotiator and a genuine spell-binder. No doubt he impressed Drury and Raney with his vision of northern industrial grandeur the same way that he overcame the scepticism of New York, Chicago and Minneapolis investors. Accordingly, the Drury government declared Backus' former properties forfeit on September 20, 1920, but on the same day in Raney's office, Backus received rights to the White Dog Rapids and a promise that the English River pulp limit would be put up for competition. On January 7, 1921, the results of the bidding were announced. Backus, as expected, won the competition with a bid of $50,000 bonus, over and above crown dues, ground rent and fire protection charges. The letter of the law has been observed, the Conservatives delighted in revealing, but its spirit had most certainly been violated. The only opposing tenders had been submitted by Backus' partner and his paper broker —hardly fierce competitors.[11]

Unfortunately, the United Farmers had compromised their attack on Ferguson's abuse of ministerial discretion by their own actions, for the English River incident was only one among several. Apparently Beniah Bowman, the Minister of Lands and Forests, promised the Spruce Falls Pulp and Paper Company sufficient timber reserves for its planned expansion in much the same way that Ferguson had guaranteed the needs of Abitibi and Spanish River. Later, when the company confronted

---

[11] For the details of the Backus agreement and its ramifications, see PAO, Drury Papers, Special Series, English River File, which contains (a) Drury's speech, (b) Bowman's statement, (c) extracts from Backus' letters, (d) Agreement, Oct. 20, 1920, conditional upon public competition, (e) Albert Grigg's memorandum, Sept. 23, 1920, (f) Grigg's official report, Dec. 28, 1920, (g) comparison of the 1914 and 1920 agreements, (h) draft speech in reply to Ferguson, (i) the Mayor of Kenora to Bowman, Sept. 29, 1922, (j) F. H. Anson's statement, (k) facts and figures of government policy, (l) summary of the English River Agreement, (m) W. E. Raney's speech at Uxbridge. For the taunting comments of the Conservatives, see PAO, Ferguson Papers, speech at Island Grove, July 20, 1923, and H. E. Wilmot, *The Backus Deal* (Toronto, 1923).

the new Conservative administration with this earlier promise, Bowman willingly supported its application: "To this I agreed at the time, and except for the change in government, the undertaking would have been carried out."[12]

By 1923 the wheel had come full circle; the United Farmers were now guilty of what they and the Timber Commission had royally condemned Howard Ferguson for doing. When Ferguson as leader of his party took his case before what he liked to call "the great Jury of the Public," he was able to turn the tables on the self-righteous Farmers; he could expose "secret deals" concluded in Raney's office in which the government "handed to a foreigner a tremendous area the size of old Ontario west of Hamilton." In rare form, Ferguson boldly slandered the Timber Commission as a "claptrap political conspiracy," accused Drury and Raney of "political knavery" for their hypocritical attempt at sullying his good name, and vilified the UFO as "intellectual and political freaks who were projected into prominence by accident and who grew out of garbage."[13] While it would be a mistake to write too much into his subsequent victory at the polls, at least it indicated that the public did not consider Ferguson to be the scoundrel that Drury and the Timber Commission were convinced he was.

This circular sequence of events demonstrated the complexity of trying to reconcile legitimate industrial demands with the essence, or even the form of democratic political control. It was an enigma, the United Farmers woefully learned, that could not be penetrated with high-minded platitudes. And the men with whom politicians had to deal made the problem that much more difficult. George H. Mead, Frank Anson, E. W. Backus, and F. J. Sensenbrenner were men with a hard edge, who knew exactly what they wanted, how to get it, and were accustomed to getting their own way. Given the initial posture of the United

---

[12] PAO, Ferguson Papers, J. Lyons to Ferguson, Sept. 26, 1925; Department of Lands and Forests, Spruce Falls File, Beniah Bowman to F. J. Sensenbrenner, June 8, 1923; F. J. Sensenbrenner to J. Lyons, Dec. 18, 1924.

[13] PAO, Ferguson Papers, speech at Thamesville, July 7, 1923; E. C. Drury, *Farmer Premier* (Toronto, 1966), pp. 109-10, 128.

Farmers' government, its rapid submission to the will of promoters such as these attests to the strength of the temptations.
However the United Farmers' interlude disclosed that open,
democratic procedures were neither adequate under the
circumstances, nor sufficient in themselves as a guarantee that
the public interest would be served. Conversely, private
negotiations between industrialists and a responsible minister,
if conducted honestly and above suspicion, did not necessarily
mean that the public trust was being sacrificed. Industrialism
confused the problem of ministerial responsibility within the
parliamentary system in a most vexing and intricate way.

Judging from their actions when they returned to power in
1923, the Conservatives had learned that they must abide strictly
by the formal rules governing political relations with industry.
Henceforth the forms of democratic procedure would be observed, but behind that façade it would still be business as usual.
Howard Ferguson, now Premier Ferguson, continued to believe
that strong, efficient, competitive (and that meant giant) paper
companies were the best vehicles of northern development.
Thus, when his government assumed power, it reintroduced
formally the policy Ferguson had followed informally in 1919.
Accordingly, the Department of Lands and Forests consigned
3,000 square miles of additional pulp limits to the Abitibi Pulp
and Paper Company "to ensure," as the 1923 *Annual Report*
explained, "continuous operation and the employment of a
large number of workmen."[14]

Shortly thereafter Spruce Falls Pulp and Paper and Backus'
mushrooming Great Lakes Paper empire received similar
privileges. Of these the Spruce Falls concession is the best
documented and permits the widest insight into the methods
and motives of the Ferguson government. Negotiations were
in progress between Spruce Falls and the *New York Times* publishing company whereby the latter would purchase one-half of
the shares in Spruce Falls and its entire newsprint output.
However, to satisfy the *New York Times* demand Spruce Falls
had to enlarge its production capacity, and to do that it had

[14] Department of Lands and Forests, *Annual Report*, 1923, p. 11.

to borrow. Whenever a pulp and paper company went into the money market investment bankers anxiously inquired as to whether the company possessed enough pulpwood reserves to guarantee near capacity production over the life of the proposed debt. No company could incur long-term obligations without being able to prove conclusively that it owned or held exclusive rights to a permanent supply of raw materials. Abitibi and Spanish River discovered this in 1919, and it was equally true for Spruce Falls in 1924. On the basis of Beniah Bowman's promise, the Spruce Falls company petitioned the new Conservative government for larger pulpwood limits. F. J. Sensenbrenner, the ever-present and persistent vice-president of the company, hovered about in the corridors of the Parliament buildings, pressing his case in writing and conversation with the Premier and James Lyons, the Minister of Lands and Forests. "As I explained to you this morning" he wrote to Lyons in mid-December 1924, "we have carried the enterprise absolutely at our own expense through the lean period subsequent to the war, but the time has now arrived when, in order to provide additional capital, further financial arrangements will require to be made, and it is essential to our interests that we should be in a position to show that we have the timber resources which will fairly justify the production of 550 tons of paper per day. . . . Following my interview with you today I saw the Prime Minister and have no doubt that he appreciates the situation as I have set it out to you. . . ."[15]

To accommodate the rapidly increasing demand for pulpwood created by the construction of new mills at the Lakehead and the expansion of older mills the government called public tenders for three huge pulp concessions in 1925, but the events that took place following the close of bidding clearly indicated that the government did not consider itself bound by the results. Officers of the Department of Lands and Forests carefully scrutinized every tender, screening out the obvious speculators

---

[15] Department of Lands and Forests, Spruce Falls File, F. J. Sensenbrenner to James Lyons, Dec. 18, 1924.

and pulpwood export promoters.[16] Yet even after this had been done it appeared that the Spruce Falls bid on the Kapuskasing pulp limit was not the highest. Nevertheless, the department recommended that Spruce Falls be granted the concession, because, as the Minister explained to Ferguson:

> They contend that they were promised the additional requirements of wood by the late Government, and there are some letters on file which substantiate their contention, and it is apparent that, in order to safeguard their present investments and carry out their original agreement with the Government, an area containing approximately the quantity of timber that they have bid upon will be required by them before they can be expected to complete their obligations.[17]

Although the government cloaked its policy with the form of democratic timber disposal technique, its intention remained, as Howard Ferguson explained to the disappointed bidders, to enlarge and stabilize the Ontario pulp and paper industry. The existing companies must be put "on a permanent basis," Ferguson reasoned: "They must have a future assured if they are to interest capital and if our forestry operations are to be carried on in a way that will secure reproduction and perpetuity."[18]

Frequent reliance upon the discretionary powers of the executive, however well intentioned or popular that recourse might be, is necessarily inimical to the principles of parliamentary democracy. On its own initiative the Ferguson government decided that the immediate objectives and neces-

---

[16] In fact the department took such a long time studying the tenders that the towns dependent upon the expansion of the mills grew restive. PAO, Ferguson Papers, Ferguson to Charles McCrae, Oct. 5, 1925; Ferguson to James Lyons, Oct. 5, 1925.

[17] *Ibid.*, James Lyons to Ferguson, Sept. 25, 1925.

[18] *Ibid.*, see correspondence between Ferguson and W. J. Boland, solicitor for W. D. Ross and I. W. Killam, Nov. 24 through Dec. 2, 1925; Ferguson to F. A. Drake, Nov. 25, 1925.

sities of the pulp and paper industry were legitimate and in the public interest. Then it threw the resources and influence of the crown into the balance on behalf of the corporations. In a very real sense the government of Ontario was, to use Howard Ferguson's phrase, the largest shareholder in the pulp and paper industry. It allowed its property to be mortgaged to New York and Chicago bankers, it legitimized the decisions of management, and stood passively by waiting for the expected employment and development dividends. It could be argued that the Ferguson government intervened rationally and beneficially to assist the creation of large, stable and efficient production units. But if that were so, then the state would have to accept a full share of responsibility for the overproduction and unemployment that resulted. Nevertheless, whether the outcome of government intervention was good or bad, those results should not obscure the fundamentally anti-democratic process that produced the government's decisions. The only difference between Ferguson's use of discretionary power in 1919 and 1925 was that in the latter case greater prudence and circumspection attended its exercise. Neither the Conservative nor the United Farmers' governments thought out the problem of accommodating their relationship with the pulp and paper industry to the principles of parliamentary government in any systematic way. Rather, under pressure from industrial promoters, government became an extension of management, bending and twisting its regulations to suit private interests.

It has been argued that the demands of industrial society upon government exaggerated the role of the executive at the expense of the Legislature. So pervasive has been that tendency in the twentieth century that it prompted one recent student of provincial government to observe:

> . . .the liberal view of the legislative branch no longer conforms to the realities of the governmental process in Ontario, and to continue to use the language of liberalism with reference to the existing situation serves only to perpetuate and heighten misconceptions. Giving lip service to such myths as "ministerial responsibility" may have some salutory psychological effect on the ministers and civil servants who are charged with a degree of discretionary authority, just as carrying on the business of

government in the name of the Crown may instill in some individuals a sense of awe and a predisposition to service. But for serious commentators on the Ontario scene to use such terms with the intent of describing actualities is at best anachronistic and at worst entirely misleading.[19]

Somewhere between William Lyon Mackenzie and his grandson one of the central principles of Ontario liberalism—responsible government—had deteriorated and the failure of the provincial government to come to grips with the dilemma of democratizing its economic responsibilities—and this has not happened to this day—contributed significantly to that decline. Industrial obligations helped hasten the rise of cabinet government; responsibility *for* an industry tended to diminish responsibility *to* the Legislature. We have noticed this dynamic emanating from a normal regulatory department of government, Lands and Forests; an independent agency with enormous delegated authority raised the dilemma of democratic accountability in its most extreme case.

## II

From the beginning of his crusade, Adam Beck endeavoured to detach the Hydro-Electric Power Commission from the conventions of parliamentary responsibility. His public power gospel stressed the fact that the distribution of hydro-electricity was after all a business function; therefore it ought to be conducted in the most businesslike fashion by an independent public corporation. There were two primary reasons for keeping Hydro out of politics, as Sir Adam often phrased it. The first was to protect the organization from what might be called the Intercolonial Railway syndrome, of loading the agency with incompetent political appointees. Hydro, if it were to deliver power at extremely low cost, would have to be the very epitome of efficiency. In the best progressive tradition the businessmen advocates of public power earnestly supported Adam Beck's

---

[19]   F. F. Schindler, *Responsible Government in Ontario* (Toronto, 1969), pp. 268-9.

contention that the patronage, waste and meddlesome political interference endured by most government departments and public enterprises simply could not be tolerated in the complex and exacting business of distributing hydro-electric power *at cost* among the factories, towns and villages of the province. The second reason was a positive variation of that proposition. In order to provide the necessary degree of expertise and efficiency, Hydro would have to recruit and claim the unswerving loyalty of a highly trained and therefore highly paid engineering staff. The devotion, hours, skill and salary demanded would necessarily exceed similar requirements in the regular public service. Moreover, Hydro as a business enterprise would also require sufficient independence of judgment in order to determine policy on the basis of economic rather than political intelligence. In Beck's view the functions of government would be limited to empowering the commission, supplying it with unlimited credit, and providing it with the weight of its legal sovereignty when the occasion demanded. The independent government agency was an ingenious device combining the public credit with the managerial efficiency of a private corporation.[20]

Although Adam Beck sat in two cabinets as chairman of the Hydro-Electric Power Commission he never held a portfolio. Whitney appointed him in 1905 as a Minister-Without-Portfolio with special responsibility for investigating the power situation; after the creation of the commission and his appointment as chairman Beck remained in the cabinet but still without portfolio. Beck's investigating commission, reporting in 1906, specifically recommended that the government avoid a departmental form of organization, and the subsequent legislation confirmed that judgment. Having thus formulated and established the principle of independence, Beck then jealously guarded it against his colleagues. In 1911 he rejected out of hand Whitney's suggestion that the commission should become a department of

---

[20] For a more detailed treatment of the rationale of the independent government agency, see Hodgetts, "The Public Corporation in Canada," pp. 51-86; Hanson, *Parliament and Public Ownership*, p. 12, and Schindler, *Responsible Government in Ontario*, pp. 69-80.

government. This would have had the effect of bringing Hydro policy and expenditures under the scrutiny of the full cabinet and, therefore, into the range of all other government programs and spending priorities. Again in 1917 the Hydro chairman categorically denied the insinuation of a government organization chart that he reported through the Attorney General's department to the Legislature. Similarly he opposed a United Farmers' suggestion, outlined after he declined their offer of the premiership, that revived the concept of a ministry of power. He insisted that it was absolutely inconceivable that a business such as Hydro could be included under the umbrella of cabinet responsibility. Hydro was not a responsible body in the manner of an ordinary government department. Rather, through the chairman, it reported directly to the Legislature. To emphasize this principle Beck refused a cabinet post—even one without portfolio—in the Hearst government. The commission began and remained an independent executive with special statutory authority.[21]

But the relationship of the commission to the government was by no means as clear cut as Beck made out. The ambivalence that he exploited most ruthlessly was that arising from the fact that Hydro was at once an agency of the provincial government and a municipal co-operative. By mobilizing his non-partisan, extra-parliamentary supporters into organizations such as the Niagara Power Union, the Ontario Municipal Electric Association and the Ontario Hydro-Electric Railway Association, Beck created a reliable and impressive power base outside of the party system which he used without conscience to bring hostile or hesitant members of government around to approving his taxing demands. By the same token, when Beck experienced difficulty keeping the municipalities in harness together, he relied upon his party and government to overrule those rebelli-

[21] PAO, Whitney Papers, Whitney to A. J. Matheson, Oct. 28, 1911; W. R. Plewman, *Adam Beck and the Ontario Hydro* (Toronto, 1947), pp. 82-5, 158, 199; Drury, *Farmer Premier*, pp. 117-18; M. Denison, *The People's Power* (Toronto, 1960), p. 144; Brian Tennyson, "The Succession of William H. Hearst to the Ontario Premiership—September 1914," *Ontario History*, Vol. LVI (1964), pp. 185-9.

ous, inferior legal bodies with the necessary bills or orders-in-council.

Adam Beck consciously installed Hydro between the municipal and provincial jursidictions where it was effectively beyond accountability to either. He ran Hydro as a curious kind of plebiscitory corporation. He would first organize his pressure groups and then the Conservative party behind the appropriate permissive legislation for his projects. Then he would pour the resources and influence of Hydro, plus his own considerable personal energies, into countless municipal by-law campaigns to win popular approval for them. With that generally overwhelming mandate to go ahead Beck would simply requisition funds from the defenceless government. If he were ever asked for a preliminary estimate or a proper accounting of expenditures, he would exclaim, to the inevitable accompaniment of the Ontario Municipal Electric Association chorus, "Hands off the municipalities!" That was Beck's favourite phrase, E. C. Drury noted caustically. "'Hands off the municipalities!' meant simply 'Hands off Beck!' and that he was answerable to no one."[22]

The Hydro chairman behaved as if his organization embodied the will of the people and merely reported to the Legislature as a matter of courtesy. However, since it was the government that passed Hydro legislation and voted Hydro funds, it was the government, in the last analysis, that bore the full responsibility for the commission—especially when obligations on this account amounted to one-half of the entire provincial debt, as they did in 1923! The provincial government had learned quickly enough how to delegate authority, but it had not discovered (nor has it yet), how to accommodate that agency with the principles and institutions of parliamentary democracy. Whatever the advantages of an independent executive such as the Ontario Hydro-Electric Power Commission, it was, nevertheless, an executive to be held accountable for its actions. If the Legislature would not or could not perform that role,

---

[22] Drury, *Farmer Premier*, p. 118; PAO, Drury Papers, Special Series, File of Municipal Resolutions.

then the political executive would have to assume ultimate responsibility, in which case Hydro became more of a department and less of an autonomous commission.

Two of Adam Beck's Napoleonic schemes, hydro radials and the Chippewa generating station, eventually led to a confrontation between the government and the commission over the question of responsibility. The genesis and evolution of both projects, which have been extensively discussed elsewhere, need only be summarized.[23] In 1912, when the commission was distributing only a fraction of the 100,000 horsepower it had contracted for, Adam Beck seized upon the idea of an electrified railway system owned and operated by Ontario Hydro with lines radiating out from Toronto to the regional cities as a sure market for his surplus power. Electric railways consumed tremendous quantities of power, and the sale of such a large block to Hydro's own transportation network would permit greater economies and even lower domestic rates. The radials would use the commission's transmission lines for their right of way, providing high-speed, clean, inexpensive and reliable transportation while at the same time exerting a stable, high level of demand for the service Hydro had been set up to provide. The idea had a natural appeal in a province where automobiles were still a rarity, which possessed only a few primitive highways and an abrasive climate. Coupled with the fervour and organizational genius of the public power movement, it soon carried everything before it. Depending upon the audience, Beck promised that hydro radials would keep the young men home on the farm (it was a time of serious rural depopulation) by speeding produce *at cost* to urban markets.[24] On other occasions he would demonstrate convincingly how commuter radials would eliminate in-

---

[23] For radials and Chippewa see Denison, *People's Power*, pp. 124-50; Plewman, *Adam Beck*, pp. 227 ff. L. A. Owen has written of the projected radials in "Sir Adam Beck and the Hydro-Electric Radial Scheme for Ontario" (unpublished master's thesis, University of Western Ontario, 1967), but this thesis makes Beck out as more of a railroader and less of a power merchant than he really was; see especially pp. 27, 176.

[24] On this point see W. R. Young, "Conscription, Rural Depopulation, and the Farmers of Ontario, 1917-19," *CHR*, Vol. LIII (1972), pp. 289-300.

dustrial slums by providing cheap, rapid transit from the city factories to neat, trim workingmen's towns in the countryside.

Radials, like Hydro itself, became something of a panacea for a host of social ills. The Ontario Municipal Electric Association immediately spawned the Ontario Hydro-Electric Railway Association to spread the gospel. Beck had legislative approval to begin preliminary surveys in 1913 and just before Whitney's death, a year later, he received permission under the Radial Railways Act to share the financing of radial railways with participating municipalities along the lines of the commission itself. Enthusiasts blackened the map with three thousand miles of projected railways which Beck reduced to a minimum initial program of three hundred miles of track. But by that time the surplus of hydro that had given rise to the scheme in the first place had been replaced by a shortage. Beck simply reversed the logic; the effect now became the cause. Radials, the surging demand for domestic and industrial power, and the optimistic projections ahead into the twenties all justified construction of the world's largest hydro-electric generating station—the ultimate monument to the public power crusade, a fitting symbol of the victory of public ownership at Niagara. A reluctant Hearst cabinet approved the project in 1916 and a series of encouraging majorities in municipal by-law votes held on New Year's Day 1917 added the required sanction from the municipal partners. On January 2, Beck announced plans for a 500,000 horsepower generating station at Queenston, and construction commenced in May. He estimated the total cost of the first stage of the radial network at $30 million and the generating installation, including the intake canal, at $20 million. Both schemes would be financed jointly by provincial and municipal borrowing which would be retired in due course by revenues.

Yet even before Adam Beck had set forth on these two bold ventures, critics had begun to challenge his financial management and question the effectiveness of political control over the operations of the commission. Much of this dissatisfaction could be traced to American utilities disturbed by Hydro's low rates and to the embattled Mackenzie group of companies; nevertheless, allowing for that bias, some of the criticism was well taken. In the first of a long series of studies commissioned by private American electrical utilities in 1912, Reginald Pelham Bolton concluded that the Ontario public power movement had " . . . fastened on the community an enormous financial burden, the effective results of which [were] inadequate and uneconomic, and the benefits such as they [were], unequally and even unfairly distributed." His report, *An Expensive Experiment*, argued that regulated private enterprise could have done the same job much more economically. He explained Hydro's apparently lower rates by the fact that the commission maintained no sinking fund to speak of and paid no taxes. Except for the sinking fund thrust, most of his accusations betrayed the venomous bias of the author and the pettiness of his source, a disaffected former employee of the commission.[25]

However, a series of biting articles written by James Mavor, a distinguished professor of political economy at the University of Toronto, and published in the *Financial Post* between July and December of 1916 could not be dismissed as easily. Certainly some of Mavor's animus could be ascribed to his friendship with many of the principals in the private power companies, some to the fact that he himself was a petty capitalist, and some to his pathological fear of socialism (he was a Russian economic historian). But by far the most important motive behind his critical attack on Hydro was a deep-seated intellectual aversion to the expansion of arbitrary state power, an abhorrence fully shared by his contemporaries Goldwin Smith and Professor A. V. Dicey. As a classical economist and as a Victorian liberal Mavor recoiled from the principle of public ownership. It defied reason and struck at the very root of liberty.[26]

---

[25] Reginald Pelham Bolton, *An Expensive Experiment: The Hydro-Electric System of Ontario* (New York, 1913), especially pp. 9, 30, 95, 181, 271. This book was serialized in the anti-public ownership journal, *Concerning Municipal Ownership*, in 1916.

[26] These articles in the *Financial Post* were reprinted as a pamphlet, unquestionably by the private utilities fighting Beck's plans to begin generating his own power at this time. For that conflict, see Christopher Armstrong, "The Politics of Federalism: Ontario's Relations with the

His laboured and often emotional essays first exposed the economic fallacies of public ownership and then bore down upon the political dangers reared by such monopolistic juggernauts as the Hydro-Electric Power Commission. By their very nature bureaucracies circumscribed freedom, he argued; they maintained themselves by forming alliances with governments for mutual permanence and promoted the subversive "illusion that politics and business are interchangeable expressions." When such bureaucracies were independent of political control they necessarily expanded the scope of discretion and narrowed the latitudes of democracy. Revising these articles into book form a decade later Mavor deplored the "enormous pile of ill-digested and incoherent" statutes that formed the foundations of the commission, each one of which closed off access to the courts. If a government had to protect itself in that manner, he lamented, "there can be no such thing as *responsible government.* . . ." Reviewing the history of the commission and the behaviour of its chairman, Mavor concluded, that " . . .the Hydro-Electric Power Commission of Ontario has from the beginning of its history been a menace to the financial credit and to the liberties of the people of the province. The chairman of the Hydro-Electric Power Commission has for the past twenty years been the Dictator of Ontario." Moreover, Mavor added, Beck had exploited and contributed to the

Federal Government, 1896-1941" (unpublished PhD. thesis, University of Toronto, 1972), pp. 209-11. The appearance of these articles as a pamphlet, *Public Ownership and the Hydro-Electric Power Commission of Ontario* (Toronto, 1917) coincided with this disallowance appeal. For Mavor's intellectual opposition to what he conceived of as the spreading "subversion of the social order," see *Niagara in Politics* (New York, 1925), p. 80; for Mavor's friendship with Canadian capitalists, see *My Windows on the Streets of the World* (Toronto, 1923), 2 vols., *passim.* Between 1902 and 1904 Mavor did some contract work for the Electrical Development Company; University of Toronto Archives, Mavor papers, G. R. Cockburn to Mavor, Dec. 15, 1903, April 2, 1904, private. There is evidence in this collection that Mavor also held stock in several South American utilities promoted by the capitalists who stood to gain most from Mavor's attack. But, as I have indicated, I do not consider these connections to be of any great significance as an explanation of Mavor's opposition to Hydro.

totalitarian propensities of his situation: "Whenever the Government . . . assumes operation of an industry, especially when to this operation there is added the incident of monopoly, there ceases to be any independent official critic of that industry. Critics," as Mavor knew from experience, "are enemies of the people. . . ."[27]

Editorials accompanying James Mavor's articles in the *Financial Post* attacked Hydro more on the level of performance than principle. Nevertheless, beneath the mound of free enterprise cant and special pleading for the private utilities,[28] there could be discerned a kernel of an argument. The *Financial Post* foresaw great risks from the "unanimity" of the Legislature: " . . . the two political parties vie with each other in protesting their solicitude for the furtherance of this particular undertaking. Herein lies great danger. There is almost entire absence of critical opposition applying to the operation of the hydroelectric systems in Ontario the same scrutiny as usually applied to public expenditure by opponents of the government in power." The *Financial Post*, like most other observers, regarded the commission as more governmental than independent. When an audit, neither expected nor authorized by the Hydro chairman, revealed that between 1911 and 1915 the commission had spent $4,190,622 more than the Legislature had voted for it, the *Financial Post* warned ominously: "The Province of Ontario will one day discover itself the victim of this hydroelectric obsession." Nor was it particularly satisfied with the McGarry legislation of 1916 that required an annual audit of the commission's accounts. In a leader headed "Curbing Sir

---

[27] See his early paper hostile to "Municipal Ownership of Public Utilities," presented to the Michigan Political Science Association, published in its *Proceedings*, Vol. IV,1904; see also *Public Ownership*, pp. 17, 27, 45; *Niagara in Politics*, pp. 8, 9, 113, 146.

[28] See, for example, Feb. 10, 1916: "Threatening British Interests." "Canadian and British money conquered Niagara and placed that power at the service of the Canadian people, and now Sir Adam threatens the British and Canadian interests concerned, with destruction through the employment of cheap, short date, Yankee money. While the Canadian and the Britisher is on the battle field his interests in his own empire are to be invaded by Sir Adam Beck through the agency of cheap neutral money."

Adam," the *Financial Post* demanded even more stringent accountability to protect the public interest: "Someone should know what Sir Adam is going to spend before the liability is incurred." And it cautioned the government and people of Ontario against writing " A Blank Cheque for the Chippewa Project":

> If the Government accedes to the request of the Hydro-Electric Power Commission it plunges the province and the municipalities into a whirlpool of debt in which these administrative bodies will. find themselves involved as inextricably as do the logs in the whirlpool at Niagara.

However biased or privately inspired these editorials against the "Hydro Menace" might have been, on this one point of political responsibility the *Financial Post* did make some valid, indeed prophetic, observations.[29]

By the end of the war others besides the obviously partisan had begun to question the wisdom of Sir Adam's schemes, especially the hydro radials. Since these electric railways had first been projected, and particularly since the latter part of the war, new factors had entered the picture to diminish the necessity for them. In the first place, wartime inflation made it practically impossible to calculate the cost of even the initial program with any degree of accuracy and some critics predicted that the original estimate of $30 million could easily double. Furthermore, railway nationalization meant that Sir Adam could no longer pose as convincingly as the people's champion, especially now that one of his certain victims would be another publicly owned railroad system, the Canadian National, which was already losing taxpayers' money. It took a giant leap of faith to justify even further duplication, but such was the power of Adam Beck that remarkably few of the converted wavered. Thirdly, disillusionment with rail transportation had finally begun to settle in. The Canadian railway crisis contributed significantly to this change of mood, but so did the disappointing

[29] *Financial Post*, Jan. 8, Mar. 25, April 15, Dec. 2, 1916; Jan. 27, 1917.

American experience with radials. Every month brought news of reductions in service, abandonments, and always staggering losses. Mass production of the automobile ultimately sealed the fate of the radials all over North America. Cars, trucks and buses were self-evidently the "coming thing," automotive transportation was well within the reach of wage-earners as well as the middle class, and people naturally began to demand better highways and secondary roads for these vehicles rather than more miles of track.

Although Beck's minions kept up the campaign for radials, the tide had begun to run noticeably against them. "Has Sir Adam Considered the Motor Bus?" the *Financial Post* asked bluntly. Even the *Monetary Times*, which usually supported Beck, felt it necessary to draw the line somewhere. And in 1917 the Canadian Society of Civil Engineers reported that no public necessity existed for the radial system, that if it were built it would operate at an annual deficit, and that the money might be better spent on roads. This study, commissioned by several Hamilton ratepayers opposed to the radials, recommended: "The amount of money named as the estimated cost of the proposed Port Credit–St. Cathatines Line would construct a system of 'Good Roads' in this portion of the Province of Ontario that would be so far reaching in beneficial effect as to be incalculable."[30] Nor could Sir Adam continue to expect automatic approval of his Hydro and radial by-laws; in spite of heavy spending by the commission the Hamilton district proved practically unmanageable and if only one of the municipal corporations along the line disapproved, then the whole project would fail.

Nevertheless, even with all of these factors turning against the great Hydro radial project, it was still too early for the major political parties to come out four square against it. Sir Adam could be a ruthless opponent, as all of his friends and

[30] *Financial Post*, Dec. 20, 1917; *Monetary Times*, Dec. 20, 1918; Col. R. W. Leonard, W. F. Tye, Sir John Kennedy, L. A. Herdt, W. J. Francis, for the Canadian Society of Civic Engineers, *Report on the Proposed Hydro-Electric Radial Railway from Port Credit to St. Catharines* (Hamilton, 1917), pp. 1-3, 30.

enemies were well aware, and he was still the most popular and powerful political figure in the province. Thus, while it is possible to note some equivocation and ever so cautious qualification of the radials in both Liberal and Conservative campaign literature in 1919, the two parties continued to vie for the honour of being the foremost friend of public ownership.[31]

Premier Hearst had never enjoyed Beck's confidence. Relations between the two men had been cool from the outset and became especially strained after the surprise audit of Hydro accounts in 1916. That year the Clarkson report identified two main reasons for the $4,190,622 excess of expenditures over the amount voted by the Legislature: "One the absence of even the semblance of legislative control over the expenditures of the Commission—in striking contrast with the complete legislative control over the expenditures of the other Executive Departments. The other the seeming defiant disobedience of the Act creating the Commissioners with their powers and duties."[32] As the *Financial Post* observed on its passage, the McGarry Act (which required the commission to submit to an annual audit) did little to improve legislative scrutiny of the commissioners' activities; it merely ensured a fairly accurate rendering of their iniquity after the event. Thus, Hydro spending continued to increase virtually at the will of Adam Beck; in the three years between 1917 and 1919 the Hearst government advanced a total of $25,972,332 to the commission, a sum exceeding 45 per cent of the government's ordinary revenue and 46 per cent of its expenditures.[33] The Premier

---

[31] PAO, Hearst Papers, memorials, annual reports, and innumerable indignant letters from the Ontario Municipal Electric Association and the Ontario Hydro-Electric Radial Association, in the Radials File. See also, Ontario Liberal Party, *Ontario Liberal Policy* (Toronto, 1919), and *The High Cost of Living, Public Ownership and Hydro* (Toronto, 1919); the Conservative Party, *Hydro Progress in Ontario: Public Ownership is Safe with the Hearst Government* (Toronto, 1919).

[32] Quoted in the *Financial Post*, Mar. 25, 1916.

[33] Plewman, *Adam Beck*, p. 477, table showing government advances by year, and Hon. James N. Allan, *Budget Statement, 1963* (Toronto, 1963), p. 65, table showing revenues and expenditures 1890-1963. In 1919 Hydro accounted for 49% of the gross provincial debt, see *ibid.*, pp. 66-7, tables showing gross and net debt, 1914-1953.

and his cabinet simply looked on helplessly as Beck extracted from them increasingly larger sums to finance his grandiose schemes and ever more exacting laws to keep the municipalities in line. Finally the long-delayed confrontation came to a head, in an election year.

After the Township of Saltfleet defeated one of his radial by-laws Beck began to see the grand design breaking up. As was his wont on these occasions, Beck laid the blame for his failure on someone else, this time his hapless Premier. "I have felt for some time that the Hydro-Electric railway projects of the municipalities were receiving but a small degree of sympathy from the members of the Government," he wrote to Hearst in mid-April. "I propose, therefore, to make such a statement and to place the responsibility for the universal disappointment at the failure . . . where in my judgment it rightly belongs. I regret the necessity for this exceedingly, but I have already allowed my sense of party loyalty to restrain me too long. . . ." Hearst was "not only surprised but dumbfounded" at what he considered Beck's totally unjustified charges of ministerial non-support. Indeed, his government had defended the radials and met their requirements to a point considerably beyond the limits of ordinary political wisdom:

> Requests have been made for legislation at the closing hours of the Session, when it was impossible that such legislation could receive the thought and attention it deserved, and at a time when I would have hesitated to allow legislation from other Commissions and Departments of Government on such important matters to be presented to the House. This legislation has sometimes been characterized as drastic and has brought criticism, particularly in view of the stage of the Session at which it was presented, but I know of no single instance in which legislation has been asked for by you that has not been secured.[34]

In reply Beck complained of the "stringent" and "exacting" terms of the original 1914 Radial Act and the complete absence of any public statement from the Premier supporting the

---

[34] PAO, Hearst Papers, Adam Beck to Hearst, April 17, 1919, personal; Hearst to Beck, April 24, 1919, personal.

Hydro-Electric Power Commission in its innumerable radial by-law campaigns. Hearst answered this letter charge by turning Beck's often-expressed wish to keep Hydro out of politics against him:

> My understanding of your attitude has been that you are anxious to keep the Hydro Radial schemes as far out of politics as possible, and I thought it would be the furthest from your desire for the Government to enter into these campaigns, making the question, as such action naturally would, a Party question, in all probability driving from the support of the by-law Liberals who would otherwise support it, and creating complications and difficulties of many kinds. If the Government is to take the responsibility for the campaigns, and make the carrying of Hydro Radial by-laws a party question, thereby constituting victories for these by-laws Government victories, and defeats of these by-laws Government defeats, then it appears to me that naturally the Government must take direct control of the whole undertaking. This we have no desire to do.

When it was to his advantage then, Beck expected the solidarity of cabinet responsibility, but all the while insisting upon the complete independence of his commission. In short, he wanted it both ways.

After reversing the independence argument on Sir Adam, the Premier added a revealing, indeed remarkable footnote:

> I might further add, if further explanation is necessary, that you have never taken me into your confidence in connection with this undertaking. I know nothing of the facts or arguments in favour of the scheme, except what I have read in the newspaper. I do not even know the names or qualifications of the experts who have reported on the scheme, nor have I been furnished with the report of these experts as to the cost of the road, the probable earnings of the road, and the other data that would be necessary for a Prime Minister or a Cabinet Minister to have before undertaking to speak on the subject and give advice to rate-payers who are assuming heavy financial obligations in the matter. Surely you would not expect a Member of Government to take part in a campaign unasked for by anyone so to do and lacking full and complete information relating to the subject.[35]

This astonishing revelation exposes the complete lack of communication and absence of trust between the government and the commission. Hearst might have thought ignorance sufficient grounds for not speaking in public on behalf of radials, but the same uncertainties should have restrained him from voting funds to the project in the first place. His confession serves as an indictment of his own conduct as well as Beck's. It is fair to conclude from this correspondence that neither the Premier nor his cabinet colleagues had any idea of what Beck was doing with his $25 million; yet they continued to vote him credit! For what was true of the radials was equally true of the enormous Queenston project. No one, not even Beck, knew its cost or had any clear idea of its optimum size. In the name of the people the Hydro-Electric Power Commission was literally running away with the provincial treasury, and no one had the courage to ask for what purpose.

Beck's forthright attempt at political blackmail actually succeeded. Hearst relented and agreed to pass an order-in-council and then a further bill at the tag end of the session, permitting Sir Adam to proceed without the approval of the yeomen of Saltfleet. Yet even the Premier's humiliating capitulation failed to soothe the Hydro chairman. To satisfy a host of niggling, pent-up grievances Beck decided to run as an independent in the general election that fall, thereby openly contradicting the Conservative campaign slogan: "Public Ownership is safe with the Hearst Government." Beck wanted his radials and his pound of flesh too.[36] After the election it was left to the United Farmers to resolve this new crisis of responsible government. E.C. Drury, the new United Farmer premier of Ontario, had always mistrusted the ambitious chairman of the Hydro-Electric Power Commission. Drury's

[35] *Ibid.*, Beck to Hearst, April 30, 1919; Hearst to Beck, May 8, 1919.

[36] *Ibid.*, Hearst to Beck, July 29, 1919; see also Hearst to Beck, August 14, 1919. For an assessment of Beck's role in the general election see Brian Tennyson, "Sir Adam Beck and the Ontario General Election of 1919," *Ontario History*, Vol. LVIII (1966), pp. 157-62, and Peter Oliver, "Sir William Hearst and the Collapse of the Conservative Party," *CHR*, Vol. LIII (1972), pp. 21-50.

intuitive scepticism of big government, debt, and bureaucracy naturally predisposed him to be suspicious of such an imperious organization. Beck, of course, had also been a potential rival for the premiership. Rather than more railways, he regarded radials as just another monstrous extravagance thrust upon unwilling taxpayers by city businessmen—Drury sought more practical objectives such as better roads and rural electrification. Since the election of the Drury government marked a complete break with the past, it provided an interlude during which these doubts, long suppressed by the tyranny of a unanimous majority, could be openly declared for the first time. From every region the Premier's correspondents questioned the mounting expense and continued necessity of the radials; the hesitancy of the *Farmer's Sun* turned to outright opposition. The executive of the United Farmers of Ontario set up the Ontario Hydro Information Association to counteract the propaganda being disseminated by the Ontario Municipal Electric Association and the Ontario Hydro-Electric Railway Association, both of which were secretly subsidized by Hydro.[37] After 1919, critics of Sir Adam's schemes were no longer confined to injured parties and the financial press. Although Sir Adam had been defeated in the general election, the government retained him as chairman of the commission largely because it was impossible to remove him. Beck was still a very powerful man, less harmful in harness than out, and continued to be the special favourite of the labour members in the coalition government. Nevertheless, the Premier served notice that his government would hold the Hydro chairman at arms' length, carefully scrutinize the estimates and expenditures of the commission, and submit its projects to a thorough-going public review.

When the bills for the Queenston generating station soared to four times the original estimates and with the municipalities clamouring for millions more in bond guarantees for their radial railways, the Drury government declared that the time had

[37] Owen, "Sir Adam Beck and the Hydro-Electric Radial Scheme for Ontario," pp. 84-5, 107; PAO, Drury Papers, C. B. Watts to Drury, Dec. 9, 1919; J. N. Taylor to the editor of the Guelph *Mercury*, Dec. 19, 1919; M. T. Buchanan to Drury, Jan. 27, 1920; Plewman, *Adam Beck*, pp. 247, 251-3.

,come for a complete investigation of the Hydro accounts, its construction program, and its relations with the government. Auditors' reports showed that Sir Adam had indulged in a great deal of estimate padding and in that manner had shifted authorized but surplus funds to unauthorized or exceptionally expensive projects. In 1919 alone he had successfully hidden over $100,000 that way! More alarming still, the auditors also discovered that by 1919 a total of $14,713,970 had been spent on the construction of the powerhouse and canal, but that the Legislature had voted only $11,075,000 for that purpose. Accountants from Clarkson, Gordon, and Dilworth estimated that another $25 million, over and above what had already been spent, would be required to complete the project. Moreover, these preliminary studies revealed that the commission had gone ahead with some radial construction without the proper statutory authority to do so, relying solely upon a verbal promise from Hearst that legislation would be introduced to legalize proceedings after the event. Thus the Drury government felt sufficiently justified, with the Queenston estimates rising above $50 million (it would ultimately cost $80 million), in calling a pause to reconsider the entire radial railway scheme. Its auditors estimated that the government would have to provide $29 million over the next two years simply to meet the commission's operating and construction expenses. If the radial program went ahead as planned, the government would have to guarantee another $25 million in Hydro bonds. Either one of these burdens would impose a strain upon the credit of the province, but undertaken jointly they threatened to plunge it into bankruptcy.[38]

Therefore, the Drury government established a Royal Commission in 1920 to report upon the prudence of the proposed hydro-electric radial railway system. In his speech defending this course of action, Premier Drury declared that the independent action of the Hydro-Electric Power Commission had, in his

[38] PAO, Drury Papers, W. E. Raney to Drury, Dec. 16, 1919, enclosing W. W. Pope's memorandum on radial railways. Drury received three reports on the Commission from Clarkson, Gordon, and Dilworth dated Aug. 22, 1918, Oct. 31, 1919, and Mar. 11, 1920.

view, plainly jeopardized an essential constitutional liberty. Under a parliamentary democracy the people vested control of taxation and spending in their Legislature; no branch of the executive possessed the right to requisition funds or guarantee bonds without the expressed statutory approval of the people's representatives in the Legislature. The arbitrary conduct of the commissioners and the extensive order-in-council provisions of the several Hydro acts thus posed a direct challenge to that important principle:

> To permit any other than the Legislature to exercise this right would take from it part of its recognized duties and deprive the people of Ontario of that one particular right—the control of public moneys—which down through hundreds of years has been tenaciously held to and done more than anything else to give the liberty they now enjoy to British people. The Government will not, under any circumstances, allow this right to be infringed.[39]

Drury promised that if the municipalities wished to go ahead with the radial program his government would not stand in their way. But he insisted that both the municipal councils and the people they represented should have a clear understanding of the total extent of their obligations before undertaking the project. In the past the only figures presented for consideration had been those of the Hydro chairman and he had a lamentable record of underestimating the cost of every plan he projected. However unpopular the steps might be, Drury was determined to obtain expert testimony from competent, impartial engineers and legislative approval as necessary preliminaries to the expenditure of millions.

After a year of hearings the Sutherland Commission reported that evidence indicated that the hydro-electric radials would never be self-supporting and might possibly endanger the other publicly owned railway system, the CNR. Furthermore, it cautioned the government against launching another large capital project until the Queenston generating station had been

[39] *Ibid.*, Draft speech on Hydro Expenditures, 1920.

completed and the final bills submitted. Noting the rapid increase in the number of motor cars, trucks and buses, the commission pointed out that expenditures on railways would conflict with the government's somewhat more urgent $25 million road-building program. Finally, it condemned the practice of guaranteeing municipal bonds and warned against incurring further obligations in view of the prevailing financial conditions.[40]

The Premier considered that his earlier opinion had been completely vindicated by the commission's *Report*. In a public speech at Glencoe he recalled the atmosphere of "indefiniteness and misunderstanding" that surrounded the question before the United Farmers came to power: "The old Government apparently afraid of the pro-radial forces and at the same time reluctantly supporting the movement on one hand while endeavouring to impede Sir Adam on the other, surrendered weakly to demands that should have been carefully considered, so that matters were more or less in a state of chaos." Moreover, a "servile majority" in the Legislature had abdicated its proper responsibility of vigilance, thereby surrendering "a very old

---

[40]  The Royal Commission was chaired by Mr. Justice Sutherland and included a carefully chosen cross-section of coalition support and opinion on the radial question: W. A. Amos, vice-president of the U.F.O., Fred Bancroft, a Toronto labour leader, A. F. MacCallum, engineer for the city of Ottawa, and Dean C. H. Mitchell (whose opinion the public power movement first sought back in 1903). For details and recommendations, see *Reports of the Royal Commission Appointed to Enquire into Hydro-Electric Railways* (Toronto, 1921). Bancroft submitted a *Minority Report* favouring radials. Sir Adam replied to the commissioners' criticisms in a point-by-point, 42-page pamphlet (printed at the public expense) entitled: *Statement Respecting Findings and other Statements contained in the Majority Report of the Commission appointed to Enquire into the subject of Hydro-Electric Railways* (Toronto, 1922). His main point seemed to be that the commission had taken the word of steam railway experts and Americans who were unfamiliar with the record of achievement and transcending virtue of the public power forces. Economics alone should not decide any issue, concluded Sir Adam: "In dealing with public problems such as the Hydro-Electric Power Commission has dealt with, the Commission has regarded that adequate knowledge of any problem in hand, coupled with zeal and enterprise for its successful solution, have been more important factors than the mere acquirement of Capital" (p. 41).

and vital principle of British government." Drury promised that at the next session his government would repeal the indiscriminate bond guarantee clauses of the Radial Railways Act, eliminate the practice of delegating authority over such critical matters to an executive body, and would thereby, he said, " . . . restore the power to vote money, [such] as the Hydro estimates, to the hands of the Legislature."[41] The promised legislation, which placed liability for the system squarely upon the participating municipalities rather than the provincial government, coupled with the Royal Commission's unequivocal warning against the folly of radial railways, effectively interred Beck's once-grand design.[42]

The turbines at the world's largest hydro-electric generating station had no sooner begun to turn than the discrepancy between its estimated and actual cost provoked another crisis. In 1922, when once again Hydro spending soared obliviously above its legislative appropriations, Drury's personal representative on the Hydro-Electric Power Commission, Col. D. Carmichael, who had been appointed primarily to rein in the ambitious chairman, submitted his resignation. "The estimates for the Queenston-Chippewa Canal have been so increased," he explained to the Premier, "that I as a member of the Commission cannot justify them to the Government." Of course Drury did not hold Carmichael responsible for the uncontrollable inflation characteristic of Hydro costs, and he refused to accept his tendered resignation. But such an event could not pass without comment. "The Hydro Commission harps upon trusteeship," Drury complained to a Hamilton audience early in 1922; "trusteeship is all right, but irresponsible trusteeship

---

[41] PAO, Drury Papers, E. C. Drury, speech at Glencoe, Aug. 24, 1921. It is interesting to note that in making these comments Drury recalled British rather than Canadian precedents; for example, see his comment on the power of the Legislature over the purse: "We know also that one king lost his head and lost it permanently because he did not regard this simple constitutional rule. We know that it was a principle insisted upon in the Commons through centuries. We know that the king comes asking the Commons for money and they vote it or not as they see fit."

[42] For the final agonies, see Plewman, *Adam Beck*, pp. 325 ff.; Denison, *The People's Power*, pp. 148 ff.

is all wrong." Soon afterwards he confessed to another gathering that neither the government nor the experts at Hydro had any clear conception of what the Queenston project would ultimately cost, and he intimated that both the politicians and the engineers had been living in a fool's paradise long enough.[43]

Once again the government had recourse to a Royal Commission to probe the estimating and cost control procedures of the Hydro-Electric Power Commission. Over and above the political advantages of avoiding a direct confrontation between Sir Adam and the government, the Royal Commission formula had other attributes to recommend it. Often the publicity function of a Royal Commission is as important as its analysis and advice. Usually the public reaction to the mere conduct of a thorough inquiry clears the way for effective remedial action and sometimes removes altogether the necessity for such action. In this respect a Royal Commission is like a coroner's inquest; it can never repair the injury, but it can alarm the spectators. Drury probably hoped that a systematic exposure of the inner workings of the commission would suitably chasten its chairman and thereby help contribute to a reassertion of political control over his activities. In any event, the Gregory Commission began its exhaustive study of the numerous Hydro construction programs within a year of a general election which E. C. Drury never expected his government to survive.[44]

When the Gregory Commission eventually reported, it condemned, as expected, the submission of unrealistically low initial estimates by the Hydro-Electric Power Commission. "Loose statements" naturally hampered rather than advanced the success of the publicly owned utility in the long run. But, the commission added, any government that accepted such estimates without thorough examination must also shoulder some

---

[43] PAO, Hydro-Electric Power Commission papers, Carmichael Collection, Carmichael to Drury, Mar. 3, 1922; Drury quoted in Plewman, *Adam Beck*, p. 297.

[44] This commission was chaired by W. D. Gregory of Toronto and included Lloyd Harris, the Brantford manufacturer, J. Allan Ross, a Toronto businessman, R. A. Ross and M. J. Haney, both engineers. For Drury's gloomy expectations, see *Farmer Premier*, p. 156.

of the blame: "No government should accept with confidence estimates prepared by a promoter of a scheme seeking support even though the promoter be a public body."

Turning to the financial aspect of Hydro's responsibilities, the Gregory Commission noted the failure of the Hydro-Electric Commission to meet its refunding obligations on time and its lack of proper sinking and contingency funds for its capital projects. The Royal Commission took strenuous exception to the unauthorized use of $1,100,000 of Hydro appropriations on radial railway projects and recommended that the amount taken should be fully restored. The Gregory Commission agreed with the Clarkson reports that the common source of these and many other difficulties could be found in the poor relations between Hydro and the government and the extra-ordinary character of the Hydro chairman. Almost single-handedly he had planned, initiated, built and defended a great and worthy public enterprise against the will of powerful interests and for that the Royal Commission extended "full and ungrudging credit." Yet at the same time the investigators could not help but deplore Sir Adam's "absolute lack of frankness," his blatant disregard of his political responsibility, and his "wholly unjustifiable" manipulation of public funds. In short, the Royal Commission reported, the chairman of the Hydro-Electric Power Commission had been "arbitrary and inconsiderate" with colleagues, governments, the Legislature and the law. "That he has kept his position notwithstanding the actions to which we have referred has no doubt been due to the fact that he has a large and devoted following and has created a political force which governments as a rule are unwilling to antagonize."

Even if the Hydro chairman had behaved in an indefensibly independent manner, the Gregory Commission nevertheless reaffirmed that the ultimate responsibility for his conduct lay with the government to which he was accountable:

If a government with the power of removal in its hands, fails to act when wrongdoing is brought to its attention, it must bear a large degree of responsibility for it and for future transgressions as well. . . . If the government is to have full and accurate information as to the Commission's operations we believe that it will have to secure this information through a representative of its own fully qualified to keep in touch with the Commission in all its branches. It cannot afford to conduct its business with the Commission as loosely as it had been conducted in the past.

Yet, even though it surveyed a mountain of evidence confirming the evil of administrative independence, and even though the final *Report* recommended a strengthening of political control over the operation of the commission, the Gregory Commission did not consider a departmental and ministerial structure suited to the operation of a public utility:

> To make it [Hydro] a department of government in the same sense that a department of a minister of the crown is a department of government would, we believe, greatly lessen its influence and efficiency. It should be kept free from the patronage hunter. If it were turned over to the patronage hunter and appointments made on purely political grounds it would receive what we believe would prove to be a fatal blow. So says Sir Adam Beck and we fully agree with him.[45]

Thus, despite the volume and detail of the various *Reports* of the Royal Commission, it could only offer some vague and inconsequential recommendations regarding this critical matter of political accountability. The Gregory Commission stopped curiously short of proposing a direct pattern of ministerial responsibility and continued to defend the independent commission form on grounds which constituted a much better argument for civil service reform than anything else. It merely recommended closer contact and greater communication between the commission and the government.

A special study of this particular problem undertaken by the Royal Commission staff suggested by implication that the

[45] See the summary of recommendations in the Gregory Commission, *Final Report* (Toronto, 1924), and the volumes of testimony and studies in the Ontario Hydro Archives. The main points are surveyed in Plewman, *Adam Beck*, pp. 353-73. The redoubtable Sir Adam replied to this Royal Commission as well in *Errors and Misrepresentations made by the Hydro-Electric Inquiry Commission (known as the Gregory Commission) respecting the Publicly Owned and Operated Hydro-Electric Power Undertaking of the Municipalities of the Province of Ontario* (Toronto, 1925).

initial relationship of the commission and government be revived. "Under the original Act the Province occupied pretty much the position of a generous parent advancing a child, but with a curb upon requests for advances and the amount of a child's expenses and provision that all income from the undertakings upon which the advances were expended should be paid over to the parent in reduction of the advances." Over time, however, the restless ambition of the Hydro chairman and the compliant abdication by the government of its rightful authority substantially altered this former dependent relationship:

> At present the relationship appears to be or is sought that the Government is an accommodating Banker, providing funds and guarantees for any and all works which a Body Corporate created by it may desire to undertake, without the Banker questioning the wisdom or expediency of the undertakings, and receiving annually the cost and expenses of the Government in raising these funds, the repayment of principal depending upon the revenues from the undertakings being sufficient to provide ample sinking funds.[46]

When Howard Ferguson returned to power he consciously strove to re-establish the old dependency. In some instances he anticipated the Gregory Commission, and in others he followed it. Whatever the recommendations of the *Final Report*, the evidence revealed during the hearings made it perfectly obvious that the time had come to reinforce the government's representation on the Power Commission, to restore legislative control of its expenditures, and generally restrain the ambition of the aging chairman. Ferguson appointed J. R. Cooke to the commission primarily, it was said, to keep Sir Adam out of trouble. Secondly, regular procedures were finally laid down governing the transferring of money from the Consolidated Revenue Fund to the commission. Henceforth the commission would be expected to stipulate the specific vote under which

---

[46] PAO, Ferguson Papers, Gregory Commission, "History Compiled by the Hydro-Electric Inquiry Commission," typescript, pp. 40-1.

its warrants were authorized. The big problem was still Sir Adam, but in Ferguson he perhaps met his match. In his own blunt and forthright manner Howard Ferguson did not shrink from bringing Sir Adam to heel if he strayed. When on one occasion the Hydro chairman independently decided upon a policy and announced it to the press, Ferguson called him up short:

> You of course realize that the general policy in connection with this work must be approved by the Government as the money is to be furnished by the Government. As I have said to you a number of times, I only intend to proceed after I have thoroughly considered each step and have been able to exercise my own judgement and approval.... It is not only embarrassing but humiliating as Prime Minister to be placed in the position where I am forced to say that I know nothing about some project for which the Government must take responsibility.[47]

Accountability to the government was one thing, but full disclosure before the Legislature was an entirely different matter. If it were proper for the executive to demand complete information before deciding policy, should the Legislature not have the same information in order to approve it? Neither the Premier nor C. A. Magrath, who succeeded as chairman upon Sir Adam's death in 1925, thought that it should. Early in 1929 some members of the Legislature asked the commission to reveal details of several of its supply contracts with Quebec power companies; Magrath demurred and Ferguson upheld him. Magrath recognized the need for a degree of openness in the conduct of Hydro affairs, but he thought that "every sensible man" would admit that complete publicity was undesirable. "A middle course must be taken," he advised the Premier, "and the problem is to find its limits." The commission differed significantly from an ordinary government department: it borrowed rather than spent public money outright; it

[47] University of Toronto Archives, Mavor Papers, H. H. MacRae to Mavor, July 9, 1923; PAO, Ferguson Papers, Ferguson to Beck, Nov. 23, 1923, personal.

was a trustee for the municipalities, and a business enterprise in its own right. Accordingly, the rules laid down for government departments could not be applied to Hydro. If the Legislature could request disclosure of its supply contracts, then contracts with its industrial customers might be next. And if that ever came to pass, Magrath warned, "industry will certainly hesitate about coming here." Private companies were not obliged to disclose their contracts and Hydro, just because it was a public corporation, should not be denied the common privilege of business secrecy in these matters. Disclosure should be left to the discretion of the commission, its chairman recommended, and if the Legislature questioned its judgment, and after the pros and cons had been fully debated and good cause established, then the commission would submit to its will. But on "sound business lines" Magrath argued that the government should protect the Commission against the meddling interference of the Legislature.[48]

The Premier, who knew something of the secrecy demanded by businessmen, concurred with the view of his Hydro chairman. "It seems difficult to get into the heads of some of the members of the Legislature,"Ferguson explained to Beck's old pressure group, the Ontario Municipal Electric Association, "a proper conception of the sphere occupied by the Hydro Electric Power Commission. I do not think that they have any special designs on the institution, or desire to see it injured in any way. They simply do not seem to understand the importance of maintaining privacy about much of its work."[49] Yet, if it was improper for the commission to keep secrets to itself, was it any less contemptible to share them only with the cabinet? Even if the government and the commission worked hand in glove that did not in itself ensure the responsibility of the commission; it might make it more likely, but not certain. The problem of political accountability remained

[48] PAO, Hydro-Electric Power Commission papers, J. R. Cooke Collection, orders-in-council for 1923-4; *ibid.*, Ferguson Papers, C. A. Magrath to Ferguson, Feb. 24, 1929.

[49] PAO, Ferguson Papers, T. J. Hannigan, secretary of the Ontario Municipal Electric Association to Ferguson, Mar. 22, 1920; Ferguson to Hannigan, Mar. 25, 1929.

unsettled even after several changes in government, a complete alteration in the personnel of the commission, and two Royal Commission investigations. And, as we shall see, that modicum of secrecy so fiercely defended by C. A. Magrath would ultimately reopen the question.

A wide field of discretion remained open to the Hydro-Electric Power Commission, the Minister of Lands and Forests, and the cabinet as a whole. Industrialism, bureaucratization, and the business involvements of the state imposed new strains upon those institutions traditionally charged with preserving democracy by exaggerating a natural inclination towards the exercise of executive power. The particularly close identification of government in Ontario with the forest products and hydro-electric industries reinforced those tendencies. The satisfaction of the legitimate demands of businessmen and bureaucrats—leaving aside their illegitimate propositions—seemed to involve an altogether inordinate degree of trust on the part of the executive and subservience on the part of the Legislature.

When a minister of the crown discovered that his obligations to an important industry dependent upon the public domain violated the spirit and letter of the law, it was the law which eventually had to give way. Sir Adam Beck's delusions of grandeur and suspicion of persecution precluded the possibility that Ontario Hydro might be easily incorporated into the traditions of parliamentary responsibility. It has often been said in jest that the worst kind of paranoid is the one who has real enemies. In Beck's defence, there were people plotting at every turn to thwart his ambitions, as he was theirs. The relevant point here is that the very antagonistic circumstances that gave rise to the institution in the first place militated against its accommodation to the openness and latent conflicts of the democratic process. Beck would never tolerate a step that could make his enterprise even more vulnerable to attack. His successors inherited this entrenched position and its state of siege mentality even though the threat had long since vanished. Now it was merely a question of taking the public into one's confidence. It might further be added that the business supporters of the concept of public ownership had such a low opinion of politics that they made a positive virtue of the independence of Hydro from the formal procedures of accountability.

In this perspective the crisis of responsibility that arose during the adolescence of Ontario Hydro followed logically from the contradictions of its birth. Easy recourse to arbitrary power constantly tested the probity, judgment and courage of ministers of the crown, not always with satisfactory results. If Ontario had once learned that responsible government could be won, it had not yet discovered that it could also be lost at this interface between government and business.

# 11
# Politics as Business

Continuous association with the problems and leading personalities of business posed a second challenge to the "responsibility" of government. Frequent discussions between businessmen and politicians necessarily exalted business opinions and discounted the views and claims of other groups within society. It is not surprising that this was the case with problems of immediate concern to industrialists such as the taxation of mining, the proration of newsprint production, and Hydro acquisitions. But it was equally true that the Ontario government's attitude towards broader social and political issues, such as unemployment, industrial unionism, federalism and public finances closely approximated business views on these same subjects. The Ontario interest in these matters was its business interest, and there were no more prominent businessmen in provincial counsels than those of the mining, forest products and hydroelectric industries. Paternal government departments and political friendships permitted businessmen to use the state to stabilize, extend and legitimize their economic power. And when their empires collapsed they called upon government to put things back together again—on their own terms, of course. After a time it became virtually impossible for anyone except a few troublesome professors and political deviants on the left to conceive of organizing these enterprises any differently than their management wished. As the largest shareholders in the resource industries, politicians were loyal management men.

A.R.M. Lower made this point in a review of the 1948 Royal Commission on Forestry *Report*: "The forests of Canada should have been vested in the people of Canada. Their being vested in the provinces simply means that they are committed to bodies which, in the subtle social sense, are essentially irresponsible."[1] Leaving aside the evident legislative unionism of his contention, Lower's diagnosis of the problem of responsibility was right on target: "Ministers of greater or lesser probity, civil servants of greater or lesser mental rigidity, come and go: the department, in so far as I can discern, goes on with a fearsome inner logic of its own." His criticism of the Department of Lands and Forests could quite easily be extended to include the Department of Mines and the Hydro-Electric Power Commission. These institutions also possessed a "fearsome inner logic" which they imparted to policy-making in Ontario. The Ontario experience seemed to indicate that responsibility *for* vast industrial enterprises narrowed the vision of government and deadened its sense of responsibility *to* other social groups. Businessmen had succeeded in generalizing their ideology, or in identifying their interests completely with the public interest, largely through their political influence. It was this imperative that ruled the administration of the mines, forests and waterpowers and dictated the provincial interest in other matters that constituted the second threat to responsible government.

---

[1] Royal Ontario Forestry Commission, *Report*, reviewed by A. R. M. Lower in *CJEPS*, Vol. XIV (1948), p. 508.

I

Mining offers the best illustration of how the managerial outlook became the government outlook. Between 1920 and 1940 the Ontario mining industry reached maturity and prospered as never before. Although there were cutbacks in the production of certain minerals, the total volume and value of the provincial mineral output rose steadily throughout the two decades:

VALUE OF ONTARIO MINERAL PRODUCTION: Selected Years, 1920-40

|  | Gold | Iron Ore | Nickel | Silver | Total |
|---|---|---|---|---|---|
| 1920 | $11,679,483 | $507,600 | $24,534,282 | $9,999,795 | $49,657,828 |
| 1925 | 30,202,357 | nil | 15,946,672 | 7,271,944 | 62,492,634 |
| 1930 | 35,886,532 | nil | 24,455,133 | 3,893,876 | 83,393,068 |
| 1935 | 78,133,624 | nil | 35,345,103 | 3,344,229 | 142,888,565 |
| 1940 | 125,574,988 | 1,211,305 | 59,822,591 | 2,127,831 | 234,209,927 |

SOURCES: Dominion Bureau of Statistics, *Canadian Mineral Statistics* (Ottawa, 1957), pp. 85-95; Douglas A. Mutch and Balmer Neilly, *Brief on Taxation on the Ontario Metal Mining Industry, 1907-1941* (Toronto, 1944), Vol. II, Schedules, nos. 6, 7, 8, 9, 19.

As this table indicates, iron mining ceased completely during the twenties, then resumed again with vigour during the late thirties; nickel experienced the ebb and flow of peacetime and rearmament; and silver production declined steadily with the gradual exhaustion of the Cobalt deposits. However, the fluctuations in those sectors were more than compensated for by the spectacular growth of the gold mining industry. In 1920 Ontario's gold mines employed slightly more than two thousand men and paid out $3,351,289 in wages and salaries. Twenty years later the industry provided employment for more than twenty thousand workers and distributed $36,593,337 in wages and salaries.[2] Throughout the twenties mining kept pace with the general expansion of the Ontario economy, then during the Depression it provided the solitary, gleaming exception amid the general gloom of unemployment and bankruptcy.

[2] Between 1920 and 1940 gold mining companies also declared $356,229,269 in bonuses and dividends. Mutch and Neilly, *Brief*, Vol. II, Schedule 19.

The Department of Mines, which E. C. Drury had elevated to a full portfolio in 1919, watched over this tremendous growth with paternal satisfaction. By its surrender of all property rights in minerals and the idea of mining its own precious metals, the state had effectively abandoned any activist pretensions it might have once had in this field. As we have seen, the possibility of public enterprise in mining existed up to 1910 but faded quickly after the closure of the Provincial mine until, by the 1930s, the suggestion of such an undertaking was immediately classified with other forms of socialist adventurism. When, for example, a usually extreme free enterprise spokesman for the Ontario mining industry proposed in 1931 that the provincial government undertake the exploration and development of some promising gold mining properties as an emergency public work, the Conservative Minister of Mines, Charles McCrae, dismissed the idea. The reasons he advanced might have been written in better times by the advocate of the scheme, Donald Mutch, for the Ontario Mining Association. McCrae pointed out that gold mining was too risky a proposition to warrant the hazard of public fortunes, that public enterprises were by definition wasteful and inefficient (though this must have startled old Conservatives and the public power veterans), and concluded, "Only in Russia does the Government mine gold. . . . It seems preferable, on all grounds, to leave the exploration of mineral deposits to be carried out by private enterprise. The fact is that the performance of Ontario's gold mines constitute their own best advertisement."[3] McCrae's deputy minister, Thomas Gibson, and his Liberal successor, Paul Leduc, fully shared his ideological antipathy towards active state intervention in the mining sector.[4]

Gradually, the provincial government removed itself to a more conventional regulatory role on the sidelines of the mining industry. The duties of the Department of Mines, as Charles McCrae defined them in 1926, were simply administrative and

[3] PAO, Henry Papers, Charles McCrae to Douglas A. Mutch, Sept. 23, 1931.

[4] PAO, Hepburn Papers, Paul Leduc to F. H. Barker, Oct. 5, 1936; Thomas Gibson, *Mining in Ontario* (Toronto, 1937), p. 64.

educational. It maintained a small bureaucracy to record mining claims, settle disputes, inspect the health and safety of miners, compile statistics and collect the Mining Tax. As an aid to the beloved small prospectors—McCrae called them "the pioneers of the industry"—the department conducted mining classes, geological surveys, published bulletins on mineral discoveries, and provided free essays at its regional laboratories. In short, the province merely disposed of its mineral domain to private developers in as orderly a manner as possible, maintained some basic promotion and inspection services, and gathered in its 3 per cent tithes from profitable ventures.[5]

Yet even this relatively remote association between government and the mining business could be used by the regulated industry to advance its private interests. There were two distinct types of problems in which the mining industry sought the ear of government. Firstly, there were domestic relations, such as provincial taxation of successful operations and the promotion of stagnant ones, wherein government measures had a direct bearing upon the profitability of enterprise. And secondly, there were external agencies, such as industrial unions and the federal government, that jointly threatened the Ontario mining companies and against which the miners hoped to mobilize the power of the provincial government. It was the responsibility of the Department of Mines and the cabinet to determine the public interest in these matters among competing desires. But both Liberal and Conservative governments seemed to place inordinate and unwarranted confidence in the counsel of their mining clients.

The domestic issue of reviving a dormant iron mining industry arose shortly after the war when the Lake Superior Steel Corporation closed its Algoma iron mines in favour of American sources of supply. This action brought iron mining in Ontario, and for that matter in all of Canada, to a complete standstill. Thus, while Ontario led the dominion in iron and

[5] PAO, Ferguson Papers, Speech by Charles McCrae, April 7, 1926; see also Thomas Gibson, *The Mining Laws of Ontario* (Toronto, 1933), Part II, for the functions of the Department of Mines and its administrative subdivisions.

steel production and contained its largest iron reserves, the province imported 100 per cent of its ore requirements from the United States. Following a conference of government officials and representatives of the metal industries, the Drury government appointed a Select Committee of the Legislature in 1922 to study this paradoxical situation and bring down some recommendations to correct it. With commendable speed the Select Committee reported that Ontario did possess sufficient iron ore to satisfy its own needs, and secondly, that the technology existed to render these low-grade, refractory ores commercially useable. To bring about this desired goal of self-sufficiency the Select Committee recommended that the Department of Mines undertake thorough studies of the known iron deposits, that it hire a fully competent mining engineer to examine the most suitable methods of beneficating those ores, and finally, the committee proposed a bounty of one cent per unit or iron produced from Ontario ore.

The chairman, Lloyd Harris, anticipated criticism of his recommended bonus by referring to the "devious ways" that assistance was being extended to almost every industry from farming through manufacturing, then added:

> Without attempting, then, to cloak our recommendation in the habit of some paternalistic experiment of questionable value [an egregious aside directed at Adam Beck], we have bluntly and directly advocated a bonus, because assistance will be available to all who produce and actually market iron ore from Ontario deposits, and at no time will the province be involved in unsuccessful development.[6]

Subsequently the Ferguson government established a bonus of one-half a cent for each unit (1 per cent) of iron contained in iron ore mined in Ontario, fully expecting that the federal government, in view of the national importance of the industry,

---

[6] *Report of the Ontario Iron Ore Committee, 1923* (Toronto, 1923), pp. 9-10; see pages 16-19 for report and recommendations of the conference that preceded the appointment of the Select Committee; see also Gibson, *The Mining Laws of Ontario*, pp. 65-9.

could be induced to make up the difference. However, the federal government declined the invitation and six years later the province assumed complete responsibility for the bounty recommended by the Select Committee. But the burden shouldered by the Ontario government was of no importance since neither the one-half cent offered in 1924 nor the full cent extended in 1930 produced the expected result.[7]

It was entirely fitting that Sir James Dunn's Algoma Steel Company—itself reorganized in Dunn's favour with the aid of the provincial government—should revive the iron mining business. Dunn and his associates had been persuaded by F. H. Clergue in 1907 to take over the bonded indebtedness of the company. When the steel company collapsed again in the Depression Dunn used his position as principal bondholder to take over complete control.[8] In 1936 Sir James decided to produce his own iron ore from his deposits north of Sault Ste. Marie, but he was not satisfied with the small bonus still being offered by the provincial government. Therefore, he approached his good friend the Premier of Ontario and asked him to increase the subsidy. Premier Hepburn readily admitted his total ignorance of the economics of the steel-making business but agreed to put himself in the hands "of those who have given this matter a great deal of thought and study."[9] One such expert, a mining engineer, recommended a bonus of $2.20 per ton of sinter to offset the competitive advantage of American steel companies. Another expert advocated $1.00 a ton. The

[7] PAO, Drury Papers, Special Series, Thomas Gibson to Drury, May 19, 1923; PAO, Ferguson Papers, Gibson to Ferguson, Aug. 2, 1929; PAO, Henry Papers, Charles McCrae to G. F. Horrigan, Aug. 10, 1931.

[8] On the Algoma Steel reorganization, see Lord Beaverbrook, *Courage: The Story of Sir James Dunn* (Fredericton, 1961), pp. 118-9, 137-8, 151; PAO, Hepburn Papers, Algoma Steel Corporation File, especially Hepburn to Ward Wright, Nov. 22, 1934 with Arthur Roebuck's comments, and J. A. Humphries (Deputy Attorney General) memorandum, Nov. 24, 1934; and PAC, Dunn Papers, Box 318, 319, especially Ward Wright to Dunn, Nov. 17, Nov. 29, 1934; Jan. 8, 1935; Newton Rowell to Dunn, Nov. 29, 1934, in Box 319.

[9] PAO, Hepburn Papers, Hepburn to James Curran, Feb. 10, 1937, private and confidential.

government finally agreed to double its present offer which paid Sir James about $1.04 on each long ton of ore raised.[10] Sir James Dunn in effect dictated the provincial government's policy on the iron bounty question—he even made the public announcement!

The Ontario gold mining companies appeared to have enjoyed somewhat similar control over the provincial government's taxation policy. Schedules for the Mines Profits Tax had remained substantially unchanged since they had been established in 1907. On profits over $10,000 and up to $1 million the province exacted a 3 per cent toll, and 5 per cent on profits in excess of $1 million. While the Conservative governments in power between 1923 and 1934 did raise the ceiling to 6 per cent on profits over $5 million, for the most part they expressed satisfaction with the contention of Ontario mining companies that they were paying enough taxes. Yet the Mines Profits Tax, while it was a tax in form, was not a tax in essence. Ontario governments had traditionally regarded mining as a special industry drawing upon the public domain (which, for essentially financial reasons, had to be entrusted to private hands), but doing so on the condition that it return a substantial portion of that natural wealth to the public treasury. For this

---

[10] *Ibid.*, D. H. McDougall memorandum, Mar. 3, 1937; James Curran to Hepburn, Feb. 13, 1937. Throughout these negotiations Sir James fed the Premier with evidence that federal discrimination existed against Ontario in favour of Maritime steel products through coal bounties, railroad subsidies and unbalanced freight rates. Sir James was understandably elated to report in 1939 that despite these biases in federal policy and with Ontario help he had been able to bid on an important international rail contract. "I think it is pretty good for our organization at Algoma right in the heart of the country," he wrote to Hepburn on May 26, 1939, "that they can pay their way to the seaboard and fight for and get as good a place in world markets as Dominion Steel which as you know lives by Ottawa subsidies. Ottawa must either stop paying the carriage on Dominion Steel & Coal products into Central Canadian markets or equalize matters for Algoma by giving corresponding subsidies to carry our goods to the seaboard so that we can get into world markets in fair competition with Dominion Steel. *It must be more important for Canada that Ontario industry reaches world markets than that Nova Scotia industry reaches Ontario markets.*"

reason the mining industry could not be compared to other industries for taxation purposes. Yet over time the word tax came to be taken literally and the schedules acquired a permanence that had never been intended.

On his return from an international mining conference in 1930, Thomas Gibson, the Deputy Minister of Mines, confidentially informed his Minister that Ontario mining taxes were amongst the lowest in the world. Gibson compared Canada with South Africa—a large gold-producing country, politically, if not culturally, akin to Canada—and reported that gold mines in that country paid taxes amounting to 35 per cent on profits. On an ounce of gold South African taxes came to $2.15, while in Ontario federal and provincial levies combined worked out to only $0.526. It is not surprising that Gibson's superior, Charles McCrae, marked the document "Not to be printed."[11]

McCrae, who held the Mines portfolio in both the Ferguson and Henry governments, considered that Ontario mines taxes were high enough, an argument for which he drew heavily upon reasoning and rhetoric supplied by the Ontario Mining Association. "Our goose is laying the golden eggs just now for Ontario and Canada," he explained to Premier Henry in 1933, "and we have [been] wise in not increasing taxation. The more the mines make the more we make, the more people are employed and the sounder is our commercial structure."[12] Could an industry ask for a better advocate as its minister of the crown? The Hepburn administration which followed not only agreed with this exceedingly generous view of the domestic provincial taxation issue, but it also undertook an energetic defence of its hard-pressed mining industry against external aggression from the federal government.

The mining industry, particularly the gold mining industry, felt itself trapped by politicians. Government fixed the price of gold and government controlled profits with taxes. Since taxes and wages were the two most significant production costs,

[11] PAO, Ferguson Papers, Thomas Gibson to Charles McCrae, Aug. 29, 1930, confidential, not to be printed.
[12] PAO, Henry Papers, McCrae to George S. Henry, Dec. 6, 1933.

and since in the case of gold, increases in these two costs could not be passed on to the consumer, inflation on either account necessarily reduced profits. For this reason the mining industry took special exception to interference in its affairs by governments and trade unions.[13]

An ardent individualism provided intellectual reinforcement for the industry's economic resentment of government intervention. The industrial symbol was the solitary prospector who made his way upward in the world through sheer wit and pluck without assistance from any quarter. That the symbol did not correspond to a reality of financial intrigue and technological intricacy attested not so much to its irrationality as to its strength and the psychological need it fulfilled. Events in an enormous game of international Monopoly had made these men suddenly rich beyond ordinary comprehension. For some, an extreme individualistic ideology performed the psychological function of legitimizing windfalls or fortunes gulled from their fellow men. Whatever the hidden psychological reasons, it seems clear that much of the doctrinaire laissez-faire outlook of the mining industry was grounded in the strident self-confidence and individualism that universally accompanied the growth of the industry.[14]

To the confidence of new wealth was added the arrogance of success amid widespread failure. When everything else had collapsed, mines continued to be, in the words of J. P. Bickell, president of McIntyre-Porcupine, "The Hinges of Prosperity." As the price of gold rose the mines were the scene of furious activity; thousands of new hands were taken on and the northern economy prospered. Yet elsewhere, in the cities and on

---

[13] On the connection between the mining barons and Hepburn's changing attitude towards unionism, see William McAndrew, "Gold Mining, Trade Unions and Politics: Ontario, the 1930's" (unpublished research paper, U.B.C., 1969), pp. 16-32; Felix Lazarus, "The Oshawa Strike," *Canadian Forum*, June, 1937; I. M. Abella, *Nationalism, Communism and Canadian Labour* (Toronto, 1973), pp. 5-6, 12-4, 19.

[14] For a development of this theme in British Columbia, see Paul Vincent Hogan, "The Myth of the Prospector in Industrial Society" (fourth year honours essay, U.B.C., 1970).

the farms, machinery stood idle and thousands were unemployed. As a consequence apologists for the industry made
all manner of self-assured claims for the miner: among others,
that he maintained the nation's credit at a critical time, that
he offered an example for all industry to follow, and that his
spirit promised hope and showed the way towards an end to
the Depression. Mining men were the leading advocates of non-
partisan political leadership to reduce government spending,
pare the public debt and debt producing social services, and
restore public confidence.[15] Some, like W. H. Wright and
George McCullagh, bought newspapers or founded movements
to publicize their views and protect their interests. Others,
like J. P. Bickell and Harry Oakes, made headlines of their
own with their airplanes, fast cars and faster company. In a
literal sense they were frontiersmen; certainly their personal
habits and the values they espoused were of the frontier.
Although restatement of these values revived old memories and
stirred a certain popular response, the old frontier virtues
seemed somehow inappropriate to the needs of a depressed
urban, industrial society.

Above all, men such as these resented government, likening
it to a great leech which sucked at the vitals of business with
its taxes and burdened initiative with a crushing mass of regulations. "Enterprise is dependent upon the expectation of profit,"
J. P. Bickell needlessly reminded the members of the Toronto
Stock Exhange in 1938: "When the state by taxation, or labour
by inordinate demands for wages, destroys the expectation of
profit, then enterprise withers and eventually dies . . . even a
strong hinge may be ruined by undue strain." At the prospect
of any new levy, Douglas Mutch and the Ontario Mining

---

[15] PAO, Hepburn Papers, J. P. Bickell, Speech to the Toronto Stock Exchange,
reprinted in its *Bulletin*, Vol. V, Aug. 2, 1938. For the most organized
presentation of this group's views on the importance of gold mining, and
secondly, on its general social and political outlook, see the work of
W. H. Moore, especially *Yellow Metal* (Toronto, 1934), and *The Definite
National Purpose* (Toronto, 1933), a scathing attack on economic planning,
Bolshevism in all its forms (trade unions included), incompetent politicians,
public ownership and the mountainous public debt.

Association raised the alarm. Improvident governments would, the spokesmen for the mining industry argued, retard and ultimately cripple their only thriving industry. In other matters the mine operators resisted the imposition of industrial standards of hours and conditions of work "on the outskirts of settled country." Mining promoters condemned securities regulation in the strongest possible terms, repeating ad nauseam the argument that strict inspection would "eventually kill prospecting." "We want the right to make our own deals, how, when and where we wish," the Ontario Prospectors and Developers Association demanded; "there is too much government in business now." Another promoter, echoing this same theme commented bitterly: "Governments had not yet apparently recognized that the finding of mines is a precarious, arduous and uncertain task, and gambling or pioneer spirit must be allowed its sway without undue regulation and unfair taxation if the vast undeveloped parts of Canada are to be made productive."[16]

For the most part, though, the mining men found that they could live quite comfortably with the provincial government; its taxes were low and it was usually controlled by easily influenced kindred spirits like Howard Ferguson, Charles McCrae, and Mitchell Hepburn. The most annoying and painful interference suffered by the mining community in what it considered to be its private, provincial affairs came from the federal government, and against this mutual enemy the miners called upon the provincial government to help with the defence. The Liberal government after 1934 was every bit as reliable as the Conservative governments that preceded it from a mining point of view. Mitchell Hepburn enjoyed the companionship of these mining men. He hunted, fished, flew and holidayed with them;

[16] Bickell, Speech to the Toronto Stock Exchange: Douglas Mutch and Balmer Neilly, *Brief on Taxation* to the Royal Commission on Gold Mining, 1943; see also, PAO, Hepburn Papers, letter from the general managers of INCO, Hollinger, Dome, Wright-Hargreaves and Lake Shore mines to Hepburn, Feb. 16, 1935, private, protesting the extension of the Industrial Standards Act; Ontario Prospectors and Developers Association brief to the provincial cabinet, April 3, 1941.

they were his regular cronies at the King Edward in Toronto, and he liked to invite them down to the farm for special occasions. As a modest plunger in mining stock himself, Mitch was beholden to his friends for more than fellowship, and they were generous supporters of the party.[17] In short, Hepburn fully shared the values and esprit of the mining milieu. From the point of view of his friends he could be counted upon to protect their interests.

Hepburn heaped praise upon the mining industry in his first year-end review. The gold mines, he pointed out, were doing more than their part in maintaining the credit of the province in the Depression. What was more, he noted in words that might have been supplied by the Ontario Mining Association, "There is a will-to-win spirit among the men searching for and developing new finds in the hinterland." However, Hepburn's support of the mining industry was more than rhetorical. He led the assault upon federal mining taxes. At the 1935 dominion-provincial conference Hepburn repeatedly demanded the immediate removal of the federal bullion tax. In this, of course, he had the full support of the mining community. Failing complete abolition, Hepburn pressed for increases in the depletion allowances granted mining companies and the transfer of 50 per cent of the federal taxes thus collected to the provinces. At a news conference after these abortive sessions with Mackenzie King and his advisors, Hepburn expanded upon the Ontario position:

> The Delegation from Ontario suggested first of all that the Dominion Government should withdraw entirely from the field of mining taxation. We pointed out that mines are exhaustible natural resources belonging to the Province, and that every dollar taken away by taxation from these mines is so much taken away from the capital of the Province.

---

[17] Neil McKenty, *Mitch Hepburn* (Toronto, 1967), p. 73. In 1935, according to McKenty, Bickell contributed $8,000, Dunn $10,000, and Sell 'Em Ben Smith $5,000 to the Liberal war-chest. For an approach to the ideology of this group, see Brian Young, "C. George McCullagh and the Leadership League," reprinted in G. R. Cook, ed., *The Politics of Discontent* (Toronto, 1967), pp. 77-102.

He maintained that over the past twenty-five years the provincial government had invested more than $100 million in roads, railroads, hydro-electric generating stations and other services in the mining districts and had itself collected only $12,200,000 during that period in return. "On the other hand the Federal Government, which has contributed nothing towards the developing of the mineral resources of Northern Ontario, collects from the very same mines yearly the sum of approximately $6,600,000. Is it fair," he asked, "for the Dominion to collect most of the taxes and to leave the Province of Ontario to bear the burden of all the expenditures?" In that same press conference Hepburn also let it be known that under provincial control alone the miners would enjoy much lower taxes: "It was never our intention to exact from them [the gold mines] the same amount that they are now paying to the Federal Government." All taxpayers should have such friends.[18]

Thereafter the Premier of Ontario reacted with characteristic petulance whenever the federal government modified any of the taxes pertaining to the mining industry. For example, a large proportion of the provincial brief laid before the Rowell-Sirois Commission studying dominion-provincial relations constituted an indictment of federal invasions of provincial tax fields. This brief, written in consultation with good friends of the mining industry, pointed out that the federal government had not only intruded upon revenue sources which had been specifically allocated to the provinces, but it also carried off the lion's share—79.2 per cent in the case of mining taxes in 1936. In the public interest, and more directly in the particular interest of the

[18] PAO, Hepburn Papers, press statement, 1934; for details of the bullion tax dispute, see Paul Leduc to Hepburn, Mar. 29, 1935 and Dec. 18, 1937; press statement, 1935; Toronto *Daily Star*, Nov. 5, 1934; Toronto *Globe*, April 26, 1935; dominion-provincial conference, 1935, *Record of Proceedings* (Ottawa, 1935), pp. 32-3; Christopher Armstrong, "The Politics of Federalism: Ontario's Relations with the Federal Government, 1896-1941" (unpublished Ph.D. thesis, University of Toronto, 1972), chapter 11, Ontario and the Reform of Canadian Federalism, pp. 522-606.

[19] PAO, Hepburn Papers, Chester Walters to H. J. Chater, Mar. 30, 1938. Chester Walters, presumably under instructions from his Premier, instructed H. J. Chater of the Treasury Department to gather statistics for the preparation of the Ontario brief to the Royal Commission. The first item on that list asked for data showing: "The Provisions of the British

mining community, Ontario called upon the federal government to respect the original spirit of Confederation by vacating
the field of natural resource taxation.[19]

The point here is not that the mining community instigated
the famous breach between the federal and provincial government during the late thirties; instead it is to be observed
how the doctrine of provincial rights directly served the interests
of the miners. Ultimately it is probably impossible to determine
the degree to which J. P. Bickell, James Dunn and the friends
of mining in the province, such as W. H. Moore, Frank
O'Connor and Arthur Slaght, influenced the Premier. How
much credit should Sir James Dunn and people like him, who
lived by provincial subsidies and aid, be given for the government's attitude towards federalism, for example? The
evidence is by no means conclusive. One can only note that
Hepburn shared the same world of robust and roistering stock
promoters and mining barons, that his circle of friends seemed
to be drawn mainly from this group of men with very particular
interests in the Ontario economy. From the Premier's friendships and the beneficiaries of his policies one can, and others
did, however, draw inferences.[20]

---

North America Act with respect to direct taxation and the natural resources
of the country belonging wholly to the Provinces." Walters went on with
a number of specific requests and concluded: "Show the part that Ontario
has played in building up Canada, and demonstrate, if possible, that, with
our share of the national income and with the financial burdens that
we have undertaken, the taxpaying capacity of the people of Ontario has
been burdened almost to its limit." W. H. Moore was a guiding spirit
in the preparation of the Ontario brief; see McKenty, *Mitch Hepburn*, pp.
158-9, and PAO, Hepburn Papers, Hepburn to Maurice Duplessis, Feb.
14, 1938, personal and confidential. For Ontario's argument for "a more
strict recognition of its clearly established legal and moral rights in the
field of direct taxation and natural resources," see the *Statement by the
Government of Ontario to the Royal Commission on Dominion-Provincial Relations*
(April, 1938), Book II, pp. 22, 34-5, 49-50, 53, 59, 60-1, 78-86, and Gordon
Conant's argument, in *Hearings*, Vol. V, pp. 7945 ff., University of Toronto
Library.

20  For the Premier's intimacy with the mining men, see PAO, Hepburn Papers,
Dunn to Hepburn, June 9, 1938, personal; Hepburn to Dunn, Oct. 12,
1938; Chrostophorides (Dunn's secretary and future wife) to Hepburn,
Nov. 4, 1938; Dunn to Hepburn, Nov. 4, 1938, personal, and Dunn to
Hepburn, May 26, 1939, personal; McKenty, *Mitch Hepburn*, pp. 68-75,
86-7, 163, 179, 183, 221-2.

At the time there was a great deal of public speculation that Hepburn's presentation to the Rowell-Sirois Commission resembled a brief for the Ontario mining industry more than a submission from the people of the province. In a rare display of unanimity both the Toronto *Daily Star* and the *Globe and Mail* condemned the tone and substance of his brief as unrepresentative of the province as a whole. The *Financial Times*, the *Financial Post*, and the *Canadian Mining Journal* questioned both the theory of federalism and the particularism of the Ontario statement.[21] *Saturday Night* saw the hand of Hepburn's notorious mining associates and disapproved wholeheartedly:

> It would be better if the Ontario mining industry, or that part of it which feels itself aggrieved by an item of new Dominion legislation, would do its own protesting upon its own responsibility rather than enlist the services of the Premier of Ontario to make the protest for it. . . . We do not think this brief correctly represents the feelings of even the majority, to say nothing of the totality of the population of Ontario.

The *Canadian Forum* spoke out with equal disdain of the "stand patism" of Ontario as illustrated by the Ontario brief:

> Mr. Hepburn, when he stood so strongly for "provincial rights," was not speaking for all the people of Ontario but only for that portion of them who have their offices in the neighbourhood of King and Bay Streets.

In its view the interests of the miners and lumber barons had once more trodden upon the larger interests of the province and the dominion.[22]

---

[21] Toronto *Daily Star*, May 2, 3, 4, 1938; *Globe and Mail*, May 4, 1938; *Financial Post*, May 7, 1938; *Canadian Mining Journal*, Sept., 1938.

[22] *Saturday Night*, May 7, 1938; "Merrily We Rowell Along," *Canadian Forum*, June, 1938. The same issue carried this memorable bit of doggerel by "A Cynic":
> The politics of Billy King
> Make honest blood to boil.
> His omissions are staggering
> His Commissions are Royal.

Plainly many observers considered that the preoccupations
of the few had been magnified into the concerns of the many.
How much of that "self-winding, self-sufficiency" reflected in
the Ontario attitude towards constitutional reform, so
eloquently despised by J. B. McGeachy and the Winnipeg *Free
Press*, could be traced back to the Premier's jovial mining
associates?[23] An industry which contributed so much to the
making of the Ontario interest no doubt had a hand in creating
its contented "milch cow" image as well. During a period of
severe social dislocation and a crisis of public finance the mining
industry could rely upon political patronage for assistance and
protection; to that extent the province of Ontario had lost its
responsible government "in the subtle social sense."

## II

Inevitably, the government of Ontario, as the largest
shareholder in the pulp and paper industry, had to bear the
brunt of its collapse. Government, which had loaned its
pulpwood so liberally to help finance the expansion of the industry during the early twenties, necessarily shared some of the
responsibility for its subsequent bankruptcy. Certainly it suffered along with the other shareholders who had risked their
capital. A province which had placed so much trust in the
promises of management unavoidably endured the consequences of management's misjudgment. The failure of the pulp
and paper industry revealed among other things that there
were two sides to a shareholder's role. In difficult times government, just like the other shareholders, had to forego its
anticipated dividends and throw its weight behind management
in an effort to stabilize prices and control output and, in the
event of total collapse, to help with the reconstruction.

Stimulated by a strong demand for newsprint and steadily
rising prices, the Canadian pulp and paper industry
experienced a period of unprecedented growth immediately

[23] Winnipeg, *Free Press*, May 4, 5, 1938.

after the war. Between 1919 and 1928 investment in the industry increased by 375 per cent and its output rose by 220 per cent. The bullish markets of the twenties provided an eager market for pulp and paper securities; investment bankers floated new companies and refinanced old ones and governments readily donated the necessary pulpwood to keep the speculative wheels turning. By the end of the decade pulp and paper ranked as Canada's leading manufacturing industry in terms of capital invested, labour employed and export value. However, in this headlong expansion productive capacity rapidly outstripped demand. Over-capacity led to a swift decline in prices. On an index of 1926=100, the contract price for a ton of newsprint slipped to 98 in 1928 and 85 in 1930. With the onset of the general business depression the bottom fell out of prices. Although the demand for newsprint remained remarkably stable throughout this period, the price index plunged to a low of 54 in 1934. A ton of newsprint which had sold at a high of $137 in 1921 brought only $57 in 1931 and only $40 at its low point in 1934.

This drastic collapse of prices provoked a major crisis within the industry. It had financed its costly expansion program largely through the sale of bonds whose retirement had been calculated on production at close to 100 per cent capacity. Falling prices and production cutbacks necessarily impaired the ability of the pulp and paper industry to meet the heavy fixed interest on its bonded debt. At 100 per cent of capacity, debt charges amounted to approximately $8.10 per ton for the most efficient manufacturers, and the cost of servicing this debt rose in proportion to reductions in output and price. The rigid capital structure of the industry thrust the burden of reducing costs to meet these interest payments upon the workers and the government, the two most easily manipulated cost components. Cutbacks and mill closures created serious unemployment problems, particularly in the one-company northern towns. The government for its part agreed to lower stumpage dues and waive forest protection laws to help effect the necessary operating economies. Notwithstanding these emergency measures, the pulp and paper industry remained hopelessly lodged between the pincers of falling prices and rising debts. In this critical situation the landlord-tenant relationship tended to shift certain duties, usually discharged by private managers, onto the provincial government. In the crisis the cabinet became in effect an executive committee of the industry.[24]

Businessmen responded to this period of economic uncertainty with the traditional countervailing devices: mergers and cartels. Voluntary restraints could minimize but not eliminate entirely the temptation of some and the ambition of other companies that led them to reduce their prices. Naturally every company wanted to operate at as close to capacity as possible and price-cutting was the most effective method of accomplishing that goal. Profits suffered, but the bond interest could at least be met. Financially weak companies desperately searching for customers and strong companies hoping to engulf their competitors freely indulged in this practice when it suited their interest. But the collective result was disastrous; it merely accelerated the downward price spiral. Mergers reduced the number and increased the size of the production units. Nevertheless, whatever stability was gained by consolidation was lost by the fact that price competition between a few large units could be just as destructive as between many small firms. Consequently, as mergers proceeded apace the leaders of the industry strove to institute formal price-fixing agreements which usually took the form of sales cartels.

In 1927 George H. Mead organized the first such cartel, the Canadian Newsprint Company, which united the three largest sales agencies with eleven pulp and paper companies controlling about one-half of Canada's newsprint capacity. This cartel, by purchasing the entire output of its eleven mills at

---

[24] For details of the rise of the pulp and paper industry and the economics of its problems, see the Canadian Pulp and Paper Association, *Reference Tables*, pp. 23 ff.; C. P. Fell, "The Newsprint Industry," in H. A. Innis and A. F. W. Plumptre, *The Canadian Economy and its Problems* (Toronto, 1934), pp. 40-53; Eugene Forsey, "The Pulp and Paper Industry," *CJEPS*, Vol. I (1935), pp. 501-9; J. A. Guthrie, *The Newsprint Paper Industry* (Cambridge, 1941), pp. 63-75, 93-126; V. W. Bladen. *An Introduction to Political Economy* (Toronto, 1956 ed.), pp. 170-208.

a fixed price, replaced competition with co-operation. The Canadian Newsprint Company steadied prices and established production quotas for the mutual benefit of its participating members. In this manner each company was protected from cut-throat competition and could be guaranteed reasonable production at reasonable prices—the most that could be expected under the circumstances. Nevertheless, several large companies refused to join the Canadian Newsprint cartel and within a year succeeded in destroying it by luring its customers away with lower prices.[25]

In the aftermath of the Canadian Newsprint Company collapse its principals approached the governments of Ontario and Quebec, urging them to persuade the independent producers to join a second cartel. William Finlayson, the Ontario Minister of Lands and Forests, reported these advances in some considerable detail to Howard Ferguson, who was vacationing in England at the time. Finlayson expressed understandable apprehension at being party to a price-fixing combination, but at the same time he thought it important that the government should throw its support behind the effort. Perhaps, he suggested, a meeting of the manufacturers, their banks and bond houses might be arranged. The two provincial governments could let it be known that they expected the representatives of industry to work out some satisfactory solution. "I thought that by doing this," Finlayson reported, "we might bring a little pressure to bear on them and get the outlaws to come in, and would at the same time not be a party to the arrangement." Although Premier Taschereau agreed to participate in such a conference, he refused to consider taking any "drastic measures" to "make more reasonable some of the '*independents*.'" He thought that the mere existence of a united front on the part of the two governments behind the second cartel would produce the desired result. After conferring with some of the Ontario paper men on his return, Ferguson reluctantly agreed to assist them. "I do not think we should allow some of these people to make use of the provincial

[25] For details, see Guthrie, *The Newsprint Paper Industry*, pp. 95-6; Forsey, "The Pulp and Paper Industry," pp. 504-5.

authority to pull their chestnuts out of the fire," he replied to his Quebec counterpart; nevertheless he recognized the importance of some kind of government leadership. Thus, with the official encouragement of the premiers of Ontario and Quebec, negotiations commenced in November 1928 towards the formation of a comprehensive price-fixing cartel.[26]

To strengthen the hand of those within the industry who were advocating a cartel as a solution to the problem, Howard Ferguson dispatched a blistering letter to Ontario's thirteen company presidents reminding them of their responsibilities to the community and their legal position *vis à vis* the state. As a matter of policy, he pointed out, the government of Ontario had distributed its pulpwood resources in such a way as to facilitate the creation of large, financially strong production units. Larger companies, the government reasoned, would be better equipped to endure the ups and downs of the business cycle and would, therefore, provide a measure of economic security to the northern towns which were almost entirely dependent upon the forest products industry. Yet despite such extremely favourable consideration from the state, the industry seemed to be bent upon its own destruction. Not even "the good sense of the people in charge of the great industry," the Premier regretted, had been able to stabilize conditions. Instead, he observed, "Methods have been pursued that have created what appears to be a situation of chaos." No government could allow such irresponsible behaviour which had already cast thousands of men out of work to continue. Ferguson reminded the executives that their legal obligations to the province, which had been set out in great detail in their pulpwood agreements, took precedence over all other considerations. The time had come, he suggested, to use this leverage to induce a steadying, rational influence into the industry's deliberations:

It is with great regret that the Government finds it necessary to draw your attention to the fact that you are under contract with this Province; that your contract contains a number of

[26] PAO, Ferguson Papers, Finlayson to Ferguson, July 19 and Aug. 3, 1928; L. A. Taschereau to Ferguson, Aug. 20, 1928; Ferguson to Taschereau, Aug. 28, 1928.

important convenants; that many of the companies are in arrears
and default had occurred with respect to a number of the conditions and obligations provided in the contracts.

This condition cannot be allowed to continue. I am, therefore,
writing you on behalf of the Government to say that unless the
people interested in the operation of this industry take some
steps to put the industry on a more satisfactory basis and improve
the present situation, the Government will be compelled to give
serious and immediate consideration to what action it should
take under existing contracts to protect the interests of this
Province, its investors, its settlers, its wage-earners, and its people
generally.

What "immediate action," the Premier wanted to know, was
being contemplated by the individual firms to meet the
industry's collective crisis?[27] Ferguson virtually ordered the
newsprint companies to co-operate in this round of price fixing
talks, or face unspecified retaliation for breach of contract.

Without doubt Ferguson's tough statement and the similar
strong language from the Premier of Quebec helped to create
the atmosphere of co-operation that prevailed in Montreal at
the end of the month when twenty-one newsprint manufacturers agreed to form a second cartel, the Canadian
Newsprint Institute. Although this body was not incorporated
as its predecessor had been, it performed identical functions.
Members agreed to co-operate and produce at under-capacity
ratings established by the institute. This central agency would
then match supply with demand and distribute tonnage among
its members according to their rated capacities. In addition
to stablilizing prices in this way the Canadian Newsprint
Institute maintained a watching brief over the entire industry
and kept both provincial governments informed of the conduct
of members and non-members alike. Only two important east-

---

[27] *Ibid*., Ferguson to Great Lakes, Abitibi, Fort Frances, Fort William, Kenora,
Spanish River, Provincial, Lake Superior, Dryden, Beaver Wood Fibre,
Abitibi Wood Fibre, Spruce Falls and Nipigon pulp and paper companies,
Nov. 19, 1928. For pained and largely inconsequential replies, see J. H.
Black to Ferguson, Nov. 20; J. S. Wilson to Ferguson, Nov. 24; E. A.
Wallberg to Ferguson, Nov. 26; F. S. Duncan to Ferguson, Dec. 4, 1928.

ern newsprint manufacturers, International Paper and Spruce Falls, resisted government pressure to join the institute.[28]

Formation of the Canadian Newsprint Institute in November 1928 represented only a tentative, far from unanimous settlement of industrial differences; it was a truce, not a permanent peace. Those within the organization could not trust each other, let alone the mavericks outside. Despite a great deal of suspicion, bickering, and dissension from the membership, the institute did succeed in stabilizing the price of newsprint—on one occasion it even won a temporary increase—and it did bind most of the industry into a hopeful, albeit reluctant, alliance.

Then in 1930 the market broke and the delicate Canadian Newsprint Institute disintegrated almost immediately. As the price of newsprint plunged relentlessly downward, driven by the Depression, by the desperation of some companies, and by the aggressive competitiveness of International Paper, over one-half of Canada's newsprint manufacturing capacity passed into receivership or underwent drastic financial reorganization. In Ontario the huge Abitibi and Backus-Brooks empires were the first to fall. Pulp mills at Espanola, Sturgeon Falls and Fort William closed down completely and other newer, more efficient mills operated at less than half capacity with only skeleton crews. Once again vicious price competition hobbled efforts directed

---

[28] International Paper, under the direction of A. R. Graustein, was in the midst of an aggressive program of expansion into Canada from its New England base. It stood to gain from the existing dislocation. The Spruce Falls Pulp and Paper Company, jointly owned by the *New York Times* and Kimberly-Clark, argued that the Sherman Anti-Trust Act prevented it from entering any formal price-fixing combination, but it volunteered nevertheless to prorate its output in accordance with institute policy. See PAO, Ferguson Papers, Rules and Regulations for the Conduct of the Newsprint Industry accepted by Twenty-one Manufacturers; A. R. Graustein to Ferguson, Dec. 11, 1928, telegram; Ferguson to Graustein, Dec. 12, 1928, telegram; Ferguson to Taschereau, Dec. 13, 1938; Ferguson to J. H. Black, May 6, 1929; Black to Ferguson, Jan. 9, 1930, private and confidential; P. B. Wilson (of the Newsprint Institute) to Ferguson, May 10, 1930, private and confidential; Black to Ferguson, Sept. 9, 1930, private and confidential; George Barber to Ferguson, Sept. 11, 1930, personal.

towards stabilizing the situation. Special deals, secret stock options, and kickbacks offered to purchasers as inducements to buy forced the real price for a ton of newsprint well below the quoted price. The disaster that had long been feared was now upon the industry.[29]

With so many firms in receivership, initiative passed to the bondholders and banks. In 1931 a Bankers' Committee was formed, consisting of E. W. Beatty, Sir Charles Gordon, M. W. Wilson, and G. F. Cottrelle, to bring about some small measure of co-operation between producers and consolidate the floundering companies into stronger units. But after a year of negotiations marked by much bitterness and rancour, the bankers threw up their hands. M. W. Wilson, the general manager of the Royal Bank of Canada, told the Commons Committee on Banking and Commerce that the committee did bring some 80 per cent of the industry to terms, but the remaining loose fish ruined that effort with complete impunity. Sir Herbert Holt in his own blunt way blamed the industrial chaos upon the "anxiety" of provincial governments during the early twenties "to start new industries, to get more money for their timber licences and employment for their people." Since politicians had created the mess, Sir Herbert continued, prime responsibility for cleaning it up lay with them too: "The only solution . . . is for the six provinces that have paper mills to get together and agree on a quota for each mill, so that one mill cannot run at 100 or 105 per cent, while another mill is running at 25 per cent." The governments involved must intervene, Sir Herbert explained, "because those newsprint fellows have never been able to get along."[30] Most businessmen agreed; compulsion was the only answer.

[29] *Ibid.*, Taschereau to Ferguson, Dec. 28, 1929, confidential; Ferguson to Taschereau, Jan. 11, 1930, confidential; Taschereau to Ferguson, Jan. 16, 1930, confidential; Fell, "The Newsprint Industry," pp. 50-1; Guthrie, *The Newsprint Paper Industry*, pp. 108 ff.; Charles Vining, *Newsprint Prorating: An Account of Government Policy in Quebec and Ontario* (Montreal, 1940), pp. 9-10.

[30] Forsey, "The Pulp and Paper Industry," p. 505; for the testimony of Holt, Wilson and others, see House of Commons, Select Standing Committee of the House of Commons on Banking and Commerce, *Proceedings*, Mar. to June 14, 1934 (Ottawa, 1934), pp. 924-6. Under question, Sir Herbert Holt eventually conceded: ". . . a good deal of the responsibility, . . . could

In 1933 the Canadian Pulp and Paper Association petitioned the federal Minister of Trade and Commerce, but H. H. Stevens rebuffed its request for assistance. The industry should not expect the federal government to act as a "fairy godmother" during this crisis, Stevens replied. Fault for the collapse plainly lay with the provinces and the promoters, the Minister explained, and he could do nothing but hope that in the reorganization that must of necessity follow more power might be given to trained operators and scientific experts and less to promoters. Ottawa seemed anxious to avoid the appearance of interfering with provincial difficulties—it had enough of its own—and short of the moral uplift of a stern lecture it could not offer any assistance.[31]

When the collapse occurred, Howard Ferguson had departed the Ontario scene for the post of High Commissioner to London. George S. Henry, the new Premier, possessed little knowledge of the pulp and paper industry and its leading figures were strangers to him—a sharp contrast with his predecessor who knew the industry from the inside out. In the bewildering confusion of a general business depression it is not surprising that the Henry administration did not know where to begin with the newsprint industry's problems. The collapse inflicted tremendous hardship upon the workingmen and tradesmen of the north, but the horrible thought that things could get worse hindered the formulation of any firm policy of dealing with the companies. If the government cancelled the rights held by companies not fulfilling their legal obligations, as Municipal Councils, Chambers of Commerce, and Trades and Labour Councils were demanding, Henry explained on one occasion, "it would not only increase the difficulty [but also] might cause a general crash."[32] The very magnitude of the disaster temporarily immobilized the government.

---

be laid...on the businessmen whose greed or avarice or design for gain led them to embark on new ventures in the Newsprint industry."

[31] PAC, Stevens Papers, Vol. 27, draft speech, Jan. 25, 1933 and attached newspaper clippings.

[32] PAO, Henry Papers, Henry to Ferguson, Mar. 18, 1931, personal; Ferguson to Henry, April 17, 1931, private and confidential; Ferguson to Henry, Dec. 24, 1932, private and confidential; J. F. Milne, city clerk, Port Arthur, to Henry, Jan. 30, 1931.

From London Howard Ferguson urged premiers Henry and Taschereau to put an end to what he called the "selfish tragic policy" being pursued by the pulp and paper companies. "I have not heard if you have taken any action to repossess yourself of the rights under your agreements and power losses," he wrote to George S. Henry late in 1932, "but I have talked to a great many people in Canada while there amongst the bankers and investors, and they all agree that drastic action must be taken to bring these people together." Industrial anarchy must be halted forthwith, he warned: ". . .if it is allowed to drift much longer paper will go to a price under this cutthroat policy from which it will take many years to recover. In the meantime, the credit of the Province, and its industries as investment opportunities, will be grievously injured." The two premiers did meet several times over the course of the next two years, but neither Taschereau nor Henry could recommend with any degree of confidence a decisive course of action. "We considered the notification of these Companies that are in default," Henry reported to Ferguson after one such conference, "but felt for the moment that the time was not opportune." Neither government was prepared to risk criticism from Canadian and American publishers that would inevitably be stirred up by any government action aimed at raising the price of newsprint. Taschereau and Henry reluctantly continued their policy of lecturing the industry on its responsibilities, a singularly vain and thankless task. The industry had become so impervious to reason that even those companies in the receivership of respected financial institutions refused to behave with honour.[33] As long as A. R. Graustein of International Paper retained the initiative as price leader and as long as fainthearted politicians could find excuses to delay the obvious, the newsprint situation could not be brought under control. But Graustein had bankers to satisfy too, and there were limits to the tolerance of Canadian governments.

Continued delinquency on the part of several Quebec newsprint manufacturers and the Ontario general election injected

[33] *Ibid.*, Ferguson to Henry, Dec. 24, 1932, private and confidential; Henry to Ferguson, Jan. 9, 1933.

a sudden sense of urgency into government-industry relations. During the 1934 campaign Mitchell Hepburn bitterly castigated Conservative mismanagement of the provincial forest resources. The government seemed content, he charged, to allow monopolists to hold vast areas of public timber in idleness while thousands of workmen and their families suffered unimaginable deprivation. Hepburn pledged that a Liberal government would undo George S. Henry's "gross betrayal of the public trust"; it would revive the forest industries, restore forest revenues, and "put the men back to work."[34] Fulfillment of sweeping promises such as these would obviously depend upon the introduction of tough legislation and the energetic use of existing executive powers.

The election gave Ontario impulsive new leadership with a broad mandate to act. At about the same time the government of Quebec demonstrated the kind of action that might be taken. When several newsprint companies announced lower prices for 1935, Premier Taschereau reacted angrily. "I have made up my mind," he declared on January 7, "that it is about useless to negotiate further with the newsprint companies. . . . Legislation is necessary and it is our intention to take such means as we may think proper to save this basic industry of Canada." The result was a powerful new Forest Resources Regulation Act which conferred upon cabinet full authority to impose heavy penalties upon any company using the public forest whose policies the government might consider to be detrimental to the public interest.[35] With the lesson of the Ontario election in the back of his mind and armed with unprecedented discretionary power, Taschereau set out to settle the newsprint situation in his province once and for all.

Despite Hepburn's declared willingness to face the newsprint crisis squarely and "to co-operate as completely as possible with the Government of Quebec," his first steps as Premier seemed

---

34 *To the Electors—A Statement by Mitchell F. Hepburn* (Toronto, 1934); *The Increased Debt and Extravagant Expenditures of the Henry Government* (Toronto, 1934); Neil McKenty, "Mitchell F. Hepburn and the Ontario Election of 1934," *CHR*, Vol. XLV (1964), pp. 293 ff.

35 Vining, *Newsprint Prorating*, pp. 12, 80-1.

to suggest the opposite. In November 1934, he tried without success to shift the burden of responsibility onto an extremely wary R. B. Bennett.[36] Then the following March Ontario declined to join Quebec in bringing down concurrent legislation aimed at strengthening political control over the pulp and paper industry. A disappointed Taschereau begged Hepburn to reconsider, but he got nowhere. "I am entirely in sympathy with your desire to obviate the self-destructive activities of the newsprint producers of the Province," Hepburn responded, "but I think more can be gained through conciliation. . . ." The united front required to rein in the anarchistic businessmen had collapsed. Taschereau had to proceed with his controversial authoritarian policy alone.[37]

In the meantime the Hepburn government tried all of the conventional expedients of a new administration. In the interests of economy Hepburn purged the civil service, especially the field staff of the Department of Lands and Forests. To put the men back to work as he had promised, he lowered stumpage dues and redistributed idle timber limits (without competition or manufacturing requirements) among eager pulpwood exporters. In the crisis the province lifted its old manufacturing condition on pulpwood and once again the rafts of raw wood began to drift southward across Lake Superior to mills in the United States.[38] These measures certainly helped create new employment opportunities in the hard-hit northern towns, but they did nothing to relieve the deep-seated distress within the pulp and paper industry. Indeed, the revival of pulpwood exports to the United States in all probability marginally aggravated matters by improving the position of American

---

[36] PAO, Hepburn Papers, Hepburn to Bennett, Nov. 10, 1934, telegram; Bennett to Hepburn, Nov. 10, 1934.

[37] *Ibid.*, Taschereau to Hepburn, Mar. 12, 1935, personal; Hepburn to Taschereau, Mar. 13, 1935, private; Taschereau to Hepburn, Mar. 26, 1935, private; George Cottrelle to Hepburn, April 15 and April 25, 1935; R. O. Sweezey to Hepburn, May 1, 1935, private.

[38] *Ibid.*, Frederick Noad to Peter Heenan, Aug. 29, 1934, private and confidential; Heenan to Hepburn, Feb. 22, 1935; Department of Lands and Forests, Woods and Forests Order-in-Council Book No. 4, p. 144.

competitors. The government of Ontario did not rediscover the need for drastic measures and close interprovincial co-operation until the stronger Quebec producers began to steal large orders from several troubled Ontario companies. Then, in its own interests, Ontario renewed the alliance with Quebec.

Talks between Peter Heenan, the Ontario Minister of Lands and Forests, and Taschereau resumed early in 1936. By February they had agreed that there must be an equitable dis-tribution of newsprint tonnage between their two provinces, that the industry must remedy its own ills, and that the gov-ernments of Ontario and Quebec would enforce such a plan once it had been worked out. In March, under orders from the provinces, the newsprint manufacturers gathered in Montreal to consider the best means to stabilize production and prices. "It is not for the Government to suggest the method. This must be found by the manufacturers themselves," Premier Taschereau instructed the committee that organized the meet-ing. But find such a method they must, he warned: "Manufacturers should realize that the Government is now in position to make its wishes felt and we would like assurance from the manufacturers that they will proceed at once. . . ." To emphasize the point the province of Ontario suddenly reversed its policy and announced the introduction of a Forest Resources Regulation Act. This overwhelming pressure produced the desired results. The manufacturers quickly formed another cartel, the Newsprint Association of Canada, whose responsibility it would be to determine the efficient productive capacity of Canadian mills and then to prorate news-print orders among the producers according to their rated capacity.

The basic concept of newsprint proration was quite simple, the president of the Association, Charles Vining, explained to Mitchell Hepburn: " . . .if a certain manufacturer has 10 per cent of the industry's total efficient capacity, his policy would be not to manufacture or contract for more than 10% of the industry's total shipments." However, the measurement of "efficient capacity" and the adjustment of tonnage from "long" to "short" companies were much more complicated and con-tentious matters than the principle. But by June 1936 the manufacturers had overcome their many differences and accepted the ratings established by the Newsprint Association of Canada. The governments of Ontario and Quebec welcomed the action and promised their full support in policing the new policy. "In accordance with our understanding with the Government of Ontario," Taschereau declared on June 2, "we shall insist that each Quebec manufacturer accept and adhere to such percentage of total business as may be found fair in relation to his capacity. Any manufacturer who exceeds this percentage may expect to pay increased stumpage rates to a degree which will make his over-production a loss rather than a gain." Hepburn agreed to proration with enthusiasm and determination. His government would not "allow its efforts to be blocked by any manufacturer who may try to obtain a selfish advantage by destructive methods. . . ."[39]

The change of government that occurred in Quebec in August tended to reinforce rather than weaken the alliance. From the outset Mitchell Hepburn and Maurice Duplessis recognized their mutual problems and the need for co-ordinated approaches towards solving them. The newsprint situation was, of course, foremost among these joint concerns. Following a series of meetings in which the two leaders established a warm personal friendship, Hepburn and Duplessis concluded a formal Interprovincial Agreement on the newsprint question on October 17, 1937. They declared that no company in either province would be allowed to overproduce or sell below the established market price. To implement that policy the two governments in effect delegated their authority to the Newsprint Association of Canada. Its proration committee was authorized "to act as the Government's referees and arbitors." On recommendations from that committee Ontario and Quebec undertook "to penalize, without further inquiry" any newsprint

---

[39] PAO, Hepburn Papers, Heenan to Hepburn, Feb. 22, 1935; Vining to Hepburn, June 1, 1936; Vining, *Newsprint Prorating*, Heenan to Vining, Mar. 4, 1936; Taschereau to Vining, Mar. 5, 1936; Hepburn to Vining, June 8, 1936, pp. 21-8, 78-9. In actual fact Vining dictated both of the letters that appeared above the signatures of the two premiers.

manufacturer who disobeyed the instructions of the Newsprint Association officials in any manner whatsoever.[40]

These early discussions on newsprint policy, plus the many more which were to follow, provided the point of departure for an exploration of a much broader community of interest. Because the two premiers shared problems in common, and because they were so much alike in personality, political outlook, and manner, they were able to reach a meeting of minds in a number of areas. As they consulted one another on newsprint matters between 1936 and 1940, they also decided upon joint approaches towards St. Lawrence development, hydro-electric questions, federal tax programs, unemployment insurance, and constitutional reform. Hepburn and Duplessis forged their "axis" (as Ferguson and Taschereau had a decade earlier) in meetings on the newsprint question.[41]

In unity there was strength and also the confidence to use that strength. It was an easy enough matter for the provinces to agree to threaten delinquents, but another matter entirely to invoke sanctions against actual offenders. However, the security of the axis gave both premiers the confidence to deal decisively with the pulp and paper companies within their jurisdictions. The self-restraint of Ontario would not be turned to the advantage of Quebec. With that confidence, the government of Ontario intervened in the affairs of the pulp and paper industry in two ways. First, it used its authority to prevent the reorganization of bankrupt companies in a way which would injure the general interest of the industry. In 1936 it ordered certain modifications in the policy of Great Lakes Paper before

---

[40] PAO, Hepburn Papers, Hepburn to Duplessis, Aug. 26, 1936, private and confidential; Vining, *Newsprint Prorating*, Interprovincial Agreement, Oct. 17, 1936, pp. 29-32.

[41] McKenty, *Mitch Hepburn*, pp. 157-9; René Durocher, "Taschereau, Hepburn et les Relations Québec-Ontario, 1934-1936," *Revue d'histoire de l'Amerique française*, Vol. 24 (1970), pp. 344-5; Christopher Armstrong, "Ontario Faces the Nation: A Study in Provincial-Federal Relations, 1927-41" (unpublished research paper, University of Toronto, 1967), pp. 21 ff.

it would permit its sale to an American syndicate. Similarly in 1940 the Hepburn government set up a Royal Commission to recommend an appropriate procedure for the financial reorganization of the Abitibi Pulp and Paper Company which would do justice to the shareholders, bondholders, the industry at large and, finally, the government. Since it supplied the bankrupt company with pulpwood and power—its two most important assets—and since the company had long been in default of its obligations on both accounts, the government, as the largest shareholder, naturally expected some satisfaction in the reconstruction of the company.[42]

But it was as policeman to the industry's proration policy that the state exercised its most profound influence. In effect, the government of Ontario became the political arm of the Newsprint Association of Canada in matters pertaining to the production of pulp and paper in the province. On the one hand the association would not exist without state support; political authority created its membership, ensured attendance at its meetings, secured accurate production statistics from each mill, and even assisted in the collection of its membership dues. But at the same time, the governments of Ontario and Quebec received their instructions from the association. When factious member companies trespassed the production limits established by the association, it requisitioned intimidating letters from the premiers, and if the non-compliance persisted, appropriate orders-in-council would be forthcoming which would raise pulpwood dues to prohibitive levels.

[42] For the Great Lakes reorganization, see Vining, *Newsprint Prorating*, pp. 14-6, 43-7; PAO, Hepburn Papers, Heenan to Hepburn, Oct. 29, 1935; Memo on Great Lakes Reorganization; Hepburn to J. L. Ralston, Oct. 30, 1935; Vining to Hepburn, Oct. 23, 1935; For Abitibi, see Lambert and Pross, *Renewing Nature's Wealth*, p. 344; Royal Commission upon the Affairs of the Abitibi Power and Paper Company, *Report* (Toronto, 1940); V. W. Bladen, *An Introduction to Political Economy*, pp. 184-9. The Abitibi affair provides one of the few documented cases of the "walking order," an order-in-council not passed at a meeting of the cabinet, but rather circulated among the required number of ministers for signature; see PAO, Hepburn Papers, G. D. Conant to Hepburn, Oct. 9, 1941.

In 1937, for example, Great Lakes Paper refused to join the association or to abide by its directives until Premier Hepburn insisted that it participate and comply. When the same company resumed its independent, overproducing ways two years later, the Ontario government responded positively to Charles Vining's request for imposition of the penalties provided for by the Forest Resources Regulation Act. The Minnesota and Ontario Pulp and Paper Company, a bankrupt American firm with mills in Fort Frances and Kenora, also had to be coerced into the association. When it disobeyed production guidelines laid down by the industry in 1939, the Minister of Lands and Forests increased its timber dues by five times the usual amount to induce its reformation. Although the penalties were stiff and the order-in-council application somewhat arbitrary, these sanctions were quietly revoked by the same method as soon as the wayward companies demonstrated a willingness to co-operate with the Newsprint Association of Canada in the future.[43]

Such outspoken advocates of free enterprise as Maurice Duplessis and Mitchell Hepburn could not exercise such over-whelming influence in the councils of industry without feeling some anxieties. By the same token, industrialists reluctantly admitted that a dose of authority eased their pain somewhat, but they considered the medicine distasteful nonetheless. Not surprisingly, proration excited the wrath of the American Newspaper Publishers' Association, which had taken such delight and profit from the disorganization of the producers. As the Canadian pulp and paper industry brought output into line with demand, the publishers angrily threatened a boycott of Canadian newsprint and on another occasion lodged a protest with the Federal Trade Commission. Officially, Ontario and

---

[43] PAO, Hepburn Papers, J. L. Ralston to Vining, Jan. 2, 1937; C. H. Carlisle to Vining, Feb. 15, 1937; Vining to Carlisle, Feb. 22, 1937; Ralston to Hepburn, Mar. 6, 1937; Carlisle to Hepburn, May 5, 1937; Vining to Hepburn, July 9, 1937; Carlisle to Vining, July 21, 1937; Earl Rowe to "Mitch," June 6, 1939, personal and confidential; Heenan to Hepburn, Mar. 24, 1939; Vining, *Newsprint Prorating*, pp. 47-85.

Quebec remained steadfast behind the new cartel despite this criticism, but privately there were some qualms in high places.[44]

By his own admission, Hepburn was "somewhat perturbed" at the prospect of the Attorney General of the United States bringing action against an alleged newsprint combine which he himself was running. Maurice Duplessis shared that uneasiness. Thus when they met in Montreal during January of 1938, the two premiers demanded assurances from Vining that his association contravened no Canadian or American laws. Notwithstanding advice to that effect, Hepburn and Duplessis set down for the purposes of the record the formal extent of their interest in the affairs of the association. This January declaration revealed a subtle shift in the rationale of political control from emphasis upon financial and production problems of the industry to the social implications of industrial dislocation. Conservation of the forests now became—in profession if not in fact—the first concern of government followed by full employment, the protection of crown revenues, and finally the prosperity of the pulp and paper industry as a whole. "You will recall," Hepburn reminded Duplessis later, "I pointed out the possibility of such action [as that being contemplated by the American Attorney General] and indicated my desire to be completely dissociated with the industry's general activities, except as their actions directly affect employment and revenue."[45] Although the premiers modified their reasons for supporting the association—largely to protect themselves against criticism and legal action—the association continued to have their full confidence and access to their executive instruments.

Without doubt government action helped to restore confidence within the industry and to settle prices. Political compulsion kept production within reasonable limits of satisfying demand and in that manner helped to moderate vicious price competition. On the index 1926 = 100, newsprint prices rose from

[44] Guthrie, *The Newsprint Paper Industry*, pp. 99-100.

[45] PAO, Hepburn Papers, Hepburn to Duplessis, Feb. 14, 1938; Duplessis to Hepburn, Feb. 14, 1938 enclosing a memorandum on their meeting, Jan. 10-11, with Vining and Howard.

57.1 ($40) in 1935 to 71.4 ($50) in 1940. The industry that had operated at about 71 per cent of capacity during the first half of the decade produced at a rate of 79 per cent during the second half. Some of the production and price increase can be charged to strengthening of demand, but the stability that characterized adjustment to these changing conditions can be attributed to the vigorous policing of the Newsprint Association and the governments of Ontario and Quebec. As economic conditions improved and as criticism of political interference grew more pronounced, the provincial governments relaxed their control over the industry—a circumstance that Charles Vining deeply regretted in his report on proration written for the information of the new Premier of Quebec in 1940.[46] But by that time another world war had created new demands for newsprint and shifted the burden of industrial stability from the provincial to the federal level. Thus, the controversial interlude of strict government control passed almost without notice as the industry geared for war and then underwent a cycle of furious promotion and construction to meet the projected postwar surge in pulp and paper consumption.

From an industrial point of view, the proration era is gone and best forgotten—an entirely understandable reaction under the circumstances. The incident represented a suspension of normal business ethics. As the League for Social Reconstruction caustically remarked: "In practice . . . our business leaders put a good deal of government interference water into their *laissez-faire* wine."[47] Certainly the state had intervened with unprecedented force and directness into the affairs of the pulp and paper industry; but it must be noted that it did so on terms dictated by the leaders of the industry itself. Government was

---

[46] Guthrie, *The Newsprint Paper Industry*, p. 248, table 14; Canadian Pulp and Paper Association, *Reference Tables*, p. 15, table 36; p. 16, table 42; Vining, *Newsprint Prorating*, p. 91 for graph showing effectiveness of political control. I must acknowledge the helpful and informative interviews on this subject granted by Mr. J. L. Hart and Mr. Robert Fowler of the Canadian Pulp and Paper Association in 1966.

[47] Eugene Forsey, J. King Gordon, *et al.*, *Social Planning for Canada* (Toronto, 1935), p. 144.

not regulating business in the public interest, but rather it was acting as the political extension of an industrial cartel. It merely assumed that the objectives of the Newsprint Association of Canada were identical with the public interest. In the light of the well-documented destruction inflicted upon the forests as a result of both public and private neglect, there is at least reasonable doubt that the interests of the association and the general public were as close as Hepburn and Duplessis made them seem. Moreover, some men and organizations seemed to be able to count on the beneficent intervention of the state more than others; the unemployed and trade unions, for example, did not receive such openhearted consideration.[48] During the 1930s the government of Ontario became, in effect, the client of its industrial tenants. Its authority *was* freely employed, as Howard Ferguson had originally feared, to snatch the bondholders' chestnuts from the competitive fire.

Nor could the official opposition be relied upon to restore the balance. Earl Rowe stepped down as its leader only to assume the presidency of Great Lakes Paper. George Drew's attacks upon government neglect and the arbitrary provisions of the Forest Resources Regulation Act gave comfort to the Ontario producers who had begun to chafe under the harness of proration once comparatively good prices had returned. Neither the majority nor the minority reports of the Select Committee Investigation of the Department of Lands and Forests produced any serious alternatives to the existing state of government-industry relations.[49] Only the Co-operative Commonwealth Federation and the intellectuals of the *Canadian Forum* and the League for Social Reconstruction seemed capable of viewing the problem with any degree of critical independence. From a socialist viewpoint public ownership of the industry seemed a reasonable and judicious extension of the principle of public

[48] PAO, Hepburn Papers, see for example, Hepburn to Hardy, July 11, 1935, private; Senator A. C. Hardy to Hepburn, July 12, 1935, private; McKenty, *Mitch Hepburn*, pp. 90-118, for hostile attitude towards labour in the Oshawa Strike.

[49] *Journals of the Legislative Assembly*, 1940, Appendix 1, for transcript of the hearings conducted by the Select Committee and its majority and minority reports; Lambert and Pross, *Renewing Nature's Wealth*, pp. 344-53.

ownership of the resources themselves. In its attempt to legitimize the concept, the *Canadian Forum* appealed to old Conservative traditions: "Think of what a material revolution might be wrought if another Beck should emerge in some province and proceed to apply to pulp and paper or to minerals the principles which Beck applied to hydro-electric power in Ontario."[50]

In 1934 it had been possible for Sir Charles Fitzpatrick, who owned a hundred and twenty-five Abitibi bonds, to inquire of the Premier of Ontario as to the possibility of reorganizing the company. "Excuse a stranger for trespassing on your kindness," Sir Charles apologized, "but there is at least a *bond of sympathy* which unites us."[51] Overlooking for the moment the possible sinister implication of the pun, that expression does convey an important truth. The "bond of sympathy" between government and industry had never been stronger than during the thirties. Owners and managers of pulp and paper companies enjoyed the protection of the state to a degree that most other classes of society did not. The legal dependence of the industry, symbolized by the landlord-tenant relationship, encouraged that reliance on the part of the businessmen and compliance on the part of the government. Because it tended to sensitize government to the problems of management, that relationship impaired the independence of government and contributed to its social irresponsibility. During and after the war professional foresters came to power within the Department of Lands and Forests. These technocrats, in the name of businesslike forest management, gradually replaced executive with bureaucratic discretion.[52] They completed the integration

---

[50] *Social Planning for Canada*, pp. 144, 259-60; *Canadian Forum*, Oct., 1933; Gerald Caplan, "The Cooperative Commonwealth Federation in Ontario, 1932-1945: A Study of Socialist and Anti-Socialist Politics" (unpublished M.A. thesis, University of Toronto, 1961).

[51] PAO, Henry Papers, Sir Charles Fitzpatrick to Hepburn, Sept. 21, 1934, personal. Although this letter was written to Hepburn it was filed with hydro-electric correspondence in the Henry Papers.

[52] Lambert and Pross, *Renewing Nature's Wealth*, chapters 18, 19, 20; Paul Pross, "The Development of the Professions in the Public Service: The Foresters in Ontario," *Canadian Public Administration*, Vol. X (1967), pp. 376-404.

government with business thinking. But such was the state forestry and democracy in Ontario that this change represented a bold step forward.

## III

No organization had more influence over the provincial government than the publicly owned Ontario Hydro-Electric Power Commission. Unlike the mining community, it did not have to rely upon a tenuous bond of friendship with members of the executive for that influence; nor did its patronage depend upon contractual relationships with the government as was the case with the pulp and paper industry. Hydro was itself a branch of the executive with delegated responsibility in all fields pertaining to the generation and distribution of hydro-electric power within the province. Since electricity affected almost every aspect of life, that was a frame of reference capable of indefinite expansion. Therefore, on account of its importance and proximity to the political executive—its only share-holders—the Hydro-Electric Power Commission exercised a preponderant influence over the Ontario government, particularly in the definition of the Ontario interest within the federation.

The requirements of expert technical and business knowledge that justified and then established the autonomy of the commission also increased the dependence of the political executive upon the integrity and good judgment of the commission as its operations grew in magnitude and expense. For, as we have already seen, the practical independence of the commission had its limits; in the final analysis the executive branch of government had to accept responsibility for its actions. The more complex the recommendations of the commission, the more their approval became an act of faith. The very size and scientific mystery of the organization inhibited constructive, independent criticism of its decisions. Yet even public corporations are subject to the follies of error, misjudgment and deceit which usually complicate human affairs. As a result of its tempestuous history, the commission had also developed a heightened instinct for self-preservation and a tradition of forceful political activism. The vigour with which the commission attacked its detractors tended to silence all but the brave. And finally, since the commission was engaged in business pursuits, it asked for and received a veil of privacy that masked its internal affairs from public scrutiny. Thus insulated against criticism, the Ontario Hydro-Electric Power Commission possessed a degree of discretionary power unequalled by any other public agency. The judgment of the commissioners ought to have been questioned constantly, but the legislative facilities for that purpose did not exist.

Practically, then, the members of the Hydro Commission had an unusual opportunity to influence the action, for good or for ill, of the members of the executive. Yet the business of the commission affected the behaviour of the government in a much more fundamental way than that. Governments might change the personnel of the commission, and the conduct of the commissioners, in turn, might contribute to a change in government; but neither adjustment could in itself alter the demands that arose from the functions of the commission. The government of Ontario, through the Hydro-Electric Power Commission, was in the power business. It was duty-bound to provide enough power to meet a variable demand by the most inexpensive methods possible. This elementary obligation was a constant in Ontario politics. If any government acted in such a way as to contradict its business imperatives, the opinions and actions of that government would eventually have to adjust to meet those realities.

Throughout the twenties the most persistent and urgent problem facing the commission was the acquisition of enough power to meet the soaring domestic and industrial demand of southern Ontario. The Queenston generating station received the last of its turbines in 1926; its capacity could not be enlarged further without a tedious renegotiation of the complicated Boundary Waters Treaty. Thus, Ontario Hydro turned to the next most readily available sources of undeveloped power, the Ottawa and St. Lawrence rivers. But interminable jurisdictional disputes between the provinces and the dominion and diplomatic manoeuvring between Ottawa and Washington effectively removed those waterpowers from immediate consideration. Howard Ferguson's determined fight against the federal government's unilateral plans for both rivers was more than just a battle about provincial rights for its own sake. Certainly he argued from a well-worn Ontario view of Confederation; but if his case was predicated upon right, it was motivated by need—a pressing need for vast quantities of hydro-electric power.[53]

To help meet the rapidly increasing demand, the commission accelerated the pace of its acquisition program. In 1921 Hydro at last acquired the troublesome Mackenzie companies and in 1925 it assumed control of twelve small companies in central and eastern Ontario. Four years later the program concluded with the takeover of two major producers, the Madawaska Power Company in the Ottawa valley and the Dominion Power and Transmission Company situated in the Niagara peninsula. However, these purchases did little to relieve the serious over-loading of the Niagara system. As early as 1923 Sir Adam Beck was giving serious thought to the "last ditch" necessity of con-structing a coal-powered thermal generating station. Such a step might remedy the problem, but it compromised fundamental principles by renewing the dependence upon American coal. Engineers on the commission staff investigated the possibility of diversions from the Hudson Bay watershed into the Great Lakes, thus increasing the flow at Niagara. Obvi-ously these were desperate measures. The most effective and economical alternative seemed to be the purchase of additional requirements from private power companies in the province of Quebec, at least as a stopgap until work could begin on the St. Lawrence.[54]

Early in 1926 Hydro's chief engineer reported to the commis-sion that within two years the demand upon the Niagara system

[53] For a detailed treatment of this phase of the federal-provincial struggle over waterpower, see Christopher Armstrong, "The Politics of Federalism," pp. 247-401.

[54] Merrill Denison, *The People's Power* (Toronto, 1960), pp. 168-79; PAO, Hydro-Electric Power Commission Papers, Cooke Collection, F. A. Gaby to J. R. Cooke, April 20, 1935 enclosing a copy of Beck to Ferguson, Dec. 2, 1924, requesting authorization to build a steam plant; PAC, Magrath Papers, Vol. 5, Memorandum Re: Quebec Power Contracts.

would exceed its capacity by 80,000 horsepower. By 1933 he predicted that this differential would increase to 630,000 horsepower. In his report Fred Gaby conceded that the St. Lawrence could easily yield that much power, but no one could predict when power from that source would become available. Therefore Gaby recommended a twofold plan: construction of dams on the Ottawa as soon as possible, and the immediate purchase of 210,000 horsepower to overcome the imminent crisis from the Gatineau Power Company in Quebec. The commission transmitted Gaby's recommendations to the cabinet and on July 9, 1926, received the necessary authorization to enter into an agreement with the Gatineau Power Company for the purchase of 260,000 horsepower.[55] After the question of jurisdiction over interprovincial waters had been settled in favour of the provinces in 1929, the commission announced construction of a massive hydro-electric project at Chats Falls to be undertaken in co-operation with the Ottawa Power Company.

Yet Ontario's insatiable demand for electricity outstripped even these elaborate preparations. The political difficulties surrounding development of the St. Lawrence still had not been overcome; it appeared as if the commission would have to postpone indefinitely its plans in that region. There was no other choice but to buy more power from Quebec, Charles Magrath explained to the Premier: "Public ownership in the electric power field will always differ from private ownership in one main feature, that is the former must always have ample supplies of power available, and must be prepared to go further than a private corporation could be reasonably called upon to attempt in meeting a demand for power." This was the provincial equivalent to John Henry Pope's famous remark: "The day the Canadian Pacific busts, the Conservative party busts the day after." A power shortage meant political ruin. Following

---

[55] PAO, Ferguson Papers, J. R. Cooke to Ferguson, Mar. 19, 1926, personal enclosing Gaby's memorandum; PAO, Hydro-Electric Power Commission Papers, Cooke Collection, order-in-council, July 9, 1926 approving Gatineau contract; Fred Gaby, *Trends of Electrical Demands in Relation to Power Supplies* (Ottawa, 1933), and *Some Interesting Aspects of the Hydro System* (Ottawa, 1931).

Magrath's recommendations, Ferguson approved further contracts with the Beauharnois Light, Heat and Power Company,
the MacLaren-Quebec Power Company, and the Ottawa Valley
Power Company to accommodate the anticipated load that
would be added during the next decade.[56] In this connection
it must be observed that the Quebec contracts depended upon
two critical assumptions, both of which proved to be incorrect:
that the demand for electricity during the 1930s would grow
at the same rate as it had in the 1920s; and secondly, that
the commission would be able to export whatever surpluses
might occur to the United States.

The second fateful decision taken by the Hydro-Electric
Power Commission at this time dealt with expansion of its
network in northern Ontario. In 1927 Howard Ferguson had
warned Magrath against such a policy, which he regarded as
little less than a direct subsidy to mining and paper companies
that were perfectly capable of looking after their own power
requirements. A year later he was still of the same mind. "As
a matter of fact," he replied to another proposal on the subject
from Magrath, "in most cases it would simply mean that the
Government was loaning money necessary for power development to private corporations and individuals, rather than to
municipalities." In rebuttal the chairman of the Hydro-Electric
Power Commission argued that the commission should plan
and direct the rational exploitation of Ontario's northern
waterpowers right from the outset rather than permitting
private enterprise to undertake uncoordinated projects that
would only have to be taken over later at much appreciated
values. With such control the provincial government could
provide hydro-electric incentives to stimulate economic growth
in the region. By acting promptly, Magrath added, the commission would also be able to forestall an expected initiative on
the part of some large American utilities. Moreover, the Hydro
chairman concluded discreetly, "I imagine that the announcement of such a policy for northern Ontario would be
met with very considerable approval throughout the prov-

---

[56] PAO, Ferguson Papers, Magrath to Ferguson, Mar. 11, 1929, Magrath
to Ferguson, Jan. 20, 1930, confidential.

ince." Before the 1929 election Howard Ferguson had been converted. Accordingly, Hydro either purchased or built a total of six generating stations in the Nipissing-Sudbury region and another on the English River.[57]

Yet for all Magrath's concern about planning, a curious and ultimately fatal inconsistency marred the government's northern hydro-electric policy. Notwithstanding the chairman's professed belief " . . .that it is almost impossible for private and public ownership to occupy the same field," the Ferguson government authorized private development of the Abitibi Canyon site on the Abitibi River by the Ontario Power Service Corporation, a subsidiary of Abitibi Pulp and Paper. In return, the commission contracted to purchase 100,000 horsepower, to build a transmission line to carry it through the rough country between Cochrane and Sudbury, where some would be sold to the International Nickel Company and the remainder to customers on the new northern system. Unfortunately, the Depression intervened and shed a lurid light upon these otherwise unremarkable technical proceedings.[58]

The sudden downturn in the business cycle confounded the calculations upon which the Abitibi and Quebec agreements had been based. Ironically, just after the conclusion of the last of the Quebec contracts industry began to switch off its motors—30 per cent of the electric motors in Toronto stood idle in 1932—and homeowners imposed rigid economies upon their domestic consumption. But as demand suddenly contracted, the supply of power steadily increased. The Hydro engineers who had estimated an 11 per cent annual growth in service over the decade watched helplessly as the extra power they had ordered surged onto the lines and the demand failed to materialize.[59] Then the Beauharnois revelations larded this

---

[57] PAO, Ferguson Papers, Ferguson to Magrath, April 13, 1927, personal; Ferguson to Magrath, Oct. 12, 1928; Magrath to Ferguson, Aug. 29, 1928, personal; Magrath to Ferguson, Oct. 29, 1928, personal and private.

[58] *Ibid.*, Magrath to Ferguson, Oct. 29, 1928, personal and private; Denison, *The People's Power*, pp. 195-6.

[59] Gaby, *The Power Situation in Ontario*, p. 10; Alexander Brady, "The Ontario Hydro-Electric Power Commission," *CJEPS*, Vol. II (1936), pp. 340 ff.

innocent engineering miscalculation with more than a hint of scandal. Evidence uncovered by federal investigators strongly suggested that political influence may have played a part in the commission's acquisition of the Dominion and Madawaska power companies and in the signing of its contract with Beauharnois.

In addition to these difficulties, embarrassing questions arose as to what the government intended to do with the 100,000 horsepower it had agreed to purchase from the Abitibi Canyon development for which there were virtually no customers. As the Henry government struggled to explain this curious anomaly, the Ontario Power Service Company collapsed. To save the project the Hydro-Electric Power Commission bought the bankrupt property—at a discount of only 10 per cent—for $18 million, an action that only heightened the government's discomfiture. Instead of a mere contract for 100,000 horsepower, it now owned the entire company, capable of generating three times as much, for whose power a market did not exist. Then, in the midst of that transaction, the opposition discovered that the Premier and the most prominent member of the commission, Arthur Meighen, each owned a quantity of Ontario Power Service Corporation bonds! George S. Henry readily confessed to the compromising circumstances, but he passionately denied the charge that a conflict of interest had influenced his judgment or that of the commission. Purchase of the property was amply justified, he explained to the Legislature in wearying detail, on strict business principles.[60]

Whatever the truth of the matter, and it will never be known, few people were willing to believe the Premier's interpretation of the affair. In one disastrous sequence of events the secrecy under which these contracts had been negotiated, the shortsighted reluctance of bureaucrats to take the people they served into their confidence, and the fundamental inconsistency

---

[60] PAO, Hepburn Papers, G. S. Henry, "The Abitibi Canyon Power Development, Reasons for its Acquisition by the Province," speech in the Legislature, April 5, 1933; McKenty, *Mitch Hepburn*, pp. 42-5; Denison, *The People's Power*, pp. 189-209.

of northern hydro-electric policy, all returned simultaneously to haunt the politicians and officials responsible.

"I have been considering the advisability of having all these items specifically given to a Commission to report on," George S. Henry confided to Howard Ferguson in November 1931. "So far as my personal relationship is concerned," the ex-Premier volunteered in reply, "these matters are satisfactory and there is nothing to worry about." He admitted that it might be difficult for "the ordinary man" to grasp the necessity for the Abitibi contract; that demanded an appreciation of the wealth and development potential of the north country:

> The Government, through the Hydro Commission, could scarcely undertake the investment of $25,000,000 from the public Treasury on the undertaking. . . . The sound and safe way is to induce somebody to put money into it and to help the enterprise by an assurance of contracts for power. The Abitibi people were, unquestionably, the proper people to whom to entrust the work. They use a great deal of power themselves, not only for ordinary purposes, but they can adjust the load by using it under their boilers. Moreover, it gave us the opportunity of linking up Northern Ontario powers with Southern Ontario power, which, in my view, is extremely important. These power enterprises must be linked together in one great network so that variations in water supply due to seasonal conditions could be overcome as well as the oscillation in industrial operations. I think the great achievement was, not only to get the Development under way, but to hook it up with Sudbury. This eventually means the elimination of private companies up in the North Country, and will put Hydro in control of the whole situation. . . . Like every other Hydro enterprise, the cost will be high at the beginning until the consumption increases. The great thing was to get the scheme under way.

As always, Ferguson retained his abiding faith that industrial expansion would vindicate his judgment. He had once before appealed successfully to the future. "So far as Beauharnois is concerned," he added, "you know the story. I never had anything to do with Aird in the remotest way, nor indeed with Sweezey, except to be present in Montreal when the contract was finally consummated."[61] As for the Madawaska and

Dominion acquisitions, Ferguson claimed that they had been undertaken on the sole initiative of the commission. Thus assured, George S. Henry decided to set up an inquiry. "The question in my mind now," he disclosed in his reply, "is how many things should be included, because I think it would be desirable to have only a short inquiry costing as little money as possible. The only need for the inquiry, so far as I am concerned, is to restore public confidence in the Hydro Commission, and even at that I do not think the confidence of the municipalities is particularly affected."[62]

Nevertheless, the Abitibi contract was not included within the terms of reference laid down for the ensuing Royal Commission. For some reason the government resisted a scrutiny of its dealings with the Ontario Power Service Corporation, even though Howard Ferguson recommended such a course: "You might better face the situation at once," he advised George Henry from London, "and agree to a committee going into the matter if they wish." But Henry thought otherwise and refused the request. For some peculiar reason the two men conducted their further correspondence on this subject in an old reliable code that Howard Ferguson had used once before, during the Timber Investigation.[63]

In the Legislature the opposition peppered the order paper with questions about Hydro as its leader, Mitch Hepburn, bounded about the province—in his own words, "like a greyhound"—spreading the message of Conservative impropriety

[61] R. O. Sweezey and John Aird, Jr., were respectively the promoter of the Beauharnois Power Company and the provincial Conservative bag-man who received the pay-off for getting the Hydro contract for it. See Canada, House of Commons, Select Committee on Beauharnois Power Project, *Fourth Report* (Ottawa, 1931) pp. xix-xxv.

[62] PAO, Henry Papers, Henry to Ferguson, Nov. 23, 1931, personal; Ferguson to Henry, Dec. 10, 1931, private and confidential; Henry to Ferguson, Dec. 24, 1931.

[63] Royal Commission Appointed to Inquire into Certain Matters Concerning the Hydro-Electric Power Commission of Ontario, *Report* (Toronto, 1932), pp. 6-7, 9-11; PAO, Henry Papers, Ferguson to Henry, Oct. 24, 1933, personal and confidential; C. C. Hele to Henry, May 28, 1934, private and confidential; Henry to Ferguson, June 21, 1934.

and ineptitude. The attack forced the government onto the defensive; Premier Henry had no choice but to set up a Royal Commission to look into the circumstances surrounding the Beauharnois, Dominion, and Madawaska deals. Predictably, the Royal Commission absolved the government and exonerated the Hydro-Electric Power Commission from any wrongdoing, but it could not silence the opposition—the evidence was altogether too tantalizing. Hepburn merely probed deeper. Why did the commission have to pay its Quebec power bills in American funds? Why did it continue to buy the power if it was no longer required? Following the collapse of the Ontario Power Service Corporation the Premier personally bore the brunt of the assault. In this attack upon the honour of George Henry, Hepburn was joined by Arthur Roebuck, who had made a specialty of Hydro criticism. Together they overturned every stone strewn along the rocky path of the Abitibi Canyon development in an effort to get to the murky bottom of the affair. Roebuck interpreted the iniquitous purchase as "The Wreck of Hydro." Hepburn called it the great Abitibi swindle: Meighen and Henry had saved their own hides by burdening the people of Ontario with a staggering load of "junk."

As the provincial general election approached in 1934, the tempo of abuse increased. Now the Liberals turned their searchlight into every corner of the commission. Hepburn and Roebuck maliciously exaggerated the salaries of Hydro's top officials and magnified the grandeur of the commission's "palatial" headquarters then under construction on University Avenue. Roebuck claimed that the commission's generating stations were running at only 50 per cent capacity while the province used up the expensive power bought from Quebec. Even so, he charged, Hydro still had a surplus of a half-million horsepower on its hands. According to Liberal critics, a politically minded commission had sacrificed the principles of public ownership and betrayed the public trust; Ontario now danced to the tune of the Quebec Power Barons. As a remedy, Hepburn promised a "Hydro Clean Up," meaning a purge of the commissioners and their technical hirelings. Nor would a Liberal government replace the dismissed personnel with partisans of its own. "A change of government will result in new Hydro Management," Hepburn vowed, "untrammelled by past entanglements and free to apply business principles to Hydro's pressing and important problems."[64]

Over the years the Ontario Hydro-Electric Power Commission had developed a paranoid reaction to all forms of criticism and had acquired the distressing habit of replying to invective in kind. Hydro was, after all, a unique and unsettling influence in the atmosphere of North American corporate liberalism and private enterprise ideology. For that reason alone the commission had its enemies. So many missiles had been launched at the publicly owned enterprise by private utilities in Canada and the United States that after a time the commission tended to assume that all criticism of its operations must, in some dark way, be prompted by vindictive "interests." Since the record and rate structure of Ontario Hydro were the most convincing arguments advanced by American Progressives on behalf of public power, the huge, privately owned utility empires in the United States had a special reason to go to any lengths to sully the reputation of the commission. The propaganda agency for the private utilities, the National Electric Light Association, mounted an insidious advertising campaign against the idea of public ownership in general and Ontario Hydro in particular. From time to time the National Electric Light Association sponsored the publication of scholarly (and therefore, by definition impartial) studies of the commission's rates, finances and technical performance, each of which purported to demonstrate the innate inferiority of public to private ownership.[65]

---

[64] For Liberal criticism of Hydro affairs, see M. F. Hepburn, *To the Electors of Ontario* (Toronto, 1934), pp. 4-5; Arthur Roebuck, *The Wreck of the Hydro* (Toronto, 1933); Denison, *The People's Power*, pp. 197-209; McKenty, "Mitchell F. Hepburn and the Ontario Election of 1934," *CHR*, Vol. XLV (1964), pp. 302-4; *Mitch Hepburn*, pp. 44-57.

[65] Richard Lowitt, "Ontario Hydro: A 1925 Tempest in an American Teapot," *CHR*, Vol. XLIX (1968), pp. 267-74; Ernest Gruening, *The Public Pays* (New York, 1933). In addition to his replies to Ontario Royal Commissions Sir Adam also found time to reply to his American critics; see for example: *Refutation of Unjust Statements Contained in a report published by the National Electric Light Association entitled "Government Owned and Controlled Compared*

In keeping with the Beck tradition of repaying detractors with interest J. R. Cooke, the chairman of the commission from 1930 to 1934, and Fred Gaby, its chief engineer, took it upon themselves to answer the charges directed at the commission and the government by the opposition. To correct the impression being created in the public mind they used their numerous public speaking engagements to explain the circumstance under which the decision to purchase power from Quebec had been taken. Up until the very end of 1930, Gaby insisted, no one could have predicted the unprecedented reversal of power consumption patterns. Hydro could not be blamed for the Depression. It had, according to the best engineering judgment available, merely tried to obtain the power Ontario needed for expansion in the most economical manner. "It is therefore unreasonable—to say the least" Gaby argued, "to assume that the commission, in 1929, before definite signs of depression had appeared, or even in 1930 before the severe and prolonged character of the depression had become evident, ought to have ceased to be guided by the experience of eighteen years, and to have based its power commitments—necessarily made years in advance—upon a foreknowledge concerning the future course of general world economic activities which neither it nor anyone else had at the time." Each of the Quebec contracts could be justified solely upon its technical merits, despite cries to the contrary.

Moreover, Hydro apologists claimed that the commission did not in fact have a crushing surplus, but rather a mere 200,000 horsepower reserve which every well-managed system required. This made it possible for Ontario Hydro to accommodate new demands instantly when the wheels of industry began to turn once again. "When a factory is ready to resume full production,"

---

with *Privately Owned and Regulated Electric Utilities in Canada and the United States"* respecting the Hydro-Electric Power Commission of Ontario (Toronto, 1922); and *Misstatements and Misrepresentations derogatory to the Hydro-Electric Power Commission of Ontario Contained in a recent report published by the Smithsonian Institution entitled "Niagara Falls: Its Power Possibilities and Preservation" under the Authorship of Samuel S. Wyer, Examined and Refuted* (Toronto, 1925).

Cooke told a Tory thinkers' conference in 1933, "it would be useless to point to potential sources of power supply and promise actual power from these sources two or three years later. . . ."[66] By normal standards, the spokesmen for the commission presented sufficient and conclusive answers to their critics. Nevertheless, the answers had to be forced from them; the commission laid its case frankly before the public only after it had become absolutely imperative to do so. Thus, Hydro's new policy of candour, because it had been initiated within an atmosphere of antagonism, appeared to be little more than overt partisanship. The travesty that would follow was the logical outcome of the earlier misguided policy that had hidden commission affairs from public scrutiny and open debate.

During the 1934 election campaign opposition criticism persisted even after the commissioners had proffered full and honourable disclosures, Hydro issued direct challenges—by name—to its detractors to correct their misleading statements of fact. Liberal provocation, compounded by Hydro's incurable persecution complex and its righteous sense of mission, all combined to transport the commissioners insensibly across that vague frontier separating legitimate educational publicity from the forbidden, indeed dangerous, realm of political activism. The logic of bureaucratic self-preservation overrode any consideration of the proper conduct of a public service agency. In 1933, for example, the commission published two detailed statements correcting accusations made by the leader of the opposition concerning its financial position and power reserves. Both pamphlets exceeded the limits of simply amending "misleading assertions": they demanded a public retraction from Hepburn. Thereafter, as the opposition shafts penetrated even deeper into the mysteries of Hydro, the publications of the commission became virtually indistinguishable from those of the Conservative party.[67]

[66] Gaby quoted from *Trends of Electrical Demands in Relation to Power Supplies*, a speech to the OMEA, Jan. 25, 1933, p. 21; J. R. Cooke's speech to the Liberal-Conservative Summer School, Newmarket, 1933, *Hydro Service Considered in the Some of its Important Economic Aspects* (Toronto, 1933), pp. 12-31.

[67] Hydro-Electric Power Commission, *Misleading Assertions that have been made*

The Hydro commissioners were genuinely convinced that all criticism of their behaviour must in some way be connected with their corporate enemies in the United States. Therefore, to confirm that suspicion, the commission hired a private detective agency to shadow and report upon the movements of key Liberals just to see how they might be associated with the private utilities. When this totalitarian measure failed to uncover the desired information, the commission merely pretended that such proof existed. In an impudent and inflammatory pamphlet entitled, *Paid for Propaganda*, the commission implied that the Liberal party was little more than a mouthpiece of the giant American utilities. "What interests would benefit from injury to Hydro?" "What interests have recently been proved to have sponsored and paid for former attacks on Hydro?" and "What steps could such interests be taking at the present time to advance their objects?" the pamphlet asked suggestively. Then on the basis of the slim evidence that Hepburn had once quoted a publication of the infamous National Electric Light Association, *Paid for Propaganda* "proved" that his disparaging remarks had been instigated by vested interests. Resting its case upon the record and on old loyalties, Hydro asked the people of Ontario to choose between Mitch Hepburn and the memory of Adam Beck: "Those who have followed Hydro matters know that the integrity of the Hydro undertaking and its administration is unassailable upon any *bona fide* basis." Trust us, the commissioners begged, and vote Conservative.[68]

But the people were in more of a mood to trust Mitch. Notwithstanding the exertions of the Hydro-Electric Power Commission—perhaps in part because of them—the Liberals

---

relating to the Power Situation in the Province of Ontario Examined and Corrected (Toronto, 1933), and *Misleading Assertions that have been made relating to the Power Situation in the Province of Ontario Have Not Been Withdrawn* (Toronto, 1933). See also the pamphlets put out by the Conservative party, *Liberalism and Leadership: Past and Present*; *This Way We Follow*; *Communism and the C.C.F.*, and *The Price of Progress* (all Toronto, 1934).

[68] PAO, Hepburn Papers; for this incredible spying episode and the even more bizarre report submitted by the detective agency, see Stewart Lyon to Hepburn, Oct. 17, 1934; Hydro-Electric Power Commission, *Paid for Propaganda: Who Instigates Attacks on Hydro* (Toronto, 1934), pp. 4, 5-9.

swept into office. To a confused, frustrated and demoralized electorate aching for leadership, Mitch Hepburn symbolized at least the expectation of action. With visible satisfaction the new Premier set about fulfilling his promise of a Hydro house-cleaning. He sacked the remaining commissioners, J. R. Cooke and C. A. Maguire, Fred Gaby, the chief engineer, and Arthur V. White, the author of *Paid for Propaganda*, and put Stewart Lyon, the faithful editor of the *Globe* in charge of housecleaning the commission. Then, encouraged by his supporters to seek sweeter revenge still, Hepburn appointed a Royal Commission to investigate the Abitibi Canyon affair and launched proceedings in the courts to recover the $4,553 of public money Meighen, Cooke, Lucas and Gaby authorized to be spent on private detectives to shadow the opposition. As this witch hunt progressed, T. S. Lyon announced his intention to renegotiate the price and quantity of power provided for by the Quebec contracts. Henceforth, he promised, the commission would go "back to Niagara" for its future power requirements.[69]

As advertised, Mitch Hepburn furnished sensational purges and a return to familiar principles. The victims cried out against the injustices they were compelled to endure in the coils of a vicious political inquisition. "The only politics they understand," snapped Arthur Meighen, "is the bar-room brawl brand." Charles Magrath wondered in as tactful a manner as possible, "Who did the loose talking?" Arthur White compared his trial with that of St. Paul and declared that he had only done his duty on behalf of what he knew to be right. In the end the Abitibi Commission exonerated Henry and Meighen from any wrongdoing but lectured them sternly for not declaring their interest in the Ontario Power Service Corporation at the outset. Chief Justice Rose dismissed the ludicrous action against Meighen, Maguire, Lucas and Gaby as being "utterly unfounded and very cruel." Arthur Meighen expected that anyone with any self-respect would have been totally crushed by the judge's remark, and he was astonished to learn that Stewart Lyon was

[69] PAO, Hepburn Papers, A. C. Hardy to Hepburn, June 28, 1934; M. J. Patton to Hepburn, July 9, 1934, strictly confidential; Theophile Meek to Hepburn, July 25, 1934; E. C. Drury to Hepburn, June 7, 1934.

anything but humiliated: "The action of which you speak," Lyon replied to Meighen, "was begun . . . to show the people of Ontario that an attempt had been made in the name of the Commission to introduce into Canadian public life the methods of European political spies and agents provocateur. . . . While the judgment of the Court would seem to indicate that there is no legal bar against the hiring by the Commission of persons who turned in such reports as were read in the Court, a very real result of the action will be that no Hydro Electric Power Commission of the future will dare to authorize or endeavour to profit politically by the operations of secret agents engaged for purely political purposes." The persecution, however much it might have been justified, did take its toll. According to Magrath, J. R. Cooke went to pieces under the strain and drove his car into a bridge.[70]

It was an easy enough matter to persecute the outgoing administrators for actual and presumed sins, but what could be done to solve the substantive problem of oversupply? Beyond altering personnel, how much freedom of action did any government possess under the circumstances? Could the contracts be changed and could Niagara yield that much power? After the swift and dramatic gestures immediately following the election, it was but a short time before the actions of even this Jacksonian administration were as thoroughly determined by the dynamics of the hydro-electric business as had been those of its predecessors.

Something had to be done immediately, Stewart Lyon warned the Premier shortly after taking charge. In 1933 the commission had lost over $6 million on account of the Quebec contracts, and the deficits were growing. The only answer as far as

[70] *Mail and Empire*, July 28, 1934; Oct. 15, 1935; *Globe and Mail*, Dec. 2, 1936; Ontario Hydro-Electric Power Commission, Annual Report, 1934; PAC, Magrath Papers, Vol. 5, Magrath to J. R. Cooke, Aug. 19, 1933 and inscription; Magrath's memoranda, Oct. 21, 1935, Sept. 26, 1939 and Jan. 1942, justifying his position; Magrath to Ferguson, Dec. 28, 1935; Magrath to Meighen, Nov. 25, 1936; Meighen to Magrath, Dec. 3, 1936, private; Magrath to White, Mar. 31, 1939, private; White to Magrath, Jan. 13, 1940; Fred Gaby, radio address, April 6, 1935, *The Power Situation in Ontario* (Toronto, 1935).

Hepburn, Roebuck and Lyon were concerned was repudiation. On April 1, 1935, Hepburn introduced a Power Bill declaring the contracts with Ottawa Valley, MacLaren-Quebec, and Beauharnois "illegal, void and unenforceable." The government agreed to continue taking some power from the Gatineau Power Company in accordance with the terms of the 1926 contract, but it demanded a revision of the other three contracts that had been negotiated much later. After four stormy sittings the Legislature passed the Power Bill as the Premier insisted it would, without dotting an "i" or crossing a "t". Using this unproclaimed bill as a trump, Hepburn invited representatives of the three companies to submit new proposals more in keeping with the needs of the commission. Though they were in a conciliatory frame of mind the power companies would not retreat as far as the Premier demanded. Accordingly, the commission severed its connections with the three companies, an action which it claimed resulted in savings of about $700,000 per month over the next year.[71] But the victory was only temporary.

There were two problems with a policy of repudiation: it was illegal, but more important, the province needed the power. As early as January 1937 the commission faced a serious shortage within the Niagara system. "Hogg [T. H. Hogg, the new chief engineer] tells me that the situation is really alarming, that the demand for power is increasing rapidly, and that we are going to be embarrassed by next fall if we have nothing further than the Gatineau 120,000," Harry Nixon impressed upon the vacationing Premier. Negotiations were underway with the Ottawa Valley Power Company, but those talks had stalled over Stewart Lyon's insistence upon a purchase clause in the agreement. In the Legislature even Liberal members were becoming impatient with Arthur Roebuck's bitter and increasingly irrational attacks on the power companies. Down

[71] PAO, Hepburn Papers, T. S. Lyon to Hepburn, personal, undated 1934; telegram to Beauharnois Light, Heat and Power, MacLaren-Quebec Power Company, and Ottawa Valley Power Company, Oct. 21, 1935; Memo on the Power Conference, Oct. 23, 1935; press release on the Cancellation and Modification of the Contracts, Nov. 3, 1935; press release re: Power Conference, handwritten, Dec. 6, 1935; McKenty, *Mitch Hepburn*, pp. 64-8.

the street at the Hydro-Electric Power Commission, communications between the engineering staff and the chairman had completely broken down. There could be no denying that technically, politically and administratively the government confronted a new hydro crisis. Then in June the Ontario Court of Appeal ruled that the Beauharnois agreement was legal and awarded the company damages amounting to $600,000.

Behind the usual bluster Hepburn was ready to compromise. But now that the province needed the power and the government had to do business with the Quebec companies, Stewart Lyon stood in the way. He had staked his career upon cancellation of the contracts—so much so that he could not see, or refuse to admit, the impending disaster. As late as September he was insisting "surely no one can believe that there is an imminent power shortage. . . ." But Hepburn, the cabinet, and now the opposition knew otherwise. On October 21 Hepburn asked for Lyon's resignation and he replaced him with a professional engineer from within the system, T. H. Hogg.[72] Political management of the commission's affairs had led directly to a critical power shortage that might easily have been avoided.

With Stewart Lyon out of the way, Hydro engineers moved quickly to avert the coming crisis. Just in time to meet the peak demand of the winter months T. H. Hogg announced that all three of the cancelled Quebec contracts had been restored. The new contracts called for the purchase of substantially the same amount of power as before, but at $12.50 instead of $15 per horsepower—and the bills were to be paid in Canadian rather than American funds. Compared with the old agreements, the commission estimated that the revision would save Ontario consumers about $17 million over the next seven years and upwards of $78 million over the entire contract

[72] PAO, Hepburn Papers, H. C. Nixon to Hepburn (in Arizona), Jan. 21, 1937, strictly private and confidential; and a second letter, same date, private; H. J. Kirby to Hepburn, Jan. 21, 1937, private; T. S. Lyon to Harry Nixon, Feb. 5, 1937, personal and confidential; T. S. Lyon to the editor of the *Brantford Expositor*, Sept. 1, 1937; Hepburn to Lyon, Oct. 21, 1937, personal and confidential; Lyon to Hepburn, Oct. 28, 1937; for the details of the shortage see T. H. Hogg to Hepburn, Jan. 21, 1937.

period. But Hydro, which had just barely escaped a shortage, now had more than enough power to meet its immediate needs. Events had come full circle; now the Hepburn government suffered the embarrassment of a surplus. As before, the commission continued to rely upon the export market to relieve some of the burden. "The cost of this reserve power," Hogg explained to newsmen, "will largely be eliminated if permission can be obtained from the Federal authorities for the export of 90,000 horsepower. . . ."[73] But for one reason or another that simple expedient eluded the commission and the government.

Mackenzie King's initial reluctance to grant such an additional export privilege provoked Hepburn's first public outburst against his former leader. Indeed, these differences over hydro-electric matters did much to exacerbate relations between the two levels of government throughout this period. Infuriated by King's apparent disregard for the interests of Ontario and determined to smash the administrative obstacles placed in his way by the federal government, Hepburn assembled a massive political alliance behind his formal application to export 130,000 horsepower which he filed on January 21, 1938. He canvassed for sympathy among members on both sides of the House, and during his talks with Duplessis over the newsprint question Hepburn won the belligerent support of the Premier of Quebec in any fight with Mackenzie King over hydro-electric exports. Hepburn confronted King with raw power—the only argument he knew—and defied him to turn down Ontario's application. But just when it appeared that Ontario had won the point—indeed, at the very moment that Arthur Slaght's bill granting an export licence was being debated in the House—the American government served notice that it would not permit the importation of power on Ontario's terms.[74] This stunning

---

[73] PAO, Hepburn Papers, press release, Agreement with Beauharnois, MacLaren-Quebec and Gatineau Power Companies, Dec., 1937; PAC, Magrath Papers, Vol. 5, Magrath to Conant, Feb. 18, 1942, personal; Conant to Magrath, Mar. 11, 1942, personal.

[74] PAO, Hepburn Papers, Geo. Lynch-Staunton to Hepburn, Dec. 16, 1937, personal; Hepburn's circular letter to federal members and their replies,

setback only widened the gulf between the province and the dominion. Hepburn interpreted the timely American intervention as conclusive proof that a conspiracy existed between Ottawa and Washington to force the province of Ontario, against its will, into an expensive St. Lawrence Seaway Development.

In 1934 when Hepburn assumed power, he declared his firm opposition to such a scheme; three years later when Franklin Roosevelt and Mackenzie King reopened discussions on the subject, the Premier of Ontario possessed even stronger reasons for objecting to it. "Having finally arrived at a tentative arrangement with respect to a settlement of our power problems with [the] Quebec companies," he replied to King's confidential inquiry, "I am advised by the Hydro Commissioners and the technicians that Ontario's power requirements have been taken care of for many, many years to come." Now that the two federal governments were eager to proceed, Ontario had a surplus of power. Yet Ottawa depended upon Ontario to undertake the hydro-electric responsibilities connected with the project. Ontario had insisted upon this point in the past; it had fought and won recognition of its jurisdiction over the St. Lawrence waterpowers. Having established the principle, Ottawa expected that the province would then co-operate to bring the plan to fruition. But the St. Lawrence did not figure as prominently in Ontario Hydro's calculations during the 1930s as it had during the 1920s. Under Stewart Lyon's direction the commission's engineers had completed feasibility studies on diverting water from the Hudson Bay watershed into the Great Lakes system. This would increase the flow over the Falls and thereby permit the commission to go "back to Niagara" for its future requirements. Instead of building costly new works on the St. Lawrence, the commission could merely expand its existing

folder V, 1938, Power Export, most dated Feb. 2, 3, 4, 5, 1938; Hepburn to Duplessis, Jan. 27, 1938; Conant to Hepburn, March 4, 1938; T. H. Hogg to W. D. Euler, Jan. 21, 1938; Duplessis, Jan. 31, 1938, personal and confidential; Conant to R. H. Elmhirst, Jan. 25, 1938; Hepburn to Duplessis, Feb. 14, 1938, personal and confidential; Duplessis to Hepburn, Feb. 14, 1938; A. G. Slaght to Hepburn, Feb. 28, 1938; Hepburn to Duplessis, Mar. 4, 1938; A. G. Slaght to Hepburn, Mar. 11, 1938.

generating facilities at Niagara Falls subject to a revision of the Boundary Waters Treaty. Again Washington—and Hepburn suspected Ottawa as well—blocked Ontario's ambition. The American government categorically refused to consider the diversion and Seaway questions separately; it wanted to re-write a comprehensive new treaty covering the entire Great Lakes and St. Lawrence system. Under such circumstances Ontario could obtain American co-operation at Niagara only by agreeing to participate in the development of the St. Lawrence.[75]

Thus, the federal Seaway proposals were diametrically opposed to the needs and desires of Ontario Hydro. The province could neither dispose of its surplus power nor win approval for the Long Lac diversion which reversed the flow of this system from Hudson Bay into the Great Lakes without first entering into a massive hydro-electric project on the St. Lawrence which would only exaggerate the former and render the latter superfluous. Ontario Hydro provided the substance of dominion-provincial disagreement; Mitchell Hepburn supplied the rhetoric. He disliked intensely the feeling of en-trapment, especially at the hands of Mackenzie King, and he expressed his displeasure in the most violent and unmistakable language. He openly accused the Prime Minister of applying a "made in Washington" policy with regard to the Seaway and blamed Ottawa for Ontario's power surplus: "This unsatis-factory condition would not obtain at this moment had you granted us, when you had the opportunity, the right to export this surplus at a profit which would have enabled us in turn to grant a further reduction in rates to the power consumers of Ontario." In February 1938, just after the Washington an-nouncement on the export question, Hepburn warned King against any intrigue with Roosevelt:

---

[75] PAO, Hepburn Papers, Hepburn to Thomas Wayling and others, Nov. 9, 1934; Hepburn to Mackenzie King, Nov. 25, 1937, confidential; King to Hepburn, Nov. 12, 1937, confidential; Hepburn to King, Feb. 14, 1938; King to Hepburn, Feb. 22, 1938; Hepburn to King, Feb. 25, 1938; King to Hepburn, Mar. 1, 1938; Christopher Armstrong, "The Politics of Federalism," pp. 345-400.

Irrespective of any propaganda or squeeze play that might be concocted by you, you may rest assured that this Government will resist ["to the bitter end" crossed out] any effort to force us to expand public funds in such an unwarranted manner or to foist upon the people of Ontario an additional burden of debt and taxation.[76]

Hepburn objected to the Seaway primarily on economic grounds. No one could predict the final cost of even the Ontario share; T. H. Hogg conservatively estimated the cost of the hydro-electric installations at $73 million (not including interest), and on top of that, taxation from Ontario would have to cover about one-half of the federal share for canals. "May I ask where the pressure is coming for deep waterways?" Hepburn inquired. He was personally of the opinion that the traffic would never warrant an enormous expenditure on canals, and even if the volume of shipping did equal federal expectations it would only further embarrass the debt-ridden CNR with competition. As far as Ontario was concerned, the Premier emphasized, "our interests are confined to power. . . ." Simply on the basis of the power surplus alone Hepburn felt justified in condemning the scheme. Hydro-electricity generated on the St. Lawrence could be sold only in New York, Quebec and Ontario. Since the latter provinces each possessed a power surplus that would continue for the foreseeable future, Hepburn concluded, "it seems clear to me that the effect of the proposed Treaty is to prepare a reserve of power on Canada's side which can be quickly brought into production when the need arises for sale to the United States."[77]

But as this pitched battle between Hepburn and King brought the Seaway talks to a complete halt, the Hydro technical staff was beginning to take a somewhat longer view of its power requirements. The demand for power had begun to climb in

[76] PAO, Hepburn Papers, Hepburn to King, Aug. 19, 1938; King to Hepburn, Aug. 30, 1938.

[77] PAO, Hepburn Papers, Hepburn to King, Sept. 21, 1938; R. H. Elmhirst to T. B. McQuesten, Sept. 19, 1938; A. G. Slaght to Hepburn, Mar. 24, 1938.

lock step with the gradual upswing in the business cycle during the latter 1930s. Moreover, engineers had a finer appreciation than politicians of the time that would be consumed between the design and construction stages of such an ambitious undertaking. Perhaps by the time the Seaway was completed Ontario would need the power. Thus, at the very moment that Mitchell Hepburn was deliberately driving nails into the federal case for the Seaway, unbeknown to him T. H. Hogg was secretly agitating on its behalf. Eventually—and sooner rather than later—the Ontario government would have to reverse itself on the question of St. Lawrence development. It was just a matter of finding the appropriate face-saving political opportunity. The war, a new power crisis, and Hepburn's overheated patriotism eventually combined to provide that occasion.[78]

Ontario politics in the thirties moved with a rhythm imparted by the Ontario Hydro-Electric Power Commission. Its mistakes had led to the fall of one administration; the imperatives of its market position manipulated the movements of another. To some observers the convolutions and reversals of government policy during this period have a certain arbitrariness about them that is most easily explained in terms of the intemperate personality of the Premier. But from the vantage of Ontario Hydro, the repudiation and then renegotiation of the Quebec contracts, and the opposition and then acceptance of the Seaway, have an inner logic. If the fact that the Ontario government was in the power business is borne in mind, then the erratic course followed by the politicians makes sense. Moreover, the relationship of power supply to demand had wider implications; the circumstances of surplus or shortage heavily influenced the provincial attitude on a whole range of vital questions. In dominion-provincial negotiations, for example, the interests of Ontario and those of Ontario Hydro were identical. The needs of Ontario Hydro, then, carried con-

---

[78] PAO, Hepburn Papers, T. H. Hogg to Hepburn, Sept. 12, 1941; Armstrong, "The Politics of Federalism," pp. 384-400; J. W. Pickersgill, ed., *The Mackenzie King Record* Vol. 1 (Toronto, 1960), p. 36; W. R. Willoughby, *The St. Lawrence Seaway* (Madison, Wisconsin, 1961), pp. 160-95.

siderable influence in the determination of Ontario's attitude towards federalism. Differences between Ottawa and Toronto over hydro-electric questions quickly became differences over constitutional questions. What is more, Hepburn's violent expression of those objections seriously impaired the success of the efforts being undertaken by the Royal Commission on Dominion-Provincial Relations to create the kind of atmosphere within which forms of federalism could be debated on their merits.[79]

At the turn of the century Max Weber pondered the question: "...how are freedom and democracy in the long run at all possible under the domination of highly developed capitalism?" and he answered: "Freedom and democracy are only possible where the resolute will of the nation not to allow itself to be ruled like sheep is permanently alive. We are 'individualists' and partisans of 'democratic' institutions 'against the stream' of material constellations."[80] In Ontario during the 1930s the intimate personal and institutional relationship of government and business magnified the task of a people, whose democratic will was weak, to oppose that stream of material constellations. During this period the province lost its responsible government "in the subtle social sense" referred to by Professor Lower.

Industrialists in both the public and private sectors were much more successful than any other groups in turning the instruments of the state to their own advantage during the Depression. Industry could expect the protection and nourishment of the state; a destitute and disorganized working force, in the name of self-reliance, was left to its own devices. Algoma Steel, Great Lakes Paper, McIntyre-Porcupine Gold Mines, General Motors and Ontario Hydro largely determined the course of public policy; in some instances these organizations even wrote the

---

[79] For a detailed explanation of the Ontario position in the Rowell-Sirois discussions, see Richard Alway, "Hepburn, King and the Rowell-Sirois Commission," *CHR*, Vol. XLVII (1967), pp. 113-41; Armstrong, "The Politics of Federalism," pp. 522-606.

[80] H. H. Gerth and C. W. Mills, eds., *From Max Weber* (New York, 1946), p. 71.

letters and statements that appeared above the Premier's signature. Together these business groups fashioned the image of Ontario. It was mutual business—mining, newsprint and hydro—that forged the axis that revolved between Hepburn and Duplessis. Businessmen and bureaucrats, men who used the words province and nation interchangeably, who believed in social laissez faire and regionalism on sound business principles, dictated the response of government to a vast array of social, economic and political problems. Provincial rights was good business, and business was politics.

# 12
# The Image
# of the State

As Ontario entered the twentieth century the old pre-industrial concept of crown ownership of natural resources was very much alive. Because the lumbermen had discovered a useful ally in the state, and because the forests rented to the lumbermen became a production source of revenue, the statist philosophy underlying the Crown Timber Act came to be applied in the regulation of waterpowers and mines as well. Thus, on the eve of intensive development, the province of Ontario exercised proprietary control over its three most important natural resources. The survival of this authority was, as we have seen, no accident, but instead a conscious choice. Looking ahead, the concept of the positive state appeared also to have much to recommend it as the basis of regulating the industrial process.

Did this tradition make any difference in what followed? Did an interventionist public philosophy significantly alter the pattern of resource development in the province from the continental norm? After surveying the record the answer must be a qualified no, the qualification being the important exception of Hydro. If anything, the proprietary relationship made it easier for business to establish a firm grip upon the instruments of the state. In this Hydro was not an exception, for it was run by businessmen, for businessmen, in what was always referred to as a "businesslike" manner.

The first and consistently most important function of the state in the industrial process was promotion, and successive Ontario governments bent their wills to this task with commendable zeal. Was it not in the interest of the landlord that his property should be productively occupied? Accordingly, bounties of one sort or another fell on demand like a warm spring rain; roads to resources were built or bonused as required; services were provided, opportunities advertised and skills imparted with an enthusiasm tempered only by the imperatives of economy. Reluctantly at first, and then more confidently, the province could even be induced to meet the challenge of hostile American commercial policies. From the outset it was readily understood that Ontario's natural resources would be exploited primarily for the American market. But who was to do battle to ensure that these products were exported in as close to their fully manufactured form as possible? The province at length took on this responsibility with a determination that varied directly with the pressure applied to it by its business clients and the rise and fall of the business cycle. Invariably, this "economic provincialism" met strong resistance in the form of the federal government which, throughout this period, tended to take a more conciliatory view of Canadian-American commercial differences. As far as help with getting on with the job was concerned, no developer could ask for a better, more attentive partner than the government of Ontario.

What then of the other side of the relationship, regulation? To what extent did the proprietary situation of the state impinge upon the development process? Here again the government proved to be more than understanding. The miners began by demanding that the state give up its proprietary pretensions entirely. They very quickly won for themselves a form of tenure more in keeping with the American pattern. As far as taxation was concerned, the miners eventually brought a stabilizing influence to bear upon the government after some dubious experiments with leases, royalties and even public ownership inspired by progressive enthusiasm and the Cobalt rush. Thereafter, mining proceeded within the lenient free enterprise, freebooting environment as elsewhere. Furthermore, the industry always seemed to be able to count upon its faithful advocate, the provincial government, to caution those improvident enough to tamper with a going concern. In mining it would seem that the regulated group experienced greater success in bringing the regulator under control than the other way around.

Something similar might be said of the pulp and paper industry's relations with the provincial government up to the Second World War. In principle, public ownership of the raw materials remained as the legal basis of the industry. However, in practice the superior legal position of the state in this landlord-tenant relationship was not used to assert any major public claim upon the resource development process. In fact, quite the reverse appeared to be the case: the position of the state facilitated the organization of a relatively small number of substantial production units. The terms and conditions of the concessions were adjusted to suit the needs of developers and the land parcelled out in such a way as to accommodate the financial requirements of expansion. When the entire industry collapsed during the Depression the governments of Ontario and Quebec readily permitted their industrial tenants free access to the coercive powers of the state in the interests of orderly reconstruction as that was perceived by the pulp and paper men themselves. Public ownership of the resource base did not necessarily imply a more systematic pursuit of conservation programs. The conservation movement, becalmed during the second decade of the century, and the fire-ravaged forests of northern Ontario during the 1930s bear witness to that. The effective demands upon the state and its forest resources were promotional and private throughout.

The rhetoric of free enterprise notwithstanding, business could not get along without the active co-operation of the state. From the exploration phase up through reorganization and concentration the state had to serve as an understanding accomplice. The values that guided government intervention in Ontario during the first half of this century have been basically those of its business clients. This, of course, was the normal state of affairs in a continental, advanced capitalist context. "Capitalist enterprise," it has been argued, " . . .*depends* to an ever greater extent on the bounties and direct support of the state, and can only preserve its 'private' character on the basis of such public help. State intervention in economic life in fact *means* intervention for the purpose of helping capitalist enterprise. In no field has the notion of the 'welfare state' had a more precise and apposite meaning than here: there are no more persistent and successful applicants for public assistance than the proud giants of the private enterprise system."[1] In Ontario a formal legal relationship between the state and its resource developers seemed, if anything, to facilitate such co-operative action.

Only in the case of hydro-electric power did public ownership of the resource provide a model for the subsequent development of the industry based upon it. In this Ontario did deviate significantly from the North American norm. But as has been suggested, retention of public rights in waterpowers, while a helpful contributing factor, was certainly not a sufficient condition for public ownership of the hydro-electric distribution and generation industry. Instead, the energy requirements of the provincial manufacturers, their fear of economic stagnation, and the metropolitan tensions of the provincial economy were far more important determinants of state intervention. Power was far too precious as an agent of industrial expansion to be left under the control of monopoly capital, Canadian or American. If the ordinary corporate instruments could not be relied upon to deliver this power on time at reasonable rates, then the state had a duty to step in and perform this function itself for the greater well-being of the economy. The strongest

[1] Ralph Miliband, *The State in Capitalist Society* (London, 1969), p. 78; see also, Gabriel Kolko, *The Triumph of Conservatism* (Chicago, 1963), pp. 279-305; James Weinstein, *The Corporate Ideal in the Liberal State, 1900-1918* (Boston, 1968), ix-xv; Martin J. Sklar, "Woodrow Wilson and the Political Economy of Modern United States Liberalism," in Ronald Rodash and Murray Rothbard, eds. *A New History of Leviathan; Essays on the Rise of the American Corporate State* (New York, 1972), pp. 7-65.

and most persistent demand for public ownership came from businessmen. Of course, the hydro-electric question split the financial sector of the business community from the merchants and manufacturers, and the brilliant political organization of the latter group at the municipal and the provincial level by a charismatic leader determined the outcome. The decentralized character of Canadian federalism prevented the former group from reversing this verdict at the federal level as so often happened in the United States.[2] This same alliance of interests sanctioned Sir Adam Beck's later drive towards a public monopoly.

Ontario Hydro never became the beachhead for an ongoing critique of industrial capitalism. Instead, the dangerous principles upon which it rested remained locked up within the confines of the commission, and the commission was allowed to remove itself as far away from politics (but not the treasury), as possible. This, it was argued, was absolutely essential if the organization were to be run in accordance with proper, businesslike principles, a key phrase. Hydro entered politics only to escape from it. In this there was a double loss. In the first place the conditions of Hydro's birth and the character of its founder prevented the accommodation of this new responsibility of state to the parliamentary system of government. Eventually the contradictions of this independent, non-accountable status practically wrecked Hydro. But the crisis of the thirties led only to the replacement of bad men by good men; it did not alter the structural relationship of the commission to the executive of the Legislature. Since then the only thought that has been given to the question has been in the direction of moving Hydro even further from the political process. Secondly, Hydro was nationalized in such a way and then managed in such a manner as to debase the concept of *public* ownership and discourage the extension of the principle. Hydro was not to be the experiment with socialized industry

---

[2] Christopher Armstrong and H. V. Nelles, "Private Property in Peril: Ontario Businessmen and the Federal System, 1898-1911," *Business History Review*, Vol. XLVII (1973), pp. 158-76.

that the power barons and James Mavor feared, but the venture in state capitalism that the merchants and manufacturers of the power legions knew it to be from the beginning. Public ownership is in itself a neutral phenomenon. Its origins, benefactors and behaviour determine its character. On close examination the much-discussed Toryism that Ontario Hydro is supposed to represent looks much like some varieties of American corporate liberalism.[3] It might as well have the same name.

After the Second World War the integration of business and the state proceeded much more quickly, under Conservative one-party government, across a much broader front and on an entirely different scale. The points of connection between business and the state multiplied as both bureaucratized their structures and professionalized their operations. This qualitatively different kind of fusion lies beyond the scope of this book and warrants study in its own right.

Perhaps no better representation of the changing scope and character of the state in Ontario can be found than the architecture at Queen's Park. The Parliament Building, compact, comprehensive, facing inward upon the Legislature at the centre, typifies the late nineteenth-century state. It could be nothing else but a government building, except perhaps a Presbyterian church. Nor was it modesty that led Oliver Mowat to exclaim upon seeing the structure in 1892, "We'll never fill it." Beck's squat little Hydro headquarters on University Avenue followed in 1916, looking like nothing so much as a bank, setting a pattern that repeated itself in the East Annex of the 1920s and the new Hydro building of the 1940s. With each step the centre of gravity shifts away from the Legislature. In

---

[3] George Grant, *Lament for a Nation* (Toronto, 1965), pp. 68-72; Gad Horowitz, *Canadian Labour in Politics* (Toronto, 1968), p. 10; Rodash and Rothbard, *A New History of Leviathan, passim*. Judging from the Ontario experience the Tory tradition has been weak at precisely that point where its apologists sense its contemporary relevance. Historically it has not been able to bring a broader range of community values to bear upon the industrial process than has Liberalism. The practice of Toryism, its anti-corporate theory notwithstanding, has always involved giving public assistance to businessmen.

the sixties government spread itself out over entire city blocks of concrete and steel. To this Hydro and Canada Square have replied with a massive concave mirror that, on a fine day, will reflect the surrounding corporate monuments, the bank towers downtown, the hotels and insurance companies nearby. The image on the outside is perhaps a fair reflection of the new state on the inside.

The habit of authority that survived from the nineteenth century did not greatly alter the pattern of resource development. It did, however, contribute to a reduction of government—despite an expansion of its activities—to a client of the business community. This need not have been so. The failure to bring the regulatory and service functions of the state into the framework of democratic accountability was the failure of parties and politicians to pursue the logic of responsible government into the industrial age.

# A Note on
# Sources

In the normal sequence of events a great deal of economic and political history ought properly to have preceded this book. As yet there is no adequate survey of Ontario political history, although the Ontario Historical Studies Series through its biographies of the premiers and these studies program promises to make up this deficiency in the near future. Similarly, the economic and business history of the province remain largely unwritten. Happily there are a few notable exceptions to this general condition. As the notes clearly indicate, I have relied heavily upon those secondary works that are available, notably O.W. Main's excellent history, *The Canadian Nickel Industry* (Toronto, 1955), Thomas Gibson's two useful compilations, *The Mining Laws of Ontario* (Toronto, 1933) and *Mining in Ontario* (Toronto, 1937), the work of Rex Lambert and Paul Pross on the Department of Lands and Forests, *Renewing Nature's Wealth* (Toronto, 1967), W. R. Plewman's chaotic but invaluable chronicle, *Adam Beck and the Ontario Hydro* (Toronto, 1947), Neil McKenty's spirited biography of *Mitch Hepburn* (Toronto, 1967), and Christopher Armstrong's soon to be published thesis, "The Politics of Federalism: Ontario's Relations with the Federal Government, 1896-1941" (University of Toronto, 1972).

Outside of the field of Canadian history I found the following books particularly useful in shaping my interpretation of these Ontario events: H.G.J. Aitken, *The State and Economic Growth* (New York, 1959), Samuel Beer, *British Politics in the Collectivist Age* (New York, 1965), Marver H. Berstein, *Regulating Business by Independent Commission* (Princeton, 1955), Oscar and M.F. Handlin, *Commonwealth: A Study of the Role of Government in the American Economy: Massachusetts, 1774-1861* (New York, 1947), Samuel P. Hays, *Conservation and the Gospel of Efficiency* (Cambridge, Massachusetts, 1959), James Willard Hurst, *Law and Economic Growth* (Cambridge, Massachusetts, 1964), Gabriel Kolko, *The Triumph of Conservatism* (Chicago, 1967), Ralph Milliband, *The State in Capitalist Society* (London, 1969) R.M. Robbins, *Our Landed Heritage: The Public Domain, 1776-1936* (Princeton, 1942), James Weinstein, *The Corporate Ideal and the Liberal State, 1900-1918* (Boston, 1968), and Robert H. Wiebe, *Businessmen and Reform* (Cambridge, Massachusetts, 1962).

For the most part this book rests upon material drawn from the splendid run of prime ministers' papers in the Public Archives of Ontario, upon the political and business collections located in the Public Archives of Canada, departmental documents, official publications, sessional papers, royal commission hearings and reports, professional journals, trade magazines, the financial and daily press. Here I will confine myself to a brief list of the principal manuscript collections and refer the interested reader to the bibliography of my thesis for a comprehensive list of primary, printed and secondary sources.

Papers consulted in the Public Archives of Canada include those of Señor Gonzala de Quesada y Arostegui, Mossom Boyd and Company, Robert Borden, the British North American Mining Company Minute Book, 1846-1910, E.H. Bronson, the Canadian Pacific Railway Company—Van Horne Letterbooks, D. W. Detwiler, James Dunn, Edward Farrer, Charles Fitzpat-

rick, George Eulas Foster, William Bell Frue, George C. Gib-
bons, G. P. Graham, Earl Grey of Horwick, Thomas A. Keefer,
Wilfrid Laurier, Charles Magrath, James Malcolm, A. N. Mor-
gan and J. J. Murphy, as well as those of C.E.L. Porteous, W. D.
Ross, Newton Rowell, Richard Scott, H. H. Stevens, Thomas
White and J. S. Willison.

The Department of Lands and Forests Collection, Woods and
Forests Report Books and Orders-in-Council Books are all in the
Public Archives of Ontario. The papers of E.C. Drury are also in
the Ontario Archives, as are those of Howard Ferguson, Casimir
Gzowski, William H. Hearst, Peter Heenan, George S. Henry,
Mitchell F. Hepburn, the Hydro-Electric Power Commission of
Ontario, Aemilius Irving, William Mulock, the Ontario
Lumberman's Association, G. W. Ross and J. P. Whitney.

In the Ontario Hydro Archives are the Electrical Development Company of Ontario, Ltd., Minute Books; the Hydro-
Electric Power Commission Collection; the Ontario Power
Company of Niagara Falls, Minutes, Directors' and Shareholders' Meetings; the Toronto Electric Light Company, Ltd., Minute Book, Directors' and Shareholders' Meetings; Toronto
and Niagara Power Company Minute Book; and the Toronto
Power Company Minute Book, Directors' Meetings.

The James Mavor, B.E. Walker and John Charlton papers are
at the University of Toronto, and the E.W.B. Snider papers are
in the Kitchener Public Library.

# Index